# The Cultures of
# Native North Americans

General editor: Christian F. Feest

# The Cultures of Native North Americans

Contributors:
Cora Bender, Christian Carstensen,
Liane Gugel, Henry Kammler,
Sylvia S. Kasprycki and Sonja Lührmann

KÖNEMANN

Endpapers
Navajo woven blanket, c. 1885.
(see page 389)
© Museum für Völkerkunde, Vienna, Austria

Frontispiece
Between flag and feather.
A young Cheyenne dressed for a powwow.
© LOOK. Photograph: Christian Heeb (Munich)

Publishing Director and Art Direction: Peter Feierabend
Project Management: Ute Edda Hammer
Assistants: Jeannette Fentroß, Ann Christin Artel
Layout: Gerald Behrendt, Carmen Strzelecki
Picture Editing: Monika Bergmann, Fenja Wittneven
Picture Assistant: Astrid Schünemann
Lithography: litho niemann & m. steggemann gmbh, Oldenburg

Original title: *Kulturen der Nordamerikanischen Indianer*

Translation from the German: Amanda Riddick, Sabine Troelsch,
and Karen Waloschek for Book Creation Services Ltd.
Editing: Lucilla Watson for Book Creation Services Ltd.
Typesetting: Gene Ferber for Book Creation Services Ltd.
Project Management: Tamiko Rex
Revision of the English text: Christian F. Feest, Sylvia S. Kasprycki,
and Russell Cennydd
Project Coordination: Alex Morkramer
Production: Mark Voges

Printed in Germany

ISBN 3-8290-2985-3
10 9 8 7 6 5 4 3 2 1

The publisher would like to thank all those individuals and institutions
who have contributed to the creation of this book for their generous
cooperation, and to their employees for their diligent work and support.

# Contents

ORIGINS
AND PAST

Christian F. Feest

# Origins and Past of Indigenous North Americans

## "Indians?"

When in 1492 Columbus mistook the people of the Antilles for natives of India, he could not have guessed how far-reaching the consequences of his error would be. More than 500 years later, the peoples of the Americas are still designated as "Indians," as if they were a more or less homogeneous population. Nothing could be further from the truth. Compared to the diversity of the ways of life that once distinguished the continent, the "multi-cultural" America of today seems rather monotonous.

Pre-European North America was inhabited by hundreds of different peoples, ranging from the civilizations of Central America (Mesoamerica) to the cultures of the Arctic coast. Some of these peoples stood at the threshold of forming states; others moved around in smaller family groupings, gathering edible wild plants or hunting game. A more sedentary existence, even if only seasonal, was made possible on the coasts and the banks of rivers and lakes by fishing and hunting sea mammals, and in inland areas by agriculture.

However, what these people had in common when compared to the Europeans who since the 16th century had been making their way into what for them was a new world, was the absence of certain achievements: the lack of animal husbandry not only meant that they depended on hunting for meat, but also that no large animals were available as transport; without the use of rotary motion there was neither wheel nor wagon, no potter's wheel, no spinning wheel, no lathe; without the ability to

control high temperatures, ores could not be smelted and thus hardly any usable metal tools produced. In comparison, the absence of true writing systems was the least of their problems. In spite of these differences, it can be claimed that some Native American peoples were culturally closer to Europeans than to some of their aboriginal neighbors.

The white conquerors and settlers, however, didn't see it this way, and the general designation "Indians" was also an indication of their lack of interest in the differences between Native American tribes. Although we have known better for a long time, there had until recently been little attempt to remove this misleading term from the vernacular and scholarly vocabularies. Coined more than 100 years ago, the term "Amerind" never quite established itself and is ultimately just another misleading generalization. More recent terms such as "Native Americans" in the United States and "First Nations" in Canada emphasize on the one hand the variety within, but on the other the differences between, the modern nation states. Peoples living on either side of the border have different names depending on where they live. The people called Blackfoot in Canada are known as Blackfeet in the United States; the Ojibwa of Canada are identical to the Chippewa of the United States (only in Minnesota are they called Ojibway or Ojibwe).

Incidentally, most of the commonly used tribal names are designations used by other peoples and originally had meanings which were not always flattering. For instance, "Mohawk" is derived from the Narragansett

"Newer Peoples," from *Systematische Bilder Galerie zur Allgemeinen deutschen Real Encyklopädie* (1825–1827).

Greater understanding of the American continent revealed to Europeans the variety and differences of its native peoples, whom from the late 18th century onward the new science of ethnology in particular sought to classify. This early 19th-century encyclopedia shows the inhabitants of northwestern America (5: Chugash, 6: Nootka) as representatives of "Mongolian and Tartar Tribes," while the famous Mohawk leader Joseph Brant (9) and a Mayoruna from the Peruvian Montaña (8) are pictured as representatives of the "American Tribes."

word meaning "cannibal," while "Sioux" is the abridged form of the Ojibwa word for "speakers of an incomprehensible language" (in a figurative sense also "snakes").

In the wake of their belated decolonization, many of the native peoples of North America have asserted their right to their own names, some of which are now officially used ( more frequently so in Canada than in the United States). As most of these self-designations mean something like "(real) human beings," those of linguistically related, but culturally and politically distinct peoples are often confusingly similar to one another. By contrast, the designation "Inuit" is now applied even to those "Eskimos" whose self-designation is different.

Henry Kammler

## Languages and writing systems

It is no longer possible to determine how many distinct languages were spoken in precolonial North America - too many have disappeared without trace. Estimates start at about 500 languages and considerably more dialects.

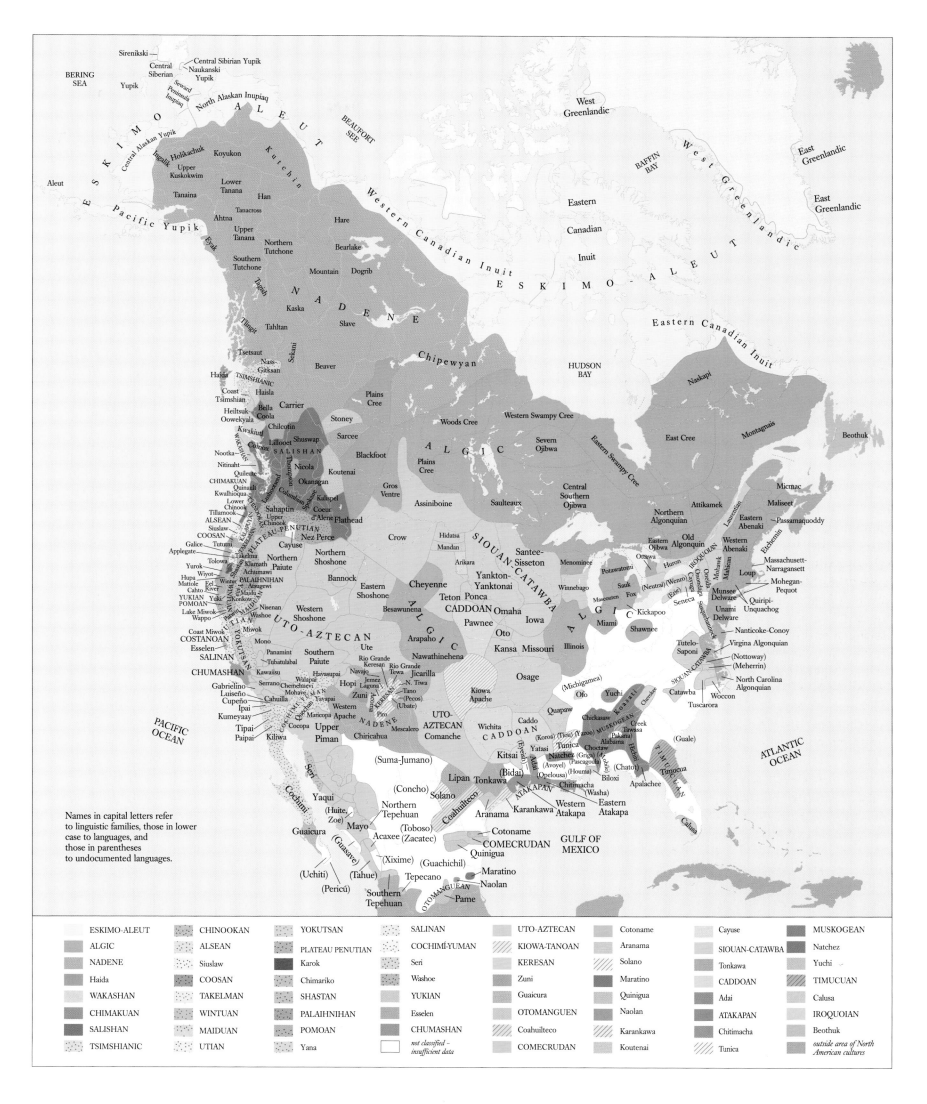

BERING
SEA

Sirenikski

Central Siberian Yupik
Central
Siberian
Seward
Peninsula
Inupiaq
Naukanski
Yupik

Yupik

North Alaskan Inupiaq

BEAUFORT
SEE

West
Greenlandic

BAFFIN
BAY

East
Greenlandic

Aleut

A L E U T

Central Alaskan Yupik

Ingalik

Holikachuk

Koyukon

Kutchin

Western Canadian Inuit

Eastern
Greenlandic

East
Greenlandic

E S K I M O

Upper
Kuskokwim

Tanaina

Lower
Tanana

Han

Eastern

Canadian

Inuit

Pacific Yupik

Eyak

Ahtna

Tanacross

Upper
Tanana

Northern
Tutchone

Hare

Bearlake

E S K I M O - A L E U T

Southern
Tutchone

Mountain

Dogrib

Eastern Canadian Inuit

Tagish

N A D E N E

Kaska

Tahltan

Slave

Tlingit

Tsetsaut

Sekani

Beaver

Chipewyan

HUDSON
BAY

Naskapi

West Greenlandic

Beothuk

Haida

TSIMSHIANIC

Nass-
Gitksan

Plains
Cree

Coast
Tsimshian

Haisla

Carrier

Stoney

Woods Cree

Western Swampy Cree

Severn
Ojibwa

East Cree

Montagnais

Heiltsuk-
Oowekyala

Bella
Coola

Chilcotin

Sarcee

Micmac

Kwakiutl

Lillooet

Shuswap

Blackfoot

A L G I C

Maliseet

Colqox

SALISHAN

Plains
Cree

Central
Southern
Ojibwa

Attikamek

Nootka

Thompson

Nicola

Koutenai

Assiniboine

Saulteaux

Northern
Algonquian

Laurentian

Eastern
Abenaki

Passamaquoddy

Nitinaht

Quileute

Okanagan

Eastern
Ojibwa

Old
Algonquin

Western
Abenaki

CHIMAKUAN

Quinault

Columbia

Kalispel

Gros
Ventre

Ottawa

Huron

IROQUOIAN

Etchemin

Massachusett-
Narragansett

Kwalhioqua

Lower
Chinook

Sahaptin

Upper
Chinook

Coeur
d'Alene

Menominee

(Neutral)

(Wenro)

Mohawk

Loup

Tillamook

Flathead

Winnebago

Mascouten

Sauk

(Erie)

Onondaga

Oneida

Mahican

Mohegan-
Pequot

ALSEAN

Cayuse

Crow

Hidatsa

Fox

Seneca

Susquehannock

Munsee
Delware

Quiripi-
Unquachog

Siuslaw

Nez Perce

Mandan

Potawatomi

Unami
Delware

COOSAN

Takelma

PLATEAU PENUTIAN

Northern
Paiute

Northern
Shoshone

Arikara

Santee-
Sisseton

Miami

Kickapoo

Nanticoke-Conoy

Galice

Klamath

Shawnee

Nanticoke-Conoy

Applegate

Tututni

Cayuse

Illinois

Virgina Algonquian

Tolowa

Takelma

Achumawi

SIOUAN-CATAWBA

Tutelo-
Saponi

Yurok

Wiyot

Atsugewi

Yankton-
Yanktonai

Teton

(Nottoway)

Hupa

PALAIHNIHAN

Eastern
Shoshone

Cheyenne

Ponca

Omaha

Iowa

(Meherrin)

Mattole

Eel
River

Maidu

CADDOAN

North Carolina
Algonquian

Cahto

YUKIAN

Yuki

Pawnee

A L G I C

Oto

Catawba

Woccon

POMOAN

Konkow

Nisenan

Washoe

Western
Shoshone

Kansa

Missouri

Tuscarora

Lake Miwok

Wappo

Arapaho

Nawathinehena

Osage

SIOUAN-CATAWBA

Coast Miwok

Miwok

Mono

UTO-AZTECAN

Ute

Rio Grande
Tewa

Jicarilla

Kiowa
Apache

(Michigamea)

Ofo

Yuchi

Cherokee

COSTANOAN

Esselen

Panamint

Southern
Paiute

Rio Grande
Keresan

N. Tiwa

Tano

Quapaw

SALINAN

Tubatulabal

Kawaiisu

Havasupai

Hopi

Zuni

Jemez
Laguna

(Pecos)

CHUMASHAN

Walapai

Serrano

Chemehuevi

Navajo

Piro

(Ubate)

Gabrielino

Yavapai

Western
Apache

Kiowa
Apache

UTO-
AZTECAN

Koasati

Creek

Tawasa

(Guale)

Luiseño

Cahuilla

Mohave

Maricopa

Comanche

Wichita

Caddo

Chickasaw

(Koroa)

(Tiou)

(Yazoo)

MUSKOGEAN

Pakana

Alabama

Cupeño

Ipai

COCHIMÍ-YUMAN

N A D E N E

Mescalero

CADDOAN

Choctaw

Hitchiti

Kumeyaay

Cocopa

Chiricahua

Kitsai

Yatasi

(Eyeish)

Tunica

Natchez

(Griga)

(Mobile)

TIMUCUAN

Tipai

Upper
Piman

Adai

(Avoyel)

(Pascagoula)

Paipai

Kiliwa

(Suma-Jumano)

(Bidai)

(Opelousa)

(Houma)

Biloxi

(Chatot)

Timucua

(Washa)

Apalachee

Seri

(Concho)

Lipan

Tonkawa

Chitimacha

TIMUCUAN

PACIFIC
OCEAN

Yaqui

(Huite,
Zoe)

Northern
Tepehuan

Solano

Coahuilteco

ATAKAPAN

Western
Atakapa

Eastern
Atakapa

Calusa

Cochimí

Mayo

(Guasave)

Aranama

Karankawa

ATLANTIC
OCEAN

Guaicura

(Xixime)

(Toboso)

Acaxee

(Zacatec)

Cotoname

COMECRUDAN

GULF OF
MEXICO

(Uchiti)

(Tahue)

(Guachichil)

Quinigua

Maratino

Names in capital letters refer
to linguistic families, those in lower
case to languages, and
those in parentheses to undocumented languages.

(Pericú)

Southern
Tepehuan

Tepecano

Pame

Naolan

OTOMANGUEAN

| | | |
|---|---|---|
| ESKIMO-ALEUT | CHINOOKAN | YOKUTSAN |
| ALGIC | ALSEAN | PLATEAU PENUTIAN |
| NADENE | Siuslaw | Karok |
| Haida | COOSAN | Chimariko |
| WAKASHAN | TAKELMAN | SHASTAN |
| CHIMAKUAN | WINTUAN | PALAIHNIHAN |
| SALISHAN | MAIDUAN | POMOAN |
| TSIMSHIANIC | UTIAN | Yana |

| | | |
|---|---|---|
| SALINAN | UTO-AZTECAN | Cotoname |
| COCHIMÍ-YUMAN | KIOWA-TANOAN | Aranama |
| Seri | KERESAN | Solano |
| Washoe | Zuni | Maratino |
| YUKIAN | Guaicura | Quinigua |
| Esselen | OTOMANGUEN | Naolan |
| CHUMASHAN | Coahuilteco | Karankawa |
| not classified – insufficient data | COMECRUDAN | Koutenai |

| | | |
|---|---|---|
| Cayuse | MUSKOGEAN | |
| SIOUAN-CATAWBA | Natchez | |
| Tonkawa | Yuchi | |
| CADDOAN | TIMUCUAN | |
| Adai | Calusa | |
| ATAKAPAN | IROQUOIAN | |
| Chitimacha | Beothuk | |
| Tunica | outside area of North American cultures | |

11

John Verelst, *Tee Yee Neen Ho Ga Row (A Mohawk visiting London)*, oil on canvas, 1710. National Archives of Canada, Ottawa, ON.

This Iroquois diplomat is holding a wampum belt in his hand. These belts were made of purple and white cylindrical beads fashioned from seashells. In the Northeast they supported the spoken word and were regarded as symbols for a treaty. Their patterns related to the stipulations of such treaties or held ritual instructions and messages that could only be "read" by the initiated. In colonial times wampum was used as a measure of value and even as a currency.

This made North America one of the areas with the greatest linguistic diversity in the world. In recent years, many linguists have become reluctant to make sweeping claims about possible relationships between languages. The most cautious among them speak of more than 60 linguistic families, a few of which consisted merely of one isolated language. Even neighboring languages could be as different from each other as German is from Chinese. More than 100 languages are spoken even today. However, many have only a few, very old speakers and are in immediate danger of becoming extinct. The distribution of these languages across the continent was far from even. In large areas where closely related languages were spoken, we can assume that their speakers spread throughout those areas within a few hundred or thousand years. This applies, for instance, to the Numic branch of the Uto-Aztecan languages in the Great Basin, to Cree and Ojibwa in southern Canada and the Athapaskan languages in the north, as well as to Inuktitut, the language of the Eskimo in the eastern Arctic. In contrast, the mountainous west of North America shows a colorful patchwork of languages, because older languages could survive in protected areas even during large population movements. The solidly Penutian speaking area in central California is probably the result of a more recent influx which pushed the Hokan speakers into marginal areas. Yuki, isolated in the middle of California, may represent the linguistic heritage of early inhabitants of the region. The Athapaskan pockets in northwestern California, however, are the result of immigration in the first millennium AD.

It is almost impossible to generalize about the native languages of North America. However, a frequent feature of these languages is polysynthesis, the formation of words containing all the elements of a sentence. In this process of "incorporation," the object of the verb is included in the verb itself – thus the Seneca word *o'gé'hnyayęn*, "I beat it with a stick" (literally, "I stickbeat it"), from *ga'hnya*, "stick," and *o'gyęn*, "I beat it." The Uto-Aztecan and Siouan languages have a range of prefixes which indicate the way in which something is performed. For instance, Shoshone *nuà*, "to move," becomes *tannua*, "to kick" (*ta*: "with the foot"), *tonnua*, "to punch" (*to*: "with the fist"), *mannua*, "push" (*ma*: "with the hand"). Often the circumstances of an action are described exactly. In Lakota, a Siouan language, the speaker must make clear whether he is using an object with the owner's permission (*ki-*) or against his will (*kiči-*): *ykíkaš-kapi*, "we are fastening it for him/with his permission," as opposed to *ykíčikaškapi*, "we are fastening it against his will." Differences in the intensity of a process can be expressed through sound symbolism, as in Winnebago *sąną* for "falling out," *šąną* for "falling down," and *xąną* for "collapsing in on itself."

Gravestone with inscription in the Carrier syllabic script, Prince George, British Columbia, 1978.

In about 1840 English missionary James Evans (1801–1846) developed a syllabary to help spread the Bible and Christian catechism among the Cree at Lake Winnipeg. The system was surprisingly simple. Every consonant was given its own geometric shape, which was turned by 90 degrees depending on the succeeding vowel – of which there are four in Cree. Other missionaries adapted the successful system to Eskimoan and Athapaskan languages such as Chipewyan and Carrier.

Systematic arrangement of the 85 syllable signs of the syllabary invented in 1819 by the Cherokee Sequoyah, by missionary Samuel Worcester in 1828.

The top row consists of the six Cherokee vowels. The columns below contain the syllables ending in the respective vowel, arranged according to the initial consonant .

The Apache are quite pedantic about the shape of an object and use classificatory verb stems to distinguish between the use of a round, rod-shaped, or animate object, or one of a mushy substance. Fourteen prefix positions to the verb's stem qualify the stem more exactly – that is, who is doing a particular activity when, in what order, and how. The number of possible combinations seems endless, but only some are actually used, presenting one of the major problems in learning the Apache languages.

Many languages also demand that the exact temporal sequence of an action ("aspect") must be expressed. Thus Eastern Pomo has *si·q'á·l*, "to call (continuously)," *si·q'álk*, "to call once," and *si·q'á·lki*, "to call suddenly."

There were no traditions of writing in precolonial North America. To a limited extent messages could be recorded or communicated through pictograms, knotted strings, or notched sticks. Some forms of writing originated in the colonial period under white influence, however, only the syllabic script invented by the Cherokee Sequoyah and those of the peoples of northern Canada have successfully been maintained.

# The "Indians" and ourselves

The "Indians" are not a people inhabiting the wide expanses of the American continent. Their place of origin and residence lies in the realm of the imagination of the Europeans (and later the white Americans) who were taken by surprise to discover "new" people in a "new" world following its discovery in 1492. With their confusing diversity and contradictions, the "Indians" quickly became the embodiment of the "other," providing a counter example of what was good and of what was bad in the observers' culture.

To those believing in progress, the "Indians" represented the "savage," living witnesses to a European past believed long overcome. "In the beginning the world was America," postulated the English philosopher John Locke (1632–1704) in the 17th century, and as late as the 19th century the Native Americans were placed within a speculative chronology of human cultural development, at best in a transitional phase from "savagery" to "barbarism." Placed in alarming proximity to the Animal Kingdom, the conception of the "beasts we call Indians" became an argument for the conquest of America. Wherever Western civilization became established the "four- and two-legged panthers" had to disappear.

To those at odds with their own culture, whether through alienation or disadvantage, the "Indians" became the representatives of a paradisical golden age. These "noble savages," untainted by the decadence of European culture, provided an ideal of a simpler but happier life, free of the constraints of society and the excesses of progress.

Still from the movie *The Silent Enemy* (1927). Canon Middleton Collection, Glenbow Archives, Calgary, AB.

In the 20th century, movies brought the fictional image of Native Americans to life. Buffalo Child Long Lance, the main protagonist in *The Silent Enemy* (1927), was himself closer to fiction than fact. Born a colored in Winston-Salem, North Carolina, Sylvester Long transformed himself into first a Cherokee and later a Blackfoot, and described his Indian childhood in his still popular autobiography. He committed suicide when his true origins became known.

Gregor Brandmüller, *Les Trésors de l'Amerique*, 1682. Musée du Nouveau Monde, La Rochelle, France.

Allegorical depictions of America in European art from the Renaissance onward also reflect the ambivalence of the Western conception of the Native American. Often the continent is depicted as the home of cannibals. Here, however, it becomes an opulent place of desirable wealth which is freely shared with others by the blond child in featherdress. Only the basket with the jewelry casket on top is truly American.

The changes in Western society's perception of Native Americans show how much the imagined world of "the Indians" is due to our own situation. While in the 19th century "the Indians" stood for exemplary courage in war, for masculinity, and for leadership, by the late 20th century they had become representatives of peace, feminism, and environmental awareness. Just as the famous "environmental" speech by Chief Seattle has never been delivered by the historic Duwamish leader but was written in 1969 by a white American for a film on environmental destruction in the United States, other aspects of the "Indian" image are also nothing but figments of our imagination.

However, these images and expectations of "Indians" have not been without effect upon the descendants of America's original inhabitants. To be recognized by whites as real "Indians", feather bonnets are now being worn by members of tribes which had never used them before. Seattle's speech has long been translated into his old language. Dissatisfaction with Christian religion and a bureaucratic health system has over the 20th century led to a profitable market for "Indian shamans" and life consultants. This illustrates how, under the prevailing influence of capitalism, spirituality and ritual have become commodities even for some Native Americans.

Given the continuing disadvantaged status of the indigenous peoples of North America, it is only understandable that many of them prefer to identify with the positive attributes of the invented "Indian" and to distance themselves from the negative. Scalping, once an indication of "Indian savagery," is now considered by Native Americans to be a white invention. And while it is neither proven nor likely that the constitution of the Iroquois League served as the model for the Founding Fathers' own constitution, this Native contribution to American political culture has already been honored in a resolution passed by the United States Congress.

Through countless books and movies, the myth of the "Indian" has been kept alive and continues to exert a considerable influence on our perception of the original inhabitants of America. It is precisely for this reason that we constantly need to remind ourselves how much this distorts our view of the manifold realities of the indigenous American.

# The Old New World: creation and knowledge

The stories of the origins of the world and the origins of humanity are as varied as the peoples of North America who tell them, and whenever the subject is the origin of humans, they always (and almost always exclusively) refer to those who are telling the tales – "the real human beings."

At the beginning of time, the ancestors of the Keresan-speaking Pueblo peoples lived together with their mother Iyatiku on the lowest level of a four-layered underworld. When the time had come to move from this white world up to the next, red world, Iyatiku made a perennially green tree grow on which humans could climb to the sky of their world. But first a woodpecker had to peck a hole through the hard top of the world so that the second level could be reached. Four years later people moved up into the blue world, then into the yellow one, and finally up to the fifth, today's world. The badger, who had dug the hole through the fourth sky, took the first look at the humans' new homeland and reported, "It is beautiful up here, everywhere there are rainclouds." Shipap, the place where people emerged from the underworld, was too sacred for them to remain there, so they moved further south. After she had given her children

her heart, the corn upon which they could subsist, Iyatiku returned to the underworld.

The Keresans live at the center of a flat, square world covered by a domelike sky. It is well ordered and well equipped for their use. At the corners of the earth are the houses of four gods, while other deities live at the six points of the compass (including Zenith and Nadir). A little nearer to the dwellings of humans are the residences of Katsina, the bringer of rain, and of Kwiraina and Koshairi, the sacred clowns.

Many other peoples of the Southwest tell of the ascent from an underworld. The Lakota of the Plains also say that they once lived as "a people of bison cows" underneath the world of today, where the master of the bison herds still makes his home. The Iroquois of the Northeastern Woodlands, however, are convinced that the female ancestor of all humans fell from the sky.

According to the creation myth of the Miwok of central California, people were made from bird feathers by Grandfather Coyote, who then scattered them across the land. Thus he created the linguistic diversity of the residents of different villages. There are various explanations of where Coyote himself came from. Some said that he had come out of a tree trunk lying in water, a piece of which was broken off by his grandson Falcon. Others reported that Coyote had arrived on a rectangular raft from beyond the ocean,

Norval Morrisseau (Ojibwa), *Creation of the Earth*. Mashantucket Pequot Museum and Research Center, Mashantucket, CT.

According to the creation myth of the Ojibwa, Nanabozho was the son of a virgin who died at his birth, and he was raised as a hare by his grandmother. He took revenge for the death of his wolflike brother on the underwater manitons. They in turn brought about a flood which forced the hero to create a new earth from a piece of mud that he was given by the earth-diver. The painting is by Norval Morrisseau (b. 1931), founder of the "legend painting" school in the early 1960s.

humanity had spread from there across the world. An unwillingness to speculate on the existence of any peoples before Adam left no doubt that the Native Americans too were descended from Adam and Noah. As early as the 16th century the scholarly Jesuit missionary José de Acosta maintained that people later to become "Indians" probably came to America via northern Asia and the then still unknown Bering Strait.

Although the indigenous Americans received these Biblical stories with friendly interest, they did not attach too much importance to them. They had learned to accept that different peoples might have different origins. What irritated them was the insistence on the part of Christians that the story of Paradise represented an exclusive truth.

This was the experience of the English trader William Henry, who in 1755 lived as a prisoner among the Seneca and felt the urge to convert the Iroquois. They listened to the story of Adam, Eve, the serpent, and the apple, and then told him of Sky-woman, the turtle, and the muskrat. Henry's mistake lay in his insistence on the universal validity of his story, which had after all been recorded in a book, while the Iroquois fable had only been passed orally from mother to daughter. At this the Seneca criticized the bad behavior of their prisoner, who did not show the same respect to their story as they had shown to his. The Bible's version might, perhaps, apply to whites, but it certainly did not apply to the Iroquois.

It was not long afterwards that the Judeo-Christian creation myth was no longer accepted

John J. Egan, *Dr. Dickeson Excavating A Mound. Section of the Egan-Dickeson Panorama of the Monumental Grandeur of the Mississippi Valley*, 1850. St. Louis Art Museum.

President Thomas Jefferson (1743–1826) was one of the first to carry out an archeological excavation in North America. However, it was only from the 19th century onward that systematic excavations, particularly of the burial and temple mounds of eastern North America gave a picture of American ancient history. At the time many Christians were alarmed by the disturbance of the dead. Today the *Native American Grave Protection and Repatriation Act* protects burial sites and ensures the reinterment of bones dug up in the past.

and that that is why the land (California's Central Valley) was likewise long and rectangular.

However, even if Coyote had perhaps been an immigrant from the Pacific region, all Native American creation myths agree that human beings were created on American soil. The whites have always seen the matter in a different light.

The Biblical myth left no doubt that the Garden of Eden lay in the Near East and that

Ernest Smith (Seneca), *The Sky-Woman*, 1936.
Rochester Museum and Science Center, Rochester, NY.

The Iroquois version of creation tells of a woman living in a village above the skydome. Her husband accused her of adultery and in anger uprooted the tree of life. He then threw his wife down through the hole in the sky the tree had left. As she hurtled toward the world ocean, she was caught by sea birds. They placed her on a piece of land built upon the back of a turtle from the mud that a muskrat had gathered at the bottom of the ocean. Until then there had only been water, but from now on the turtle and the earth on its shell grew and grew and became the home of Sky-woman and her descendants, the human race.

as literal by the whites either. This development was not the result of turning to another mythic truth, but the recognition that many aspects of the Biblical story could no longer be reconciled with growing scientific knowledge.

Paleface scientists have ruled out a specific American origin for the American peoples – and that quite simply because America was never home to the great apes from which humans could have evolved. Discoveries in the Old World of hominids millions of years old overshadow the skeletal remains found in the New World that date back scarcely more than 10,000 years.

Although the proof is inadequate, the Bering Strait land bridge, which emerged when sea levels were much lower during parts of the Ice Age, stands practically uncontested among all the possible ways of entering the New World. Only via this route could large groups of people have moved on dry land from Asia across to America and populated the double continent within a few thousand years. As recently as 60 years ago this time span was considered to be 2,000 years, and initially many scientists even found it difficult to accept that the first humans had reached the continent 12,000 years ago. Later this figure became a new dogma in North American archeology and was defended even after much older discoveries had been made, particularly in South America.

Since this consevative estimate can no longer be defended, the Bering Strait theory as the only explanation has also become a little shaky. However, since prior to 25,000 years ago no land bridge existed we would have to make the assumption of immigration across water, however unlikely for that period. Even so, it is certain that the movements of people into America took place over a long period of time and that the immigrants from Asia were not one homogeneous population. By the time the land bridge had been submerged by rising sea levels there were definitely boats in the area of the Bering Strait and the Aleutians to connect the Old World and the New.

These results of scientific research present the indigenous population with a two fold problem.

Firstly, archeology seems to undermine the foundations of the traditional world view that rests on the simultaneous creation of a people and their land. Secondly, Native American politicians see the idea that their ancestors may also have been only immigrants to the New World as a threat to their exclusive land rights.

Christian fundamentalists too have never accepted science's claim to truth and continue to demand that religious and scientific versions of creation be equally taught in schools. Native Americans can therefore count on sympathy for their rejection of the Bering Strait theory and for their insistence on the truth of their myths.

# The new peoples

The fateful relationship between the original inhabitants of North America and the settlers who arrived from Europe is usually (and not unreasonably) presented as a conflict that destroyed whole populations. However, this view does not take into account and indeed overlooks the development of new peoples through the meeting of old and new. This applies not only to Native American peoples, such as the Delaware or the Seminole, who evolved out of the merging of previously independent groups, but also to associations between indigenous Americans and new settlers.

In the colony of New France in what is today Canada, the interest of the fur trade in the local population was at least equal (if not greater) to the requirements of the relatively small group of French settlers. Marriages between traders and indigenous American women created kinship ties useful to the exchange of goods and offered hope for the integration of indigenous groups into colonial society in the long term. Often the traders found the lifestyle of their new relatives more attractive than that of the colonists and did not return to the French settlements.

Thanks to their upbringing, the Métis, the children of these unions, were ideal mediators between the two different cultures. Over time they developed their own way of life and even their own language (Michif), which combined French nouns with Cree verbs.

Peter Rindisbacher, *A Halfcast and his Two Wives*, watercolor, c. 1825.

The Métis united the heritage of two cultures not only in their origins and language but also in their attire and lifestyle. Their Catholic faith did not prevent them from marrying several wives, especially as their success in trade often gave them the means to support a large family.

In the 19th century a large number of these Métis lived as bison hunters and traders in the area around the Red River of the North, but they were soon pushed further west by advancing settlers. Although they were sometimes joined by originally English or Protestant "Halfbreed" families, the Métis kept their identity as Catholic hunters, fishermen, trappers, and farmers. When their rights were ignored during the founding of the province of Manitoba in 1870, they rebelled under the leadership of Louis Riel (1844–1885) and achieved legal recognition of their "native" land rights. However, like other indigenous peoples the Métis were heavily discriminated against in the distribution of land. At the same time their share of Manitoba's population fell from 82 percent to only 7 percent between 1870 and 1885. Conflict broke out again in 1885 in the province of Saskatchewan. Louis Riel, who had dreamed of autonomy for the Métis, was apprehended and finally executed.

Only in 1982, nearly 100 years later, did the Canadian constitution finally recognize the Métis as an indigenous people with corresponding rights. Today about 100,000 "historic Métis" live in Canada's Prairie Provinces, although more than one million consider themselves to belong to this particular group.

In the English colonies south of Canada traders also married into the indigenous tribes. Yet their descendants did not become a separate people but often formed the upper class of their tribes.

Life was far more complicated for the descendants of marriages between indigenous people and the Africans who had been brought particularly as slaves to the southern colonies of North America. While the Cherokee, Creek, or Choctaw, for instance, became slave-owners themselves, other peoples chose to harbor runaway slaves.

The race laws passed from the 18th century onward classified the descendants of unions between Native Americans and Africans as "persons of color," who were deprived of most rights, and many tribes distanced themselves from this class of person in order to avoid losing rights themselves. As "persons of color" these mixed bloods were not allowed to marry whites, voluntarily avoided all too close contact with Africans, and thus became isolated groups, whose members almost exclusively married among themselves.

Especially after the American Civil War of 1861–1865, and increasingly over the last 30 years, many of these new peoples declared themselves to be "Indians," mostly without official recognition as "tribes" from the federal government, and also without indigenous rights (the status afforded to the Métis). Their number probably also exceeds 100,000.

Haliwa festival, North Carolina, 1973.

Only about 50 years ago a local population in north-central North Carolina split into an African-American and an "American Indian" group. The latter initially called themselves Haliwa (after the counties they lived in, Halifax and Warren), were recognized as Native Americans by the state of North Carolina in 1965, and regard themselves today under the name of Haliwa-Saponi as the descendants of a pre-European population. Their annual festival is the most visible expression of the maintenance of this recent tradition.

Benjamin West, *Sir William Johnson, Bt*, oil on canvas, c. 1776. Andrew W. Mellon Collection, National Gallery of Art, Washington, DC.

As superintendent of the Northeastern Indian department in British North America, the successful land speculator William Johnson (1715–1774) was the direct representative of the Great White Father in London. Thanks to his close relations with the Mohawk (he had eight children with the sister of Chief Joseph Brant, and lived with another Mohawk woman after the death of his white wife), the British crown was supported by the Iroquois in driving the French out of North America.

whites had in mind. Rather it referred to the generosity of fatherly love that brought with it expectations of presents and liberal supplies of desirable goods. Growing dependency on these products – iron tools, firearms, glass beads, textiles, and not least alcohol – together with inferior military strength and declining population levels also frequently led to a political dependency of the "red children" on their "white father." A Supreme Court ruling of 1828 described the legal relationship between the United States government and those tribes living on the land claimed by the United States as its own territory as one resembling that of guardian and ward. A separate legal identity for the tribes was combined with marked limitations on independent decision-making. The situation has basically remained unchanged to the present-day.

As long as there were competitive conflicts between the colonial powers or even among the different English colonies in North America, indigenous groups with some political skill were able to negotiate special rights for themselves. The central regulation of "Indian affairs" by a federal agency – the Bureau of Indian Affairs (BIA) set up in 1824 in the War Department – left no room for special solutions. Further, its legal and administrative treatment of all "tribes" as indigenous peoples came to be called officially as if they were all the same, despite their many differences and conflicting interests, contributed to the creation of a shared "Indian" identity.

Although there were subtle differences in the way that the Spanish and Mexicans, French, Dutch, Swedes, Russians, British, Canadians, and Americans acted, the goal of each nation's policy regarding the "Indians" was to secure and justify the seizure of the continent. This took place against the backdrop of the Christian mission to convert, "civilize," or Europeanize the indigenous population, with the long-term aim of assimilation with equal rights into the ruling society. There were basically only three ways of achieving this common goal, all of which were tried at different times and in different variations over the course of the next 500 years: violence, deportation, or autonomy.

# The Great White Father

In political terms, most indigenous American societies were organized not on the basis of a common territory but rather on that of kinship. Even though the form of political order might differ greatly, the pattern of family relations provided a widely accepted frame of reference for establishing or expressing political relations. Depending on their relationships to one another, friendly or allied tribes often referred to each other as "elder brother" or "younger brother," "grandfather," "cousin," and so on. The best way of making peace was to adopt the enemy, thereby creating ties of kinship.

This principle was also applied to relations with the white colonies and the subsequent nation states. Kings living in far-away Paris or London, and later the president of the United States, were warmly described as the Great White Father. However, most of the time this did not correspond with the patriarchal role the

George Winter, *Council Assembly in Keewaunay*, 1837. Indiana University Museum of Art, Bloomington, IN.

The policies regarding Native Americans that were made in capital cities far from actual needs had then to be explained and enforced in "Indian" country. In 1837, by Lake Keewaunay, a government delegation tried to convince the Potawatomi of the necessity of selling their land in Indiana and moving westward. However, the government agents seem as uninterested in the entreaties of the Potawatomi speaker as most of the audience, who can probably guess that their fate is sealed anyway.

Premeditated genocide was carried out only rarely, when the goals of civilization and a peaceful coexistence seemed impossible. More frequently, a blind eye was turned on privately organized violence against indigenous peoples – and with that the murder of whole populations. The exclusion and deportation of peoples to their designated reservations gave them a higher level of independence, but could often only be achieved by force.

Although autonomy was often the explicit goal of Indian policy, it regularly collapsed in the face of an insatiable land hunger on the side of the whites. The attempt, to virtually force integration into the white man's world by destroying the old political structures and replacing traditional cultures with Western values proved finally to be no less fatal as a deadly embrace. The real miracle is that so many indigenous Americans have managed to survive this treatment.

# This land is your land, this land is my land ...

The history of America is also the history of Native American land loss. In the United States, less than two percent of the land, mostly of below-average quality, now belongs to tribes. However, that land is an important link between its current inhabitants and their past sovereignty. It is hardly surprising that land rights continue to be at the center of controversy between Native Americans and federal and state governments.

When appropriating American land, the Spanish claimed the right of conquest, justified by the original inhabitants' refusal to convert voluntarily to Christianity. The other colonial powers did not shrink from the use of violence either. However, the British in particular also concluded treaties with the previous owners, either to justify their conquests after the event or to avoid the higher costs of a war. Basically those affected had little choice but to agree to hand over their land. On the Atlantic coastal plain there are still some reservations today which were established by such colonial treaties.

The United States and Canada adopted the British practice of acquiring land by treaty. The United States concluded a total of some 800 treaties with various tribes, but only half of these were ratified by the Senate to come into force. Settling indigenous land rights in the Union's southern states had become a particularly pressing issue in the early 19th century because of the plantation owners' insatiable hunger for land. The *Indian Removal Act* of 1830 allowed the deportation of all tribes living east of the Mississippi to an "Indian Territory" in today's Oklahoma and to Kansas. Only a few groups in the Northeast escaped such a fate. The majority were forced to move westward, despite resistance and with enormous losses on the "Trail of Tears," as the survivors of this forced removal later called this traumatic experience.

While the United States abandoned treaty making in 1871 and regulated further land issues through executive order, Canada, independent since 1867, concluded eleven collective treaties with tribes in Ontario and the Prairie Provinces between 1871 and 1921. In British Columbia and in the Yukon and Northwest Territories the issue of land has to this day remained largely unresolved. Only in 1971 did the United States set up legal regulations regarding Native American land rights in Alaska, which they had purchased from the Russians in 1867 without regard to the peoples living there.

In Canada, the reserves that were established as a result of these treaties were often quite small, as their size was determined by the number of families currently living there. To achieve the rapid assimilation of the "Indians," the United States passed the *General Allotment Act* in 1883, on the basis of which the reservations (and therefore the tribes) were to be disbanded.

Andrew Standing Soldier (Oglala Lakota), *The Land of the Free*, 1964. John Borman Collection, Fort Collins, CO.

The Lakota did not have to walk the Trail of Tears, as their reservations lay in their territory. Nevertheless, these former bison hunters, forced by the army to abandon their extensive traditional hunting grounds, saw this as proof that America was a Land of the Free only for the whites.

Instead, every family was to receive a private plot of land, which would make them into free and independent citizens living from their farming activities. This goal was never achieved, and the law was not applied to many reservations because of previous bad experiences. Even so, two thirds of reservation land was lost this way: any land that remained after allotment was given to whites by the federal government, and often impoverished indigenous American owners of small plots found themselves forced to sell them.

In 1946 the United States government set up the Indian Claims Commission to fulfill all outstanding treaty obligations, and to settle all disputes over illegally seized land. This was to thank Native Americans for their contributions in World War II: the slate should be cleared before reservations were to be abolished once and for all through the so-called termination laws. However, the implementation of this plan led to serious economic problems, as the sudden loss of subsidies, tax exemption, and collective land ownership was a heavy blow to the economic welfare of the tribes affected. As a result the "termination" was partially withdrawn by the federal government. For instance, the Menominee of Wisconsin achieved the restoration of their reservation and of the tribe's old status in 1973 after violent protests. On the other hand, the Klamath tribe in Oregon officially ceased to exist in 1958.

The current number of legal disputes arising from questions of land ownership makes it clear that this problem is far from being relegated to past history.

### Reservations

Not all of the reservations, of which there are over 2,000, are shown, especially in Canada. Nunavut Territory in northern Canada, inhabited by 25,000 people (of which 85 percent are Inuit), covers about 772,000 square miles. Formed out of the old Northwest Territories in 1999, it became an autonomous region as a result of the new Canadian aboriginal land rights policies, since 1973.

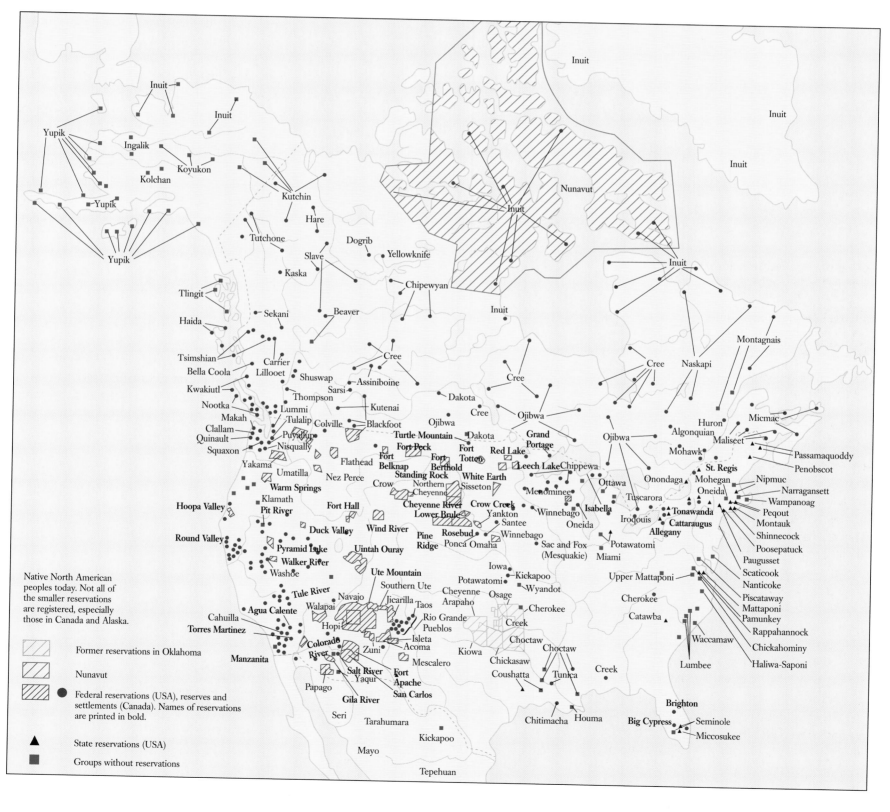

# On the warpath

Control over land was the greatest source of conflict between the old and the new Americans, but it was not the primary reason for warlike encounters. Just as the Europeans were torn between the "noble" and "savage" aspects of the "Indians," so the native populations saw the Europeans as suppliers of incredible new goods, but also as unpredictable and therefore dangerous strangers.

In pre-European times, raiding for booty (including women) was as valid a reason for war as wanting to wreak revenge or gain supernatural powers and social status. When the white newcomers did not as expected generously give out their amazing goods as presents, and instead charged high prices for them, theft or robbery of these goods seemed absolutely justified.

The whites, highly sensitive in matters of property, usually reacted with military punishment against not only the suspected perpetrators but their whole group. In return, an attack by a band of Native American warriors on an isolated house on the border could be revenge for the killing of a member of the tribe, even though the victims of that retaliatory attack might have not been personally involved in the killing in any way.

Although possessing superior arms power, the white armies were usually too small for real wars of conquest, especially in colonial times. Moreover, it was not in the tactical interests of most indigenous peoples to engage battle in an open field where superior military equipment

*Ira Hayes Ready To Jump* (1943). National Archives and Record Service (Washington, DC.).

The photogenic Pima Ira Hayes gained national fame through another photograph which shows him, together with four other soldiers, raising the Stars and Stripes on the volcanic Japanese island of Iwo Jima, which had been stormed on February 19, 1945. Although it was posed, the photograph was to make clear that the Indians were now finally US citizens and that the enemy was no longer a domestic one. Ira Hayes died an impoverished alcoholic in 1955 at the age of 32.

would have come into its own. Long before the Vietnam War, the colonists learned that a guerrilla war can often work in favor of the weaker party.

Aztec Mexico could only be conquered by a handful of Spanish troops because they received help from Mexican enemies of the Aztecs. Likewise, it would have been hard for the whites in North America to achieve their goals without the support of Native American allies. Such alliances were often initiated by the indigenous partners who expected to gain their own advantages in the battle against their enemies.

Military resistance to the conquerors nearly always came too late. In 1622, some 15 years

after the English colony of Virginia was founded, the coastal Algonquians revolted against the colonists and killed more than a quarter of them. However, the remaining three quarters were victorious, and their retaliatory war contributed to the reduction in the native population, which 50 years later was at a twentieth of its original level. One of the reasons for the revolt's failure was an Algonquian's betrayal of the plan to the Virginians, a sign that many could no longer imagine a life without the material goods of the whites.

The uprising staged by the Dakota in Minnesota in 1862 to drive out the whites, who were already numerically far superior, was also betrayed. The exemplary punishment for the deaths of more than 500 whites was the public execution of 38 suspected leaders and the exile of the surviving Dakota from Minnesota.

The Pueblo revolt of 1680 was a partial success, as the Spanish were chased from their colony along the Rio Grande. However, they did return twelve years later and reestablished their hegemony.

The native scouts who were so useful to the United States army in the Indian wars of the second half of the 19th century were only the beginning. The end of armed conflicts between the tribes and the whites represented a real problem to the men belonging to societies where honors won in warfare were an important means of gaining social status. Already in World War I a large number of Native American men served voluntarily in the same army that their fathers had fought against. Today, the number of Native American soldiers, particularly in special units, is disproportionately high.

Edgar Paxon, *Custer's Last Stand*, oil on canvas, 1899. Buffalo Bill Historical Center, Cody, WY.

The Battle of the Little Bighorn, at which superior numbers of allied Lakota and Cheyenne under the leadership of Crazy Horse and Gall destroyed the Seventh Cavalry Regiment under Lieutenant-Colonel George Armstrong Custer, has become legendary for both winners and losers. While patriotic Americans see the military failure of the popular Custer as a heroic feat, for many Indians the victory remains to this day proof of the possibility of successful resistance against the Americans.

## Administered Indians: The Indian Bureau

In 1999, the agency celebrated its 175th birthday, making it 25 years older than the Department of the Interior, of which it is now a part. Like all long-lived branches of public administration, it also is in some respects independent of day-to-day politics: Presidents, Secretaries of the Interior, and political administrators come and go, announcing new visions and promising reforms, whereas the employees dealing with the practical aspects know better, and much stays the same as it always has been. The institution in question is the Bureau of Indian Affairs (BIA), the US agency for indigenous Americans. It was established in 1824 as part of the War Department: it was the soldiers on the western frontier who had the most contact with the Native Americans. However, the equation of "Indian Affairs" with war did not favorably impress those affected, and when a separate Department of the Interior was founded in 1849, the Bureau of Indian Affairs was placed under its charge. The new department was also responsible for public land, so the administration of the reservations seemed to fit in rather well with this.

In the long run the double task of holding in trust indigenous land and safeguarding the public welfare of US citizens frequently led to conflicts of interest, in which the Indians usually were the losers. The War Department, incidentally, was not happy about losing its responsibility for Indian affairs; it was still the army that had to maintain order in Indian country, where the government's agents may have had considerable authority but could actually do little without support from the military.

Far away from Washington, the badly paid Indian agents working at the "frontier of civilization" operated under rather loose supervision, providing ideal conditions for mismanagement and corruption. Often, goods reserved for the tribes were exchanged for less valuable items, or sometimes never

Charles A. Zimmermann, *Annuity Payment Scene at La Pointe, Wisconsin*, c. 1871. Minnesota Historical Society, St. Paul, MN.

It was the agent's task to pay out the annuities as promised in the treaties. Critics saw the threat of Native Americans' growing dependence on government welfare payments, which would reduce their willingness to earn their own living. The possibilities for paid jobs or establishing businesses on Indian reservations were, and are, extremely limited.

even reached their intended recipients. These positions were great opportunities to get rich, and were popular as sinecures given by politicians to loyal supporters. Many of the agents were correct and responsible federal employees who took their task of "civilizing" the Indians seriously, but others, who abused their position, tainted the Bureau's public image.

The situation was particularly bad under the former Civil War general President Ulysses S. Grant (1822–1885, in office 1869–1877). Part of his "peace policy" was the allocation of reservations as mission areas among the various Christian denominations, with the government agent of the same faith. This reduced the agents' independence and increased the effectivness of safeguards against abuse.

Employee of the Oglala Sioux Tribe, Pine Ridge, South Dakota, c. 1990.

Since the tribal administrations have increasingly taken over tasks previously carried out by the BIA, they have become one of the most important employers in Indian country of the USA. However, as long as income is spent mostly outside the reservation, for lack of adequate facilities on the reservations themselves, economic development cannot take off.

At the same time Grant appointed his former aide, the Seneca Ely S. Parker, as the first Native American to run the BIA. His leadership was so unpopular that it was nearly 100 years before another Native American was appointed to this position in 1965. Since then, however, this post has been firmly in Native American hands.

In Grant's time, indigenous employees in the Indian Service were practically unheard of. This changed during the "Indian New Deal" of the 1930s, when the newly established, partly autonomous tribal administrations created jobs on the reservations, and the BIA also increasingly began to employ Native Americans. Since 1972 they have even enjoyed positive discrimination in appointments and promotions, and today they represent the majority of employees. Soon after, as a reaction to the militant protests against Washington's Indian policies, the head of the BIA was given the status of a deputy Secretary of the Interior.

As the tribes' self-administration expanded – although often accompanied by cuts in its financial and other means – the BIA gradually lost its power and developed into a service organization for the tribes. Although often demanded, its abolition is unlikely as long as there are indigenous peoples in the United States who retain a special legal status.

Occupation of the Bureau of Indian Affairs, Washington, DC., 1972.

Inspired by the Poor People's March of the black Civil Rights Movement, a coalition of Native American groups organized the Trail of Broken Treaties in 1972, which led from the West Coast to a large demonstration in Washington. Accommodation was a problem, so the demonstrators simply occupied the unpopular Indian Bureau. After one week's siege the occupiers left, taking many documents with them. However, the BIA also survived this crisis without undergoing any major changes.

# Nations and citizens

The modern term "nation" is closely associated with the political form of the state, which hardly existed in native North America. However, under the more general meaning of "independent political community," there were hundreds, perhaps even thousands, of "nations," especially since many "peoples" consisted of numerous such "nations," some of which were comprised of only a few families. This was all too complicated for the colonizers who came into contact with these groups, and whenever possible they treated "peoples" or "tribes" as political units with whom, for example, treaties could be concluded. For them, the consent of one single chief or a handful of chiefs was enough to bind a much larger number of independent "nations" to such an agreement.

During the 19th century, "tribe" became the term employed in the United States by the parties in a land cession treaty. The jurists, who tried to define their legal situation often only after the treaties had created these groups, devised the term "domestic, dependent nations." On the one hand this emphasized the traditional sovereignty of these communities, and on the other it clearly underlined their political dependency on the modern nation-state which made them "wards" of the federal government.

With regard to their sovereignty, they were in a position superior to the states of the Union who were prevented from any active

Federal fishery agents and Native American fishers, British Columbia, 1978. Photograph: Wayne Leidenfrost. Vancouver Province, Vancouver, BC.

There were hardly any treaties made during the 19th century on the Canadian west coast in British Columbia. Nevertheless, federal regulations limited indigenous fishing rights to fishing for own use only. After a tightening of these regulations in 1968, police often raided native fishermen. Only in the 1990s did the Canadian Supreme Court uphold the original indigenous fishing rights, as these had never been limited by contract.

involvement in Indian affairs. Thus, until today the tribes and their reservations enjoy special rights as an expression of their remaining aboriginal sovereignty, and are only subject to federal law. These special rights include freedom from taxation. The establishment of separate tribal courts and police forces is also a vestige of earlier autonomy.

Dependence on the federal government is shown by its role as trustee for tribally owned land, which is to protect it against a sell-out. This role of guardian gives the government a special responsibility, which used to express itself through well intentioned but often menacing involvement in the tribes' internal issues. With the implementation of self-determination policies in the late 1970s, the federal government increasingly withdrew from this educational aspect of its parental role.

Already in the middle of the 19th century some treaties contained a clause which provided for an allotment of tribal lands to individual members and the dissolution of tribal lands. At the end of a lenghty period of protection, the individuals were to become tax-paying American citizens. This practice then became the essential provision of the *General Allotment Act* of 1883. However, implementation was a slow process, and a law passed in 1924 made all "Indians" American citizens, even if they were still members of tribes. Soon after, it was recognized that the dissolution of the tribes had been a mistake, and another law, the *Indian Reorganization Act* of 1934, was passed to allow tribes to reestablish themselves or even to organize themselves from scratch, on the condition that they adopt a democratic constitution. This often led to conflict between the remaining traditional chiefs and the elected tribal councils.

Although denied the right to vote in a number of states (such as Arizona) until after World War II, Native Americans as US citizens now enjoy universal civil rights, some of which are in conflict with traditional ways of life. For example, the right to freedom of religion is a contentious issue for the Pueblos who are governed by traditional priesthoods, since adherence to the old religion

**Cut Finger (Southern Arapaho) signs the Declaration of Allegience at El Reno, Oklahoma, June 21, 1913. William Hammond Mathers Museum, Indiana University, Bloomington, IN.**

Like many philanthropists of the time, the department store millionaire John Wanamaker (1838–1922) and his son Rodman (b.1863) regarded the discrimination against Indians as disgraceful for American civilization. To improve their situation, the Wanamakers sponsored an expedition in 1913 through the western reservations to collect oaths of allegience to the United States so that the signatories could obtain citizenship. However, the majority of Native Americans had to wait another 11 years.

is considered to be an important part of their identity. On the other hand it has been found necessary to protect by law the free exercise of traditional religions.

Sylvia S. Kasprycki

# In the shadow of the cross

"When they arrived they had only the Book and we had the land; now we have the Book and they have the land," is the polemical comment that the Sioux writer Vine Deloria Jr. (b. 1933) made in 1969 on more than four centuries of missionary work in North America.

For a long time missionaries were seen as self-sacrificing benefactors and saviors; today many critics – and not only Native American ones – regard them as collaborators with the colonial powers, who paved the way for the submission and exploitation of native societies. The spread of the Christian message among the indigenous inhabitants of the New World did indeed often serve to legitimate the appropriation of land by the conquerors, just as missionary assimilation programs directly or indirectly furthered colonial interests.

However, a sweeping condemnation of all Christian missions does not do justice to the complexity of historical events, nor does it take into account that, in earlier times, attempts to

**Père Nicolas Point: *The Art of Conversion* (1841–1846). Archives des Jésuites, St. Jêrome, QC, Canada.**

Communicating the canon of faith was made difficult not least by language barriers. The use of visual aids to explain more deeply the Christian truths was therefore a popular method trusted by generations of missionaries, regardless of the cultural context of pictorial displays. "I tried very hard to speak to them through pictures," was how the Jesuit Nicolas Point (1799–1868) described his missionary strategies in the mid-19th century. "While the truths found entry to their souls through the eyes, the great virtues filled their hearts."

allow "pagans" to be blessed by God's mercy and become part of a civilization considered to be superior came as much from a humanitarian ideal as do today's claims for religious freedom and cultural equality. The missionaries' innocent contribution to "cultural genocide" lay primarily in the fact that their religious convictions were so closely linked with their own cultural values.

Christianity and "civilization" were almost inseparable concepts, and conversions were not only about introducing a new faith but also about the use of the plow, the adoption of European forms of political organization, clothing, and living, and even the acceptance of new habits of hygiene. Missionaries often tried to realize their utopian ideals of a Christian way of life without the dark sides of civilization precisely in those isolated settlements which were later often overrun by colonial expansion.

How the conversion into civilized Christians was to be actually affected, remained a matter of contention among the many and various denominations: whereas in the 16th and 17th centuries the Franciscans dominated in the southwest and the Jesuits in New France – they were soon succeeded by others, such as the Puritan missions in New England and the Moravian Brothers in Pennsylvania and Ohio – the number of religious groups wishing to contribute to the harvest of Indian souls rapidly increased together with the exploration of the continent. This frantic missionary competition, joined in the 19th century by the Russian Orthodox church (in Alaska) and the Mormons among others, was temporarily stopped when the denominations were given mission monopolies on the reservations under President Grant. Although this regulation was in effect for

Tabernacle decorated with quillwork on birch bark. Ottawa, Cross Village, Michigan, 1848. Museum für Völkerkunde, Vienna, Austria.

Material objects as expressions of cultural values played an important role not only in missionary programs of civilization but also in the practice of religion itself. The use of indigenous materials and techniques for the production of church furnishings and other sacred objects led in many places to a distinctive material culture of Indian Christianity which often expresses the fusion of traditional ideas with Christian thought.

only a few years, it is still reflected in part today in determining the leading the denomination on each reservation.

The reactions of the peoples affected were as varied as the innumerable missionary projects, and they did not simply adopt the stance of passive victims. As long as they more or less retained their way of life, they quite frequently rejected the missionaries altogether. In most cases it was the existential crisis into which many groups were drawn by contact with other cultures that increased their willingness to scrutinize the new religion.

Whereas for some, complete conversion to Christianity and to the way of life connected with it represented a survival tactic in a world increasingly dominated by whites, others were interested only in particular aspects, such as the suspected usefulness of the strange rituals involved in healing the sick.

Elsewhere traditional faiths and Christianity continue to exist side by side up to today. In spite of violent suppression by the Spanish, the Pueblo people of the Rio Grande, for example, still practice their religion in strict separation from Catholicism, which they also practice. Only in a few specific cases, such as in the Peyote religion, did traditional and Christian theories and practices combine to form new, syncretic systems of faith.

Henry Kammler

# A hard schooling

The colonial administrations of North America had little interest in the education of indigenous peoples, and the plans of missionaries to turn Indian children into Christians in seperate schools were not all that promising, as their ideas of education and upbringing were very different from those of the original Americans. For them, corporal punishment of children was mostly unheard of, and misbehavior was usually corrected through derision or the withdrawal of certain benefits.

The different spiritual ideals of education were rooted in the different concepts of different cultures. Unlike the white redeemers, the Native Americans regarded children not as empty containers to be filled with knowledge as effectively as possible, but as autonomous beings who could also possess powers beyond the influence of their parents. A rich store of oral traditions should teach youngsters the rules of behavior without overt coercion.

The missionaries managed to establish at least a few day schools. With a school in each of his fourteen parishes in Massachusetts, John Eliot (1604–1690) was highly successful from 1649 onward among the Wampanoag. His converts even printed their own books.

In the early 19th century the Choctaw and Cherokee established their own schooling systems. By 1853 the Cherokee had 21 schools as well as two colleges with a total of 1,100 students. When this bilingual education system was broken up in the early 20th century, illiteracy was almost unknown among them – a condition not matched by the American school system of the time.

During the final phase of the Indian wars, the American government began to take measures for the education of the minority which was to be assimilated as quickly as possible. The omens were telling: Major Richard H. Pratt (1840–1924) applied the experiences of reeducating Indian prisoners of war in Fort Marion to the boarding school he founded in 1879 in Carlisle, Pennsylvania. It became the

The martyrdom of Jesuit missionaries among the Iroquois. Etching after a painting by Grégoire Huret from François du Creux, *Historiae Canadensis*, Paris 1664. Bibliothèque Nationale de France, Paris, France.

"We all believe in the Great Spirit, but different are the ways leading us to him," was how the Menominee leader Souligny expressed his rejection of a Capuchin preacher's attempts at conversion. Tolerance toward alternative ways of accessing the supernatural was typical of many indigenous religions and contrasted with Christianity's claim to universal validity, for which missionaries were even prepared to suffer a martyr's death.

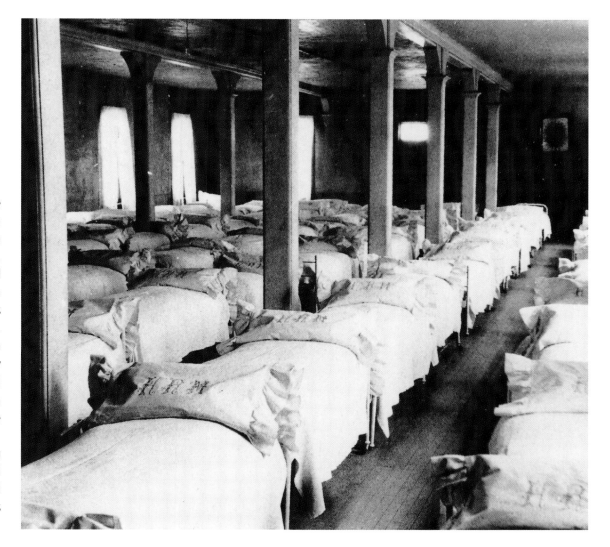

model for many schools throughout the United States and Canada, where children were isolated and persistently alienated from the cultures of their parents. Lack of funds, incapable staff, military drill, violence, and racist ignorance were the order of the day in these schools, which were mostly run by various churches on the behalf of the government. Interpreting Pratt's battle cry "Kill the Indian and save the man!", school personnel saw themselves on the front line of a war, the goal of which was to civilize the Indians. Any breach of the rules, such as speaking one's native tongue, was met with draconian punishment.

Only from the 1930s on was the schooling system gradually relaxed and adapted to local conditions. In Canada it only became at all possible for Indians to attend public schools beyond the eighth grade in the late 1940s.

The establishment of tribally operated schools on a contract basis with the federal government – starting in 1965 with the the Rough Rock Demonstration School among the Navajo – opened an entirely new chapter in Native American education. For the first time Native Americans regained control over their own education. Many indigenous communities decided to follow this path during the years that followed.

In 1969 the Navajo set up the Navajo Community College in Tsaile, a mixture of trade school and high school which also offered preparatory courses to college. Recognizing the developing educational needs, the *Tribally-controlled Community Colleges Act* of 1978 paved the way for Indian colleges. Sinta Gleska College, founded in 1970 and a university since 1992, situated on the Rosebud reservation, became the first Indian college to award a Master of Arts in 1989.

Not all of the 31 Native American colleges in the United States are on reservations. The Native American Educational Services in Chicago, for example, serves the city's large Native American population, while also supporting educational enterprises on reservations in Montana, Dakota, and Wisconsin.

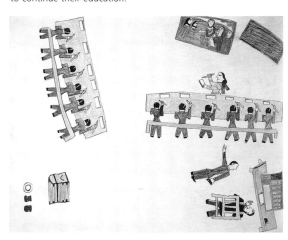

# Red Jacket and the missionary

## A speech (1805)

Red Jacket (c. 1756–1830), a member of the Seneca Wolf clan, was given the rank of merit chief because of his abilities as a speaker and received the name Sagoyewatha ("the one who keeps them awake" – like the howls of wolves keeps human beings awake). His American contemporaries too regarded him as the epitome of a skilled orator, and printed versions of his speeches were met with well-intentioned interest, even though they hardly contained a good word about the whites and their culture.

The following text is Red Jacket's answer to the missionary Joseph Cram's request to build a mission among the Seneca on the Buffalo Creek Reservation. In spite of Red Jacket's rejection, the Presbyterians did open a station in Buffalo Creek in 1811. Their following grew quickly, and in 1827 the Christian party of the Seneca, by now in the majority, were able to depose Red Jacket, a decision that, ironically, was reversed by the Indian Office of the United States so heavily criticized by Red Jacket.

Friend and Brother! It was the will of the Great Spirit that we should meet together this day. He orders all things, and he has given us a fine day for our council. He has taken his garment from before the sun and has caused the bright orb to shine with brightness upon us. Our eyes are opened so that we see clearly. Our ears are unstopped so that we have been able to distinctly hear the words which you have spoken. For all these favors we thank the Great Spirit and him only.

Brother! This council fire was kindled by you. It was at your request that we came together at this time. We have listened with attention to what you have said. You have requested us to speak our minds freely. This gives us great joy, for we now consider that we stand upright before you, and can speak what we think. All have heard your voice and all speak to you as one man. Our minds are agreed.

Brother! You say that you want an answer to your talk before you leave this place. It is right that you should have one, as you are a great distance from home, and we do not wish to detain you. But we will first look back a little, and tell you what our fathers have told us, and what we have heard from the white people.

Brother! Listen to what we say. There was a time when our forefathers owned this great island. Their seats extended from the rising to the setting of the sun. The Great Spirit had made it for the use of Indians. He had created the buffalo, the deer, and other animals for food. He made the bear and the deer, and their skins served us for clothing. He had scattered them over the country, and had taught us how to take them. He had caused the earth to produce corn for bread. All this he had done for his red children because he loved them. If we had any disputes about hunting grounds, they were generally settled without the shedding of much blood. But an evil day came upon us. Your forefathers crossed the great waters and landed on this island. Their numbers were small. They found friends and not enemies. They told us they had fled from their own country for fear of wicked men, and had come here to enjoy their religion. They asked for a small seat. We took pity on them, granted their request and they sat down amongst us. We gave them corn and meat. They gave us poison [spirituous liquor] in return. The white people had now found our country. Tidings were carried back and more came amongst us. Yet we did not fear them. We took them to be friends. They called us brothers. We believed them and gave them a large seat. At length their numbers had greatly increased. They wanted more land. They wanted our country. Our eyes were opened, and our minds became uneasy. Wars took place. Indians were hired to fight against Indians, and many of our people were destroyed. They also brought strong liquors among us. It was strong and powerful and has slain thousands.

Brother! Our seats were once large, and yours were very small; you have now become a great people, and we have scarcely a place left to spread our blankets; you have got our country, but are not satisfied; you want to force your religion upon us.

Brother! Continue to listen. You say that you are sent to instruct us how to worship the Great Spirit agreeably to his mind, and if we do not take hold of the religion which you white people teach, we shall be unhappy hereafter; you say that you are right, and we are lost; how do we know this to be true? We understand that your religion is written in a book; if it was intended for us as well as you, why has not the Great Spirit given it to us, and not only to us, but why did he not give to our forefathers the knowledge of that book, with the means of understanding it rightly? We only know what you tell us about it; how shall we know when to believe, being so often deceived by the white people?

Brother! You say there is but one way to worship and serve the Great Spirit; if there is but one religion, why do you white people differ so much about it? Why not all agree, as you can all read the book?

Brother! We do not understand these things; we are told that your religion was given to your forefathers, and has been handed down from father to son. We also have a religion which was given to our forefathers, and has been handed down to us their children. We worship that way. It teaches us to be thankful for all the favors we receive; to love each other, and to be united; we never quarrel about religion.

Brother! The Great Spirit has made us all; but he has made a great difference between his white and red children; he has given us a different complexion, and different customs; to you he has given the arts; to these he has not opened our eyes; we know these things to be true. Since he has made so great a difference between us in other things, why may we not conclude that he has given us a different religion according to our understanding; the Great Spirit does right; he knows what is best for his children: We are satisfied.

Brother! We do not wish to destroy your religion, or take it from you; we only want to enjoy our own.

Brother! You say you have not come to get our land or our money, but to enlighten our minds. I will now tell you that I have been at your meetings, and saw you collecting money from the meeting. I cannot tell what this money was intended for, but suppose it was for your minister, and if we should conform to your way of thinking, perhaps you may want some from us.

Brother! We are told that you have been preaching to white people in this place: these people are our neighbors, we are acquainted with them: we will wait a little while and see what effect your preaching has upon them. If we find it does them good, makes them honest, and less disposed to cheat Indians, we will then consider again what you have said.

Brother! You have now heard our answer to your talk, and this is all we have to say at present. As we are going to part, we will come and take you by the hand, and hope the Great Spirit will protect you on your journey, and return you safe to your friends.

*(Indian Speeches; delivered by Farmer's Brother and Red Jacket, two Seneca Chiefs.* Canandaigua, New York, 1837).

George Washington peace medal, 1793.
National Archives of Canada, Ottawa, ON.

As the Spanish, French, and British had done, the Americans presented to allied chiefs medals picturing the Great White Father. Because of "the high value the Indians attach to these tokens of friendship," said Thomas McKenney (1785–1859), the first director of the Indian Office, hardly anything concerning the Indians could be achieved without them. The Indian shown has dropped his battle ax in favor of the peace pipe; the background promises an attractive future as a farmer.

George Catlin, *Red Jacket*, watercolor, 1827.
Thomas Gilcrease Institute of American History and Art, Tulsa, OK.

Red Jacket owed the name by which the whites knew him to a red uniform jacket that a British officer gave him as a present in the American War of Independence. Although in subsequent negotiations he never missed an opportunity to criticize the government-sponsored "civilization program," during his visit to Philadelphia in 1792 he received the great peace medal from President Washington (1732–1799), which he wore with great pride even 30 years later.

ARCTIC

Sonja Lührmann

# Arctic Ocean and foggy coast – a cold home

Drifting icebergs in a fiord near Ilulisat (Jakobshavn), on Disko Bay, western Greenland.

On much of the western coast of Greenland the water, warmed by the Gulf Stream, never freezes. Blocks of drift ice usually result from the calving of glaciers.

Inhabitants of temperate zones imagine the Arctic either as a useless desert of ice and snow or as the last wilderness where animals and plants can live undisturbed according to natural cycles. But for the Eskimo and the Aleut this land is home, a place where over centuries their ancestors developed the techniques necessary for exploiting the surprising diversity of resources that exist in these harsh conditions. At the turn of the millennium, these citizens of the United States, Canada, and Greenland have also come to face the consequences of the Arctic's widespread image as an empty, uncultivated land. To governments, the military, and commercial firms, the huge expanse of the icy north seems an ideal place for dumping toxic waste as well as for the ruthless exploitation of mineral resources. Meanwhile, environmental activists have attempted to protect the seemingly untouched, paradisiac wilderness by also attacking the traditional hunting and fishing rights of the original population.

Cultural boundary
International border
State border
Present woodland
Forest tundra
Glacier
Pack ice

150 miles

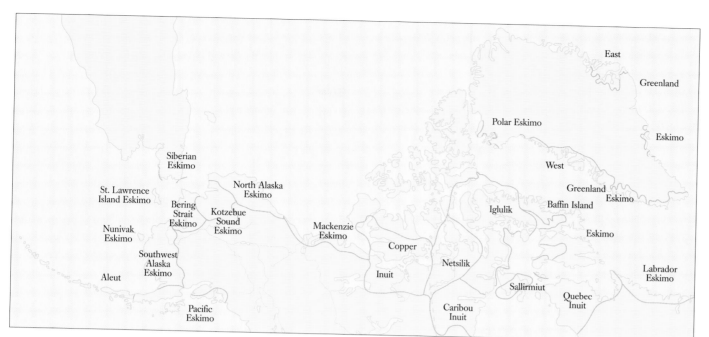

**Peoples of the Arctic.**

The ethnic designations on this map refer mostly to linguistic boundaries or geographical zones. The groupings relevant to the current population range from the old hunting groups and today's village communities, through regional corporations and development agencies, to state and federal governments and the Inuit Circumpolar Conference, an international association of the Inuit and Yupik of Greenland, Canada, Alaska, and Siberia.

East Greenland

Polar Eskimo

Eskimo

Siberian Eskimo

West Greenland Eskimo

North Alaska Eskimo

Iglulik

Baffin Island

St. Lawrence Island Eskimo

Bering Strait Eskimo

Kotzebue Sound Eskimo

Mackenzie Eskimo

Copper

Eskimo

Nunivak Eskimo

Southwest Alaska Eskimo

Netsilik

Labrador Eskimo

Aleut

Inuit

Sallirmiut

Quebec Inuit

Pacific Eskimo

Caribou Inuit

**The edge of the ice sheet.**

The edges of the ice sheet covering Greenland and Baffin Island push out into the ocean as glaciers. There, in a process known as calving, fragments break off and are released into the sea; the largest of these continue to drift south for a long time.

dess et Lith par Choris      Lith de Langlume

# The conquest of the far north

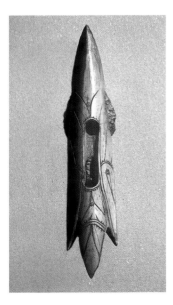

Inuit harpoon point made of walrus ivory and flint, St. Lawrence Island, c. AD 200. University Museum, University of Alaska, Fairbanks, AK.

The holes in the point of a toggle harpoon serves for the attachment of the line which when pulled turns the point sideways in the prey's flesh. Stone blades set in slits on the side give the point its actual sharpness. Harpoon points as used in various Bering Sea cultures in the first millennium AD are attractively shaped and feature engraved decoration. Perhaps the idea that the beauty of the weapon would please the animals and contribute to the hunter's success was already held then.

The home of the Eskimo and the Aleut stretches from the Aleutian Islands in the northern Pacific across the coastal areas of Alaska and northern Canada all the way to Greenland. The ancestors of these people were some of the last immigrants from Asia. Although it is unclear whether this migration took place as early as 8,000 years ago or no more than 5,000 years ago, it can safely be assumed that there were Aleut and Eskimo cultures in Alaska by the beginning of the 3rd millennium BC.

From a starting point more than 4,500 years ago, large parts of the Arctic were occupied for the first time by human settlers. Archeological finds of objects belonging to what is known as the Arctic Small Tool tradition, spreading from Alaska to the eastern Arctic, point to an original population of hunters who, having adopted the Asian bow and arrow, mainly followed the musk ox, but also exploited the resources of the ocean.

The later Dorset culture seems to have started with the onset of a colder climate around the middle of the 1st millennium BC, much further south around Hudson Bay. It already carried unmistakable Eskimo features: People hunted sea mammals using harpoons and lived in semisubterranean earth houses. The people of the Dorset culture introduced the general use of objects such as stone lamps, in which blubber was burned, and blades of ground slate, which became typical of the Eskimo.

At about the time of the Dorset culture, new ways of life adapted to the proximity to the ocean developed in Alaska, apparently under renewed influences from Siberia. It was from here that, from the end of the first millennium BC, the last great eastward migration began. The newcomers,

recognizable as the ancestors of today's Inuit, came equipped with boats and improved harpoons and lived largely from hunting whales and other large marine mammals. This Thule culture, named after a fabled land which according to Antique legend lay in the far north, was able to spread rapidly during this relatively warm period. Due to the mild climate there was much open water, making it easier to hunt whales from boats.

Around AD 1200 the Thule culture had reached Greenland. Many Arctic islands that had been abandoned by their inhabitants in the previous cold phase were settled again. The surviving Dorset communities adopted the Thule people's achievements and also, it seems, their language, which forms the basis of modern Inuktitut. The rapid advance of the Thule culture is the main reason for the great homogeneity of Inuit languages from Alaska to Greenland.

Before the Thule culture reached Greenland, the resident Dorset population had already met Norman settlers. Erik the Red, banned from Iceland for committing murder, founded the colony of "Greenland" on the island in AD 986, establishing the first trading links between Europe and parts of America. The Vikings settled briefly on the coast of Labrador, where they exchanged iron tools for furs and probably also tried to mine for copper and iron. At the beginning of the 11th century, Erik's son Leif Eriksson, who had been raised as a Christian in Norway, founded the first church among the still pagan Normans of Greenland, who gradually converted to Christianity.

In the late 15th century, following a worldwide climatic cooling and the gradual decline of the colony in a Greenland that was no longer green, where animal husbandry and other activities were no longer possible, contact with Europe ceased. The settlers either died from diseases caused by nutritional deficiency, intermarried with the Inuit, or were killed by them. By the time the Danish missionary Hans Egede (1686–1758) came to Greenland in 1721 expecting to convert the Catholic Normans to Protestantism, he did not find them, and instead founded the Godthåb settlement and with it a new Danish colony.

# There is no one Eskimo culture

Although the culture area of the Eskimo and the Aleut is usually thought of as the Arctic, not all peoples mentioned here lived within the Arctic Circle or even in snow and ice all year round. On the islands named after them as well as on the neighboring Alaska Peninsula, the Aleut lived in relative ease in a climate which due to the warm ocean currents was mild, although very humid. An ice free sea gave them the opportunity to hunt whales, sea lions, and other kinds of seal, as well as to catch fish.

The Koniag and the Chugach ("Pacific Eskimo") on the Pacific coast of southern Alaska settled partly in wooded areas similar to the adjacent culture area of the Northwest Coast. Here meat from sea mammals as well as plentiful salmon could feed permenant settlements of several hundred people. The river deltas of the Yukon and the Kuskokwim offered the Yupik a wide range of water fowl and game as well as the annual runs of salmon heading upstream to higher forested regions, where they spawned in clear freshwater lakes.

The Inupiaq, who lived on the northern shores of the Bering Sea and the coast of the Arctic Ocean subsisted primarily on whales and had developed great skills in hunting them. Toward the end of the 19th century, Inupiaqs were hired on various occasions to assist American whalers in their work. The latter often took them to the estuary of the Mackenzie River in northern Canada, where they intermarried with the local population, whose numbers had been severely reduced by disease. Their present-day descendants refer to themselves as Inuvialuit.

Far away from the warm ocean currents, the Copper Inuit, the Netsilik, and the Iglulik of the central Canadian

Opposite page (above):

Louis Choris, *View of the harbor at Onnalaschka* **(Kapitanskaya haven)**. Color lithograph from his *Voyage pittoresque autour du monde*, Paris, 1822. University of Washington Libraries, Seattle, WA.

The climate of the Aleutian Islands is marked by the mild ocean current, but also by frequent rain and powerful storms. On these grassy islands without large game, both food and wood for houses and tools came from the ocean. The settlements of earth houses lay in protected bays of river deltas. Illyulyuk (today Oonalaska) became one of the main supports for the Russian colonization of Alaska as well as a supply harbor for travel in the North Pacific and northward toward the Bering Sea and the Arctic Ocean.

Family from Ilulisat (Jakobshavn), West Greenland, 1877. Rautenstrauch-Joest-Museum für Völkerkunde, Cologne, Germany

The man Okabek, the woman Maggek, and their daughters Ane and Katarine formed the core of a troupe of Eskimo who were displayed in Germany in 1877/8 as curious inhabitants of the North. All of them are wearing the short Greenlandic parkas which had come into fashion since the 19th century. The woman's married status is indicated by her topknot.

Arctic were exposed to the harshest climatic conditions endured by any polar population. Storms whipped the open plains, and not infrequently temperatures dropped to below minus 60° F. Over the duration of their short summer, small family bands of Copper Inuit and Netsilik moved slowly across the tundra in pursuit of caribou, the wild American relatives of the Eurasian reindeer, which flock northward in summer and return south to the treeline in winter. At that time, the people would move on to the icy surface of the frozen ocean, where several family groups would settle together in large winter villages of igloos. Here they lived mostly by hunting seal. Camouflaged in white fur, the hunters waited at the animals' breathing holes in the ice and with some luck were able to harpoon their prey.

Nightmute fishing settlement, Alaska, c. 1975.

To this day, many Yupik spend part of the year in coastal fishing camps consisting of tents or smaller houses. The people of Nightmute, in the interior of Nelson Island, use Umkumiut, on the Bering Sea. Driftwood logs were once the only wood available on this treeless tundra.

Kuugmiut woman with oil lamp, Wainwright, North Alaska, 1921. Denver Museum of Natural History, Denver, CO.

The invention of the oil lamp made it possible to obtain light and heat without using precious supplies of wood, thus making life in the Arctic much easier.

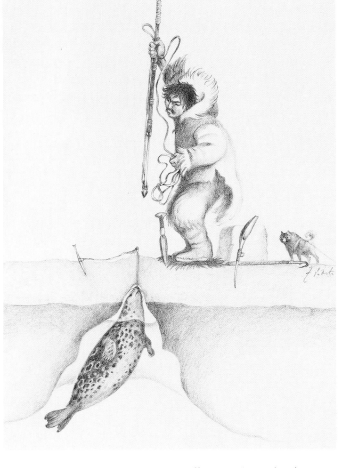

Seal gnawing at the ice to make a breathing hole.

Seals gnaw a breathing hole in the ice from below. As they must prevent it from freezing over, a hunter can be sure that some prey will surface for a breath of air and to maintain the hole. A tiny exhalation gives away the seal's presence. Polar bears are able to smell animals beneath the ice; humans place a tiny stick in the hole to indicate when the prey is there.

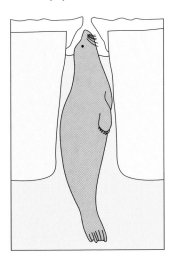

On Baffin Island, home of the Iglulik, the older, more experienced hunters hunted walruses on the ice floes, while inland the younger men with their families tried to get as much meat from the caribou and musk ox as they could before returning to the coast in the fall. Here they would spend the winter on the ice, living in large communities. The seasonal movement between summer hunting grounds and winter settlements ended for the Inuit in the 20th century, as they settled permanently near missions, trading posts, and military stations.

The Inuit of Labrador, east of Hudson Bay, also moved inland during the summer and returned to the icy coast as the days grew shorter. In this dark season, veiled by the northern lights, they would spend their time hunting seal, catching birds and fish, and dancing and storytelling. However, the distances that they covered in their seasonal wanderings were shorter than those of the caribou hunters of the central Arctic.

The Greenland Inuit were restricted to the coastal strip, and therefore to the consumption of aquatic animals, by the uninhabitable glaciers covering the greater part of their island. They hunted several types of seal, walrus, and sometimes whales.

From a linguistic point of view, Aleut is but a very distant relative of the Eskimoan languages, which themselves are by no means uniform. Spoken by peoples living west and south of the Bering Sea, the five Yupik languages are spoken from western and southern Alaska to the opposite Siberian coast. They are bordered to the north and east by the six Inuit-Inupiaq languages spoken across northern Canada all the way to Greenland. These languages are so similar to

each other that, with a little effort, a Greenlander can communicate with a Canadian Eskimo.

The terms Yupik, Inupiaq, and Inuit are derived from the word for "human being," *yuk* or *inuk*, respectively. In Alaska the collective term for the Yupik and Inupiaq is "Eskimo." This description is considered derogatory by many in Canada, where the term "Inuit" is officially preferred. In this book, "Inuit" is applied only to those peoples who refer to themselves by this name in their own language.

From the late 18th century until 1867, when it was sold to the United States, Alaska was the easternmost extremity of the Russian empire, which really managed to control only the southern coastal areas. Aleut, Koniag, and Yupik hunted sea otters and other fur animals for the Russians. On the eastern side of the continent, Danish, Dutch, and British whalers appeared around Labrador and Baffin Bay as early as the 17th century.

For a long time, the Inuit of the central Arctic only intermittently encountered ships on daring expeditions searching for the Northwest Passage, the legendary northern sea route to Asia. After 1900, increasing numbers of fur traders found their way to this isolated area. It was only after World War II that radical changes in northern Canada and Alaska were brought about by the construction of military installations in the course of the Cold War and the commercial exploitation of Arctic oil and gas resources.

However, the original inhabitants of the Arctic generally remained the majority population in the area. Therefore, regional autonomy, established in Greenland in 1979 and in Nunavut in the former Northwest Territories of Canada in

Eskimo beside his winter stores.

In the icy temperatures of the Arctic, prey animals froze very quickly. Although the food did not spoil in this natural freezer, these winter supplies had to be kept in pits, rocky recesses, or under heaps of rock to protect them from raids by hungry sled dogs or other predators.

The *Neptune* in winter quarters at Cape Fullerton, 1903/04. National Archives of Canada, Ottawa, ON.

Even the *Neptune*, anchored in the Iglulik area, was transformed into a snow house in this landscape of snow and ice that made such great impressions on travelers. The people who seemed literally to live in the snow embodied the archetypal Eskimo in the European imagination, although only a small proportion of the inhabitants of the Arctic built permanent winter dwellings out of snow.

1999, offers the opportunity of intergrating indigenous languages and traditions in the political structures.

In the early 1990s, Alaska was home to about 4,400 Koniag and Chugach, 2,600 Aleut, 27,000 Yupik, and 16,500 Inupiaq, while there were 31,000 Inuit living in Canada and 46,400 in Greenland. Additionally there were around 900 Yupik and about 300 Aleut on the Russian side of the Bering Strait. At the time of the first contact with Europeans, numbers are estimated at 75,000 Eskimo in total and 10,000 to 12,000 Aleut.

# Between ocean and tundra

**Eskimo in Canada.**

An Eskimo hunter and his kayak form a close-knit unit. These excellent navigators often spent hours in their fast vessels, never losing their orientation even when they could no longer see land. As a sports boat the kayak attracted much attention in Scotland, when in 1815 in Leith the Greenlander Hans Zakæus won a race in his kayak against a whaling boat with a crew of six strong oarsmen.

*Five men in three kayaks, fishing on water near the shore.* Drawing by Henry W. Elliott, 1872. National Anthropological Archives, Smithsonian Institution, Washington, DC.

The Koniag shown here avoid the danger of capsizing while fishing for halibut by using two kayaks to support each other, with one man ready to beat the strong fish to death immediately. The men's waterproof jackets are made out of gutskin and are tied to the manholes of the kayak so that no water could enter the vessel even if it capsized. In this event the paddlers would right the kayak by executing the famous Eskimo roll. On a hunt for sea mammals in the western Arctic, the man sitting in the front of a two-hole kayak would hold the harpoon, while the one in the back would paddle.

The migrations of whales through the ocean, of salmon upriver to their spawning grounds, and of herds of caribou between their winter and summer pastures make the Arctic a great provider of seasonally varying but generally reliable food sources. To make the best use of this, most human inhabitants of the Arctic also undertook seasonal migrations between the different fishing and hunting grounds on the coast and inland on tundras and by rivers. In all these areas, their survival depended upon the use of particular techniques, tools, and rules.

## The ocean: cornucopia and freeway

In Greenland, the seal hunt was an important part of gathering food all year round, although the seasons defined its operation. In winter, seals could be caught only on the surface of the ice, using a method typical of the Inuit. Motionless and holding his lethal harpoon, the hunter would wait, often for hours, at a breathing hole until a seal came up for air. This required immense patience, for seals can stay under water for 20 minutes and have numerous breathing holes, making it practically impossible to predict when they will appear at a particular spot near the surface. To increase the likelihood of a strike, the men would often encourage their wives and children to take up position at other breathing holes and make a lot of noise so as to drive the animals away. Eventually the seals would come up at that breathing hole where the hunter was lying in wait.

In summer, seal and other smaller sea mammals such as the sea otter were hunted from kayaks. Used all over the Arctic, this boat consists of a wooden frame covered with leather, with a circular opening in the center for the paddler. (In Alaska kayaks might have two openings, and in colonial times there were even three for the transport of passengers.) These holes can be closed watertight around the paddler, who himself wears a waterproof jacket made of seal gut or skin, leaving only his hands and his face exposed. Such protection was an important prerequisite to avoid the constantly present threat of freezing to death.

Their remarkable construction alone makes kayaks fast and easy to maneuver, but their full potential is really brought out by the skill of the paddler. The best-known technique is undoubtedly the Eskimo or kayak roll, when the paddler of a capsizing kayak saves himself from drowning by swinging himself and the boat back to an upright position.

In a volume of the yearbook *Atuagagdliutit* ("Shipping Around the Coast"), published in Greenland since 1861, the seal hunter Petrus Lynge from Napassok, western Greenland, described in the late-19th-century for his fellow countrymen the arduous process of learning this art: "Father forced me to learn capsizing and coming up again as befitted a true kayak man. I was close to tears out of unwillingness, but I made no objections, as he was my father, after all. He carried out the training himself and started by tipping me to the side while holding on to the stern-post of my kayak. However, if I hesitated and could not be bothered to start throwing myself around, he would do it for me and would hold me under water for not exactly a short time until he allowed me to come up again. In this way he continued the practice until I got as far as looking forward to it and at last learned how to come back out my own strength."

Lynge also had good advice for those unable to manage the Eskimo roll, which indicates just what strong nerves were expected of a man floating upside down with his head in cold water: "At this point I want to give my opinion on leaving or not leaving the kayak when it has capsized. In my view, if there is the possibility of help from another kayak man, then you should not crawl out under any circumstances until the other has reached you, as this makes the work of the one who has come to your aid much less difficult. [The one who has capsized sticks his hand or his paddle out of the water, and the helper grabs hold of the

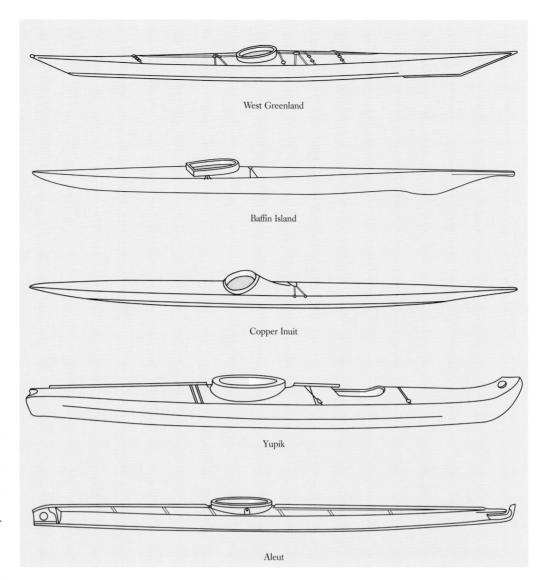

West Greenland

Baffin Island

Copper Inuit

Yupik

Aleut

hand and pulls him back to an upright position.] It also reduces our own suffering considerably, as we will not be as wet and cold as if we had been outside of the kayak in the water. I have had an experience in this regard and at the time when I had not yet learned to get back up by my own strength."

In the hunt for larger prey – such as whales and in particular the gray whale, the humpback whale, the beluga whale, and the narwhal – groups of hunters went out in *umiaks*, large, open boats made of leather that could each hold up to 50 people, with the oarsmen sitting along the vessel's sides. The frame of an *umiak* consisted of driftwood and whale bone (it took a while to collect enough of these valuable construction materials) covered with walrus skin. The large vessels were also the most important means of transport along the coasts or up fiords and rivers. They could carry all household goods and the greater part of the family as well as any kayaks not in use.

Types of Eskimo and Aleut kayaks.

The Yupik model shows the raised bow typical of southern Alaskan kayaks as well as a second seat for a passenger in front of the paddler's cockpit. The Aleut kayak is called baidarka and is distinguished by a forked bifid bow.

Kayak model of the eastern Arctic type (Greenland and Labrador). Canadian Museum of Civilization, Hull, QC.

The hunters kept all their equipment under the straps on the boat's surface. It remained secure even when the kayak capsized and the paddler had to perform a kayak roll. Behind the seat is a bladder float for harpoon hunting, while the harpoon itself is at the front on the right. At the back there are two multipronged bird spears.

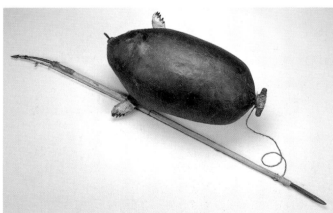

Harpoon with float made of seal skin, probably from Alaska, c. 1900. Canadian Museum of Civilization, Hull, QC.

This air filled float connected to the harpoon prevented the prey from going under water and sapped its strength. At the same time it marked the animal's location. The orifices (limbs, anus, neck) are tied with string. The nub at the front is shut by a wooden plug which can be pulled out so that the float can be inflated.

The invention of the toggle harpoon made hunting from boats considerably easier. This type of harpoon consists of a spear with a point that can be disconnected from the shaft. Once lodged in the animal's body, the point can be twisted by the hunter pulling on the harpoon's line so that the animal cannot escape. After the point is disconnected, the shaft through which the line is threaded also lies at right angles to the animal's axis and provides another obstacle to escape, as does the inflated float made of seal skin which makes it impossible for the prey to dive away. Still in use today, this type of harpoon is particularly effective in waters with drifting ice floes, where a long shaft with a simple hook would simply break off.

The Aleut and Koniag hunted whales from their kayaks. The danger of a single kayak being pulled under water or out to sea by a harpooned whale, however, posed too great a risk. So, using a spear, they tried to cause fatal injury to the animal, in the hope that the cadaver would then be washed up on the beach. The chances of success in killing the whale were heightened by rubbing poison on the tip of the spear.

Inuit on the hunt.

From the modern boat that has replaced the kayak and the *umiak*, the Inuit hunter is ready to launch his sharp-bladed harpoon at a seal, while the man standing behind him holds the line. The skin of large seals is so thick that it can be split lengthwise and can only be pierced by a heavy harpoon or by bullets shot from a gun.

Opposite page (left):

Principle of the toggle harpoon.

The point of the harpoon penetrates the skin and blubber, while the foreshaft and shaft disengage, leaving the point connected to the line (a rigid shaft would be broken by the seal's violent struggles). The animal dives away quickly, thereby pulling on the line, which makes the harpoon's tip turn like a toggle in the flesh. Now there can be no escape, for even when the hunter lets go of the line, the float attatched to it marks the location of the seal.

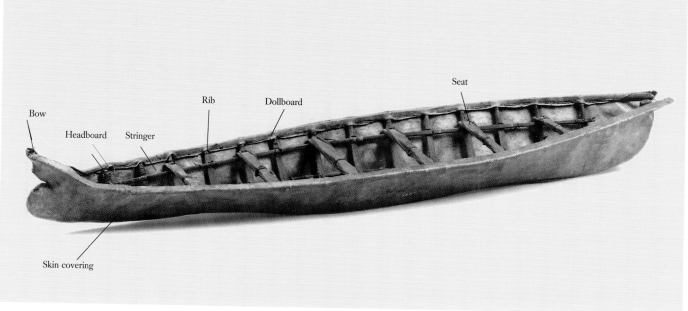

Bow

Headboard    Stringer

Rib    Dollboard

Seat

Skin covering

Model of an *umiak*, Yupik or Chugach, southwestern Alaska, c. 1900. Rautenstrauch-Joest-Museum für Völkerkunde, Cologne.

Although generally referred to as a woman's boat, as women did not use kayaks, the umiak also served men on whale hunts. Umiaks were also used when settlements were moved; laden with household equipment and also extra kayaks, they were rowed by women, who sat facing the stern.

"Seal party" of a family in Tunuak, Nelson Island, Alaska, c. 1975.

A Yupik family celebrate their son's first successful seal hunt with a seal party, where the meat is distributed into the guests' pails. Older people, who no longer hunt, are particularly well supplied on such occasions.

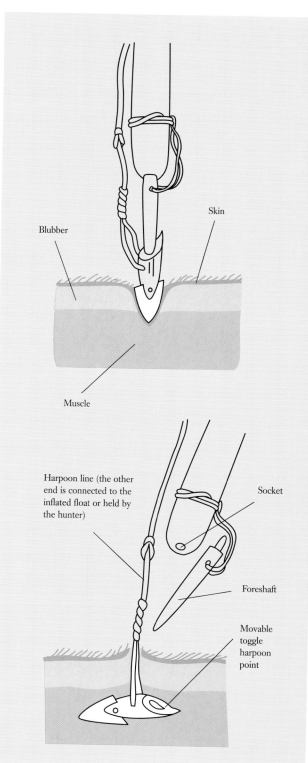

Blubber

Skin

Muscle

Harpoon line (the other end is connected to the inflated float or held by the hunter)

Socket

Foreshaft

Movable toggle harpoon point

# On the trail of the caribou

Chasing herds of fast-moving caribou would hardly have been a promising endeavor. Instead, hunters preyed on them along their migration routes. By closely observing weather conditions and the movement of the herds, and being guided by oracles of shamans, who had been asked for their advice, they decided on the most advantageous locations for hunting.

In the central Arctic, hunters preferred to move to shallow parts of lakes and rivers on the tundra, where the caribou could easily be killed from a kayak as they crossed the water. To steer herds toward particular fords, hunters used *inuksuit* ("they look like people"), human-size piles of stone which lined a path narrowing in a V-shape. Shying away from their supposed captors, the caribou would keep to the track set out for them, which steered them to a particularly advantageous point on the river. Slowed down by the water, the animals could easily be killed by piercing

their sides, and as the carcasses did not sink immediately, a large number of caribou could be caught in this way, the bodies being gathered up after the hunt was over.

When there were no *inuksuit*, women and children would take on the role of beaters. When there were no appropriate stretches of water, the hunters would build a stone enclosure into which the animals would be driven and where spears could be hurled at them more easily. The drawback of hunting on open ground or even at narrow passes was that the animals, often only injured, would run off with the valuable arrow or spear points in their bodies and often die much later, of advantage only to wolves and arctic foxes.

The Eskimo also made use of plants as food resources. From the ocean, women gathered various kinds of seaweed, which was dried for storage. On land they dug up starchy roots, and moss containing vitamins was widely used as an accompaniment to meat and fish. The Eskimo's vitamin and mineral supply was relatively balanced, except in times of scarcity. Meat was largely eaten fresh and raw, making

Fleeing caribou.

These wild reindeer nicely show their soft, cloven hoofs, which prevent the animals from sinking into the snow in winter and into mud in summer. Snowshoes, which are a great advantage for the Inuit when they hunt other deer, which sink into the snow, are of no use to the hunters here.

optimal use of its vitamins. Seal oil was used as a source of
vitamins, as medicine, for preserving dried meat and fish,
and last but certainly not least as fuel for oil lamps.

However, contrary to a widespread assumption, the
Eskimo did not eat only raw meat. Food was cooked, even
if only slightly, using oil lamps or fires fueled by oil and
bone. In the treeless areas of the Arctic, driftwood would
have been far too precious to use as firewood.

Even those groups who did not migrate between the
coast and the interior often maintained close relations with
the residents of other areas. The Nunamiut of inland Alaska,
and the Caribou Inuit west of the Hudson Bay, lived inland
all year round only coming to the coast to trade with the
local population, exchanging caribou skins for seal oil,
which they needed as a source of fat and fuel.

The Nunamiut's trading partners were the whale-hunters
living on the coast between Point Hope and Point Barrow.
In spring, they went out in umiaks to catch the whales
which came close to the coast in channels carved out of the
ice by warm ocean currents. Even today, in spite of a
general ban on whale-hunting the inhabitants of these
villages catch a few whales every year as part of a quota
agreement, not only to supplement their meat supply, but
also to strengthen community ties by the ritual sharing of
the catch.

Team of dogs.

In the eastern Arctic, dogs are usually harnessed on seperate lines attatched to the sled in fan-shape. This method offers no major advantages or disadvantages compared to harnessing dogs in pairs, although their pulling power is not used to its optimum.

A sled made of fish.

In many parts of the Arctic this only happens in emergencies, but in the central Arctic, where wood is scarce, a sled improvised out of frozen fish is an everyday affair. The fish are wrapped in two wet seal skins (top) and the two rolls are tied as tight as possible (center). Ribs made of antlers or bone are then attached to connect the two rolls (below). The runners are covered with a mass of moist ground moss and doused several times in water, which freezes immediately and forms a smooth surface. This is polished with a piece of wet bear fur to reduce friction as much as possible. Upon arrival, the sled can be eaten.

# Across the ice – at twelve dog power ...

Dog sleds were once important means of transportation for nearly all Eskimo groups. The sled frames were made of driftwood or bone and had runners fashioned of the same materials, although in emergencies the inventive inhabitants of the Arctic made improvised runners out of leather that was rolled up when wet and then frozen, or even out of frozen fish.

A team of dogs was an essential part of every household. A responsible owner would care well for his sled dogs, feeding them with an appropriate portion of the hunt to ensure a reliable means of transportation. The tough, thick-coated huskies were bred by the Eskimo for the purpose of drawing sleds, and much time was spent on their training.

Assembling a team of up to twelve dogs required special care. The dogs had to be well trained and the hierarchy within the pack firmly established. Any fights within the team led at the very least to a lot of tangled-up leads. The lead dog was especially important, serving as a guide for the others to follow. An unreliable team could mean death for the driver.

Dogs were also loyal helpers, locating seals' breathing holes, which were often covered with snow, or scenting musk oxen, polar bears, or snowy owls, all of them desirable prey for the Eskimo. The sedantery Koniag and the Chugach of south Alaska and some of the Yupik on the Bering Strait, however, also regarded dogs as a source of fresh meat, as here the dog sled played a far less prominent role. In South Alaska, which is relatively free of snow, dogs were used as pack animals for hunting on land. Larger distances, on the other hand, were usually covered by traveling on water.

In winter people lived on their stores of food, continued with a little hunting and fishing with nets under the ice, and took the opportunity to travel by sled across areas and rivers that were too difficult or even dangerous to negotiate during summer, in order to attend feasts and ceremonies being held in other villages.

## From dried meat to canned fish

Today, the yearly round and the various tools in use are different. Most families live in permanent settlements equipped with electricity and provided with schools and social institutions. The dog sled is popular for sport among whites too, but as a practical means of general transportation it has been replaced by the snowmobile (or "metal dog"), just as motorboats and guns have also come into general use. This means that, to supply a family with meat and fur from the hunt alone, large amounts of capital are required. Income from casual work or welfare payments is used to purchase hunting equipment, and sometimes a family member will hold one of the few permanent jobs in the village.

In southern Alaska and Greenland, commercial fishing is of great importance: together with work in fish canneries it provides cash, while seals are caught for private consumption. Young people often spend most of the year at far-away schools, and then return in summer to participate in their families' hunting and fishing trips. Although living a more settled life, many families, particularly in rural areas, are able to satisfy their taste for traditional food and to soften the impact of high unemployment in this way. However, in the cities of Alaska, Canada, and Greenland increasing numbers of Eskimo make a living entirely from wage labor and have access to their traditional diet only through relatives they may have still living in the "bush."

Colony of sea lions on the coast.

In spring, thousands of sea lions gather on the rocky coast of southwestern Alaska. The Aleut, Koniag, and Chugach regarded them as a welcome change in diet during their short stay in Alaska and hunted them on land.

## By Alaska's rivers

In the inhospitable central Arctic, land and sea are covered with ice and snow for up to nine months of the year. Spring and fall were particularly hard for the Eskimo, as moving around during these seasons was beset with hidden dangers. Heavy ice floes would drift too close to each other for kayaks to be able to get through, and wet snow and melting ice made travel by dog sled difficult and often risky. In the fall the ice cover was often unpredictably thin, and dogs teams could easily fall through into the icy waters beneath.

In summer, lasting from June through September, the salmon hunters of southern Alaska would pitch camp by the deltas or riverbanks where large families would catch salmon in weirs or nets and dry them for the winter. The sea lions and seals that came to the coast in spring to warm themselves in the sun were easy targets for the hunters' ready harpoons.

Women would spend the fall gathering sweet berries to provide a vegetable accompaniment to an otherwise rather monotonous diet consisting almost entirely of animal flesh. Migrating birds would return to their breeding grounds in the early summer. They were hunted with spears and bolas made of leather strings, with stone or bone weights at the end, that could be hurled at the prey. Fur-bearing animals were caught in various kinds of traps, and sea otters killed with spears wielded from kayaks.

Meat hanging out to dry outside a house, Nuuk, Greenland.

For many Greenlanders, the meat from their own hunt is still an essential part of their everyday diet. This is also the case in Nuuk (Godthåb), the capital city of Greenland, where meat hung up to dry on the outside of houses is an everyday sight.

**Herd of musk ox by the Coppermine River, Northwest Territories, Canada.**

When they sense danger, the healthy adult animals form a circle to protect the young and the weak inside. This keeps wolves at bay, but not people with guns. The Eskimo used to avoid the musk ox, who also played little part in their mythology. Today their numbers are so reduced that they are very rarely seen.

**Selling the musk ox heads, Kalaaliaraq, Greenland, 1994.**

Hunting musk ox with traditional Inuit weapons was a dangerous undertaking. After the gun was introduced musk ox became easy prey, because their typical response to an attack is not to flee but to build a solid line of defense to protect the weaker animals. Although not originally their home, some musk ox have been introduced to southwestern Alaska, where an Eskimo cooperative sells knitwear made from their wool.

## Female survival arts

"When a mother loses a husband, she can sew, or she can get food by begging or working for it. But when a husband loses a wife, he can't do anything."

This is how Bessie Ericklook, from Nuiqsut in northwestern Alaska, evaluates the contributions of women and men to their life together. Sewing is so important because making clothes that could give protection against the extreme cold was essential to survival in the Arctic. A man's hunting skills were nothing without a woman who could supply him with clothes.

The Arctic and Subarctic were the only areas in North America where the indigenous inhabitants made tailored clothes to fit the body exactly. Eskimo women spent much time and creativity in making clothing such as the parka or anorak – words that have entered the vocabulary of European languages – out of single pieces of fur cut exactly to the individual wearer's measurements. The *ulu*, or woman's knife, was used for cutting out the pieces for a garment, and bone needles and animal sinews were used for sewing.

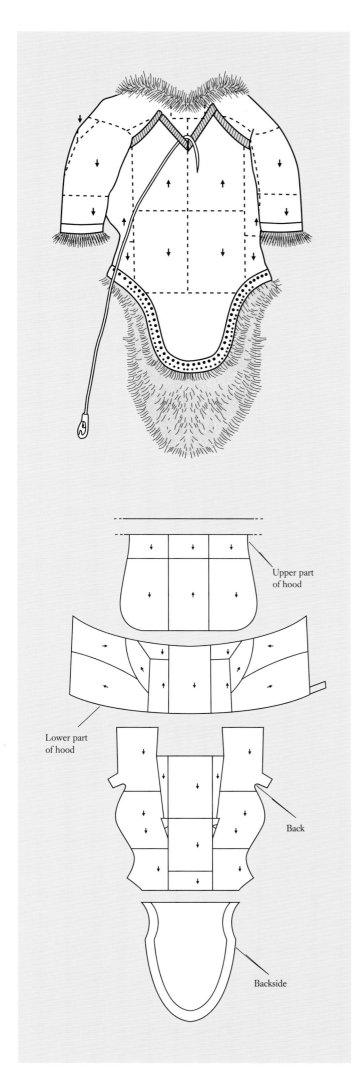

Upper part
of hood

Lower part
of hood

Back

Backside

In winter, central Arctic men and women wore double-layered anoraks, the inner layer next to the skin with the fur facing in for warmth, and the outer layer with the fur facing out. The latter was often decorated with bands and patchwork made of different furs to impress both other people and hunting prey. The decorative borders indicated the wearer's exact origins. Women wore anoraks with particularly wide hoods in which they could easily carry small children on their back.

Protective talismans and amulets were worn over the inner anorak. The warmest anoraks were made of two layers of caribou skin, for long-time protection against temperatures as low as minus 60° F for a longer period of time. All sewing work on the fresh caribou skins had to be completed before the move to the winter ocean ice, as it was believed that mixing the hunt of land animals with that of sea mammals would bring bad luck. Seal skin was also used for pants and for summer anoraks.

White Alaskans called the Eskimo's boots *mukluks,* after the Yupik word for the bearded seal whose skin was used to make them. The sole was made of rawhide, turned up at the sides to keep out water. Clothes for the upper body were taken off as often as possible – and always indoors – and turned inside out in order to allow condensation and sweat to dry off. Through slow movements sweating was kept to a minimum, because frost penetrating through moist layers of leather down to wet skin could mean death by freezing.

The Yupik, who lived in a milder climate, wore less tightfitting clothes. Their parkas reached below the knee, and on the lower body they wore leggings and boots made of fur or fish skin. Socks, woven of grass and changed frequently, absorbed sweat from the feet, as wet feet are particularly susceptible to freezing. Waterproof parkas made of strips of sea lion gut or fish skin were worn in wet weather. They were also part of the equipment for hunting in a kayak; the hunter fastened the bottom seam to the kayak's cockpit's rim to protect his whole body against the waves. On the Aleutian Islands, this item of clothing (called *kamleika*

An *ulu,* the woman's knife and a universal tool. Smithsonian Institution, Washington, DC.

The *ulu* was used for cutting up meat, scraping animal skins, and cutting pieces of leather to measure, and as a knife when eating. This specimen has a metal blade and an ivory handle. Originally the blades were made of slate, while the handle could also be worked in bone or wood.

Left:
Pattern for a woman's parka made from the skin of 22 eider ducks, Belcher Island, Quebec.

The Inuit women of Labrador displayed masterful skill in making parkas from bird skin, which produces very light clothing. The separate parts, otherwise usually cut from caribou or seal skin, had to be put together from the individual small bird skins. The feathered side was always turned inward. The little arrows indicate the direction of the feathers. The tails that are sewed onto the bottom seam symbolize the female reproductive organs.

A woman cutting small leather pieces from caribou skin.

Modern and festive clothing is often pieced together from different types of fur to form a decorative pattern.

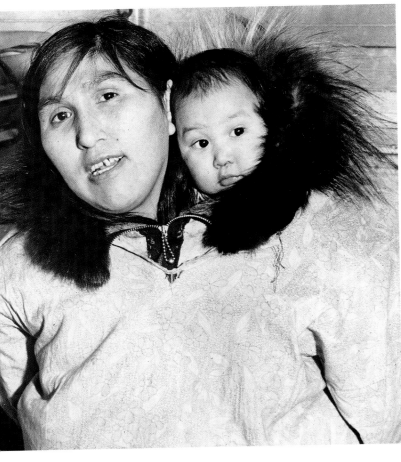

by the Russians) formed part of the taxes that the local inhabitants had to pay the Russian colonial authorities. While the men hunted sea otters, the women made parkas and *kamleikas* to equip their men and the Russian traders for the coming year. Even after the spread of European clothes, the *kamleika* remained in use as an effective rain garment.

The clothes of the Aleut, Koniag, and Chugach were even lighter than those of the Yupik. Men and women wore long gowns without hoods. They were made of entire bird skins sewn together. In colonial times the use of such clothing increased as the furs of sea otters, which had been very popular, had to be delivered to the Russians. According to early descriptions, the Aleut often went barefoot when it was not too cold, before they were introduced to Russian and Siberian boots.

The social hierarchy of these Pacific groups – there were rich village chiefs who inherited their position, as well as commoners, and a small number of slaves – was also expressed in aspects of their clothing. Members of the upper stratum sported special costumes and ornaments, such as colorfully painted hunting hats decorated with ivory figures, to distinguish themselves from the general population and from the slaves.

# Igloo and Qasgiq – houses and their inhabitants

## Built of snow ...

*Igloo* is the Eskimo word for "house" and by no means refers only to the domed habitation of snow blocks that is generally regarded as the typical Eskimo residence. Most Eskimo spent the winter in stone, wooden, or earth houses, and passed the summer in tents made of caribou skin. Nevertheless the snow igloo justifiably enjoys a high level of recognition: discovering the principle of the true vault in the Arctic ice independently of the architects of the Old World can be seen as nothing less than a cultural-historical masterstroke. Standing on the inside of the future house, the igloo's builder positions row upon row of snow blocks, reducing the radius toward the top of the dome. The final snow block must be inserted from the outside. Small igloos such as these could be put up in a very short space of time and made a passable winter shelter. In the more permanent settlements of the central Arctic the igloos measured over six feet across and were inhabited for several months.

## House and boat

Eskimo households were organized around the women. Apart from the *ulu*, the women's knife, a married woman's important possessions included a lamp, which was central

Building an igloo, Whale Cove, Nunavut.

For shelter against bad weather two hunters can build an igloo out of the hard-packed arctic snow in less than an hour. First they mark out the hut's circumference then, using their snow knives, they cut the first snow blocks from within the circle. This makes the floor of the igloo slightly lower than the surrounding ground level.

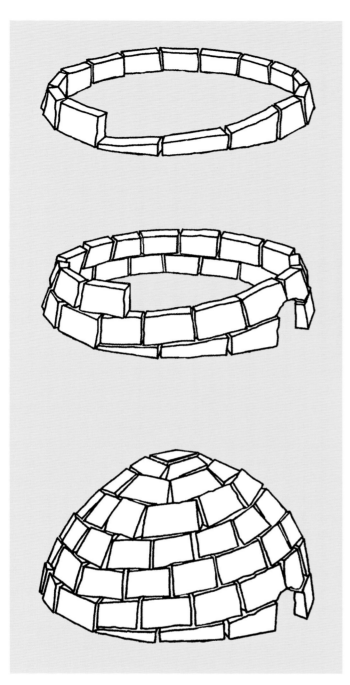

to the household: it took the form of a stone bowl in which seal oil was burned. This lamp was essential in every winter dwelling both as a stove and as a source of light and heat.

Winter houses were built of stone and grass sods in Greenland, of snow in the central Arctic, and of earth and wood in Alaska, where they were semisubterranean. They usually housed several families. The Koniag lived in virtual village-houses; each family had its own room, which was reached from a central room accessible through a hatch in the roof. A house like this could contain 40 or more residents. Yupik women shared a large house with their sisters, each of whom had her own oil lamp for cooking. The house consisted of a single semisubterranean room and was entered through a low tunnel. Yupik men and boys resided in the *qasgiq*, an assembly house of which every village would have at least one, and only came on visits to the house of their wives, mothers, or sisters.

The Inupiaq whale hunters around Point Barrow on the northern coast of Alaska also had such men's houses, which were called *qarigi* in their language (a word that corresponds exactly to the Yupik *qasgiq*). Every *qarigi* belonged to an *umialik* ("owner of an *umiak*"). *Umialiks* were successful whale hunters and leaders of their chosen umiak crew. They controlled the distribution of the meat of the killed whale among crew members and their families and were often decision makers in important questions of everyday village life.

Just as the *umialik*'s boat secured the basic foods, and the men had a space in society in the form of the *umialik*'s assembly house, the *umialik*'s wife also had an extremely important role to play. Not only was she responsible for the boat's equipment, she contributed through magic to the hunt's success. She was thought to be spiritually related to the *umialik*'s prey, so during the hunt she had to lie down at home and be as still and as resigned to her fate as the

Igloo construction, the keystone.

The shelter is nearly finished: only the final block is not in place. The igloo's dome shape makes the structure so stable that a person can walk on top of it without it caving in.

Wooden snow shovel with leather handle. Canadian Museum of Civilization, Hull, QC.

Its blade reinforced with bone, the shovel is used to pile up snow on the outside of the igloo so as to improve insulation.

Building a snow house.

To build an igloo, blocks of snow about one foot long are stacked up on each other in spiral fashion (top). When the second layer is finished, a low entrance is carved out (center) so that the Eskimo architect can check his work from outside. The final block at the top is slotted in from outside (below). Finally the entrance is constructed as a tunnel and cold trap, if the ground allows it. Cold air from outside sinks into this depression, while the interior of the igloo is heated by the oil lamp and body heat. The subterranean entrance is a piece of technical knowledge that might have been lost. When in about 1860 Canadian Eskimos from Baffin Island settled among the Polar Eskimo in Greenland, they reintroduced the cold trap (as well as the kayak, which was no longer built because at one time all the old men who were able to do this had fallen victim to disease). Up until then the houses of the Polar Eskimo had been much colder than those of the Baffin Islanders.

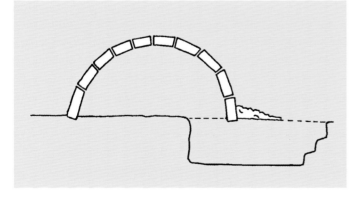

Semisubterranean houses in Hooper Bay, Yukon Delta, c. 1910. Glenbow Archives, Calgary, AB.

Earth houses featured a long tunnel serving as porch, cold trap, and storage space. Houses like these provided good protection against cold and storms, but because of their small rooms and inadequate ventilation, became increasingly close and stale over the winter. During the thaw the ground and the walls turned muddy. The missionaries who worked among the Yupik from the late 19th century onward preached against these earth houses, which they considered unhygienic.

John Webber, *Inside of a House in Oonalaska*, pen and ink wash and watercolor, 1778. Mitchell Library, State Library of New South Wales, Sydney, Australia.

Unlike the Yupik, the Aleut entered their houses through the roof. This drawing shows the individual families' areas in the rectangular house separated by mats. After making contact with the Russians, the Aleut began to build houses influenced by the Russian model, with doors on the side and floors covered with wooden planks instead of grass.

hunters hoped the whale would prove to be. Her contribution was to influence the whale's behavior. If, during the hunt, the woman made a sudden, jerky movement, or if she irresponsibly tended to her everyday chores, everyone was convinced that the whale would be driven away.

When white whale hunters and traders arrived in the area around Point Barrow at the end of the 19th century, many of the Inupiaq's *umialiks* were able to extend their power, becoming middlemen in trade and arbitrators in conflicts with the whites.

## Partners and spiritual relatives

The Canadian Inuit had virtually no social group beyond that of individual families. The winter villages were smaller than those in Alaska and in summer their inhabitants dispersed into family groups camping in tents. However, even here there were subtle forms of authority, usually exerted by the older men over the younger, which not all young hunters found easy to accept.

There was a constant threat that the communities would break up into individual households, families of umiak crews, or the members of a *qasgiq*. In the short term, it was in any case easier for very small groups to exploit effectively certain ecological niches. However, counterbalancing these tendencies toward dissolution was a network of partnerships that linked people in ways that went beyond family and residential groups.

Partnerships could take several forms. The Inuit of the central Arctic had a complex set of regulations dictating how a woman was to distribute the different parts of a seal caught by her husband to households linked in a partnership. The hunter's own household received little, but was entitled to identical pieces from any partner's prey. Men had partners who would mock each other in singing competitions but who would also confirm their friendship through the exchange of gifts. As such partnerships also served the exchange of spiritual powers between families, there were times when two married couples would swap partners for sexual intercourse. The children of both couples regarded each other as direct siblings, and in this manner a few more knots were added to the network of social relations.

In spite of occasional armed conflicts, trade between the Nunamiut of the inland and the coastal population of northern Alaska was possible because every Nunamiut had a trading partner at the coast from whom he expected friendly treatment. A transgression against partnership rules, such as the refusal of help when it was needed, was more than a mere breach of good manners, and those forgetting their duties could even face being ostracized from society. The partnerships had to be reliable, for often life quite literally depended on them.

A further relationship going beyond generation and

Types of Greenlandic houses. Copperplate etching by J. M. Fosie from Hans Egede, *Det gamle Grønlands nye perlustration*, Copenhagen, 1741. The Library of Congress, Washington, DC.

The work of the Danish missionary Hans Egede includes an illustration showing different types of Greenlandic dwellings and activities at the time. While one man is hunting sea birds from his kayak using a spear with an inflated float, other hunters have caught some seals and are carrying their boats ashore on their heads. Behind the rectangular winter houses made of earth and stone, some *umiaks* and a sled have been put out to dry. Three leather tents illustrate the people's summer dwellings, the snow house a temporary winter shelter.

family boundaries rests on the belief in a name-soul which enters a newborn some time after a person's death. To this day children in Greenland are given the name of a recently deceased local person to help the disembodied name-soul become reincarnated. As the relatives of the former bearer of the name are now akin to spiritual relatives, the circle of people from whom help and support can be expected is once again extended. In the eyes of the Eskimo, a child becomes a human being only after it receives a name.

Reconstruction of a Greenlandic winter house, Nuuk, 1994.

Today, Greenlanders live in Scandinavian-style wooden houses or concrete buildings. This reconstructed winter house shows the old technique of building with grass sods and stone. Hans Egede described the interior of such houses in 1741: "Every family has its own room. This is separated from the others by a post in front of a plank bed, which also supports the roof. The women sit on the bed and busy themselves with sewing or whatever else they have to do. The men sit with their sons at the front end of the bed and have their backs turned to the women."

# Human and nonhuman beings

## World of souls

"The greatest peril of life lies in the fact that human food consists entirely of souls," Ivaluardjuk, an Iglulik, explained to the Danish ethnologist Knud Rasmussen (1879–1933) in 1921. Like people, animals too had an *inua* (plural *inue*), a resident-like soul who gave them breath and a personality. However, not every animal had its own *inua*: rather, every species had a communal or central *inua*, who was responsible for deciding whether or not animals would give themselves up to hunters.

The goodwill of the animals' *inue*, and therefore people's survival, could only be secured by following rules such as not allowing the consumption of seal and caribou meat at the same time (products from the sea and the land must not be put together), or showing respect to the killed animals by placing a handful of snow in a dead seal's mouth to quench its thirst, for example.

Because there were so many different taboos in Eskimo life, no single individual could possibly know them all, so that hunting misfortunes were to a degree unavoidable. Similar to the way in which human name-souls were reborn from generation to generation, the number of animals who carried their species' *inua* was also limited. If it was pleased with how it was being treated, this same *inua* incarnation would return to the hunter year after year in a renewed physical form.

In Alaska, a hunter's outward appearance also played a prominent part. Decorated harpoons and clothing

Painted wooden hat decorated with walrus ivory, seal whiskers, and glass beads. Aleut, early 19th century. National Museum of Scotland, Edinburgh.

Hats made of carved wood had several uses. They protected the eyes from the bright sunshine, which was also reflected by the water, during a hunt in a kayak. The Yupik also believed that the hunter in a hat with such an extended brim looked like a water bird to seals, allowing him to approach and catch them. Among the Aleut, such elaborately decorated hats also signified the wearer's high hereditary status in his village.

were intended to attract sea mammals, while the low-brimmed wooden hats worn by the Aleut and the Yupik made a hunter in a kayak seem like a water bird. Reporting on Greenland in the 18th century the missionary Hans Egede observed that "they put on their best clothes for the whale hunt, as if for a wedding. Otherwise the whale would avoid them, for he cannot tolerate impurity."

The Koniag on the southern coast of Alaska carried out special ceremonies relating to the whale hunt. Only specialists were involved who had songs to lure whales and to influence the direction of ocean currents so that a dead whale would drift in to the beach and not be carried out into the open sea.

The whale hunters also appear to have owned the recipe for a poison that was rubbed on harpoon points to help kill the whale. The hunters conducted their rituals in caves where the mummies of previous whale hunters were kept as well as amulets which the whale hunters took with them when out at sea but which were not supposed to get wet under any circumstances. Both the Koniag and the Aleut accorded mummy burials to members of the upper social stratum; the deceased's personal household goods, their ornaments, and most especially their cult objects (such as wooden figures which would help to procure the benevolence of the souls) and masks were placed in the graves with them.

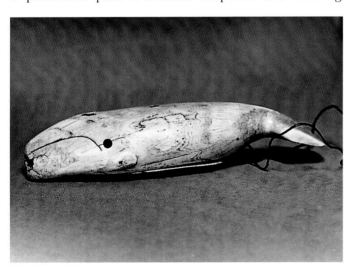

Wooden container for harpoon points in the shape of a whale. North Alaska, before 1900. The Field Museum of Natural History, Chicago, IL.

The equipment of an Inupiaq *umiak* included a number of ritual objects to guarantee the success of the hunt. The harpoon points kept in a container like this one had symbolically already hit their target. Whale-shaped amulets, made partly of transparent quartz to sharpen the owner's vision, were also carried. Before going out on a hunt, all the equipment was ritually cleansed and displayed.

Opposite page:

Feast after the annual whale hunt in Point Barrow, Alaska.

At this celebration a real specialty is being dished out in large quantities. It is "rotten" whale blubber, known as *muktuk*. The sharp taste of this delicacy is comparable to refined blue cheese, which for European gourmets is as far from being considered spoiled as *muktuk* is for Arctic ones. The original inhabitants of Alaska have the right to catch a certain quota of whales without coming into conflict with international protection agreements.

Yupik masked dance in the *qasgiq* of Qissunaq, Alaska, 1946. Alaska State Museum, Juneau, AK.

With their gentle movements, the unmasked women in the background provide a contrast to the often dramatic gestures and jumps of the masked men. The dance shown here was performed for the 1946 Walt Disney movie *Alaskan Eskimo*. The documentary presented an apparently dying culture and its disappearing customs to an American audience. It was also the first time in 20 years that the local priest had allowed the Yupik to carve masks and to perform a dance.

# Guests, ghosts, and gifts

For the Yupik, winter was the time for a series of ceremonies, held in the *qasgiq* under the leadership of a shaman: masked dancers, wooden puppets worked by strings that made them appear to float through the room, drums, and song made for dramatic performances.

The Messenger Feast opened the winter celebrations. In preparation for this event, two men would be sent to a neighboring village both to invite the inhabitants and to deliver a list of presents their hosts would like to receive from them. The invited people replied with their own wish list, and at an agreed time they would arrive at the host's *qasgiq* to sing and dance for them and to exchange gifts. Armed clashes between Yupik villages were not unknown, and these feasts too were something of a competition where both sides tried to outdo each other through displaying and giving away wealth, and in the creativity of the songs they composed. A similar but more playful exchange of wish-list gifts took place within a village between the men of the *qasgiq* and the women.

The week-long Bladder Festival honored the souls of seals killed over the year. Their bladders, which were considered to be the seat of the seal's soul, were inflated, hung up in the *qasgiq*, and honored with song, dance, and various offerings of food. The hunters underwent a ritual cleansing in the smoke of wild celery, so that they could enter a new hunting season harmoniously. On the final day, young men took the bladders down from the chimney in

the *qasgiq*'s roof and carried them off to the sea, where they let out the air and dipped them into the water through a hole in the ice, so that the souls would return the next year as living seals.

During the Feast for the Dead, the souls of those who had died in the previous year were served food, and presents were given out in their name. Their relatives would perform particular rites at the graves before once again gathering to eat and dance.

The Great Feast for the Dead was held every year by a different village in the region, as it was a very costly undertaking. The dead were symbolically invited to eat with the living. At the celebratory meal, families would symbolically dress their dead relatives in new clothes by giving clothes as presents to their namesakes, as these were considered the reincarnated name-souls of the dead.

The Inviting-In Feast took place at the end of the series of ceremonies, when supplies in a village were beginning to run short. All supernatural beings were invited to the *qasgiq* to share the meager remains of their supplies. This sacrificial gesture served to establish a kind of partnership with the supernatural beings, reminding them of previous support, and asking them to grant another successful hunting season.

Curtailed by missionaries at the beginning of the 20th century, some of the dance festivals are now being revived, as even the churches increasingly recognize them as valuable. As a result of Russian colonization, the Koniag are Orthodox Christians and have blended their masked dances with Russian folk beliefs in the *maskalataq* customs. In the period between Christmas and New Year, young men wearing masks made of pillowcases portray Herod's henchmen. Going through the village in search of the Baby Jesus, they enter houses, where they eat, drink, and dance.

In northern Alaska, where whales were caught by an *umiak* team, the hunting season began in March with a ceremonial launch of the repaired and ritually cleansed boats, and closed in June with a feast at which the *umialiks'* families handed out meat and oil and gave thanks to the whales' souls.

The first catch of the year of any species of animal was also usually cause for celebration. On the Pacific coast, for instance, there was the ceremony of the first salmon catch, at which specific women of high standing prepared the fish, served the food to the community, and finally ritually threw the fish bones back into the water so that the fishes' souls would return the following year, intact and in new bodily form.

*N⁰ 4. I. Miriggiô misigititauvok, tokussardllune umartardllune, ûlang miunigdlo Kristumiunigdlo okalugdllune.*

## Lady of the ocean, Lord of the winds

The rituals of the Canadian Inuit were far less elaborate than those of the Alaskan Inuit described above. There were numerous but informal occasions for singing and dancing. Altogether, the shaman was more at the foreground of rituals. Men and women could become shamans. Female shamans were usually healers and fortunetellers. When hunting went badly male shamans tended to travel to the bottom of the ocean to visit the goddess Sedna, the ocean's *inua* and therefore also the ruler of sea mammals. Here they would ask her to release the animals.

Sedna was not particularly fond of humans, as her life on earth as a woman had ended in a particularly cruel way. In a fierce storm she had been pushed out of an *umiak* to save the lives of the others on board, and when she tried to hold on to the boat's edge, the crew cut off

her fingers. Since then she had lived in a house at the bottom of the ocean, ruling over the sea mammals into which her severed fingers had been transformed. Whenever her hair had become dirty with human errors and with the transgressions of taboos, she would hold back the animals until the shaman combed her hair clean and thus pacified her. This only brought success if all the village members had previously publicly confessed their mistakes.

The search for secret breaches of taboos was also central to healing the sick. In front of witnesses the shaman asked the patient to admit to any errors that could have led to his or her condition – for instance, not carrying out the cleansing rituals after the death of a relative, or a woman eating forbidden foods after giving birth. Once the transgression had been recognized, the shaman could set about removing the illness.

However, in serious cases the shaman was sometimes forced to retrieve the soul from the realm of the dead. For this journey, as for that to visit Sedna, he needed the help of his guardian spirits, whom he had acquired during his career after receiving instructions from an experienced shaman. The spirits also helped him predict the future and influence the weather.

Sila (meaning "air" and "mind"), the *inua* of the air, was, like Sedna, another important power whose goodwill the Inuit could not always count on. He ruled over the weather and the winds, among other things. Creation myths or the belief in a god directing the fate of the world, were unimportant in the Arctic. In a few areas the missionaries tried to reinterpret Sila (or his Yupik equivalent Ellam yua) as the Christian God, an idea which today's Christian Eskimo like to use to defend their ancestors from the charge of having been polytheistic heathens. Indeed, many of today's Arctic church communities stress the similarity between traditional and Christian values, ideas, and behavior.

Aron of Kangeq (Inuit), *Imaneq tells of his visit with God*, watercolor, 1858–1860. National Museum of Greenland, Nuuk.

The Christian Inuit have an ambiguous attitude toward shamans. On the one hand, shamans' practices were often equated with the work of the devil; on the other, there are many stories of healing, "good" shamans who predicted the coming of Christianity or who let themselves be baptized. Here, Greenland hunter and self-taught artist Aron of Kangeq (1822–1869) depicts the shaman Imaneq, who has returned from a visit to heaven, preaches on God's magnificence, and sends men to Nuuk in the middle of winter to fetch a priest for his baptism. Miraculously, the ice broke to make way for their kayak.

Yupik Amanguak mask, Kuskokwim, Alaska. Ethnologisches Museum, Staatliche Museen zu Berlin – Preussischer Kulturbesitz, Berlin, Germany.

Yupik masks were customarily destroyed or buried after the ceremony for which they had been made. However, on their travels through western Alaska collectors acquired them as ethnographic material. The European Surrealists were greatly fascinated by the combination of human and animal features and grotesque shapes. The masks' human faces represent *inue*, or animals' souls. According to the collector of this mask, the hands signify the power of the shaman to attract hunting prey.

Caribou antler decorated with relief carvings, Abverdjar, Igloolik, Canada, Dorset culture, c. AD 1000. Cambridge University Museum of Archaeology and Anthropology, Cambridge, England.

Excavations at various sites have revealed caribou bone carvings from the Dorset period which are entirely covered with human faces. This theme, whose deeper meaning is unknown, has been taken up again by contemporary Inuit carvers.

Davidialuk Alasua Amittu (Inuit), *Woman with katyutayuk*, soapstone, c. 1969. Canadian Museum of Civilization, Hull, QC.

Many first-generation soapstone carvers grew up in hunting camps. Dealing with the past through art helped them adjust to life in the planned settlements in which they were placed in the 1950s, partly to save them from starvation but also to underline Canada's claim to the far north. In this sculpture Davidialuk (1910–1976) depicted the meeting between a woman and one of the many spirits inhabiting the world of the Inuit. A *katyutayuk* can be a large cannibalistic monster, but may also appear as a dwarf, breaking tools in the igloo at night and generally making mischief.

# Soapstone, ivory, wood – the arts of the Arctic

"Inuit are not considered terribly important to Canada, except as squatters in the interests of Arctic sovereignty and producers of stone carvings to show off at world fairs."

This sarcastic remark, made by Canadian sociologist Marybelle Mitchell (b. 1940), reflects the ambivalent position of the Inuit and contemporary Inuit art. In many Arctic settlements, carving is the most important source of income. However, in many museums and galleries of southern Canada, Inuit stone carvings are turned into symbols of national identity, which legitimizes itself partly through the incorporation of its indigenous heritage. Mitchell recognizes the similarity between the role of those Inuit who were settled on previously uninhabited Arctic islands in order to justify Canada's claim to these areas, and that of the stone carvers who learned their new craft from Canadian teachers at the same time. In both of these cases, the underlying aim is the consolidation of the Canadian state: in the one case this is achieved by territorial means, in the other by establishing the claim to a pre-European identity.

Although it features motifs from Inuit traditional life and can therefore be sold as an archaic art form, soapstone sculpture is actually of quite recent origin, and has only

been practiced on a noteable scale since the 1950s. For a long time before that the soft stone had been used for making oil lamps and cooking pots. Carvings, however, were made of bone and walrus ivory.

From the Dorset culture many depictions of animals have survived, and they can be connected to shamanistic ideas of souls traveling in animal guise. The first miniature depictions of birds and people appeared in the Thule era alongside decorated everyday tools. The Eskimo decorated hunting equipment in particular with depictions of their prey or of wolves and arctic foxes in the belief that some of the characteristics and powers of these animals would thus be transfered to the tools. There is also a long tradition of painting everyday objects and amulets with the silhouettes of spirits and animals.

The creation of smaller carvings made of walrus ivory showing scenes from everyday life, spread in Alaska and Greenland after stimulation by contact with the whites, whose constant appetite for souvenirs provided the Eskimo with new sources of income.

Soapstone was used only rarely for such pieces until Canadian artist James Houston (b. 1922) came to Quebec and the Northwest Territories in 1948. He encouraged the use of soapstone as a material for carvings and worked to

Opposite page:

Aka Høegh (Inuit), *Vision-Insight*, relief sculpture carved into the rockface at Qaqortoq, southern Greenland, 1993.

Greenland artist Aka Høegh (b. 1947) experiments with a localized art form in this rockface installation *Stone and Human*. It was created in the framework of the Scandinavian sculptors' symposium of the same name.

Walrus ivory bow from a bow drill, Baffin Island, probably c. 1800. Canadian Museum of Civilization, Hull, QC.

With the aid of straps strung on bows made of bone or walrus ivory, drills were rotated to make tools and fire. These bows are often decorated with scenic depictions. On this one there are summer tents at both ends; on the left, hunters in kayaks pursue a caribou, while on the right, a battle is fought with bows and arrows. Conflicts with other Eskimo groups or with their southern neighbors were frequent, but decreased over the 19th century as large numbers of people fell victim to European diseases.

Hunter with two birds, walrus ivory, Bering Strait Eskimo, Nome, Alaska, 1904. Panstwowe Muzeum Etnograficzne, Warsaw, Poland.

The Yupik and Inupiaq in Alaska have a tradition of walrus ivory carving dating back several thousand years. Spurred on by the demands of traders and a market that developed from the Alaskan gold rush of the late 19th century, the carvers produced not only everyday tools but also figurines to appeal to the collecting interest of their new clientele.

market these soapstone carvings in the south. Through government sponsored workshops established in the Canadian Arctic, as well as by means of a book of motif patterns that was published by Houston, the art of carving quickly spread, and since 1957 workshops for print graphics have also developed in some places following Houston's suggestions.

Many villages have founded cooperatives which handle the sale and marketing of all products from the north, but which are also the primary purchasers of artists' work and often maintain a store. Most attempts at developing trades other than arts and crafts have met with failure because of the high cost of transportation and production in the north. The boom in soapstone sculptures on the Canadian art market of the 1970s was a lifesaver for many of the cooperatives.

Many of today's leading Inuit artists began their work predominantly with the motive of earning money. By refining their techniques – soapstone being initially an unusual material for representational carvings – they developed their own styles and also higher standards of work. Because it is uneven in hardness and texture, soapstone presents a challenge and often dictates particular shapes. On the other hand, being quite a soft material to work with, it is easy to cut, carve, and file.

The blessing of carving and making souvenirs is also a curse for some. Dust from soapstone, inhaled by carvers and their families as they work in crowded rooms, has been shown to pose an alarmingly high health risk. In addition, resources are diminishing, forcing artists to look for other materials.

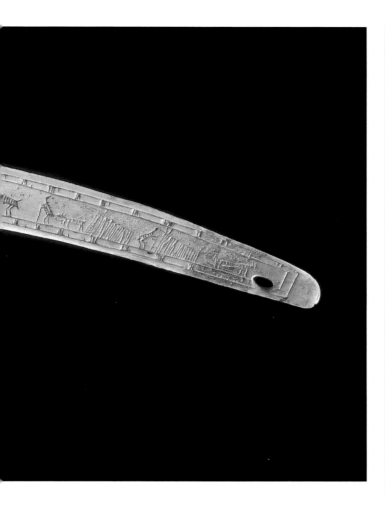

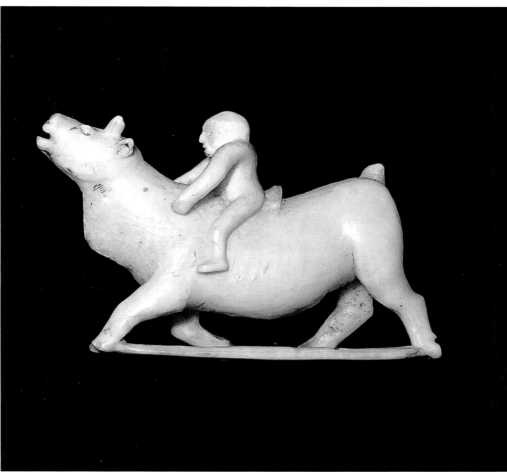

Reindeer rider, walrus ivory, Bering Strait Eskimo, Nome, Alaska, 1904. Panstwowe Muzeum Etnograficzne, Warsaw, Poland.

In 1891/92, on the initiative of missionary Sheldon Jackson, herds of domesticated Siberian reindeer were brought to northern Alaska to turn the Eskimo hunters into herdsmen. Thus the Inupiaq also came to know the Old World relative of the caribou, which could be used to pull sleds and even for riding.

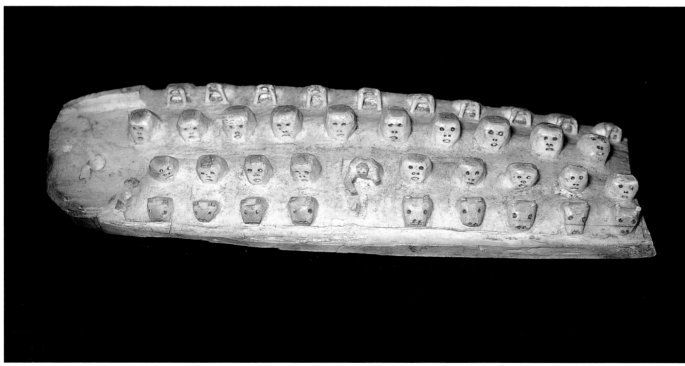

Animal and human heads, walrus ivory, Bering Strait Eskimo, Nome, Alaska, 1904. Panstwowe Muzeum Etnograficzne, Warsaw, Poland.

In earlier days the foreshafts of harpoons and the toggles of harpoon lines were sometimes decorated with the carved heads of the expected prey. Here, heads of seals, humans, and walruses are neatly aligned. The meaning of this carving – if there was one – is unknown.

In Alaska Yupik masks carry a symbolic function similar to that of Canadian Inuit carvings. Today their production has once again increased, although they are made mostly as wall decoration, without holes for the eyes. Together with reproductions of Tlingit crest poles from southern Alaska, they decorate the offices, airports, and concert halls of the United States' most northerly state. The indigenous heritage of Alaska is thus on public display, but is also appropriated by mainstream American society as part of their own heritage, as if colonization had never happened.

A similar situation applies to the walrus ivory carvers of Greenland. Since the 1950s, they have been using the increasingly rare material to produce figures of *tupilaks*, grotesque and malicious magic animals, carved to satisfy the collectors' market. African ivory, which had been used as a substitute, can no longer be imported under the current wildlife protection laws.

# The Aleut – between the continents

In the late 19th century, the majority of Aleut were able to read and write in their own language using the Cyrillic alphabet, prayed in Aleut in the Russian Orthodox churches, and made a living from hunting fur animals to supply American traders of the Alaska Commercial Company, successor to the Russian-American Company, a Russian fur trading consortium. The identity and history of the Aleut, a people living on a group of islands between Asia and America, mirrors the dual colonial history of Alaska, which was under Russian control from the late 18th century to 1867 and was then sold to the United States.

Together with the Koniag, the Aleut were the group most affected by Russian rule in Alaska. During this time their population, which originally stood at 10,000–12,000, shrank to about 2,500. Many, especially children and the eldery, fell victim to outbreaks of smallpox; several hundred men drowned on long hunting expeditions commanded by the colonial administration; and many villages faced starvation in winter as, instead of storing up reserves of meat in summer, the men were forced to hunt sea otters for their fur.

After 1867, the Russian system of pressing men into service for sea otter hunting was replaced by a dependency on American trade goods. The new masters, initially represented only by the traders of the Alaska Commercial Company, but later also by teachers, Protestant missionaries, and government officials, looked down on the cultural heritage of 100 years' contact between Aleut culture and the Russians. The descendants of Russian-Aleut marriages, the so-called Creoles, had held important posts in administration, education, and the church in Russian America (Alaska). To the Americans, such a "halfbreed" was worth even less than a pure Aleut, and American Protestants regarded the Russian Orthodox church that had become the Aleut's traditional religion as little more than superstition. Sheldon Jackson (1834–1909), a Presbyterian minister and from 1885 to 1908 also Alaska's first

John Hoover (Aleut), *Shaman in the Form of an Eagle*, sculpture in wood, 1973. Heard Museum, Phoenix, AZ.

Little is known of the Aleut's pre-Christian beliefs. Artist John Hoover (b. 1919) attempts to approach these through his bird figures whose significance is suggested by mythical texts, parkas made of bird skin, beak-like hunting hats, and other aspects of traditional art. While teaching at United States Air Force schools in East Asia, he also learned local techniques of working with wood: a new variation of the role of Aleut culture as a bridge between America and Asia.

Commissioner of Education, considered both the Orthodox faith and the multilingualism in schools and church services to be obstacles to the assimilation of the indigenous population. The Orthodox parish schools were gradually replaced by government-sponsored Protestant mission schools, where the only language spoken was English – as was customary all over the United States – and the use of Aleut was punished.

Initially American companies had made quick profits from their relentless pursuit of seals and sea otters around the Aleutian Islands, but the turn of the 20th century was a time of economic downturn. As the stocks of fur animals were exhausted, the sea otters and the valuable seal colonies on the Pribilof Islands had to be protected through international agreements. Many trading stations were closed, leaving the people with no source of cash income.

The Aleut were hit even harder by World War II. After the Japanese had abducted the entire population of the Island Attu, the United States Navy ordered the evacuation of all indigenous inhabitants of the archipelago - whose loyalty may have been in doubt - in 1942. While 10 percent of the 881 Aleut evacuees died because of the inadequate sanitary conditions in the south Alaskan camps, American soldiers willfully destroyed houses and plundered churches. The village of Atka was burned down before the eyes of its residents without their being given the chance to save their possessions for the evacuation.

For decades, the Aleut received no compensation whatsoever either for the destruction of their houses or for the islands that were closed off completely as military training areas during the Cold War, or contaminated with the remains of ammunition and fuel. In connection with the compensation for the United States citizens of Japanese origin who were interned during World War II, the Aleut were finally awarded a sum of $12,000 per person in 1988.

The militarization of the Arctic and the ensuing environmental damage were a direct result of Russian-American rivalry for the area. With the end of the Cold War, Alaska hopes to play a central part in peaceful trade in a new North Pacific economy. In this context, the Aleut, with their blend of Russian and indigenous traditions, could be a model of cultural exchange across the Bering Strait.

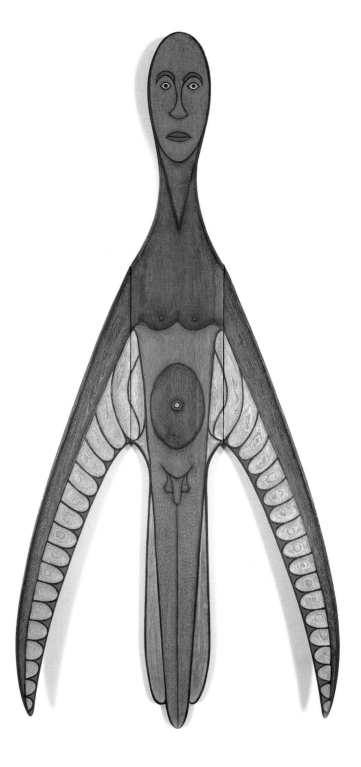

Main street of Unalaska, c. 1890. Elmer E. Rasmuson Library, Erskine Collection, Alaska and Polar Regions Department, University of Alaska, Fairbanks, AK.

Unalaska's most important institutions in the late 19th century were the Orthodox church, whose towers can be seen in the background, and the Alaska Commercial Company (ACC), which took over the properties of the Russian-American Company after 1867. Orthodox priests often accused the Americans of exploiting the Aleut population and of encouraging the consumption of alcohol, but they also depended on ACC ships for visiting their parishioners, who were scattered across half of the island chain. Sometimes American traders in turn, asked the priests to encourage their parishioners to adopt a more zealous work ethic.

# The Yupik – salmon fishing in transition

The Yupik in the Alaskan Yukon-Kuskokwim delta are the salmon eaters among the Eskimo, even though their local environment offers them not only salmon but also a wide range of water fowl and other prey. Here, in the Arctic's most densely populated area, there has always been a close, ritually maintained bond with this most important food source that reliably returns every year. In the eyes of the people this bond was marked by mutual obligations and respect. However, changes in Yupik life brought about by contact with whites also included a changing relationship to salmon.

Moving to the summer fishing grounds was something that extended family groups looked forward to, an escape from the villages that had become stuffy and crowded over the long winter. During the whole dark season the women had made strips of seal leather or willow bark into string, which they tied together to form nets. Now the first task was to repair the weirs. The rows of vertical wooden posts blocking off part of the riverbed had to be renewed, and cone-shaped fish-traps made of willow twigs were placed between the posts. Between June and August five different varieties of salmon would make their way up the river to their spawning grounds, and the fishers would be kept busy transferring their catch to the shore from the traps and from the nets which were used from kayaks.

The first salmon to be caught was ceremonially honored so as to attract more fish. The drying racks quickly filled up with the shimmering reddish salmon fillets. Stores of dried fish caught and preserved in the summer and fall fed the family and its dogs over the winter, but also became a desirable trade good around the turn of the 20th century, when increasing numbers of white traders, prospectors, and trappers arrived and needed food for their sled dogs.

Skinned salmon drying on wooden racks at the site of the catch.

Both the native and white inhabitants of Alaska's "bush" enjoy the right to catch salmon for their own use.

Toksook Bay Village, Nelson Island, Alaska, c. 1975.

In Alaska, where no treaties were made with the native population and no reservations established, indigenous communities are only organized as villages. According to ANCSA (the *Alaska Native Claims Settlement Act*), every village could choose its land, which was then transferred to a corporation in which every village inhabitant became a shareholder. Every village also belongs to one of 12 regional corporations; Toksook Bay, for instance, is part of the Calista Corporation. These corporations usually sponsor community welfare and health services and cultural institutions (community centers and in certain places elementary schools and libraries as well). ANCSA brought greater autonomy, but also caused legal conflicts as to whether villages can still claim tribal rights such as freedom from taxes and their own jurisdiction.

This greater demand was met by the use of the fishing wheel, newly introduced from China; fitted with two pails and turned by the flowing water, it lifts the salmon that are swimming upstream out of the water. When the pails are directly above the axle, the fish then slide down into a trough leading to a large container. This method makes it possible to catch far more fish without human effort than by using traps and nets, which regularly have to be emptied and put back into place. However, to protect salmon stocks, today only members of indigenous communities are allowed to use this device and then only for their own subsistence use.

From the 1920s on, motorboats allowed many fishers to monitor their fishing sites from their villages, making the scattered fishing settlements redundant and allowing the men to come home every evening. The women stayed in the village with their children for the whole of the school year and worked in fishing less than before. The definition of gender roles therefore came closer to the ideal of the nuclear family that the missionaries were aiming for in their attempts to dissolve the men's houses and the households of related women. Gradually, more and more married couples moved into single-family above-ground houses.

As the value of salmon increases in a market expanding beyond regional boundaries, outsiders join the competition for this resource. In 1973 commercial fishing licenses were distributed: those who do not inherit them and are unable to buy such a licence are excluded from the salmon trade. For this reason, many Yupik defend the legal guarentee which gives subsistence fishing priority over commercial fishing.

Anuska Petla, a Yupik from New Stuyahok on the Nushagak River, told an investigative committee in 1984: "All the meat and all the fish that we eat every year per household would come to about $6,000 to $7,000, and I know we can't afford it. I mean, most of us can't afford it ... because there's not enough jobs for everyone."

Even the seemingly harmless practice of sport fishers who catch fish and then release them again is strongly criticized by the Yupik. From their point of view, this insulting treatment of the fishes' *inua* (called *yua* in Yupik) will finally drive them away.

Maintaining a connection with the land on the basis of mutual respect rather than on a basis of commercial exploitation is made more difficult by the legal regulation of native land ownership in Alaska. The 44 million acres given to indigenous ownership under the *Alaska Native Claims Settlement Act (ANCSA)* of 1971 did not go to tribes but instead to the corporations that the indigenous communities had been turned into and whose shares, as of 1991, can also be sold following a majority decision. Just as communities based on kinship have been turned into economic enterprises, so hunting grounds which were once crucial to a whole way of life have now become capital to be invested in profit-oriented development.

# Inuit – roads toward autonomy

Ane Martinsen, Kipisillit, West Greenland, 1991.

The power to name places is one sign of sovereignty over an area. Since Greenland's autonomy, local Greenland names for towns and villages are increasingly preferred over Danish ones; Godthåb became Nuuk, and Julianehåb became Qaqortoq. Ane Martinsen, the Greenlander pictured above, holds a bag featuring both the Danish and the Greenland names for the country. The Inuit of Nunavut and Quebec have followed this example, and now English- and French-speaking Canadians also have to get used to Inuit names.

Dissatisfaction with the legal resolution of land claims has led to attempts by Alaska Natives to win greater political as well as economic autonomy. The Canadian Inuit face similar issues: as in Alaska, no treaties on land cessions were made in northern Canada in the 19th century, and the situation regarding ownership of land and natural resources has been as unclear as the rights of the indigenous population.

As in Alaska, the discovery of oil in the Arctic Ocean attracted great interest in the economic exploitation of the North, and settling the original inhabitants' claims suddenly seemed necessary. Plans by the Quebec provincial government to build enormous dams for hydropower stations east of Hudson Bay met with protests from the Inuit and the Cree, leading to the 1975 James Bay and Northern Quebec Agreement.

In return for allowing large areas of their territory to be flooded, the Inuit and the Cree were granted exclusive hunting and fishing rights in the remaining areas and the right to autonomy in certain sectors such as education and health. Similar to Alaska, the $90 million compensation paid to the Inuit for the transfer of land rights went to a development corporation, Makivik, established with the aim of working toward the region's economic independence. Makivik operates an airline as well as several enterprises within the building and tourist industries. In some areas it is competing with older cooperatives, so that Quebec's Inuit now have two kinds of economic organization but no common political representation.

A similar ruling of 1984 applies to the Inuvialuit at the Mackenzie River. However, the share companies were granted ownership of more land, but mainly without rights to the minerals and other natural resources that make the area so attractive to firms from the south.

The Inuit from the eastern part of the Northwest Territories won far more political concessions. Not only did the Inuit obtain ownership of 772,000 square miles (only ten percent of which includes sub-surface rights to natural resources) an area the size of Germany, but the Northwest Territories have even been divided. In 1999 the northeastern part, consisting of the islands of the Arctic Archipeligo and the northwestern coast of Hudson Bay, became Nunavut, of whose 22,000 inhabitants 17,500 are Inuit. Inuktitut is the second official language, and elected governments will most likely consist mainly of Inuit.

The founding of Nunavut does not imply ethnic autonomy for the Inuit, detached from other residents of the area. All of Nunavut's residents have the same political rights, and the same laws apply to all. However, the Inuit make up the majority of the population in a large area, a situation unique among native North Americans. They want to use this to set up a political structure within the framework of the Canadian constitution, but based on their own values and traditions, even though in Inuit culture there are no precedents for an administration going beyond individual settlements. Financially, however, Nunavut will remain strongly dependent on the Canadian federal government, and its own income could only be generated through the exploitation of natural resources, which would not only cause environmental problems but also encourage a greater number of whites to settle in the area.

Only the Inuit in Greenland have greater independence. The island has been running its domestic affairs independently of Denmark since 1979, and has left the European Union so as to protect its fishing rights. Since then, the Inuit dominate politics and are working for a united national identity for Greenland, for instance through the development of a single national language based on the West Greenland dialect. This new language is used in newspapers, books, electronic media, and parliamentary debates, and is also the language of instruction in schools.

MIK choir from Greenland at a performance in Hørsholm, Denmark, 1991.

The up-and-coming nation of Greenland also expresses its unity and uniqueness through its traditional dress, which is based on a mix of West Greenland and Danish forms and patterns. At celebrations, dances, and choral concerts this costume stands for a supraregional Greenland identity.

Opposite page:

Kayaks laid up to dry, Nuuk, Greenland, 1997.

Even when it is thickly greased, the leather covering the kayaks soaks up some water and makes the vessel impossible to maneuver after 48 hours at the most. With every last space taken, this drying rack on the coast near Nuuk, the capital of Greenland, shows that the vessel has lost little of its appeal.

Father and son return from a successful seal hunt, Foxe Basin, Canada.

In addition to government school, today's Inuit boys still have to learn in the school of life. The skills and knowledge that a father can pass down to his young son cannot be learned at any public school, but are essential to his future survival. The North still offers almost no employment other than hunting and fishing. Whether the boy will become a good kayaker is another question. However, in this age of outboard motors and snowmobiles, this is no longer an issue for most of the Canadian Inuit.

# The rise and fall of the fur trade

Neither the American Arctic nor the adjacent Subarctic forests were particularly appealing to white settlers. The area's attractions lay in its great resources of furs, which could be sold at high prices in Europe.

From the 17th century onward, various trading companies spread through the Subarctic, moving northward and westward out from the Atlantic coast and the areas around Hudson Bay. After periods of fierce competition for key areas in the skin trade (beaver, marten, mink, and others), the Hudson's Bay Company (HBC), founded in 1670, secured a monopoly in Canada after buying up its greatest rival, the North West Company, in 1821. In certain parts of the North the HBC was even charged with administrative functions by the British crown.

For its operations the HBC depended on binding the leaders of smaller hunting groups to its stores by offering such goods as metal tools, firearms, clothing, glass beads, fabric, and tobacco. In comparison, the Russian-American Company, in control of what was then the Russian colony of Alaska between 1799 and 1867, used a mixture of military coercion and diplomatic cooperation to commit leading Aleut and Koniag families to providing crews for the annual sea otter hunt.

During the 19th century, the native population of both areas increasingly specialized in the hunt for fur-bearing anomals and became more dependent on trading, posts even for food supplies. When shrinking animal stocks and falling prices forced many trading posts to close at the end of the century, many families suffered economic hardship.

At this time, the HBC moved some of its business from the Subarctic to the Arctic. The trade in arctic fox fur

flourished between 1920 and 1930, as the fur was very fashionable in Europe during this period. In the years after World War II the Hudson's Bay Company gradually metamorphosed into a chain of supermarkets and department stores, and for a long time was the greatest trader in Inuit carvings.

Today only a few Eskimo trappers can make a living from the fur trade alone, even when there are enough animals. The market in seal skins from Greenland and Canada collapsed in the late 1970s after a campaign in which the media was effectively used to expose and frequently distort the facts of the seal hunt on Newfoundland, turning the European and American public against the wearing of furs. In the name of animal protection, many environmental organizations overlooked the needs of those people who depended on the fur trade for a living.

In 1996 Larry Merculieff, an Aleut, described in a newspaper interview the protest against the seal fur harvest on the Pribilof Islands in the Bering Sea – hunting carried out by local people in the service of the United States government – and the effect it had on the islands' inhabitants: "People were really filled with fear. We were getting hate mail from all over the world as a result of full-page newspaper ads that characterized our people as brutal, bloodthirsty killers of animals."

Today both legislators and environmental activists increasingly differentiate between commercial fur-hunting and hunting for subsistence food supplies where furs are only a by-product. The European Union's embargo on the furs of young seals does not include the products of the traditional Inuit hunt, and the furs of adult seals are legally imported as before. However, this does nothing to reverse the decline in demand for sealskin coats. No purchaser can tell, whether the furs these items are made from come from self-sufficient Inuit trappers or profit-hungry white hunters.

SUBARCTIC

Tundra and taiga in the fall, Denali National Park, Alaska.

Tundra with trees and ground cover in the transition zone to the taiga in Denali National Park, Alaska.

Opposite page:
Peoples of the Subarctic.

At the time of the first encounters with Europeans, no more than 60,000 people may have inhabited the whole of the Subarctic. The tribal boundaries marked on the map should not obscure the fact that people mostly lived in small family groups moving across the thinly populated area, sometimes with a "multicultural" membership. Today the Cree, the region's largest indigenous group, alone number more than 60,000.

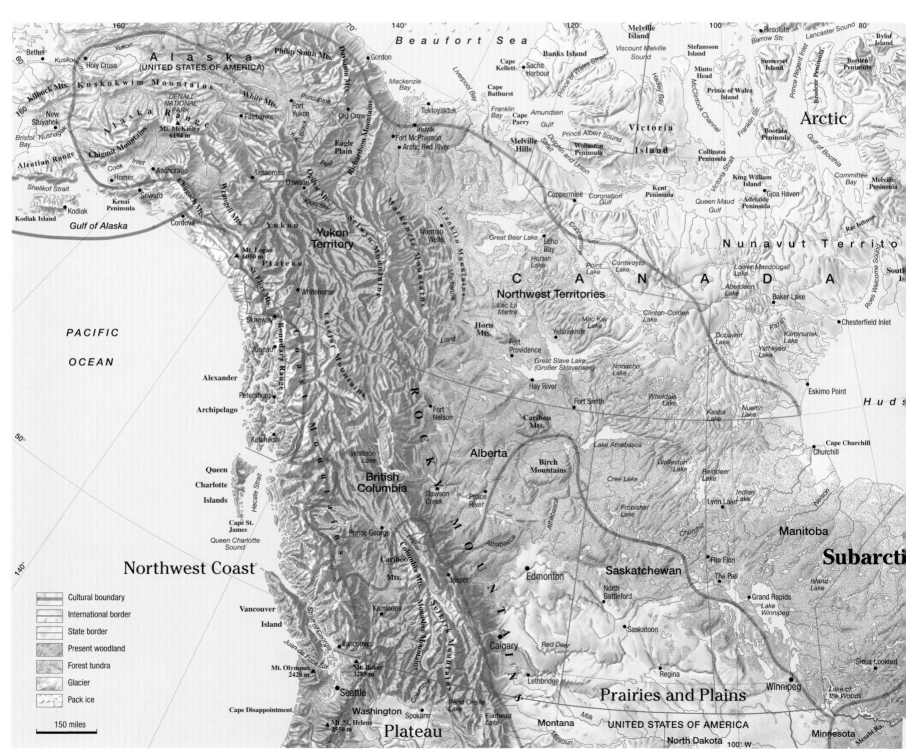

Cultural boundary
International border
State border
Present woodland
Forest tundra
Glacier
Pack ice

150 miles

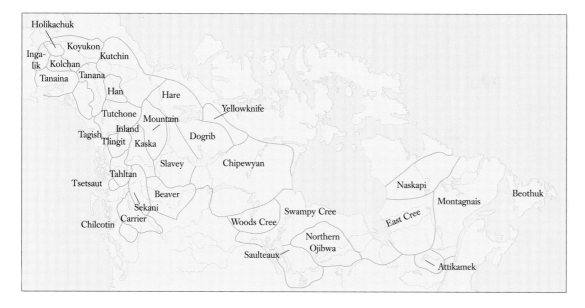

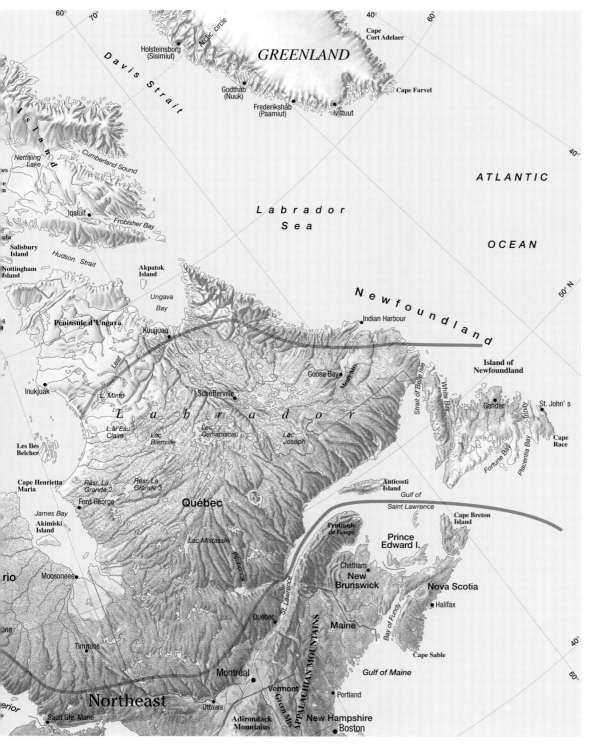

Sonja Lührmann

# In the northern forests

The Subarctic, an expanse between the treeless areas of the Arctic permafrost zone and the temperate belt encircling the globe, is covered with dense coniferous forest. In Canada and interior Alaska, subarctic spruce woods interspersed with birch, willow, alder, and pine cover a seemingly infinite area of more than two million square miles. Icy winters with heavy snowfalls alternate with short summers during which there is no escape from the buzzing swarms of mosquitoes that mercilessly attack any warmblooded animal.

Of course, this large region is by no means homogeneous. The area of the Mackenzie Plains and the Canadian Shield acts like a rocky tray, carrying the forests that stretch from the Atlantic coast of Canada to the Rocky Mountains. Here, the land is relatively flat, having been scoured by Ice Age glaciers which, as they retreated, left troughs in the rock which are now filled by 100,000 lakes, large swamps, and the tightknit network of rivers that drain these depressions. Toward the north the density of trees gradually decreases and the terrain turns into arctic tundra. In the west, the Rocky Mountains are the northernmost ranges of the Cordilleras, running the length of the continent down to Tierra del Fuego like its backbone. Between British Columbia and eastern Alaska these mountains and the high plains that they surround show subarctic characteristics, but as altitude increases trees become fewer, the terrain finally turning to treeless fields of snow and rock. Between the northern ranges the Yukon and Kuskokwin rivers run from central Alaska to the Bering Sea, whereas on the side facing the Pacific Ocean the mountains form steep cliffs with a low-lying coastal plain only around Cook Inlet.

Previous pages:
Mount McKinley, Denali National Park, Alaska.

Rising to a height of 20,320 feet, Mount McKinley towers majestically over the autumnal treeless tundra of Denali National Park.

"First Coming-out" ceremony, East Cree, Quebec, c. 1990.

"They let him go outside" is the literal translation of this East Main Cree ceremony held when little boys and girls have learned to walk. The children are led out of the tent by their parents and taken to a nearby decorated tree. The boys are equipped with toy guns, the girls with small axes, and both imitate gathering wood and hunting, tasks they are expected to perform as members of their society. Back in the tent, they present their grandparents with their "prey." The ceremony ends with a feast and thanksgiving to the child for providing the meal.

Opposite page:
Charles A. Zimmermann (1844–1909), Two Ojibwa, Minnesota, c. 1870.

The hunter squarely trudges through the snow on snowshoes, yet is still faster than any stag or moose, which sink into the snow. He wears a woolen blanket around his hips as well as a hooded jacket made of the same material. Both men display the typical Ojibwa hairstyle, with plaits and a strand of hair sticking up.

## Peoples and languages

The names of the indigenous peoples of the Subarctic – such as Cree, Chipewyan, and Slavey – might be interpreted as an indication of clear demarcations between tribes. In fact, these names relate purely to linguistic boundaries, not to the identity or self-designation of these people whose social and political life was generally focused on much smaller groups.

The native populations of the Subarctic are divided into two linguistic families. In the east, from the Labrador peninsula along the southern coast of Hudson Bay down to northeastern Alberta, Algonquian languages are spoken. Strictly speaking there are only two of these: the ten dialects of the Cree-Montagnais-Naskapi language extend like a chain from western Canada to the northern Atlantic coast in the north; while to the south, Ojibwa is spoken in eight dialects.

Both languages reach beyond the Subarctic: speakers of Cree and Ojibwa also live in the Plains, and a large portion of the Ojibwa people live in the Northeast, having ventured further north and west only in the last 300 years.

Distinctions between these dialects tend to be rather fluid, especially as fluency in several languages is widespread in those areas that are located along a linguistic boundary. Even today, many Algonquian-speakers can speak both Cree and Ojibwa (mostly in several dialects) as well as being able to communicate in English or French, or both. Furthermore, in some communities there is such a marked difference between the language of the old and the language of the young that it is possible to speak of generation dialects.

Northwest of the Algonquians live the speakers of the region's 23 Athapaskan languages, which are also partly divisible into dialects. In the Northwest Territories of Canada, *dene* ("human beings," or *deneza*, "real human beings"), the term used by most Athapaskans to designate themselves, has become today's collective political term for all the groups united within the Dene Nation, among which, however, the Alaskan Athapaskans do not count themselves. Traditional terms often provide useful clues about the relationships that existed between the various groups. For the Athapaskan Chipewyan, the world was neatly compartmentalized, at least in this respect: the Cree were just "enemies," and in a simple distinction, the Copper Inuit were referred to as "tundra enemies." On the other hand, their Athapaskan neighbors, who were also potential marriage partners, were given descriptive names. For instance, the Beaver were "the ones living by the beavers," and the Slavey were "those living by the great river" (the Mackenzie).

The Cree took their revenge by creating many of the names that are still used today, as missionaries and traders passed through their area first and simply translated the Cree descriptions, such as Slavey (the "slaves") and Dogrib ("the side of the dog"). The latter name shows the Cree's fascination with the Dogrib's origin myth. This tribe believed that they were the descendants of two boys and a girl whose father was a dog and whose mother was banished to the wilderness as punishment for this unnatural union.

The linguistically isolated Beothuk of Newfoundland, once a tribe of only a few hundred and the sole masters of this big island, are an exception among Subarctic peoples. Following campaigns to push them out or drive them to extinction, this people ceased to exist as early as the 19th century, with no noteworthy records having been made of their culture and language.

The inhabitants of the Subarctic were entirely dependent on hunting and were thus confronted with highly insecure living conditions. Famines occurred not infrequently when hunting was unsuccessful or when stores had been raided by wolves, bears, or enemies. For their survival most peoples of the area concentrated on hunting land animals, complemented by some fishing.

However, the inhabitants of the coastal areas at either extremity of the Subarctic, the Beothuk of Newfoundland, and the Tanaina of southern Alaska, focused on the ocean for their food supply, living mostly on fish, sea mammals, and crustaceans.

# Hunters and entrepreneurs

It was only the fur trade with Europeans which enabled the hunters of the Subarctic to go beyond merely assuring their survival, and to acquire riches in the form of glittering glass beads and colorful woolen fabrics, and to make their life easier with metal tools and firearms. The price for this was the change from hunting for food to specializing in the supply of animal furs to a distant European market, and a growing dependence on items supplied by the whites.

In the east, the British Hudson's Bay Company (HBC) competed for trade with the native hunters first with French traders and later, after France's loss of New France to Britain, with French Canadian traders. In Alaska, on the other hand, the Russian-American Company held a trading monopoly until the United States purchased the area in 1867. The competitive situation allowed fur hunters to play off various traders against each other, but also rapidly led to overhunting in many areas. Once a company had gained a foothold in an area rich in resources, it was quick to exploit it to the full before any rival could move in to do the same.

In addition to useful tools, the traders brought deadly diseases to the North, especially smallpox, measles, and tuberculosis. The smallpox epidemic of 1781/82 claimed up to 90 percent of the population of certain Chipewyan and Western Woods Cree groups. Neighboring tribes used this opportunity to push into these depopulated territories, especially if at an early stage they had acquired firearms from the whites, as did many Cree communities. With such a strategic advantage, they expanded their territories at the expense of their neighbors.

The fur trade in Alaska and the Canadian Rockies was oriented toward the Pacific coast. Peoples of the Northwest Coast acted as middlemen and attempted to prevent any direct contact between Europeans and the Subartic fur hunters.

However, in many areas of the northwestern Subarctic, discoveries of gold provided the main attraction for hordes of whites who also brought lasting changes to the lives of the native population, as in the Carrier and Chilcotin areas of British Columbia in 1862 or in the Han territory as a result of the 1898 Klondike Goldrush. Droves of fortune seekers made their way up the rivers of gold to stake their claims. Organized gangs controlled the life of the mushrooming prospector towns. Smallpox, which wiped out the majority of Chilcotin in 1862, diphtheria, tuberculosis, and venereal diseases spread rapidly, and alcohol was omnipresent. The Klondike madness itself passed after a few years, but there were lasting consequences for the Han. Numerous mixed marriages had been made, and a money economy had pushed aside the traditional economy of barter. Missionaries began to work particularly hard among the Han as they recognized the widespread moral corruption prevalent in the goldrush settlements.

Today, most peoples of the Subarctic live in larger, permanent settlements, with hunting and fishing providing only a small part of their food supply. Especially the measures to develop the North have increased the integration into the nation states of Canada and the United States. Everyone uses airplanes and snowmobiles as a matter of course, and Dene and Cree children watch MTV, while their mothers struggle to make the welfare check last to the end of the month. The North offers little opportunity for employment, and the jobs that are available – in forestry, road construction, or mining for oil or uranium – are dangerous and damaging to health.

The boarding school system which was in place for generations brought two different results. Many young people returned to their homes feeling uprooted and unable to speak their mother tongue. Conversely the shared experience of boarding school forged a new consciousness of a common fate as the original inhabitants of the North that crossed tribal boundaries. Today, political associations successfully fight on issues of land rights and the long-term effects of environmental exploitation of the North. School education has been moved back to the home villages, and local committees set the curriculum and determine how state subsidies should be used to develop the North.

Oil pipeline near Paxon, Alaska. The zigzag pattern protects the pipeline from earthquakes.

Like endless snakes, the oil pipelines have eaten their way through the subarctic forests. The numerous bends balance out the strains of extreme changes in temperature that make the material expand and contract. In the permafrost zone the ground softens only on the surface; even so, the whole construction has to be supported by posts deeply anchored in the ground to prevent it from sinking into the summer morass. The building and maintenance of these pipelines has connected many previously isolated native settlements to the national economy. To a limited extent they also offer employment opportunities.

# Hunting for a living – between feast and famine

When the French Jesuit father Paul Le Jeune (1592–1664) spent the winter of 1634 with the Montagnais, he aroused his host's disapproval by not indulging in the banquets which took place daily at the beginning of winter, and to which he had to contribute. Le Jeune saw his own reserves dwindle, and the time of carefree overeating was soon followed by hunger. "As to the chase, the snows not being deep in comparison with those of other years, they could not take the elk, and so brought back only some beavers and porcupines, but in so small a number and so seldom that they kept us from dying rather than helped us to live." Deep snow was essential for a successful moose hunt, for the animals could then move only slowly, and it was easier for hunters wearing snowshoes to catch them. The priest's host encouraged him: "Thou wilt be sometimes two, sometimes three or four days without food; do not let thyself be cast down, take courage; when the snow comes, we shall eat."

## Scarcity

Although the extremes of winter famine and times of abundance were accepted as unavoidable by Le Jeune's host, to many European visitors they seemed to be a result of waste and neglect in making provision. However, the mobile life led by the small groups of hunters and their families did not allow for large-scale storage of food. People tried to assure adequate food supply not solely through preservation, but also by a precise knowlege of their prey's habits and a special relationship with its supernatural "owners." These were always given thanks for a successful hunt and were honored in a festive, communal meal at which the prey was served. As Le Jeune observed, the weather was crucial to the hunt's success, so people attempted to influence it, too. The Cree,

Frederick Whymper, *A Co-Yukon Deer Corral*, from F. Whymper, *Travel and Adventure in the Territory of Alaska*, New York, 1869.

The two rows of shrubs leading to the entrance of a caribou corral of the Alaskan Koyukon could stretch for several miles. If the caribou tried to escape, they would be caught in the nooses placed between the fence posts. The hunters would take up positions behind trees and mounds of snow into which crenelations were made.

A CO-YUKON DEER CORRAL.

Herd of caribou in the valley of the Porcupine River, Yukon Flats, Alaska.

In the flat landscape of the tundra, approaching a herd of caribou without being seen was a great challenge for hunters – especially in spring, when the cows give birth to their calves.

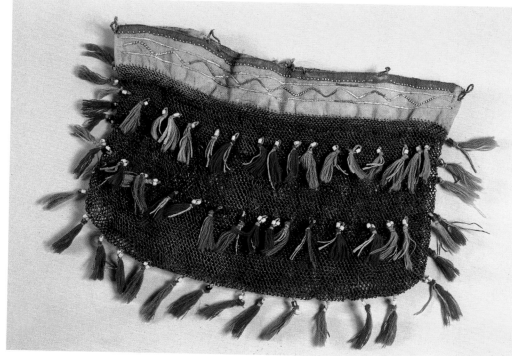

Hunting bag made of babiche, Hare, before 1860. National Museum of Scotland, Edinburgh, Scotland.

Net-like bags woven out of babiche (thin strips of semitanned caribou or moose hide which are twisted into strings) were strong yet very light. They were used to carry smaller prey, which would spoil less quickly as the air could circulate and the blood could drip through the netting. Babiche was also used for stringing snowshoes and for making snares and nets. By the same technique strips of rabbitskin were woven into warm blankets and jackets.

the Montagnais' westerly neighbors, would throw a winterly, snow-white rabbitskin into the fire so that winter, angered by the treatment of his friend, would send down snow.

In emergencies, people had to make do with eating rabbits and other smaller animals caught in traps, or survive on fish caught in nets hung below the ice instead of consuming the larger game. For this reason, fishermen would make holes in the ice at regular intervals. With a long pole they led a long line from hole to hole beneath the ice, anchoring it at each hole. The net could then be threaded along the line under the ice in order to catch the fish.

As emergency rations, tree bark and the leather used in clothing and tents were often the last resort to stave off agonizing hunger. The meat of fur-bearing animals, whose carcasses were usually burned outside the camp, sometimes served as food in difficult times, too. Small game and fish were also taken by women and children when the men were absent from the camp, hunting or trapping, for a period of time.

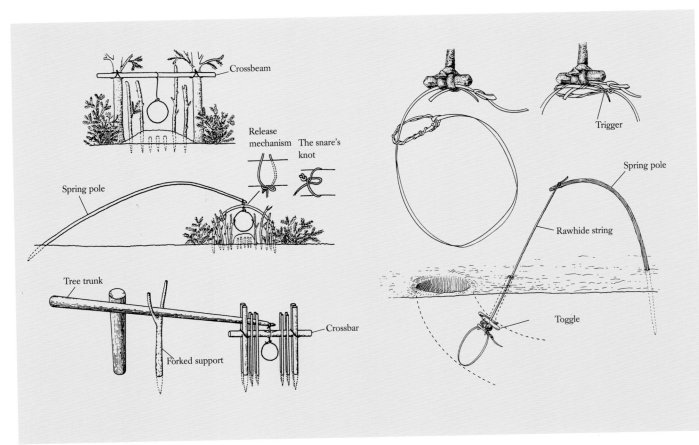

Crossbeam

Release mechanism

The snare's knot

Spring pole

Tree trunk

Forked support

Crossbar

Trigger

Spring pole

Rawhide string

Toggle

**Snares of the Subarctic.**

Like all traps, snares are automated hunting mechanisms set into motion either by the prey itself or by weights or spring poles.

Top left: a noose is suspended in an artificially narrowed passage in a game trail. The fox, for whom it is intended, jumps over a small pile of moss beneath the snare and draws the wire noose tightly round its own neck.

Center left: the noose is fastened to a spring pole which is prevented from springing back by an attached toggle. When a rabbit jumps through the small opening in the fence, the toggle is dislodged and the power of the spring pole is released and tightens the noose around the rabbit.

Right: the Tutchone chipmunk trap operates in a similar way. Here, a camouflaged noose has been placed near the exit of the chipmunks' lair. The mechanism is set off by the animal entering or leaving.

Bottom left: in this bear trap, the noose is attached to a tree trunk that serves both as a lever and a weight to operate the device, whose power is released when the crossbar is touched.

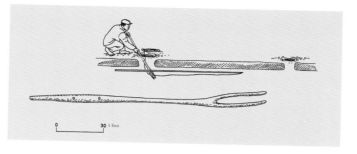

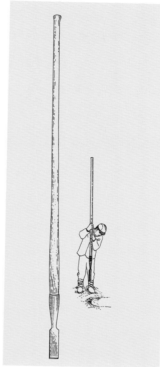

# The forest's richly set table

The range of available food was more varied in summer. Caribou appeared in larger herds, especially during their migrations between winter and summer grounds, and could be hunted down at river crossings, snared in the forest, or chased into corrals built from trees and bushes. In the Subarctic, traps are finely tuned to the way of life of particular animals, and are technical masterpieces of adaptation to the environment. Snares or deadfalls in particular were constructed for specific animals whose habits had been observed by hunters over a period of time. There were even traps for large animals, such as bears, in which a falling tree trunk would kill the animal that touched the bait.

With the help of dogs, bears could also be tracked down to the caves where they hibernated, or they could be taken by surprise in the berry groves where they went to fatten up for the winter. The fall was considered the best time for hunting bears, because then the prey was particularly fat and tasty. The hunters would try to kill the bears with spears or catch them in traps. In a direct confrontation with these raging beasts it was essential for a hunter to keep calm. If a bear stood up on its hind legs, its blows were dangerous, but it could not move as quickly. Now the hunter could seize the opportunity to run past it and pierce the animal's heart with his weapon.

In the Canadian forests, the Slavey and Beaver hunted the forest bison, which unlike its relatives on the Plains did not live in large herds but alone or in small groups. Moose too were hunted in this area, as they wandered mostly alone through the forests during the warm season.

A number of Alaskan peoples, such as the Ahtna and Tanana, could generally make a good living from salmon fishing. Like salmon, various kinds of whitefish in the Mackenzie River provide another reliable source of food at spawning time. During this period larger groups of people, who would have to spend the rest of the year scattered across the land in order to survive, came together at the weirs. The situation was similar in other parts of the Subarctic, where fishing in the summer brought with it a longer period of a more sedentary life and therefore allowed for a richer social life to be enjoyed.

Vegetables made up only a small part of the Subarctic diet, but the different types of blueberries, bilberries, and currants offered a most welcome change and addition to the meal, while dried berries could be preserved for a long time. They were also mixed into the standard preserved food, pemmican, which consisted mainly of pound dried meat mixed with bone marrow and fat. The bast of certain trees was eaten in the spring. The idea of boiling birch sap to make a syrup probably originated with the employees of the fur trading companies who were familiar with the maple syrup from further south.

Opposite page, bottom:
A Carrier fisherman secures his catch. Bulkley River, near Moricetown, British Columbia, c. 1995.

The Carrier spear and lift the jumping salmon out of the river with an iron hook attached to a detatchable foreshaft. A leather strap connects this foreshaft to the long pole. The Carrier are named after one of their customs: widows carried the ashes of their dead husbands with them on their backs. They call themselves Dakelhne ("those who walk on the water"), as they nearly always used their boats for moving through the branched-out network of rivers and lakes in their homeland.

# Of bones and dreams

A Tanaina story from southern Alaska tells of a young man who always carelessly broke and threw away the bones of the caribou he had killed. As a result, he was harassed by mice: they drove him away from his meals, ate the animals in his traps, and prevented him from sleeping at night. Later, he saw the mistress of the caribou in a dream. She showed him the terribly crippled animals whose sufferings were caused by his carelessness. She explained to him that the animal souls who had to slip into animal bodies formed from broken bones would never be able to return as prey.

Every species of animal hunted was living in some way under the protection of a master or mistress of the animals, and humans had to be on good terms with them if they wanted to be lucky in the hunt. Furthermore, every animal had its own soul. "The animal and its spirit are one and the same thing," a Koyukon explained to anthropologist Robert K. Nelson. "When you name the animal, you are also naming its spirit. That is why some animal names are *hutlanee* (taboo) – like the ones women should not say – because calling the animal's name is like calling its spirit. Just like we do not say a person's name after they die ... it would be calling their spirit and could be dangerous for whoever did it."

Hunting success could be guaranteed only by observing numerous rules. Among the Athapaskans of the north-western Subarctic, the hunter would dream of the animal's tracks before the hunt. In this way the animal's soul was showing him that it was ready to give itself to the hunter. Among the Algonquian peoples, the task of dreaming about the prey was usually assumed by a seer to whom the hunter had turned. Caribou also announced themselves to the Athapaskans through songs which would be on the hunter's mind after he had woken up. However, these songs could also point to broken taboos, if for instance, a menstruating

**Antler silhouette before sunset.**
Many Subarctic hunters placed caribou antlers on special constructions and decorated them with colored ribbons and the skulls of smaller mammals. As well as showing respect to the prey, this would secure future success in hunting from the master of the caribou.

woman had eaten fresh caribou meat. The hunter established a personal relationship with the animals and referred to the expected prey in terms of kinship or even as a lover.

Every hunt was preceded by a steam bath in the sweat lodge, to ritually cleanse the hunter. Anyone going hunting would announce his intention obliquely, saying "I am going to look for moose tracks," rather than "I am going to hunt moose." A killed animal's name was never used in its presence so that its soul would not be angered; a circumlocution was employed instead. Among the Koyukon the red fox would become "many tracks." Women were not allowed to call the brown bear by its name; they used the description "those who are in the woods." In English they spoke only of the "large animal." A fish was placed in the mouth of a wolf, and a bone in that of a fox to feed and appease their souls. One would break the hind legs of

snowshoe hares before bringing them into the house so that their souls would not hop around the house and cause damage. Many animals regarded having their bones chewed by dogs as particularly insulting, which is why dog food usually consisted of fish.

The tasty meat of the beaver was very popular everywhere, but the animal commanded respect for its lifestyle (calling someone "beaver" was high praise), and it had to be specially treated. Its throat must never be cut, nor its eyes injured. The Koyukon threw the bare bones back into the water with the plea "may you return next year."

Fish were also said to possess spiritual powers. Koyukon children had salmon tails hung around their neck as amulets against misfortune. The season's first catch of whitefish was eaten by the whole camp together, ensuring that not a single bone came loose from the fish's spine and that after the meal the whole skeleton was thrown back into the river.

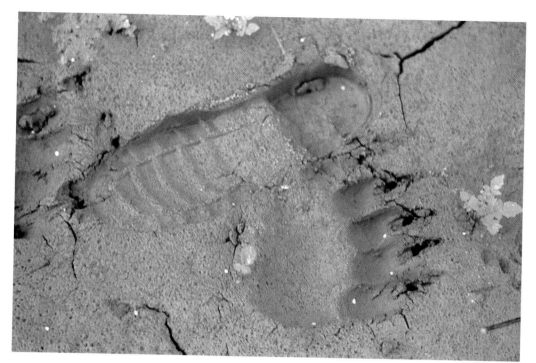

Footprints of bear and human in the mud.

Here the paths of a black bear and a human have crossed. Although the black bear is the smallest of the American bears, the inhabitants of the Subarctic attributed special magical powers to it. Much of its behavior appeared very human to them. As a conciliatory gesture, Attikamek hunters in Ontario placed a tobacco pipe in the mouth of a killed bear so that it could inhale the sacred smoke one last time.

Drawings of animal tracks (bear).

Tracks of the black bear and the grizzly bear showing their difference in size.

Opposite page:
Grizzly bear standing upright in the grass.

Standing on its hind legs, a grizzly bear can be up to 9 feet tall. The mighty bear and humans kept out of each other's way as much as possible.

# Grandfather bear

A virtual cult surrounding the bear hunt developed in the Subarctic. Black bears in particular were said to possess great powers. According to some Algonquian groups, they did not even need the protection of a master. They were considered to be man's closest relatives, able to understand the hunter's every word and even interpret his every thought. For instance, if a Montagnais-Naskapi hunter had discovered a bear's cave during the winter, he stood in front of it and shouted, "Grandfather, come out!" several times. If the bear did not appear, it was left in peace, as it was obviously not ready to give itself up to humans.

When a bear was killed, the team of hunters would smoke in honor of the dead animal and its soul, and would also put a little of the sacred tobacco in its mouth. Then they removed the stomach and small intestine from the animal's belly (the stomach was used as a container for the drained fat), which was then neatly sewed up again. Unlike other large game, the prey was not cut into pieces there and then but only in the village, where unmarried women were not allowed to see the bear.

In the hunter's dwelling, the bear, unlike other species, was flayed from the head downward, with a piece of the heart thrown into the fire as a sacrifice. Then a bear feast was called, at which the guests took their places according to rank.

The cooked bear's head and its front paws – spiritually and physically the most powerful parts of its body – took up an honorary guest's position, so to speak. In order of rank, men bit off pieces of meat after speeches had been addressed to the bear. All members of the group, including women and children, were allowed to eat the meat from the animal's back parts. The feast only finished when all the meat had been eaten.

It was followed by the bear's ritual funeral, a gesture of reconciliation. Those parts to be used in future (claws, teeth, bones to be used as scrapers, bearskins) were ritually cleansed. The skull was painted with red and black dots, and together with the front paws it was wrapped in birch bark and placed in the branches of a tree. The other bones had to be whole so that the soul could reconnect with them. They too were buried where they were safe from dogs.

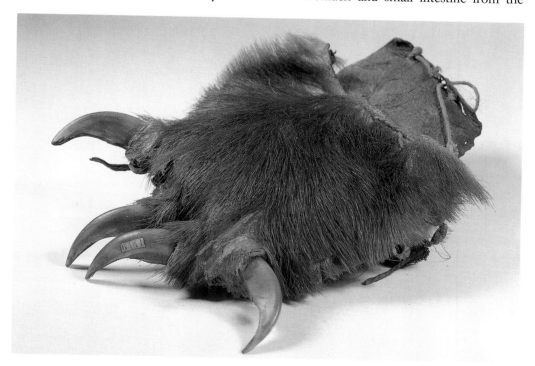

Grizzly bear paw. Rautenstrauch-Joest-Museum für Völkerkunde, Cologne, Germany.

Bear's paws were thought to contain particularly strong magical powers. It is unclear exactly what this paw was used for; it could have been part of a hunter's magical equipment. Naskapi hunters carried the lower lip or the tongue of a bear as an amulet for hunting magic.

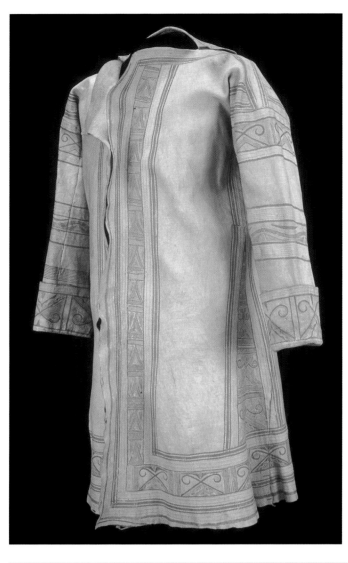

## Spirit helpers, tent shakers, and dreamers

Simply observing general rules was not enough to achieve hunting success. Every person possessed their own magical powers, which they had obtained through contact with the spiritual world. Animal spirits would appear in dreams or in visions brought about by a long period of fasting, and would teach the hunter songs or practices which could effectively be used in hunting, war, or healing the sick. Both men and women could practice divination. A very popular method was the use of the shoulder blade of animals, such as the caribou or the beaver, which would show cracks when placed in hot ash. These cracks were interpreted as maps indicating the current location of prey.

Some people obtained particularly great spiritual powers in visions and used these not only for themselves but also for others. These specialists, who received compensation for their services, had different techniques and areas of expertise. The tent shakers of the Algonquians, for instance, put up cylindrical tents with an opening at the top. From here they would call on their spirit helpers, whose arrival would announce itself through a palpable trembling of the tent. The onlookers would listen to the spirit helpers' conversations in a language only understood by the tent shaker. Sometimes the outline of one of their body parts would even become visible on the wall of the tent. Under the instructions of their client, the tent shaker would then

Painted Naskapi coat, early 18th century. Canadian Museum of Civilization, Hull, QC.

Decorative and religious elements often overlap. Made of finely tanned white caribou leather, Naskapi tailored coats were painted by the women with colorful line patterns inspired by the men's dreams. At the same time, their stylized form followed a traditional canon and has no apparent connection with the dreams. It was assumed that the caribou would be pleased by these beautiful coats and would be attracted to such finely dressed hunters.

Kutchin sled bag belonging to Episcopalian Archdeacon Hudson Stuck, c. 1900. University of Alaska Museum, Fairbanks, AK.

The Kutchin used the richly decorated "sled bags" to carry their Bibles as they made their way to church services. The Christian missions were not always greeted with enthusiasm by the fur traders, as converted Native Americans tended to spend more time with the priests at the trading posts instead of quickly selling their furs and returning to the hunt again. However, many missionaries settled at trading posts during the 19th century, Anglicans mainly to the east of Hudson Bay, French-speaking Catholics to the west. In Alaska, several Protestant churches became active after the sale of the Russian colony to the United States

ask the helpers about lost objects, how people away from the community were doing, where game was currently to be found, or why someone had become sick.

This concentration on hunting success and the interest in personal spiritual power instead of trust in one god presented the Christian missionaries with some problems. Father Émile Petitot, who lived among the Athapaskans around Great Slave Lake during the 1860s, told of a discouraged hunter who complained that since he had allowed himself to be baptized, the moose he was hunting only made fun of him and would not let him catch them. As a result, Petitot decided to hand out pictures of saints or prayers written on scraps of paper as lucky amulets for hunting. He found himself in a conflict of conscience when trappers for whom he had prayed attributed their success in fox hunting not to God but rather to the priest himself, asking him to continue dreaming for them.

His Dene converts recognized Petitot in terms of their culture as a dreamer (*naachin*, translated by them as

"prophet"). The Beaver *naachin* receive songs in their dreams through which they give support to others. They have a particularly important task to perform, that of dreaming of songs which will safely accompany people to heaven after their death.

This is how *naachin* Charlie Yahey described this task to anthropologist Robin Ridington: "There is no ladder into the sky. The ghosts have to make it on their own. There's a road to the sky – *yagatunne*. You've got to be good to make it. It used to be that people who dreamed about heaven put water and feathers upon the people's heads so they could go straight to heaven – just the way the priests baptize."

In this way, the dreamers of former times assimilated themselves into the Christian world view. The pre-Christian Athapaskans strongly believed in reincarnation. As caribou hunters, the Chipewyan identified so strongly with the wolf – also a caribou hunter – that they believed that wolves could be reborn as humans and humans as wolves.

Shoulder blade oracle of the Mistassini Cree, Quebec, 1969/70.

Among the Mistassini and other East Main Cree, the shoulder blade oracle is used not only for locating game but also to predict the weather, health, and other events. Other oracles (broken or found animal bones, or gazing into a vessel filled with water) may also complete the information gathered from observing the environment. Dreams and unusual shapes and sounds that the hunter had noticed also became subject to interpretation, mirroring people's endeavor to control their natural environment.

# Soft gold

Winter was considered to be the best time for hunting beaver by many peoples, not only the Red River Saulteaux here depicted. As the waters iced over, the rodents' mobility was limited to the small areas around their elaborate lodges. After blocking the entrances, hunters could break open the lodge and kill its inhabitants with spears. Nets also brought good hunting results. They were attached under the water's surface in front of the lodge's entrances. The beavers got entangled in them and drowned.

Before the arrival of the whites, the inhabitants of the Subarctic had little use for most fur animals. Beavers and hares were the only animals caught for both their meat and their furs. Only the European traders' demands made Algonquians and Athapaskans also hunt marten, mink, fox, and otter. Beaver skin, from which the fashionable beaver hats were made, however, remained the most important exchange commodity by which the value of all other goods was measured.

Shortly after establishing a trading post, the traders would usually complain that the hunters were not bringing enough skins. The hunters' need for trade goods, especially metal goods, was quickly met, and they continued to spend most of the year hunting caribou and moose as they had before. This kind of hunting could not easily be combined with trapping. The Chipewyan, for instance, who hunted caribou in the border areas between forest and tundra, could take part in the fur hunt only when they moved further south into coniferous forests where fur animals lived. Groups who opted for a more intensive fur hunt soon also depended on traders for some of their food supplies.

The supply of the trading posts offered hunters further opportunities for profit beyond the fur trade. In the late 18th century, the Assiniboine and some of the Cree began to supply the Hudson's Bay Company (HBC) posts southwest

Hare inspecting a stretched beaver pelt, from J. Savishinsky, *The Trail of the Hare* (1974). Photograph: Joel Savishinsky.

The prices paid for one beaver skin depended not only on the quality of the fur, but also on its treatment. Thoroughly cleaning the skins and drying them evenly on circular frames was the responsibility of the women. The men were responsible not only for hunting but also for trading.

Skins of red and arctic foxes and of other fur-bearing animals are hung up for an auction.

Today, many subarctic Native Americans and Métis combine trapping in winter with jobs in forestry or other branches of the economy. Only the middlemen still live exclusively from the fur trade.

themselves, but the so-called "Made Beaver" (MB), a unit into which all types of fur were converted. Sometimes the HBC even issued coinlike tokens worth one MB that functioned like cash.

For instance, in 1715 at the York Factory trading post in Hudson Bay, one beaver skin was worth a hand-held mirror, a small powder keg, or eight awls. One gun was worth thirteen skins of prime quality.

Among the Algonquians, individual families had the exclusive right to set traps in a certain area. This practice apparently became common after the results of over-hunting of fur-bearing animals had been experienced. The establishment of family hunting territories helped to prevent the extinction of the desirable fur animals, for the family's hunters would closely observe the stocks and had a personal interest in protecting them.

Hunting was still allowed everywhere, but setting traps was permissible only on a family's own land or in another territory on the owner's invitation. In practice, such invitations were frequent – for instance, when two men decided to set up two trap lines close together for security and companionship.

In this way animals living in the unused areas could start to multiply again. Even within a hunting territory certain species were protected when their numbers decreased – a measure that could more easily be taken in a territory owned by one family than in an area with several families competing for returns. The HBC's attitude to such practices was basically positive, but if several trading companies were actively engaged in a region, they often required of the trappers the rapid exploitation of resources in order to leave as little as possible from which their competitors could profit.

of Hudson Bay with bison meat, thus moving their hunting territory from the forest to the northern Plains. Some families stayed at the trading posts for most of the year. The men delivered meat to the traders, while the women produced warm clothes for them.

In remote areas beyond the reach of the fur traders, other groups acted as middlemen. For a long time, the Chipewyan profited from the trade with their northwesterly neighbors, the Athapaskans, for whom the white man's goods (metal tools, cloth, glass beads, and later also guns and ammunition) were particularly valuable, as they had no direct access to them.

Native trappers exploited the competition between different trading companies in order to drive up their prices or achieve better conditions. The traders were under additional pressure from price fluctuations on the European market, which they could not pass on to the hunters, who had no conception of such processes. A trader who gave his clients credit in the form of food and hunting equipment in the fall ran the risk that in the spring his debtors would take their furs to another trading station. Efforts to abandon the credit system were made after 1821, when the HBC had gained a monopoly over wide areas, but many traders realized that a family without provisions spent too much time hunting for food and thus neglecting trapping. The currency in this credit system was not the beaver skins

# Scattered survival, communal affluence

*Skin lodges of the Dogrib Indians in front of the HBC's fort on Great Slave Lake, 1895–1901. Northwest Territories Archives, Yellowknife, NWT.*

Tents were best suited to the nomadic way of life of the caribou hunters. In winter, caribou furs rather than bare skins covered the tent poles, as these offered better protection in cold weather. During summer, all social life – cooking, eating, gossiping, gambling, smoking, sewing, repairing tools, and so on – took place outside the tents anyway. The canvas tent covers used later were an inadequate substitute, particularly because of their poor insulation, but they eventually established themselves as the standard, as they were easily available.

The subarctic environment could not sustain larger groups of people over a long period of time. Therefore for the greater part of the year the northern Athapaskans and Algonquian found it necessary to live in small groups of a few families, each one usually consisting of an experienced hunter, and his relatives by blood and through marriage. One or two nuclear families would live in a dome-shaped or conical tent (*wigwam* in most Algonquian languages) covered with birch bark or caribou skin.

A newlywed couple would usually join the woman's family for a certain period of time, but afterward the choice of which family the couple would go with was relatively free. In some northwestern tribes, the husband would spend a year of bride service in his in-laws' household. Good hunters could sometimes afford to have two wives, who were often sisters.

These extented families would only gather into larger groups, whose members were likewise partly related to each other, at certain times of the year. Occasions for such assemblies were provided when it was necessary for a large number of people to work together, such as for the caribou hunt in the fall or for catching salmon at the time of their spawning runs. These meetings also offered the opportunity to see relatives and friends again, to find marriage partners, or to join another group when the large gathering of a few hundred people broke up again. The anthropological term for this type of local organization is "band."

In the fur trade era, this communal economic activity was increasingly replaced by gatherings at the various trading posts in early summer, when the trappers sold their catch of the hunting season. The number of people connected through common trading posts could often be significantly higher than that of the hunting bands of former times.

There was no formal position of chief, but only particularly experienced and successful hunters around whom their followers would gather. The groupings of the northwestern Athapaskans stand in contrast to such impermanent communities. Here, descent followed the maternal line, and in several places the position of chief was hereditary.

The Hudson's Bay Company (HBC) interfered in the existing political structures, especially in the early days, by giving preferential treatment to some leaders and giving them luxury goods as presents in order to persuade them to return with their followers for the coming year's trade. Only gradually did the role of such trading captains merge with that of the chief, whose authority traditionally rested purely on his hunting skills and on the modest wealth arising from these.

Abel Chapman tells of the situation of his grandfather Abraham Beardy, chief of the York Factory Cree in the first half of the 20th century, who every spring collected his people's best furs and sold them to the HBC. "Then what he received would go towards their credit and the rest is left on their account ... That money that he looked after in the accounts was for everybody, for all his people, so when a family ran short of food, money was taken from this account and food was puchased for them ... He would get the councillors to go and give the family this food. This was always available, and also if there was to be a wedding, money was taken for food." Once he had distributed all the meat and the skins caught by hunters from his family among the members of the groups that he led. Now, in contrast, the chieftain was in charge of the profits made from the fur trade.

Societies in the northern Rocky Mountains and Alaska had a significantly more hierarchical structure. Permanent caribou fences cut off the animals' escape routes during the hunt, and they were controlled by chiefs who could order members of their group to construct and maintain them. The salmon runs in the rivers provided an opportunity for a more sedentary lifestyle during the summer. At their fishing grounds, the Tanaina erected square houses with walls made of strips of bark or constructed of logs laid horizontally between corner posts, while during the winter they lived in leather tents. In the mountains, some houses were partly set into the ground, with gable roofs made from tree trunks, which thanks to the warmth from the earth, never got as cold as the thin and drafty tents.

Storehouses were an essential part of every settlement. They were usually either simple platforms or small houses on stilts, which kept food supplies reasonably well protected from the village curs and from other thieves such as foxes and raccoons. Here provisions could be dried in the summer and stored frozen in winter. Such "Indian freezers," in which smoked fish, dried meat, and dried berries are stored, can still be found situated next to the log cabins which are the homes of many Athapaskans today.

Hare summer camp at Great Bear Lake, 1969. Northwest Territories Archives, Yellowknife, NWT.

For many Athapaskans today, summer and early fall have remained the fishing seasons, when people spend the longest time in a larger group. Children are on their summer vacations and return from their boarding schools in the south. In addition to fishing there is also paid employment to be found with the local fur trader or at the mission.

# Moccasin, toboggan, and snowshoe

Almost every part of the caribou and moose was used. Bones and antlers supplied tools, the stomach could be used as a bowl, the brain served for tanning leather. As material for clothing the ruminants' skins, were nearly as important as their meat.

Athapaskan men wore long-sleeved, knee-length shirts with pointed hems, and under them, particularly in winter, leggings to which moccasins were often directly sewn. Women dressed similarly, but their shirts reached to their calves and the hems were straight. The Chipewyan's name derives from the Cree term for "pointed furs" describing this traditional Athapaskan clothing. The clothing of both sexes was originally decorated with bands of colored porcupine quills, and with leather fringes.

Men's clothing among the Algonquians consisted of leggings, a breechclout, and a shirt. A leather coat was worn over this in winter. The women's dresses were held up by shoulder straps and had detachable sleeves.

Mothers carried their children on their backs in baskets of birch bark or simply in a cloth attached with a strap. In the eastern Subarctic, moccasins were made from one piece of leather shaped to fit the foot with only two seams, one from the instep to the toes and another one at the heel. Hard soles were unnecessary on the soft forest floor. In the west, a gusset was added in front of the instep. Today *mukluks*, colorfully embroidered boots modeled on those of the Eskimo, are also part of the ethnic costume there.

Large animal skins, and later the woolen blankets supplied by the Hudson's Bay Company (HBC), served as coats. The furs of small animals were rarely used; only rabbitskin was cut into small strips and used for making blankets and coats. This practice also gave the Athapaskan Hare their name. Leather coats open at the front probably followed European models, as did new kinds of caps, shawls, and bags, often richly decorated with glass beads in geometric or floral patterns.

Whereas smaller game was carried in hunting bags, larger prey was generally brought back to the camp by means of carrying straps. In winter a toboggan (like "moccasin," a word from the Algonquian languages) was used for transporting heavy loads. This was a sled without runners made of one or two thin boards bent up and over

William G. R. Hind, *Louis' Wife with a Group of Montagnais Squaws*, watercolor and gouache, 1861/62. Dalhousie Art Gallery Collection, Halifax, NS.

The Montagnais, who call themselves *ilnu* ("humans"), had been in contact with French settlers and missionaries since the 17th century, and quickly replaced their leather clothing, which required much effort to make, with imported textiles. Here, English-born painter William Hind (1833–1889) depicts Montagnais women whom he met on an expedition through Labrador in 1861. The caps, based on regional French traditions, and the hair tied into knots over a small wooden board soon became typical of the Montagnais and were regarded as traditional dress.

*Tennanah Tribe: Man and Woman,* from Ivan Petroff, *Report on the Population, Industries, and Resources of Alaska,* Washington, 1884.

For a long time, the central Alaskan Tanana's access to European goods depended on the Kutchin and Koyukon middlemen who operated from Fort Yukon and Nulato. Around 1880, when this illustration was made, the use of glass beads for decorating clothing was gaining popularity among the Tanana. The man's shirt shows both the traditional hem ending in a point and the shoulder pieces and a bib embroidered with beads that were modeled on English hunting shirts.

at the front, and pulled by people or dogs. The Siberian-style dog sleds introduced to Alaska by the Russians were popular in the Subarctic, too, until the advent of snowmobiles. However, the most important means of transportation in winter were undoubtedly snowshoes, which bear a faint resemblance to tennis rackets. They consisted of a bent wooden frame and strips of untanned hide woven together which supported the foot and prevented the wearer from sinking into the snow. Using a pole for support, people made their way through the snow with their legs apart. This required considerable effort, but, thus equipped, they were still much faster

Opposite page, above:
Making moccasins, a woman's task.

Making moccasins is one of the
traditional crafts that is still alive in
the Subarctic, unlike others – such
as canoe building – that have been
forgotten. The sole and sides of a
moccasin are made from a single
piece of leather. Before the upper
cover and the optional side cuffs for
protecting the ankle are attached, they
are decorated with glass beads or
embroidered with moose hair or silk.

Opposite page, bottom left:
Cree or Métis embroidered
moccasins, c. 1880. Rautenstrauch-
Joest-Museum für Völkerkunde,
Cologne, Germany.

The floral patterns embroidered in
silk on the U-shaped instep follow
European models. The Métis and their
Cree and Ojibwa wives contributed
much to the spread of this style. The
high cuffs provided effective protection
against the snow and could be snuggly
tied with a leather band at the front.

Opposite page, bottom right:
Naskapi painted leggings of caribou
leather, Labrador, c.1800.
Ethnologisches Museum, Staatliche
Museen zu Berlin – Preussischer
Kulturbesitz, Berlin, Germany.

Made from a single piece of leather
sewn together at the side, these
leggings were attached to the belt by
straps. The way that they are painted is
reminiscent of the Naskapi's coats, and
like these probably also served to win
the approval of the caribou who would
then agree to let themselves be killed
by the hunter.

Man with dogs harnessed to
toboggan, Ndilo, Yellowknife.
Northwest Territories Archives,
Yellowknife, NWT.

While sled dogs and sleds with runners
became popular in the Alaskan
Subarctic, in Canada the dogs were
harnessed to toboggans. Shortly before
entering a settlement, the toboggan
driver would cover the dogs with
blankets decorated with bells and
glass beads and attach upright poles
with colorful woolen tassels to them,
to make a good impression on his
neighbors. The inhabitants of the
Subarctic loved color and were ready
to spend huge amounts on colored
glass beads, which were a status
symbol. Fur traders complained that
rich chiefs would put aside hundreds
of furs just to obtain particular types
of glass beads.

than the four-legged animals which inevitably sank into the snow. Only snowshoes made it possible for people to move camp or to catch up with the fleeing game even in the deepest of winter.

In shape and size, snowshoes differed considerably between Subarctic peoples, depending on their intended purpose. The Cree had rounded snowshoes designed for hunting in open country, and long, heavy ones with the front bent upward with which they were able to break a trail through deep snow in the forest. Children were often given small, round snowshoes as soon as they were able to walk.

The Kutchin fashioned their long snowshoes with rounded fronts in two distinct sizes. The smaller ones were used on well-trodden paths, while the larger variety, which was as long as the wearer was tall, were perfectly adapted for hunting in the bush. The Tanaina were experts in producing different thicknesses of weaves each particularly appropriate for a different kind of snow.

Along with snowmobiles, snowshoes are still widely used today. However, for many of the subarctic settlements which cannot be reached by road, the airplane serves as the main connection to the outside world, and has now become an essential means of transportation for both people and goods.

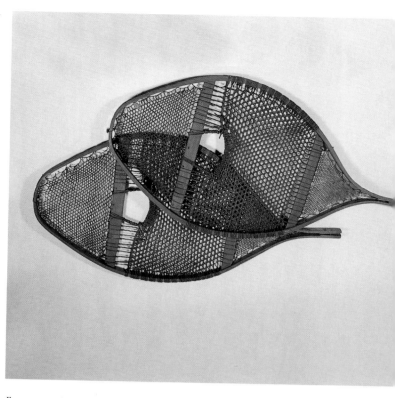

Frame snowshoes of the eastern Subarctic, c. 1880. Rautenstrauch-Joest-Museum für Völkerkunde, Cologne, Germany.

Two crossbars reinforce the frame made from a piece of wood softened in steam and bent into an oval shape to form the "swallowtail" snowshoes typical of the eastern Subarctic. In the 19th century the Huron of Lorette produced snowshoes on a commercial basis for white Canadians .

Trunks of birch trees.

Birch bark is very resistant to decay, rotting more slowly than the wood, so that when a birch falls over, the hollow bark remains the longest. According to Ojibwa beliefs, Nanabozho, the mischievous culture hero, made use of this when he was fleeing the thunderbirds whose children he had killed. When the thunderbirds were already so close that he could almost feel their claws in his back, he saved himself by hiding in a hollow birch. The thunderbirds left him alone, as they regarded the birch as a creature of their own kind. When the danger had passed, Nanabozho crawled out from his bark cover and announced that from then on, people were to use and honor the birch. If they wanted to store anything, they could use birch bark as packaging material, but they had to make an offering of tobacco to the tree.

Western Woods Cree bucket made of birch bark (*makuk*), Saskatchewan, c. 1910. Ethnologisches Museum, Staatliche Museen zu Berlin – Preussischer Kulturbesitz, Berlin, Germany.

The container is sewn from just one piece of birch bark and is reinforced by wrapped twigs along the edge. The upper half shows a sawtooth decoration of thinner bark. The strap is made of leather.

# "The most precious tree of the Northwest"

"Beneath the bark of the birch one finds an excellent natural tinder, the only kind used throughout the north," reported the Dene's missionary Petitot in the 19th century. "The bark is used to make vases, boxes, all kinds of tools, lightweight boats, and roofs for the huts. The birch's wood, very hard, finely grained like boxtree and at the same time very flexible, serves for the manufacture of snowshoes, seats, sleds, ribs for canoes and boats, drums, rattles, and a multitude of other things. Finally, the sap of this precious tree, which is gathered in spring and prepared like that of the *acer* and the *negundo* (two types of maple), turns into a syrup which is kept in a barrel until the following year."

Best peeled in spring when the sap is rising in the trees, fresh birch bark is easily bent, folded, and used for sewing. It is light, stable, and waterproof. Boats made from birch bark, with their flat keels and shallow draft, are suitable for use in shallow waters, and thanks to their light weight, they can be carried past rapids or from one river to another over the watersheds that are such a common feature in northern Canada. In the summer a bark boat is by far the fastest and most comfortable means of transportation for anyone traveling on the taiga's waterways.

An Algonquian bark boat measured between 12 feet (for one person and baggage) and 20 feet (for several passengers). The trading companies ordered larger boats to transport goods and crews. To make a boat out of bark, several smaller pieces of bark were sewn to a central strip the length of the keel. These smaller pieces added sufficient width for the bark to be folded in over both sides of the boat. Wooden ribs bent into shape over steam and two poles reinforcing the rim of the boat formed a loose frame. The boat's outer cover of birch bark was sewn to the frame with splints made from spruce roots. Finally, the seams were sealed with pitch obtained from spruce trees.

The Athapaskans in the southwestern part of the Mackenzie Plain also made boats from a single piece of spruce bark held in shape by a few ribs. The boats made from this brittle material did not last long, but were quicker to build.

The outer cover of wigwams was sewn together from several strips of birch bark similar to that used for the sides of boats. When a camp was taken down, the bark was kept for future use.

Birch bark was also the raw material employed for making items such as plates, bowls, pails, berry baskets,

Model of a Beothuk birch bark boat, c. 1820. National Museum of Scotland, Edinburgh, Scotland.

Many Europeans who used these light bark boats for the first time were frightened by their lack of stability on the water. Unpracticed users easily capsized. For this reason, the Beothuk always carried stones in their boats as ballast. Using different types of these canoes, they traveled both on inland waters and on the ocean. Boats of the type shown here were used particularly for inland travel, and models of them were often buried with the dead. In an oceangoing canoe, Beothuk paddlers could cover as much as 40 miles a day.

storage vessels, baby carriers, and other utensils. Placed over an open fire, bark vessels would have burned, so instead red hot stones were put into the water to bring it to the boil. Although metal, chinaware, and plastic have replaced bark objects in practical use, vessels made of bark have remained an important part of folk art to this day.

To make a container, the bark is folded and sewn together with root splints. The rim is often reinforced with a wooden hoop. Decorative patterns can be scratched into the darker inner surface of the bark, which in the case of most vessels is on the outside, so that the lighter outer surface of the bark becomes visible.

The Koyukon of northern Alaska paid similar respect to this tree as they did to their prey. According to their beliefs a birch must never be peeled in the winter, as this would bring severe frost to the region. Also, anyone who had left shavings of birch trees lying around carelessly or had burned them after carving would no longer be able to find any suitable birch trees for carving.

*Cree Indian settlement on the Jack Fish River, Lake Winnipeg*, 1884. Peabody Museum, Harvard University, Cambridge, MA.

Birch bark was used for building dome-shaped and conical huts as well as boats. Spruce bark could also be used to cover houses, but unlike birch bark it was not sewn together in strips but applied in single pieces. However, spruce bark easily becomes brittle in severe frosts.

Opposite page, below:

Birch bark vesell, Carrier, Upper Skeena River, British Columbia, c. 1920. Canadian Museum of Civilization, Hull, QC.

Techniques for decorating birch bark differed between the Algonquians and the Athapaskans. The Algonquians created positive patterns by scraping off the layer of dark bark around a stencil so as to produce a dark pattern on a lighter ground. The Athapaskans achieved the opposite effect by scratching the pattern into the bark freehand, giving this part a lighter tone than the rest.

# Kutchin – border lands

The Kutchin, in Canada also known as Loucheux, are Athapaskan groups who inhabited a large area from the Mackenzie Plain in the east over the northern Cordilleras to the Yukon valley. They lived on the border between the more sedentary Alaskan Athapaskans with their more complex social order (hereditary chiefdom), and the less formally structured Canadian groups. At the same time, their territory bordered the Inuit area to the north.

Their relation with the Inuit can only be described as one of fragile peace. Both sides liked to trade with each other, but also repeatedly tried to improve on their own balance of trade through raids and kidnapping women. These conflicts even led to shifting borders between the two populations. In the early 19th century, the Kutchin still lived far to the west, on the southern slopes of the Alaskan Brooks Range, but were driven away from there by the inland caribou hunting Inupiaq.

War was also waged against other Athapaskan groups and was a way of achieving status in society. The leader, who was chosen just before going to war, was usually younger than the chief of the hunting group. The position of chief itself often passed from father to son, as it required not only experience and skill in hunting, but also considerable wealth, thus enabling the chief to attatch a following to himself which would then take part in such communal enterprises as building weirs or erecting caribou corrals, as well as claim the chief's support in times of need.

A good hunter brought in a large amount of prey, which in turn required much labor in the form of cleaning and tanning the animal skins and making clothes out of them. Therefore a wealthy man was usually head of a large household, with two or three wives. A chief's first wife

Delta of the Mackenzie River, Inuvik, Northwest Territories, Canada.

The border between the territories of the Kutchin and the Mackenzie Delta Eskimo is at the confluence of the Mackenzie and Peel rivers. From here the delta, with its countless branches, stretches out to the coast of the Arctic Ocean. With its drainage area including British Columbia, Alberta, and Saskatchewan, the Mackenzie is the Subarctic's greatest river. In summer, melted snow swells the river to 20 times its winter volume.

Frederick Whymper, *Fort Yukon: Hudson's Bay Company Post,* from F. Whymper, *Travel and Adventure in the Territory of Alaska*, New York, 1869.

From 1847 Fort Yukon was the gateway for new cultural ideas among the Kutchin. Trade with the Hudson's Bay Company brought not only Scottish fiddle music, of which modern versions are regarded as typical of Athapaskan culture, but also influences from distant Native American cultures. The Kutchin heard from the trading post's Cree employees about the trickster Wisakechak (known in English as Whisky Jack), whom they incorporated into their own collection of stories as Vasaagijik. Visaagijik now competes with Raven for the role of the deceitful and greedy trickster.

enjoyed high status, but held no formal position of political leadership. A high bride price was generally required for marriage to daughters from good families, which is why such women were often the target of kidnapping across tribal boundaries. Sometimes such a woman would end up living with several men, as none of them could afford to pay the high price for the bride on his own. A newlywed couple would usually join the bride's family.

Membership in one of the three clans, which also defined social ranking, was passed down through the female line. Members of a clan were said to have particular attributes. For instance, members of the Naatsaai clan were considered to be tall, dark-skinned, and passionate. Marriages could only be made outside one's own clan.

To hold a feast in memory of the dead, similar to the potlatch of the Northwest Coast, a wealthy man needed the support of his relatives and followers. About a year after his or her death, the deceased would be honored with a festive meal to which members of other clans who had helped with the funeral were also invited. The guests received presents such as caribou skins (later also trade blankets), ornaments, and tools, which were hung out on a fence for public exhibition.

In 1932 a Kutchin from the Peel River in Canada summed up the contents of the songs performed at such occasions in the following manner: "Sorry about good friend is dead – how good man he is – never come back again – I wish his luck come to us." In spite of these affirmations of mourning and farewells, the belief in reincarnation was and is widespread among the Kutchin. According to their belief, an indefinite number of the living are reincarnated souls.

To the Kutchin, the borderline between human and animal becomes blurred in the case of the caribou, to whom they feel closely related even though they hunt them. They believe that, from mythical times onward, every human being has carried a piece of caribou heart in their breast, and caribou have a partly human heart. Members of the three clans feel a special connection with particular animals (for example, the highest-ranking clan is associated with the raven), but individuals can also obtain a personal guardian spirit who will appear to them in dreams. However, such a spirit cannot be gained through conscious effort.

The Kutchin found themselves on the border in their history, too. Russian goods came up the Yukon and were sold on by the Kutchin into the hills or to the Inupiaq. In 1847 the Hudson's Bay Company (HBC) coming from the continent's interior founded Fort Yukon in Kutchin territory, on land claimed by the Russians. When Alaska was sold to the United States, the post had to be moved across the border into Canada. However, Fort Yukon remained as a Kutchin settlement.

Today, nation-state citizenship defines the organizational structure of Kutchin villages. Since the regulation of land rights which took place in 1971, every village in Alaska is now a landowning joint-stock company, while the indigenous population in the Canadian Yukon Territory are still currently in negotiation over their claims for land rights. However, the six contemporary Kutchin (Gwich'in in Canada) tribes have developed a strong sense of unity.

# Around Great Slave Lake

Before the arrival of the whites, the Chipewyan, the linguistically related Yellowknife, Dogrib, and Slavey, all living around Great Slave Lake, traded with each other, intermarried, and stood in close though not always friendly relation to each other. The Yellowstone in particular had desirable goods to offer their neighbors, as the pure copper found in the ground of their territory could be hammered into blades and other tools without heating.

The Yellowknife were named after the copper found on their territory, which provided the material for knives, arrowheads, and ornaments. According to legend, the metal was discovered by a Yellowknife woman escaping from Inuit captivity, who found a mountain glowing red. When she showed the place to other Yellowknife men, they raped her and she retreated into the interior of the mountain. From here, she gave copper only to those who brought her an offering.

When the Northwest Company founded a settlement on the lake's southern shore in 1786, relationships between neighbors were reorganized. Before the trading post was established, some Chipewyan groups had controlled the intermediate trade between the Great Slave Lake and the Hudson's Bay Company (HBC) to the south. Later, the Yellowknife became middlemen for the Dogrib and Hare living in the northwest, and often used their privileged position to intimidate and raid their neighbors.

In 1823 the Dogrib wreaked revenge by mowing down Chief Long Leg's camp. One fifth of the Yellowknife, who numbered only 150, were killed.

The establishment of scattered HBC trading posts in the northwest gradually made middlemen redundant, and in the second half of the 19th century life around the lake became peaceful again. Dogrib families joined Chipewyan hunting groups and vice versa, while Yellowknife families assimilated into both neighboring groups and ceased to exist as an independent people.

At the end of the 19th century, the Athapaskans adopted a more sedentary way of life. Initially, log cabin villages developed on the shores of the lake, with the inhabitants fishing in summer and migrating into the interior for winter trapping. At Christmas and Easter, and for the distribution of treaty annuity rations in July, families from several villages would gather at Fort Resolution on the southern shore or at Fort Rae in the north. Instead of moving to the tundra to hunt caribou, people concentrated on trapping for fur, but continued to live in purely indigenous communities.

Even in the 20th century, isolation and inadequate supply led to serious epidemics (influenza in 1928, measles in 1948). In addition, fur prices fell after World War II, making the fur trade less attractive, and so there came the desire to connect to national progress. Gradually people settled permanently around the old trading posts rather than living from trapping in the bush. This development was supported by the Canadian government's decision to assume responsibility for education and health in the north and to make welfare payments. The Athapaskans found little employment in the expanding mining and timber industries,

*Akaitcho and his Son*, color lithograph of 1821 after R. Hood. National Archives of Canada, Ottawa, ON.

By supporting the fur trade, Akaitcho, chief of several Yellowknife groups, controlled the meat supply of several trading posts and the intermediary trade with his neighbors. As a result he built up a large following. This portrait of him and his son was made during John Franklin's expedition of 1819 to 1822, to which he provided valuable services. When, from 1823 on, the Dogrib attacked the Yellowknife's dominance and finally gained ascendance, Akaitcho's following was reduced to a few families.

On the shores of Great Slave Lake, Fort Smith, Northwest Territories, Canada.

Covering more than 10,000 square miles, Great Slave Lake is Canada's second-largest lake and the deepest in North America. While its eastern arm reaches into the tundra of Dogrib territory, its southern shore, inhabited by the Slavey and Chipewyan, is a wooded area.

Opposite page, bottom:
Interior of a Dogrib tent, after Émile Petitot, 1864, from É. Petitot, *Autour du Grand Lac des Esclaves*, Paris, 1891.

The woman on the left and the man behind the fire wear richly decorated knife sheaths round their necks. The two figures on the right are wrapped in woolen blankets of the kind provided by the HBC. The copper kettle in the right foreground is also evidence of the influence of traders. According to their own tradition, the Dogrib are descendants of a Yellowknife woman who married a dog.

and even then it was only seasonal as both were forced to cease operating during the tundra's icy winters. Most lived off state welfare supplemented by some hunting or trapping.

Tensions and jealousy arose in relation to the Métis, the descendants of mixed marriages between white traders or coureurs de bois and Native American women, and to the "Non-Status Indians" (who are denied recognition and therefore rights as members of Canada's First Nations by the government because of a lack of documented native descent). These people were not accounted for in the treaties with the Dene and could not make use of the services (such as healthcare) guaranteed there. However, they often spoke better English than the Athapaskans with recognized "Indian status" and therefore had easier access – although not without discrimination – to paid employment, making them socially superior to the Dene.

Not only the Métis complain about treaties No. 10 (1907) and No. 11 (1921). The treaties state that, after selling their land, the indigenous population could retain only hunting rights and small reservations – which were never established in the Northwest Territories. Witnesses, however, insist that the sale of their land was never an issue raised with the Athapaskans, and that it was only a pact of friendship. Since 1970, representatives of the various tribes have united in the Indian Brotherhood of the Northwest Territories (today called Dene Nation). Together with Métis organizations, they fight for their land claims and negotiate with the Northwest Territories and the Canadian federal government about the possibility of regional autonomy similar to that of the Inuit.

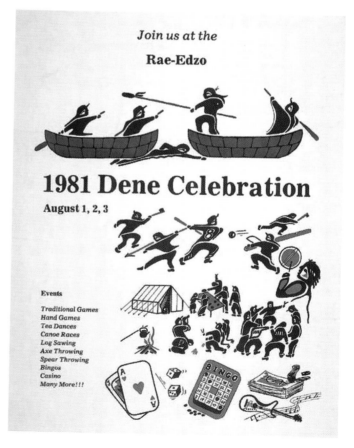

"Join us at the Rae-Edzo 1981 Dene Celebration."

Since the 1899 and 1921 treaties with the peoples around Great Slave Lake, annual celebrations were held at the trading posts of Resolution and Rae on the occasion of the distribution of rations promised by the government. Festivals such as the Dene Celebration follow the tradition of these "treaty days," with traditional and modern entertainments ranging from boat races to ax throwing to bingo.

# Cree – hunters and bureaucrats

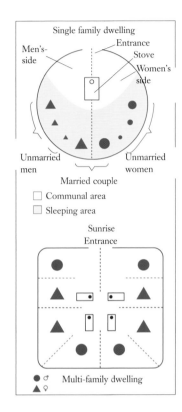

Single family dwelling

Men's side · Entrance · Stove · Women's side

Unmarried men · Unmarried women

Married couple

☐ Communal area
☐ Sleeping area

Sunrise
Entrance

Multi-family dwelling

● ♂
▲ ♀

**Cree dwellings.**

Mistassini Cree houses follow strict gender divisions. In the single-family tent, which is inhabited for the greater part of the year, the women sleep on one side, the men on the other. Both sexes also keep their equipment on their side: the food stores on the women's side, hunting equipment and traps on the men's. Only the fire is a neutral space, with both sexes gathering around it. The oldest unmarried woman of the family prepares the meals, while the married woman is responsible for tanning and processing leather. The entrance faces towards the water in summer, and to the east in winter. Used for part of the winter, tents housing several families are partitioned into single units which are organized like the tents for single families. Every unit has its own stove. The units are arranged in such a way that members of the same sex sleep on both sides of a wall. If there is an odd number of family units, an improvised extension is added.

**Preparing a meal in a Cree hunting camp, c. 1990.**

All prey from a communal hunting expedition is shared equally, regardless of the success of individual participants. However, the meal is usually prepared by the individual families on their own fire.

Over the centuries, the Cree became involved in all aspects of the great fur trade in their wide-ranging territory on both sides of James Bay, in the forests on the western shores of Hudson Bay, and on the northern Plains. They acted not only as trappers, but also as suppliers of provisions, carriers and oarsmen for the trading posts (the huge shipments of goods had somehow to be transported), and used their position to act as middlemen for groups living in the hinterland. Thanks to careful preservation of fur animals in family hunting grounds, the fur trade, together with big game hunting, formed the economic basis for the communities east of James Bay for more than 300 years.

Their close connections with the fur trade also gave the Cree a special position in the province of Quebec. Their land, administered directly by the Hudson's Bay Company (HBC), as well as the entire coast along Hudson Bay and the Canadian northwest, only became part of Canada in 1870. Quebec took on the administration of its northern areas in 1912, but concluded no treaties with the indigenous population. The Cree villages were declared reservations and placed under the authority of the Department of Indian Affairs and Northern Development (DIAND), the Canadian equivalent of the United States Bureau of Indian Affairs. As in the United States, it was primarily a trust administration of the land and the tribes' economic resources, as well as an institution executing the government's policies on Native Americans. The English-language education in DIAND schools continued the trend set by trade with the HBC and by Anglican missions, namely a stronger orientation toward the English-speaking part of Canada rather than the French-speaking part. In the last referendum concerning the secession of the predominantly French province of Quebec, it was the Cree votes that kept the province in the Canadian federation.

In 1975, the James Bay Cree were together with the Inuit partners in the James Bay and Northern Quebec Agreement. This arose from Quebec's plans to build hydro-electric power stations in its northern areas to export electricity to the United States, which met with resistance from the Native populations concerned. The agreement gave the Cree local autonomy and ownership of land

Peter Rindisbacher, *Cree Indians at York Factory*, c. 1821. National Archives of Canada, Ottawa, ON.

A Cree family returns from the hunt for the Hudson's Bay Company's York Factory on the west side of Hudson Bay. The man wears a "chief's coat," a uniform coat that the HBC gave to loyal trading partners among their chiefs who brought their followers to the trading posts. In spring and fall, flocks of migrating ducks and geese amply supplied both families and trading posts.

Below left:
Lubicon Cree house with frame for drying skins, c. 1990.

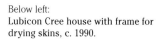

Their isolated territory offers the Lubicon Cree little alternative to hunting and trapping, a life that is now threatened by oil and timber companies working on their land. The Lubicon Cree are not even entitled to shares in the profits of these uninvited guests, as their land claims are not recognized. In 1982 Chief Bernard Ominayak described the desperate situation of his people to a parliamentary commission. "Oil companies level our trap lines and use sticks from our traps as road markers. Moose, our main source of meat, have practically disappeared in our area since the onset of development activity....Trails which our people have used for centuries are being made into private oil company roads; posted with 'No Trespassing' signs and protected by gates and guards."

Below right:
Oil pump in Lubicon Cree territory, c. 1990.

Like the James Bay Cree in their fight against damming projects, the Lubicon Cree in Alberta attracted the attention of support groups in the 1980s when they effectively used the media to protest against oil and timber extraction on their land, which they had never given up. In 1899 this small group had been overlooked by the whites in their treaty negotiations covering the whole of the Canadian Northwest. The mistake was recognized in 1939, but to this day this group of about 500 people has not received its own reservation.

around their villages. For the first time, the hitherto independent families united on a regional level, economically in the Cree Regional Economic Development Corporation, politically in the Grand Council of the Cree, and educationally in a Cree education authority. The prospect of employment in these newly developed offices encouraged young Crees for the first time to complete their schooling.

The Cree are still passionate hunters trying to secure a living through hunting. Cree politicians repeatedly describe this as part of their own identity, even though there are obvious contradictions between the market-oriented exploitation of the land and an ecological bond to nature. The James Bay Agreement created a support program for hunters which guarantees a minimum income for families living from hunting. In this way, subsidies for hunting decrease the number of welfare claimants. In 1996/97, 1,742

adults made use of this program, representing 38 percent of all James Bay Cree of working age. Most of them are married couples with small or even grown-up children, who spend the winter in the bush, or those who have relatives to look after their school-age children.

The James Bay Agreement also created stronger links to southern Quebec. On the one hand, sports fishermen and hunters from southern cities present increasing competition for the Cree; on the other, fish are affected by the damming of rivers, which in many places have been contaminated by industrial sewage carrying mercury and other heavy metal compounds. The even greater autonomy demanded by Cree organizations would not change their dependency on income from the electrical power, logging, mining, and tourist industries. It would, however, give those directly affected a greater voice in decisions concerning the direction that economic development should take.

# NORTHEAST

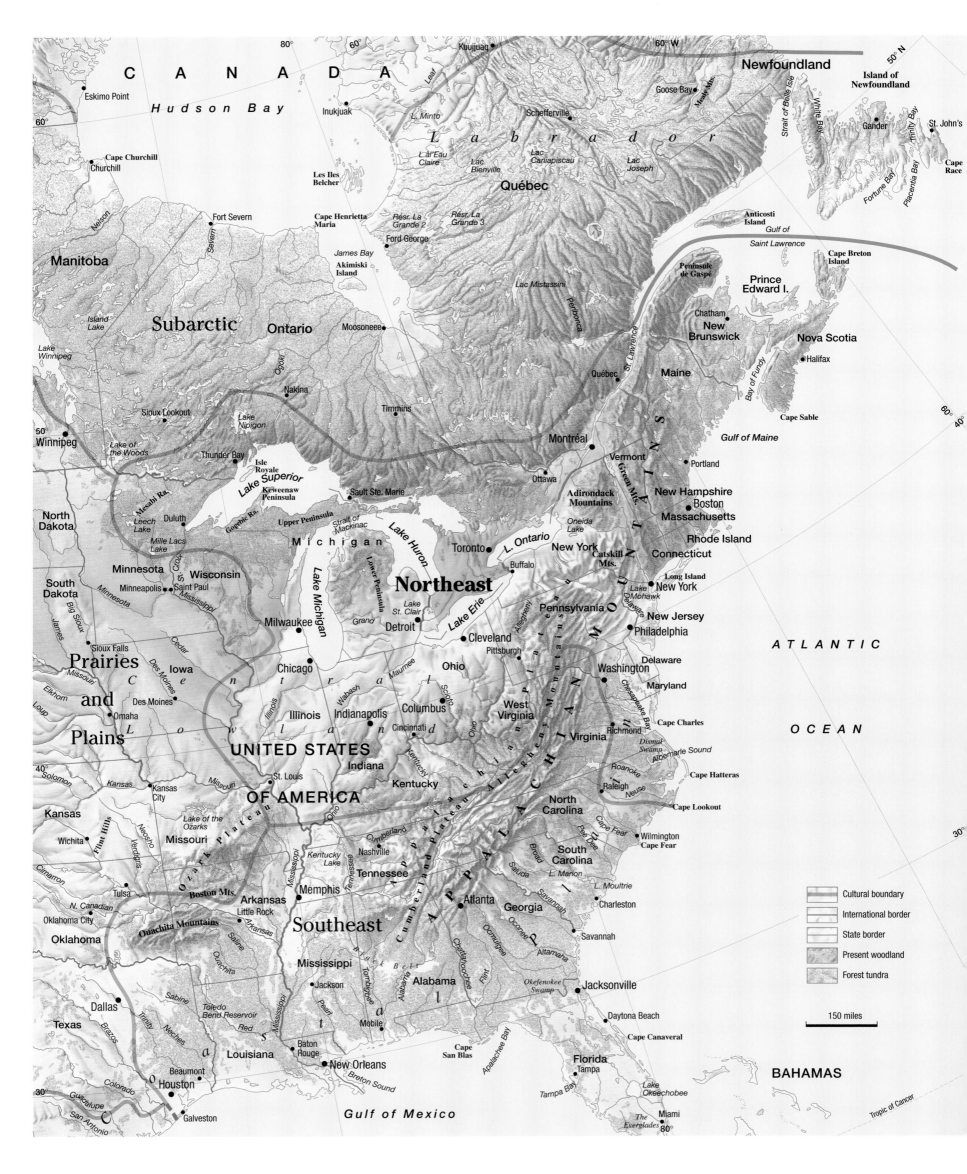

Previous pages:
Hudson highlands north of West Point, New York State.

The Hudson River was an important gateway for the Dutch and later English colonists pushing forward from the Atlantic coast into the lands of the Iroquois. In 1802 the United States built its military academy on the lower Hudson, once the land of the Munsee-speaking Esopus and Wappinger. It was here that many officers serving in the Indian Wars in the West were educated.

Atlantic coast, Cape Breton Island, Nova Scotia.

Behind the narrow rocky strip of the windswept northern Atlantic coast is an expanse of wooded hills which in some places reach all the way to the sea. In the rough climate of these latitudes, the availability of seafood, complemented by deer and moose hunted inland, provided a diet rich in proteins. Huge schools of herring and smelt gathered here in the spring, while shellfish, cod, eel, and other fish provided for a good summer on the coast. On the outlying islands people took out birds' nests from the huge bird colonies settling there.

Sylvia S. Kasprycki

# The forests of the Northeast

Between the skyscrapers of the cities on the Atlantic coast and the endless wheatfields of the Ohio valley, there are today few natural landscapes to remind us of the virgin nature of the American Northeast – that "vast expanse of woods, relieved by a comparatively narrow fringe of cultivation along the sea, dotted by the glittering surfaces of lakes, and intersected by the waving lines of rivers," through which Natty Bumppo, Chingachgook, or Uncas, the heroes created by James Fenimore Cooper (1789–1851), made their way along narrow paths.

Of course, the forests of the Northeast did not remain untouched by their original inhabitants either, who planted fields and raised settlements in forest clearings, thereby not only exploiting but also altering their natural environment.

However, it was only European settlement that brought about large-scale forest clearances, an intensive timber industry, the draining of marshes, the introduction of plants from the Old World, and last but not least ushered in urbanization, all of which made long-lasting changes to the original landscape.

Almost the whole region between the East Coast and the Mississippi Valley was once covered with forest. Oak, chestnut, and hickory made up the greater part of the deciduous forest; further north it became a mixture of maple, birch, beech, and hemlock fir. In the higher altitudes of the Appalachians, the boreal coniferous forest of the neighboring Subarctic reached like a raw tongue down to the temperate latitudes. In the plains south and west of Lake Michigan the forests opened out into parklike lands whose grassy clearings formed a transition to the prairies of the West. The humid continental climate of the region that lay between the Subarctic in the north and the subtropics in the south brought summer temperatures ranging from moderately warm to hot, and, particularly in the north, winters characterized by heavy snowfall.

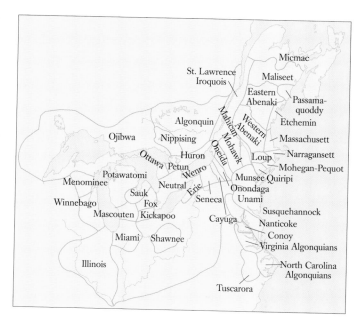

Peoples of the Northeast.

The Northeast was populated mainly by speakers of Algonquian languages, whose eastern branch along the Atlantic coast was separated from its western relatives by various Iroquoian peoples. In the western Great Lakes area, the Siouan-speaking Winnebago had largely adopted the lifestyle of their Algonquian neighbors. Scarcely any reliable information exists about the original inhabitants of the Ohio region. Many of the names on this map group together a large number of independent, sometimes even hostile tribes purely on the basis of close linguistic relations. On the other hand, some of these independent peoples spoke the same language: the Sauk, Fox, and Kickapoo used different dialects of the same mother tongue, as did the Ojibwa and Ottawa.

This environment suited many animal species. Apart from deer, wapiti, black bear, raccoon, beaver, and many other fur animals, all not only suppliers of vital proteins but also of furs and leather for clothes and containers, there were large wildcats such as the lynx and the puma. Particularly in Algoquian mythology, the puma plays an important role as the "Underwater Panther" that rules the underworld. As late as the 17th century bison, generally regarded as the typical inhabitants of the grassy plains of the American West, could still be found east of the Appalachians; by the 19th century only few remained in the western part of the culture area east of the Mississippi.

The versatility of the natural environments of the Northeast contributed to the different cultural and economic developments in each region. It also greatly influenced the history of European settlement. The first attempts at colonization were made along the Atlantic coast, whose northern section features many rocky bays and outlying islands but which further south expands into lowlands divided by the estuaries of tidal rivers. Separated from the interior by the Appalachians and their foothills, the coastal region, with its favorable climate, was also attractive because of the proximity of the ocean with its abundant food resources.

Further north, the valley of the St. Lawrence River provided another gateway for European exploration of the continent. The river drains the five Great Lakes – the vestiges of Ice Age glaciers – into the Atlantic Ocean.

Swamp, Point Pelee National Park, Lake Erie, Ontario.

Marshland and swamps characterize the landscape in many parts of the coastal plain but can also be found in other areas of the Northeast. The rich vegetation of this wetland biotope is an ideal environment for nesting water birds, and offers shelter to many types of smaller mammals, such as beaver, otter, and muskrat.

Wolf River, Wisconsin.

The numerous rivers in the area of the Great Lakes provided an intricate transportation network that served trade between tribes already in pre-European times. In this type of environment, the lightweight boats made from birch bark were an ideal means of transport, as they could also be easily carried around rapids or over portages, the land bridges between waterways.

This waterway offered a convenient way around the Appalachians, which in some places rise to a height of 6500 feet, and as a watershed divide the region into a smaller eastern and a greater western part. The fertile valleys of the Ohio and its tributaries, which established a connection to the traffic artery of the Mississippi, attracted a seemingly never-ending stream of white settlers hungry for land. The waters had already been important for transportation before the arrival of the whites. These waterways were complemented by innumerable beaten paths whose names, such as "Great Warriors Path" or "Ambassadors Road," indicate that they were particularly important in warfare.

The plants of the Northeast, by no means homogenous across the region, were no less diverse and provided the indigenous residents with part of their diet, but also with medicines, building materials, textile fibers and other raw materials, dyes and tanning agents, and with a range of ingredients for use in hunting magic or love potions. In the early 20th century, the Menominee of Wisconsin still knew of about 130 plants that could be used for medicinal purposes, as well as nearly 50 plants that boasted edible fruits, roots, or leaves.

More recent research credits the Iroquois with knowledge and use of some 450 medicinal plants, which, however, represents the collective knowledge of about 80 informants from different reservations in Canada and the United States.

# Burial mounds and their builders

During their advance into the region beyond the Appalachians, white settlers encountered hundreds of prehistoric earth mounds and ridges, sometimes of impressive size. Educated Americans of the time generally assumed the builders of these mounds to belong to a lost civilization, variously attributed to the Phoenicians, Egyptians, Scythians, the lost tribes of Israel, or Celts, who had somehow landed in the New World.

The commendable natural historian Benjamin Smith Barton (1766–1815), who was one of the first explorers of the mounds in the Ohio Valley and prepared quite detailed descriptions of them, even posited the theory that these earthworks had been built by Vikings who had emigrated from Scandinavia to Mexico, there becoming the Toltecs before bringing their culture to this part of North America. Such fantastical views were fed not least by the disparaging attitude taken toward the local indigenous populations, who were unable to explain these monuments and who were considered to be incapable of such cultural achievements. At best, their ancestors were held responsible for wiping out the "mound builders" – which also served to justify policies of suppression and removal of indigenous groups.

Most of the new arrivals to the area, however, gave no thought whatsoever to the origin of the archeological monuments they destroyed when laying out their fields. In around 1840 an English traveler described his impressions of the town of Circleville on the Scioto River in Ohio which had been founded at the beginning of the 19th century in the middle of an archeological ring-wall encompassing a four-hectare ceremonial center. "So little veneration ... have the Americans for the ancient remains ..., that ... Circleville is soon likely to lose all traces of its original peculiarities. ... Though the octagonal building still remains, the circular streets are fast giving way, to make room for straight ones, and the central edifice itself is already destined to be removed, to give place to stores and dwellings; so that in half a century, or less, there will be no vestige left of that peculiarity which gave the place its name."

By contrast, Thomas Jefferson (1743–1826), third president of the United States, had a mound of this type on his Monticello country estate in Virginia carefully excavated, layer by layer, already in the late 18th century, making him a pioneer in American archeology.

Systematic and scientific research into the burial mound cultures set in only in the mid-19th century and resulted in the conclusion that they had indeed developed from older cultural traditions of local origin. The early ancestors of these people had lived from hunting, fishing, and

gathering, but more than 3,000 years ago showed initial signs of a sedentary lifestyle. Grave goods also testify to wide-ranging trade connections and to a distinctive cult of the dead.

## Adena and Hopewell

On this basis, the two main cultures of what is known as the Woodland period of the Northeast, Adena and Hopewell, developed in the first millennium BC. Their populations grew not only native plants such as sunflowers, goosefoot, and marsh elder, but also squash and corn, cultivated crops originating in Central America. Together with intensive food gathering, the gradually increasing importance of agriculture supported a sedentary way of life and promoted population growth in these societies. A distinctive ancestor cult also seems to have evolved, for some of the dead were buried at great expense in mounds that sometimes towered more than 65 feet high. These striking burial mounds have yielded revealing artifacts from which a vivid picture of the daily life in these communities can be reconstructed.

The Adena culture flourished in southern Ohio between about 500 BC and AD 100. Its population lived in relatively small villages, engaged in vigorous long-distance trading, and exhibited pronounced differences in social standing, as marked by the different methods of burial. While the majority of the dead were cremated and buried in pits, conical mounds, often enclosed by low earthwork walls, were erected as monuments above the graves of high-status individuals. Their remains were placed in log tombs which were often burned before the construction of the burial mounds.

The mounds were not raised in a single operation; instead successive layers were added over longer periods of time until the mounds reached the height of what today would be approximately a seven-story building. The aristocratic dead received gifts of ornaments and ritual objects for the way. These included tubular tobacco pipes and small stone tablets with stylized depictions of birds of prey or geometrical motifs. Remnants of dyes found on the stone tablets point to their use as stamps for decorating clothes or perhaps for body painting. Strangely, ceramics, then already widely known in the region, do not feature among the grave goods.

In the final phase of the Adena culture, a new population migrated from present-day Illinois to the Ohio valley, bringing with it the Hopewell culture (200 BC to AD 500). The bearers of this culture apparently developed some interest in astronomy and erected complex arrangements of earthworks, often aligned with the constellations, as well as large burial mounds in the Adena style. In contrast to the great variety of Adena burial methods, the magnificent grave goods buried with high-ranking persons are so homogeneous throughout the Hopewell area that their spread across a wide-ranging trade network is highly probable.

Hopewell artists and artisans manufactured luxury goods and tools from materials that would have been quite exotic to them. Translucent mica from the southern Appalachians they cut into ornaments, and they hammered cold copper (and more rarely silver and meteoric iron) from the Great Lakes into tools, ceremonial objects, and ornaments. Found in its pure state in some deposits, this metal did not need to be melted out of ore and was made supple for use by heating followed by rapid cooling. Obsidian (black volcanic glass) from the Yellowstone region was used for making blades which served ceremonial purposes or as an expression of wealth.

Helmets decorated with pieces of mica, copper breastplates, earrings, bracelets, and necklaces made of silver and freshwater pearls were found in great quantities in graves and obviously formed part of the splendid attire of high-ranking men of the Hopewell era. Some of the dead were even given copper noses. Tobacco pipes fashioned in animal shapes were also found as gifts in countless graves. Naturalistic terracotta figurines showing the clothing, hairstyles, and other details of the everyday, and otherwise little-known, aspect of this culture provide archeologists with important information about the actual use of many of the articles that have been found.

The disappearance of the mound builders was not due to their being exterminated by "barbaric Indians," as had been assumed in the 19th century, but rather to a change in their living conditions. A cooler climate after AD 400 made the cultivation of corn less attractive than the hunt, whose yield had markedly improved through the growing use of the bow and arrow as a effective hunting weapon. At the same time, the old elite lost its importance, and so the elaborate cult of the dead, and the artistic grave goods, soon became things of the past.

Human effigy pipe, Adena culture (c. 500 BC to AD 100). Ohio Historical Society, Columbus, OH.

This unique Adena tobacco pipe carved in slate stands in the tradition of the tubular stone pipes that were in use before local tobacco, which also grew wild, was cultivated in the Northeast. The pipe depicts a human figure in a breechclout, with spool-like earrings that may indicate high status. Magnificent ear ornaments of this kind are also known from the Hopewell culture, and particularly from the civilizations of Central and Southern Mexico.

# Unequal neighbors

When in 1524 the Florentine seafarer Giovanni da Verrazano (c. 1480–?1527), on behalf of the king of France, was searching the Atlantic coast of North America for a western sea route to Asia, he was greeted "cheerfully" and with "great shouts of admiration" by the inhabitants of Narragansett Bay (the Narragansett or Pokanoket) – probably also because of the brass bells and glass beads that he gave them. However, only a little further northeast, on the coast of Maine, he found "no courtesy" among the Abenaki. To barter, they retreated to a cliff from which they lowered a basket filled with their goods, for which they wanted only knives, fishing hooks, and other metal tools in return. As a farewell, the Abenaki let the surprised visitors know of their scorn in no uncertain terms by "exhibiting their bare behinds and laughing immoderately."

Verrazano's report makes it clear that in the first years of contact with European sailors the original inhabitants must already have formed an ambiguous impression of their pale-faced visitors. No wonder: in the area of present-day New York State, Verrazano himself had robbed a woman of her child; the woman could only save herself from capture by shouting loudly.

## Involuntary messengers

For more than a quarter of a century before Verrazano's arrival, curious or simply avaricious seafarers had haunted the coast, taking men, women, and children from that area and bringing them back to Europe, where they were exhibited as curious examples of the savagery of America's inhabitants or sold into slavery. Rumors of these and other outrages committed by the foreigners soon spread, but the temptation of European trade goods, which were often ascribed a supernatural origin, proved in most cases to be stronger than any fear of, and disgust with, their producers.

Some of the indigenous Americans who were shipped to Europe were trained as interpreters and were used to help the travelers find their way around the New World. In 1534 the French explorer Jacques Cartier (1491–1557) took two sons of Donnaconna, a leader of the St. Lawrence Iroquois, back to France with him and, in keeping with his promise, returned them the following year. When in 1536 he once more reached the mouth of the St. Lawrence, he again invited the two and their father to Europe, where they died before their planned return. It was the fantastical reports of these three Iroquois about the legendary kingdom of Saguenay, rich in precious metals, which led to the foundation of the first, short-lived French colony on the St. Lawrence River between 1538 and 1543.

In about 1560, the Spanish took the brother of a chief from the coast of what is today Virginia to Mexico, where Don Luis de Velasco, viceroy of New Spain, ordered his Christian education and gave him his aristocratic name. In 1566, the Virginian Don Luis traveled to Spain and lived there at the expense of Philip II until 1570, when he was given permission to take a group of Spanish Jesuits to his native country. However, instead of acting as their intermediary, Don Luis had them murdered after a few months. When in the following year a supply ship appeared in Chesapeake Bay, several Virginia Algonquian men dressed in the Jesuits' cassocks waved from the shore, but the Spaniards were not deceived by this stratagem and did not go ashore. In 1572, a punitive expedition avenged the missionaries' deaths and rescued the only survivor (the servant Alonso), thus putting an end to the dream of a Spanish colony north of Florida.

In November 1620, Puritan religious refugees who had initially fled from England to the Netherlands founded the first New England colony on Plymouth Rock. They were helped by a Pokanoket called Squanto (d. 1622), who had been carried off to England in 1614, and they chose as the location of their new settlement an area of the Pokanoket territory that had shortly before been depopulated by an epidemic disease. Unlike Don Luis, Squanto lived up to the hope placed in him, teaching the starving settlers how to cultivate corn, showing them the best places to fish, and negotiating peaceful relations between them and his chief Massasoit.

## The race begins

Gradually, more and more European colonies gained a foothold on the East Coast, often supported by the interests of some of the local peoples in regulated access to the whites' trading goods, but also always threatened by the hostility of other aborigines toward the strangers.

The British founded the colony of Virginia in 1607, with the first settlement Jamestown in Chesapeake Bay. Here and in the other British colonies, which by the end of the 17th century covered the entire coast from North Carolina to Maine, interest in utilizing the land for agriculture was far greater than in trading with the indigenous neighbors.

Two smaller trading powers, the Netherlands and Sweden, also attempted to gain a foothold in the New World early on. In 1624, the Dutch established themselves in what is today New York State. Their main interests lay in the wealth of fur-bearing animals, which they hunted themselves or bartered for with the neighboring Algonquians. They pushed up the Hudson River all the way to the territory of the Iroquoian Mohawk, whom they equipped with firearms, thereby smoothing the way to their absolute control of the fur trade in the Northeast.

The colony of New Sweden, founded on the Delaware River in the year 1638, was forced to surrender to the Dutch a mere 17 years later. However, the Dutch likewise finally lost the race for the American Northeast: in much the same way as they had incorporated New Sweden, their colony, the New Netherlands, fell to the British in 1664.

Until 1763, the British and the French (who had established themselves in the colony of New France in present-day Canada in 1609) remained the only European

colonial powers in the Northeast, and their rivalry for dominance also directly affected the indigenous populations. The French sphere of influence reached from the St. Lawrence River as far as the western Great Lakes, while that of the British covered all of the central and northern Atlantic coast.

As the British came to the country primarily as settlers, violent clashes with the Algonquian peoples on the coast were inevitable. Those not carried off by European diseases sooner or later rose up against the colonists, who claimed ever larger areas of their territory (for instance, in Virginia in 1622 and 1644–1646 and in New England in 1675–1676), but they always remained unsuccessful and were eventually forced onto small reservations.

For the peoples in the interior, above all for the Iroquois, the presence of the whites on the coast offered the opportunity to strengthen their position vis-à-vis their neighbors. For them, the profits of trade outweighed the disadvantages of contact with traders and settlers, especially as the frontier of European settlement was moving westward only very slowly.

The main interest of the French definitely focused on the fur trade and the conversion of the native population, which had generally been neglected by the British. Their small settlements on the St. Lawrence River stood on land from which the original Iroquoian inhabitants had already disappeared by the beginning of the 17th century. Particularly the Huron and the Algonquian peoples living in the western Great Lakes region were pulled onto the French side and acted as their partners in the fight against the British and their allies. Even after the Huron had been driven out by the Iroquois League in 1649, the well-armed Chippewa were initially able to prevent the dominance of the Iroquois from posing too great a threat to French interests.

Joseph Wabin, *Kaskaskia man*, watercolor, 1796. Départment des Cartes et Plans, Bibliothèque Nationale de France, Paris, France.

The Kaskaskia were one of several independent tribes (like the Peoria, Michigamea, Cahokia, and others) who because of their common language were grouped together as "Illinois." In the 17th century, they inhabited large parts of what today is the state that bears their name. As enemies of the Iroquois, the Illinois and the closely related Miami tribes soon sided with the French. In the 18th century they sustained the loss of a major part of their population through disease and war, as well as of their allies through the British defeat of the French. The Kaskaskia then allied themselves with the colonists in the American Revolution, but were soon after forced westward by the anti-American Shawnee. Today, the descendants of the Illinois and of two Miami groups live as "Peoria" in Oklahoma.

Below:
George Winter, *No-taw-kah, Kee-waw-nay, July 17, 1837*, watercolor, 1837. Tippecanoe County Historical Association, Lafayette, IN.

In the early 19th century, politically independent groups of Potawatomis – sometimes associated with the closely related Ojibwa and Ottawa – lived widely scattered across Michigan, Indiana, Illinois, and Wisconsin. Many of them were relocated to Iowa and Kansas between 1836 and 1841. Others fled to Ontario or joined the Kickapoo or the Menominee over the next few decades. At the beginning of the 21st century, about 15,000 Potawatomi recognized by the United States government live in Oklahoma, Kansas, Wisconsin, and Michigan.

Opposite page, below:
Winnebago men playing the moccasin game, Wisconsin, c. 1890. State Historical Society of Wisconsin, Madison, WI.

According to their own oral traditions, the Winnebago stayed behind in the vicinity of Green Bay in Wisconsin when their closest relatives, the Iowa, Oto, and Missouri, moved further west beyond the Mississippi. As part of the removal policies of the 19th century, the Winnebago were likewise driven out of their old homeland. After an odyssey through Minnesota and South Dakota a part of them ended up on a reservation in Nebraska. Others managed to avoid removal by retreating to small forest settlements in Wisconsin; at the beginning of the 1960s they were even recognized as a separate tribe by the federal government. Today the Wisconsin-Winnebago officially call themselves "Ho-Chunk," a shortening of their traditional name, which means both "the great voice" and "the great fish."

## The Fleur-de-lis, the Cross of St. George, and the Stars and Stripes

From 1740 onward, the conflict between the colonial powers shifted to the Ohio region south of the Great Lakes, with its mixture of indigenous peoples and those which had been pushed westward from the east. In 1760, with the help of the Iroquois, Delaware, and Shawnee, the British finally managed to defeat the French and to take over their Canadian possessions.

To appease the growing resistance of the indigenous peoples in the Ohio region, the king of England promised, in a proclamation of 1763, to respect the region west of the Appalachians as Indian land and to allow no European settlement to take place there. The white inhabitants of the colonies, constantly intent on expanding their developing economy, were highly indignant at this restriction of their expansionist desires. Their discontent with the colonial corset of an imposed western border, trading restrictions, high taxes, and limited political rights led to growing resistance to the mother country's policies, which finally resulted in the outbreak of the American War of Independence (1775–1783).

For the Northeast, the British troops' defeat by the militias of the evolving United States meant the end of the stability brought about by the outstanding geopolitical role played by the Iroquois. After the American Revolution laid waste to the Iroquois territory and divided their confederacy, all dams seemed to break. Settlers and land speculators poured into the lands between the Appalachians and the Mississippi, occupying the territories of the native peoples living there, most of whom understandably had supported the British and therefore suffered ruthless treatment at the hands of the Americans.

Military resistance to American rule and their incessant westward advance flared up only occasionally, the last time in 1832 in the war led by the Sauk leader Black Hawk, who fought against the planned removal of all indigenous peoples still remaining east of the Mississippi to the as yet unpopulated West. This policy particularly affected the tribes who lived in Indiana, Illinois, and southern Michigan and Wisconsin. The groups based in northern Michigan and Wisconsin, on the other hand, received small reservations mostly on or near their old territories.

After four centuries of intense and not always peaceful contact with the whites, the living conditions of the native peoples still surviving in the Northeast have changed considerably. Today the dense forests that once covered the region have almost completely disappeared, many Native American communities lie within largely urbanized areas, and only a few have managed to carve out for themselves a niche in the employment market.

Even though the tribes of the Northeast have maintained, or rediscovered, a strong awareness of their peculiarities, ultimately the true variety of their original cultures can be perceived only by looking back into the past. This, however, is often distorted by the lack of understanding contemporary observers displayed toward lifeways that were alien to them.

Christian F. Feest

# The settler and the princess

In the winter of 1608, in the Virginian village of Werowocomoco, the residence of the ruler Powhatan (c. 1547–1618), an Englishman lay in chains. He was waiting for the end of a long ceremony whose meaning he could only imagine, but which obviously focused on him. Finally the prisoner was led to the mighty Powhatan's house, more than 50 yards long, where a large gathering had already assembled. The ruler sat enthroned on a pedestal covered with fur. The stranger's head was placed on a flat stone, and a lusty warrior was already raising his heavy club, when suddenly Powhatan's favorite daughter, the 12-year-old Pocahontas (1595–1617), burst from the circle of spectators and threw herself over the condemned man. Without really knowing what had happened, the stranger was soon free to return to Jamestown, founded only eight months before as the bridgehead of the first successful English colony in North America.

The prisoner was Captain John Smith (1579–1631), who in spite of his youth had already fought as a mercenary

Simon van de Pass, *Matoaka alias Rebecca*, 1616. Copper engraving from John Smith, *General History of Virginia*, London 1624. Library of Congress, Washington, DC.

The king of England is said to have been annoyed that the commoner John Rolfe married the daughter of the "King of Virginia." Of course, the Virginia Company of London did everything to make the 21-year-old Pocahontas appear like a real princess as defined by the conventions of the time, even though as a child she had performed cartwheels naked in Jamestown, much to the delight of the English settlers. The engraving – the only portrait of her made in her lifetime – was accordingly widely distributed.

Chief Tecumseh Deerfoot Cook (second from right) and three other Pamunkeys pay the annual tribute to the governor of Virginia, c. 1930.

Powhatan's other children fared far worse than Pocahontas. After an unsuccessful uprising in 1622, they became the target in several wars of extermination and were finally forced onto reservations by the colonists. Since 1677 the Pamunkey have paid the governor of Virginia an annual tribute in the form of game. Threatened by race laws which gave them few more rights than the descendants of African slaves, in the late 19th century the Pamunkey performed a play about John Smith's rescue as a reminder that Pocahontas had been one of them.

against the Turks and had twice been saved from seemingly hopeless situations by exotic women. The fact that Smith recounted at length his miraculous rescue by the chief's daughter only 17 years later, when Pocahontas was not only widely known but also dead, has made many historians doubtful of the story.

It can be supposed that what Captain Smith interpreted as his approaching execution was in fact nothing more than an adoption ritual, a symbolic killing of the Englishman that had to precede his "rebirth" as a member of the ruling family. With this adoption, Powhatan presumably wanted to establish bonds with the leader of the English colony: in exchange for two cannons and a millstone, Powhatan offered his newly adopted son Nantaquod control over a part of southern Virginia.

However, contemporaries do confirm that as a bearer of peace (perhaps acting on the orders of her father) Pocahontas contributed much to the survival of the weak colony in its first years. Pocahontas spent much time in Jamestown, warning the settlers of potential dangers and sometimes even supplying them with food when they fell upon times of hardship. Unpopular among the other colonists as well, the overbearing, boastful Captain Smith soon returned to England, and Pocahontas no longer appeared in the colony after her reputed marriage to a young warrior. Without the mediation of the young Pocahontas, the colonists soon became embroiled in a hopeless war with Powhatan, who on losing his adopted son obviously saw no other way of controlling the settlers peacefully.

In 1613, another Englishman, Captain Samuel Argall (d. ?1626), was in search of provisions for the colony near today's capital Washington when by chance he encountered Pocahontas, who was the guest of the chief of Patawomeke, lured her to his ship, and took her back to Jamestown as a hostage. Pocahontas put up no resistance at all; in fact, once in the colony she quickly converted to Christianity and was baptized.

More than that, Rebecca, the new name of the first indigenous Anglican, accepted the marriage proposal made to her by the widowed English settler John Rolfe (1585–1622). Despite the fondness that may have existed between the two, it was first and foremost a political marriage. Powhatan sent one of his brothers to represent him at the wedding, but maintained the peace established with his relatives by marriage to his death in 1618.

In 1616, the Virginia Company, which under a Royal Charter was in charge of this colonial venture, brought Pocahontas, John Rolfe, and their newly-born son Thomas over to London, where she attracted much attention as the Virginian princess, and was also introduced at court. However, when the family decided that they would return to Virginia, Pocahontas, only 22 years old, fell ill and died from "the fever" on the not yet departed ship and was buried near Gravesend, on the Thames.

Twice widowed, Rolfe returned to Virginia alone. His later fame was based on his introduction of the cultivation

of South American tobacco in Virginia, which formed the basis for the later prosperity of the colony. Thomas, who had stayed in England, followed him across the Atlantic only later, as a young man. To this day, many prominent Virginian families claim they can trace their blue-blooded descent from the regal house of Powhatan through this son of Pocahontas.

Later, in the mythology of the young United States, Pocahontas became the heaven-sent savior of the colony who through her marriage seemingly provided a justification for the violent takeover of land – just as if two royal families had willingly united their territories to create a new empire.

As with the "Indian" in general, Pocahontas again and again had to fulfill the new needs of a changing American society. She turned from being seen as the tool of providence and the unspoiled, romantic "child of the wilderness" into being interpreted as a modern "woman of enormous power and intellect" in the late 20th century, finally being portrayed in the Walt Disney Studios' animated cartoon (1995) as a potent symbol of red and white living peacefully side by side.

Victor Nehlig, *Pocahontas and John Smith*, oil on canvas, 1870. Museum of Art at Brigham Young University, Salt Lake City, UT.

The American ideology of the 19th century turned the story of Pocahontas into a national origin myth. The indigenous Virginians are here portrayed in the style of the Plains tribes who at the time of painting put up the kind of threatening resistance to the United States' expansion in the West from which the noble Pocahontas had saved John Smith and the first English colonists in North America in January 1608. Powhatan, who would in reality have been in his sixties, is shown as a hero in the prime of life.

George Catlin, *Ten-squát-a-way*, watercolor, c. 1830. Thomas Gilcrease Institute of American History and Art, Tulsa, OK.

The Shawnee Prophet, as Tenskwatawa is often called, had poked out one of his eyes as a child with an arrow. When American artist George Catlin (1796–1872) painted him in 1839, the now 55-year-old man lived in Kansas after returning from exile in Canada in 1825. In the question of land concessions, Tenskwatawa now supported the American policy of forced resettlement of the eastern tribes in the West, contrary to the views of his brother Tecumseh, who had been killed in 1813.

Christian F. Feest

# Tecumseh, the prophet's brother

Much of what has been written about the Shawnee Tecumseh (c. 1768–1813) is founded on hearsay and assumption. Was his mother a white prisoner? Did he receive a basic course in political education and Christian neighborly love from pioneer girl Rebecca Galloway, whom he is said to have adored? Was he even a freemason? He is supposed to have abolished in his tribe the torture of prisoners of war, and to have very nearly succeeded with his great plan of a "united Indian front" against the land-hungry Americans.

Tecumseh, one of the most famous Native Americans, is a man without a face. As in the case of Crazy Horse, the Lakota of whom there is also no verified portrait, this fact has contributed to the sweeping role of imagination in the development of the Tecumseh myth.

There are few facts. His father, a warrior, died in 1774, when Tecumseh ("the panther who jumps across the sky") was about six years old. As his mother, a Creek from the South, returned to her home a few years later, the boy grew up in the care of his sister in Ohio. In the late 18th century, this area was inhabited by a colorful blend of different tribes and splinter groups, some of whom had been driven out of their previous homelands by the whites and were now standing in the way of the advancing Americans. In the company of his brothers he gained experience in warfare early on, but did not distinguish himself particularly.

This changed only in 1805, when his younger brother Lalawethika ("the noisemaker," 1775–1836), a notorious drunkard, when lighting his pipe fell into such a deep trance that he was taken for dead. On regaining consciousness he told of his visit to the Master of Life and of the teachings he had received there. The only chance the indigenous Americans had of returning to the happy state that they enjoyed before the arrival of the whites was to be found in complete abstinence from any of the seductive things offered by the traders: alcohol, metal tools, and textiles. Even traditional practices like witchcraft and polygamy had to be abandoned. Finally, according to the directions he received in the vision, all dogs had to be killed. Tenskwatawa ("the open door"), as Tecumseh's brother now called himself, had been granted the gift of prophecy. A solar eclipse in 1806 which he had predicted convinced even the most doubtful. The new doctrine quickly spread throughout the region and was to contribute to Tecumseh's reputation as well.

In the following years, Tecumseh also proclaimed teachings directed at an intertribal audience. However, Tecumseh turned the Master of Life's instruction to respect the earth into a political message. The tribes should in future hold their land in common and stop any further land cessions to the Americans. For the whites he summed up his guiding principle in a handy formula : "The earth is my mother, and on her bosom I will rest." This pronouncement by Tecumseh in 1810 is the oldest evidence of an indigenous notion of "Mother Earth" in all of North America, and Tecumseh may be seen as the originator of the concept.

His attempt to unite the tribes of the Midwest and the South in one mighty alliance found little success. He aroused greater interest among the British in Canada, who were still mourning the loss of their former colonies and who saw the Shawnee and his supposed hordes of warriors as allies in their fight against the United States. At the start of the British-American War of 1812 (1812–1814) Tecumseh and his braves stood firmly on the side of the British. When the British had virtually lost the war on the northern front and were retreating, Tecumseh tried to encourage them to fight against the Americans one more time. At the Thames River, however, the British army quickly retreated and left the battlefield to Tecumseh, where he lost his life on October 5, 1813.

Even in death Tecumseh left no trace. His corpse ended up in a mass grave. Indigenous mythology on the other hand maintains that his body was never found.

Ferdinand Pettrich, *The Dying Tecumseh*, marble, 1856. National Museum of American Art, Smithsonian Institution, Washington, DC.

Already during his lifetime, even Tecumseh's American opponents praised his extraordinary military and political genius – of course also to emphasize their own achievements. After Tecumseh's death, his former enemies considered him worthy of a marble statue, especially as every victory over him counted more if his abilities were portrayed as superhuman. Colonel Richard Johnson (1780–1850), who killed Tecumseh in his final battle, used this in his 1836 campaign for vice-president, while William H. Harrison even became president in 1840 as the victor at Tippecanoe.

Tippecanoe Battlefield, Indiana.

In 1808, Tenskwatawa founded the village of Prophetstown near the present Lafayette, where the Tippecanoe joins the Wabash River. Three years later, the village was attacked during Tecumseh's absence by troops led by the governor of Indiana, William H. Harrison (1773–1841). The prophet's claim that his followers were invincible soon proved to be mistaken; the battle was lost and Tenskwatawa's military career came to an end.

Chippewa farmer, Wisconsin, c. 1930. State Historical Society of Wisconsin, Madison, WI.

The introduction of plowing as part of the American "civilization" programs was difficult because of men's reluctance to take on traditional female tasks such as working the fields. When missionary Jedediah Morse (1761–1826) tried to encourage the Oneida men to work the fields, he was told that "Only women and hedgehogs have been made to scratch the ground." On the other hand, the goal of turning the Native Americans into model farmers in the Western mold was in many places thwarted by the very consequences of Indian policies. Too often, reservations were in areas whose unfavorable climate and barren soil could hardly produce the agricultural yields that were necessary for survival.

# Between wood, water, and clearing

Covered with forest and traversed by rivers, the Northeast with all its regional differences provided its inhabitants everywhere with ample game, fish, and wild plants as the basis of their subsistence. Moreover, the climate afforded nearly everywhere 120 successive frost-free days, the minimum requirement for a reasonably reliable cultivation of corn.

The rich aquatic resources had long made a largely sedentary existence possible for the peoples living on the shores of the Atlantic and the Great Lakes, while in the wetlands of the western Great Lakes area fishing and gathering wild rice enabled the Ojibwa, Menominee, and other tribes to develop an economy based on provision and storage, and therefore to remain longer in one place in large groups. The cultivation of corn, beans, and squash, which was gradually adopted in the Northeast only after AD 900, therefore brought no radical changes in the living conditions, but rather strengthened the seasonal sedentism, while hunting and gathering continued to be important.

Nevertheless, the extent to which agriculture was practiced defined the different conditions for cultural developments. Among the Huron and the Iroquois, nearly half the total food supply came from this resource, while in the area of the western Great Lakes it provided less than 20 percent of the necessary provisions. Only the Micmac on the northern Atlantic coast practiced no agriculture at all.

## Corn – the daily bread

In the general framework of economic activities, men and women pursued different tasks. The women supplied vegetable foods by growing corn, squash, and beans, and by gathering wild fruit and roots. The men, as hunters and fishers, were responsible for the not always reliable provision of meat and fish. However, men also cleared the fields and sometimes helped with the harvest, while old men and children aided the women in gathering. All further processing of food – not only the vegetable food but also the game brought home by the men – lay in the hands of the women.

Where the cultivation of corn formed the basis of subsistence, the villages were inhabited throughout the year, and were only moved when firewood had become scarce and the soil of the fields that lay within walking distance around the village had become exhausted. This usually occurred approximately every 10 to 20 years. The villages were relocated only a few miles away, just far enough from their former location to ensure a sufficient supply of firewood for the next few years.

To make a clearing in the forest, the trees were stripped of crown, branches, and roots and left to rot, while the undergrowth between what remained was burned, the ashes of the burned plants nourishing the ground. Except in New England, where dead fish were thrown onto the fields, other forms of fertilization were unknown, because there were no large domestic animals to supply manure. Afterward, a stick would be used to dig holes in the ground at regular intervals for planting seeds. The plantations, measuring up to several square miles in area, provided the Huron with two or three years' supply of corn, which was stored in the houses or in pits dug in the ground and later used either for bartering or as emergency provisions in times of shortage.

Beans were often grown in the same field, climbing up the corn stalks and enriching the soil with nitrogen, as occasionally were squashes, whose large leaves prevented the ground from drying out. Sunflowers were planted separately, and their seeds were used for oil but also to make flour.

The women tending these fields took such care in their weeding that missionary Gabriel Sagard, who lived among the Huron in the 17th century, often mistook the neat rows for paths and regularly became lost in the cornfields when trying to make his way to neighboring villages. The Iroquois also used the corn husks to make ceremonial masks (the "Husk faces" or "bushy heads"), mats, baskets, sandals, and other useful household items.

Ernest Smith (Seneca),
*The Three Sisters*, watercolor, 1937.
Rochester Museum and Science
Center, Rochester, NY.

The Iroquois regarded corn, squash,
and beans as sacred gifts from the
Creator. They worshiped them as
benevolent beings and held rituals
in their honor during the growing
season and at harvest time in the fall.
According to the stories told by the
old people, the plants in the fields
could sometimes be heard talking to
each other. (Busy among the squashes
shown in the picture is one of the
"Little People," who are the humans'
invisible friends and who look after
the growth of plants.)

Sawmill on the Menominee
reservation, Neopit, Wisconsin,
1989.

While agriculture never really caught
on among the Menominee, lumbering
has developed into a leading branch
of the economy since the late 19th
century. Profits from the Neopit
sawmill, erected in 1909, financed
the building and maintenance of a
hospital as well as various social
programs. The sawmill is one of the
reservation's most important
employers, and its forward-looking
management is today committed
to observing limits of timber cutting
and to regular reforestation.

The manner of their fishing

## Man cannot live on corn alone ...

Even in the villages with the most productive fields, the inhabitants always depended on hunting for their meat supply. During the growing season, the forests near the settlements served as hunting grounds. Winter expeditions, during which men were away from home for weeks or months, often took the hunting parties to faraway regions.

For some peoples, 90 percent of the meat they ate came from white-tailed deer, and hunters killed hundreds of them, often in communal drives. There was even the occasional war fought over areas that boasted dense deer populations. The moose hunt also played an important part in the provision of meat, particularly in the northern parts of the Northeast. Black bears, hares, beavers, muskrats, partridges, wild ducks, turkeys and huge swarms of passenger pigeons completed the variety of meat. The porcupine provided the quills that the women used to decorate clothes and pouches.

On the northern Atlantic coast, hunting sea mammals, especially seals, was one of the men's most important tasks. Seal oil was a desirable trade good. Of course, beached whales were not scorned either, and active whaling was carried out at least in the area around Long Island.

In the western grasslands, where the culture area of the Northeast merges into that of the Prairies and Plains, the communal bison hunt, which was conducted in the late fall, was the climax of the economic year for the numerous Illinois and Miami tribes. In this area hunters also had the opportunity of taking the pronghorn antelope.

Apart from bow and arrow (and later guns), slings and traps were also employed as hunting tools. In communal drives, the hunters surrounded the herds with bush fires or drove them into funnel-shaped fences, where the quarry could easily be killed in large numbers. Hunters would also surprise game animals at their watering holes, where they were blinded by the light of the hunters' torches.

Good runners wore out their prey in an unrelenting pursuit to exhaustion. In this they were given an advantage in the winter over the run down animals by their snowshoes as, unlike the hoofed animals with their thin legs, runners wearing snowshoes did not sink into the deep snow.

A successful hunter needed not only detailed knowledge of the territory and the behavior of the animals, but also sharp senses, physical strength, stamina, and patience – qualities developed in play from early childhood. Ritual preparation with fasting and prayers as well as respectful treatment of the killed prey and thanks-giving sacrifices guaranteed him the benevolence of the supernatural powers, without whose blessing even the most capable man would be denied success. Therefore, the bones of the quarry were carefully buried rather than being left to the dogs, and a piece of the killed animal was thrown into the fire as a sacrifice.

A hunter distributed his prey among relatives and the needy, gaining high prestige in return. Like war, hunting provided an arena in which men could aquire fame and honor. Considering its economic importance and the effort and privation connected with it, hunting was by no means the enjoyable leisure activity that casual European observers sometimes took it for.

John White, *The Art and Method of their Fishing*, watercolor, 1585/86. Department of Prints and Drawings, British Museum, London, England.

The indigenous methods of inshore fishing were varied. The North Carolina Algonquians, for instance, erected weirs near the shore, or caught their prey with spears and nets from a dugout or wading through the shallow water. At night, the animals were lured by the glow of the fires on board the fishing boats. The diet was enriched by gathering mollusks and crabs that had washed ashore.

Seth Eastman, *Spearing Muskrat in Winter*, watercolor, c. 1850. Afton Historical Society, Afton, MN.

Smaller animals such as muskrats, otters, or beavers were preferably hunted in winter, when they spent most of the time in their burrows and were easy prey. In summer, hunters lowered the water level by draining the beavers' dams to expose their lodges. However, the thick winter coat of the beaver brought the hunters greater commercial profit. In the second half of the 18th century, one beaver pelt was worth an iron knife; an ax cost twice that much, and a gun could be exchanged for 20 pelts.

Production of maple sugar by the Ojibwa, Red Lake, Minnesota, 1939. National Archives and Records Administration – Central Plains Region, Kansas City, MO.

The production of maple syrup by thickening the trees' sap was already known to indigenous peoples in pre-European times. However, further processing on a larger scale only became possible after the traditional bark vessels were replaced by metal kettles. These had a much greater capacity and could be heated directly over the fire. The main product was granulated sugar, made for trade and for the peoples' own consumption, but the thick syrup was also left to solidify in wooden molds or quickly cooled in the snow to produce a malleable, chewy candy popular not only with children.

When a German traveler in the mid-19th century asked if there were good hunting grounds in the next world too, a Chippewa answered no, with the dry comment that there would be no more work for him there.

Of course, the pots of the Woodland women were filled not only with corn, beans, and meat, but also with fish. Trout, carp, pike, herring, sturgeon, and various other kinds of fish supplemented the range of foods all year round, although fishing was most productive at spawning time in the spring and in the fall.

The tools used for fishing were spears, hooks made of bone or copper, and nets made of Indian hemp (later of commercially manufactured yarns) weighted with stones and equipped with wooden buoys. In the northern regions of the Northeast, fishermen made holes in the ice in winter and tried to bait the fish by making small wooden dummies dance in the water. White observers were often openly admiring of the skills of Native American fishermen in the area of what is today Sault Sainte Marie in Michigan, who balanced their boats in the dangerous rapids and infallibly retrieved dozens of whitefish (which to this day are a specialty of the region) with their dip nets.

Women and children spent the summer and fall gathering groundnuts, Jerusalem artichokes, and other bulbous vegetables, as well as hickory and walnuts and other edible plants. In certain areas acorns were also collected and soaked in liquid to remove their bitterness. Blueberries, raspberries, cranberries, and wild grapes were dried to make preserves and later added to corn and meat dishes to vary the flavor.

In present-day Wisconsin and Minnesota, wild rice, a species of grass growing along the shores of countless shallow, limy lakes, was one of the main foods. The time of the plants' maturation in the fall was ascertained by close observation and was announced by a rice chief in the harvest camp. A few days before the rice was ripe, the bark boats were maneuvered into the rice fields claimed by the respective families. Using a stick, the women would bend the stalks over the edge of the boat, and brush them in a glancing stroke with a second stick to knock the seeds from the ears. If the wild rice was already completely ripe, the slightest touch could empty the ears, and the seeds were easily lost. Unripe grains, on the other hand, could hardly be removed at all. This particular harvesting technique ensured that enough seeds dropped into the water to germinate the following year and therefore always guaranteed a reliable harvest. Once it had been dried and parched over the fire, wild rice was stored in pails made of folded birch bark, and could thus be preserved over long periods of time.

In early spring, entire families would migrate to groves of sweet maples, where the sap rising after the end of the frost was tapped, thickened in large kettles over the fire, and finally pounded in wooden troughs to produce sugar. Maple sugar served as seasoning, as candy, and also for emergency rations, but above all it was a trade good to be sold or exchanged for other foods and commodities. Considering the huge amounts of this foodstuff produced every year – in 1847 the Ottawa alone processed about 150 tons – the production of maple sugar represented a lucrative economic activity.

# From longhouse and wigwam

## The mighty chief

In the late winter of 1608, Chief Powhatan, surrounded by his concubines and dignitaries, and in repose on a bed of mats and cushions embroidered with pearls, received a delegation from the English colony recently founded on his land. This "great king" had every reason "to carry himself so prowdly," for as the English later reported, his subjects regarded his wishes as law, since not merely "as a king, but as halfe a God they esteeme him."

At this time, Powhatan's empire included nearly all of Virginia and represented the highest developed form of a hierarchical political structure in the Northeast. Supported by an influential priesthood and a council of advisers, Powhatan ruled over 30 chiefdoms, which he had brought under his control before the arrival of the Europeans by military threats or forcible subjugation.

The chiefs of these territories were all bound in obedience to his superior rule and to the payment of tributes. In strategically important places, Powhatan filled the positions of the district chiefs with his own sons and in particular his younger brothers. According to the rules of heritage along maternal lines, they (followed in turn by the sons of his sister) were destined to be his successors.

Moreover, Powhatan created social bonds through marital politics by choosing his wives from different areas of his empire. His marriages lasted only until the first child was born, after which the woman and her offspring would return to her home, where she was free to remarry. Powhatan's authority found its expression in a series of ceremonial offices, such as presiding over religious celebrations or the execution of criminals, and in the great public deference shown to him by his subjects. Chiefs, priests, and other members of the ruling class also enjoyed economic privileges granted by him in the form of trading monopolies and tributes.

## The politics of persuasion

Not in all societies of the Northeast did political leaders possess such sweeping powers. The small independent kinship groups of the Micmac were headed by leaders whose authority rested solely on their age and experience, and whose influence was limited to their own kindred. In the tribal societies of the Iroquois and the Huron the chiefs' authority likewise depended not on absolute power, but rather on their own personal influence and on their ability to convince others of their point of view.

Among the Huron, every village consisted of the members of various clans, whose membership was inherited along maternal lines. Each of these clans was led by a civil chief and a war chief, whose offices were hereditary in certain lineages of the clan, but who were also chosen on the basis of their achievements or

John White, *Secoton*, watercolor, 1585/86. Department of Prints and Drawings, British Museum, London, England.

The coastal Algonquians lived in mat-covered buildings with barrel-shaped roofs similar to the longhouses of the Iroquois. Raised platforms along the walls were used as storage space and for sleeping on. Unlike in neighboring villages, the loosely grouped houses of Secoton were not enclosed by palisades. Planted at different times, the corn plants standing in the village's fields were at different stages of growth and were protected from rapacious birds and other animals by guards sitting on shaded platforms in the fields.

Mesquakie (Fox) wigwam, Tama, Iowa, 1978.

Under pressure from government programs, indigenous buildings on the reservations, regarded as "backward," gradually gave way to houses of European style. Nevertheless, in many places the wigwam long remained the preferred type of residence, sometimes being converted from a traditional winter house into summer quarters. As an emblem of cultural identity it is still in temporary use today, even if the choice of building materials – in this case, canvas and plastic – has adapted to modern conditions.

proven skills. The civil clan chiefs discussed the affairs of the village with the elders in daily council meetings, chaired by the head of the most influential clan who acted as village chief and also represented the community in its external relations. Councils of war, however, convened only on given occasions.

The village chiefs formed the superior council of each of the four Huron tribes, which in turn was led by a tribal chief. In the council of the Huron tribal federation, every clan chief apparently had a seat and a vote. The purpose of these assemblies on the various political levels was to reach unanimous decisions, which would affect the opinions of the rest of the population, but would by no means be regarded as binding by everyone.

There was always the danger that some villages would break away from the consensus and act on their own initiative, threatening laboriously worked out compromises. In explosive political situations – such as the massive Iroquois aggression in 1648 and 1649, which ended with the Huron being driven out – the elaborate and ritualized process of decision-making in these councils at times proved far too cumbersome to bring about the rapid and purposeful action required in these circumstances.

While Powhatan's centralized chiefdom is sometimes wrongly described in historical reports as a confederacy,

real tribal federations could be found in the Eastern Woodlands. In the case of the Wabanaki confederacy, the alliance of the Micmac, Maliseet, Passamaquoddy, and Abenaki in the late 17th century can be understood as a reaction to the threat posed by colonial expansion.

The Iroquois League, founded in the early 16th century, long before European powers had established themselves in North America, is of much older origin. The alliance put an end to the bloody civil wars being fought between the culturally and linguistically closely related peoples of the Mohawk, Oneida, Onondaga, Cayuga, and Seneca, and developed into a forceful regional power, which later proved to have considerable influence on the fortunes of the European colonies.

# Longhouse and wigwam

Emblem of the League of the Iroquois, the "builders of the longhouse," was the typical elongated dwelling of the Iroquois villages which was inhabited by several nuclear families related through the female line. The houses, which were up to 65 yards long, consisted of a simple framework covered with elm bark and had a ridged roof. Inside, individual families lived in partitions along the walls and opening onto the central aisle, and shared a fire with the residents of the opposite partition.

The second characteristic type of dwelling of the Northeastern Woodlands was better suited to the seasonal mobility of other peoples. The dome-shaped wigwam (from the Algonquian term for "house") consisted of a framework of saplings set in the ground to a circular or oval plan, bent inward and tied together with bark fibre cords. Horizontal poles were attached to strengthen the frame, and an opening was left for the entrance.

The structure was covered with bark or reed mats arranged in shingled layers so that the rainwater drained off. Low wooden platforms lined up along the walls served as beds, while mats and furs laid out on the ground provided comfort for the inhabitants at other times. The women needed only a few hours to put up such a house; when the camps were broken up, the mats and pieces of bark could simply be rolled up and carried along to the next destination.

# Love and marriage

## From the autobiography of a Fox woman (1918)

The lives of the great chiefs had long fascinated the whites. It was only anthropologists who began to take an interest in the living conditions of "ordinary" people and of women. The autobiography of a Fox woman, an extract from which is quoted here, presents one of the oldest of these ethnological texts and furthermore can be taken as being particularly authentic. The account given by the woman was taken down in the syllabic script used by the Fox by Harry Lincoln, a Fox informant working for linguist Truman Michelson, who subsequently translated it.

The following extract ends with the woman's marriage, urged by her mother, to an unloved man whom she could only leave five years later, after the death of her mother. A year after the divorce, she married her former lover, by then a widower, and they lived very happily together until his death. Her third husband was lazy and gambled, but after several miscarriages she had her longed-for children with him. After his death she remained a widow, as her children could now look after her.

When I was eighteen, in the spring at the time when people begin to pick strawberries, I accompanied a young woman when we were strawberrying. "We will see one," she would say to me. Then she would say to me, "I am just joshing you." As a matter of fact she and one young man had made arrangements to see each other over there.

Soon he came over there. They were well acquainted with each other and treated each other kindly. She was helped by him when she was picking strawberries. She kept coming to me to get me to go with her some place. Soon he came with another young man. Then this young woman got me to talk to his fellow young man. "He will not do anything; you may talk together quietly," that woman told me. As often as we went anywhere those men came. Finally I surely began to talk to that young man. And then we four went around together a great deal. It surely was enjoyable to hear them say funny things. Then it was that I always wished to see him right away when I went anywhere, that is after I had seen him.

Of course many men tried to get me to talk with them. Soon it was known what kind of a person I was. My, but they scolded me severely. Another young man had been selected for me to take as husband. The other one and I were already well acquainted.

"You had better take a husband right away," I was told, "When you are twenty, you shall take a husband, I told you formerly when I was instructing you. And I forbade you to go around with immoral girls. Surely you are already not doing right. I desired to see you well-married while I was still living. But now I do not expect you to be well-married to one man. The father of the one with whom you talk is evil. Your lover might beat you. That is the way his father is. He is always beating his wife. And when anything is taking place, he will not allow his wife to go there. Moreover, that man is extremely lazy. That is why I think the son will be like that. He is always merely walking around. I have never known him to do any work. If you took him as your husband, you would probably then be taking care of him. He would cheat you, for you already know

Fox woman weaving a band of glass beads. Photograph: E. A. Rinehart, 1899. Museum für Völkerkunde, Vienna, Austria.

"When I was twelve years old ... a small belt of yarn was put on the sticks for me. 'Try to make this one,' I was told. I began to try to make it. Later on I surely knew how to make it. Then I kept on making yarn belts. My mother was pleased when I learned how to make anything."

how to do all the work that belongs to us women. You really must not take him for your husband. You must take the other one as your husband, the one with whom I think it proper for you to live. You must stop talking with the one you are trying to love. If, however, I learn that you talk again with him, you will cease to have control over any of our things. I shall not believe anything you say to me. Now I know in the past, that you listened to what I told you. That is why I believed you when you said anything to me. And this. As many things as you have learned to make, I am very proud of them. That is why I would forbid you to go around with immoral girls. Surely as soon as you began to go around with them we found it out. You are no longer afraid of men. You formerly were afraid to go anywhere because of them. But now you always desire to go somewhere. You will be thought of as naught if you are immoral. The ones who are moral are those whom men want to live with. And they will only make sport of the immoral ones. That is why they bother them, to have a good time with them, not to marry them. You might as well quickly take as your husband the one whom I permit you," I was told.

I was nineteen years old. Then I made up my mind to begin talking with the one I was permitted. I did not like him very well. I thought more of the other one. Always I would think, "Would that I might talk with him." I really couldn't stop talking with him. I worried about him. And I again went around with the one I was permitted, when I went anywhere. Later on I became acquainted with him. But I always thought more of the other one, the one they hated on my account.

Soon the one I was permitted began to try to have me accompany him to his home. He always asked me to go with him whenever I saw him. Then I said to him, "I am very much afraid of your parents." "Well, I will go with you to your home," he said to me, "we do not speak a different language, so it is not right for us to be afraid of each other. As for me, I am not afraid of your parents. For I have done nothing evil to you. As long as we have been talking together, I have been quiet with you. You know it too. I intend that we shall live quietly with each other. I always think, 'Oh that she were willing.' You are the only one with whom I wish to live. I shall treat you very nicely. Whatever you tell me, I shall do. And I shall always work. And I shall not hate your parents. I am not fooling you. What I say to you this day, I shall surely do," he said to me. Soon I consented. At night we departed. When it was daylight, I was rather ashamed to go where we lived with him. The next day when he was seen, he surely was treated very nicely, for I had taken for a husband the one they had wished me to.

Then he gave me his horse, and the clothing which he used at dances, his finery. And I gave that horse to my brothers. Soon my mother-in-law came to summon me. "Go over there," my mother said to me. I departed. When I arrived there, "Right here," I was told. "Sit down," I was told. I sat down comfortably. Well, they began to clothe me in finery. I was clad all over in finery. Then, "You may also take this kettle home," I was told. There were also some dry goods in it, and a bridle was in the kettle. I had a very large bundle on my back when I departed. I arrived where we lived clad in finery. My mother looked at the bundle. When she saw the bridle she said, "Now you have two horses. If you had taken the other man as your husband, you wouldn't have been given anything."

Soon I likewise was told, "I say, you take this to them." Food was placed in a sack, mattings, and several belts of yarn were tied around them. Then we were through with the wedding ceremonies. And then only the relatives of my husband gave me each something, usually dry goods. And I would take a sack or basket full of food, beans, pumpkins to his people, and mattings and corn.

Surely my husband for a long time treated me nicely. And my mother strongly forbade me to keep on talking with the other one. She watched me closely. But I couldn't stop thinking of him, for he was the one I loved. I did not love my husband. That is why I always thought of the other one.

Truman Michelson, ed. "Autobiography of a Fox Woman,"
*40th Annual Report of the Bureau of American Ethnology*, Washington 1925.

Studio portrait of a young Fox woman, Tama, Iowa, c. 1900.

"[After the death of the second husband] for four years I remained single, showing how sorry I was for my husband. If I had had a child I should have never married again. As it was, I was too much alone all the time. 'That is why,' I thought, 'I am always lonely.'"

Samuel Marsden Brookes, *Menominee Men*, oil on canvas, 1858. Milwaukee Public Museum, Milwaukee, WI.

With the exception of the moccasins, which continued to be made of leather, by the mid-19th century the whole attire of the Menominee and other peoples of the Northeast consisted of cotton and wool cloth. In spite of these changes, the garments' cut and decoration remained in many cases an expression of cultural independence and identity. Turbanlike headdresses following the model of the Five Civilized Tribes of the Southeast likewise spread as a temporary fashion among the peoples of the western Great Lakes area.

# Body art

In contrast to the originally very plain dress of the peoples of the Northeast, the inhabitants of the Woodlands paid great attention to the care and decoration of their bodies. They shaved off body hair with a sharp seashell or obsidian blade, or pulled it out with tweezers made from two shells. As protection against cold, sunburn, and insects, both skin and hair were thickly rubbed with bear or raccoon fat. The red color sometimes mixed in with the grease literally made their wearers "redskins."

Men's heads were adorned with headdresses made of upright feathers, or roaches of red hair from deer tails attached to a base of Indian hemp. Women wore their hair loose or tied into one or two heavy braids. Many men shaved all or part of their scalp, usually leaving a long strand on the crown (the "scalp lock"). The Jesuit missionary Joseph-François Lafitau (1681–1746), who lived among the Iroquois from 1712 to 1717, gave a detailed description of the hairstyle of young Iroquois, which fascinates young people of today's subcultures as much as it captivated the 18th-century observers:

"A young Iroquois then, to adorn his head, cuts his hair on one side as long as the breadth of two fingers from the skin and lets it grow to its full length on the other side. Next, to arrange it, after greasing and combing it well, he puts on top of his head two or three little topknots in the form of tufts to which he ties, with a little worked leather, a little piece of white wampum; and he passes through the base of the middle tuft a feather tube adorned with different colors. He has drawn up the hair in the direction contrary to its growth on the shaven side. He braids that on the opposite side and gathers it under his ear with a ribbon knot. He makes another little braid in the middle of his forehead which he lets hang over one of his eyelids and ties on the side."

To the eye of a European observer, such clothing, ornaments, and body decoration seemed at best an exotic display of color, and at worst an expression of backward barbarism. Native American contemporaries could read the other's social prestige from it and could also recognize in aspects of clothes and accessories various allusions to the wearer's relationship to the supernatural.

The clothes that a woman made to meet the personal requirements of the family (but also for ritual gifts, payments of atonement, or for exchange) testified not only to her diligence and skills. This activity was also a way of obtaining considerable social prestige. Special creativity in decorating garments was regarded as a sign of supernatural blessing, and often originated in dreams or visions which were also the source of artistic innovations.

Male dress accouterments primarily pointed to the wearer's hunting and war achievements. For instance, eagle feathers in a headdress, cut in a certain way, could indicate how many enemies a warrior had killed or injured, and whether he had suffered any battle wounds. Well into the 19th century, a man's attire also reflected his skills in hunting and in trapping, for many of the goods acquired through the fur trade were immediately incorporated into the traditional clothing ensemble.

In addition, the outer appearance mirrored the current social situation. In mourning for the dead, the closest relatives of the deceased dyed their faces black, neglected bodily hygiene, and wore shabby clothes, and only after a year's mourning or more were they dressed in new clothing by their relatives. People's everyday clothes differed markedly from the magnificent attire displayed on ceremonial occasions. The gradual Westernization of everyday clothing coincided with a flourishing of decorative techniques, which found their brilliant expression in festive attire and served as a visible sign of ethnic identity.

Unknown artist, *Fox Warrior*, watercolor, c. 1730. Cabinet des Estampes, Bibliothèque Nationale de France, Paris, France.

Made from deer hide and skins, the pre-European clothing of the Northeastern peoples was often limited to a breechclout (or short wraparound skirt) and moccasins. If necessary, leggings and a leather cape worn around the shoulders were added to this outfit. Tattoos, in which pigments were inserted into the skin with bone needles, and body painting with mineral pigments or charcoal were widespread, and to differing extents popular among both sexes. However, the use of the skin for the expression of personal identity soon lost its importance, as many whites regarded tattooing as an indelible mark of "savagery." The Iroquois of the 17th century were still described and portrayed as walking galleries of a highly developed art of tattooing, but a few generations later no trace of this remained.

Left:
Miami woman's skirt with silk ribbon appliqué, c. 1830. Cranbrook Institute of Science, Bloomfield Hills, MI.

Native Americans were fascinated by glass beads, silk ribbons, silver ornaments, small brass bells, metal cones, and other prestigious trade goods. Part of the reason for this lies in the similarity of the color, luster, or texture of many of these materials to substances such as copper, meteoric iron, crystal, or seashells, which in traditional culture were held in high regard because of their association with the powers of the underworld. Their innovative incorporation in local forms of dress and ornament brought about characteristically indigenous styles of clothing.

Huron moccasins decorated with moosehair. Huron, 1800. Rautenstrauch-Joest-Museum für Völkerkunde, Cologne, Germany.

The word "moccasin," today part of the general vocabulary, comes from the Algonquian languages, where it designated the footwear typical of the Northeastern Woodlands, made from one piece of soft leather. While moccasins made for everyday use were usually quite plain, those worn for special occasions were elaborately decorated with dyed porcupine quills or moosehair. Even Europeans, especially those who made their living in these woods, such as fur traders, appreciated the advantages and comfort of this footwear. The broad ankle flaps of these shoes are very typical of the Northeast.

Chippewa offering tree, Wisconsin, 1930. Milwaukee Public Museum, Milwaukee, WI.

In times of sickness and need, cloth, glass beads, and other objects were hung from a tree or wooden pole as a communal sacrifice to arouse the supernatural beings' compassion. "I have seen an idol set up in the middle of a village; and to it, among other presents, ten dogs were offered in sacrifice, in order to prevail on this false god to send elsewhere the disease that was depopulating the village. Every one went daily to make his offerings to this idol," Jesuit priest Claude Allouez (1622–1689) lamented in the 17th century about what he considered "superstitious" customs. Missionaries looked upon this "idolatry" as a veneration of the devil, taught to the "savages" by Satan himself.

# Thunderbirds and underwater panthers

Just as, in the economy of the Northeast, hunting and agriculture complemented each other, so the world view of the peoples of the region also incorporated features connected to both hunting and planting. Hunting (and war) required the immediate and personal relation of humans to the powers ruling the world outside the village, while the sedentary life near the fields was characterized by a need not only for fertility but also for greater social order. The individual quest for help from supernatural powers stood opposite the communal ritual to secure an existence led by native priesthoods.

For many peoples of the Northeast, the universe basically consisted of an upper and a lower half separated by the earth afloat in the ocean. These three spheres – sky, earth, and underworld – were each ruled by different supernatural beings. Where there was a belief in a creator, who resided in the uppermost heavenly sphere, he played only a minor role in everyday religious life, as he was simply too far removed from earthly matters. Only under Christian influence did the Creator – often equated with God by missionaries – assume tangible form in people's faith. The Iroquois, for instance, originally imagined that the world was created for humans in mythical times by a pair of contrary twins. Over time, the twin who was connected with the sky, Tharonhiawagon ("He holds the sky"), turned into the

Creator sky god, while his twin brother Tawiskaron ("Flint") became the devil-like embodiment of evil.

## Manito

Of greater consequence for an individual's everday life than the far away Creator were the countless non-human beings believed to inhabit the entire cosmos. In the Algonquian languages they were mostly designated as *manito*. They manifested themselves in animals, plants, cosmic phenomena, and even in some objects.

The cultural goods that could be acquired by trading with the whites but that could not be manufactured by the Algonquians themselves also fell into the *manito* category. The Ojibwa, for instance, called the desirable glass beads of the whites "little *manito* berry" and referred to woven cloth as "*manito* fur." The Narragansett of Rhode Island also considered the ships, the houses, and the plows of the English settlers to be *manitowok*. However, the Algonquians did not regard the ghosts of the dead as *manito*.

As supernatural beings, the manitos were beyond human comprehension, and could harm, help, or bestow special talents on people. The powerful thunderbirds of the upperworld, who created thunder by beating their wings and whose eyes hurled bolts of lightning, were particularly revered as patrons of warriors, and they also provided farmers with the desired rain. Their archenemies, the underworld's horned snakes and long-tailed underwater panthers, were considered by the people to be particularly dangerous, but were also seen as donors of hunting success and abundant food resources.

The hunters particularly venerated the masters or owners of the animals who represented the supernatural prototype of every single species and from whom the species constantly renewed itself, thereby providing humans with essential foods. Every year a hunter would sacrifice the first animal of a species that he had killed to its supernatural owner.

The green corn ceremony traditionally held by the agricultural Iroquois and Delaware at the beginning of the harvest season was a thanksgiving from the whole community to the Creator himself for the fruits of the earth that he provided. In this ritual, the world was symbolically renewed. All fires were extinguished, and then rekindled by means of a fire drill, even in times when lighters or matches had become available.

## How culture came to the people

Most peoples ascribed to a culture hero the original arrangement of the world for the use of humans. For the Micmac and Maliseet-Passamaquoddy it was Gluskap who gave the world its current appearance. After he

had created the tribe of dwarfs living in the rocks, and given life to the fairies who bewitch humans with their songs, he took his bow and shot arrows into the trunks of evenly grown ash trees, from which emerged the first human beings: beautiful men and women with skin the color of hazelnuts and shiny black hair.

Gluskap not only taught the humans the arts of survival, such as the use of tools and weapons, and how to create a family, but also repeatedly intervened in human history as their savior. For instance, when a giant frog drank all the world's water and caused a widespread drought, Gluskap killed it, and the water returned. Some thirsty people jumped into the water to enjoy it and immediately turned into eels, lobsters, and frogs, who are now regarded as relatives of humans. Although Gluskap disappeared at some point, the Micmac believed that he would return to offer his help when people fell upon hard times.

In the Great Lakes region, the culture hero is the "Great Hare" Nanabozho, who was believed to possess supernatural abilities and powers of transformation. As a real trickster he often behaved in childlike, foolish, or even rude manner, but he also created all kinds of useful things and finally founded the "Medicine society" for the benefit of the people. Whole myth cycles, whose dramatic narration would take up many evenings, tell of Nanabozho's adventures in an endless chain of linked episodes. The corresponding mythical figure of the Sauk, Fox, Kickapoo, and Potawatomi was not identified with the hare, and bore the untranslatable name Wisakeha.

This trickster's character is illustrated by a story that the Ojibwa told the German traveler and geographer Johann Georg Kohl (1808–1878) in the mid-19th century. It concerns the origin of *kinikinik*, a mixture of willow bark and other plant products that was used as a substitute for tobacco:

"On one of his wanderings, Menaboju was once lying by his camp fire, but, to his annoyance, his tobacco-pouch was empty. When a savage cannot smoke he goes to sleep, and so did Menaboju. But he lay so awkwardly, that, in his dream, he rolled too near the fire, and burnt all his back and loins. He woke up, yelled, and rushed, tortured by pain, through the bushes. Some of these bushes, which he grazed, received the singed odour of the demi-god's scorched skin, and thus became perfumed, and henceforth suited for smoking. These now supply the Indians with kinni-kannik. And thus poor Menaboju had to suffer like a martyr, in order that his children, the Indians, might never henceforth fall into the dilemma in which he found himself. They now find tobacco everywhere in the forests and shrubs."

In his memoirs, the Ojibwa writer and Methodist preacher Kahgegagahbowh a.k.a. George Copway (1818–1869) described the vision he had experienced as a 12-year-old boy:

"I saw, in my dream, a person coming from the east; he approached, walking on the air: he looked down upon me, and said, 'Is this where you are?' I said 'yes.' 'Do you see this pine?' 'Yes, I see it.' 'It is a great and high tree.' I observed that the tree was lofty, reaching towards the heavens. Its branches extended over land and water, and its roots were very deep. 'Look on it while I sing, yes, gaze upon the tree.' He sang, and pointed to the tree; it commenced waving its top; the earth about its roots was heaved up, and the waters roared and tossed from one side of their beds to the other. As soon as he stopped singing, and let fall his hands, every thing became perfectly still and quiet. 'Now,' said he, 'sing the words which I have sung.' I commenced as follows:

'It is I who travel in the winds,
It is I who whisper in the breeze,
I shake the trees.
I shake the earth,
I trouble the waters on every land.'

While singing, I heard the winds whistle, saw the tree waving its top, the earth heaving, heard the waters roaring, because they were all troubled and agitated. Then said he, 'I am from the rising of the sun, I will come and see you again. You will not see me often; but you will hear me speak.' Thus spoke the spirit, and then turned away towards the road from which he had come. I told my father of my dream, and after hearing all, he said, 'My son, the god of the winds is kind to you; the aged tree, I hope, may indicate long life; the wind may indicate that you will travel much; the water which you saw, and the winds, will carry your canoe safely through the waves.'"

George Copway, *The Life, History, and Travels of Kah-ge-ga-gah-bowh (George Copway), a Young Indian Chief of the Ojibwa Nation, a Convert to the Christian Faith, and a Missionary to His People for Twelve Years*, Philadelphia, 1847.

# Guardian spirits

The ritual of acquiring a guardian spirit, the Jesuits in New France observed, consisted "in each one's making for himself, in his early years, a god which he reverences for the rest of his days." Among many Algonquian peoples in particular, the highly personal, lifelong relationship formed during the vision quest in puberty was indeed of great significance for an individual. Boys, and more rarely girls, had to spend several days at an isolated place without food or water until a supernatural being showed pity and promised the fasting youth support for the rest of his or her life. Certain songs, medicines, or objects (sacred bundles) symbolized this personal relationship and the spiritual power that the being would also make available in the future. The sacred bundles were among a person's most important possessions.

In the western Great Lakes area, not only such personal bundles were known but also bundles owned by associations or kinship groups, which originated in a vision of an ancestor or of the association's founder. Ceremonies relating to them were held annually for the benefit of the whole community. Among the Virginia and North Carolina Algonquians, instead of the individual vision quest a ritual was performed during which a group of adolescents were symbolically killed and administered drugs to eradicate their memory. After nine months of isolation and teachings by the priesthoods, the young people were reborn as religious or political leaders.

Plate 55

Drawn by Capt. S Eastman, U.S.A

## Calling the spirit helpers

Apart from the priests who had inherited their office or who had been specially trained, all over the Northeast there were also persons who had been given special individual abilities by the supernatural powers which they devoted to the service of the community. Much as in the Subarctic, some of these were tent-shakers, specialists in the diagnosis and treatment of disease who could also predict events, recover lost objects, or gather information about faraway people.

To conjure up his spirit helpers, in particular the turtle, the tent-shaker would withdraw into a cylinder-shaped tent open at the top, which he had built at dusk. When night set in, he began to sing and beat the drum to call the spirit helpers. Their arrival communicated itself to the bystanders as the structure started to shake when the supernatural beings arriving one by one settled on the tent poles. Their voices could be heard by everyone, but only the tent-shaker could interpret the content of their messages.

In 1764 the fur trader Alexander Henry (1739–1824) was witness to such a ceremony in Sault Sainte Marie, during which the turtle spirit flew at the request of the tent-shaker to Fort Niagara and Montreal to find out about the movements of the British troops. He returned with the information that boats full of British soldiers were already on their way, and recommended immediate peace negotiations, advice which the Ojibwa wisely followed. This took place against the background of the final surrender of Canada by their French allies in the previous year, which left the Ojibwa and Ottawa, enemies of the British, in a hopeless military situation.

Apart from its practical results, the ritual also served to strengthen faith in the supernatural powers by providing empirical knowledge. Nevertheless, skeptical white observers constantly searched for rational explanations of these events. They attributed the voices of the spirits to the arts of a ventriloquist, and the swaying of the tent to the efforts of the ritualist, yet at times had to tell of predictions which were amazingly accurate. At the end of the 19th century, a Catholic missionary voiced his suspicions that perhaps the devil, "the father of all humbug," was from time to time involved after all.

It was not only the supernaturally gifted medicine men, however, who were responsible for healing the sick, but also medicine societies which did not originate from visions, but had been set up in mythical times by the culture hero or Creator. The best-known, apart from the Algonquian Medicine society, was the False Face society of the Iroquois, whose members personified the spirits of the forest in spring and fall ceremonies. At these events, they wore

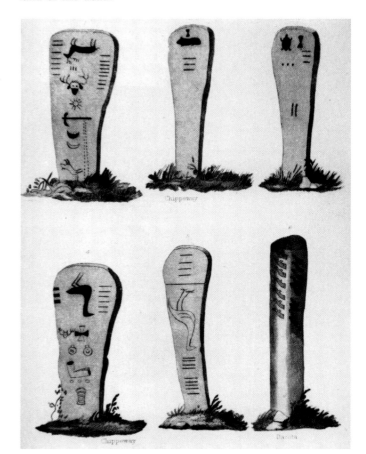

wooden masks painted black or red with characteristically distorted expressions which were regarded as the living embodiments of these beings and were offered sacrifices of tobacco and food.

## The path to the afterworld

The Algonquians of the western Great Lakes claimed to have firsthand knowledge of what awaited people after their death and how they should imagine the world beyond – from those who had already been there. Occasionally, it happened that an individual's soul who in serious illness had set off on the path to the shadowlands did not meet with a friendly reception there, but was sent back so that the survivors could tell of their experiences.

There was also no need to fear ultimate judgment of one's actions in life, as unethical behavior brought about disease and other punishment already in this world – punishments which might include the loss of a beloved relative or bad luck in hunting. In the land of the dead, however, good people as well as wrongdoers were received on equal terms.

The funeral rites of the Menominee, Chippewa, and related peoples reflected their belief in a dual soul. Clothes, weapons, tobacco pipes, and other funeral gifts were intended to facilitate the way to the afterworld for the "vital soul," which had its seat in the human heart and was responsible for the body's vital functions. On the other hand, the "free soul" living in the head, which formed individual consciousness and could leave the human body in dreams, tended to linger near the graves for a while. To prevent these ghosts from finding their way back to their wigwams and disturbing those they had left behind, the dead were carried out of the house through a hole in the wall, and the relatives made detours when returning from the funeral in order to confuse the ghosts.

Food left by the graves satisfied the hunger of these souls until they finally left the world of the living for good.

Before a soul could celebrate its reunion with dead relatives and join their dances, it had to travel a path full of obstacles. Its journey lasted four days, leading past a giant strawberry whose temptation it had to resist, and across a raging river, which it had to cross on a slippery tree trunk or on the back of a snake. Those who fell were lost forever and condemned to haunt the forest as restless ghosts, or were lost in the emptiness between this world and the realm of the dead. Those who safely reached the shore were rewarded with an eternal life of joy and affluence in the land of the dead.

The Tombe of their Cherounes or cheife personages, their flesh clene taken of from the bones saue
the skynn and heare of theire heads, w^th flesh is dried and enfolded in matts laide at theire
feete. their bones also being made dry or couered w^th deare skynns not altering
their forme or proportion. With theire Kywash, which is an
Image of woode keeping the deade. ~ ~ ~ ~ ~ ~

9

Paul Kane, *Indian Encampment on Lake Huron*, oil on canvas, 1845. Art Gallery of Ontario, Toronto, ON.

Birch bark was an ubiquitous and versatile resource in the material culture of the Ojibwa and their neighbors. It was used to make cooking vessels and containers of all kinds, it was a medium for pictographic records, and could be rolled up to make torches. Large pieces served as building materials to cover the conical or dome-shaped wigwams, or for the construction of boats, whose seams were caulked with resin and which, in spite of their light weight, had remarkable carrying capacity.

Opposite page, below left:
Southwestern Chippewa bandolier bag decorated with glass beads, 1885. Detroit Institute of Arts, Detroit, MI.

In the course of the 19th century, shoulder bags richly decorated with glass beads, whose wide variety of geometrical patterns later gave way to naturalistic floral motifs, developed from being articles for everyday use to prestige objects and an indispensable part of male ceremonial dress. They are sometimes called pony bags or friendship bags, as the Chippewa regularly exchanged these highly desirable trade goods for the horses of their western neighbors, who were otherwise regarded as enemies.

# Totems and Medicine society – the Ojibwa

While in the mid-17th century many indigenous peoples struggled for survival in the face of epidemic diseases and mounting assimilation pressure from white society, the Ojibwa's contact with French fur traders triggered population growth and territorial expansion. At the time, hunting and fishing characterized the way of life of the Ojibwa, who had only recently emerged through the amalgamation of several smaller local groups. The French simply named them Saulteurs, "the people from the waterfall," after the falls of the St. Mary's River connecting Lake Huron and Lake Superior, the area originally inhabited by the Ojibwa.

As skilled hunters and trappers they soon secured a leading role in the fur trade, and with the expansion of trading routes they quickly spread across a huge region, which in 1830 reached from Ontario in the east to the plains of Manitoba and Saskatchewan in the west. This geographical expansion led to different economic and cultural adaptations. While the northern Ojibwa (Saulteaux) developed a lifestyle suited to their subarctic environment, the Plains or Bungee Ojibwa adopted cultural elements of

their western neighbors. For the groups referred to as Chippewa, who had moved southwest into what are today the states of Wisconsin and Minnesota, the harvesting of wild rice became central to their economy. With about 200,000 tribal members in the United States and Canada, the Ojibwa (many today prefer their own term Anishnabe, "the original people") are one of the most populous indigenous groups in North America.

European travelers, traders, and missionaries seldom failed to comment on the Ojibwa's social structure, which they usually only partially understood. The Ojibwa were divided into patrilineal clans named after animals, which reminded the Europeans of the coat of arms of aristocratic families in the Old World. In fact, the term "totem" designating such a "coat of arms" is related to the corresponding Ojibwa word meaning "relative" or "family emblem."

A Chippewa story tells of five original totems (catfish, crane, bear, loon, and marten), whose creation goes back to the visit of five mythical beings in ancient times. By the 19th century, their number had increased to more than 20

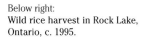

Alice White Cadotte gathering wild rice, Lac Court Oreilles reservation, Wisconsin, c. 1941. Milwaukee Public Museum, Milwaukee, WI.

Wild rice "had been put in Nett Lake and other lakes and rivers, when the land was formed for the Indians," Nett Lake Chippewa Bill Johnson declared in 1947. Like the Menominee and others, the Chippewa considered wild rice to be a gift from the supernatural powers that had been brought to the world by the culture hero. This interpretation is mirrored in the ceremonies surrounding the harvest. Prayers before the season of maturity were to guarantee a rich harvest and good weather, while after the harvest the supernatural donors were given thanks in a communal feast.

Below right:
**Wild rice harvest in Rock Lake, Ontario, c. 1995.**

Since wild rice has also become a specialty in American cuisine, the Chippewa suppliers have been hit by powerful competition from the commercial cultivation of wild rice in California. The grains harvested by traditional methods find little sales beyond the local markets.

among the Minnesota Chippewa. The members of these kinship groups were closely tied to each other through reciprocal rights and obligations, but at the same time alliances with other groups were promoted by the rule prescribing marriage to a partner from another clan. The confusion over the meaning of the term "totem" was caused by some historical observers who erroneously also used it to denote the personal guardian spirits which manifested themselves to adolescents during their vision quest. As most of these spirits appeared in animal form, they were often mistaken for the totems displayed in many places, for instance on grave posts.

Apart from the important individual relationships with supernatural beings, the Ojibwa also communicated with the supernatural through the communal rituals of the Medicine society (Midewiwin, "the society of the Mide"), which focused on healing the sick, preventing disease, and spiritual regeneration. The members of this society were made up of patients as well as healers (Mide priests). The latter possessed secret medical and ritual knowledge and belonged to one of the higher of the four (sometimes eight) grades into which the Midewiwin was divided. Every progression to a higher rank required an initiation and involved a long apprenticeship to deepen the understanding of the creation myth as well as herbal and medicinal expertise. The society's traditional store of knowledge, but also some songs and mythical texts, were recorded in pictographic writing on rolls of birch

bark, which were used as teaching aids when instructing the candidates. On account of their special knowledge and the cost involved in its acquisition, the Mide priests enjoyed high social prestige. If someone felt unwell and then dreamed that membership in the Midewiwin would heal them, they would apply to be admitted to the society, and against payment were initiated into its basic secrets.

At the society's assemblies, usually annual or biennial, the official admittance of such novices was part of the public "Medicine Dance," which took place in a long wigwam. The initiates were dramatically shot by older members, with cowry shells magically catapulted from the medicine pouches made of animal skin. They were then brought back to life through the powers of medicine. While this ritual was intended to demonstrate the potency of the secret healing powers, especially to the uninitiated audience, the actual healing took place in private.

# Scalp, stake, and adoption

Courage, magnanimity, and the proverbial ability to endure pain dominate the romantic image of the "Indian warrior." Evidence of these qualities can be found in numerous historical reports, even though contemporary white eyewitnesses tended toward a less blissful view of Native American warfare, whose motives and procedures clearly differed from the European practices of the time. Accounts of surviving prisoners of war usually focused on the cruel treatment of the victims, and the indigenous tactics of surprise attack followed by a quick retreat was often held in low regard by the whites and considered "deceitful."

The European military strategy of sending soldiers in well-ordered formation to their deaths as cannon fodder, employed well into the 20th century, made little sense in societies where wars were usually not waged for territorial conquest but rather provided an arena in which men could prove their courage, resourcefulness, and leadership qualities, and thereby achieve high social prestige.

Although economic interests such as defending trade monopolies did play a part, the "mourning wars" of the Iroquois, Huron, and other peoples of the Northeast were aimed primarily at taking revenge for killed tribal members. Their enemies' scalps would "dry the women's tears," and prisoners of war would be adopted in order to replace the dead. Only increasing involvement in colonial wars, the scalp bounties and other economic incentives offered by the European powers, and not least the increasing spread of firearms gradually changed the character of indigenous warfare.

## On the warpath

Usually a war party was formed at the instigation of a leader who would also take charge of the venture. A war expedition was deemed successful if the warriors managed to approach enemy villages or camps without being noticed, and to attack them with the least possible casualties on their own side. The attackers did not normally lose time by looting, as they could easily be ambushed on enemy territory.

With the scalp trophies, taken from the heads of their dead victims by a quick cut and a strong pull, and, depending on circumstances, a number of captives, the warriors retreated without delay. This type of warfare did not aim at the total destruction of the enemy, but simply at the restoration of the social balance which had been upset by the death of members of the tribe.

When a bewildered French officer asked some successful allied warriors why they were already on their way back home, they answered, "We have taken enough prisoners." Outright wars of extermination took place only in Powhatan's chiefdom in Virginia, which was ruled with an iron fist.

## Adoption or death

While the victorious men were joyously received on their return, the prisoners of war had to run the gauntlet and suffer all kinds of maltreatment. The final decision over their fate came from the women, who could choose from among these men a replacement for their husbands or their sons killed in war. In the case of an adoption, the prisoners would take on all the rights and obligations of the dead family members

Iroquois scalping a white prisoner of war, from Jacques Grasset de Saint-Sauveur, *Encyclopédie des voyages*, Paris 1796. Bibliothèque des Arts Décoratifs, Paris, France.

The drama in this picture hardly makes up for its lack of realism, revealed both by the landscape of palmtrees in the background and by the fanciful depiction of the scalping process itself. Such gruesome pictures of bloodthirsty savages contributed considerably to the cliché of the barbaric Indians held by the general public. However, this should not lead to the frequently voiced assumption that scalping was another European invention that only spread in North America in colonial times.

Peter Rindisbacher, *Chippewa Scalp Dance*, watercolor, c. 1829. Joslyn Art Museum, Omaha, NE.

After a successful war expedition, the scalp trophies, carefully mounted on hoops and often decorated, were ceremonially passed from hand to hand. In 1855, the German traveler Johann Georg Kohl (1808–1878) witnessed the excitement in a Chippewa camp over a recently taken Sioux scalp, and the enthusiasm of those "who also wished to enjoy the happiness of fondling it for a while at their fire, and listen to the accurate account of the foray."

whom they were now replacing. The less fortunate among them, who were not accepted into the tribal community, suffered a long and very painful death at the stake, which had the character of a human sacrifice and was connected with fertility rites.

The transition between periods of war and peace was marked by particular ceremonies, which on the one hand prepared the warriors for combat by mobilizing supernatural help and spurring on their belligerent spirit, and on the other hand celebrated the warriors' solemn reintegration into everyday life after their return from war. The sexual abstinence observed in the meantime emphasized the difference between the life-giving power of the woman and the male activity of killing in hunting and in war, and thus accentuated the separate yet complementary domains of both sexes.

Left:
*Nakaw, or Wood.* Winnebago (holding a Calumet). Lithograph after a painting of 1828 by Charles Bird King from T. McKenney and J. Hall, *History of the Indian Tribes of North America*, Philadelphia 1838.

Decorated with bird skin and eagle feathers arranged in a fan shape, the ceremonial pipe (*calumet*, after the French term for the long stem) was regarded as a symbol of peace, and was smoked and passed around at the conclusion of treaties and trade agreements. The calumet ritual, which was described by European observers as early as the 17th century, forged fictive kinship ties to strengthen alliances. It was widespread, especially in the Mississippi Valley and in the region of the western Great Lakes.

*Nawkaw*

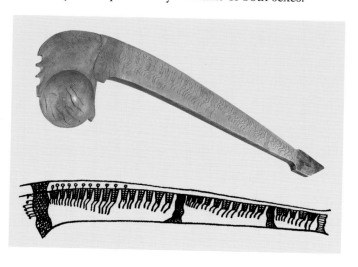

Far left:
Ball-headed club from the area of the Great Lakes, 18th century. Canadian Museum of Civilization, Hull, QC.

Before the introduction of iron axes (tomahawks) and knives, the wooden ball-headed club, sometimes armed with bone or stone points, was the traditional weapon for close-range combat in the Eastern Woodlands. The pictographs etched into the shaft identified the owner's military achievements and supernatural helpers; left at the scene of battle, the weapon thus virtually served as the warrior's "calling card."

The Americans' victory in the War of Independence spelled the end for the geopolitical role of the Iroquois, their wars, and trading interests, and threw them into a deep existential crisis by which the men were particularly affected. Deprived to a large extent of their traditional roles as hunters, warriors, and traders, they were forced to stay in the village communities, which were dominated by women, or to work as performers in traveling circuses or as scouts for fur-trading companies. This rampant feeling that their world had come to an end showed itself outwardly through increasing violence and alcohol abuse. New hope was raised by the instructions to reform Iroquois society which had been received by the Seneca chief and prophet Ganeodiyo or Handsome Lake (c. 1733–1815) from the Creator in several visions, and which he successfully spread through his preaching. The new Longhouse religion combined traditional and Christian values, turned against alcohol and witchcraft, encouraged the men to become farmers, and gave the Iroquois identity a new stability under the changing circumstances.

# The longhouse and its residents – the Iroquois

In the first half of the 17th century the Dutch, and the French advanced into the interior from the bridgeheads of New Amsterdam on the Atlantic coast and Quebec on the St. Lawrence River in search of animal furs and human souls. Unknowingly they were thus entering an invisible house 300 miles long, reaching from the Mohawk River valley in the east nearly all the way to Niagara Falls.

It was a typical Iroquois longhouse; however, its five fireplaces were not shared by families living on either side of the central aisle, but by five tribes, the speakers of languages which were related though partly mutually unintelligible. At one end, the Mohawk were guarding the eastern door; in the west the Seneca carried out this important task to protect its inhabitants, while the Onondaga held special responsibility as keepers of the central fire. These were the three "older brothers" or "uncles," who because of their male activities as warriors and politicians embodied the paternal side of the tribal family. As "younger brothers" or "nephews," the Oneida

and Cayuga represented the maternal side. They were all Onkwehonwe ("real people"), together they were Hodenosaunee ("the ones from the longhouse"), and united they were practically invincible.

## The Tree of Peace

It had not always been that way, however. The ancestors of the Iroquois had come around AD 900 from the Pennsylvanian Appalachians to the fertile lowlands south of Lake Ontario, where their cornfields produced prodigious harvests and could feed a rapidly growing population. The Algonquian peoples who had lived here previously were beaten in battle and either driven from the area or assimilated into the societies of the new arrivals. When the "Little Ice Age" began in the 14th century and the harvests declined, internal conflicts increased markedly. Archeologists have found clear

Those Iroquois who had emigrated to Canada after the American Revolution made their reservation by the Grand River the new center of the confederation, with its own league council, an institution also retained by those who had remained in New York. On both sides of the border, the Canadian and United States governments (in 1924 and 1934, respectively) attempted to replace the hereditary chiefs with democratically elected tribal representatives; however, alongside these new tribal councils, the traditional league council remains in operation to this day.

William Berczy, *Joseph Brant*, oil on canvas, c. 1807. National Gallery of Canada, Ottawa, ON.

The Mohawk Joseph Brant or Thayendanegea (1742–1807) was the grandson of one of the "Four Kings of Canada" who had visited London in 1710. Although he himself did not hold one of the 50 inherited chief's titles, he was an "honorary chief" on the basis of his personal abilities and was a close ally of the British in the fight against the French. Contrary to the Iroquois League's decision to remain neutral, Brant also fought on the British side during the American Revolution and moved with his followers to Canada after the British defeat, thus causing the tribal federation to break apart. For this reason, two Iroquois Leagues have officially existed since 1803: one with its traditional seat in Onondaga, the other one on the Canadian side, with its main seat in the Onondaga longhouse on the Six Nations Reserve near Brantford, Ontario.

indications for wars between the related tribes, which is exactly what Iroquois traditions describe. In a display of unbridled aggression, tribe fought against tribe, village against village, neighbor against neighbor. The oral tradition relates that "everywhere there was peril and everywhere mourning."

In these troublesome times, an unmarried Seneca woman who had found refuge among the Huron gave birth to a son. In a dream, a messenger of the Creator announced that her son Deganawida had been chosen to raise up the Great Tree of Peace. The child's grandmother attempted in vain to drown the bastard baby in the wintry ice water, and it was this miraculous invulnerability which later helped Deganawida to convince the Mohawk of his divine mission as the messenger of peace. Among the Mohawk he allied himself with Hiawatha, who had fallen into deep despair because of his daughters' death which had been caused by a sorcerer.

Deganawida used the wampum beads discovered by Hiawatha to make strings with which, among other things, he wiped away the mourning man's tears, unstopped his ears, cleared his throat, erased the yellow spots caused by mourning from his chest, wiped the bloodstains of the sorcerer's wicked deed from the cornhusk mat, dispelled the darkness, caused the sky to shine, leveled the earth over the daughters' grave, and dispelled the insanity caused by grief. With this sequence of ceremonial acts, Deganawida established a ritual through which the Iroquois would "raise up" their future chiefs in place of their deceased predecessors, thereby establishing a chief in the position rightfully belonging to his clan. The successor would bear the same name title as his predecessor and was therefore the same person in a new guise.

Assisted by Hiawatha, Deganawida now formulated the Great Law of Peace which would end the war among brothers. Together the two traveled through the land of the

Iroquois to spread this law. The only resistance came from Thadodaho, a powerful chief and sorcerer of the Onondaga who suppressed his own people.

According to the story, only after Hiawatha had combed out the snakes living in his hair, did Thadodaho come to his senses, and Deganawida made him the first among equals of the 50 chiefs of the Iroquois League that had finally been established. Then they threw all of their weapons into a pit and planted the Tree of Peace on top of them: the future proverbial hatchet was buried.

The Great Law regulated the relations of the five tribes among each other, their representation in the League council, the specific tasks of the clans, and the religious ceremonies. The positions of the 50 chiefs in the council had to be filled by certain clans, which in each tribe were allocated to two halves or moieties. During the mourning ritual of "raising up" the chief, the moiety from which the new chief did not come was responsible for organizing the ceremony.

The Great Law also determined the relationships to other peoples who were offered a place in the shade of the Tree of Peace as long as they acknowledged the superiority of the five founding tribes. Around 1722, the Iroquoian Tuscarora, who had been driven out of their homes in North Carolina, were accepted as the sixth nation in the League without representation in the council. Other non-Iroquoian groups were also adopted and more or less intergrated into the League.

By uniting their strengths the "Five (or Six) Nations," as they were called by the Europeans, gained military ascendancy over their neighbors, a key political role in the colonial conflicts of the North American East, and special interest from the whites in the peculiarities of their culture.

Caroline Parker, a Seneca Iroquois woman, New York, 1849. Photograph after a lost daguerreotype. Southwest Museum, Los Angeles, CA.

What today is regarded as the traditional costume of Iroquois women – dresses made of textiles and decorated with beadwork – did not develop until the 19th century. Caroline Parker was the sister of General Ely Parker (1828–1895), the first indigenous head of the Bureau of Indian Affairs in Washington. Ely Parker was also the main source of information for lawyer Lewis Henry Morgan (1818–1881), whose book on the Iroquois provided the springboard for his theory of the development of human society, which later greatly influenced Karl Marx (1818–1883) and Friedrich Engels (1820–1895). Marx and Engels claimed that the Iroquois federation was an early forerunner in the formation of states, and that clan ownership of land was a step toward the development of private ownership of the means of production, and therefore of class society.

Street in the Mohawk settlement of Kahnawake, Quebec, c. 1990.

While most Iroquois were fighting the French in the 17th century and were rejecting any attempts at conversion by the Jesuits, several Mohawks and Oneidas moved to French mission stations near Montreal. These included the mission of Lac des Deux Montagnes (known to the Algonquian as Oka, and to the Mohawk as Kanehsatake), where they lived together with Algonquian groups, as well as Sault Saint Louis (Kahnawake), founded in 1676. In about 1750, some Mohawks moved away from Kahnawake and founded Saint Regis (Akwesasne, today a reservation on both sides of the American-Canadian border) further upstream. After their conversion to Protestantism in the 19th century, many of the Iroquois living along the St. Lawrence River became followers of the Longhouse religion in the 20th century.

The lengthy wars fought in the 18th century led the Iroquois far into the South and West in the course of military campaigns often lasting several years. These wars gave them (also known under their Algonquian name "Mingo," used particularly for the Iroquois living outside the League in the Ohio region) a dubious reputation for extraordinary cruelty. The name of the Mohawk even derives from a word from the now extinct language of the Narragansett, which translates as "cannibals."

## Mohawk, myths, matriarchy

At the same time, the Iroquois became the epitome of skilled diplomats, gifted speakers, and insightful critics of European culture, and found admirers and imitators among educated and disgruntled Europeans. As early as 1712, the Irish satirist Jonathan Swift (1667–1745) reported from London of "a race of rakes called the Mohocks [Mohawks] that play the devil about this town every night, slit people's noses and beat them etc." The Iroquois have thus been a symbol of alternative youth culture for longer than just the last few decades, when the "Mohawk" haircut became a trademark of the punk scene. The Iroquois also continue to this day to be regarded as a perfect example of a matriarchal society, and their tribal confederation as a direct model for the American constitution.

Considering a union of the English colonies as early as 1754, Benjamin Franklin (1706–1790), one of the architects of the American constitution, remarked that it would be strange if "six nations of ignorant savages" could form a solid and lasting association while a dozen English colonies found the very same impossible. However, this only referred to the federation and not to the constitution, which indeed cannot be compared to that of the United States. Unlike the American representatives, the 50 League chiefs by no means fairly represented the whole population. The Seneca, always the largest tribe, only provided eight chiefs, while the Cayuga, at best numbering a third of the Seneca, came up with ten, and not all clans were represented in the League's council. Also, these representatives of the people were not elected, but were chosen by the matrons (the eldest women of rank) of the clans in which their office, including their name title, was passed down. Finally, the League's council did not reach decisions by a majority vote, but had to negotiate until unanimity had been obtained. Furthermore, not even these decisions could be enforced, but were dependent on the tacit consent of the people.

Above all else, the fact that women could appoint and in cases of incompetence recall the chiefs was taken as proof of an Iroquoian "matriarchy." This right – and duty – resulted from the fact that the clans, whose membership was inherited matrilineally, were the owners of all names and name titles (though of very little else). At the same time, the Great Law also required the matrons to award these titles to someone, as otherwise they would be declared dead and their family extinct. It is not by coincidence that the Iroquois referred to dependent tribes as "women" when they took away their independent political rights.

This, however, does not mean that Iroquois women necessarily held an inferior position. They had their own councils and women's associations, and as owners of the house and of the land that they farmed, they played an important part in both domestic and economic life. As one house would be inhabited by related women and their husbands, the men often remained outsiders in the household, and many marriages fell apart as a direct result of this. Finally, the hunters' and warriors' long periods of absence from the village also strengthened the female position. This does not make the Iroquois a matriarchy, but rather a society with a relatively egalitarian gender status, which is rare enough in the world.

Just as the idea of Iroquois "matriarchy" inspired the founders of the American women's movement as early as the 19th century, so the peace movement of the 20th century made frequent reference to the Great Law of Peace of the warlike Iroquois.

Mohawk ironworkers Angus Mitchell and Joe Jocks with a colleague on a building site in New York, c. 1950.

When a bridge crossing the St. Lawrence River near Kahnawake was built in 1886, the local Mohawk discovered their talent for carrying out the dangerous work of building steel structures at dizzying heights. Since then Iroquois bolters and riveters have helped to erect many of North America's skyscrapers, at the same time finding a niche in the employment market, which requires the daring of a hunter or warrior and is well paid.

Group of Iroquois ironworkers working on a bridge, c. 1930.

As early as 1709, the English surveyor John Lawson (d. 1711) admired the ease with which the Iroquoian Tuscarora – at that time still living in North Carolina – could balance on the tree trunks that served as bridges: "They will walk over deep Brooks, and Creeks, on the smallest Poles, and that without any Fear or Concern. Nay, an Indian will walk on the Ridge of a Barn or House and look down the Gable-end, and spit upon the Ground, as unconcern'd, as if he was walking on *Terra firma*."

Captain Noel Marshall and his wife (Micmac), Nova Scotia, c. 1978.

As early as the 19th century, long coats of dark cloth fashioned on the model of British uniforms, with collars, lapels, and shoulders trimmed with red fabric and decorated with glass beads and silk ribbons, were part of "traditional" men's dress, just as the typical woolen hoods were part of women's clothing. The curvilinear beaded designs may derive from the painted motifs on the original leather garments. Today, these dress items are worn on festive occasions and testify to the Micmac's traditionalism and pride in their own identity.

# Sagamores and hieroglyphs – the Micmac

When at the beginning of the 16th century Breton fishermen searching for new fishing grounds reached the North Atlantic coast, the Micmac were living as hunters, fishers, and gatherers in the region south and west of the Gulf of St. Lawrence, the "happy land" that their culture hero Gluskap had created for them in mythical times. The dense forests of their homeland were full of moose, caribou, and bears, which they hunted in smaller family groups during the fall and winter. In spring and summer,

when great quantities of sturgeon, trout, herring, salmon, and smelt, as well as a variety of shellfish, were available, they gathered in larger numbers in their established camping grounds along the rivers and on the coast, where seal and walrus were also hunted. This was the time when the sagamores, the heads of individual family groups, met for political deliberations. It was also the season for communal festivities, the cultivation of family relations, and for courtship.

Marriages served to establish alliances between family groups, or strengthened existing relations. For the sagamores, the network of kinship ties formed the basis of their power and influence. Marriages were therefore often arranged by the parents of the two future spouses. As the woman would later move to the man's household and her labor be lost to her own family, the bridegroom was obliged to spend one or two years of "bridal service" with his in-laws. During this time he lived in their conical bark tent and hunted, fished, and worked for the household as if he were part of the family, although he was allowed no sexual contact with the bride. A feast at which the bridegroom served the guests with the yields of his hunting marked the formal end of this bridal service and the beginning of the marriage.

After marriage a woman continued to exercise control over her own possessions, so that divorce, which could be initiated by either the man or the woman, was relatively unproblematic. Any subsequent marriages took place without much ceremony. Some men married a second wife, for instance the widow of a deceased brother.

In the world of the "L'nuk" ("human beings," the Micmac's original self-designation), supernatural power could manifest itself in all aspects of creation, which therefore deserved respect. Supernatural beings appeared to an individual in dreams and offered their protection and support.

The Micmac's amazement at the first European ships, which they initially took for floating islands covered with trees and inhabited by hairy bears, soon gave way to the recognition that the strangers were human, and to pronounced interest in their material goods. However, when they departed, the French, Basque, and Portuguese visitors left more behind than their iron axes, copper kettles, and numerous Basque loan words. In the centuries that followed, dramatic population decline caused by imported diseases, increasing dependency on the fur trade, in which the Micmac tried to maintain their position as middlemen for the tribes in the interior, and entanglement in the colonial conflicts between the French and the British threatened their physical and cultural survival. Their alliance with the Maliseet, Passamaquoddy, and Abenaki was one of the strategies for maintaining indigenous autonomy in the face of a changing political and economic order.

The Catholic missions exerted considerable influence early on. Although they undermined traditional culture on the one hand, they also contributed to finding a new identity on the other. The baptism of the great sagamore

also the internal stability of communities. The invention
of the Micmac "hieroglyphs" played an important
part in the history of Christianization. This non-
alphabetical script containing more than 5,000 characters
was developed in the 17th century by the missionary
Chrétien Le Clercq (c. 1630–1695) as an aid to memorizing
prayers, hymns, and the catechism, and was received
with great enthusiasm by the Micmac. With the liturgical
texts recorded on birch bark, they were able to practice
and maintain their religion even in the absence of
Catholic priests, and they also turned it into a
form of cultural resistance against the Protestant
British authority.

As late as the second half of the 19th century, the
Baptist missionary Silas T. Rand (1810–1889) attributed
his own failure to the unbroken influence of their
"peculiar characters," which he denigrated as "one of the
greatest literary blunders ever perpetrated." To this day,
Catholicism forms an important part of the group identity
of the Micmac living on several reserves in Nova Scotia,
New Brunswick, Prince Edward Island, Newfoundland,
and southeastern Quebec.

Membertou, who was greatly feared for his supernatural
powers, was celebrated in 1610 as the first conversion, but
the Micmac probably regarded it primarily as a means of
forming a political alliance with the French. However,
Christian ideas soon replaced the old religious beliefs. Their
additional task as functionaries of the congregation
strengthened the traditional leaders' position and therefore

# The lost country – the Delaware

In the popular imagination, the sale of Manhattan for "a handful of glass beads" is regarded as one of the most profitable real estate deals in history – and for many it is also an example of how the original inhabitants were cheated.

Strictly speaking, the payment was in trade goods to the value of 60 Dutch guilders, which according to a conversion more than 100 years old but still cited in this context, is said to have been equal to $24. However, the

Munsee, ancestors of today's Delaware, who sold the granite island to the Dutch in 1626, must at the time have considered the desirable European goods sufficient compensation, while for the latter the deal did not turn out to be as advantageous as they initially had expected. Barely four decades later New Amsterdam was conquered by English colonists and renamed New York.

The oral tradition of the Delaware, however, tells of real deceitfulness on the part of the European settlers when it came to the acquisition of their land. After they had granted a piece of land "just as much as a bullock's hide would cover" to a group of Dutch, the latter cut the hide into a narrow strip so as to encompass the greatest possible area.

A century later, the sons of William Penn, founder of the colony of Pennsylvania, with unparalleled ruthlessness cheated the Delaware out of their land in Pennsylvania. In the infamous Walking Purchase Treaty of 1737, the Delaware ceded a piece of land, the length of which a man could walk in a day and a half. However, they had not reckoned with the slyness of their treaty partners, who provided three runners specially trained for running the distance as fast as possible and without a break, on a path that had already been cut through the forest.

Thus the Delaware's ancestors, in one way or another, lost their old homelands on the Delaware River, whose English name eventually came to designate a people that only emerged in the 18th century from the union of several displaced groups. The originally small and independent local groups of this region, who soon became known to the Europeans by dozens of names, spoke different dialects of two eastern Algonquian languages, Munsee in the north and Unami in the south. The Unami-speakers called themselves Lenape ("real people"), still the preferred self-designation of the Delaware today. They hunted and fished, with individual families claiming the right to certain areas, and cultivated their cornfields near their villages in summer.

The leaders of these groups, men from influential families, carried out ceremonial functions, acted as political representatives, and discussed the fate of their people with other men in council. From time to time, smaller local groups would join up in order to organize large hunting expeditions, to defend themselves against enemies, or to conduct diplomatic negotiation with the Europeans or with their indigenous neighbors.

The larger political body of the "Delaware" only emerged during their gradual migration to the upper Ohio Valley, although not all of the local groups joined it, and often splinter groups broke away. The Iroquois, who had already made tributaries of some Munsee and Unami groups in the mid-17th century, and in whose territory Delaware refugees settled in the 18th century, "made women of them," which meant that they had no right to cede lands or wage war, and that their diplomatic relations with the whites were controlled entirely by the Iroquois.

The Delaware regained their political status as "men" only in the American Revolution, which, however, also contributed to their division into several factions and to

Gustav Hesselius, *Tishcohan*, oil on canvas, 1735. Historical Society of Pennsylvania, Philadelphia, PA.

Tishcohan (or Tishecunk) was one of the Delaware leaders who fell victim to the Walking Purchase Treaty of 1737. Two years before, the Penn family had commissioned the Swedish artist Gustav Hesselius to portray him and fellow chief Lapowinsa. For the sitting, Tishcohan was draped in a blue woolen blanket and wore around his neck a tobacco pouch made of squirrel skin, in which he also kept a clay pipe that he had obtained through trade with the English.

their further scattering. A neutrality agreement of 1775 with the rebelling colonists was followed in 1778 by the first formal treaty of the United States with an indigenous people, in which the Americans guaranteed the Delaware land rights in their new homeland. After Delaware groups sympathizing with the British had withdrawn to western Ohio, American militia took revenge on the peaceful groups that had been converted to Christianity by the Moravian Brethren, and in 1782 killed some 90 Delaware Christians in a massacre in the mission village of Gnadenhütten in eastern Ohio.

Still in the 18th century, several Unami and Munsee groups retreated to the Canadian province of Ontario, some under the leadership of the Moravian Brethren, some as followers of the Iroquois. Others moved to Missouri in what was then Spanish Louisiana. The last Unami still living in New Jersey left their reservation in 1802 and joined the Stockbridge in New York, the latter a mixture of Mohegan-Pequot and Mahican, who in 1823 migrated to Wisconsin under the protection of the Iroquoian Oneida.

The majority of the Delaware followed the emigrants who had settled on the White River in Indiana around 1780 upon the invitation of the Miami, but in 1818 they were driven away from there into Missouri. Some groups moved from there to Arkansas and Texas; others received lands in Kansas in 1829, which they later exchanged for a reservation in Oklahoma in 1867. Today the Delaware live widely scattered across different parts of Canada and the United States as Delaware, Munsee, or Unami. Their fate strikingly illustrates the history of loss of land, relocation, and changing identity that similarly affected the destiny of so many other peoples of the Northeast.

Earnest Spybuck (Shawnee), *Oklahoma Big House Ceremony*, watercolor and crayon, 1912. National Museum of the American Indian, New York, NY.

The Big House Ceremony celebrated in the fall was central to the religious life of the Delaware. It emerged from the fusion of the old rituals of vision quest and harvest festival. Accompanied by two singers and a drum, the older men danced round the two central fireplaces for twelve nights and recited the visions that they had received in puberty. A final prayer of thanks and a ritual meal ended the ceremony, which was last held in Oklahoma in 1924.

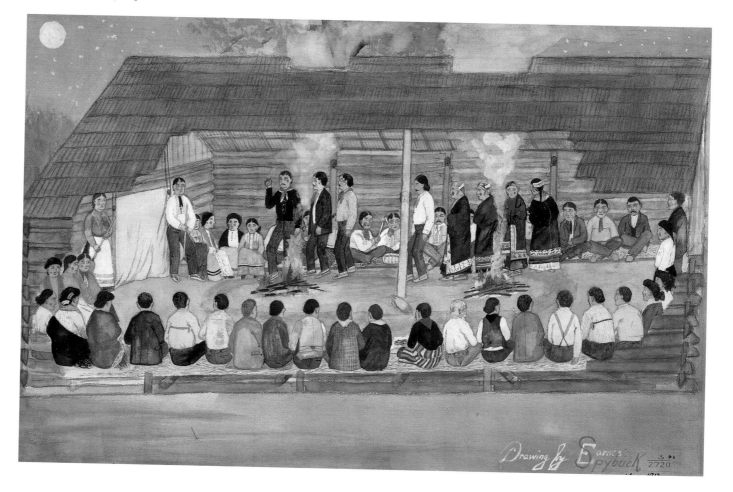

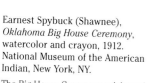

SOUTHEAST

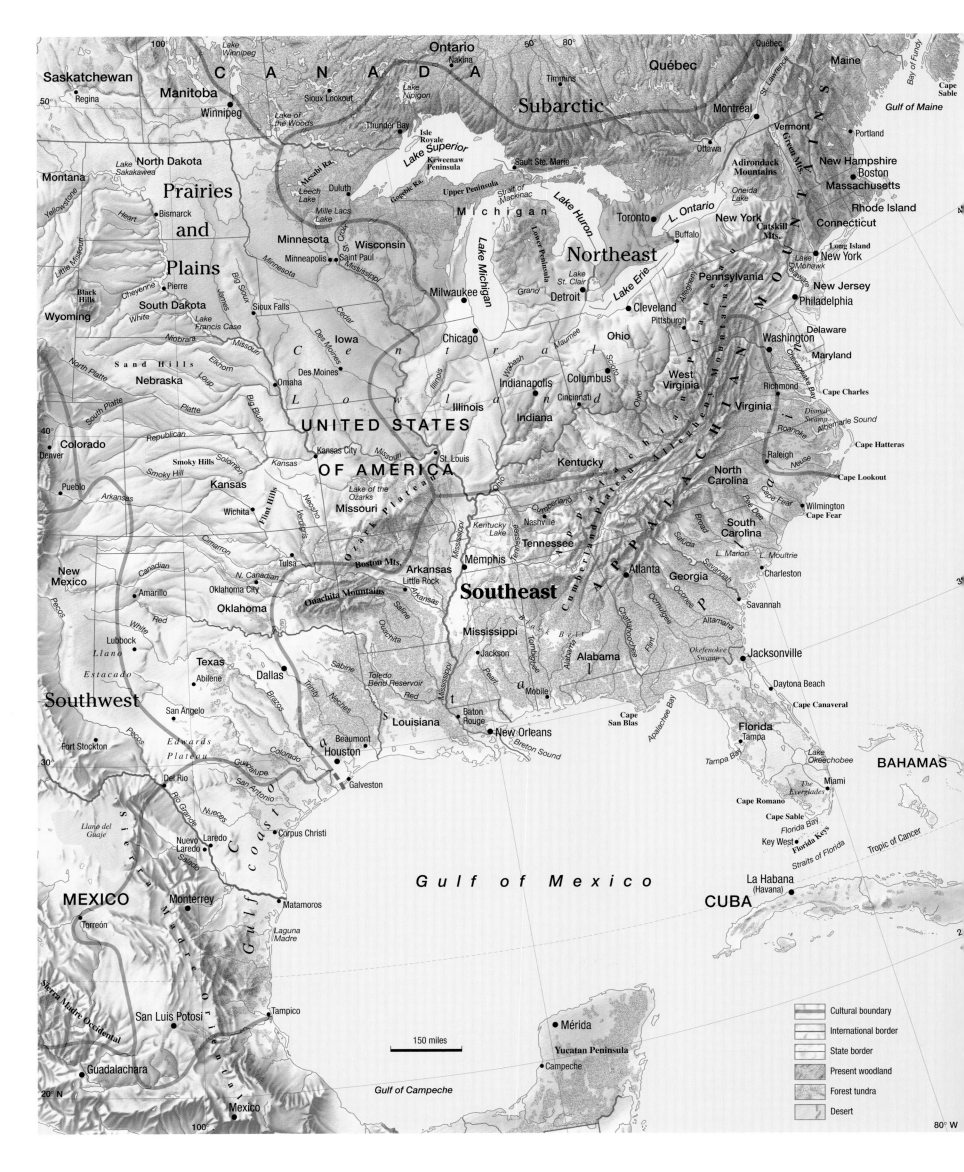

# Swamp forests and red earth

Sylvia S. Kasprycki

Sluggish rivers meander through the lowlands of the coastal plain that forms one of the major geographical areas of the North American Southeast and covers more than three quarters of this region. It stretches along the Gulf and Atlantic Coasts and also includes the lower Mississippi Valley and the Florida peninsula. To the northeast, the area reaches to North Carolina, while in the north it encompasses a large part of the southern Appalachians. The region west of the Mississippi was inhabited by agricultural peoples and forms a transition to the Great Plains. The culture area of the Gulf Coast represents a separate border zone of the Southeast, covering the southern coastal regions of present-day Texas and the areas on the lower Rio Grande. Little is known of the original inhabitants of this region.

The rivers, whose deposits have built fertile alluvial floodplains, feed the innumerable swamps of the lowlands, whose vegetation supplied the local populations with valuable raw materials. The rot-resistant wood of the cypress proved to be a useful material for house posts and dugouts, while cane was used for making mats, baskets, sieves, weirs, and many other items. Today, the Everglades in Florida, a national park dedicated to the protection of the unique fauna and flora, have become a tourist attraction.

Previous pages:
Palmettos and pines in Everglades National Park, Florida.

Palmetto leaves served as roof coverings and as a material for plaiting. The fruit of some kinds of palms were also eaten.

Above right:
Coastline of the Gulf of Mexico in the area of the Everglades, Florida.

Home to alligators, flamingos, pelicans, and pumas, the swamps of the western Everglades were once utilized by the Calusa. In the 19th century, the Seminole used these inaccessible swamps as a place of refuge in their wars against the United States army and as a hideout to escape the impending removal to Oklahoma.

Peoples of the Southeast and the Gulf Coast.

The heartland of the Southeast, from the foothills east of the Appalachians to the Mississippi and the Gulf of Mexico, was inhabited by speakers of Muskogean languages. They included the Seminole, who evolved in the late 18th century from Creek and Hichiti refugees in Florida. Adjoining this Muskogean core to the northeast were Siouan speakers, of whom only the Catawba have survived into the present on a reservation in South Carolina. The Iroquoian Cherokee lived on the southern slopes of the Appalachians. Except for the linguistic family of the Caddo at the western edge of the region, the other languages spoken here, such as Yuchi and Tunica, have no known relatives or, like Cusabo and Calusa, are impossible to identify because of a lack of written records. The Seminole and other "new peoples" such as the Lumbee do not appear on this map. Most of the very few linguistic data on the peoples of the Gulf Coast, recorded prior to their destruction, are inadequate, so that in most cases nothing can be said about their linguistic affiliation. Of eight languages (Karankawa, Aranama, Cotoname, Comecrudo, Coahuilteco, Solano, Naolan, and Maratino) it can at least be assumed that none of them were related to each other. Only two peoples at the edges of the Gulf region can be classified as part of a greater family. The Lipan were an Apache group, while the Pame, the only independently surviving people of this region, are a member of the Otomangue language family of Mexico.

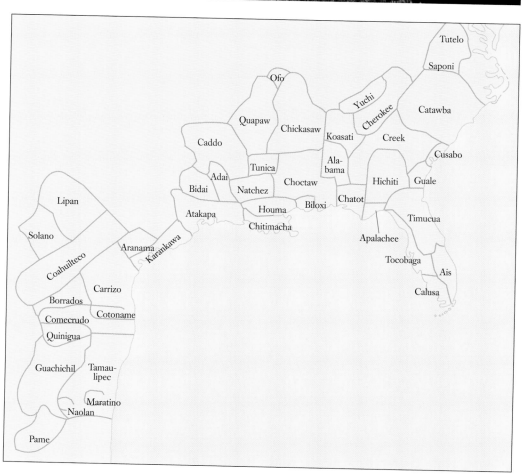

The coastal lowlands border on the piedmont plateau south and east of the Appalachians. The rivers abruptly fall from this hilly region down into the plain along a marked shelf known as the fall line. Long before the Europeans arrived, this area was settled by populous tribes who knew how to make use of the natural resources of the lowlands as well as of the piedmont, and particularly of the ideal conditions for fishing at the waterfalls.

The hill country forms a pedestal of the densely forested southern Appalachians, whose ranges reach their highest peak in Mount Mitchell, at 6684 feet. Only few passes allow transit across the mountain ranges, which run northwest to southeast, are divided by valleys and plateaus, and up to the 19th century formed a barrier hard to surmount for white settlers, who could only skirt it to the south.

With the exception of the coniferous forests of the higher altitudes, the oak and hickory forests of the Northeast also cover the greater part of the Southeast. In the coastal regions they are replaced by pines and scrub oaks, while further south magnolias, cypresses, palmettos, and cane make up the region's typical vegetation. The western coast of Florida is lined with mangroves. By burning the underbush, indigenous peoples already in pre-European times created grassy clearings in the originally wooded areas of the Appalachians and the piedmont, which facilitated the hunt for deer and the occasional forest bison.

Apart from deer, the most important game, these regions were inhabited by wapitis, bears, and many smaller fur animals such as the opossum, beaver, raccoon, and muskrat. Turkeys were present everywhere and provided meat and feathers. Huge shell middens testify today to the importance of this source of food to the original inhabitants of the land.

Migratory waterfowl, for whom the Mississippi Valley is the main flight route, still spend the winter in the coastal marshes, and in the piedmont huge swarms of

passenger pigeons darkened the sky, before they became extinct at the beginning of the 20th century. Alligators were once hunted on the Gulf Coast and in Florida. Today they are a protected species, and men of the Seminole – the only tribe now living in Florida – wrestle with them on alligator farms to provide entertainment for tourists.

The climate of the Southeast, ranging from temperate to subtropical, is marked by mild winters and humid, hot summers. Southwesterly winds bring much rain, especially in the warm season. Temperatures in the higher altitudes of the Appalachians are cooler, but summer rains are frequent there too.

The long growing season and the fertile red soil of this region favored intensive agriculture by the indigenous population. The plantation economy introduced by the whites thoroughly changed the natural environment, and it is doubtful whether the original inhabitants, nearly all of whom were either exterminated or driven away, would still recognize their old homeland if they were to see it today.

The region of the Gulf Coast to both sides of the lower Rio Grande differs markedly from this general characterization of the Southeast. Today the Rio Grande constitutes the border between Texas and the Mexican state of Tamaulipas. The coastal plain around its delta extends up to 120 miles into the interior, with the foothills of the Sierra Madre Oriental as its western border. Many long, narrow islands lie off this part of the Gulf Coast, and protect the branched-out lagoons behind them.

The grasslands of the northern coast turn into the typically Texan savanna in the west and south. In the south, the hot and humid coastal plain reaches down to the area of the Mesoamerican civilizations, while in the north it merges into the Mississippi delta and its numerous branches. Here the plain borders the North American region that is most clearly influenced by the Mexican civilizations.

None of the glamour of its two culturally flourishing neighbors – the chiefdoms of the Southeast on one side, Mesoamerica on the other – seems to have made any impression on this geographical intermediary. In fact, it was condescendingly described as a "cultural sink." Instead of urban life supported by agriculture, this provincial area was only populated by hundreds of small groups of hunters, fishermen, and gatherers.

Spanish moss on trees, Louisiana.

Spanish moss, a species of Tillandsia growing on trees, is found throughout the coastal plain, and like the magnolia is characteristic of the Southeastern landscape. Indigenous peoples used the plant for tinder and as raw material for making cordage or clothing.

Town Creek Mound with reconstructed temple, North Carolina, Mississippian tradition, c. AD 1300–1400.

While some of the towns of the Mississippian cultures were densely populated, and with their places of pilgrimage gave rise to urban life, others were merely ceremonial centers. The Town Creek site was used as such for about 100 years by people living scattered in smaller fortified villages where they worked their fields. In this reconstruction, the grounds feature not only a rectangular temple on a platform mound, but also palisades and defensive towers.

# Temple mounds and towns

Their rulers were revered as gods and were ceremonially carried on a litter, and in their temples, life-size wooden sculptures guarded the bones of their aristocratic ancestors. Although their treasures were only made of copper, mica, and freshwater pearls, even the Spanish conquistadors of the 16th century, disappointed in their search for gold and silver, were impressed by the magnificent chiefdoms that they encountered in the course of their campaigns of conquest.

These highly developed societies, doomed as a result of their contact with the whites and their insidious diseases such as smallpox and measles, were the descendants of a cultural tradition that had emerged in the middle Mississippi Valley in about AD 1000 and which had many local variations spread along the rivers over the whole of the Southeast. Its characteristic features, such as its religious architecture and imagery, reflect influences from the Mesoamerican civilizations that had apparently been conveyed by long-distance traders. The result, however, was clearly not a poor imitation of the faraway civilizations, but an independent local development.

The economic basis of Mississippian cultures was provided by the intensive agriculture in the fertile alluvial lowlands. Here, corn, beans, and squash, all of them cultivated plants of Middle American origin, were grown alongside older local plants such as sunflower, goosefoot, and marsh elder. Fishing and hunting deer, smaller animals, and aquatic birds also made significant contributions to the diet.

People settled in scattered villages and compounds along the river valleys which would give them the best possible access to all these food resources. The focal point of the social and ceremonial life as well as the seat of political authority, however, were the urban centers, which were linked by changing alliances or tributary relationships.

Often surrounded by fortifications and moats, these towns of differing sizes were ceremonial centers with a square for religious rituals, ball games, or council meetings, surrounded by temple mounds, public buildings, and often also conical burial mounds. The temple mounds took the form of truncated pyramids, and were built by

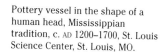

Engraved shell gorget, Mississippian tradition, c. AD 1300–1500. Frank H. McClung Museum, University of Tennessee, Knoxville, TN.

A recurring motif in the pictorial language of the Southeastern Ceremonial Complex, whether found on embossed copper plates or on shell gorgets like this, is the stylized figure of a warrior wearing a falcon costume. In a dancing or fighting pose, he brandishes his ceremonial club, and wears an elaborate headdress and a characteristic foreheadlock. Frequently the warriors depicted also hold a trophy skull and have bird's talons for feet.

Pottery vessel in the shape of a human head, Mississippian tradition, c. AD 1200–1700, St. Louis Science Center, St. Louis, MO.

The occurrence of the motif of the severed human head in the artifacts of the Mississippian tradition points to the prehistoric custom of head-hunting, which was widespread throughout the Southeast. The ritual taking and preserving of heads (like the later practice of scalping) was connected to ideas about fertility. This effigy vessel shows the closed eyes and sewn-up mouth of a trophy head, in addition to face paint and ears pierced in several places for the attachment of ornaments.

piling up basketfuls of earth in the course of several stages of construction. Ramps led up to the top of the pyramids, which were surmounted by the temples and residences of rulers. In its heyday, Cahokia, the largest and most widely known Mississippian metropolis, located east of present-day St. Louis, had a population of more than 10,000. Etowah in Georgia, Moundville in Alabama, and Spiro in Oklahoma were other important centers of urban life.

At the top of these hierarchical societies stood the chiefs, whose positions were inherited, as were those of the religious functionaries and political office holders, who came from families of the highest rank. The bones of the members of this elite were placed next to those of their ancestors in the temples, where their official insignia, weapons, and other symbols of authority were also kept. A far-reaching long-distance trade network supplied the raw materials needed to produce these luxury items or these objects themselves, and centers of local craft specialization developed in the cities.

Moundville, for instance, is well known for its high-quality pottery wares, which were distinguished at the time not only for the innovative shape of their bottles, dishes, and stirrup-shaped vessels, but also for new decorative techniques such as polychromy and negative painting. Etowah artisans produced embossed copper objects of choice quality, whereas engraved shells were the hallmark of Spiro.

Naturalistic human sculptures and monolithic ceremonial axes are among the finest stone carvings. Linking all these various visual forms of expression in the late Mississippian period is the iconography of the Southeastern Ceremonial Complex, a shared system of beliefs, cult objects, and religious symbols, which revolved around concepts of agriculture and fertility, chiefdom and social status differences, and warfare and warriors.

# Civilization and tears

The "discovery" of the New World was soon followed by the first Spanish expeditions to plunder its treasures. However, these explorations on the southeastern coast of North America, rather than finding the expected riches, met with open hostility from the indigenous inhabitants and ended in disaster.

Juan Ponce de León (c. 1460–1521) discovered Florida in 1513 and then in 1520 planned to establish a colony there, but he was wounded in fighting against the local inhabitants and died shortly afterward in Havana. Eight years later, Pánfilo de Narváez (c. 1470–1528) was to continue the colonial project with 400 men, but after the loss of his ships he and his men were finally forced to make for Spanish outposts in Mexico by sailing along the coast in self-made boats. In the fall of that year, the boats, which proved impossible to maneuver, were wrecked off one of the islands near the coast of Texas.

These events brought the Gulf Coast in spite of its isolated location to European attention early on. Although the resident Karankawa considerably cared for the shipwrecked men from Narváez' expedition, only four survived in the end – and about half the host population lost their lives to an imported intestinal infection.

One of the surviving Europeans, Alvar Núñez Cabeza de Vaca (c. 1490–c. 1557) wrote a lengthy account of the six years that he spent on the Gulf Coast and in the adjacent interior before he and his three fellow sufferers embarked on a grueling two-year journey to central Mexico. Despite all that it omits, Cabeza de Vaca's report still has more to tell us than any record made by the French and the Spanish in the borderlands between New Spain and Louisiana in the course of the next 300 years.

The fantastic reports of the expedition into the interior of southeastern North America between 1539 and 1543, led by Hernando de Soto (1486–1542), who also did not live to see his expedition return home, likewise did little to encourage colonization of the region. Only the founding of a French Huguenot colony in Florida in 1564 renewed the interest of

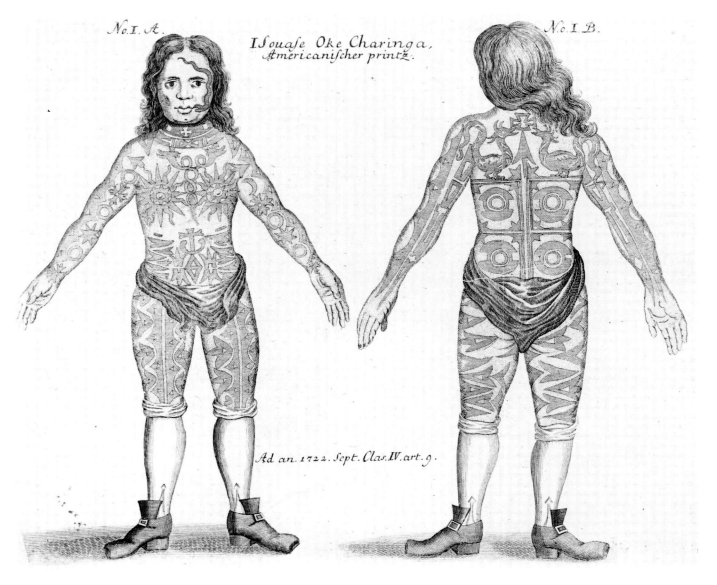

*Souase Oke Charinga, an American Prince*, copperplate engraving from J. Kanold and J. Kundmann, *Sammlung natur- und medecin- wie auch hierzu gehörigen Kunst- und Literatur-Geschichten*, Leipzig-Bautzen 1722. Österreichische Nationalbibliothek, Vienna, Austria.

In 1722, the citizens of various German towns had the opportunity of paying a small fee to gape at "two famous savage Indian Princes," who were "greatly admired everywhere for the decorations found all over their bodies." The viewers were told that the tattoos marked their kinship affiliations and the "triumphant victories achieved in war by their ancestors." The two Creeks had been brought to Europe by Captain John Pight, who had taken part in the Yamassee War and knew how to exploit the exotic attraction these two young men presented in Europe.

the Spanish, who a year later expelled the French and from their base in St. Augustine began to colonize and set up missions in Florida.

British advances in the late 17th and early 18th centuries led to the establishment of colonies in North and South Carolina and in Georgia. In 1682 the French also returned, entering the Southeast from Canada via the Mississippi, claiming Louisiana for the French crown, and establishing a colonial administration in 1711.

Over the next 50 years, the Spanish, British, and French fought for supremacy over the indigenous peoples of the Southeast, and for control of the booming trade with the native populations. When France lost its American territories in 1763, the Spanish took over as rulers of the area west of the Mississippi, while the British gained eastern Florida from Spain and western Florida from France. After the American Revolution, Florida was ceded to Spain, until the region finally became part of the United States in 1819.

Culture contact and European colonization had a devastating effect on the indigenous peoples living on the coast. Epidemics decimated local populations at an alarming rate. The kind of diseases involved cannot always be certainly identified, as the old sources often only speak of a mysterious "fever" that carried off great numbers of people. In addition, Spanish and British slave hunters kidnapped many Native Americans for the Caribbean slave markets.

By the 19th century, many of the original inhabitants had disappeared from the Gulf Coast and the adjacent interior in present-day Texas. By 1858, the last Karankawas were wiped out by the French privateer Jean Lafitte, who had settled on one of the islands in 1817, by Texan settlers, and by Mexican border troops.

## Resistance and assimilation

Military resistance against white claims of supremacy and the involvement in colonial power struggles took a heavy toll on the peoples of the Southeast. The war against the Tuscarora in North Carolina of 1711–1713 and the subsequent Yamassee War in South Carolina opened the gates of the interior for British settlement. While the Tuscarora fled north to seek the protection of their Iroquoian relatives, the Yamassee were completely wiped out and many of them ended their days in slavery. The 1729 Natchez rebellion in Louisiana was also put down, by the French with the help of their Choctaw allies, and the surviving Natchez dispersed.

Nevertheless, competition between the colonial powers initially strengthened the position of tribal confederations such as the Creek or the Choctaw in the interior of the region. These peoples benefited from the new materials and technologies that were introduced by the Europeans, and also from the economic prosperity brought by the deerskin trade. At the same time, their physical distance from the European settlements reduced the immediate impact of colonialism. The culture of the conquerors was even more

acceptable where a mixed-blood elite of the descendants of marriages between Scottish traders in particular and local women exerted its influence. Thanks to these circumstances, the Cherokee, Choctaw, Chickasaw, Creek, and Seminole were known as the Five Civilized Tribes.

The introduction of African slaves by the European colonists had its repercussions for the indigenous peoples. In the wake of race laws, which only distinguished between "white" and "colored," some of the already decimated groups were threatened with the loss of their special legal position as "Indians," which at least gave them internal domestic autonomy as dependent nations. On the other hand, keeping black slaves soon became a common practice among the Five Civilized Tribes, where slavery had pre-European roots. Close contacts with Afro-Americans as well as whites soon led to the emergence of a mixed population, which often preferred to be identified as "Indian." The Lumbee developed in this way, and today are one of the largest population groups with a Native American identity in the United States.

A. de Batz, *Bride-les-Bœufs, Chief of the Tunica*, watercolor, c. 1732. Peabody Museum, Harvard University Cambridge, MA.

The Tunica chief displaying the trophy scalps of three Natchez warriors suspended from a pole is shown here with the widow and son of his predecessor, who had been killed by the Natchez. The depiction illustrates the hostility between the two peoples, which also emerged during the great Natchez uprising against the French, when the Tunica sided with the whites. The Tunica's descendants now live in the Red River area of Louisiana.

Valjean Hessing (Choctaw),
*Choctaw Removal*, watercolor, 1966.
Philbrook Museum of Art, Tulsa, OK.

The Choctaw were the first of the Five
Civilized Tribes to be removed to
Oklahoma, on the basis of a treaty
signed by a small group of leaders
against the will of the majority of their
people. In October 1831, 4,000 people
set off on foot, on horseback, or in
wagons along the bitter way to the
West, and further mass removals
followed in the ensuing years.
Hundreds died on the way of disease,
starvation, cold, and exhaustion.

## The Trail of Tears

In the early 19th century, a series of treaties between the United States and the Five Civilized Tribes caused the indigenous land base to crumble away. In the face of the white settlers' insatiable appetite for land and the growing economic importance of cotton, there was increasing political pressure to resettle the local populations in an "Indian Territory" west of the Mississippi, a move that was allegedly also to protect them from the evils of "civilization."

While some tribal leaders viewed a removal to the West as the inevitable means of securing the cultural survival of their people, others signed these treaties purely out of personal greed. Even without the stipulations of the treaties, 5,000 Cherokees had voluntarily emigrated to Arkansas and Texas before 1820. The removal of the majority of the population of the Five Civilized Tribes to Oklahoma, however, was enforced by the army after the *Indian Removal Act* had been passed in 1830. In 1831, the army began to drive the Choctaw from their villages, and to transport them on steamboats and overland to the Indian Territory. The Chickasaw and the Creek followed in 1836, after their flaring resistance had been brutally suppressed. The deportees were allowed to take only about 30 lbs of personal belongings with them, and even that seemed "excessive" to some congressmen. In the winter of 1838/39, some 7,000 soldiers drove the remaining Cherokees westward. Starvation, exhaustion, and shipping catastrophes cost innumerable lives. Today, this exodus is generally referred to as the "Trail of Tears."

Some Cherokees hid in the mountains of North Carolina, as did some Choctaws in Mississippi. Larger groups of Creeks fled to their Seminole relatives in the Florida swamps, who put up fierce resistance to American expansion in three wars (1817–18, 1835–42, and 1849–58), until their deportation to the Indian Territory in 1856.

## Survival and new identity

Most of the smaller groups remaining in the Southeast (including in addition to the remnants of the Five Civilized Tribes also such less well known peoples as the Catawba in South Carolina, the Houma in Louisiana, and the Alabama in Louisiana and Texas) avoided the forced removal, and instead continued to live on state reservations, purchased land, or as illegal squatters near their former homes.

In the west, the Five Civilized Tribes had to rebuild their communities under great difficulties, and were then forced, after all their efforts, to dissolve their own governments when the state of Oklahoma was established in 1906. They were given permission to reorganize only in 1938, under the *Oklahoma Indian Welfare Act,* which had been passed to alleviate the adverse effects brought about by the enforced dissolution of their polities.

Until the 1960s, the descendants of the Choctaw remaining in Mississippi found themselves in a very difficult situation. After the Civil War they had managed to survive by living as sharecroppers, but although an agent of the Bureau of Indian Affairs was supposedly put in charge of their welfare in 1918, little was done to alleviate their poverty. The lack of educational facilities available to them also meant that even in the 20th century a surprisingly large proportion of Choctaw could not speak English. Since the 1960s, however, the Mississippi Choctaw, headed by an efficient tribal government, have performed a veritable economic miracle. Programs providing employment training, and the establishment of a business park – a multimillion-dollar enterprise under tribal control – have brought work and wealth. They are proud of their tradition and have in many ways been able to exploit the best of both worlds to their advantage.

The Cherokee are also divided into the group that emigrated to Oklahoma, and the descendants of those tribal members who remained in the Southeast. The two groups reassembled for a symbolic joint council meeting in 1984, 146 years after the Trail of Tears. In addition, tens of thousands of people who identify themselves as Cherokee live scattered across the United States, and many more – including many Afro-Americans – claim Cherokee ancestry.

For a long time, the chiefs of the Oklahoma Cherokee were appointed by the government and were businessmen assimilated into mainstream society, who had hardly any links with the 50-odd impoverished communities in which the old language and many aspects of traditional culture have survived. Today the Oklahoma Cherokee elect their chiefs themselves, among whom Wilma Mankiller (b. 1945), the first woman in such a position, was particularly popular. A qualified lawyer, she had early become involved in the Indian civil rights movement and had actively supported the spectacular occupations of Alcatraz (1969–1971) and Wounded Knee (1973).

After 500 years of culture contact, the situation of the indigenous inhabitants of the Southeast has changed in many respects. Some peoples, such as the Timucua, Calusa, or Cusabo, have completely disappeared from the map. Others have lost their earlier identity, merged with neighboring groups, and then reappeared out of obscurity under a new name. Most of those who survived into the 19th century were removed to Oklahoma. All of them were forced into a minority status and into economic dependence on the white world that surrounds them. In spite of their widely differing fates and survival strategies, they share the miracle of having survived against all expectations and against all odds into a present marked by their rediscovered pride in their separate identity.

Left:
*Lipan warrior*, after a lost photograph of 1842 from *Magasin pittoresque*, Paris 1870. Österreichische Nationalbibliothek, Vienna, Austria.

Together with the Spanish advancing from the south, the equestrian Lipan, the most southeasterly Apache group, drove the Coahuilteco and their neighbors from the northern Gulf region since the late 17th century. This portrait is a rare illustration of the costume worn by a Lipan killed in battle in Mexico in 1842. Together with the manikin, made in 1857, it was destroyed when the royal armories in Madrid burned down in 1884. The descendants of the Lipan now live on the Mescalero reservation in New Mexico.

Right:
John White after Jacques Le Moyne de Morgues, *Of Florida* (Timucua woman), watercolor, c. 1586–1588. Department of Prints and Drawings, British Museum, London, England.

Jacques Le Moyne (c. 1533–1588) made many drawings of Timucuas while living in the French Huguenot colony established in northern Florida in 1564. Later, these pictures were widely distributed as engravings and contributed to the contemporary European image of the indigenous North Americans. Under Spanish rule, the agricultural Timucua, who were organized into several chiefdoms, converted to Christianity, but until the beginning of the 18th century became the victims of deliberate raids by the British and their Creek allies. Some of the Timucuas were enslaved; most of the rest were killed, leaving only a few survivors.

# Town fields and deer hunting

As elsewhere throughout indigenous North America, subsistance activities among the peoples of the Southeast were subject to a division of labor by gender. Hunting and fishing were the responsibility of the men, agriculture and food gathering that of the women. Men did, however, help out in the fields during the planting and harvesting seasons, and they were also responsible for clearing the fields before cultivation could begin.

All economic activities were governed by a seasonal cycle, which also determined the social and ceremonial events of the year. During the warmer months, from March onward, the fields were tilled, the foods that grew naturally within the proximity of the settlements were gathered, and small animals were hunted. When the harvest had filled the granaries in the fall, religious ceremonies and games were held, before the return of migratory birds from the north heralded the onset of winter. At this time the majority of villagers set out on winter hunts to more distant regions. In the spring, sturgeon, herring, and other kinds of fish were caught in great numbers during the spawning runs and supplemented the now diminishing food supplies.

The fields of a "town" (a term often used for the dispersed settlements) were situated on the fertile alluvial lands along the rivers. Such grounds were well drained and easy to cultivate with wooden hoes and digging sticks. The crops that were planted included several varieties of corn, beans, squash, and sunflowers. Although the fields were divided into allotments for each family, all crops were communally cultivated, including those on the fields of the chief, provided that he was not supported by the payment of tributes. Women also often maintained additional small gardens near their compounds, which were located above the flood plain. Fertilizers were not used, but the weeds plucked from the ground were sometimes burned on the fields. Corn was planted by making rows of

holes with digging sticks and inserting kernels of corn into them. Apart from weeding, the most important task was hilling up the earth around the growing corn stalks. Field watchers – mostly old women or children – would sit on roofed platforms and chase away voracious birds and other harvest thieves such as deer, rodents, and pigs.

In some parts of the Southeast, extended frost-free periods made possible two harvests within a single season. The Timucua in Florida planted their corn in March as well as June. Some groups, like the Choctaw, regularly sold or exchanged their corn surpluses. Farming was not, however, an equally important source of subsistance in all regions alike. The Calusa, who lived largely on fish and shellfish were able to develop and maintain a stratified society governed by a chiefly elite without the benefit of agriculture.

The cultivation of figs, peaches, and watermelons was adopted from the whites during the early colonial period. Attempts by the American government, however, to introduce plows were generally unsuccessful. They were predominantly employed by the mixed-blood elite who also used African slaves for the cultivation of cotton.

Wild vegetables, roots, berries, fruits, and seeds were abundantly available during various times of the year. An especially important source of starch were wild sweet potatoes and the tubers of various kinds of greenbrier, which the Creek called red *kunti* and which were best gathered during the cold months. The white *kunti* of the Seminole contained a toxic substance, so that it first needed to be dried or parched to become edible. Other important foods were nuts, which were gathered in the fall in large quantities and from which oil was extracted, as well as clams and other shellfish. During times of shortage, acorns were sometimes eaten, which first had to be soaked to rid them of the bitter taste of tannic acid. Salt was extracted from salt-pans and salt springs or obtained through long-distance trade. Otherwise, the ash of certain plants was used as a salt substitute.

The diversity of fish that were caught throughout the year in both coastal waters and inland rivers was matched by the diversity of fishing methods. The fishermen would stand in the water or in canoes and target their catch with bows and arrows, fish spears, or dip nets, skills that required a keen eye and a sure hand. Fish dams built of stones and fish fences constricted the freedom of movement of the fish, making it easier to catch plenty of them. The Choctaw used bloody bison hides to lure fish. Fishnets to which clamshell sinkers were attached and fishhooks made of bone were also commonly used. Larger species of fish, such as sturgeon, were sometimes caught with lasso-like nooses.

Throughout the Southeast, deer were the main source of animal protein. Only the Caddo, and other inhabitants of the westernmost parts of the region bordering the Great Plains, relied just as much, or even more, on bison as a food source. Bears were hunted not only for the meat they provided, but chiefly for their fur and their fat. They were sought out during their hibernation, after they had retreated to hollow tree trunks or caves, whence they were driven out by fire. When they stood on their hind legs as a threatening gesture, they were killed with spears (later also with rifles).

The peoples of the Gulf Coast and of southern Florida also hunted alligators and sea cows, and occasionally even whales. In addition to big game, a number of small animals contributed significantly to the meat supply. Turkeys, opossums, raccoons, and other small mammals were hunted in much the same way as were deer, that is with the help of dogs, fire, snares, and traps.

Passenger pigeons, an important source of fat in the Carolinas, were hunted both at night and during the day. At night, they were first blinded by torches, and afterwards knocked down with long poles from the trees in which they roosted. In daytime hunts, the low-flying flocks were targeted with blunt arrows and wooden throwing sticks. According to contemporary witnesses, the flocks of pigeons were so dense that "they obstructed the light of the day."

## The raw eaters of the Gulf Coast

In order to exploit the available natural food resources, the peoples of the Gulf region, in particular those living inland, needed to be extremely flexible, since fish and mollusks were the only resources constantly available on the coast and along the Rio Grande. Equipped with bows and arrows, they hunted deer, peccaries, bears, hares, turkeys, and even rats and more rarely bison (which originally came all the way to the coast). In the 18th century, the region's inhabitants began to hunt wild horses and the cattle kept by the Spanish.

Among the wild plants were found not only a variety of edible roots and tubers, but more importantly cactus fruits, mesquite beans, and the fleshy-leafed maguey agave. The Spanish called the peoples of the Gulf region Comecrudo, meaning "Raw Eaters," which, however, is more indicative of the European prejudices than of the traditional methods of food preparation employed by the local populations. The notion that the Karankawa were cruel cannibals can also be relegated to the realm of legend.

The simple dugout canoes that were used in the lagoons were just as important to the coastal dwellers as the narrow trails that facilitated penetration of the inland regions. The women fashioned small, dome-shaped dwellings, that were sometimes scarcely more than a windbreak, but were easy to erect and to dismantle. The fact that coastal people used pottery vessels lined with asphalt is indicative of the more sedentary lifestyle of the fishermen.

## From hunting to animal husbandry

Dogs were the only domestic animals kept in the Southeast and were used in hunting and as pack animals. Dog meat was generally consumed only on ceremonial occasions. While most of the turkey population in this region lived in the wild, they were attracted to the outskirts of villages by the surrounding cornfields. Thus, they can be seen as being semi-domesticated. Similarly, people attempted to lure red deer to the vicinity of the village by regularly making clearings

and thus providing them with an attractive habitat. The peoples of the Southeast remained reluctant, however, concerning the adoption of European domestic animals.

Horses were sometimes used as pack animals, and their meat was considered to be a delicacy. Pigs, which had first been introduced to the region as a mobile source of meat for Spanish expeditions, were often left to roam freely and were hunted whenever the need arose. The only precaution required was to keep them away from the fields as the corn ripened. It was not until the late 18th or 19th century that cattle farming was introduced to some of the Five Civilized Tribes to compensate for the dwindling returns of the hunt.

By conserving and storing food, it was possible to balance the uneven supply throughout the seasons. Corn was dried on racks or in hot ash, but was also pounded to meal, and kept either in granaries or, less frequently, in underground storage pits. Squash was cut into long strips and dried, as were berries and fruits. Fish, deer, and bison meat was also dried, or smoked, or sometimes salted, while bear fat was kept in clay pots, gourd vessels, or bags made from animal skins.

Jacques Le Moyne, *Methods of Hunting Deer*, copperplate engraving from T. de Bry, *America*, Frankfurt 1591. British Library, London, England.

While fire was used to encircle game in most of the communal drives in the fall or early winter, the challenge of individual hunting was to get as close to the animal as possible so as to have a greater chance of killing it with bow and arrow. So adept were some hunters in the most common and effective method of disguise – using deer masks or entire deerskins – that they were themselves at risk of actually being taken for prey by other hunters and thus injured or even killed.

# White and red

Travelers visiting the territory of the Five Civilized Tribes in the 18th century, found that the "towns" of these peoples had nothing in common with European towns. Their dwellings, mostly compounds consisting of several buildings, were often widely scattered and sometimes grouped into small hamlets situated among the fields. Each compound included a cooking house that also served as a winter residence, a summer house, a two-story granary with an open loft, and in some cases a storehouse for animal hides. The winter houses were often circular and were normally built on a low platform; the walls were made of vertical poles, the insides and outsides of which were partially plastered with limey clay. Around 1775, the natural scientist William Bartram (1739–1823) described a Yuchi town on the Chattahoochie River as follows: "The habitations are large and neatly built; the walls of the houses are constructed of a wooden frame, then lathed and plaistered inside and out with a reddish well-tempered clay or mortar, which gives them the appearance of red brick walls, and these houses are neatly covered or roofed with Cypress bark or shingles of that tree." The airy summer houses, with roofs and walls of grass, palm-leaf mats or bark were rectangular and sometimes open on the gable side. The upper floor of the granaries also served as a living and meeting room.

A. de Batz, *Temple of the Savages ... Hut of the Chief*, pen and ink, 1732. Peabody Museum, Harvard University, Cambridge, MA.

In the hierarchically structured societies, architecture was one way of expressing status differences. Temples and the dwellings of leaders were positioned on higher ground at the center of the settlement. They differed in size and often in construction from the houses of the rest of the population. The mat-covered temple of the Acolapissa in Louisiana was crowned with three carved birds on perches, encased in a woven structure spiked with reeds. Reed mats also covered the roof of the residence of the Acolapissa chief, the walls of whose house were meticulously plastered with clay both inside and out.

In the midst of such a rural idyll, every "town" also had a public square enclosed on all four sides by covered platforms on which in the summer the townspeople would take their seats (according to clan membership) for festive occasions. There was also a meeting house in which councils were held and visitors received and entertained.

During times of peace, a white flag would fly over the Cherokee meeting houses, near which lived a priest-chief, three other priests, and a secular representative. These officeholders and the representatives of the seven Cherokee clans formed the leadership committee for the council meetings attended by the entire population of the town. The highly respected senior men of the community played a very important part in these deliberations. They were also known as "beloved men," and indeed without being loved they would not have had much influence on the affairs of the town. They personified the ideals of harmony, purity, and a balance of interests. In order to reach unanimous decisions during council meetings, they needed to be good speakers as well, since neither their position nor that of the clan representatives or the priest-chiefs allowed them to force their will upon others.

Everything was different in times of war. A red flag would fly over the meeting house, and everyone knew that the wartime order was in force. Leadership of the war administration was in the hands of four officeholders drawn from among the beloved men, older men who possessed the secret knowledge of the war ritual. These four men served as war chief, war priest, war speaker, and doctor, and were in turn assisted by a war council consisting of clan representatives. Wartime dictated a strict hierarchical order, a state of martial law, as it were, and order could be enforced when necessary.

Among the Creek, red and white also stood for war and peace. However, whereas among the Cherokee the whole village was organized according to either "white" or "red" principles as the occasion required, all Creek clans, villages, and even entire subtribes belonged to either the white or the red side. During peacetime, those who belonged to the white group played the leading role. Conversely, the red group took charge during times of war. The white and red towns made up opposing teams during ceremonial ballgames and also avoided intermarriage.

Until the late 18th to early 19th century, none of the Five Civilized Tribes had a central government. Such an institution did, however, become necessary in order to safeguard their rights against the pressures of white society. The two chambers of their legislative body were modeled on the American system. The Creek had a "House of Kings" (senate) and a "House of Warriors" (house of

Seminole chickee, Florida, c. 1921. National Anthropological Archives, Smithsonian Institution, Washington DC.

In the warm climate of Florida, the Seminole did not need winter dwellings. They lived (as some still continue to do today) in *chickees* the whole year round. These are light timber dwellings built on a raised platform and with a palmetto-thatched roof, which are open on one or more sides and provide shelter not only against sun and rain, but also against soil moisture. The space between the ceiling and the roof was used as a storeroom for household items and other possessions.

Cherokee blockhouse, North Carolina, 1888–1893. National Anthropological Archives, Smithsonian Institution, Washington DC.

In the 19th century, indigenous forms of housing, the walls of which were made of wattle and daub, were gradually replaced by European building forms. In many parts of the Southeast, the indigenous inhabitants built shingle-roofed blockhouses of the kind also used by the white rural population. These houses consisted of one or two rooms and normally also had windows and a chimney.

representatives), in continuation of the opposition between "white" and "red" organizational forms.

Some peoples of the Southeast, such as the Natchez, Calusa, and Timucua, had developed a different form of political order: centralized chiefdoms, in which dynastic families ruled with coercive power. Their political and judicial authority as well as their economic and religious privileges were derived from their special relationship with supernatural beings. They exacted tribute payments from their subjects, who were also required to pay their respects in accordance with court etiquette. The aristocrats were often distinguished from commoners by their clothes, ornaments, and insignia.

## Matrilineages and clans

With the exception of the Yuchi and Quapaw, the peoples of the Southeast reckoned their descent through the maternal line. All individuals who could be traced back to a genealogically known female ancestor formed a matrilineage that owned common property and special rights. Several such lineages that were considered to be of common mythical origin would, in turn, make up a clan, which might be named after an animal, a plant, or a natural phenomenon. The number of clans ranged from seven among the Cherokee to three dozen among the Creek.

The women within a lineage, their husbands from other clans, and their unmarried sons lived together in one place. The families that made up a clan, on the other hand, were scattered among several villages. When people undertook a journey, they could therefore expect hospitality from their clan relatives in other villages, but not all clans were represented in all villages. Clan members were not only obliged to extend mutual aid and assistance, they also had to avenge the killing of another clan member. In such a case, they would first attempt to call the offender himself to account. If he eluded them, the murderer's entire clan would be made liable for the crime.

Clan affiliation also affected the choice of a spouse, since marriages within the clan were prohibited. Even marriages between relatives belonging to different clans were usually avoided, because such marriages did not create new social bonds. Although it would have been quite possible to marry into the father's matriclan, the Creek ridiculed such

François Bernard, *Choctaw Village near Chefuncte*, oil on canvas, 1869. Peabody Museum, Harvard University, Cambridge, MA.

As this view of a Choctaw village of the mid-19th century shows, the rectangular, open summer houses were still being used at the time, even though European-style block-houses were already being built (possibly to replace the old winter houses). While several villagers lounge on the seating and sleeping benches, the women in the foreground appear to be busy making vegetable dyes for the reeds used in basketry.

Karl Bodmer, *Choctaw Camp on the Mississippi*, watercolor, 1833. Joslyn Art Museum, Omaha, NE.

Windbreaks that were quickly built from locally available materials served as temporary shelters during hunting trips or while traveling. They also protected the fireplace from wind and rain. On a visit to a Choctaw camp near Mobile in Alabama in the mid-19th century, Swedish traveler Frederika Bremer (1801–1865) observed that at some distance from the domestic domain of the women the men had built "between some trees a screen of foliage and twigs," behind which "they dress, paint, and decorate themselves."

marriages. "He has fallen into his own *sofki* pot," they would say, meaning that a person had acquired what indeed he already possessed.

Creek, Choctaw, and Chickasaw clans were, in turn, grouped into tribal moieties, within which marriage was also prohibited. Such moieties had predominantly ceremonial responsibilities, such as the burial of the opposite moiety's dead among the Choctaw. There are indications that, in the Southeast, this dual organization can be traced back to an opposition between dominant local and subjected foreign groups. In this respect, the tribal moiety system is related to the existence of a two-caste system among the Chitimacha (nobility and commoners), in which, however, marriages were expressly forbidden outside one's own group. Even in the absence of distinct class differences, the hierarchical order of individuals and kinship groups was often of considerable importance.

Unless they were adopted, prisoners of war who were not members of a local kinship group possessed no rights whatsoever and were treated as slaves. The Choctaw even demanded of such prisoners that they behave like dogs, guarding their masters' houses, barking at strangers, and chewing bones.

There was a rather marked separation of male and female spheres of life. On the one hand, there was a clear division of labor according to gender, on the other hand, men moved to the household of their wives, but remained virtual outsiders. Not only among the Creek was it the women who dominated the household, while the men were in charge of the public arena. Often, men and women even took their meals separately. In one variant of the ceremonial ballgame, the men competed against the women; however, while men used the racket also used in other variants of the game, women threw the ball with their hands. Among the Koasati, and other Muskogean peoples, each gender even had its own language. The men would either add an s to the female versions of the words or replace the last consonant with an s. Whereas female Koasati for "he said" is *kaa* and "we will peel it" is *molhíl*, the male forms of these words are *kaas* and *molhís*.

Although cornfields, houses, and other family possessions belonged to the women, men held the majority of political offices. The most prominent exception is found in the aforementioned chiefdoms of the Natchez, Calusa, and others, where aristocratic women were able to take on positions of leadership.

Some of the peoples of the region, such as the Timucua and the Natchez, are said to have had male transvestites (berdache) – men who wore women's clothing and performed women's tasks. They also had certain other obligations, such as burying the dead, treating the seriously ill, and carrying loads on the war path. To these transvestites were obviously attributed healing and magical powers, but they were also avoided and made to perform the most arduous and unpopular tasks.

Alfred Boisseau, *Louisiana Indians Walking Along a Bayou*, oil on canvas, 1847.
New Orleans Museum of Art, New Orleans, LA.

Only wealthy men could afford more than one wife. In societies where men lived with the families of their wives, they generally chose sisters or cousins as additional wives. The wives of a Choctaw man each lived in different houses, often several miles apart. Polygamy was far more common among the Yuchi, where the women moved to their husband's village. Permission for a second marriage had to be obtained from the first wife, who otherwise could leave her husband or punish him as an adulterer.

# A life of avoidances

Life among many of the peoples of the Southeast began by proverbially taking the plunge. When a Cherokee or Creek child was born, it was immediately submerged in cold water, an act which marked the beginning of a lifelong striving for physical and spiritual purity. During pregnancy, women were not allowed to eat fish and deer meat, and they also had to heed other rules that all served to safeguard the healthy development of their children. Childbirth generally took place in the same remote house to which women also retreated during their menstruation. During infancy and early childhood, all children were cared for by their mothers. Later, the girls would be entrusted to the care of the women of their clan, while boys were instructed by their male relatives as to their future duties as hunters, warriors, and politicians.

Her first menstruation signified a girl's first step into adulthood – although there were no celebrations to mark the event. Since menstruating women posed a danger to the ritual purity of others, they took care to remain strictly isolated.

Surprisingly similar restrictions were imposed on men who took part in war parties, which were indicative of a man's adult status, but also carried the danger of being contaminated by strangers, death, and enemy blood. On their return from war, Chickasaw warriors retreated from the community for a period of four days, gathering around a purifying fire and drinking laxative beverages. Choctaw men who had taken scalps were not allowed to comb their hair for a whole month, and instead used head-scratchers – just as was the case with menstruating women or young Creek men during initiation.

Before going on the war path, Creek men would retreat to the town's meeting house, fasting and purifying themselves under the supervision of the war chief through the consumption of an emetic made from rattlesnake root. In order to achieve a state of purity, warriors were not permitted, among other things, to have sexual intercourse or to consume alcohol bought from the whites.

War enabled men to gain status, which was expressed in the form of war names awarded to warriors during special ceremonies. The names that the Creek assigned to their

Karl Bodmer, *Choctaws at New Orleans* (detail), watercolor, 1833. Joslyn Art Museum, Omaha, NE.

Children were generally given a great deal of love and attention, and were breast-fed by their mothers for several years, or at least until such time that a second child was conceived. Although naughty behavior was not tolerated, it was generally punished only lightly, such as by scratching the surface of the child's skin with a needle. What was considered to be a far more effective disciplinary measure was to humiliate children by making fun of them or publicly compromising them. The Choctaw, Chickasaw, and Natchez tied small wooden boards or little pillows filled with sand to their infants' foreheads in order to flatten them in accordance with the reigning ideals of beauty.

*New-Orleans T. 1833.*

warriors were part of a system of ranked titles owned by individual clans, and which could be acquired on the basis of bravery and merit. Women appear to have kept the same name throughout their lives.

Even though both the men and women of most Southeast societies enjoyed sexual freedom prior to marriage, the act of adultery was considered a grave crime, for the punishment of which a man could have his ears cut off. When a couple married, it was generally the man's lineage that contributed to the gifts to the lineage of the bride, which among some peoples had to be repeated in symbolic form every year. In societies in which men married into their wives' households, marriages often did not last very long, and divorce was not an uncommon occurrence. In such an event, Creek men were obliged to leave the conjugal household, and women, for their part, were obliged to refrain from remarrying for a period of four years (a rule that applied likewise to widows). Among some peoples of the Southeast husbands were required to avoid their mothers-in-law. Creek men and their mothers-in-law were not permitted to speak to one another; the Choctaw even forbade eye contact between the two. Wives, on the other hand, never uttered their husband's name, referring to them only in his relationship to their children (for example, "the father of my son").

When someone died, the relatives entered a time of mourning, during which they blackened their faces, cut off their hair, neglected their dress, and renounced all forms of pleasure. They would affirm their loss through loud wailing

and lamenting, for which helpers were sometimes hired. Through a series of rituals, mourners were eventually and gradually released from their obligations. Creek widows were expected to mourn for a period of four years before they could return to normal life. A widow could, however, be prematurely released from mourning if, in the tradition of the levirate, the sister of her deceased husband gave her another brother to marry. This act would renew the alliance with the kinship group which had been severed through the death of her husband. One of the customs related to the ritualized lamentation of the dead was the greeting of tears practiced by the Caddo, Timucua, and other groups. When people had not seen each other for a long time, they would greet one another with tears in remembrance of those who had died in the meantime.

The Choctaw laid their dead, with the deceased's possessions and food sacrifices, on a scaffold until their flesh was sufficiently decomposed for the "bone collector" or "buzzard man" (as the Chitimacha called him) to remove it from the skeleton, which he did to the accompaniment of the mourners' wailing. The clean bones were put in boxes and kept in special bone houses. When the ceremonies for the dead were held in spring and fall, the members of each moiety of the village would alternately dance in honor of the other moiety's dead and bury their bones. Under the influence of Christian missionaries, the Choctaw adopted the practice of inhumation in about 1800.

To touch the dead was often considered to mean risking contamination. Among the Creek, once all hope of curing a diseased person had been lost, a grave was dug and the dying person prepared for burial, so that they could be interred immediately upon their death.

Seminole grave houses near Wevoka, Oklahoma, 1981.

In the chiefdoms of the Southeast it was only the common people who were buried, while the bones of leaders were laid to rest in temples. Among the Cherokee, Creek, and Seminole, by contrast, simple burials appear to have been the general custom. Even today, the Oklahoma Seminole continue to build traditional grave houses consisting of a wooden framework and asphalt shingles and standing over graves that are aligned on an east–west axis.

# Body painting and ruffled shirts

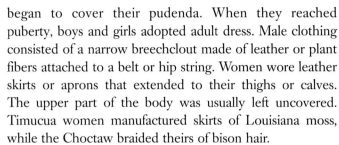

Karl Bodmer, *Tshanny (a Choctaw)*, watercolor, 1832.
Joslyn Art Museum, Omaha, NE.

European fabrics and garments, considered to be exotic, were received everywhere with enthusiasm. A "bit of cloth over their private parts, a shirt of English make" and "a sort of cloth-boots," a British officer commented in the late 18th century, in addition to leather moccasins, were in great fashion among those Cherokees who could afford them. Elaborate turbans, sometimes adorned with metal rings or ostrich feathers, ornaments produced by European silversmiths, and a woolen blanket used as a cape supplemented the typical male attire.

When, in the early 19th century, the delegates of the Five Civilized Tribes negotiated the fate of their peoples with government representatives, their outward appearance hardly differed from that of their white counterparts in the discussions. For the mixed-blood elite, at all events, European dress had long become the usual everyday attire, and even "traditionalists" had incorporated ruffled cotton shirts and European fabrics into their typical costume. Little remained of the sight that the indigenous inhabitants of the Southeast had presented to the first white visitors.

In the warm climate of the region few demands had been placed on clothing. Small children ran around naked until the girls reached the age of about eight and

began to cover their pudenda. When they reached puberty, boys and girls adopted adult dress. Male clothing consisted of a narrow breechclout made of leather or plant fibers attached to a belt or hip string. Women wore leather skirts or aprons that extended to their thighs or calves. The upper part of the body was usually left uncovered. Timucua women manufactured skirts of Louisiana moss, while the Choctaw braided theirs of bison hair.

People went around barefoot most of the time. Soft-soled moccasins and leather leggings were put on only when traveling or in periods of cold weather. Fur and leather robes, some of which were painted, were also used as protection against the cold. European observers marveled not only at the softness of the tanned leather, but also admired the exquisitely fashioned capes of turkey, duck, or swan feathers worn by the native people.

The Southeastern peoples living on the eastern border of the Prairies, such as the Caddo and Quapaw, used not only deer hide, which was the principal source of clothing material, but also bison leather for their winter garments, and on special occasions wrapped themselves in painted bison leather robes. Among some of the peoples that inhabited the Rio Grande delta on the coast of the Gulf of Mexico it was customary for the men to go naked until the end of the 18th century, and they only relinquished this "costume" under the influence of Spanish missionaries. The women are said to have worn grass skirts.

Head coverings tended to be worn only on special ceremonial occasions. This was partly due to the fact that men's hairstyles could be quite elaborate and sometimes served to indicate special social status. Frequently they included partial removal or close cropping of the hair. Timucua men tied their hair into a conical, helmet-like bun. By contrast, women's hairstyles were less extravagant. Their long hair was tied into knots or they let it fall loosely over their shoulders. In some tribes, such as the Seminole, the particular hairstyles worn by the women served to distinguish them as married or unmarried.

The cloth garments introduced by European traders quickly became a part of everyday dress, which thus met European standards. Men started to wear pants with a shirt or jacket, the length of which was often indicative of their social status. Jackets were tied at the waist with a braided sash, to which matching knee bands were chosen. In accordance with European moral codes, women began wearing short blouses and long skirts.

The scanty dress originally worn by the inhabitants of the region was generally offset by elaborate bodily adornment. Both men and women tattooed their faces, limbs, breasts, and backs. Contemporary observers compared the artful

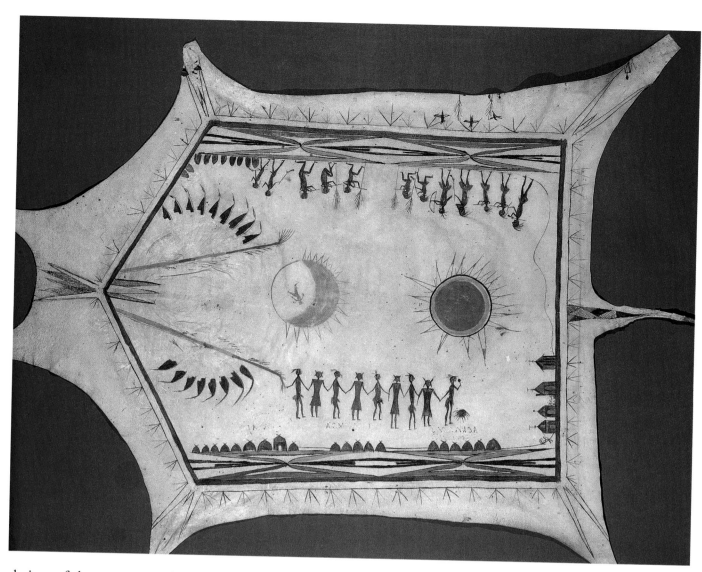

designs of these tattoos with "mezzotintos" (engravings), declaring that the "painters of Europe could not improve upon it."

As indelible markings, tattoos generally indicated an individual's permanent social attributes, such as membership in a class or a kinship group, or achievements in war. Men would also paint their bodies on certain occasions, such as on war parties and during ballgames, or just purely for the sake of adornment. Red, the most prominently used color, was obtained from iron-rich earth and later from imported vermilion; other colors likewise consisted of mineral pigments. According to their ideal of beauty, Natchez women and their neighbors would blacken their teeth every day with an ash mixture. For many peoples of the region, bodily hygiene also included the removal of body hair with clamshell tweezers.

Both men and women wore necklaces and bracelets made of shell, bone, or pearls. Silver gorgets and bracelets purchased from traders gradually replaced the traditional copper ornaments worn by people of high rank.

Men and women pierced their ears to attach strings of pearls, animal claws, bird's talons, and the like. The men of the Creek and their neighbors slit their ears in order wear a profusion of ornaments. Nose plugs and rings were exclusively worn by men and had only limited distribution.

# Green corn and world renewal

The Cherokee believed that, at the beginning of time, a firmament of solid stone arched over the unfathomable depths of the ocean. When the birds and animals that lived together in the confinement beyond this canopy wanted more room, little Water Bug dived to the bottom of the sea and brought to the surface soft mud. Flapping his wings, Buzzard used this mud to fashion the mountains and valleys of the earth. To provide light for the earth island that floated on the ocean and that was suspended from the sky by four strings, the original beings set the sun into motion in its daily orbit. Soon, plants and animals inhabited the land.

The peoples of the Southeast told a variety of stories about the origin of humankind. According to a Choctaw legend, their original ancestors had ascended to the world from the sacred mound Nanih Waiya in northeastern Mississippi. The Yuchi, on the other hand, saw themselves as children of the sun, since they originated from a drop of blood that fell to earth from this celestial deity.

The myths that tell of supernatural beings or of the origin of ceremonies, traditions, and the social order of men, were considered to be sacred, and were told only under very specific circumstances. The Natchez, as many other peoples of North America, narrated their myths exclusively in wintertime and during the hours of darkness. Since the time of their contact with the whites, Christian ideas have left their mark on these sacral stories, while black slaves added African elements to those groups of tales told as a form of entertainment and involving the incredible adventures of Hare, the trickster.

The Seminole and some other groups also had stories explaining the origin of races. Attempts by the Creator to

Cherokee men performing the traditional eagle dance, North Carolina, 1932. National Anthropological Archives, Smithsonian Institution, Washington, DC.

The eagle dance symbolized the reestablishment of peace subsequent to victory over an enemy, and it was originally performed as an act that sealed peace treaties and friendship pacts. Participants carried gourd rattles and dancing wands adorned with eagle feathers, the design and significance of which were similar to that of the calumet even though they lacked a pipehead. Like other rituals associated with death, the deceased, and ghosts of the dead, the eagle dance was held only in winter, for it caused frost and thus endangered the growth of corn.

Choctaw dance group from Conehatta at the Choctaw Fair, Mississippi, 1976.

When the world was created, supernatural beings gave the Choctaw their songs and dances as a gift. Present-day public displays of dances are no more than a remnant of the traditional dance repertoire, whose songs, musical style, and instruments (including the typical concussion sticks) have been passed down over generations in a surprisingly conservative fashion, although their religious character was lost with conversion to Christianity.

bake a human made of clay failed twice. The first human was too pale, the second too dark. Only his third attempt was successful, producing the perfect red man. Of the three boxes that he offered his creatures to choose from, the white man selected the one that contained feathers, ink, and paper; the red man the one that held tomahawks, knives, and bows; thus the black man had no choice but to take the one filled with axes and hoes with which to work the ground.

Once the earth had been created, the universe consisted of three worlds. The upperworld, situated above the sky, represented order and stability and was inhabited by Sun, Moon, Thunder, and other benevolent supernatural powers, most of whom had a human appearance. Conversely, the underworld represented the principle of disorder, inversion, and change, and was home to a range of dangerous monsters. The Seminole believed the Water Puma, with its long fishlike tail, reigned over the beings of the underworld. The Cherokee feared Uktena, a mighty being with a snake's body, deer antlers, and the wings of a bird. The earth, or middle world, was shared by humans and unpredictable, gnomelike "Little People" as well as various other kindly disposed or evil beings.

The four cardinal points of the earth were often thought of as individuals and were associated with colors and with social values. They were part of a system of polar opposites such as above/below, east/west, north/south, fire/water, and man/woman, the balance of which was considered a prerequisite for the order of the universe. Thus, the life of indigenous peoples was decisively based on the principle of keeping separate those things and deeds that belonged to opposite categories. Thus fire, as the sun's representative on earth, was never extinguished by water, as this was a substance associated with the underworld. The only exception to this rule were the burial rituals, during which this very act symbolized death.

# Priesthood and temples

Two groups of specialists acted as mediators between mankind and the supernatural world. Priests were trained for their duties during a strict apprenticeship and were sometimes selected on the basis of their kinship affiliations. Their duties included healing the sick by applying the medical knowledge that they had acquired, practicing preventive medicine in the form of rituals that provided spiritual purification, and conducting rites in the temples or "town houses." The second class of religious specialists was endowed with the innate power to see into the future, to diagnose the cause of disease, to recover lost or stolen objects, and even to influence the weather. Among the Creek, it was the younger of twins who were often credited with such abilities and thus were predestined to become fortunetellers (*kila*, "the knower").

The temple religions were of special importance within the hierarchically structured societies, such as those of the Natchez or Calusa, where they served to legitimize the authority of the ruling family. The worship of carved replicas of deities or natural objects (notably stones) regarded as sacred and kept either in or near the temples was a widespread feature of these religions. Other objects of sacred nature, from personal charms to medicine bundles, however, were also common throughout the Southeast. Objects of European origin, of which the mode of manufacture was inexplicable to the indigenous people, were often included in this group of sacred objects as well. A stone column bearing the coat of arms of the king of France, erected in 1562 by a French explorer in Timucua territory, was receiving worship and food offerings on the part of the Timucua, when the French returned two years later. Similarly, reverence was accorded the copper and brass plates, probably left behind by unsuccessful Spanish conquistadors who crossed Creek territory in the 16th century, which were eventually incorporated into the town bundles kept at the central temple of the Creek of Tukabahchee.

A number of smaller ceremonies and games were generally held in preparation for the most important ritual event of the year that was celebrated in one form or another by all the peoples of the region. The Green Corn ceremony was held in July or August when the first cobs were ready to be eaten. More than a harvest festival, this ceremony was foremost a ritual of regeneration and spiritual purgation, as is expressed by the Creek term *poskita* (literally "to fast"). In preparation for the ritual, the public buildings surrounding the ceremonial site were repaired and villagers cleaned their compounds. Men stayed away from their women and observed certain food taboos. The four-day (sometimes eight-day) ritual began with a day of council, followed by a day of fasting, on which participants consumed nothing but four servings of "Black drink" that caused vomiting and cleansed their bodies and souls. On this day, a village's sacred objects

William Bonar, *A Draught of the Creek Nation* (detail), pen and ink drawing, 1757. Public Record Office, London, Great Britain.

The ceremonial center of every Creek "town" consisted of a heated winter council house ("hot house" or "rotunda"), a rectangular square in which all public social events and religious ceremonies were held, and a ball field ("chunkey yard") with a central goal post, which served as an arena for games and dances. During times of war, this was where prisoners of war were tortured to death.

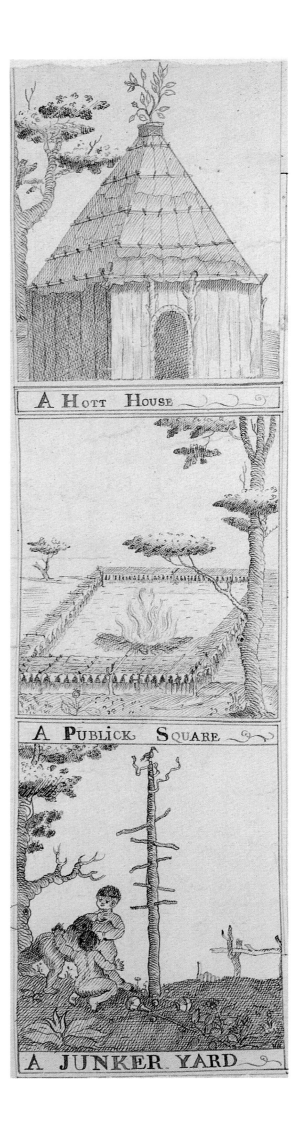

A HOTT HOUSE

A PUBLICK SQUARE

A JUNKER YARD

Jacques Le Moyne, *How Those From Florida Council on Important Matters*, copperplate engraving from T. de Bry, America, Frankfurt 1591. British Library, London, England.

The ultimate objective of all rituals was to maintain spiritual purity or to recover such purity after it had been polluted. Sweat baths and the ingestion of emetics were means of physical and spiritual purgation. At important events such as council meetings or religious ceremonies, men drank a decoction of holly (*Ilex vomitoria*) that had the color of strong black tea, prepared in accordance with special ritual directions, and known to the Europeans as "Black drink."

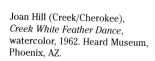

Joan Hill (Creek/Cherokee), *Creek White Feather Dance*, watercolor, 1962. Heard Museum, Phoenix, AZ.

A variety of ceremonial dances are still held as part of the Green Corn ceremony. The Feather Dance, a male dance, is performed in honor of birds, who are called at the beginning of the dance. The leading dancers are members of the Bird clan, and they also make the dancing wands used in the performance. By moving the wands during the dance, the feathers attached to it create the impression of a flock of small birds appearing above the dancers' heads.

would be exhibited, new titles were publicly confirmed, all crimes (with the exception of murder) committed during the past year were forgiven, old pots were broken, all fires were extinguished, and the ashes carefully removed. The third day was a day of celebration. Copious amounts of the new corn were prepared and, after a sacrifice of the first field fruits, eaten in a communal meal. The highest priest then kindled a new fire on the public square, whence the women carried it into each household. On the last day of the Green Corn ceremony, everyone painted themselves with white pigment and took a ritual bath in the river. Daily ballgames and nightly dances, at which the women would set the rhythm of the songs with turtleshell rattles attached to their legs, accompanied the whole ceremony which purified, fortified, and reconciled the people as they entered the new year. Green Corn dances are still commonly held in many parts of Oklahoma.

As the "little brother of war," the ceremonial ballgame was played with a high risk of injury, and was subject to ritual regulations similar to those that applied to war itself. Prior to a game, players refrained from all sexual activity and heeded a variety of food taboos. They often drank an emetic beverage in order to cleanse themselves from within, pricked their upper arms and lower legs, and applied consecrated water to the wounds. The object of the game was to maneuver the ball into a goal or onto a central goalpost by means of two racket-like sticks.

Jacques Le Moyne, *Solemnities at the Reception of the Queen by the King* (Timucua), copperplate engraving from T. de Bry, *America*, Frankfurt 1591. British Library, London, England.

Public events in the chiefdoms of the Calusa, Timucua, and their neighbors had a formal ceremonial character which served to emphasize the political authority and social status of the ruling class. The chiefs wore special headdresses, feather fans, and arm and knee bands made of pearls as insignia of their power. A widespread symbol of sovereignty throughout the region was the wooden stool, on which chiefs and their wives seated themselves in the midst of their subjects.

# Princes of Florida – the Calusa

In the spring of 1895, while cutting peat on his property in Key Marco on the southwestern coast of Florida, a settler uncovered some archeological remains. In spite of technical difficulties and financial straits, the scientific excavation of the grounds which eventually took place about a year later was crowned with success.

Wading side by side in deep pools of mud and exposed to swarms of mosquitoes, the scientists unearthed what the tannin-containing peat had preserved for centuries. Even though a quarter of the objects made of organic materials were destroyed during their recovery and only half the artifacts survived the following days of being exposed to light and air, 11 barrels and 59 crates filled with tools and ornaments made of shell, wooden

vessels, clubs, spears, masks and ceremonial objects, bone needles and weapons, and cordage and nets of plant fibers eventually found their way to American museums – remarkable testimony to a vanished culture, which has left equally remarkable traces in the historical record.

Our knowledge of Calusa culture is based mainly on late 16th-century Spanish accounts. Key Marco was only one of the central settlements of this chiefdom, whose ruler resided in the capital of Calos, situated north of Key Marco, which was also the scene of short-lived colonization and missionization attempts by the Spanish conquerors. In contrast to their northern neighbors, the Timucua and other highly developed societies of the Southeast, the lifestyle of the Calusa was founded not on agriculture, but primarily on intensive exploitation of the ocean as a source of food. Fishing, the gathering of shellfish, and the hunting of sea mammals and turtles formed the economic basis for their sedentary lifestyle, the concentration of large populations, and the development of a hierarchically structured political system.

Calusa society was headed by the ruler in Calos, to whom the chiefs of the subordinate settlements paid tribute in the form of feathers, mats, deerskins, food, captives, and the gold and silver salvaged from Spanish shipwrecks. These leaders were often married to women from the ruling family, while the supreme chief himself chose his wives from among the nobility of the satellite towns under his rule.

The Spanish missionaries were concerned not only about the practice of polygamy, but also about the custom of sibling marriage, a privilege of the chiefs. This practice, considered incest by the whites, served as a means of maintaining the purity of royal blood within Calusa society. When a chief, his (principal) wife, or one of their children died, some of their followers or their sons and daughters were sacrificed. Noble

dignitaries held political offices – the highest office being that of an advisor and representative of the chief – and they enjoyed special privileges, as did priests, healers, and religious functionaries.

The sovereign was also the supreme commander of the Calusa warriors, whose reputation as fine archers was confirmed by the Spanish. War was an important means of maintaining political and economic control and it ensured a supply of captives, who were often used for human sacrifices in religious ceremonies on the temple mounds. In their accounts, Spanish administrators and missionaries drew only a very incomplete picture of such rituals and of the underlying religious concepts, some of which was esoteric knowledge that only the priests and chiefs possessed.

Even though the Calusa were successful in their resistance to the Spanish, they ultimately shared the fate of many societies of the Southeast who were forced to yield to the onslaught of European settlement. In the 19th century, the last surviving Calusas were incorporated by the neighboring Seminole and Miccosukee.

Right:
Wooden sculpture of a feline being, Key Marco, Florida, 15th century. National Museum of Natural History, Smithsonian Institution, Washington, DC.

As in other stratified societies, the production of cult objects and luxury items was probably assigned to specially trained craftspeople. Wood was worked with tools made of clamshells and barracuda or shark teeth. The grooves that resulted on the surface of a carving were then carefully smoothed with sand or fishskin. This kneeling feline figure is one of the most impressive and renowned examples of Calusa visual art.

Fare right:
Painted wooden tablet depicting a woodpecker, Key Marco, Florida, 15th century. Florida Museum of Natural History, Gainesville, FL.

Even though the Calusa stood in the Mississippian tradition, they developed independent forms of artistic expression which only resembled those of the Southeastern Ceremonial Complex to a limited extent. Like the painted wooden masks recovered in Key Marco in 1896, which, according to Spanish descriptions, were kept in the temple and worn only during special ceremonies, the painted tablets probably also played a part in Calusa religious life – one, however, of which we have no knowledge today.

Making the Natchez Language Recordings in 1931, from Charles D. Van Tuyl, *The Natchez*, 1979. Oklahoma Historical Society, Oklahoma City, OK.

Today, several hundred people trace their origin to Natchez ancestors who had come to Oklahoma with the Creek or Cherokee. While their unique culture has long vanished, some of them still regularly gather for dances on their own ceremonial ground. With the support of several surviving speakers, linguistic research could still be carried out in the 20th century. Today, Natchez is considered to be extinct.

# In the shadow of the Great Sun – the Natchez

In the early spring of 1725, two musket shots ended the uneasy silence in the villages of the Natchez, and loud wailing arose everywhere. Tattooed Serpent, the war chief and brother of the ruler Great Sun, was dead, and his wives and closest followers prepared to accompany him on his journey to the afterworld. Great Sun, too, announced his intention to take his own life and follow his brother by having all fires extinguished. It was only with great effort that the French colonial officers managed to swerve his resolve. Dressed in his finery, his face painted red, and equipped for his final journey with headdress, moccasins, and his weapons, Tattooed Serpent lay in state in his house for three days. In a festive procession headed by a priest, six temple guards finally carried his body to the temple, in front of which mats had already been spread out for those individuals who were destined to join him in death. Having sat down on the mats, they were administered a drug prepared from tobacco, and as soon as they lost consciousness, were then strangled by their relatives. One couple had previously

killed their infant and thrown it onto the ground before the passing litter in an act of sacrifice.

After Tattooed Serpent and his wives had been buried in the temple, his house was burned to the ground. The bodies of the others who had been killed were taken back to their native villages to be buried. Several months later, their bones would be exhumed, cleaned, and stored in baskets in the temple.

Although the French, who first reached the lower Mississippi Valley at the end of the 17th century and there made contact with the Natchez, were themselves well acquainted with a strict social hierarchy and the courtly etiquette that it demanded, they found the latter's peculiar rules of marriage and descent no less disturbing and fascinating than the human sacrifices described above. Natchez society was divided into two classes: the aristocracy, among whom one distinguished between the ranks of "Suns" and "Nobles," and the common people ("Stinkards"), for whom it was possible to attain the higher status of the "Honored." The men and women of the aristocracy were obliged to choose their spouses from among the commoners. According to matrilineal rules of descent, the children of an aristocratic mother automatically inherited her status; the children of an aristocratic father, however, were born into the next lower rank.

Social advancement from the status of a commoner to the ranks of an "honored" person was possible either through exceptional achievement in warfare (such as the taking of scalps) or through the ritual sacrifice of a close relative on the occasion of the burial of a "Sun" (as was performed by the couple who sacrificed their newborn child to Tattooed Serpent).

Great Sun sat atop the social pyramid as an absolute ruler, upon whose death the office passed to the son of his eldest sister, White Woman. The Suns of the ruling family traced their lineage back to the Sun deity, whose son had once descended to earth to bring the Natchez their laws, customs, and ceremonies, after which he had retreated into a stone which had since been worshiped as a sacred shrine. An eternal flame burned within the temple in honor of the Sun. It was carefully looked after by temple guardians, who could expect to be severely punished if it ever died out. Every morning and every evening, Great Sun and his wife visited the temple to pay homage to their deity.

Only a few years following Tattooed Serpent's death, the French brutally suppressed the Natchez rebellion against their colonial rule, thus dealing Natchez culture a fatal blow. Great Sun and his family were sold into slavery, and all remaining survivors dispersed. They were later taken in by the Creek and Cherokee, whose fate they would ultimately share, and whom they accompanied 100 years later on their Trail of Tears to the West.

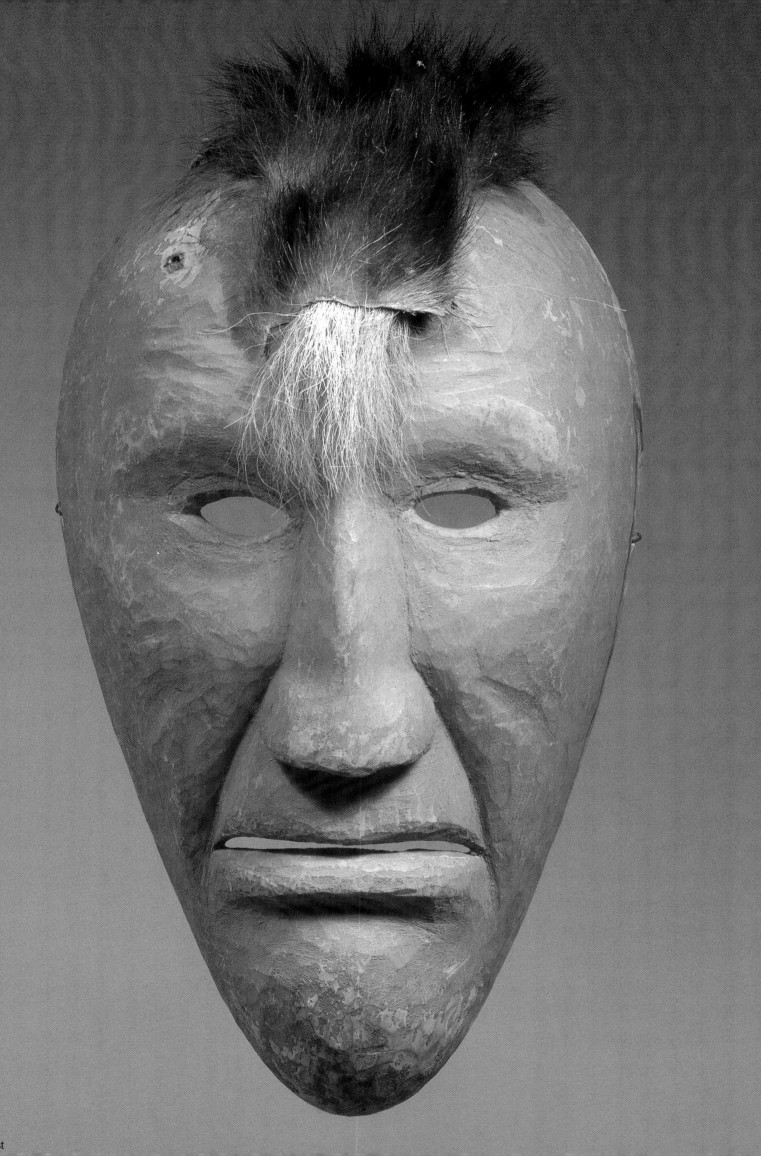

# The Cherokee
# – beloved men and raven mockers

The wooded region in the southern Appalachians that around 1700 was home, hunting ground, and farmland to some 20,000 Cherokee, covered 40,000 square miles – so that the population density was one person per two square miles. Forty "towns" were situated in river valleys separated by mountain ranges and formed three districts, whose inhabitants each spoke a distinct dialect. While there was a sense of shared identity (especially since all Cherokee belonged to one of seven clans), each town was ultimately independent, governed by its peace and war organizations under the leadership of the "beloved men."

Soon after the inception of close contacts with the Europeans in 1673, a flourishing trade developed. The first treaties were signed, and the Cherokee became so involved in the wars of the British against the peoples of the piedmont that warfare became their "beloved profession." In 1721, 37 chiefs accepted a proposal by the governor of South Carolina to make the tribe a kingdom. In 1750, a peace council for all Cherokee was created, which was modeled on the system of unanimity and harmony practiced in the "towns." However, since young men thirsting to distinguish themselves could not be kept from going on the warpath by words alone, war chiefs (and later even young warriors) were admitted from 1768 to the tribal council.

In the American Revolution, the Cherokee fought on the side of the British. When the United States won the war, the Cherokee were seen as allies of an enemy power; the economic prosperity of their slave-owning upper class was another thorn in the side of the American plantation owners. For better protection against the risks of this situation, a group of influential Cherokees began to boost the powers of the tribal leadership. A constitution adopted in 1828 provided for a national chief, who together with a national council governed the Cherokee people.

The introduction of plow farming also weakened the towns. The larger fields no longer needed to be farmed collectively; new homes were built far from the town center and closer to the fields. Although the Cherokee continued to uphold the principle of unanimity, factional disputes on the tribal level could no longer be contained – especially with respect to the issue of the removal to the West demanded by the United States. While those opposed to removal were in the majority, those in favor (who saw emigration as the only way to save the nation) signed the treaty by which the Cherokee territory was sold. After resettlement in 1838, tension within the Indian Territory escalated when the leaders of the protreaty faction were murdered by their opponents, and when the "old settlers" who had emigrated before 1830 could not agree with the newcomers on the way the community should be organized.

## Witch hunt

The old social order based on harmony and unanimity would have been doomed to fail due to a lack of enforcement, but anyone who voiced disagreement risked being accused of witchcraft. After removal, the persecution of political opponents accused of witchcraft reached epidemic proportions, as did the active use of magical means to achieve earthly goals. It was thought that witches could change their shape at will and that they usually lived alone (though surrounded by a whole menagerie of dogs, owls, wolves, and lizards). Vampirelike night stalkers, or "raven mockers," were especially feared. They would appear in the guise of a firebird, trailing a track of sparks across the night sky and cawing like a raven. Witchcraft was commonly considered to be an innate capability, but similarly devastating effects could be achieved by black magic, the secret knowledge of which had to be learned from a master. After the invention of Cherokee syllabic writing, a regular literature of magic formulas and instructions on black magic was produced.

Victory over evil was not always as simple as it is portrayed in the myth of the primeval monster Stone-Clad, the enemy of hunters, whom a medicine man deprived of his powers by lining up seven menstruating women along his path and then impaling him with seven poles. When Stone-Clad was burned on a pyre, he recited his magic songs as he was dying and thus revealed the secret of evil to mankind.

John Ross

# Guerrillas in Florida
# – the Seminole

Indignation sparkled in Osceola's eyes when the representatives of the American government assembled at Camp King in 1835 pressed the leaders of the Seminole to recognize a treaty that was to seal the ultimate sellout of their lands in Florida. A contemptuous smile on his face, he pulled his dagger and with the words "There is my mark!" thrust it into the detested document with such force that the blade almost passed through the table. That, at least, is how a well-meaning contemporary reporter described the young war chief's heroic gesture. This "novel mode of signing with a steel pen" set an unmistakable signal. Many similar legends are still told by his descendants. It is indisputable that Osceola (c. 1803–1838) became the symbolic figure of the Seminole's armed resistance against their white suppressors, a fight recorded in the annals of history as the Second Seminole War. It cost 1,500 American lives, and depleted the American treasury by $20 million.

Only in the late 18th century did a separate Seminole people come into being when various Creek groups, together with the surviving Yamassee, Appalachee, and others, settled in northern Florida – a region previously depopulated by epidemics and war – and there gradually attained political autonomy. The name "Seminole" derived from the Muskogee word *simanôle* ("runaway"), which in turn can be traced back to the Spanish word *cimarrón*, meaning "wild" or "feral." The speakers of the two related languages Muskogee and Hichiti eventually joined forces

Fred Beaver (Creek/ Seminole), *Florida Seminole Women Daily Life*, watercolor, c. 1962. Philbrook Museum of Art, Tulsa, OK.

The typical patchwork style that has become the distinguishing feature of Seminole costume only evolved during the 20th century when sewing machines became increasingly available. While the older decorative technique of appliqué work consists of sewing cut and folded pieces of fabric onto garments to form certain patterns, in patchwork the pieces making up the designs (rows of geometric motifs) are part of the garment's structure.

with black refugee slaves, the demand for whose extradition ultimately resulted in the First Seminole War (1817–1818). At the end of the war the Seminole were assured by treaty of a reservation in central Florida. However, in 1832 the American government forced several of their leaders to sign a second treaty, according to which all Seminole were to be removed to the Indian Territory in Oklahoma. Since the majority of the population did not accept this treaty, Osceola managed to unite numerous scattered Seminole groups against the American forces. The murder of Indian agent General Wiley Thompson (1835) and the annihilation of an army unit under the command of Major Francis L. Dade (known as Dade's Massacre) triggered the longest and most expensive Indian war ever fought by the United States. It brought disaster to a number of commanding officers who had taken into account neither the hot and humid climate and the inaccessible Florida terrain nor the guerrilla tactics of the Seminole. When Osceola was finally captured while bearing a white flag of truce, even those sections of American society hitherto unsympathetic toward the cause of the Indians condemned this act of betrayal. Osceola died in captivity in 1838, a "hero of liberty." When the end of the war was declared in 1842, most of his comrades-in-arms had already been deported to the West as prisoners of war. The majority of those who remained in Florida, and who once more rebelled against the United States in the 1850s, finally emigrated to Oklahoma as well.

While the Seminole population there shared the fate of other tribes removed to the region, the few who survived and remained in Florida retreated to the swamps, living in relative isolation and economic independence as hunters, trappers, and traders (of feathers, furs, and alligator skins) until the end of the 19th century. White settlers eventually forced them onto reservations, where they now live as two federally recognized tribes. Since 1965 the Miccosukee Tribe of Indians of Florida exists alongside the Seminole Tribe itself. The Miccosukee claim to represent the remnants of the pre-Seminole population of Florida. The sale of arts and crafts, services in the tourist industry, casino gambling, and the introduction of cattle-breeding have recently opened up new economic opportunities for the Seminole and the Miccosukee.

George Catlin, *Osceola*, oil on canvas, 1838. National Museum of American Art, Smithsonian Institution, Washington, DC.

"He wore three ostrich feathers in his head, and a turban made of a vari-coloured cotton shawl – and his dress was chiefly of calicos, with a handsome bead sash or belt around his waist," so George Catlin described his model. "In stature [Os-ce-o-la] is about at mediocrity, with an elastic and graceful movement; in his face he is good looking, with rather an effeminate smile; but of so peculiar a character, that the world may be ransacked over without finding another just like it. In his manners … he is polite and gentlemanly, though all his conversation is entirely in his own tongue; and his appearance and actions, those of a full-blooded and wild Indian."

Opposite page:
Billy Bowlegs, daguerreotype, 1852. Florida State Archives, Tallahassee, FL.

Billy Bowlegs (c. 1810–1864), whose war title was Halpuda Mikko ("Chief of the Alligator clan") was one of the Seminole leaders who, after Osceola's death, continued to fight against the United States until the very last warrior had surrendered to the American forces. In 1856 he and his people moved to Oklahoma, where he died soon after his arrival. In this portrait he is wearing a feather-decorated turban, silver gorgets, and a shoulder bag adorned with glass beads.

PRAIRIES AND PLAINS

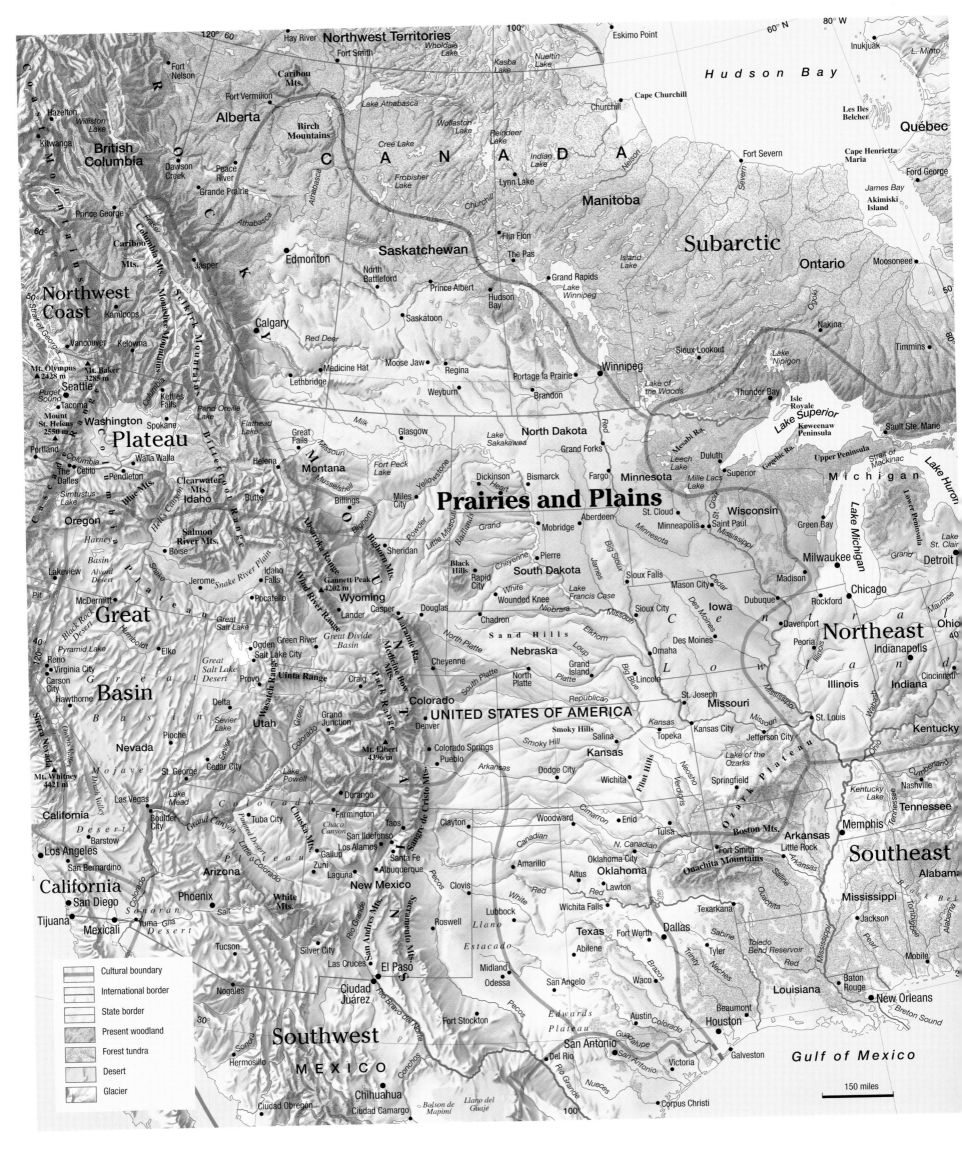

**Hudson Bay**

Inukjuak
L. Minto
Eskimo Point
Cape Churchill
Churchill
Les Îles Belcher
Québec
Cape Henrietta Maria
Ford George
James Bay
Akimiski Island

Northwest Territories
Hay River
Fort Smith
Wholdaia Lake
Kasba Lake
Nueltin Lake

Fort Nelson
Caribou Mts.
Fort Vermilion
Lake Athabasca
Wollaston Lake
Reindeer Lake
Indian Lake
Nelson
Fort Severn

Hazelton
Williston Lake
Alberta
Birch Mountains
Cree Lake
Frobisher Lake
Churchill

Kitwanga
British Columbia
Dawson Creek
Peace River
Grande Prairie
Athabasca
Flin Flon
The Pas
Grand Rapids
Island Lake
**Subarctic**
Ontario
Moosoneee

Prince George
Athabasca
Manitoba
Lynn Lake
Lake Winnipeg
Nakina

Cariboo Mts.
Jasper
Saskatchewan
North Battleford
Prince Albert
Hudson Bay
Sioux Lookout
Lake Nipigon
Timmins

**Northwest Coast**
Kamloops
Calgary
Edmonton
Saskatoon
Grand Forks
**C A N A D A**

Vancouver
Kelowna
Red Deer
Medicine Hat
Moose Jaw
Regina
Portage la Prairie
Brandon
Winnipeg
Lake of the Woods
Thunder Bay
Isle Royale
Sault Ste. Marie

Mt. Olympus 2428 m
Mt. Baker 3285 m
Seattle
Tacoma
Kettles Falls
Lethbridge
Weyburn
**Lake Superior**
Keweenaw Peninsula
Upper Peninsula
Strait of Mackinac

Mount St. Helens 2550 m
Washington
Spokane
Walla Walla
Flathead Lake
Great Falls
Milk
Glasgow
North Dakota
Red
Minnesota
Duluth
Mesabi Ra.
Leech Lake
**M i c h i g a n**
Lake Huron

**Plateau**
Portland
The Dalles
Pendleton
Blue Mts.
Helena
Montana
Musselshell
Missouri
Fort Peck Lake
Lake Sakakawea
Heart
Dickinson
Bismarck
Fargo
Minnesota
St. Cloud
Minneapolis
Saint Paul
Mille Lacs Lake
Superior
Green Bay
Lower Peninsula
Lake St. Clair

Oregon
Clearwater Mts.
Idaho
Billings
Yellowstone
Miles City
Powder
Little Missouri
Grand
**Prairies and Plains**
Aberdeen
Mobridge
Wisconsin
Milwaukee
Lake Michigan
Detroit

Harney Basin
Salmon River Mts.
Boise
Helis Canyon
Absaroka Range
Bighorn Mts.
Sheridan
Black Hills
Cheyenne
Pierre
Big Sioux
James
Mason City
Cedar
Madison
Rockford
Chicago

Lakeview
Alvord Desert
Jerome
Snake River Plain
Idaho Falls
Pocatello
Gannett Peak 4202 m
Wyoming
Bighorn
Wind River Range
Black Hills
Rapid City
South Dakota
White
Wounded Knee
Lake Francis Case
Sioux Falls
Iowa
Dubuque
Davenport
**Northeast**
Ohio

McDermitt
Black Rock Desert
**Great**
Pyramid Lake
Reno
Humboldt
Elko
Great Salt Lake
Ogden
Salt Lake City
Green River
Great Divide Basin
Lander
Casper
Douglas
Niobrara
Chadron
Sand Hills
Missouri
Sioux City
Des Moines
Omaha
Peoria
Indianapolis
Indiana
Cincinnati

Virginia City
Carson City
Hawthorne
**Basin**
Nevada
Pioche
Delta
Sevier Lake
Provo
Uinta Range
Craig
Medicine Bow Mts.
Cheyenne
North Platte
South Platte
Platte
Grand Island
Lincoln
St. Joseph
Des Moines
Illinois
Kentucky

Sierra Nevada
Mt. Whitney 4421 m
Mojave
St. George
Cedar City
Sevier
Utah
Wasatch Range
Green
Colorado
Grand Junction
Park Range
Denver
**UNITED STATES OF AMERICA**
Republican
Big Blue
Kansas
Topeka
Kansas City
Jefferson City
Missouri
St. Louis
Wabash
Ohio

Owens Valley
Death Valley
Las Vegas
Lake Mead
Colorado
Durango
Farmington
Mt. Elbert 4396 m
Colorado Springs
Pueblo
Smoky Hills
Salina
Kansas
Smoky Hill
Arkansas
Dodge City
Wichita
Springfield
Lake of the Ozarks
Ozark Plateau
Kentucky Lake
Nashville
Tennessee

Los Angeles
Barstow
Boulder City
Tuba City
Painted Desert
Chaco Canyon
Chuska Mts.
Los Alamos
Taos
San Ildefonso
Santa Fe
Clayton
Woodward
Enid
Cimarron
Tulsa
Boston Mts.
Fort Smith
Arkansas
Little Rock
Memphis

San Bernardino
**California**
San Diego
Phoenix
Arizona
Little Colorado
Gallup
Zuni
Laguna
Albuquerque
New Mexico
Canadian
N. Canadian
Oklahoma City
Oklahoma
Ouachita Mountains
Saline
**Southeast**
Alabama

Tijuana
Mexicali
Sonoran Desert
Gila Desert
Yuma
Salt
White Mts.
Clovis
Pecos
Amarillo
Altus
Lawton
White
Red
Red
Wichita Falls
Texarkana
Ouachita
Mississippi
Alabama

Nogales
Tucson
Silver City
Las Cruces
El Paso
Rio Grande
Sacramento Mts.
Roswell
Llano Estacado
Lubbock
Texas
Fort Worth
Dallas
Tyler
Toledo Bend Reservoir
Jackson
Black Warrior
Tombigbee
Mobile

Ciudad Juárez
Rio Bravo del Norte
Fort Stockton
Pecos
Edwards Plateau
Midland
Odessa
San Angelo
Abilene
Waco
Sabine
Neches
Trinity
Brazos
Louisiana
Baton Rouge
New Orleans
Breton Sound

**Southwest**
30°
**M E X I C O**
Sonora
Hermosillo
Ciudad Obregón
Chihuahua
Ciudad Camargo
Conchos
Bolson de Mapimí
Llano del Guaje
Rio Grande
Del Rio
San Antonio
**San Antonio**
Nueces
Colorado
Guadalupe
Austin
Victoria
Corpus Christi
Beaumont
Houston
Galveston
**Gulf of Mexico**

150 miles

Cultural boundary
International border
State border
Present woodland
Forest tundra
Desert
Glacier

60° N
80° W
120°
60°
100°
60° N
80°
50°
40°
100°

Liane Gugel

# On the Great Plains

The popular image of "the Indians" as proud warriors and bison hunters, with streaming feather bonnets – men like Sitting Bull, Red Cloud, or Crazy Horse – emerged in the 19th century, when the struggle of the peoples of the Prairies and the Plains for their freedom made the headlines of American newspapers and when some voices (if only here and there) were heard calling for an end to the brutal war. While Buffalo Bill's Wild West shows as well as countless novels and movies of the 20th century have underscored this image, they have rarely contributed toward painting an unstereotyped picture of the ways of life of the peoples of the Prairies and Plains in all their diversity.

The peoples of the Prairies and Plains.

As the transition between the Prairies and the Plains is a gradual one, it is difficult to categorize many of the inhabitants of the region as either Prairie or Plains people. There are distinct similarities between groups that inhabited the border areas and those of the neighboring regions. Over time, many of the peoples of the region moved (more or less voluntarily) to other areas, and the development of the bison hunting culture led to new fusions and fissions. At the beginning of the 18th century, The Suh'tai joined the Cheyenne; the Crow separated from the Hidatsa in 1670.

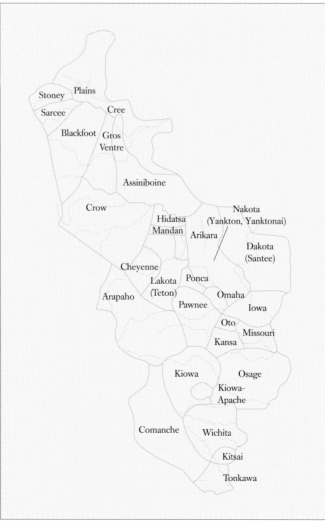

Herd of bison in Yellowstone National Park.

The disappearance of the great bison herds around 1880, was a turning-point in the history of the peoples of the Plains. "When the buffalo went away," Crow chief Plenty Coups recalled, "the hearts of my people fell to the ground, and they could not lift them up again. After this nothing happened." Sitting Bull was of much the same opinion: "A cold wind swept over the prairie when the last buffalo fell … a wind of death for my people."

Previous pages:
Grasslands in South Dakota.

A boundless sky extends over the grasslands of South Dakota. Cold winters and hot summers are the rule, but because rainfall fluctuates strongly from one year to the next, the Plains may take on various hues of green and brown.

# Plentiful Prairies, meager Plains

Extending over an area of one million square miles, the Prairies and Plains region, often subsumed under the term Great Plains, are one of the largest areas of grassland on earth. They extend westward from the Mississippi valley to the foot of the Rocky Mountains, and from the central Canadian provinces almost as far south as the Rio Grande in Texas.

The Prairies, the eastern part of this grassland region, were originally a tallgrass steppe with an abundance of herbs and flowers interspersed with smaller wooded patches. Their soil is dark, almost black, and very fertile. Today, the Prairies are considered to be the breadbasket of North America. These soils were only taken under cultivation by white settlers, whose plows were needed to cut through the dense network of roots. The peoples of the Prairies, however, planted corn and beans in the alluvial soils of the meadowlands along the rivers. Archeological finds confirm that the peoples of the eastern Prairies, in the transitional zones to the Woodlands of the east, were already practicing this type of horticulture around AD 250. Later it gradually spread westward, ultimately becoming the basic form of subsistence for the tribes of the western Prairies in about AD 1000.

In the western part of the Great Plains, the Plains in the narrow sense of the word rise to 6,000 feet where they adjoin the Rocky Mountains. An annual rainfall averaging less than 20 inches is only able to support a short-grass steppe with few trees. Because of extreme climatic conditions (cold winters in which temperatures often dropped to minus 20°F and snowstorms swept over the land, and scorching summers that desiccated the earth), the indigenous peoples of the Plains were unable to raise crops.

This general picture of the Prairies and Plains should not, however, obscure the fact that they constitute a region of far greater diversity. For instance, the northern parts and the interspersed highlands (such as the Black Hills, the Ouachita Mountains, or the Ozark Plateau) are more humid and are wooded in parts, while the landscapes in the south (such as the Llano Estacado) often have an arid, even desertlike character. Groves of willow, poplar, ash, and elm extending along the many rivers, all of which flow into the Missouri and Mississippi, not only provided sufficient firewood, but also offered shelter from the icy-cold winter storms.

## History

Before the introduction of horses by the Spanish in the 17th century, the Plains were only sparsely populated. The horticultural peoples of the Prairies and the hunters of the Great Basin and the Plateau only rarely advanced into this region. When they did, it was to hunt pronghorn antelope, bison, and elk. From about 1720, this situation

**Badlands in winter, South Dakota.**

The rugged landscapes, in whose soft surface the rains have drawn deep furrows and where hardly a plant can grow, appeared too inhospitable even for the Lakota, who were accustomed to dry steppes. Convinced that this, the largest expanse of eroded land in the world, was inhabited by supernatural beings and that lonely wanderers could easily become lost, they named the region "Badlands." During times of conflict, however, (for example, at the climax of the Ghost Dance crisis of 1890) this labyrinth of rocks served as a place of refuge from persecution.

The dammed Missouri near Mobridge, South Dakota.

In the 20th century, the construction of numerous dams for hydroelectric power plants significantly changed the face of the Missouri River. The fertile alluvial lands along its banks have been submerged, as have the tree populations, some of the tops of which jut out of the waters of the artificial lakes. Not far from the spot shown here, the town of Mobridge has erected a monument to the former archenemy Sitting Bull, who, toward the end of his life, witnessed the beginning of the great changes affecting his homeland.

was to change radically. The formerly almost deserted Plains were gradually populated. The introduction of horses allowed some of the peoples coming in from the west (the Comanche), the north (Athapaskan groups), and the east (Siouan and Algonquian tribes) to make bison hunting the very basis of their livelihood. The new culture that thus evolved also influenced the life of the sedentary peoples along the rivers, some of whom began to give more importance to hunting than to crop cultivation, and who accordingly began to replace their pit houses during the summer months with leather tents so as to be likewise able to follow the herds.

However, the culture of the bison-hunters was short-lived. No more than about 100 years after it had started to evolve, epidemic diseases and wars led to a rapid decline in population, and the culture ultimately collapsed when by about 1885 white hunters exterminated the bison herds.

In 1541, just a few decades after the European discovery of the New World, when the Spanish expedition led by Don Francisco Vásquez de Coronado (c. 1510–1544) first brought Europeans to the Plains region, the local cultures still presented a completely different picture, since they had not yet been introduced to horses. Coronado had traveled to the Pueblo region in the hope of finding the golden cities of

Cibola, but instead discovered only adobe houses. Spurred along by native reports, he continued with renewed hope of finding great treasures as far as the Kansas River. What he did find were immeasurable expanses of steppe and the Wichita, modest horticulturists who lived in grass-covered houses. The disappointed members of his expedition forced him to return to Mexico. Coronado thus barely missed an encounter with the expedition led by Hernando de Soto (1486–1542) that was advancing into the country from the east and that had just as little success finding the legendary golden lands of the north.

For a while, Spain lost interest in North America, and only a handful of settlers and missionaries remained along the northern border of the white settlement in the Pueblo region and present-day Texas. Although the Spanish attributed little significance to their sporadic encounters with the inhabitants of the Plains and rarely reported about them, they had a lasting impact on the peoples of the Prairies and Plains: it was the stray horses from the Spanish settlements of the Southwest that brought radical change to the traditional way of life. The Plains provided an ideal habitat, in which the swift herd animals - known as "mustangs" in their naturalized state - could flourish. The peoples of the southern Plains were quick to recognize the usefulness of horses, and began to steal them from the Spanish in the south or even to exchange them for children abducted from enemy tribes. Another way of acquiring horses was to catch wild mustangs and break them in, for which some groups developed a special skill.

The French first advanced from their colony in Canada into the northern Prairies and Plains as fur traders. After the establishment of the colony of Louisiana on the lower Mississippi in 1682, the French represented a growing competition for the Spanish in the south. When France was defeated by England in 1763, the Spanish were quick to seize the opportunity of taking possession of the territory extending from the Mississippi to the Rocky Mountains

Karl Bodmer, *The Missouri Below the Mouth of the Platte*, watercolor, 1833. Joslyn Art Museum, Omaha, NE.

As one went further upstream along the Missouri, the groves of trees, which lined the fertile banks of the river gradually disappeared and were replaced by the undulating grasslands of the hinterland. Those who farmed on these lands also had easy access to the hunting grounds.

George Catlin, *Breaking down the Wild Horse [among the Comanche]*, color lithograph, 1844.

Wild horses were chased until their mounted pursuers got close enough to cast a rawhide lasso around their necks. The stranglehold of the noose would bring the horse to the ground, and its front legs were tied together while another noose was placed around its lower jaw. With the leather rope stretched taut, the catcher would move up close to the horse until he could put his hand on its eyes and blow into its nostrils, thus breaking the resistance of his captive and future companion.

Alfred Jacob Miller, *Interior of Fort Laramie*, watercolor, 1837. Walters Art Gallery, Baltimore, MD.

Trading posts were places for the exchange of goods and information. They were considered to be neutral ground on which even enemy peoples normally maintained peace. Their fortifications served to protect the valuable goods of the White Man, but they also offered protection to intrepid travelers in an environment that could be fraught with danger. Outposts of "civilization" such as Fort Laramie in Wyoming were later sometimes used as military facilities.

and from the Gulf of Mexico to the Canadian border. The trade in Euro-American goods – first of all horses and guns – fueled the rivalry between tribes and triggered massive shifts in population. In the early 18th century, for example, the military supremacy of the Osage and Comanche, who thanks to their stable trade relations with white traders were rich in horses and guns, forced the Wichita to relinquish their traditional territory in Kansas and to relocate further south in present-day Texas. But the Wichita, too, would ultimately profit from trade with the whites, for they would soon adopt the role of middlemen between the Comanche and the French.

Considerable trading had taken place between the peoples of the Prairies and Plains even before the Europeans arrived. Once horses had been introduced, had spread, and had become the primary means of transportation, trade between tribes promoted the development of common cultural ground, since it was not goods alone that were exchanged, but also ceremonies, songs, dances, and legends. The villages of the Arikara, Mandan, and Hidatsa farming communities evolved into important trade centers. To enable them to cultivate their manifold trade relations, these groups were often versed in many languages. They exchanged products of their fields – corn, beans, squash, and tobacco – for the goods produced by the hunters of the Plains, such as bison hides, bows made

of the horn of the bighorn sheep, and nutritious dried meat. Because the introduction of horses enabled even nomadic peoples, who traditionally followed the bison herds, to possess and transport larger amounts of goods, the existing trade network spread ever further.

At the same time, the coveted products supplied by Euro-American fur traders further encouraged economic exchange. They erected trading posts and created their own supply routes. However, the diseases introduced along these routes (notably smallpox, measles, and whooping cough) brought doom to the indigenous peoples, in particular to sedentary groups, whose populations dwindled at an alarming rate. In 1837, for instance, an outbreak of smallpox wiped out about three quarters of the population of the Mandan which before 1790 stood at approximately 8,000. Although the influence of the old trading centers and of the original middlemen waned as the whites achieved increasing dominance, the indigenous groups remained actively engaged in trade. The Blackfoot, for example, managed for a long time to prevent white traders from supplying weapons and ammunition to their enemies. Other groups, such as the Eastern Shoshone, tried to gain control of the trade with groups inhabiting the marginal zones of the Plains, far from the major trade routes.

In 1803 the United States purchased Louisiana from Napoleon, who had succeeded in getting back the colony from Spain only three years earlier, but who needed the funds for his war coffers. Now the only obstacle that stood in the way of rapid United States expansion and settlement of the West were the peoples of the Prairies and Plains. In the first half of the 19th century, however, the Americans did not yet consider the spacious grasslands to be particularly inviting for settlement. Their policy, therefore, was to forcibly remove the tribes remaining east of the Mississippi to Oklahoma and Kansas, thus permanently concentrating the indigenous peoples in a compact "Indian Territory" and making room for the rapidly expanding farming economy and for industrialization. Some peoples of the Prairies and Plains were later also moved to the Indian Territory. Today, Oklahoma is the state with the largest indigenous population (close to 300,000) in the United States. The forced relocations have made Oklahoma home to 38 different peoples.

The massive influx of settlers into the Plains region which began in 1848, was triggered by the great Californian gold rush and by the incorporation of Oregon into the United States, and was further accelerated after 1860 by the construction of transcontinental railroads in a spirit of patriotic enthusiasm. This new situation soon destroyed all plans for an Indian Territory and increased pressure on the indigenous peoples to sell their lands, relinquish their cultural heritage, and adapt their lifestyles to conform to those of white farmers. Even those who tried to evade these oppressive policies were soon left with no choice. Their lands were divided by fences into pastures and intersected by railroads that restricted the freedom of movement of game and hunters alike. The military mercilessly persecuted all Native American groups who dared to stray outside their reservations. By 1885, professional white hunters had almost wiped out the entire bison population. Deprived of their source of food, the last free hunters of the Plains were compelled to submit to the agencies of the Bureau of Indian Affairs, where they were forced to subsist on government charity in the form of salted meat, flour, sugar, coffee, and discarded textiles.

Opposite page:
Little Wolf, a Sicangu Lakota, demonstrates the sign for "riding" in sign language, 1908. Hamburgisches Museum für Völkerkunde, Hamburg, Germany.

The diversity of languages and the frequency of contact between the tribes in the Plains and Prairies region resulted in the evolution of a sign language, in which the speakers of different language groups were able to communicate. The signs used were not universally valid: different signs for the same term often existed in different regions.

"Parading Indianness" at the Crow Fair, Montana, 1978.

At the closing parade of the annual Crow Fair, held every August since 1898, it is still possible to encounter the feather-bonneted equestrian inhabitants of the northern Plains and the adjacent Plateau, who in the 19th century had shaped the Western image of "the Indian."

# Grasslands and cornfields

Opposite page:
Painted bison robe, northeastern Plains, c. 1840. Museum für Völkerkunde, Frankfurt, on loan to Deutsches Ledermuseum, Offenbach am Main, Germany.

The pictographs that men painted on their bison robes illustrated their war deeds, their spoils (notably scalps, weapons, and horses), and the gifts they had distributed. Other robes depicted stylized motifs with symbolic meaning for their wearers. In addition, these garments would sometimes be adorned with bands and disks of porcupine quill or glass bead appliqué, which were made exclusively by women.

Seth Eastman, *Indians Travelling*, watercolor, 1850. Afton Historical Society, Afton, MN.

"A family who owned horses or to which many strong women belonged," missionary Samuel Pond (1808–1891) explained, had an added advantage over the semisedentary Dakota in the prairies of Minnesota. On hunting expeditions, they would be the first to arrive at the campsite and could choose the best site for their tipi (the poles for which were not transported, but were newly fashioned at each site). The women owned the tents and were in charge of the transportation of all loads, while the men were free to go hunting.

## "Mysterious dogs" and bison

Bison have been hunted in the grasslands of the Great Plains for thousands of years, but it was only the advent of horses that made exploitation of the countless herds all the more attractive. When the peoples of the Prairies and Plains still followed the herds on foot, they were obliged to undertake long and arduous journeys between the available water sources at which the animals regularly gathered. On such journeys it was also impossible to carry more than the bare essentials. Horses made it much easier to move camp; they also enabled people to use more effective hunting methods and thus improve their quality of life. In addition, their use had a major impact on the practice of warfare; in contrast to the hunting groups who used horses, sedentary horticulturists and their villages were easy prey for surprise attacks.

It was these advantages that convinced the traditional farming peoples of the Eastern Woodlands (such as the Cheyenne) to leave their cornfields behind, move west, and turn to hunting bison. Some groups had less freedom to decide on such a course, being forced by their better-armed eastern neighbors to leave their territory and head west. It was apparently for similar reasons that the Comanche moved from the Great Basin to the southern Plains in the 17th century. Other peoples, such as the Sarcee, emigrated from the subarctic forests of Canada to the Plains. Thus, during the course of the 18th century, the Plains region, which until then had been populated by only a few groups, was transformed into a melting pot of diverse cultural traditions.

Horses also changed the social values of the peoples of the Plains and Prairies. Before they were introduced, people were forced to keep their possessions to a modest minimum, so that few inequalities existed between the wealthy and the poor. This status quo was fundamentally changed with the advent of horses. Prosperity was now measured by the possession of horses. Those who had none, or who had poor horses, were at a disadvantage in matters of hunting and depended on the generosity of wealthy horse owners, a generosity that was paid for by faithful allegiance. Since, with few exceptions, it was only the Comanche who bred horses, other groups resorted to theft and barter as a means of acquiring horses of their own.

When the Prairie and Plains peoples first gained knowledge of horses through their contact with Europeans and with neighboring peoples, they were both amazed and filled with admiration. Since none of their languages included a term to describe this animal, and since it replaced dogs as a beast of burden, the Lakota, for one, called it "mysterious dog" (*šunkawakán*). Dogs were, of course, capable of carrying only light loads, sometimes with the aid of a travois. Horses, however, could transport long tent poles, heavy loads, or even the disabled and elderly.

Thus, the Prairie and Plains people had occasion to be very grateful to their horses. They carved and publicly displayed memorial sticks in honor of horses that were wounded or died on the battlefield or during a hunt. The Mandan so cherished these animals that they even allocated to their favorite horses a special compartment within their earth lodges.

Around 60 million bison are estimated to have populated the grasslands and forests of North America before the arrival of the Europeans. By the end of the 18th century, bison were considered to be extinct in the east. From 1860, the herds were systematically slaughtered by professional hunters as a source of food for the settlers trekking across the country on their way to the West, for leather to make transmission belts for the newly established factories in the Midwest, but also as a way of depriving the indigenous population of their main source of sustenance. In 1870, about 4.5 million bison still grazed on the Great Plains; ten years later, they were almost extinct. Today several protected herds still exist in national parks and others are kept by individual tribes. In recent years, there have been many calls (especially by Native Americans) to declare parts of the Plains and Prairie region a protected zone for bison and to allow the former grasslands to regenerate. Whether this dream of repopulating the region with bison is feasible depends predominantly on the willingness of white farmers to cooperate and of the government to provide the necessary financial backing.

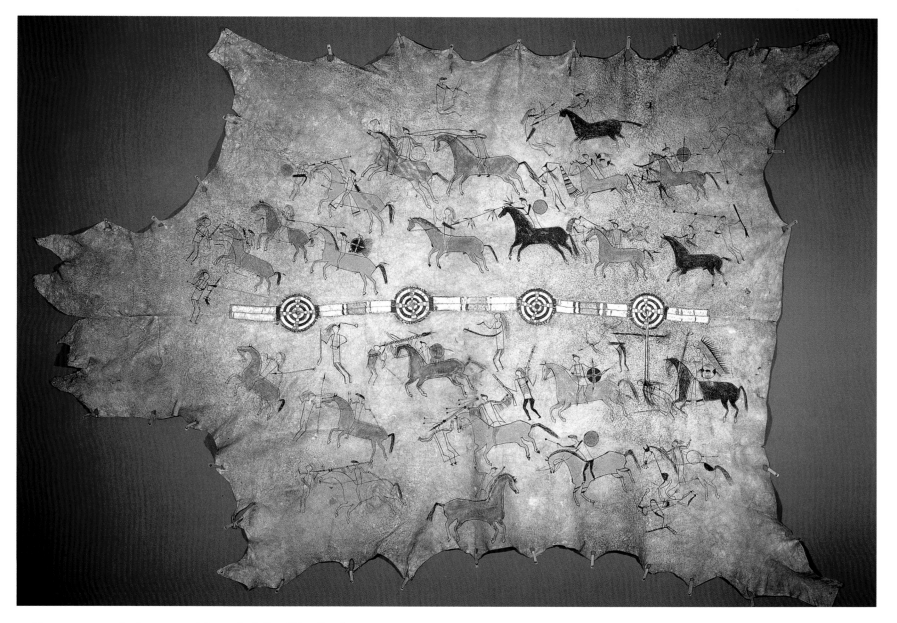

Since most of the necessities of daily life (food, clothing, and household goods) were provided by the bison, many myths and religious ceremonies surrounded these animals, their reproduction, and their status as game. Among the Blackfoot, a women's society, on the last day of their annual assembly, would imitate a herd of bison traveling to a watering hole. The women wore headdresses made of bison hides. Having come to rest at a selected spot (as would bison), they were driven back to their ceremonial lodge by men reenacting a bison hunt. This "hunt" was performed, prayers were held, and offerings were made to ensure the success of the hunt, on which the community were so heavily dependent.

There was also a direct link between the bison herds and the political organization of Plains tribes. In early summer, when huge herds gathered to migrate north, the families of hunters who had lived scattered throughout the area during winter would also gather in large camps of several thousand people. This was the time of communal hunts, of feasts, and of reunion. When the animals retreated in small groups to their sheltered winter grounds, the hunters were likewise forced to break up their summer camps and move to small camps in the sheltered woods along the rivers.

Stone bison figurine, northern Plains, late prehistoric period. Glenbow Collection, Calgary, AB.

Bison meat was consumed fresh, dried, or in the form of pemmican. Untanned hides were used to make moccasin soles, parfleches, or shields. The lighter summer hides were also used to make clothing, tents, and bags of all kinds, and winter hides for robes and bedding. Bison stomach pouches served as receptacles for water or for cooking, and the animal's sinews were used for sewing or to make bowstrings. Bison wool was spun and twisted to make yarn or rope. Bison horn was fashioned into spoons and their bones were used to make skin scrapers or awls. Their hooves were used to make glue, and their brains and livers provided tanning paste. Bison hides were used to make round-hulled boats. Since timber was scarce, the hides were also dried and used as fuel.

# Bison hunting

Bison hunting was a vital element not only in the lives of the Plains people, but also in those of the Prairie tribes who were primarily farmers. All the peoples of the grasslands were also dependent on pronghorn antelope, wapiti, other species of deer, and bighorn sheep as a source of meat and raw materials.

In the old days, bison were predominantly hunted in communal drives or by stealing up as close as possible to the animals (disguised in an animal hide) in order to place a good shot at close range. These methods continued to be used by groups such as the Cree and Assiniboine who had few horses. In the winter, men would follow bison tracks on snowshoes made of wooden frames strung with strips of rawhide that prevented wearers from sinking into the snow.

Horses brought considerable change to these hunting methods. Some animals were trained especially for bison hunting. They needed to be quick and maneuverable and to have sufficient stamina and courage. They were well cared for and were an extremely valuable trade item. Often, several hundred hunters would set out together from the large camps. It was particularly important to young men to return as successful hunters. But because they lacked the necessary experience, foresight, and patience, male military societies would act as hunting police. They were responsible for maintaining strict order, and without their organizing skills, many such large-scale hunts would surely have been unsuccessful. Hunt leaders were elected, and scouts were sent out to search for bison herds.

Once the signal was given, the hunters would encircle the herd. When it came to killing the animals, however, each hunter was left to the devices of his own courage and skill. Killing them with a bow and arrow meant having to get dangerously close to these massive beasts

of shoulder height. The men would attempt to gain on a runaway animal from an angle to their rear using the horses that were specially trained for such maneuvers. When they had come into the right distance between themselves and the animals, they would shoot their arrow directly into the heart located behind its shoulder blade. Normally a single arrow was not enough to kill a bison. Any further attempts to target the animal, however, could easily be thwarted by a counterattack by the beast. Hunters were often wounded and even paid for this dangerous method of food procurement with their lives.

While arrowheads and spearheads made of stone and bone were eventually replaced by metal ones, traditional bows remained in use even after firearms were introduced. In contrast to complicated muzzleloaders, they allowed shots to be made in quick succession, and they did not cause the animals to flee in panic at the noise. Bows needed to be small and easy to handle on horseback. To compensate for their small size, powerful bows were made of wood or of pieces of horn of the bighorn sheep that had been welded together by heat, and to which layers of sinews had been glued. By the time repeating rifles and pistols became available, bison were almost extinct.

Skinning and butchering was women's work. The meat not eaten immediately was cut into thin strips, dried on frames, and either stored in folded parfleches or processed into pemmican. For the latter, dried meat was roasted and ground by the women in a rawhide bowl using a stone or stone hammer until it was broken up into fluffy fiber. Hot fat and marrow were added to make a dough. The dough was kneaded, and with dried berries was formed into small blocks or cakes which became very solid. Pemmican was not only a nutritional dish; preserved, it could be kept for several years, thus ensuring that food supplies would be available in winter or on the warpath, when fresh meat was scarce.

Before the Europeans introduced copper or iron pots, people used pouches made of animal stomach or leather as

Left:
Head-Smashed-In Jump, Alberta.
During the summer months, hunters would often drive whole herds over a cliff ("buffalo jump"). Two rows of men would form a funnel into which another team of hunters would drive the animals. Prairie fires or walls of stone, bush, or tree stumps were used now and then to steer the herds to their ultimate death. Other hunters would wait at the foot of the cliff to kill the surviving animals.

George Catlin, *Buffalo Hunt Under a Wolf-skin Mask*, oil on canvas, 1854. Ethnologisches Museum, Staatliche Museen zu Berlin – Preussischer Kulturbesitz, Berlin, Germany.
Stalking bison required not only good hunting skills, but considerable courage as well. Hunters would often disguise themselves in wolf skins or bison hides, approaching from a direction downwind of the animals in order to get as close as possible without being noticed. Since a single hunter could easily frighten the herd and cause a stampede, jeopardizing the success of a communal hunt, this method was generally not used during the big summer hunts.

cooking vessels, which were either lowered into pits or attached to willow frames. They were filled with water that was heated by means of hot stones, and the cooking ingredients added. Other domestic utensils included horn spoons, wooden bowls, animal-bladder water pouches, shell or flint knives (later, made of metal), and fire drills, which were later replaced by the flint and steel strike-a-lights commonly used at the time.

## Planting and harvest

The cultivation of crops, especially corn and beans, was a matter of survival for the tribes of the Prairies. But even for the bison-hunting tribes, cultivated produce bought or stolen from their farming neighbors was a welcome part of their diet. The sedentary groups, in turn, procured most of the meat that they required by hunting methods that were very similar to those of the Plains peoples. The relative importance of hunting

or farming, however, varied considerably among the various peoples. The Pawnee, for example, who depended equally on hunting and farming as a means of subsistence, set out on their summer hunting expeditions in mid-June and only returned to their villages in September to harvest their crops. At the end of October, when the crops had been brought in and stored, they departed again on winter hunts, returning in spring to plant fresh corn.

The Mandan, Hidatsa, and Arikara, by contrast, lived mainly from the cultivation of corn, beans, squash, and sunflowers – the cultivation of which was the responsibility of the women. Big summer bison hunts, which were village rather than tribal affairs, were scheduled so as not to interfere with the work required in the fields. In addition to the big hunts, one-day hunting expeditions took place in the immediate proximity of the settlement. Thus, it was important to perform attraction rituals that would bring the bison herds as close as possible to the village.

Crow women tanning hides, 1902. Denver Public Library, Denver, CO.

The difficult and arduous task of processing and tanning hides to make leather was carried out by the women, who were highly esteemed for this skill. The skins were stretched out on the ground or on a wooden frame, and remnants of flesh and fat were removed from one side and the hair from the other with special scrapers. The hides were tanned by rubbing them with a mixture of fat, liver, and brains, watering them, wringing them out, and then rolling them up into a bundle. After a certain time, the shrunken skins were unrolled, pulled back into shape, and softened by stretching them over a pole or a taut rope.

A whole range of ceremonies served to secure an abundant harvest. Corn was the most important cultivated plant, and a variety of species were raised. (One difference between them was the color of their kernels.) Only species of corn that were resistant to frost and drought could grow at all in the harsh climate of the upper Missouri region. The crops also needed to mature within no more than two to three months.

Before new seeds were planted, the women would loosen the soil of the riverside fields with hoes and digging sticks. The fields were previously cleared of trees, bushes, and grass with the aid of axes or by burning. Old fields were soon exhausted and new ones had to be laid out frequently, so that the fields in use were not always within close range of the villages. It was therefore often necessary for men to accompany the women to the fields to protect them from possible enemy assaults.

By May, the small fields were sufficiently prepared, so that the corn seeds could be planted. When the corn began to ripen, it was important to protect it from crows, horses, but also from hungry boys. For this purpose elevated platforms were erected along the edge of the fields, from which young girls kept watch. Older women often kept the girls company to make sure that they were not secretly approached by some admirer. (Young men and women had few opportunities for confidential encounters.)

The cornfields could thus grow during the summer. Since food stores were almost empty by then, the first tender green corn was harvested at the beginning of August. It was cooked or roasted, and any surplus stored. The main harvest was in September or at the beginning of October. The ripe cobs were shucked, spread out on a rack to dry, and threshed with sticks. The women then ground the corn with wooden mortars and pestles; the resulting cornmeal was used to make bread and other foods or was stored in underground storage pits along with other provisions such as beans, squash, and sunflowers.

The women would also gather the wild fruits and berries that formed a significant part of everyday diet. Except for medicinal plants, men generally did not participate in gathering. Large amounts of prairie turnips and various other tuberous roots were extracted from the ground in the early summer with digging sticks. Since they were ideal for storing, most of them were kept as winter food for the time when people had the greatest need for the nutrients and vitamins they contained. The dried tubers were braided into strands in a fashion

"I am an old woman now. The buffaloes and black-tail deer are gone, and our Indian ways are almost gone. … Often in summer I rise at daybreak and steal out to the cornfields; and as I hoe the corn, I sing to it, as we did when I was young. No one cares for our corn songs now."

(Buffalo Bird Woman, Hidatsa, 1921)

very similar to way the garlic is often strung. They were soaked in water or grated and added to corn soups or venison stews. Although the women knew exactly where to forage for prairie turnips, climatic conditions in some years could often make it very difficult to find sufficient amounts of this food plant. For this reason, they would often dig out the nests of mice and other rodents that hoarded large quantities of small tuberous roots (for example, the so-called ground beans) and seeds. As it was mostly the old women whose range was restricted by age who procured these foods, the myths of the northern Plains peoples often contain witty episodes about the eternal enmity between old women and mice.

On the northeastern edges of the Prairies, the Dakota, Plains Ojibwa, and Plains Cree also harvested the seeds of the aquatic grass known as wild rice. Fish was another source of food for them, especially at times when meat was in short supply. For most of the Plains peoples, however, fish was only a very minor part of the overall diet, except for the Mandan and Hidatsa whose country abounded in lakes plentifully stocked with fish.

When the reservations were established, the government introduced new foods and crops, including potatoes, wheat, and watermelons. Although it was initially rarely used, wheat flour soon became one of the main staples. Along with meat and corn, the fried flat-cake bread (fry bread) for which it was used is still today one of the most important elements of a "traditional" meal. Especially the former hunting peoples do not, however, grow their own wheat or other crops, since the reservation lands are generally either entirely unsuitable or can only be made sufficiently fertile with the help of large-scale irrigation.

The peoples of the Plains and Prairies still frequently engage in hunting (though not, of course, of bison). On the reservations, fresh venison is just as popular as hotdogs and hamburgers. Unfortunately, however, their hunting rights, reserved to them in the old treaties, often give rise to fierce disputes between Native American and white hunters.

Rodeo at the Crow Fair, Montana, 1978.

Rather than becoming farmers, many of the former bison hunters showed an inclination for cattle breeding, which was also better suited to the natural conditions of the dry steppe. The American government supported this choice only half-heartedly, because the large herds necessarily would have been tribally owned, and therefore contrary to the policy of strengthening the personal profit motive through the allotment of land for farming. Today, there is no longer any conflict between "cowboys" and "Indians," as many Native Americans have themselves become cowboys.

Opposite page:
Hidatsa woman working in a cornfield, 1912. Photograph: Gilbert Wilson.
Minnesota Historical Society, St. Paul, MN.

Mandan and Hidatsa women often performed household and field chores together. The most important agricultural utensils were digging sticks, hoes (the blades of which were fashioned from the shoulder blades of bison or wapiti), rakes made of wood or antlers, and threshing sticks. Land, utensils, earth lodges, and household equipment were jointly owned by the women of an extended family and were generally passed down from a mother to her daughters.

# Paris of the Prairies

Paul Kane, *Big Snake, a Blackfoot Chief, Recounting His War Exploits*, oil on canvas, 1848. National Gallery of Canada, Ottawa, ON.

The decoration of painted bison robes and of other garments had symbolic meaning that often is no longer known. Strips of ermine apparently symbolized the swiftness and courage associated with this aggressive weasel and thus that of the wearer of the shirt. The tufts of hair attached to the "scalp shirts" worn by a group of Lakota political leaders are not those of their enemies, but from fellow Lakota, and served as a reminder of the responsibility that leaders had toward their people.

Throughout the world, clothing not only provides protection against the elements, but has always served as a means of expressing social and personal identity: it is no coincidence that the saying "The tailor makes the man" has become so popular. Because of the differences in climate within the Great Plains and the diversity of peoples who inhabited the region, it comes as no surprise that there was a multitude of regionally diverse forms of dress. The many different costumes worn by the various peoples, meant each group could compare, be inspired by, and adopt the dress styles of neighboring groups. At the height of the bison-hunting culture in the early 19th century, the upper Missouri region, with its colorful mixture of tribal wear, was a veritable "Paris of the Prairies."

Throughout the Prairies and Plains, deer, pronghorn antelope, bighorn sheep, and bison leather were the main materials used in clothing, which was made by women.

The everyday attire for men generally consisted of moccasins, leggings that extended from heel to hip, a breechclout, a leather shirt usually made of two animal skins folded and sewn together at the top, and a bison robe made of bison hide or leather. The women normally wore moccasins, knee-high leggings, a leather dress, and also a leather robe. Everyday clothing was simple and functional, and not necessarily decorated. It was uncommon to have more than one set of clothes. The more one owned, the more burdensome it was to move camp. Hence, people only accumulated the bare essentials. Everyday clothes did not generally serve to emphasize social differences.

The clothing worn on festive or ceremonial occasions, however, was very different from the plain everyday attire. It was adorned with porcupine quills, later with glass beads, horse hair, feathers, fur, or painted decorations. Richly adorned shirts, bear-claw necklaces,

Thomas Easterly, *Kun-zan-ya, Wife of Mahee*, Iowa. Handcolored daguerreotype, 1849. Missouri Historical Society, St. Louis, MO.

By the mid 19th century, textiles had been introduced and had widely replaced leather as a material for clothes in the eastern border region of the Prairies, since imported fabrics were more valuable and thus expressed the wealth of the people who wore them. The woman in this portrait is wearing a woolen blanket, in place of a traditional leather robe. As among the peoples of the neighboring Northeast, frilled blouses made of printed cotton were worn in combination with a wraparound skirt.

Plains Cree woman's dress, c. 1840. Canadian Museum of Civilization, Hull, QC.

An older form of the woman's dress of the northern and central Plains, one that was outmoded after 1850, consisted of an animal skin folded over to make a tube, with a side seam and a single shoulder strap. The decorative section across the chest and upper arm is made of leather thongs wrapped with porcupine quills. It features stylized bison heads, a motif pointing to the symbolic link between women and bison.

sexes in society and often displayed an individual's personal achievements. Since generosity was regarded as one of the greatest virtues in indigenous societies, men rarely neglected to paint on their robes a list of the gifts that they had made. Depictions on clothes also included war deeds and less often a person's visionary experiences. In contrast to those painted by men, the motifs painted on robes by women consisted of stylized symbolic forms, the meanings of which are often unclear.

Most moccasins were made of an upper part of soft leather and a rawhide sole. Sometimes this footwear was made from a single piece of soft leather, the soles of which, however, were not very durable. Many of the old moccasins displayed in museums clearly show how economically people used the raw materials at their disposal. Many of these shoes have rawhide soles made of discarded parfleches.

In winter, people would sometimes have footwear made of a single piece of bison hide. The women of some of the southern Plains groups favored a bootlike shoe that consisted of moccasins and leggings sewn together in one piece. These peoples also ornamented their garments with pigments and fringes rather than with the porcupine quills and glass beads that were so common further to the north.

and feather ornaments were worn by men as visible signs of the wearer's high standing or as insignia of office.

On public occasions, respected warriors and hunters, leaders of men's societies, and religious dignitaries would wear garments and adornments that proclaimed their social standing or their achievements. Each detail of their dress identified their special merits. For example, horse tracks painted onto shirts or leggings might represent the successful theft of horses. The costumes of tribal members with fewer heroic war or hunting deeds to their name, who held no office, or who were simply still too young to possess any distinctions, were much less elaborate.

On the ceremonial garments worn by women, it was generally the yoke-shaped shoulder sections that were adorned with porcupine quills, glass beads, wapiti teeth, or dentalium shells imported from the Pacific coast. While northern Plains Cree and Plains Ojibwa women traditionally wore shoulder-strap dresses, often with a sort of little jacket consisting of two sleeve sections joined together, before 1850 women in the southern Plains normally wore a costume consisting of a leather skirt and a poncho-style cape. Wichita women often wore no upper garments, thus exposing the tattoos that decorated that part of their bodies. From about 1860, and probably as a reaction to the prudishness of the whites they too began to wear full-length leather dresses in which skirt and top were firmly joined to one another.

While men wore shirts and women wore dresses, a further clear distinction was made between male and female clothing in the decoration on the bison, wapiti, or deer skins; these adornments clearly reflected the roles of both

**Tipi camp at a powwow.**

Leather tents have not been made on the Plains for about a century, and because the nomadic way of life in the region was forcibly brought to an end, the tipi no longer plays a role as a form of year-round housing. However, these ingenious tents are increasingly being used at powwows, especially in summer, when visitors travel from afar, as they stand for traditionalism and, increasingly, a Panindian identity.

# Tipi and earth lodge

The differences in the economy of the Plains and the Prairies peoples were clearly reflected in the respective types of their housing. The bison hunters of the Plains lived throughout the year in conical tents, or tipis (from the Lakota word *tipi*, "dwelling"), while the corn farmers on the Prairies dwelled in permanent settlements that they left only to go on hunting trips.

The hunters' mobility was facilitated by the ingenious construction of their tipis, which could be quickly set up and dismantled, which were easy to transport, and which

also provided protection as much against the heat of summer as against the cold of winter and could equally withstand violent storms. The advantage of tipis compared to the conical tents commonly built in the Subarctic lay in their cover, which fitted snugly around a framework of slender poles.

This cover was originally made of bison hide. From about 1870, when the bison herds began to dwindle and commerce with white people increased markedly, canvas became a more popular material. Leather tents rarely lasted for more than two years because of the extreme temperature to which they were exposed. They were owned by women, who made them by sewing together about 12 bison hides.

Tanning the hides was an arduous and lengthy procedure which women seldom performed on their own since they could generally count on the assistance of other female relatives or friends. Sewing the hides together was another communal task which concluded with a feast provided by the future owner of the tent. Among some peoples – the Cheyenne and Arapaho, for example – the activities involved in making and decorating tents and their furnishings were regarded as sacred and had to be performed by women's societies.

Covers of bison leather could weigh between 100 and 110 lbs, too heavy a load to transport when, before the introduction of the horse, dogs were the only available draft animals. This is why tents in the old days were noticeably smaller than those used later on. Naturally, the size of a tent is also dependent on the number and wealth of its inhabitants and on its purpose: council or ceremonial tents which could hold 50 or more people were much larger than those made for domestic use.

Some peoples used three, others four poles tied together below their tops for the basic structure of the tent, which bore the weight of the other poles. The cover was fixed to the ground with heaps of earth, stones, or wooden pegs, and the front was closed with wooden pins; the oval entrance was covered by a flap. Of course, the Plains people had rules of decorum. Visitors were expected to make themselves known before entering, which they did either by a greeting, by coughing, or by scratching the cover. An open flap was a sign of welcome.

Ventilation was regulated by means of smoke flaps which were adjusted according to wind direction and which could be closed in bad weather. By lighting a small fire and using sufficiently dry firewood, it was even possible to avoid any smoke being created, so that the smoke vent could be kept closed. Because good

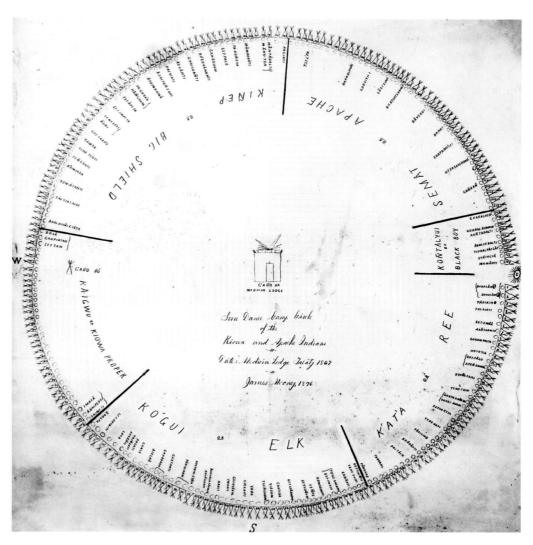

firewood was always difficult to find in the steppe, people began to use an entirely different fuel – dried bison dung, of which there were always plentiful supplies in the summertime. A tipi's entrance always faced east, toward the rising sun. Because it symbolized renewal and life, the east was the cardinal point to which prayers were most often directed.

The first thing that a visitor would see on entering a tipi was the decorated leather tipi curtain that hung from the tent poles from a height of about 6 feet. The curtain insulated the tent against the heat of summer and the cold of winter and formed a separate compartment where people could store their possessions. The backrest was another ingenious construction. Made of around 200 willow sticks joined to form a kind of mat which rested on two legs of a tripod, it was the ideal form of seating which could be rolled up for easy transport.

The sole source of light and heat in the tent was the central fireplace. Cooking was usually done outside the tent in a designated cooking area. The fires, both inside and outside the tipis, were meeting places for family and friends. This is where stories were told, heated debates conducted, where meals were shared, or where people simply relaxed after a strenuous day.

The most widespread of the Prairie peoples' permanent forms of housing was the round earth lodge, which was built partly into the ground and featured a domed roof which was also covered with soil. Generally, earth lodges

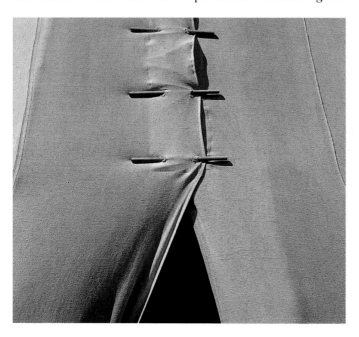

*Sun Dance camp circle of the Kiowa and Kiowa Apache Indians*, 1867. Drawing by James Mooney. National Anthropological Archives, Smithsonian Institution, Washington, DC.

The center of a summer camp circle was often taken up by a council tent, where the leaders of local groups and respected warriors could assemble, or (as here) where ceremonies could be conducted. Each local group was allocated a particular place within the camp circle which indicated the group's status within the tribe. The group with the greatest social standing (frequently the group with the most highly regarded leader) was given a place of honor opposite the opening in the circle.

Fastening of a tipi cover above the entrance, 1987.

Modern covers are made from lengths of canvas which are sewn together by machine. However, the simple and practical method of fastening the tent with wooden pins continues to be used as it was when people still lived under bison hides.

Seth Eastman, *Dacotah Village*, watercolor, c. 1850. Afton Historical Society, Afton, MN.

The permanent villages of the Dakota and their neighbors consisted of summer houses with walls and ridged roofs lined with elm bark. The buildings could be up to about 30 feet long, and provided housing for four or more related families, while also serving as winter bases from which people went on extensive hunting trips with their tipis. In hot weather, social life was conducted in the shade of the drying racks in front of the entrances of the buildings.

ten years. Earth lodges were built without using nails or studs, and their construction, including preparation (gathering building materials) could take a week. This was always a communal task although, as with the tipi, women assumed most of the responsibility for construction. Helpers were rewarded with a feast given by the earth lodge's future owners.

In addition to earth lodges and tipis numerous other house forms existed in the grasslands, which were influenced by climate and available building materials. The Plains Ojibwa and the Plains Cree occasionally lived in Subarctic-style bark- or mat-covered tents, and the Osage in domed houses with circular, oval, or rectangular floor plans. Rectangular houses with ridged roofs are known from the Quapaw and Santee (Dakota), and grass-covered roundhouses with pointed roofs among the Wichita and their relatives.

Villages were always located near rivers, where fuel and grazing for horses was in sufficient supply. The permanent settlements of the village tribes along the Missouri were located in areas which could easily be defended against attack and reinforced with palisades and ditches. A plaza in the center of these villages usually served as a dance and ceremonial area. Midway through November the inhabitants moved to winter villages in nearby woodlands where there was a plentiful supply of firewood and adequate protection from the cold. They did not move back to their summer villages until the end of February or the beginning of March.

There were major social and political differences between the Prairie and Plains peoples. Thus Prairie tribes featured social orders which were based on the

were 9 feet high at the center, 5 to 6½ feet high at the outer walls, and about 50 feet in diameter, thus providing enough space for a family of ten. Council and ceremonial lodges were large and could generally hold up to 100 people.

When the weather was bad a bison hide or a "bull boat" (a circular, lightweight willow-frame boat covered by a stretched bison hide) was attached to the smoke hole as protection against wind and rain. The roof was generally a popular place for people to congregate, and was therefore subject to great wear. However, regular repairs ensured that earth lodges could last for seven to

Karl Bodmer, *Interior of a Mandan Earth Lodge*, pen and ink with watercolor, 1833/34. Joslyn Art Museum, Omaha, NE.

In the center of every house was a fireplace, near which cooking utensils were kept. Backrests and hides provided residents and visitors with a warm place to sit. Beds were arranged along the outer circle of roof supports and next to the entrance there was a space for dogs, bull boats, gardening implements, and fuel. The interior of an earth lodge might also contain a sweat lodge and storage pits, and sometimes even stables for horses. The domestic shrine where sacred bundles were kept was situated at the rear of the house.

stability of permanent communities and favored the inheritance of offices within a family, whereas the way of life of the bison hunters in the Plains necessarily led to a high value being placed on individual achievement and social mobility. The forms of social and political structures therefore tended to be much more formalized and complex among the Prairie tribes than among those of the Plains.

Kinship was the dominant principle which gave cohesion to society. The kinship groups of the Prairie peoples were organized as clans, membership of which was inherited either through the maternal or the paternal line. Led by men of high status, clans performed important political and religious functions which complemented each other, thereby promoting the unity of both village and tribe. For example, clans regulated marriages, hunting and the cultivation of corn, and were also prominently involved in the ceremonial life of the community.

Every clan of the Siouan-speaking Osage in the southern Prairies had its own religious leader who participated in the village council together with the other clan leaders. Generally, religious leaders inherited their office from a close relative and their main task was to attend to the relations with other tribes and with supernatural forces. Only they could declare war and set the time for military action, since the success of war parties depended on the assistance of supernatural forces. The leader of a war party was nominated by the village council and had to perform certain rituals, he therefore had to be selected from among the clan leaders. Osage villages were divided into two halves (moieties) of approximately equal size, which took responsibility for peace and war, respectively. All clans belonged to one of the two moieties, the leaders of which came from among the group of clan leaders. They were responsible for maintaining harmony and prosperity, arbitrated in disputes, and led the bison hunts. At the tribal level, the tribal council, consisting of representatives from each clan, made all the important decisions.

Unlike the farming peoples, the bison hunters of the Plains were organized into local groups made up of families attached to a successful leader. Members of local groups regarded one another as relatives, though they were not always able to prove their genealogical kinship. It was not unusual for a family to leave its local group and join another.

The Cheyenne, for instance, were divided into ten politically independent local groups of some 300 members each, which only met in summer for the big hunts and ceremonies and went their own ways in the fall. The core of these local groups was made up of one or several groups of related families. The men who led these local groups commanded a great deal of respect, but had to prove their leadership constantly by achievements in the chase and in war, by generosity and by oratorical skills. If they were unable to fulfill the group's expectations, they would be replaced by another respected member of the tribe. They were primarily responsible for maintaining

peace and ensuring prosperity, sometimes by providing assistance to the less prosperous through gifts or hospitality. Furthermore, these leaders could become members of the tribal council or lead a men's society. In the tribal council, which was the real seat of power, members known as "peace chiefs" were elected to serve terms of approximately ten years. Their main task was to ensure the wellbeing of the tribe, and they also had to settle conflicts, conduct ceremonies, and in summer to maintain order in the camp and during the hunt. They were supported by men's societies which could use physical force to execute orders and whose leaders were responsible for war and foreign policy.

Since about 1860, the confinement to reservations has necessitated changes in housing, settlement structure, and social organization. Tipis and earth lodges have gradually been replaced by wooden log or frame houses, although tents are still popular summer residences. Despite massive cultural change, the kinship system, which ensures mutual assistance and cooperation, remains an important social signpost. The only officially recognized, albeit controversial, tribal governments are now the democratically elected tribal councils in which, since the 1980s, women have increasingly participated.

Reconstruction of a Wichita grass house, Anadarko, Oklahoma, 1976.

The construction of the grass houses of the Wichita and other southern Caddo was similar to that of earth lodges. A circle of roof supports was erected, over which rafters made of saplings were bent to form a slightly pointed dome. Smoke from the central hearth seeped out through the covering of grass. Like that of many types of buildings elsewhere, the design of the grass house, which had been a gift from the Creator, reflected the architecture of the cosmos.

Modern Blackfoot house, Starr, Montana, 1990.

When bison hunters were forced to give up their nomadic way of life, they began to live in American-style timber houses. These lightweight constructions are barely adequate to withstand the harsh winters in the northern Plains and are expensive to heat: the government does not subsidize the building of the much warmer log cabins, because it regards them as "substandard." Isolated houses are frequently still not connected to the water pipes or power lines. Compact settlements which were built to alleviate this problem are at risk of becoming rural slums.

Ponca woman holding a child on a cradleboard, c. 1900. National Anthropological Archives, Smithsonian Institution, Washington, DC.

Infants spent a major part of their first year in a carrier, which was usually made of a wooden frame fitted with a leather bag. Children were named shortly after birth and were often given the names by relatives, who were thus obliged to offer gifts to the child and its parents. Sometimes children were named after siblings who had been killed in war. These names were kept until a special occasion would justify the adoption of a new name.

# Man's worlds – woman's worlds

The stereotype of the "Indian," shaped by the indirect encounter with bison-hunting cultures through literature and the cinema, gives the impression that it was a man's world, a world in which women spent their lives in a menial position in the shadow of their men. This image is deceptive: as elsewhere in North America, the men

and women of the Plains and Prairie peoples fulfilled complementary roles which were valued equally in society. A woman's sphere of influence included childcare, gathering, preparing, and storing food, making clothing, tents, and implements, and transporting household goods when the camp was moved. Men were responsible for hunting, warfare, trade, and political matters. Because this meant that men would frequently be away from the community, women's importance in domestic and public life increased. By becoming members of women's societies, women could further enhance their social standing. At the same time, the reputation of their fathers, husbands, brothers, and sons also influenced their status.

The basis for the different lifestyles of the sexes was laid at an early stage. Adolescent boys were taught to ride and given the responsibility of looking after the horses. Fathers, uncles, and grandfathers made bows and arrows for them, taught them how to hunt, and encouraged them to kill small animals and birds, thus preparing them for their role as hunters and providers. By the age of about 13, boys took part in their first bison hunt. If a boy proved to be a successful hunter, his father would give a horse to a poorer member of the village or would organize a feast during which the child's success was publicly announced.

By the time they reached the age of 15, most young men could look back on their first experiences as warriors. Going on the warpath normally required prior visionary experiences, for which a young man would withdraw to an isolated spot where he fasted and prayed until a merciful supernatural being, usually in the form of animal, revealed itself. This guardian spirit would teach him a song, which the young man could use in the future to summon the supernatural, and would reveal to him the ingredients and preparation of a "medicine" whereby special powers were transferred to the visionary. The first vision left a particularly deep impression on a young man, because the transfer of knowledge and special powers did influence the rest of his life. If a young Lakota man dreamed of wapiti medicine, no woman would be able to withstand his amorous advances; if lightning featured in his vision, it was a sign that he was to become a sacred clown and had to behave contrary to every rule or even had to change his social gender. The songs and medicines obtained in visions provided protection in times of crisis, and Plains people also regarded them as decisive for their success in the hunt or in war. On his return from such a vision quest, a young man would seek out a religious specialist who would help him interpret his vision and prepare the medicine. Men sought visions especially prior to any important event for which they required supernatural assistance.

The education of girls was in the hands of their mothers, aunts, and grandmothers. Toys made for girls included dolls, cradleboards, and miniature tents, all of which prepared them for their future roles as mothers and housewives. The physical maturity of a young woman was closely connected to her social and ritual status. At their first menstruation, for instance, Lakota girls were taken to a separate tent where an older female relative would instruct them in their duties as future wives and mothers.

Cheyenne painted woman's robe, second half of the 19th century. San Diego Museum of Man, San Diego, CA.

In contrast to young men, Cheyenne girls were the subject of a ceremony in which the critical transition from childhood to adulthood was supported by instruction of the young women. The ceremony announced the girls' sexual and social maturity and thus their marriageability. After these ceremonies women were permitted to wear robes decorated with a pattern expressing the symbolic connection between the life-giving nature of women and bisons.

The social transition to womanhood occurred during a special ceremony at which prayers were said to White Buffalo Calf Woman, a mythical being of the Lakota, which included a request that the young woman be blessed with many children and that she be helped to lead a responsible and virtuous life. From that point onward she would retreat each month to the menstruation tent where she could relax and be taught by older women how to improve her artistic and craft skills. These rituals and menstruation taboos emphasized the great importance of such abilities as childbearing, and referred to the temporary power of women during menstruation which was incompatible with the power of men. For example, if menstruating women touched ritual objects or weapons, the objects would lose their supernatural power. Conversely, men were not permitted to enter the special tipis erected for childbirth until four days after the birth, as a precaution to ward off evil from mother and child.

Societies also served to teach and train young people. Among agricultural peoples older members of women's societies taught new members the numerous rules and methods required to cultivate the fields and for gardening; men's societies prepared young men for their roles as hunters, warriors, and politicians by organizing competitions and relating the myths which contained a society's secret knowledge about the world.

Marriage was commonly arranged by a couple's parents and sealed by an exchange of gifts or a celebration. A young couple's place of residence was determined by various factors, including the rules of descent. Where descent was reckoned through the father, as it was among the Blackfoot, a couple would generally move in with the groom's family. In other societies – for example, among the Crow, whose social order was organized along matrilineal lines – the young couple moved in with the bride's family. These rules were not immutable, however. For instance, among

Charles Deas, *Sioux Playing Ball*, oil on canvas, 1843. Thomas Gilcrease Institute of American History and Art, Tulsa, OK.

Games were also gender-specific. The Dakota's ball games were played by the men of different villages or by two teams selected from the same settlement. The women's version of the game was played with sticks that were bent at one end rather than the racket-like sticks of the men's game. The men's most popular game of chance involved guessing the arrangement of marked gaming sticks hidden inside a moccasin, whereas the women played dice with plum stones.

the Blackfoot, if the bride's father was a successful hunter, a young couple could also erect their tent near that of the bride's family. Most marriages were monogamous, although a man's marriage to several women was seen as desirable. It was only the wealthy men who could marry and feed several women; they in turn contributed to his wealth because they could process more hides, which could be traded for other goods. In order to avoid jealousy between co-wives, men would often marry sisters, so that existing family ties might prevent conflict arising between the women. Typically such marriages occurred between a man and his brother's widow (a levirate marriage) or between a man and his wife's widowed sister (a sororate marriage), thereby maintaining the link between families that had originally been forged by marriage.

Marriages could also be dissolved. If a woman wanted to divorce her husband, she could literally "show him the door" since she owned the tipi. She would pack up his personal possessions and leave his luggage by the entrance. When a husband came home he had no choice but to take his belongings and leave. The woman would usually move back to her family, who supported her until she eventually remarried. In the event of divorce, small and adolescent children generally stayed with their mother, whose authority within the household tended to be greater than her husband's.

Among some of the peoples of the Great Plains there was a third gender, the so-called berdaches. Among the

> "When white women get near the time in life when they will no longer have their moon [menopause], they get depressed and frightened. Many of them feel that their lives are over. In our way, I looked forward to that time when I didn't have to worry about getting pregnant, about caring all the time for young children. In our way, we look forward to it because it is the time when we can pursue other things full-time, become a medicine woman or [traditional] artist if it's our calling. Prior to that time, our powers of creation are too strong. Because we can make new people, our spiritual powers are greater than men's. After that time, we can hold the pipe, work with the sick, be a doctor if that is our calling."
>
> (Darlene Young Bear, Minneconjou Lakota)

Hidatsa, men who dressed and acted like women as a result of particular dreams were regarded as being holy. Among their ceremonial duties was the selection of the central post for the Sun Dance hut (the summer Sun Dance was the most important annual ceremony in the calendar of most of the region's peoples) and participation in all the important ceremonies of the Holy Women society. Berdaches generally lived with older men, worked in the gardens, ran households, and were thought to be particularly talented at women's crafts, in which they tried to outdo real women. They frequently adopted orphans or juvenile prisoners of war, and bequeathed to them their possessions and ceremonial knowledge.

Gender roles in the indigenous societies changed as a result of their contact with whites. In the early 19th century, the increasing importance of the fur trade caused a deterioration in the position of women. They had to produce more furs for trade, which only helped the men garner additional profits. On the other hand, the crisis caused by the collapse of the bison hunting culture, by the extermination of the bison herds, and by the end of the wars had its greatest effect on men, whose self-image suffered while women's lives were initially relatively unaffected. Women maintained their traditional roles as mothers and wives and their growing economic independence enhanced their social standing.

Men, however, still find themselves in a less secure position, with few job prospects on the unemployment-ridden reservations, and therefore unable to improve their status and sense of self-esteem. Women, by contrast, are much more likely to have a secure income because, in general, the government's welfare is more often paid to women as the effective heads of households. Because of their roles as mothers, women's ties to their homes and families tend to be stronger than those of their husbands. They have easier access to permanent, if badly paid, jobs in schools, in hospitals, and in the inflated administrations on the reservation. Because men are either looking for work or have to work outside the reservation, they are often obliged to stay away from their communities for long periods.

The Crow Berdache Finds Them and Kills Them, 1928. National Anthropological Archives, Smithsonian Institution, Washington, DC.

The berdaches among the Crow became transvestites not as a result of dreams, but by personal inclination. They were highly regarded, were thought to be talented craftsmen, and fulfilled the function of mediators between their community and the supernatural. Berdaches formed distinct social groups with their own leaders and generally did not have permanent relationships with men. White society refused to accept the lifestyle of the berdaches, who were singled out for particular pressure from agents, teachers, missionaries, and doctors.

# War – a matter of honor

Opposite page:
Mountain Chief (Blackfoot)
holding a horse effigy, 1913.
Photograph: Joseph K. Dixon.
National Anthropological Archives,
Smithsonian Institution,
Washington, DC.

Unlike the carved staffs made
to commemorate horses injured
or killed in war, the Blackfoot
used wooden effigies of horses
to distinguish successful horse
thieves. They were also used in
victory celebrations in order to
demonstrate dramatically horse-
theft as a strategic masterpiece.

War was a determining factor in the life and history of
the Plains and Prairie peoples. The mounted bison
hunters, who availed themselves of vast tracts of the
Great Plains during the 18th century, drove their
competitors from their traditional hunting grounds.
They regularly attacked and raided the corn farmers'
riverside villages. Yet only a century later, long before
the process of mutual displacement among the tribes
had come to an end, the hunters had themselves
become the prey and unsuccessfully attempted to stem
the flood of white settlers and resist the army that
protected them.

The importance of warfare to the bison hunters was
based not only on their initially aggressive and later
defensive struggle for the resources. Because of their
nomadic way of life, they could possess only modest
material wealth – except for the ownership of horses,
which represented a mobile form of capital. Since the
possibilities of transferring possessions and social status
to their offspring were limited, reputation and influence
depended mainly on individual success in the hunt and
especially on war deeds.

War was a matter of honor. A relative slain by enemy
warriors provided due cause, as did the theft of horses
and insults. Skirmishes were also possible on hunting
trips when members of different tribes pursued the same
bison herd. War was not, however, a continuous series of
pitched battles, but short, targeted raids – often at dawn –
when horses were stolen, women abducted, and enemies
killed or wounded.

Yet killing was not the primary aim: to touch an
enemy in battle was regarded as a far more honorable deed
because of the greater risk that it entailed. The warriors
generally withdrew as swiftly as they came. The revenge
of adversaries was fully expected, though many years
could pass before it occurred. Nevertheless, it was also
possible to settle conflicts by exchanging gifts with
the enemy.

Despite their apparently arbitrary nature, military
conflicts were in the long run also about control over
particular territories and their food resources, and could
lead to hereditary enmity between tribes. The Lakota,
who forcefully pushed into the northern Plains in the
18th century because they were themselves being
pressed hard by the better armed Ojibwa, were in almost
constant conflict with all their neighbors. Not until the
early 19th century did they establish a lasting peace
with the Cheyenne and Arapaho, while the Crow and
Pawnee remained their sworn enemies.

The fights against indigenous enemies were often
valued more highly than those against the white
Americans, even after the latter posed the far greater
danger. Other strategic alliances were forged in the
southern Plains. Thus the Kiowa, Kiowa-Apache, and
Comanche joined forces in order to fight their American,
Mexican, and indigenous enemies.

All the peoples of the region had a graded system of
war honors – personal achievements regarded as
extraordinary and thus publicly acknowledged. They
determined a man's place in society. The rank order
of honorable deeds varied from people to people. The
most important battle deed among the Blackfoot was
the capture of a rifle, while the theft of a horse was so
common that little value was attached to it. For the
Mandan, the greatest honor lay in tracking down a
single enemy, and killing and scalping him. However, the
Mandan view of this matter was exceptional, since
touching the enemy – the coup (the French word for
"blow") - generally earned the greatest renown because it
required the greatest courage to get within striking range
of the enemy.

Precise rules governed the evaluation of a coup or any
other war honor. The Omaha ranked honors on the basis

Horned bonnet of the Strong Hearts
warrior society owned by Opomika,
of the Hunkpapa Lakota, North or
South Dakota, before 1871. Museum
für Völkerkunde, Vienna, Austria.

Among the Plains peoples, as in many
other cultures around the world, horns
symbolized political or spiritual power.
Headdresses featuring whole or split
bison horns and a variety of trailers
were widespread in the 19th century
as the insignia of particular warrior
societies. Among the Lakota, horned
bonnets with frontlets of trimmed bird
quills and fitted with a leather or
fabric trailer and long leather fringes
identified the leaders of the Strong
Hearts, one of the warrior societies
that could perform policing duties
when ordered to do so by their
political leaders.

of whether the touched opponent was uninjured, wounded, or already dead. The Comanche permitted two, the Pawnee three, and the Lakota four warriors to "count coups" on the same enemy, with the first contact made earning the greatest honor. Coups could be made with the bare hand, with a weapon, or by using a specially prepared coup stick. After a fight, the warriors' possibly competing or contradictory claims were publicly discussed before a war deed was officially recognized as an honor. At least during the reservation period, when it became increasingly difficult to perform war deeds, war honors could even be bought among the Comanche.

Plains warriors documented each of their deeds of war by means of special insignia – such as a decorated feather, a particular face painting, or a conspicuous item of clothing – which were demonstratively exhibited on special occasions. Members or leaders of men's societies were entitled to wear other insignia such as feather head-dresses, horned bonnets, or roaches made of dyed deer hair. The headdresses symbolized the wearer's political influence, but they also held great spiritual power and were therefore carefully stored and looked after.

With the establishment of reservations, intertribal conflict came to an end and the headdresses lost their religious and military meaning. Feather headdresses, however, regarded as sacred by the Blackfoot, because according to their myth they had been the bison's gift to humans, became the universal symbols of "Indian" identity and spread far beyond the borders of the Plains and Prairies region. A historical tradition of the Oglala Lakota relates how their tribe's first feather headdress was acquired in 1797, when a warrior took it from a slain Blackfoot.

The public enumeration of war deeds during larger meetings, celebrations, and parades served to preserve the memory of the honors earned. Among the Crow, only those warriors who could prove that they had performed all four honorable deeds – a coup, the seizure of a rifle or bow, the theft of a tethered horse from an enemy camp, and organizing a war party – could become a respected leader or chief (*bacheeítche*, literally "good man").

A young Mandan returning from his first glorious war party with, for instance, a handsome booty of horses, was not only rewarded with a new name that reflected his experiences; his newly acquired social status and economic success also meant that he would suddenly be inundated with offers of marriage by the parents of unmarried girls.

War parties were usually small, since it was easier to feed small groups and detection by the enemy was more difficult. They were generally led by an experienced and well respected man who displayed clear leadership qualities, and who could be expected to be successful thanks to the strong war medicine that he had acquired in a vision. The decision to wage war was taken by him, and it was his powers of persuasion that ensured that sufficient volunteers joined him in battle. Since a primary consideration was to return from war without major losses, any bad omen, such as a

Depiction of war honors by White Swan (Crow), paining on muslin, c. 1890. Denver Art Museum, Denver, CO.

Pictorial records of their exploits were originally drawn by warriors on leather, but later also on paper or fabric. The hero is recognizable by his clothes or the pattern of his shield. White Swan (usually shown wearing a green shirt and a red feather) defends himself in a gun battle against three enemies and subsequently kills a fourth. Later he is seen reconnoitering a camp in his role as army scout; he is wounded, is taken away on a travois, and kills another enemy.

portentous dream, could cause the men to lose courage, so that the undertaking would have to be deferred. Among some peoples, war parties did not set off until a supernatural being had expressly announced a successful outcome in a dream or vision.

Scouts played an important role on the war path. If a party was in enemy territory, scouts would leave the group in order to reconnoiter the area. As it was always possible that enemies were in the vicinity, the scouts had to move with extreme care. Abandoned camp sites, the dead embers of a fire, footprints, and hoof marks were scrupulously examined. Such tell-tale signs enabled the scouts to assess the distance of hostile war parties and to inform their own side about the opponent's numerical strength. Scouts were highly respected, but were especially prone to fall victim to the enemy, while their comrades were able to withdraw in time.

Thorough planning and extensive preparations were required before a war party could set off: war songs and dances had to be performed and the power of the war medicine summoned. However, secular activities were also included in the preparations. Women made spare clothing and an extra pair of moccasins for their men. Nonperishable foods such as pemmican had to be carried in sufficient quantities as it was inadvisable to create additional tracks by hunting inside enemy territory. Ceremonial objects such as war pipes, which had to be taken along, had to be prepared by the "pipe keeper" and by other specialists. The custom of taking a war pipe into battle was based on the meaning ascribed to smoking: the ascending smoke was believed to transport the warriors' prayers to their guardian spirits, on whose protection the success of the undertaking depended. If a young warrior did not yet possess his own medicine, he would borrow one from an older successful man, who was then richly rewarded in return. Among the Blackfoot, a medicine or a replica of it could even permanently change ownership.

The leaders of local groups did not always condone the warlike activities of the young hotheads in their camps. If such was the case, they tried to prevent a war party from setting off, if necessary by calling on the camp police organized by the men's societies. For this reason, belligerent leaders and their followers would often steal out of the camp under cover of darkness.

For hand-to-hand combat – which could bring great honor and which was therefore consciously sought – warriors used clubs, the stone heads of which were attached with rawhide to wooden handles. In the more heavily forested west and north of the region, where wood was plentiful, clubs were entirely made of wood and either had ball-shaped heads or were shaped like gunstocks. Bows and arrows were carried around in leather

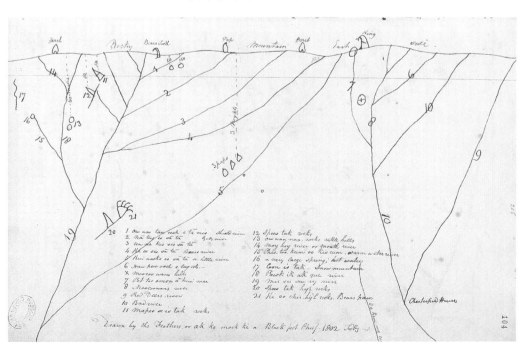

quivers and remained in use even after the introduction of firearms, since loading a rifle while on horseback was extremely difficult. When white traders first introduced muzzleloaders among some of the peoples, their advantage probably lay predominantly in the panic that was caused by their noise and the muzzle flash among peoples to whom firearms were still entirely alien. In general, rifles were status symbols for their owners with little practical usefulness. Not least, rifles were thought to possess spiritual powers beyond the effect of gunpowder and lead; in Lakota, for instance, a rifle is called *mazawakan*, which translates as "incomprehensible iron."

Women captured in war were generally accepted into the victorious group and became integrated into the community through marriage. Male prisoners, on the other hand, suffered quite a different fate and were frequently subjected to torture. Those who survived the torture then faced a bleak future as prisoners. The men were subjected to ridicule because they were forced to perform women's tasks, fetch water, and gather firewood. Very few prisoners ever escaped. Prisoners could also be adopted if, for instance, a couple had lost a grown son in battle and wished to mitigate the painful loss – especially from an economic point of view – by means of adoption.

Although war was, in the main, dominated by men, women could also enter battle alongside their husbands and brothers. In some areas, they were even permitted to count coup and to acquire war honors. Furthermore, the ceremonies of many women's societies directly concerned war, especially when they included dances performed in honor of returning warriors. Through visions, individual female members of some of these societies could even become authorized to make war medicine or to prepare shields for the warriors, thereby creating a clear link between the female and male spheres of power.

Since World War I, service in the United States army has been regarded by many descendants of the 19th-century mounted warriors as an opportunity to preserve the ancient ideals of valor and courage in a new era. Today Native Americans are proportionally over-represented in the armed forces, which may reflect the more favorable career opportunities linked with the military as well as a traditional sense of honor. Among some peoples this has even brought about the emergence of new societies (like the War Mothers of the Cheyenne), which honor returning soldiers with ceremonies and solemnly welcome them back into the community.

Crow shield cover depicting dragonflies, c. 1850–1880. Field Museum of Natural History, Chicago, IL.

Rawhide shields or their soft leather covers were often decorated with motifs based on visions. Among the Crow, up to four identical shields could be made and passed on to other warriors. The protection that this afforded was regarded as emanating from the supernatural power of the motifs rather than as inherent in the shield itself. Dragonflies were hard to catch and therefore widely used as a symbol of invulnerability.

Opposite page:
Ak Ko Mock Ki (Blackfoot), Map of the eastern side of the Rocky Mountains, 1802, from Peter Fidler's journal of exploration. Hudson's Bay Company Archives, Winnipeg, MB.

Maps drawn on the ground enabled scouts to transmit to the warriors who followed them their observations on the particularities of the landscape, campsites, or traveling times. Pictographic messages were also exchanged by warring groups to boast about their exploits in war or to enter into peace negotiations. Their excellent knowledge of the geography was reflected in the maps that they produced to help white people find their way.

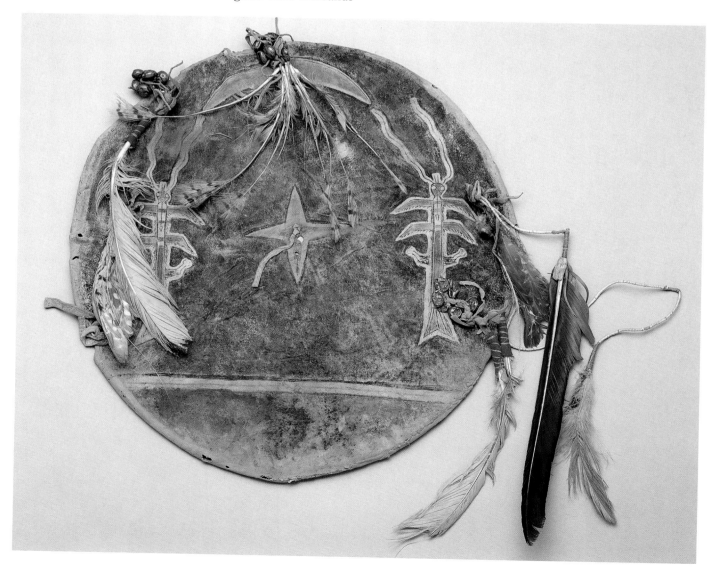

Karl Bodmer, *Dance of the Mandan Women of the Ptihp-tack-ochata Band,* 1883, from Prince Maximilian of Wied, *Reise in das Innere Nord America,* Koblenz, 1839–1841.

The ceremonies during which membership to the White Buffalo Cow Women was passed to the next generation took place in the late fall after the group had moved to their winter village. On payment of the transfer fee, the "mothers" prepared the equipment required by the society. The novices chose their future lead dancer, who wore a white buffalo robe and carried a bundle that helped to attract the animals.

# Dog Soldiers and Buffalo Cow Women

Many of the peoples of the Prairies and Plains were not only divided into local kinship groups and clans, but also had organizations termed "associations" or "societies." To be accepted into these societies, prospective members had to pass tests or perform certain deeds.

As warfare affected all aspects of what was an already insecure daily life, a system of men's societies, with responsibility for defending and ensuring the internal security of the villages, developed in the region of the Plains and Prairies. As military societies they prepared young men for armed conflict or assumed the role of a police force to ensure that hunting, the relocation of a camp, and the Sun Dance and other ceremonies ran smoothly, thus serving the entire community. Among the Plains peoples the public activities of these associations were restricted to the summer months, when people lived together in large groups.

Thus the associations, consisting of members of all constituent groups of the tribe, promoted the cohesion of the family groups, which were separated from one another for most of the year.

The men's societies of the Mandan, Hidatsa, Blackfoot, Arapaho, and Atsina, and the women's societies of the Mandan and Hidatsa, represented age groups. New members (usually on reaching sexual maturity) would join the lowest age group, that is, the youngest society and the lowest in the hierarchy. After about six years, they graduated to the next age group; ideally, therefore, they passed through every stage of their lives as members of a group of people of the same age.

Every age group had a particular name, and among all five of the peoples with age-grade societies, there were societies of young men whose members were known as "Dogs" or "Kitfoxes." The highest age group for men was the Buffalo Bull society, which consisted of older, highly respected men. Among the Mandan and Hidatsa, the highest age group for women was called "White Buffalo Cow Women."

Each age group had the right to perform particular dances and songs and to wear certain insignia particular to the group. The acquisition of rights from the next higher age group, to which the younger group aspired, required the payment of substantial admittance fees, in the form of horses or rifles, to their predecessors. This buying and selling primarily concerned the acquisition of non-material property, such as the ceremonial knowledge required to perform dances or songs that defined the social and religious position of the age group. Joint ownership of dances and songs and the society's name promoted the group's overall sense of solidarity, which was emphasized by the members' duty to stand by their fellows in times of crisis.

By contrast, the men's societies of the Crow, Lakota, Assiniboine, Cheyenne, Arikara, and Pawnee were not tied to age groups. Among the Crow, young men generally joined the association to which close clan relatives (such as the mother's brother) also belonged. When societies wished to fill a place left vacant by a deceased member, they could recruit new members, who were paid by the association for joining it. The Cheyenne men's societies, however, demanded an admittance fee in the form of horses or rifles. Although existing members could invite others to join, men normally decided to join the society to which their fathers had belonged and they would initiate

matters themselves. The Pawnee men's societies were of a primarily religious nature and were entrusted with keeping the tribe's most important sacred bundles which embodied the integrity of the entire nation.

The Blackfoot, Arapaho, and Atsina women's societies and the White Buffalo Cows of the Mandan and Hidatsa contributed to the successful outcome of hunting expeditions, and thus to the survival of the community, mainly by ritually attracting bison herds. To this purpose they performed masked dances during which they imitated the behavior and movements of the animals.

The women's societies' fertility rituals promoted the fecundity of animals, of wild plants and, among the agricultural Mandan and Hidatsa, of the fields. These women's societies and the men's highest-ranking age groups – the Buffalo Bulls – were closely linked, their social standing in the community was comparable, and they complemented each other since women lured bison cows and men lured bulls.

Central to the Lakota, Cheyenne, and Arapaho women's societies was the preservation of sacred knowledge pertaining to porcupine-quill or glass-bead work. A comparison with guilds of master craftsmen is not entirely inappropriate since this sacred knowledge included the secular technical expertise required for the production of these magnificent crafts as well as the deeper meanings attached to the various symbols and colors used. Other women's societies celebrated men's roles as warriors and organized ceremonies to honor the fighters.

With the demise of the bison hunt and of tribal wars, most societies lost their importance. However, new groups have emerged; women's groups that try to combat social problems such as employers' discrimination against women, sexual abuse, and drug and alcohol addiction, by invoking ancient values play an increasing role in the social life of many peoples today and derive themselves explicitly from the historical women's societies.

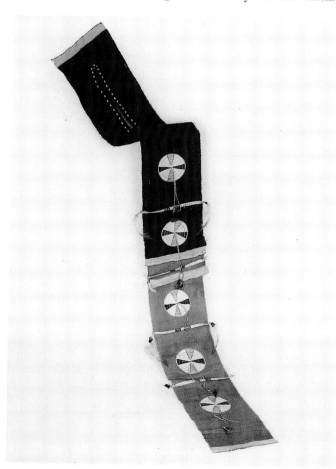

Samuel Seymour, *Dog Dance in a Kansa Indian Lodge*, 1819. Beinecke Rare Book and Manuscript Library, Yale University, New Haven, CT.

Among most Prairie and Plains peoples there were men's societies, like the Dogs or Kitfoxes. Their relative position within age-group systems could fluctuate enormously. If one age group did not sell its existing ownership rights when it purchased those of another group, it could acquire control over several societies; but the next group down could also acquire ownership rights of this society from another tribe or of an older age group. The rank order could also be affected when societies died out.

Sash of the Dog society, upper Missouri, c.1830. Ethnologisches Museum, Staatliche Museen zu Berlin – Preussischer Kulturbesitz, Berlin, Germany.

Societies competed to distinguish themselves in battle. Floor-length sashes formed part of the equipment and insignia of their courageous leaders. The hems of these sashes were staked to the ground in battle, thus making it impossible for the men to withdraw, and unless they were freed from this position by other warriors they could only leave the battlefield either victorious or dead.

# The mysterious in the world

Common to all the Prairie and Plains peoples was a belief in a supernatural, mysterious power that existed in the world and that could be experienced and used by humans. The Lakota, for example, called it *wakan* and the Crows *baaxpée*. Anything that the Lakota found difficult to understand – supernatural beings, powerful objects ("medicines"), and also infants, since they could not speak – they regarded as *wakan* ("sacred, incomprehensible, or supernatural"). *Wakan*, finally, were the powers that could be acquired by encountering supernatural beings in visions. The *baaxpée* of the Crow could also be acquired in dreams and visions and increased by ceremonial acts. *Baaxpée* could be transferred onto objects and thus passed on to other people.

Access to these powers was achieved through visions, which especially men attempted to secure by fasting and inflicting physical torments upon themselves in isolated places. Another way of obtaining supernatural powers was through spontaneous visions, for which no prior preparation was required. Naturally, this never occurred on days when nothing out of the ordinary happened. Spontaneous visions were generally triggered by crises like enemy attacks or the affliction of a close relative by a serious illness and required a large measure of experience in contacting the world of the supernatural. Such abilities were generally available only to older men and women or religious specialists, and earned them a great deal of respect from their fellows.

In the course of a vision instructions were received from one's guardian spirit on which medicine would have to be prepared in order to secure the spirits' assistance, power,

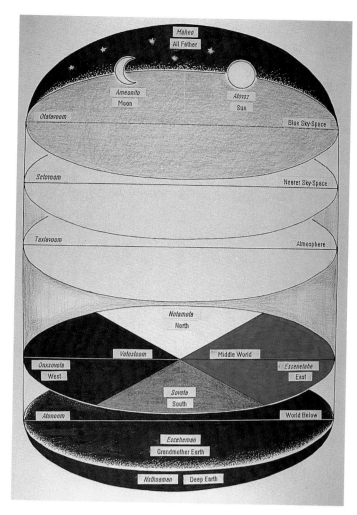

and protection. This personal medicine was kept as a bundle in special places inside the tipi or earth lodge, or carried in small pouches. In addition to these bundles expressing the personal relationship between their owners and the beings revealed in the vision, many peoples, local groups, villages, clans, or societies also had collectively owned bundles. These were usually derived from the encounter of the group's founder with a supernatural being. The myths and songs relating their creation contained the history of the people to which they referred and were passed on from generation to generation. Because of their great importance such bundles were kept and protected by highly respected individuals. Numerous duties befell those who held this office, which was often inherited within particular families. The myths and songs pertaining to the bundles had to be learned, and certain taboos and food restrictions observed. Yet the keepers of such bundles were generally happy to make these sacrifices as the temporary possession of the bundle made them highly regarded members of the community.

Religious specialists – predominantly men, more rarely women – had one or more spirit helpers with whose assistance they could perform extraordinary feats, including healing the sick, finding lost objects, and predicting future events. Their help was sought when an individual's own abilities were exhausted. These specialists formed a religious elite which also preserved the traditions and led the most important ceremonies.

Many Plains and Prairie peoples also had secret societies, made up of men, women, or both. These societies were not identical with the age groups found among some of the peoples. Their supernatural knowledge – for example, their medicinal expertise – was either inherited from close relatives or acquired through visions. The knowledge that they shared was kept secret from non-members. Secrecy was important since possession of this knowledge could entail status, influence, and economic advantages. When a patient was cured of an illness, members of the secret

society would be paid in the form of a meal, a bison hide, or even a horse.

Before a healing ceremony was held, the patient and healer would withdraw to a sweat lodge. Sweat lodges were especially constructed circular huts where water was poured over red hot stones in a central depression in the floor. The interior of the lodge rapidly filled with hot steam, which cleansed the whole person, including the soul. To increase sweating, the leader of the ceremony fanned the hot steam in the participants' direction. Even if the heat in the lodge became unbearable and the steam was hot enough to scald, lifting the mat which closed the entrance to allow fresh air to enter was not highly regarded.

Dried sagebrush placed on the hot stones filled the sweat lodge with a pleasant aroma that was considered sacred and an aid to communication with the spirit helpers. During the steam bath, guardian spirits were asked to assist in the healing ceremony that would follow. Sweating was also used as a ritual for cleansing and for spiritually purifying people before religious ceremonies or going on the war path. Healthy people also liked to enjoy regular steam baths after which they jumped into cold rivers to cool down.

Tobacco smoke was another means of communicating with the supernatural. Many Prairie and Plains peoples kept their own tobacco gardens, others made use of wild tobacco species or obtained the sacred tobacco in trade from other groups or from white people.

Pipes were often richly decorated with feathers and bird skins. They consisted of a wooden stem and a carved

bowl, usually made of red catlinite, most of which was taken from a quarry in Minnesota, a neutral place of asylum and peace that was accessible to all nations. Since tobacco smoking served as an invocation of supernatural beings, any major activity, such as the initiation of war or peace, was supported by its practice, whereby a pipe would be passed from mouth to mouth. This ritual linked the participants with the supernatural beings because their thoughts, words, and prayers were transported by the smoke to the beyond.

## Vault of heaven, death, and the hereafter

Although all the peoples of the Great Plains regarded humans, animals, and plants as parts of a whole, their ideas regarding the world and its origins diverged markedly. For instance, the Pawnees believe that the world resembled an earth lodge. The celestial vault was seen as resting above the earth, which was structured by its cardinal points, and was supported by four star deities which assisted the creator god Tirawahat in his protection of the Pawnee. On the other hand the Crow, like the majority of Plains peoples, had no real conception of a pantheon of separate, distinctively individual deities, and in their myths the same deities generally appear in different manifestations. Exceptions are Morning Star, Thunder (in eagle form), and Sun. Although many prayers and offerings were directed at Sun, most Crow regarded the mythical Coyote as the Creator, although they barely acknowledged him in their prayers and rituals.

Just as conceptions of the world differed, ideas regarding the soul and the realm of the dead also varied from people to people. Common to all Prairie and Plains peoples was the belief in an afterlife. Many peoples distinguished between free souls, which journeyed to the hereafter or the realm of the dead, and life souls, which were tied to the body and roamed the area near the funeral site as ghosts, and were thus greatly feared. On the Great Plains, people also yearned for a perfect world: they believed that life in the hereafter was like life on earth, though happier, more prosperous, and without hunger, danger, and sickness.

## New teachings – new hope

By the late 19th century the bison had largely been exterminated, land and freedom were lost and the great herds of horses owned by the once proud horsemen had been confiscated. The peoples of the Prairies and Plains experienced an existential crisis. Yet they clung to hope, and this was fertile ground for the emergence and spread of new religious movements.

After their final defeat in about 1875, the Kiowa and Comanche, who were resettled to a reservation in western Oklahoma in 1867, developed a religion at the center of which stood the communal ritual consumption of the peyote cactus. This consciousness-altering plant, which grows especially in northern Mexico where it has long been in ritual use by the Huichol, Tarahumara, and Cora, was thought to possess divine properties and the capacity to cure the sick. The new religion rapidly spread across the Great Plains, its success partly explained by its similarities

to the earlier vision quests. In many places, Christian elements, including the belief in a Great Spirit and its equation with God or Jesus, were absorbed into the Peyote religion. The Christian churches, followers of traditional religions, and the government, all decisively rejected the new religion. In 1918, the adherents of the Peyote religion founded the Native American Church in order to be recognized as a church organization. This church is now the largest Panindian religious community in North America. Use of the peyote cactus, which is classed as a controlled substance under narcotics laws, is legal only within the context of their ceremonies.

A messianic movement that promised salvation and came to have a lasting influence on the fate of the Plains peoples, particularly the Lakota, was the Ghost Dance. This was rooted in the Prophet Dance of the Plateau region, a world-renewal cult, which had reached the peak of its popularity in the Great Basin and California around 1870.

Following a vision received in 1889, the Paiute prophet Wovoka announced an imminent reunion with the ancestors which could be achieved by dancing and peaceful coexistence with the whites. Wovoka was soon visited by representatives of numerous Plains peoples who derived hope from his teachings. However, some of the desperate Plains peoples interpreted his message as a proclamation of the end of white supremacy and a call to resistance. Wovoka's original dance was transformed by the Plains tribes into a Ghost Dance during which participants went into states of trance and saw their relatives in the hereafter in the company of the Messiah. The hope for a world renewal, a disappearance of the whites, for the resurrection of the dead, and for a return of the bison came to a swift end in the terrible bloodbath of Wounded Knee perpetrated by the United States army in the winter of 1890 to suppress the religious movement that was regarded as dangerous.

Today the coexistence of traditional and Christian religions is frequently encountered on the reservations as a result of culture change. Approximately 90 percent of the Lakotas now belong to official Christian churches, while combining to varying degrees their Christianity with traditional religous practices and the Peyote religion.

*Ani'qu ne'chawu'nani'* –
Father, have pity on me,
*Ani'qu ne'chawu'nani'* –
Father, have pity on me;
*Awa'wa biqāna'kaye'na* –
I am crying for thirst,
*Awa'wa biqāna'kaye'na* –
I am crying for thirst;
*Iyahu'h ni'bithi'ti* –
All is gone – I have nothing to eat,
*Iyahu'h ni'bithi'ti.* –
All is gone – I have nothing to eat.

(Arapaho Ghost Dance song)

Arapaho Ghost Dance shirt, c. 1890. Kansas City Museum of History and Science, Kansas City, MO.

The Ghost Dancers of the Plains wore ceremonial shirts and dresses made of buckskin or white muslin and decorated with geometric or naturalistic designs which referred to the renewal of the world or were meant to protect wearers from the bullets of their white oppressors. Among the Lakota, these shirts and dresses were exact copies of the clothes of the deceased friends or relatives who appeared to them in their visions.

Karl Bodmer, *Mandan Dog Sled*, watercolor, 1834. Joslyn Art Museum, Omaha, NE.

Dogs have been kept as domestic and useful animals for over 7,000 years in North America, where they were used for hunting or to transport loads and, in some areas, even as food. Local breeds resemble both the wolf and the coyote, from which they have descended. Among the Hidatsa they are regarded as a gift from Yellow Dog, the son of a Hidatsa woman and a mythical wolf, whose "medicine" was the first dog. The howling and barking of dogs was thought to be directed at Yellow Dog, who retired to the sky after his death.

# First Man and the Okipa ceremony of the Mandan

Around the middle of the 18th century, French traders first reported encountering Siouan-speaking Mandan in several villages along the upper Missouri near the mouth of the Heart River. After epidemics caused a drastic reduction of their population in the late 18th and early 19th centuries, the remaining Mandan established the village of Like-a-Fishhook together with the two other village tribes of the region, the Siouan-speaking Hidatsa and the Caddan-speaking Arikara. For a while, part of their ceremonial life was kept alive, although population decline induced some changes. The Hidatsa helped the Mandan to perform their ceremonies, but overall control remained with the Mandan. With the disappearance of the bison and in the wake of United States policy designed to eliminate the cultural heritage of the tribes, the ceremonies began to lose their importance in the late 19th century.

The religious aspirations of the Mandan were centered on the acquisition of supernatural powers through the vision quest, self-torture, or the ritual transfer of such power, and its preservation in medicine bundles belonging to individuals, the tribe, clans, or societies. Unlike personal bundles, which tended to be made as the result of visions, collective bundles and related secret rituals had mythical origins. Oral traditions explained the creation of the bundles and told how the sacred objects had been transferred by mythical beings to certain Mandan, such as the founders of clans.

To maintain the powers that were received from supernatural beings, renewal rites were required, because over time the powers were gradually decreasing through use, and thus had to be recharged, so to speak. In a ceremony at which, in the case of a clan bundle, only senior members of the respective clan and the keeper of the bundle were permitted to be present, the bundle was opened, the relevant myths were retold, and the supernatural beings awakened through prayer and asked for protection and assistance in order to renew the power of the bundle.

If a person present wished to have a share in this power and if the owner of the bundle was willing to sell, a bundle could be purchased. Naturally, the transfers of a bundle and the associated knowledge of myths, songs and rituals related to it could only occur in exchange for appropriate remuneration and within a strictly ceremonial context. Since the compensation in the form of horses or bison hides was extremely high, the bundles tended to be the property of families which had large herds of horses. Families which owned tribal as well as clan bundles were among the most wealthy and had a particularly high status in society.

The Mandan's most important annual event was the Okipa ceremony which revolved around the tribal Okipa bundle. It took place during the summer and was designed to secure good hunting, prosperity, and the transmission of Mandan oral traditions to the next generation.

At the center of the ceremony was the dramatic reenactment of the creation of the world. First Creator created the world and all its peoples. He covered the whole earth, except for a small hill, with water. As he walked along the water he met First Man (Númank Máxana). Then the two of them met a pair of ducks that at their request dived into the water and collected a small amount of dirt from the bottom of the sea. First Creator used some of it to make the south of the earth, and First Man used the rest to make the north. First Creator created human beings, bison, and streams on his side, while First Man created wapiti and lakes on his. One day, First Man met a bison bull who taught him how to cultivate tobacco. In order to thank him, First Man decided that human beings would have to dedicate special ceremonies to the bison. First Creator and First Man visited the Mandan in their village and acquainted them with the Bison Dance and the Okipa ceremony, which they were to perform whenever they lacked meat. One day, four medicine men who were angered by the way that some younger Mandan had maltreated bison calves sent a great flood. The Mandan asked First Man for help. He built a dam that saved the Mandan from the flood.

Another dramatic event of the creation myth was the quarrel between Spotted Eagle (Hoita) and First Man which resulted in Spotted Eagle locking all the animals into a hill in his fury. First Man released the animals and thereby saved the Mandan from starvation.

George Catlin, *Interior View of the Medicine Lodge, Mandan O-kee-pa Ceremony*, oil on canvas, after 1832. National Museum of American Art, Washington, DC.

The pale light entering the earth lodge through the smoke hole illuminates the beginning of the Okipa ceremony. The impersonator of Spotted Eagle is seated in the center, close to the fireplace, and recites prayers in front of an altar made of human and bison skulls and a scaffold on which various ceremonial objects are kept. Sacred turtle drums are positioned in the foreground to the left and right of the hearth. The young men who have prepared themselves for their self-torture by fasting sit largely naked along the wall on which shields, weapons, and medicine bundles are hung.

The performance of the myths, songs, and rituals pertaining to the bundles was a prerogative of religious leaders who acquired their secret knowledge by inheritance or by purchase.

The Okipa ceremony took place in a ceremonial lodge near the village plaza, which could be distinguished from other buildings by its flat entrance area. It represented the mythical mountain in which Spotted Eagle had once imprisoned the animals until they were released by First Man. The family of a high-ranking member of the clan to which, according to tradition, First Man had once belonged, normally inhabited the lodge, but left it for the duration of the ceremony. The owner of the earth lodge was charged with taking care of the ceremonial objects required for the Okipa during the rest of the year.

A post painted red that stood in the village plaza symbolized the body of First Man as well as that of all deceased Mandan. It was surrounded by boards, the Ark of First Man, to commemorate the dam that was erected by the culture hero in order to protect the Mandan's ancestors against the impending flood.

First Man and Spotted Eagle, who directed the ceremony in the ceremonial house, were incarnated by the keepers of the bundles of the same name; all other representatives of mythical beings were selected by the guardians of the respective bundles. This included, among others, the actors of eight bison bulls, to whom bisons had to appear in a vision prior to the Okipa, the players of two eagles, two female mythical figures, swans, snakes, hawks, black bears, grizzlies, beavers, and wolves as well as the mythical figures of First Creator and Foolish One.

Since women were not permitted to enter the ceremonial house, men also played the parts of female figures. Eight singers were also among the active participants. Every Mandan village contained everything required to stage the Okipa (a ceremonial lodge, a First Man clan, the Ark singers, and bundles); only the turtle drums once given to the Mandan by First Creator and First Man were tribal property, kept in one village, and loaned to other villages when required. Each Okipa was organized by a man who was instructed to do so in a vision. Since he had to present the ceremonial leaders, who were regarded as teachers, with gifts in return for their ritual teachings, wealth was an important precondition for the performance of this duty. He, together with the keepers of the First Man and Hoita bundles, the eight singers and all previous organizers of the ceremony together formed the so-called Okipa society.

The ceremony was opened by the owner of the First Man bundle. In the presence of all the ceremonial leaders he related the creation story in a special ritual language, which was understood only by the initiated. With his costume and the ceremonial objects from the First Man bundle he brought back to life such mythical events as the threatening flood and the adventures of First Man.

Young men were encouraged to fast during the four days of ceremony, because visions experienced during the Okipa ceremony were thought to be particularly plentiful and desirable. Recognizable as embodiments of bison by their bison headdresses, the young men and the Okipa Maker (the organizer of the ceremony) moved to the Ark where prayers were said to First Man and where he was asked for his continued assistance, for good hunting, and for well-being.

During the course of the four-day ceremonial, the buffalo dancers' appearances became increasingly frequent: on the first day they danced only four times, on the last day 16 times. During the second and third days, the number of dancers incarnating the mythical beings also progressively increased. They streamed out of the ceremonial lodge like the animals kept in captivity by Hoita in the myth. This was concluded by a simulated bison hunt in which four bison dancers were symbolically "killed" by hunters.

The acts of self-torture performed by men, particularly during the second and fourth days, were similar to those performed by the Sun Dancers of other peoples. Participants drew wooden skewers through the skin of their backs and chests to which they attached straps connected to the central framework of the earth lodge. The dancers then had to free themselves of the straps by leaning further and further back until the flesh gave way. The last Okipa ceremony took place in 1890 after the United States government imposed a ban on its performance.

Today most Mandan live together with the Hidatsa and Arikara on the Fort Berthold Reservation in North Dakota. In the 1950s vast tracts of the reservation were flooded after the construction of a dam. The flood which played such an important role in Mandan mythology, now became a reality for them. At the place, where formerly had stood the village shrine of the Mandan village Ruhptare, there is now another, temporal source of power - a hydroelectric power plant.

Naming ceremony at a Pawnee earth lodge village, Loup Fork, Nebraska, 1871. National Anthropological Archives, Smithsonian Institution, Washington, DC.

Among the Pawnee names were the codified expression of personal goals and achievements, the meaning of which remained incomprehensible to outsiders. Names were announced during a public ceremony, but never used in daily life. A Pawnee priest explained that "the people who desire to have a name, or to change their name, must strive to overtake in the walk of life an upper level, such a one as these ancient men spoken of in the [name changing] rituals had reached, where they threw away the names by which they had been known before (to achieve something new and elevated)."

# The morning star sacrifice

From the 17th century onward the Caddoan-speaking Pawnee inhabited their earth lodge settlements in the Platte River region of Nebraska, grew corn, and hunted bison. Four groups (the Skidí, Chauí, Kit'kaháxki, and Pítahauírata) formed independent political units, which regarded themselves as linked by virtue of their common use of the Caddo language, albeit in slightly divergent dialects, and their similar cultures.

The Pawnee originally had a complex social, political, and religious organization which can best be reconstructed on the basis of historical and ethnological records concerning the Skidí. Their system of organization was based on several sacred bundles owned either by the village or the tribe and the associated ceremonies, which were dedicated mainly to the fertility of their cornfields and success in the hunt, but also in war. The bundles, in which the powers of the sky were united, were thought of as gifts from the star deities to mankind. They were kept by political leaders and entrusted to the safekeeping of their wives. Bundle ceremonies were the responsibility of the priests, who were specially trained to perform these rituals.

One of the rituals involved a sacrifice to the morning star, the origin of which is contained in the creation myth: the creator god Tirawahat had instructed the male Morning Star to beget the first human being by the female Evening Star. Evening Star tried in vain to prevent it, and gave birth to a daughter. Her defeat put an end to Evening Star's claim to power and, as a sign of male supremacy, Morning Star demanded the periodic sacrifice of a girl. From time to time he would appear to a warrior in a vision and order him to capture a girl of about 13 years of age from an enemy camp. The search for a victim was embedded in extensive ceremonies that the visionary had to learn from the keeper of the Morning Star bundle.

The sacrifice itself did not take place until the spring following the capture of a girl. Until that time, the keeper of the Wolf Star bundle (the wolf represented death and the renewal of the world in the spring) looked after the girl, who was dressed in clothes taken from the Morning Star bundle and was treated with the greatest consideration: it was hoped that her submission to the sacrifice would be voluntary.

Petalesharo (Pawnee), color
lithograph after a painting by
Charles Bird King, from T. L.
McKenney and J. Hall, *The
Indian Tribes of North America*,
Philadelphia, PA 1836

When the first reports of the
Pawnee's human sacrifices
reached the American East
Coast, they appeared to confirm
the worst fears about the barbarism
of the indigenous population.
Thus, when in 1821 the young
Skidí warrior and chief's son
Petalesharo, who had risked
his life in 1817 in preventing
the sacrifice of a Comanche
girl and generally wished to
abolish the practice of human
sacrifice by his tribe, visited
Washington, he was received
with great enthusiasm.

The appearance of the morning star (Venus) in the sky
with a red halo was the sign for the ceremony to begin in
the visionary's earth lodge, during which the keepers of
bundles represented the star deities associated with their
respective bundles. Following dances, songs and prayers, a
scaffold was made out of four different kinds of timber, each
of which represented a different cardinal point – northwest,
southwest, northeast, and southeast – as well as a sacred
animal and its power.

On the fourth day of the ceremony the girl was given
new clothes to wear for her last role, and the right side of
her body was painted red like Morning Star while her left
side was painted black like Evening Star. All male villagers
then took part in the subsequent procession to the place of
sacrifice. There, the girl climbed onto the scaffold and was
tied to it. Then the keeper of the southeast bundle touched
her with a burning rod, and finally she was killed by the
keeper of the northwest bundle who shot an arrow through
her heart.

After the keeper of the northeast bundle had made a
cut above the girl's heart and smeared his face with her
blood, the keeper of the southwest bundle and the other
participants shot arrows into the girl's body. The girl's
blood was dripped onto bison meat, a ritual for securing
future hunting success. Now the village was filled with joy:
exuberant dances and an exceptional sexual permissiveness
symbolized fertility and the hope for a good harvest and for
successful hunting. Now Morning Star would assist the
people in both war and in peace; fertility and the renewal of
life were now assured.

*Petalesharo*

In the early 19th century some people among the
Pawnee began to voice the opinion that the human
sacrifice should be abolished. Despite such growing
opposition, the priests maintained that the morning star
sacrifice was necessary to ensure the continued existence
of the Skidí. The last known case occurred in 1838,
shortly after the outbreak of a smallpox epidemic which
the priests interpreted as Morning Star's warning that
the bloody custom must continue. Yet even the sacrifice
was unable to prevent the devastating epidemic from
running its course.

A comparable ceremony in which a boy was sacrificed
(according to myth, the first boy resulted from a conflict
between the sun and the moon) and which was closely
connected to the cultivation of corn is known only
through oral tradition and was probably abandoned
before the arrival of the Europeans.

Frame for offering to the morning star, engraved silver, 1821. Nebraska State
Historical Society, Lincoln, NE.

The reverse of a medal awarded to Petalesharo for his brave intervention against
human sacrifice bears the only known depiction of the sacrificial scaffold used
by the Pawnee. It corresponds exactly to the sacrificial scaffolds for the arrow
sacrifice of ancient Mexico known from Mixtec pictorial manuscripts, and from
archeological finds at the prehistoric site of Spiro in Oklahoma. The obverse
shows Petalesharo with the Comanche girl and bears the inscription, "To the
Bravest of the Brave."

# "Great Sun Power!
# I give you my life today"

Ceremony of erecting the Sun Dance Lodge, Piegan Reserve, c. 1910. Provincial Archives of Alberta, Edmonton, AB.

The central post of the Sun Dance lodge was especially important. A group of men were instructed to fell a tree, which they attacked as if it were an enemy while reciting war deeds. The raising of the post at the ceremonial site was accompanied by the same songs as those chanted on arrival at an enemy camp. Offerings of cloth and children's clothes were draped on the post, and like the prayers directed at the sun promised good fortune.

The Blackfoot (whose self-designation is Nitsitapi, "real people"), a loose confederation of Siksika ("black-footed"), Piegan (Pekani), and Blood (Kainah), are the westernmost members of the Algonquian language family and the largest people of the northern Plains. In the early 18th century they were already encountered by white people as bison hunters near the northern reaches of the Saskatchewan River, where they may have lived for some time previously. In the 19th century large parts of Alberta and Montana formed part of their territory, which was gradually reduced to the four current, non-contiguous reservations in the United States and Canada.

As for most other Plains peoples, the Sun Dance was the Blackfoot's most significant collective ritual of the year,

during which almost all important dignitaries (such as the bundle keepers) and organizations (especially the societies) had specific ceremonial functions. Unlike most bundle ceremonies, which were dedicated to the welfare of their owners, the Sun Dance served the good of the entire tribe. It differed from the Sun Dances of other peoples in that it was organized by a woman who during a period of crisis, such as a serious illness, had vowed to act as the medicine woman during the next Sun Dance. She carried full responsibility for the ceremony's success and she and her family were obliged to provide extensive services such as supplying food and drink for the numerous participants. A woman could only become a medicine woman if she led a virtuous life, which particularly entailed fidelity to her

husband. She also had to be wealthy since she needed to purchase the Natósi ("medicine man") bundle from the previous owner, which contained the headdress which medicine women had to wear during the Sun Dance. In addition to the sacred headdress, the medicine woman wore a bison robe, a dress made of wapiti leather, and bracelets made from wapiti teeth. The robe was decorated with symbolic representations of the moth, mediator between the powers of the sky and mankind, and the morning star, the source of power and protection. The robe was thus an impressive depiction of the close links that existed between supernatural power and the way in which it could be conveyed.

The medicine woman and her husband, who acted as her assistant in the rituals, shared the prestige that she earned by making her sacrifice for the good of the community.

At the beginning of summer, the future medicine woman and her husband invited all the local groups to a camp, in the vicinity of which people gathered in early June for a communal bison hunt. The ceremony began with a fast by the medicine woman and with the erection of a sweat lodge. After that, the camp was moved three times before reaching the predetermined place where the ceremony was to take place.

On the fifth day of the Sun Dance, in the fourth camp, the opening and ceremonial transfer of the Natósi bundle took place, and the ceremonial lodge was constructed. The fifth day was thus the climax of the Sun Dance. Since rain would have disturbed the ceremony, ritual dances were performed by people who in visions had acquired the ability to control the weather, and who now asked the sun to contribute to the success of the ceremony. The right to perform as a weather dancer had to be purchased from previous holders of this special office. Usually, however, it remained with the same people for several years before they passed it on to other interested parties.

Self-torture was another feature of the fifth day and was conducted in the ceremonial lodge. By comparison with other peoples, such as the Lakota, this physical sacrifice played a lesser role among the Blackfoot. It was always preceded by a vow of endurance should the prayers directed to the sun be heard. Young men in particular liked to subject themselves to the torment in order to improve their social standing.

After the young men had completed a period of fasting in preparation for the ceremony, small wooden skewers attached by straps to the central post of the sun lodge were inserted through the skin on their chests. The dancers

Victor Pepion, *Sun Dance*, tempera, 1956. Department of the Interior, Indian Arts and Crafts Board, Washington, DC.

According to reports, the practice of self-torture was introduced by young warriors who had participated in an Arapaho Sun Dance and who therefore regarded themselves as having acquired the rights to this ceremony. Usually, small wooden skewers were inserted through the skin of the chest and were attached by straps to the central post. After embracing the central post and praying to the sun, the young men danced away from the post and repeatedly leaned further and further backward until the skin tore and they were freed.

prayed to the sun, and danced for many hours, moving toward the post and back again, pulling with their entire weight against the straps as they retreated, thus stretching the skin further and further until it finally gave way, tearing and freeing the dancers.

Triggered by hunger, thirst, and pain, some participants experienced visions during the dance while others retreated to a place where they could be alone. Small pieces of the flesh torn out during the torture were offered as sacrifices to the sun. The dancers, whose physical sacrifice caused the supernatural powers to be merciful, thus provided the assurance for the security and survival of the entire group.

On the following days, the men's societies and, among the Blood the Mátoki women's society as well, appeared and performed their own rituals, which concluded with the sacrificial offering to the sun of such ritual objects as rattles, fans, and embroidered leather bags, which were tied to the central post. Now the societies had to provide everyone present with food and drink. The medicine woman and her husband participated in all these rituals, although they had already handed over the direction of the Sun Dance to the officers of the societies. On the eighth day the Sun Dance ceremony was over and the camp was struck.

Although the United States government banned the Sun Dance in 1881 because of the bloody sacrifice, it continued to be widely performed in secret. The ban no longer exists nowadays and like many other Plains peoples the Blackfoot have succeeded in keeping their Sun Dance tradition alive. The ceremonies are still being held, although no longer every year.

Blackfoot (Blood) painted parfleche, c. 1885. University of Pennsylvania Museum, Philadelphia, PA.

"Parfleche" is a broad term for the various rawhide containers made and decorated by women and used across the entire region of the Prairies and Plains. More specifically it refers to the folded bags used to keep and transport clothing or food. The word derives from French (*parer*, to parry, and *flèche*, arrow) and refers to the earlier use of rawhide to make shields.

"Great Sun Power! I give you my life today, because I have always been a pure and honest woman. I promise now to eat with you and with the Underground Spirits, that my grandchild may recover. I am praying also for these children standing before you, that they may grow and be strong, that they may have long life and may never suffer from hunger. Hear us and pity us!"

(Sundance prayer by Awasaki for her grandchild, c. 1900)

# Seven in a circle

In its broadest sense, Sioux is the name given to the largest language group of North America's Great Plains, to which numerous peoples other than the Sioux belong. The word also refers to a people, the "real Sioux," who comprise seven independent groups and whose members speak three different dialects. The Teton, the westernmost of the groups, speak the Lakota dialect, the Yankton and Yanktonais speak the Nakota dialect, and the Mdewakanton, Wahpeton, Sisseton, and Wahpekute speak Dakota. It is centuries since the Sioux lived and hunted together in the forests of the Eastern Woodlands, and yet they speak of themselves as the people of the "seven council fires" (*oceti šakowin*), which – if one were to think of them in spatial terms – were ordered as in a camp circle. In the 19th century the place of honor on the western side of this circle was taken by the Lakota-speaking Teton; previously, when they all still lived together, this place was reserved for the Mdewakanton, one of the Dakota-speaking tribes.

The Teton came to the Plains to hunt bison in the 18th century, and they fought as allies of the Cheyenne for their position between the Black Hills and the upper Missouri, which was ideal for hunting bison and as a base from which to launch raids on their neighbors. The Teton had long been far too numerous to be able to function as a tribe, but

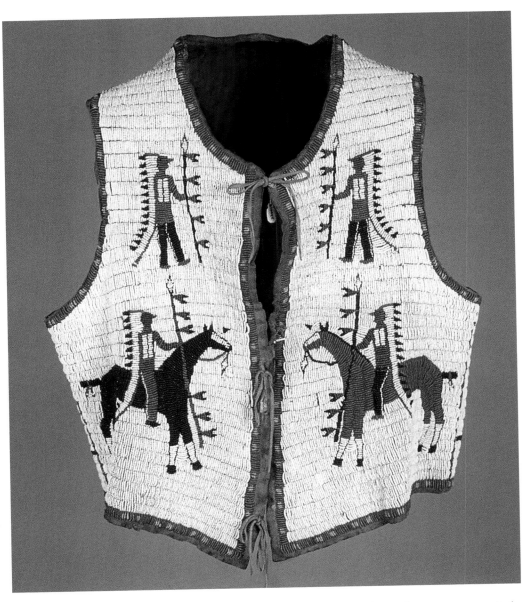

Lakota man's waistcoat with glass bead decoration, c. 1890. Haffenreffer Museum of Anthropology, Bristol, RI.

Glass beads were purchased from traders and represented wealth. beadwork took time, although it was not quite as time-consuming as the earlier practice of using porcupine quills. Waistcoats covered with beaded decorations therefore demonstrated both the wearer's wealth and the industriousness of his wife (or wives). The depictions of warriors in full ceremonial dress follow the style of drawings made by men to commemorate their war deeds.

Lakota doll, buckskin and bead appliqué, c. 1890. Plains Indian Museum, Cody, WY.

Mothers made dolls dressed in minute copies of traditional dress for their children – and, since the establishment of reservations, for white customers. Here the 19th-century form of breastplate made from industrially manufactured bone beads is imitated by porcupine quills. The dolls served to prepare children for their adult lives through role play, and to remind white people of the rapidly disappearing "savageness" of their Native American neighbors.

they too continued to think of themselves as a camp circle consisting of seven autonomous divisions: the Oglala were the protectors of the Black Hills, where according to myth the Lakota had originated, and thus were allocated the western place of honor opposite the camp circle's opening in the east; the Hunkpapas and Sihapsas were situated to either side of the opening; and the Sicangu, Itazipco, Minneconjou, and Oohenonpa filled the spaces in between. Ideally, each division in turn consisted of seven independent tipi divisions (*tiospaye*), which themselves were made up of several camps.

Early contact with white traders was generally peaceful, and familiarized the Lakota with the white man's goods which people were beginning to rely on. When in the 1840s settlers and gold diggers passed through the land of the Lakota on their way to Oregon and California, conflicts flared up and, to protect the settlers, the army established a garrison in Fort Laramie in 1849; this former fur-trading post was the first of many strongholds in the area.

This development disturbed the Lakota as much as did the decline of their game animals and the increasingly frequent epidemics, especially measles and smallpox, which they were powerless to avert. The Fort Laramie treaty (1851) promised them goods and services valued at $50,000

in return for allowing settlers unhindered passage through their land. However, not all constituent tribes and tipi divisions were informed of this agreement or indeed felt themselves bound by it. Many regarded the American-backed nomination of Conquering Bear, a Sicangu, as "Chief of all Lakota" as equally meaningless because it contradicted the Lakota's political system, in which this kind of central leadership was unknown. The government, however, was looking for cooperative leaders with whose assistance successful agreements could be reached.

The violence escalated on both sides, reaching a climax with the Sioux wars of the 1860s, when Red Cloud, of the Oglala, and Sitting Bull, of the Hunkpapa, achieved partial success against the army. In 1868 the end of the fighting seemed to have come with the Fort Laramie peace treaty, which Red Cloud could celebrate as a victory. The terms of the treaty created a large reservation within which the army had to relinquish all its forts. However, in 1874, gold was discovered in the Black Hills, and the Lakota's insistence that their borders should be respected fell on deaf ears. In 1875 the treaty-breaking government decided to sever the Black Hills from the reservation and ordered the Lakota to leave their western hunting grounds by the end of January 1876 and to withdraw to the remaining reservation land. A faction of the Lakota, led by Sitting Bull (who refused to accept the treaty of 1868 in any case) and Crazy Horse, refused to obey this order from the government. On June 25, 1876, while attempting to drive the unwilling Lakota back onto the reservation, the army suffered a disastrous defeat at the Little Bighorn, although it ultimately succeeded in achieving its goal. In 1877 Sitting Bull and his followers fled to Canada, and Crazy Horse was stabbed to death on the reservation by another Lakota.

On the reservation the Lakota depended on government food rations and were subjected to a rigorous program of "civilization": men were taught agricultural skills and children were sent off to boarding schools. Despite continuing resistance, the government finally managed to break up the Great Sioux Reservation and to begin with the allotment of the land in severalty.

The Lakota still regard the Black Hills as sacred land and themselves as their guardians, so that the Black Hills are an important point of reference for their cultural identity. Their exclusive use rights, granted to them by the treaty of 1868, continues to be the object of a dispute between them and the United States government.

Although in 1980 the courts recognized that the annexation of the Black Hills was a gross infringement of law, they merely awarded the Lakota compensation of $17.6 million plus interest which, with the addition of 105 years worth of interest, produced a very large sum of money indeed. Despite the poverty on the reservation, the various Lakota's tribal councils decided not to touch the money and to insist on the return of the Black Hills. Thus the Sioux wars of the 19th century still have not come to an end.

The Big Foot Ride in South Dakota, 1990.

In 1973, when the radical American Indian Movement occupied the site, a new dimension was added to the trauma experienced in 1890 at Wounded Knee, when the United States army massacred the predominantly unarmed Lakota led by the Minneconjou chief Big Foot. What was planned as a media-friendly confrontation with the army became a protracted civil war on the reservation. A commemorative ride on the 100th anniversary of the massacre organized by victims of the civil war was to contribute to overcoming a painful past.

# The death of Sitting Bull

Christian F. Feest

Before the break of dawn, the Indian police arrived in the small settlement near the Grand River in South Dakota to execute an arrest warrant. The uniformed men forced their way into two adjacent log cabins inhabited by Sitting Bull and his last two wives. He was not particularly surprised when they awoke him, and he did not resist. He merely asked for his wife to be allowed to collect his clothes from the other house. She also took that opportunity to wake the rest of the camp, which included the closest relatives and supporters of the Hunkpapa Lakota leader. When Sitting Bull came through the door, flanked by commanding officer Lieutenant Bull Head and police deputy Shave Head, his friends were already assembled in front of the house and challenged him to resist the public authority. It has even been said that even his 14-year-old son called him a coward.

Suddenly Sitting Bull's body guard Catch the Bear opened fire on his old enemy Bull Head, who, even as he fell, managed to fire at the prisoner as did Red Tomahawk, the policeman standing behind Sitting Bull. The shooting, during which Sitting Bull's followers retreated to a nearby woodland, lasted for an hour and cost the lives of Sitting Bull, seven of his supporters, and five policemen. The battle did not end until the army intervened. Although they would have liked to conduct the arrest themselves, they had remained in the background until then. James McLaughlin, the Indian agent of the Standing Rock reservation, had persuaded them that it was important for Sitting Bull to be arrested not by whites but by his own people. After all, nobody wished him to become a martyr. Yet for those who regarded the Indian police as nothing more than the agent's henchmen, that is what nevertheless happened.

Sitting Bull's death on December 15, 1890 put an end to an unusual life. He was born in 1831, the only son of an influential Hunkpapa family, not far from the place where he was to die. Although everyone called him Hunkesni ("slow") because of his ponderous manner, he was the fastest runner of his age group and killed his first bison calf at the tender age of ten. By 14 he had counted his first coup by touching an enemy in the thick of combat. It soon became apparent that he also had a particularly close relationship to the supernatural world, which made him a visionary and holy man (*wicasa wakan*).

In 1889 Sitting Bull recollected that "When I was a child the Sioux were the masters of the world. The sun rose in their country and went to rest there as well. They sent ten thousand horsemen into battle." Half a century later, the former bison hunters and warriors had become recipients of the United States government's charity: the bison were no more, the Lakota vanquished, and the Great Reservation founded in 1868 broken up.

J. Steeple Davis, *The Death of Sitting Bull*, wood engraving from Edward S. Ellis, *The Indian Wars of the United States*, Grand Rapids, MI 1891.

Sitting Bull's death freed the white settlers on the western borders of the United States from a constant threat. In the East Coast cities, on the other hand, the event was regarded as a sign of the government's misguided Indian policy. This contemporary illustration shows Sitting Bull dying astride his horse like a true hero; like a real "Indian" he wears a feather headdress and lives in a tipi.

Sitting Bull had never trusted the whites. While other leaders signed treaties with them, he led a bitter war against them which caused his friends among the Lakota to call him the "head chief of all the Sioux" – a position which did not exist in the Sioux tradition – thus deepening the cleft between the progressives, who advocated the white American way of life, and the traditionalists. His eminent position was the ultimate cause for his undeserved reputation for having brought about the victory of "the Indians" over the white army at the Battle of the Little Bighorn (1876). In 1877 he led his followers into exile in Canada. Queen Victoria's subjects, however, were not pleased to see this political asylum seeker, and limited his freedom of movement without supplying him and his tribe with rations. In 1881, after selling all their possessions and even eating their horses, Sitting Bull and his last followers surrendered to the Americans at Fort Buford, North Dakota. After the Great Sioux Reservation was divided in 1889 and the already meager rations were cut, a period of hopelessness and despair set in; by 1890 many Lakota were ready to believe the prophets of the Ghost Dance who proclaimed the return of both bison and ancestors, as well as the disappearance of the whites. Fearing a Sioux uprising and wrongly suspecting Sitting Bull of being the leading force behind the conspiracy, the army put his name at the top of their blacklist.

His death at the hands of the reservation police did not come as a surprise to Sitting Bull himself. A lark had told him many years previously that "The Sioux will kill you."

| Iki cize | A warrior |
|---|---|
| waon kon | I have been. |
| wana | Now |
| hena la yelo | it is all over. |
| iyto tiye kiya | A hard time |
| waon | I have. |

(Song composed by Sitting Bull after the negotiations about the allotment of the reservation, 1889)

Opposite page:
Sitting Bull and his nephew One Bull, 1884. Library of Congress, Washington, DC.

Sitting Bull adopted One Bull, his sister's son, after his first son died in 1857. Together with his favorite nephew he fought the whites, together they went into exile in Canada after the Battle of the Little Bighorn, and together they were interned in Fort Randall on their return to the United States. One Bull slept through the killing of his adoptive father: by the time he reached the log cabins, it was all over.

# Sitting Bull replies

## An interview in exile, 1877

In 1877, following the embarrassing defeat of the United States army by the Lakota and Cheyenne at the Little Bighorn, Sitting Bull and his followers fled to Canada after having been chased back and forth across the Plains for six months by Colonel Miles. Canada allowed the refugee to enter the country but would not recognize him as a "Canadian Indian." A government delegation traveled from Washington to persuade him to return to the reservation, and it was accompanied by American reporters who wanted to hear from Sitting Bull's own mouth who he really was. Until then the public had had to depend on rumor and speculation for information.

The official negotiations were unsuccessful. Sitting Bull did not wish to return to the United States. He was all the more talkative with the journalists and provided a taste of his talent for self-presentation, which was confirmed on numerous subsequent occasions. The interview was conducted by Jerome Stillson for the *New York Herald* in the presence of a Canadian officer, two interpreters and a stenographer. This is a brief extract:

"You are a great chief," said I to Sitting Bull, "but you live behind a cloud. Your face is dark; my people do not see it. Tell me, do you hate the Americans very much?"

A gleam as of fire shot across his face.

"I am no chief."

[...]

"What are you?"

"I am," said he, crossing both hands upon his chest, slightly nodding and smiling satirically, "a man."

[...]

"You say you are no chief?"

"No!" with considerable hauteur. "Are you a head soldier?"

"I am nothing – neither a chief nor a soldier." "What? Nothing?"

"Nothing."

"What, then, makes the warriors of your camp, the great chiefs who are here along with you, look up to you so? Why do they think so much of you?"

Sitting Bull's lips curled with a proud smile.

"Oh, I used to be a kind of a chief, but the Americans made me go away from my father's hunting ground."

"You do not love the Americans?"

You should have seen this savage's lips.

"I saw to-day that all the warriors around you clapped their hands and cried out when you spoke. What you said appeared to please them. They liked you. They seemed to think that what you said was right for them to say. If you are not a great chief, why do these men think so much of you?"

At this Sitting Bull, who had in the meantime been leaning back against the wall, assumed a posture of mingled toleration and disdain.

"Your people look up to men because they are rich; because they have much land, many lodges, many squaws?"

"Yes."

"Well, I suppose my people look up to me because I am poor. That is the difference."

[...]

"What is your feeling toward the Americans now?"

He did not even deign an answer. He touched his hip where his knife was.

I asked the interpreter to insist on an answer.

"Listen," said Sitting Bull, not changing his posture but putting his right hand out upon my knee. "I told them today what my notions were – that I did not want to go back there. Every time that I had any difficulty with them they struck me first. I want to live in peace."

"Have you an implacable enmity to the Americans? Would you live with them in peace if they allowed you to do so; or do you think that you can only obtain peace here?"

"The White Mother [Canada] is good."

"Better than the Great Father [the United States]?"

"Howgh!"

[...]

"Do you expect to live here by hunting? Are there buffaloes enough? Can your people subsist on the game here?"

"I don't know; I hope so."

"If not, are any part of your people disposed to take up agriculture? Would any of them raise steers and go to farming?"

"I don't know."

"What will they do, then?"

"As long as there are buffaloes that is the way we will live."

"But the time will come when there will be no more buffaloes."

"Those are the words of an American."

"How long do you think the buffaloes will last?"

Sitting Bull arose. "We know," said he, extending his right hand with an

Thomas Stoneman (Yanktonai), *The Arrest and Death of Sitting Bull*, drawing on oilcloth, c. 1925. State Historical Society of North Dakota, Bismarck, ND.

Over 30 years after Sitting Bull's death, one of the Lakota police officers involved in the bungled arrest drew a picture of the dramatic events: the Ghost Dancer's tent and dance area can be seen behind the two log cabins, gunmen in the lower foreground and right are firing on the police detachment, and the army intervenes from above. At the center of the scene, Sitting Bull is seen dying between policemen Bull Head and Shave Head. His corpse is shown again at the bottom of the picture; a policeman, enraged by the death of five of his colleagues, has used an ox yoke to smash his head.

impressive gesture, "that on the other side the buffaloes will not last very long. Why? Because the country there is poisoned with blood – a poison that kills all the buffaloes or drives them away. It is strange," he continued, with his peculiar smile, "that the Americans should complain that the Indians kill buffaloes. We kill buffaloes, as we kill other animals, for food and clothing, and to make our lodges warm. They kill buffaloes – for what? Go through your country. See the thousands of carcasses rotting on the Plains. Your young men shoot for pleasure. All they take from dead buffalo is his tail, or his head, or his horns, perhaps, to show they have killed a buffalo. What is this? Is it robbery? You call us savages. What are they? The buffaloes have come North. We have come North to find them, and to get away from a place where people tell lies."

[...]

"I was born on the Missouri River; at least I recollect that somebody told me so – I don't know who told me or where I was told of it."

"Of what tribe are you?"

"I am an Uncpapa."

"Of the Sioux?"

"Yes; of the great Sioux Nation."

"Who was your father?"

"My father is dead."

"Is your mother living?"

"My mother lives with me in my lodge."

"Great lies are told about you. White men say that you lived among them when you were young; that you went to school; that you learned to write and read from books; that you speak English; that you know how to talk French?"

"It is a lie."

"You are an Indian?"

(Proudly) "I am a Sioux."

[...]

"I am a man. I see. I know. I began to see when I was not yet born; when I was not in my mother's arms, but inside of my mother's belly. It was there that I began to study about my people."

[...]

"I was," repeated Sitting Bull, "still in my mother's insides when I began to study all about my people. God (waving his hand to express a great protecting Genius) gave me the power to see out of the womb. I studied there, in the womb, about many things. I studied about the smallpox, that was killing my people – the great sickness that was killing the women and children. I was so interested that I turned over on my side. The God Almighty must have told me at that time (and here Sitting Bull unconsciously revealed his secret) that I would be the man to be the judge of all the other Indians – a big man, to decide for them in all their ways."

"And you have since decided for them?"

"I speak. It is enough."

(*New York Herald*, November 16, 1877)

# The lords of the Southern Plains and their shrinking land

George Catlin, *His-oo-sán-chees, the Little Spaniard*, watercolor, 1836. Thomas Gilcrease Institute of American History and Art, Tulsa, OK.

Until the 19th century the Comanche were split into three to six politically independent groups whose names ("root eaters," "woodland people," or "bison eaters," for example) originally pointed to their different ways of life. Links with the Spanish were the result of temporary alliances, but also of prisoners being taken during raids in Mexico. As a child of mixed ancestry, Little Spaniard had to show particular bravery to prove that he was a real Comanche.

Among the first to adopt the horse and to begin a new life as mounted bison hunters were the Comanche (whose self-designation is Numunu, "the people"). They split from the Northern Shoshone in Wyoming in the 17th century and advanced into the southern Plains. Their position of supremacy, which they swiftly achieved, prevented the advance of both the Spanish (with whom they temporarily had peaceful relations) from the Southwest, and the French from the north.

In 1790, after many years of armed conflict, the Comanche and the Kiowa finally negotiated a peace settlement. Other than these allies, the Comanche had few friends among the neighboring Ute, Cheyenne, and Osage. The Comanche's advance had had a particularly

adverse effect on the Apache. They lived along the southern and western borders of the territory of the Comanche, and were pushed by them southward and westward. In about 1830, the land of the Comanche, commonly known as Comancheria, stretched from the Arkansas River to the northern Mexican settlements, and from Taos in New Mexico to eastern Oklahoma.

In 1835, after the establishment of the Indian Territory and the resettlement of the Five Civilized Tribes (Creek, Cherokee, Choctaw, Chickasaw, and Seminole) in Oklahoma, the Comanche signed an agreement with the United States. This was a promise to share their hunting grounds with the migrants from the east and to cease their incursions upon the white people who in increasing numbers were crossing their land on their way to the Californian gold fields and to Oregon. This treaty did not hold for long. The Comanche's enmity toward their new neighbors grew in parallel with the increasing scarcity of game animals. At the same time tensions with Texan settlers mounted as their rapid expansion forced peoples like the Wichita and Lipan further into the Comanche's hunting territory.

Under the terms of the Medicine Lodge treaty (1867), the Comanche were to surrender most of the area under their control, thereby conceding to the growing pressure from settlers and the United States army which protected them. In return, the Comanche were given a reservation in southwestern Oklahoma that they were to share with the Kiowa and the Kiowa Apache. Although not all local groups were present at the signing, in the eyes of the whites the agreement also applied to those groups who rejected the terms of the treaty and life on a reservation.

Soon after the reservation was established, the Fort Sill Indian agency responsible for the Comanche began its first attempts to make farmers out of them. The Comanche, however, showed scant interest in this activity, and most decided to live outside the reservation which they only visited to receive the annuity that had been promised to them by the treaty. When these annuities were dramatically reduced in 1869, many Comanche found raids a much more profitable source of income. As a result the government ordered the army to take all the Comanche to the reservation or to kill them if they refused to go along. After some painful defeats, most local groups gave up their resistance and allowed themselves to be settled on the reservation.

Not long afterward, a new conflict arose when cattle farmers used reservation land to graze their animals; the case was resolved to the detriment of the Comanche. A drought in 1881 and the repeated reduction of food rations, without which survival was impossible since the

Comanche women and children eating beef, c. 1895. National Anthropological Archives, Smithsonian Institution, Washington, DC.

The government food rations promised by treaty were insufficient for the requirements of the inhabitants of the reservation. Since the rations were extremely meager and were often delivered far too late, if at all, many suffered from hunger. At first the Comanche rejected the alien salted beef, and would leave the reservation with a military escort to go hunting, but found it increasingly difficult to find game. Survival without food rations had become impossible.

Comanche painted leather coat, Texas, c. 1830. Staatliches Museum für Völkerkunde, Dresden, Germany.

Examples of open-fronted leather coats in the style of uniform coats were found in various parts of the Plains in the 19th century. Some are merely fashionable reflections of military attire, while others betray their use by native scouts or ancillary troops in the service of the army. Despite its cut, the depiction of two scalps on the front and of a bison on the back of this Comanche coat leaves no doubt as to the traditional orientation of its wearer.

disappearance of the bison, prompted the Indian Agent to allow cattle farmers to drive their herds through the reservation in return for their supplying the Comanche with beef. The farmers agreed to this because it legitimized what they were already doing and, empowered by this policy, it was not long before they began to use the reservation as permanent grazing land. The Comanche were powerless in the face of this lasting abuse of the agreement.

It was during this period that the Comanche found renewed vigor in the Peyote religion which they hoped would help them to overcome the extreme existential crisis into which their new circumstances had plunged them. Quanah Parker (c. 1845–1911), probably the most influential Comanche leader of the period, contributed to the spread of the new religion in the Indian Territory. The introduction of a tribal police force (1878) and a tribal court of justice (1886) served to adapt life on the reservation to the new circumstances facing the people.

The decision by the United States government to allot the reservation lands to private ownership was regarded as unfair by the Comanche. Every member of the tribe was given 160 acres of land; the remaining reservation territory was handed over to new white settlers in 1901 and 1906. Tribal institutions like the police and the court of justice were dissolved. Today most Comanche live in and around Lawton, Oklahoma. The tribe has around 10,000 members (there were 2,700 in 1950 and 12,000 in 1840), of whom only about 8 percent – and all of them over the age of 60 – are fluent in their mother tongue. In 1993 the Comanche

Language and Cultural Preservation Committee was set up with the aim of remedying this situation; preschool classes were organized to teach young children the indigenous tongue. The committee also publishes a regular newsletter in Comanche which is distributed free of charge.

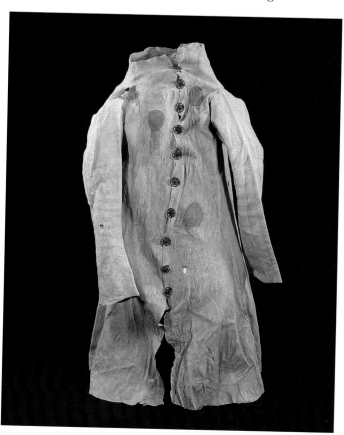

PLATEAU

Christian Carstensen

# Fishing for salmon and hunting bison

Even today, the wintertime landscape is buffeted by fierce winds bringing snow and ice from the north. Temperatures are way below freezing; both flora and fauna seem to be in profound hibernation. But inside the houses of the Yakima, Nez Perce, and Kalispel – insulated by an outer layer of tule matting (tule is a type of bulrush) – and the wooden plank houses of the Wasco and Wishram the young and the old once gathered around warming fires, to hear the storytellers' tales. In an animated, melodramatic style, using all the narrative means at their disposal, they would tell of the origin of the world, the advent of the animals, and the appearance of humans on earth. They taught the assembled children (as well as adults) about the routes taken by the Columbia and Fraser rivers, how the cliffs of the huge mountains in the east (the Rockies) and the snow-covered volcano cones projecting from the Cascades in the west had been created in mythical "pre-history."

These geographical cornerstones mark a culture area that is known today as the Plateau and which adjoins the Great Basin in the south. It extends over the US states of Montana, Idaho, Oregon, Washington, and the Canadian province of British Columbia. Whereas most of the northern part of the Plateau region is covered by coniferous woods, the south is a hilly, dry country of open steppe (also called a "high desert") covered with sagebrush and some light stands of trees, and divided by extremely deep gorges. One of these is Hell's Canyon, part of which reaches down some 7900 feet, surpassing the Grand Canyon in depth. Because of the continental climate, summer temperatures can reach 115° F, while the winters bring icy storms. Owing to the two large river systems, and thus the abundant water resources, this region was more densely populated (around three people per square mile) than the Great Basin in the south.

Previous double page:

Painted Hills, Oregon.

The region's steppes and forests, river valleys, and mountains offered the inhabitants of the Plateau very diverse living conditions.

Top:

The Rocky Mountains near Banff, Alberta.

The Rocky Mountains form the eastern border of the Plateau region. In winter the Kutenai crossed the mountains to hunt bison in the wooded valleys.

Peoples of the Plateau.

The majority of peoples that inhabit the Plateau belong to the linguistic families of the Interior Salish (in the north) and the Sahaptin (in the south). But there are also Athapaskan (Nicola), Chinookan (Wasco, Wishram), and linguistically isolated groups such as the Kutenai, Cayuse, Molala, and Klamath (Plateau Penuti). The latter two groups probably have distant links with the Sahaptin. Around 1775, the overall population stood at 90,000, a number that was likely to have been significantly higher before the spread of epidemic diseases.

Paul Kane, *Spokane Chief
Tum-se-ne-ho, The Man Without
Blood*, watercolor, 1847. Stark
Museum of Art, Orange, TX.

The Salishan-speaking Spokane
played an important role in trade
between the Great Plains and the
Plateau, and their language served
as a lingua franca in the northwestern Plateau region. The pierced
leather shirt worn by the "Man
without Blood" symbolized the fact
that supernatural powers had been
bestowed upon its wearer, which
made him bullet-proof.

Winter storytelling among the inhabitants of the Plateau was conducted in a range of languages that differed greatly from one another. For the most part, the languages of this region belonged either to the Salishan or the Sahaptian family of languages. The exceptions were the Athapascan Nicola in the north (a people incorporated into the neighboring groups of the Thompson during the period 1850 to 1890) and the linguistically isolated Kutenai, Klamath and Modoc, Molala, and Cayuse. Speakers of the Chinookan languages, the Wasco and Wishram, were related to the peoples of the southern Northwest Coast.

The Wasco and the Wishram were unable to understand their Sahaptin-speaking neighbors, the Celilo (Wayampam), who lived no more than six miles away, and thought their language to be extremely difficult to learn and speak.

Stone arrowheads from the big-game hunters of the Clovis era (11,600–10,700 BC), sandals made of sagebrush approximately 10,000 years ago and found near Fort Rock in Oregon, and the remains of salmon caught at around the same time and found near the Columbia River all confirm a long history of human habitation in the region. Yet the seminomadic annual cycle, during which the

Opposite page:
Flathead Lake, Montana.

The name of the Salish of western Montana was later extended to include the great language family to which they belong. The official designation of the tribe ("Flathead") is the translation of a name they had oddly enough been given by their neighbors – even though they did not practice the head deformation, common among many peoples dwelling further westward. Flathead Lake forms the northern boundary of the reservation in which they live today.

peoples of the Plateau lived in permanent settlements during the winter and camped in various locations during the summer to hunt, fish, and gather plants, appears to have evolved only at the beginning of the second millennium AD.

As in the neighboring Plains region to the east and in the Great Basin to the south, the advent of horses around 1730 decisively changed the life of Plateau peoples. Longer distances could now be covered in a comparatively short period of time, and larger quantities of goods transported. The inhabitants of the eastern Plateau (such as the Nez Perce) increasingly undertook journeys across the Rocky Mountains into the hunting grounds of the bison-hunting Plains peoples. This led to an increased exchange of goods and ideas. Enhanced mobility and combat efficiency caused methods of warfare to undergo fundamental changes. In the western part of the Plains, the Blackfoot had joined larger groups and pressed upon the Flathead and Kutenai of the eastern Plateau. Horses had become a visible symbol of wealth and prestige, and therefore the subject of raids. The increased danger posed by an enemy who practiced mounted warfare forced the Plateau peoples to form larger alliances.

**Fishing platform near Sherar's Falls, Deschutes River, Oregon.**

In 19th-century treaties, the United States granted the peoples of the Plateau fishing rights beyond the boundaries of the reservations. To this day, the residents of the Warm Springs, Umatilla, and Yakima reservations still fish at Sherar's Falls.

**Dry Falls on the Columbia River near Coulee City, Washington.**

Dry Falls is situated near the trading site of Soap Lake, the center of the former territory of the Salishan-speaking Sinkayuse. During the last Ice Age, water plunged more than 300 feet down this precipice, which is more than two miles wide. The caves carved out by these waters offered the ancestors of the Sinkayuse a spacious refuge. Such is the aridity of the region in summer that there is no more than a strip of green vegetation in the immediate proximity of the water.

**Drylands near Fort Rock, Oregon.**

Large expanses of the southern part of the Plateau are covered with lava. Typical for this region are bunchgrass steppes with typical stands of sagebrush.

A delegation of Umatilla, Walla Walla, Cayuse, and Palouse in Washington, 1889. Photograph: C.M. Bell. University of Oregon Library, Eugene, OR.

Although they spoke different languages, the Cayuse and the Umatilla and Walla Walla traditionally maintained good relations, coexisting on the same reservation since 1855. One of the key tasks involved in maintaining relationships with the outside world was in the hands of the Métis. They not only served as interpreters (as here, the standing figure on the left), but also assisted both the agents and the chiefs on the reservation, became speakers for their community, and often paved the way for the missionaries.

The inhabitants of the Plateau heard of the arrival of whites on the American continent long before any direct contact was made. Efficient trade routes meant that goods of Euro-American origin (such as Spanish coins or copper cauldrons) had found their way to the upper course of the Columbia River, as Meriwether Lewis (1774–1809) and William Clark (1770–1838) – the first official American explorers of the region – were astonished to learn when they crossed the region from east to west in 1804. The peoples whom the expedition encountered were not particularly surprised to see them, since their prophets had already heralded the coming of men with pale, hairy faces. Smallpox and other epidemic diseases were further harbingers anticipating the arrival of the whites (even though the connection was made only retrospectively). The last quarter of the 18th century saw these diseases killing almost half the population of some regions.

The aim of constructing the first settlements in the Plateau region (for example, Fort Nez Perce in 1818, later renamed Fort Walla Walla) was to support trade and missionary endeavors. Christianity proved to be so attractive to the Plateau peoples that in 1831 a delegation of Nez Perce and Flatheads went to St. Louis to request that missionaries be sent to them.

Generally, the whites were initially tolerated and accepted, primarily as trading partners, by local populations. However, the peace soon vanished when, from 1842, an increasing number of immigrants made their way across the Oregon Trail. Groups such as the Cayuse and Nez Perce resisted the takeover of their territory by the settlers. Subsequent to their military defeat, however, they were forced onto reservations, as were those groups that had ceded their territories in 1854–55 and, for the most part, had thus abandoned their traditional way of life. Today, the situation on the reservations is much the same as that in other parts of the country, though there are some differences. The Warm Springs Reservation in central Oregon, for instance, is a prime example of the successful and independent development of an autonomous administration and economy. Despite the advent of modernity into this world, the inhabitants of Warm Springs have to this day upheld the old tradition of storytelling.

Paul Kane, *Falls at Colville*, oil on canvas, 1847. Royal Ontario Museum, Toronto, ON.

The importance of fishing was reflected in the numerous techniques that were used. The Colville used fishing spears and woven fish fences, often with built-in fish baskets, to catch the fish as they struggled up the Kettle Falls. Here a man dispatches his catch with a fish club; behind him are the platforms from which the fish were hauled in with dip nets. Gill nets, fish fences, stone fish dams, fishing hooks, and poison were also used.

# The big net

When, after long winter months, the yearned-for spring finally came, it marked the beginning of a new annual cycle. The inhabitants of the Plateau now began to gather the first vegetable foods; these were mostly roots – a large array of lomatium (parsley family) or wild Indian celery, "Indian carrots" (also of this family), and bitterroot (of the purslane family). A little further into the cycle, they would gather a variety of liliaceous plants – for example, camas in the south and common dogtooth violets and "Indian potatoes" (in no way related to real potatoes, but considered to belong to the pink family). These plants were only allowed to be extracted once the "first root" ceremony had been duly performed. This ceremony, in which thanks are given to the Creator for making these foods available, is still conducted today. Digging up the roots with a digging stick, and processing what had been gathered was the task of the women, for it was the women who knew where to find prolific quantities of these plants both within and outside the vast expanses

of the present reservations. Today, however, the root-gathering women often encounter signposts saying "Private Property! No Trespassing!", erected by white property owners along the fences bordering their land.

Before the advent of the automobile (much less of four-wheel-drive vehicles), it could take days for groups to reach the respective spots and begin digging and gathering (since horses were not available throughout the Plateau region). These groups would normally remain in one area for one or two weeks before heading on to the next location where food plants were ripe. They did not merely extract the plants; the produce needed to be washed and either pared and cooked (like the bitterroots) or cooked in a hole in the ground for a period of several days before it was edible and could be dried and preserved (like the camas).

In spring, the new growth was still fresh and tender, so some of it was eaten raw. A favorite vegetable to this day is the cow parsnip, or Indian stick celery, that grows in many areas and is peeled and consumed raw.

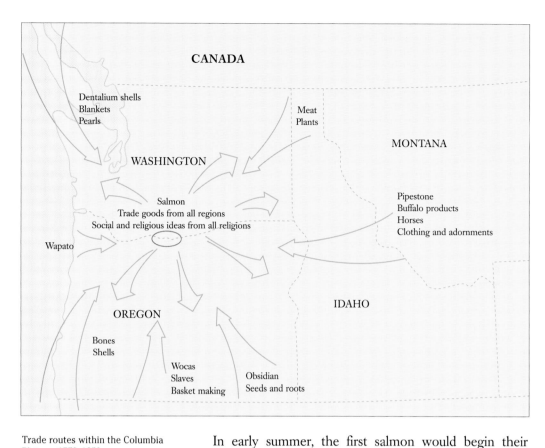

CANADA

Dentalium shells
Blankets
Pearls

Meat
Plants

WASHINGTON

MONTANA

Salmon
Trade goods from all regions
Social and religious ideas from all religions

Pipestone
Buffalo products
Horses
Clothing and adornments

Wapato

IDAHO

OREGON

Bones
Shells

Wocas
Slaves
Basket making

Obsidian
Seeds and roots

Trade routes within the Columbia
Plateau, 1750–1850.

Sites located near rapids or near
waterfalls (such as The Dalles or Kettle
Falls) and offering good fishing
grounds have always been popular
trading centers. The Columbia River
provided ideal access to the Pacific
coast, to the northern Plains, and to
the Great Basin. Mussel and snail
shells, obsidian, dried roots, bison
and local salmon products, and
bartered slaves or those captured
from other tribes were among the
most important trade items. In
addition, ideas of all kinds also
spread along these trade routes.

The upper course of the John Day
River, Oregon.

The Blue Mountains and Ochoco
Mountains in the south of the
Plateau receive more rainfall
than the rest of the region. Here,
the steppe gives way to the
woodlands that dominate in
the higher territories.

In early summer, the first salmon would begin their struggle against the rapids to reach the spawning grounds in the upper reaches of the tributaries of the Columbia and Fraser rivers. In the past, the men would gather in throngs on the slippery rocks along the routes, wielding dip nets and spears with which to catch the salmon in midair when they tried to jump up these natural obstacles. The largest specimens of chinook (king) salmon, a type of Pacific salmon, weighed as much as 100 lbs; the local rainbow trout might weigh up to 40 lbs; and a type of sturgeon caught predominantly in the Snake River could weigh as much as 250 lbs. At those locations that had no natural fishing platforms, wooden platforms were constructed, from which it was easy to get close to the fish. The fishermen would throw the wriggling fish caught up in their nets onto the platform or rocks, where they were gathered and processed by other members of the family. At Kettle Falls, in the region now within Washington state, the Colville, Spokane, and neighboring Salishan-speaking peoples used woven fish fences and fish baskets, from which the salmon could not free themselves once they had jumped into them.

Among the Wasco the community elders were allowed to pick out the best fish from the first day's catch. It is estimated that the inhabitants of the Plateau region consumed around 500 lbs of salmon annually per head.

The fishing grounds along the Columbia River – in the proximity of the Dalles in Oregon and around 10 miles further upstream near Celilo – were particularly popular and yielded such vast catches that even visiting fishermen were tolerated. The salmon that passed through these waters until well into October would do so in huge numbers. By the time they reached the upper course of the river, they had lost much of their bodyweight, but were not yet exhausted by their arduous journey against the currents. These once-powerful rapids have since disappeared under the waters of an artificial lake, and the inhabitants of the Yakima, Warm Springs, and Umatilla reservations had to endure long court battles (and even fist fights) against white fishermen before they were finally allotted their share of salmon, for not all whites were willing to accept that native peoples should enjoy special rights. The number of salmon that complete the journey up the Columbia or Fraser rivers has long been reduced. Very many do not even survive their encounter with the trawlers in the Pacific.

It had already come to the attention of pioneer explorers Lewis and Clark during their travels in 1804 that, having crossed the Rockies, the further west they went, the more the indigenous groups relied on salmon fishing. The peoples along the Columbia, in particular the Wasco and Wishram, as well as the Yakima (who now call themselves Yakama), Warm Springs, and Walla Walla were better off than the inhabitants of the northern Plateau. During the course of a year, five different types of Pacific salmon plus rainbow trout passed along the river and provided inhabitants with regular food supplies. Hence, famines were rare. The fish appeared in such huge numbers that the fishermen were able to dry and pound them, and then sell and barter them in hundredweight bundles. This processed product is referred to as salmon pemmican, a term derived from the name of the process by which the Plains peoples dried and pounded bison meat and then mixed berries into it.

The people of the Fraser River country were unable to depend on fish to the same extent as those along the Columbia as generally only one type of salmon passed through their waters to the spawning grounds. Because salmon have a four-year life cycle, the number of fish that travel through the waters during any season can fluctuate.

Salmon fishing was subject to a similar ritual to that of the gathering of roots and tuberous plants. Only when the obligatory ceremony had been conducted could fishing begin. The same applied to the berry harvest in late summer.

The most popular berries were the fruits of the elder tree in the northern Plateau and cranberries in the south. "These are wild ones, good ones, they were gathered; not those raised and canned ones," explained Myra Shawaway during a banquet at Warm Springs, referring to the cranberry sauce served with the cake. She went on to explain that a ceremony had first been held to bless the fruit, after which several days had been spent laboriously picking the berries before they were dried and stored for winter. In former times, the berries would be preserved by smoldering them over a fire. Today, they are stored in freezers or preserved in pots and bottles.

Lake Simtustus, Warm Springs Reservation, Oregon.

The artificial lakes built by the whites in their ongoing attempts to exploit hydraulic power have changed the landscape in many parts of the Columbia Plateau.

Opposite page:

Lillooet (Stl'atl'imx) drying berries, 1954. British Columbia Archives, Victoria, BC.

The annual food cycle began in February or March, when in their winter villages people would conduct ceremonies honoring the major food plants and the salmon before setting out on the journey to the rivers. When, toward the end of April, the abundance of fish in the rivers began to wane, individual families traveled to places where roots and game were in plentiful supply, returning to catch salmon in June. Summers were spent on higher grounds, hunting and gathering foods. In the fall, the families returned to the river valleys yet again to catch salmon and to trade. In mid-November they returned to their winter villages, supplementing their winter food supplies by hunting and fishing.

**Horses on the Warm Springs Reservation, Oregon.**

In the modern-day Sahaptin language, dogs, which were known to the people long before horses, are referred to as "little horses." This shift in meaning makes it clear how significant a role the horse has played for the inhabitants of the Columbia Plateau over the past 300 years.

When a young man killed his first deer, this was celebrated by a "first killing" ceremony in which the novice gave away the animal that he had killed, the weapon that he had used, and the clothes that he had worn to hunt. The guests invited to this thanksgiving ceremony received gifts and were served a plentiful feast, for this was a special event in the life of a young man – to return to his village with his first deer. A similarly proud achievement among the women was when a young woman filled her first basket with the fruits of her labor (the roots extracted from the ground). While hunting was not as important a task in the western and southern regions of the Plateau as it was in the other parts, it still carried considerable prestige. Most hunting was done in the fall. The most popular game was white-tailed and mule deer as well as wapiti. Black bears were also commonly hunted for their fur. Small hunting parties would share the work by dividing into groups – one group would drive the animals in the direction of the other group poised in their hideouts, ready to attack. Several members of the hunting party would don animal furs, in an attempt to get as close as possible to their prey.

When horses spread throughout the Plateau during the first half of the 18th century, summertime bison hunting became part of the annual food cycle of eastern Plateau groups such as the Flathead, Pend d'Oreille, and Nez Perce who dwelled beyond the Rockies. They prized bison hides, a sought-after trade item within the Plateau region.

Although the region's inhabitants did not always live in peaceful coexistence, they were linked by an extensive trade network that spanned the Great Plains all the way to the Northwest Coast and California. The most prominent transregional trading centers were situated at the best fishing sites along the Columbia River – near The Dalles and Celilo for the Wasco and Wishram and the ancestors of

the people of Warm Springs. Thousands of people would gather there during the summer, to fish, trade, gossip, and gamble. Chinook traders from the coast, who maintained links with the coastal trading centers brought clams, fish oil, wapato roots, and goods of European origin such as glass beads, all of which they gladly traded for dried salmon from the Wasco and bison hides, furs, horses, and camas roots from the Walla Walla and Umatilla. From the south, the Klamath and Modoc brought enslaved women and children abducted during raids on the north Californian Shasta, Achumawi, and Atsugewi; Salishan-speaking visitors bartered with their woven mats and tanned hides. Chains of 40 dentalium shells were used as a means of exchange on the Northwest Coast and along the lower course of the Columbia, and were themselves sought after as a trade good east of the Dalles. They were a popular adornment all the way into the Plains.

The hustle and bustle of trading ceased in winter. During summer, the inhabitants of the Plateau would travel from one place to the next, seeking out locations at which food was being gathered or hunted. In winter, they returned to their villages to spend the long evenings in storytelling and conducting the special midwinter ceremony.

"When I grew up, things were different. There was a lot of berries, a lot of game, fish, everything. But now everything is gone – roots, berries ... they don't grow no more. That's because when they are ripe, nobody prays when they grab the berries to put 'em in their mouth; they just go in there and eat off the bushes. It's the same with roots. The oldtimers believed they had to pray for everything before they tasted it. But now, they don't believe in anything anymore ... now you believe in the other way, not in our Indian ways."

(Agnes Vanderburg, Flathead, 1995)

# "Indian giving" and democracy

Trade was often not limited to the mere exchange of goods. In the Plateau so-called "Yahlupt" trading partnerships existed, which were far more than a simple commercial association determined by economic interests. When, for instance, an Umatilla was prepared to form a trading relationship with his Wasco partner, he would offer him a gift. At the close of negotiations, the host would offer a return gift of a value equaling that of the original gift. The guest would be entertained with food and drink. Women conducted negotiations in a similar way. This custom resulted in widespread networks being established between members of various Plateau peoples. Such relationship networks remained stable as long as the gifts offered were mutually considered to be adequate. But as soon as the whites joined this system, difficulties arose: in 1843, Jason Lee, a missionary at the Wascopam Mission on the Columbia River, accepted the gift of a horse from a Native American, but was incensed when, after some time had elapsed and no gift was forthcoming from the white man, a cow was stolen from him in return.

In addition to such partnerships, there was everyday bargaining for individual items when goods would be laid out in front of people's homes and potential buyers would stroll by to look. Bargaining was popular among the people of the Plateau. Travelers to the region became aware of this, since the prices they were expected to pay for food were so high.

A peaceful exchange of goods between the Spokane traders and a group of Yakima could prove short-lived. If their paths crossed again, such encounters could spark war. But just the opposite could also occur.

Men and women had equal status, in the broadest sense of the term. While men hunted, fished, and went to war, the women would gather plant foods, so that each gender contributed equally to the sustenance of their communal livelihood. The women owned the foods, and were allowed to sell surplus supplies for their own benefit. The property thus amassed belonged to them alone, making women independent of their male partners. Single mothers have long been a common phenomenon in the Plateau region.

Yet the family was important to Plateau inhabitants. The family unit comprised not only immediate family members (such as father, mother, and children), but also grandparents, aunts and uncles, and cousins. A young person's first marriage did not generally last long, for it was normally arranged by the family, who would instigate a cycle of "gift" negotiations, similar to exchanges between trade partners, which was strengthened by the the marriage of their children. Divorce was simple: both parties would pack their possessions and part, possibly joining a partner

whom they had chosen for themselves. In this case, the family would refrain from becoming involved.

Home was where a family had their permanent winter village. The family and the village to which the family belonged were the centerpiece around which the life of Plateau peoples revolved. Family ties, however, were not indefinitely binding. Those who moved to another village were likely eventually to join the kinfolk resident in that village – that of their cousins or spouse, for example.

At village meetings, the entire adult population would be involved in making important decisions and electing leaders. Sometimes the members of neighboring villages would also take part in these processes. Elected chiefs felt allegiance to no higher entity (such as the "tribe"). The number of signatures on the treaties with the United States is accordingly large, since all the village chiefs of a given region needed to be included in the agreements.

The introduction of horses changed this grass roots form of democracy. As the threat posed by mounted aggressors increased, the small communities of old – especially those in the eastern Plateau region – were forced to amalgamate to form larger bands. Conversely, horses also helped sustain such large groups, since members could now travel longer distances to procure food for the extended group. These large communities gave rise to a development in which power became concentrated in the hands of only a few leaders. The influence of neighboring peoples from the Northwest Coast was noticeable in some bands, such as the Shuswap or the Wasco and Wishram. An aristocratic class evolved, setting itself apart from the commoners and slaves and gaining more influence over village matters.

Kutenai bark canoe, c. 1900. Canadian Museum of Civilization, Hull, QC.

The canoe used by the Kutenai is as unique in the Columbia Plateau region as their isolated language. Typical of the entire region, however, is the fact that men and women worked together as equals (when steering their vessels through the water, for instance). Both genders had an equal amount of socioeconomic influence, each owning their own property and each contributing to the procurement of food. Men and women each conducted their own ceremonies to ensure prosperity. While it was the men who held most political offices, they relied on the counsel of their women.

Opposite page:

Wishram bride, 1911. Photograph: Edward S. Curtis. University of Washington Libraries, Special Collections Division, Seattle, WA.

First marriages were normally arranged by parents or grandparents and were sealed by the exchange of goods. If the prospective marriage partners did not agree with the choice that had been made for them, the family would accept their choices to the contrary. Because of the young marriageable age and the independent status of women, the majority of first marriages were not particularly long-lasting. If one of the partners packed their possessions and left, the couple was considered divorced. The family then had little influence with respect to the choice of a new spouse.

Pit houses, which were sunk into the ground to a depth of about three feet, were about 50 feet in diameter and could accommodate 15 to 30 people. The floor plan was rectangular, circular, or oval. The roof was supported by beams extending from the edge of the pit to the smoke hole in the center. This frame was covered with poles, pine needles, and grass, to which, in humid climates, cedar bark and earth were also added. Entry was through the smoke hole by means of a ladder.

Opposite page:

Rosie Ross with a basketry cradle. Lillooet, British Columbia, 1978.

The demands of 19th-century settlers and tourists were met by women producing basketwork trays, cups, and bottles. Yet, a decline in gathering lowered the demand for receptacles in which to gather and store food. While the few skilled basket weavers that remain enjoy high standing, they can scarcely make a living, despite the high prices their work fetches. Profits from basket weaving compare unfavorably with income offered by other employment.

# ... and water boils in the basket

Although the various peoples of the Plateau had much in common in socioeconomic terms, there were considerable variations between them, especially in their material culture. In the case of dwellings, not only were there differences between summer and winter houses, and changes brought by the advent of the horse, but also each of the peoples often had their own characteristic building style. In the western part of the Plateau, the Wasco and Wishram lived in winterproof timber houses with vertical walls, sometimes additionally covered with bark, whereas the ancestors of the Yakima found protection against icy winter temperatures in earth houses, the lower halves of which were sunk into the ground.

During the 19th century, longhouses became a popular form of dwelling among Plateau inhabitants. Their design consisted of an A-shaped framework of poles that resembled an extended version of the tipi used by the Plains peoples. This frame was then covered with several layers of tule (bulrush) matting sewn together. In damp or rainy weather, this material would swell, thus closing all gaps and crevices through which cold winds would normally pass. During the warmer months, the mats would dry out again, re-creating the gaps, through which a cooling breeze could pass. Entering a longhouse, you would first find yourself in an anteroom, a sort of airlock that was also used as a larder. A second door led to the living area, in the center of which the fires of each family burned. A slit at the top of the dwelling, some 10 to 12 feet above ground, served as a smoke outlet.

A dwelling that housed grandparents, parents, and children could be extended as often as necessary to

accommodate additional members joining the family through the marriage of children or if the parents' siblings moved in.

As bison were increasingly hunted, the tipi, a cone-shaped pole tent covered with bison hide, became a more common form of dwelling, its popularity spreading from the east throughout the Plateau. This popularity was due to the fact that a tipi could be quickly erected and dismantled and was easily transported by horse.

The tule mats used for houses also had a variety of other uses, for example to extract the fat from salmon by soaking it up. When the thanksgiving ceremonies were held in spring, they were followed by a feast. Since the longhouses contained neither tables nor chairs, those attending the feast sat on the ground; tule mats spread out in long rows functioned as tablecloths on which the food was served.

We can still marvel today at the baskets woven by the Plateau peoples. Because they were not familiar with the art of pottery, they even used watertight basketwork receptacles for cooking. Rocks would be heated on the flames and, when red hot placed in the cooking basket, thus bringing its liquid content to a boil. When gathering roots and berries women wore special baskets on their hips and then emptied the contents of these into larger basketwork receptacles.

The baskets were commonly made using a traditional method of decorative folding (imbrication) that gave their outer surface a scaled look. With the advent of the fur trade

Joanna Meninick (Yakima), 1987.
Basketwork hats in the shape of truncated cones were a characteristic element of Yakima women's dress, and are today often worn at powwows as an expression of identity. The formidable skills involved in weaving with root splints and bear grass were long expected to become extinct. They are, however, now being cultivated anew, and courses are being given to preserve the art.

Umatilla Council Lodge, c. 1900. Photograph: Major Lee Woodhouse. National Anthropological Archives, Smithsonian Institution, Washington DC.

In the past, missionaries and government representatives attempted to dissolve or weaken extended families. They condemned polygamy, encouraged small families, and promoted the erection of solid-construction houses that were much less easily extendable than the traditional mat-covered houses. Despite their efforts, extended families have retained considerable importance. Family members support one another economically and jointly hold weddings and funerals.

and of animal husbandry and crop cultivation, traditional materials were replaced by corn leaves, cotton, and wool, and commercial colors extracted from bark, lichen, moss, and fruits were replaced by commercial dyes.

In the southern Plateau, basketry hats were often worn, predominantly by women. In the past, they were part of everyday dress; today they are worn only on special occasions as a symbol of tribal affiliation. Basket weaving, long looked down upon as being old-fashioned and far too time-consuming, has regained popularity among a growing number of enthusiasts who are being taught the skills anew in night classes and weekend courses.

Gambling has a long tradition on the Plateau. Today tribal governments use casinos as a means of raising much-needed funds for the budgets of their reservations. One of the traditional games still commonly played at any large gathering is the stick, bone, or hand game. Accompanied by chanting and rhythmic drumming, two players in a team each conceal two sticks, one marked, the other unmarked. The opposing team must guess which hand is holding the unmarked object (normally a piece of bone about three inches long). Larger sticks are used as counters and are won or lost after each turn at guessing until one team ultimately owns all eight to eleven sticks. Individuals watching the game, and also the teams themselves, place high bets on who will win each round.

## Old-One teaches the people the use of ornaments

Ntce'mka was travelling through the Shuswap country in search of his wife, who had been stolen from Lytton by a cannibal. Old-One was also travelling in the Shuswap country at this time, and one night wandered into Ntce'mka's camp [...] Ntce'mka did not know him; but, seeing that the old man had a very dignified and wise appearance, he treated him very kindly. [...] Ntce'mka was surprised when the stranger recognized him, and told him all about himself and where he would find his wife. When about to depart in the morning, Old-One pulled out four small bundles and gave them to Ntce'mka. They consisted of porcupine quills, scalps of the red-headed woodpecker, eagle tail-feathers, and dentalium shells. He said, "Hitherto the value of these things has not been known, and people have not used them. Henceforth they will be much used and highly prized by all peoples for decorative purposes." In this way people first learned the use of these things, and afterwards became accustomed to decorate their persons and clothes with them.

(James A. Teit, *Mythology of the Thompson Indians*, New York 1912)

# Seven Drums

"The 'sweat lodge,'" an old Nez Perce woman explains, "served both spiritual and physical well-being. The old people believed in spiritual beings; they sometimes sang their medicine songs there and then cleansed themselves and their spirits ...They hoped to become good human beings through their spirit, which is why they purified themselves inside and out. They always called it *kheeln* – Old Man [the Creator]; and they called the sweat lodge *kheeln* as well, so they said, since they prayed to him."

In the old times, the healers of the Plateau region were wealthy people, but they also lived dangerously. They had magic powers and, thanks to the spiritual helpers at their personal disposal, they were able to heal the sick. They were just as able, however, to make the healthy sick. The fees that they demanded for healing ceremonies were very high, and they required payment in advance. If their patient died, they would of course refund the payment. "This is necessary for their own security," missionary Daniel Lee wrote in 1844, "for otherwise they might be charged with having caused his death [and this] will probably be followed with his death by the relatives of the deceased." And if the healer had a rival who would be glad to be rid of the competition, then it could almost certainly be expected that his days were numbered.

All things in this world, so it was believed, were endowed with a power, a living soul, and were also connected to one another. The supernatural beings that were the source of this power had already existed on earth in the days when the world as we know it was still being created. (This, at least, is the substance of the many myths told in wintertime.) These supernatural beings now influenced the present world, and anyone who set out on a personal vision quest might be fortunate enough to win the support of one of these spirits for his personal protection and well-being. Before making contact with them, it was necessary to undergo a process of thorough (chiefly spiritual) purification, for which people would retreat to the sweat lodge. In the heat of the rising steam and in the darkness of that room, they would pray, chant, give thanks, and appeal

Medecine d'Ignace

for help, and the ways of the world would be explained to young people. This ritual remains almost unchanged today.

During the first few decades of the 19th century, missionaries were generally welcomed among the native peoples. Native leaders were keen to exploit the mysterious "mighty powers" that the whites commanded. But the new religion, to some extent amalgamated with their own, also introduced a different set of morals and values. Missionaries were adamant about banning polygamy and forcing Christian values on the indigenous peoples. These principles were vehemently emphasized by the white Christian churches and the American government, who forced them on those living on the reservations.

Even before the whites appeared in the Plateau, its inhabitants were aware of their imminent arrival. There were prophets among the Nez Perce, Umatilla, Yakima, and Kutenai who would fall into a trance or state of unconsciousness and after a time wake up, endowed with inspiration and prophecies. One such prophet was Smohalla (c. 1818–c. 1907), who received visions in the 1860s and who later became head of the Washat (or Seven Drums) religion. His teachings consisted of strict rejection of the whites and their influence on traditional life. Despite its disapproval by Catholic and Protestant missionaries and by the American government in the 19th century, the Washat religion survived and is still practiced by the peoples of the Plateau region.

Visitors to major festivities on reservations in the Plateau region generally come into contact with the Washat religion. Services honoring the Creator are held on Sunday mornings, thanksgiving ceremonies are conducted in spring and summer, public meetings are opened with a prayer, ceremonies are held at which traditional names are bestowed upon people, weddings take place, and funeral ceremonies spanning several days are held for the deceased. Washat is considered the "traditional" Native American religion of the Plateau region. Elements of Christianity have been incorporated into it. Although for some time Washat took something of a background position, the revival of Native American values over the past 20 years has led to the religion again being attractive to new followers, many of whom use this faith to help them escape alcohol and drug addiction.

Washat – the Seven Drums religion – is named after the following ritual: At the upper, western end of a longhouse (today a hall is used), eight men and women rise, and seven of them each take a drum. The eighth takes a bell and proceeds to set a rhythm, which the drummers take up and to which they begin to chant. The remaining participants rise and take up the chanting, swinging their right hands up and down in front of their chests to the rhythm of the bell. After several minutes the chanting ends with a loud and joint "Aaaauuuu," at the shout of which everyone stretches their hands up high. When this prayer has been chanted, the dancing commences.

Nicolas Point, *The Medicine of Ignace*, c. 1842. Midwest Jesuit Archives, St. Louis, MO.

In order to attain supernatural powers, the Cœur-d'Alene chief Ignace retreated to the seclusion of the mountains. In the background is the sweat lodge in which he prepared himself for his vision quest by fasting and praying, and thus beseeching the favor of a guardian spirit in animal form that would bestow upon him extraordinary hunting prowess. The missionary Nicolas Point (1799–1868) saw no contradiction between practices of this kind and the belief in patron saints (such as St. Hubertus, patron saint of hunters).

Following pages:

Smohalla and his followers in Priest Rapids, Washington, 1884. Eastern Washington State Historical Society, Cheney Cowles Museum, Spokane, WA.

The best-known prophet in the Washat religion was Smohalla, a Wanapam (a neighboring group of the Yakima). His teachings, in which he fiercely opposed adopting the ways of the white man and demanded a return to old traditions, fanned the flames of late 19th-century indigenous rebellions such as the Nez Perce war of 1877. This chief and his followers were not only strongly condemned by the missionaries, but also imprisoned by Indian agents and punished by being deprived of rations.

# The Thompson are called Nlaka'pamux again

Nlaka'pamux woman extracting roots from the ground, 1897. Photograph: Harlan L. Smith. American Museum of Natural History, New York, NY.

When the women dug up roots, they generally extracted only the larger plants, thus safeguarding future harvests and increasing the productivity of a location. Roots such as the camas (high in carbohydrates) were cooked for a period of approximately two and a half days in earth ovens and – if not eaten immediately afterward – placed on mats to dry before being stored in baskets and bags. They would be made edible again by being soaked in water or cooked in a stew.

"Thompson" is not the name by which the indigenous inhabitants of the region surrounding the junction of the Thompson and Fraser rivers, in southern British Columbia, like to be known today. More than 5,000 of them live there, approximately the same number that dwelled in the region around 1850, according to an estimate made retrospectively by the ethnologist James A. Teit in 1908. The modern-day Nlaka'pamux Nation occupies a conglomeration of eleven minor reservations located around the town of Lytton. This alliance of reservations has elected a joint tribal government, primarily in order to coordinate economic and social programs.

The peoples of this region were given the name Thompson by the whites because, during the winter months, they dwelled along the rivers named Thompson and Fraser. They considered themselves as belonging together, spoke a common language, and traced their existence back to the same origins, outlined in a comprehensive cycle of myths. The slight differences between the northern (Upper) and southern (Lower) Thompsons were due to the differing environments in which they lived. The southern part of the region had deep gorges with steep, densely wooded cliffs in which rain clouds would hang. Their main source of food was the salmon caught at sites to which individual families

Pubescent Nlaka'pamux girl in ceremonial attire, 1914. Photograph: James A. Teit. Canadian Museum of Civilization, Hull, QC.

During the first four days of their puberty ritual, girls would wear a cone-shaped headdress made of twigs of the hemlock tree, bound together at the stem, and totally covering the upper part of their bodies, except for an opening for their faces. The shape of this headdress replicated that of the huts made of hemlock branches that were built especially for the girls at the onset of their first menstruation.

Rock painting near Pavilion, British Columbia.

The rock paintings in the border region inhabited by the Thompson, Shushwap, and Lillooet play an important role in the vision quest practiced most prominently by these groups. During the period of preparation for their vision, the young Salish would use red pigments to draw pictures of their dreams, their experiences, and desires on rockfaces and stone blocks. This example shows drawings of a bird, bear paws, and human figures.

had the exclusive fishing rights. The northern parts, by contrast, were among the most arid in all of what today is British Columbia. Game was a much more common source of food in this area.

Some villages consisted only of two or three pit houses on the banks of the river. These houses could accommodate as many as 30 people, if an extended family was particularly large. Such families might include slaves, whom the Thompson regularly procured by abduction from their neighbors, the Lower Lillooet and Shuswap.

The Thompson acknowledged as their chiefs only those with exceptional skills in hunting or warfare. Especially suited individuals were elected to the office of chief. However, they solicited the support of the other members of the village in all matters, so as not to act solely on their own authority. Those who proved generous came to be highly respected and thus had greater influence on community issues, a circumstance also fostered by a broad kinship network.

Children led a largely unsupervised life. It was merely expected of them that they rise early, wash regularly with cold water, and stop playing when the sun set. Whoever disobeyed the latter rule, it was said, would be carried away by owls, and put into a basket of snakes and other reptiles.

Puberty was a time of trial for both boys and girls. During their first menstruation, girls would retreat from the community for four months and live alone in a hut set apart from the rest of the village. This period of initiation involved many a night outing, to train the perseverence and skills needed as adult women. During the first four days, they were required to wear a headdress made of hemlock twigs, were not allowed to wash themselves, and were only permitted to drink water through tubes made of goose or swan bones. Should they touch the surface of a creek, it was believed that it would dry up.

A boy's initiation into manhood began when he first dreamed of an arrow, a canoe, or a woman. He too retreated from the community, fasting, spending time in the

sweat lodge, honing his practical skills, and waiting for his future guardian spirit to reveal itself to him.

The Stein River Valley, in which the western tributary of the Fraser created an impressive landscape of rapids and caves, was a popular place of reclusion – a fact to which an array of rock drawings bears witness. It was no surprise, therefore, that plans by the British Columbia government to authorize commercial logging in this region, announced in 1976, met with opposition. The Nlaka'pamux, increasingly aware of their traditional heritage, were outraged. In 1995 their protests were successful, not least thanks to the support received from environmental activists, and parts of the region were declared a protected area.

> In the morning, an old man holds a sermon for the young, explaining what they need to do. They will spend their life there [in the Stein Valley], and God will help them and give them strength. The Indians hold claim to this site, since, for thousands of years, it has been their university. We teach our youth to worship things. [...] The Stein Valley can be likened to Mount Sinai or Rome for the Catholics. These are holy sites.
>
> (Annie Zetco York, Nlaka'pamux)

Alfred Jacob Miller, *Nez Percé*, watercolor, 1837. National Archives of Canada, Ottawa, ON.

While the name Nez Perce was introduced by 18th-century French traders (but has long been subjected to English pronunciation), it is actually based on a self-designation meaning "The People Who Pierce Themselves." Having relinquished their nose ornaments prior to 1850, the Nez Perce adopted several elements of their dress, adornments, and hair styles from the neighboring Plains.

# Horsemen, warriors, and strategists

The Nez Perce were renowned horsemen, fearless warriors, and clever strategists. They formed the protective southeastern flank of the Plateau. From the south the tribes of the middle Columbia River Valley were threatened by the Shoshone and Paiute, and from the north by the Blackfoot.

Their traditional homelands were along the lower reaches of the Snake, Clearwater, and Salmon rivers in the present states of Oregon, Idaho, and Washington. They became renowned mostly due to the fate of Chief Joseph and his band from the Wallowa Valley in Oregon in 1877. The present Nez Perce reservation is in Idaho, where approximately half of the 3,000 registered members live.

The Nez Perce speak a Sahaptian language and form a linguistic group with their western neighbors in Oregon. They originally lived in small, independent villages along the rivers, forming larger subgroups when necessary.

The introduction of horses greatly changed their lives. The story of the arrival of horses in their world is told to this day – not only among their own people, but also among the neighboring Umatilla. Once upon a time, a band of warriors from these two tribes sneaked up to a group of enemy Shoshone and saw horses for the first time. The warriors were so taken by these strange animals that they decided that they wanted some at any cost and thus approached their enemies in peace the next day. They asked to be given a stallion and a mare. At first, the Shoshone refused. Only when the warriors offered all their clothing and weapons in return for the horses did their trade partners agree. Two horses were brought home in triumph.

The Nez Perce are still considered good horse breeders, and in the past specialized in breeding Appaloosas. Once horses had been adopted in the Plateau region, every tribesperson was soon as secure on horseback as they had previously been on foot. Bison hunting beyond the Rocky Mountains was now a regular event, with the Nez Perce leading groups of up to 1,000 Plateau dwellers into the new hunting grounds. Their allies were the Flathead and, in the Plains, the Crow, who were happy to have support in their battle against the Blackfoot and Lakota.

The influence of Plains culture to which the Nez Perce (and, through them, other peoples of the Plateau) were thus subjected was quick to develop and fundamental in nature. Bison hides now covered their lodges, replacing tule (bulrush) mats, the importance of salmon fishing declined, and the splendid feather headdresses that were produced in the Plains for "export," adorned the men's heads. Horses became a valuable possession, and varying levels of affluence soon arose among the Nez Perce. Those who possessed hundreds, or even thousands, of horses not only had valuable stock at their disposal, but also commanded respect and had significant influence on the decisions made in councils held by the village, the subtribe, or the tribe.

The Nez Perce evolved to become intermediary traders who traveled to the major trading centers along the Columbia River with goods (such as bison hides) from the Plains. They exchanged their goods for the much-cherished salmon pemmican. Thanks to their military and economic supremacy, neighboring bands entered close alliances with the Nez Perce; the Cayuse even went so far as to give up their own language.

Grandparents and their grandchildren generally had a warm, close relationship. The younger generation considered their grandparents to be equals with whom they played and romped around. They reciprocally addressed one another by the same term. Grandparents taught

children the rules of conduct. The relationship with parents, on the other hand, was formal, and based on great respect.

The prerequisite of success in any area of life was that an individual had the support of a personal guardian spirit and supernatural powers at their disposal. The more support an individual had, the greater was his or her success and status. To gain such support, youths set out to selected sites in the wilderness in search of visions. There they would fast, pray, and live in the hope of being endowed with their own song with which they would later call upon their guardian spirits.

Even today, political life is based on the lingering contrast between tribal members who are Christians and those who adhere to tradition, the influence of the latter having markedly increased.

Left:

Eliza Spalding, *Protestant Ladder*, ink and natural pigments on paper, c. 1842. Oregon Historical Society, Portland, OR.

Among the displays with which Catholic and Protestant missionaries hoped to promote the conversion of indigenous "heathens," the "Ladders" enjoyed exceptional popularity. This version, done for the Nez Perce by Eliza Spalding, wife of the missionary, depicts the Apostles as Protestant priests and Martin Luther, among others, situated between the straight path to heaven and that on which the Pope lands in hell.

Gustavus Sohon, *Hal-hal-tlos-tsot, "Lawyer,"* pencil drawing, 1855. Washington State Historical Society, Tacoma, WA.

Not only the cylinder hat as a dignified symbol of chieftainship, but even the chieftainship itself was often the result of culture contact. The high status of persons like Lawyer (c. 1795–1876), who signed the treaty of 1855 as the "Supreme Chief" of the Nez Perce, was triggered by a need on the part of the American government for transparent hierarchies when it came to the cession of lands or contentious issues. Thirty years later, the same government complained that the immense powers of tribal chiefs were detrimental to the progress of civilization.

# Chief Joseph – Thunder Rolling Over the Mountains

"Hear me, my chiefs! I am tired; my heart is sick and sad. From where the sun now stands I will fight no more forever."

These words, probably the most famous historical words ever spoken by a Native American, were that of Nez Perce chief Hinmató Wyalahtqit ("Thunder Rolling Over the Mountains") on October 5, 1877, the day he surrendered to United States officers General Oliver Howard and Colonel Nelson Miles in the Bear Paw Mountains in northern Montana. He and the 87 warriors, 184 women, and 147 children that made up his exhausted band were less than 40 miles away from the Canadian border, behind which they had hoped to find safety from their pursuers and a fresh start. They had already covered a distance of 1,200 miles, their torturous trek having started in mid-June of that year from their home in the Wallowa Valley in northeastern Oregon.

Hinmató Wyalahtqit was born in 1841, in the region that, because of its breathtaking landscapes, is today known as the Switzerland of North America. Since his father was one of the first Nez Perce to be baptized by missionary Henry Spalding (1803–74), when he received the name Joseph, he, the son, was named Chief Joseph junior (1841–1904) by the whites. Having converted to Christianity, Joseph senior (c. 1788–1871), chief of the Nez Perce in the Wallowa Valley, later reconverted to the traditional Washat, or Seven Drums religion. He was disappointed by the missionaries; they continued to bring ever more whites into the country and appeared to be immune to the epidemic diseases afflicting the indigenous people, and the rough manner with which they treated the natives made them increasingly unpopular.

Other Nez Perce chiefs, however, adopted the Christian faith as well as the system of government determined by the missionaries and the American government under which Hal-hal-tlos-tsot, or Lawyer, was declared Supreme Chief. Even though Lawyer, according to traditional Nez Perce law, only actually represented half of the Nez Perce population, he signed a treaty in 1863 in the name of all Nez Perce (despite being unauthorized to do so), according to which his people's once extensive territory was reduced to a small reservation.

Traditionally oriented Nez Perce chiefs such as Joseph senior did not accept this treaty, since they had no intention of forfeiting the lands pledged to them by the treaty of 1855. According to the treaty of 1863, the home of Joseph's band was outside the planned reservation borders, and the government authorized white settlement on that land. Joseph senior died in 1871. His son, elected as his successor, refused, as had his father before him, to leave his traditional home in the Wallowa Valley and settle among the Christian "Treaty Indians" on their reservation in Idaho. For some

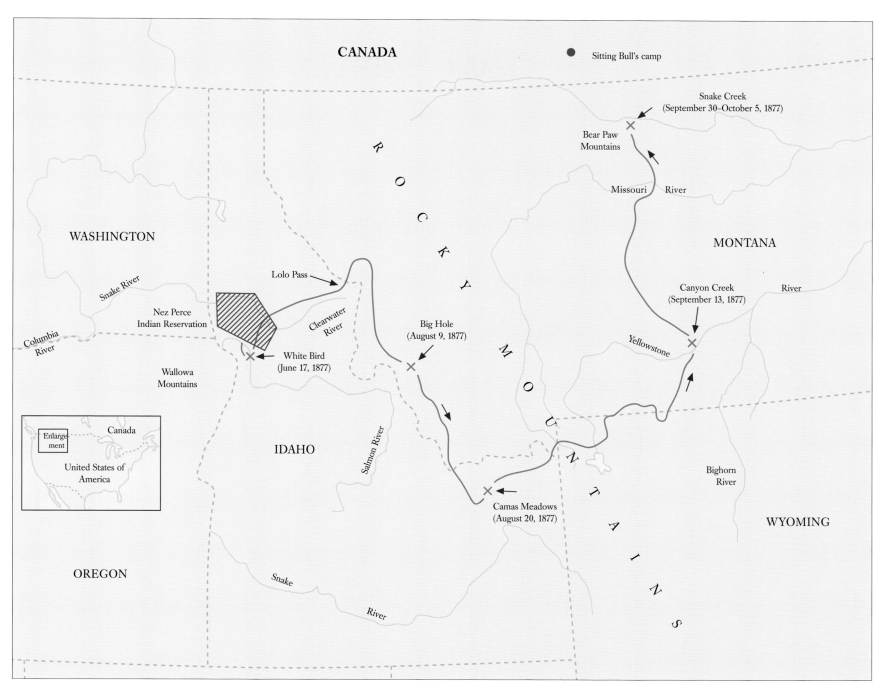

Map of the Nez Perce War, 1877.

CANADA

Sitting Bull's camp

Snake Creek
(September 30–October 5, 1877)

Bear Paw
Mountains

Missouri    River

ROCKY

WASHINGTON

Lolo Pass

MONTANA

Canyon Creek
(September 13, 1877)          River

Snake River

Nez Perce
Indian Reservation

Clearwater
River

Big Hole
(August 9, 1877)

M
O
U
N
T
A
I
N
S

Yellowstone

Columbia
River

White Bird
(June 17, 1877)

Wallowa
Mountains

Enlarge-
ment

Canada

United States of
America

IDAHO

Salmon River

Bighorn
River

WYOMING

Camas Meadows
(August 20, 1877)

OREGON

Snake

River

Plateau    267

Map of the Nez Perce War, 1877.

After the Crow had refused to support the Nez Perce in their resistance, their only hope was to flee to Canada, which had several months before become the refuge of Sitting Bull. Even though the Nez Perce and the United States army fought several battles in Idaho and Montana from June through October 1877, American officers were most impressed by the way Joseph's people repeatedly managed to keep out of reach of the far more powerful military.

Opposite page:

Chief Joseph, presumably in 1884. Denver Public Library, Denver, CO.

On his visits to Washington in 1879, Joseph, or Hinmató Wyalahtqit ("Thunder Rolling Over the Mountains"), was given a friendly reception. Despite the fact that philanthropic organizations, the press, and the public at large had bemoaned his fate, Joseph's attempts to obtain permission to return to his own reservation were in vain.

time, he and his band were able to resist the increasing pressure to which they were subjected by the advancing settlers – but only until 1877, when General Howard set a final ultimatum for the band to resettle.

Joseph and his council wanted to continue negotiations. In an act of revenge, however, some of the younger warriors killed several settlers, so that the Nez Perce, having hitherto maintained peace with the whites, had no choice but to leave their homelands and thus preserve their freedom. Hoping to be able to live among the allied Crow as bison hunters, they marched across the Rockies to the east. Upon arrival, they realized that they could hope for no support from these people. Some of their former friends had, in fact, been hired by the United States army as scouts for the campaign against them. The Nez Perce considered their flight to British Canada to be a last resort in their search for freedom.

Notwithstanding their skill and several skirmishes during which the United States army suffered severe losses at the hands of the Nez Perce, Joseph and his band were

ultimately forced into military captivity. Burdened with the many injured and with exhausted and emaciated women and children, it was no longer possible to flee. More than 150 Nez Perce had already died. Joseph's aspiration to return to the Wallowa Valley and keep his territory proved futile. The army transported the survivors to Oklahoma, where almost a quarter of them died of malaria. In 1885, after Joseph had made several trips to the capital city, Washington, his people were allowed to return to the Northwest, to the Colville Reservation in Washington state. There, until his death in 1904 and despite much harassment from the administration, Joseph remained a tenacious believer in the traditional way of life.

Joseph realized the futility of any hope of returning to the Wallowa Valley when he traveled there on a visit in 1900. During the 23 years of his forced exile, the whites had fenced in the entire region and turned it into farmland. Hence, here, as in other regions of the North American continent, there remained little room for the free-spirited lives of those who had once reigned here.

Chief Joseph, 1903. Photograph:
Edward S. Curtis. National
Anthropological Archives,
Smithsonian Institution,
Washington DC.

His advocacy for peace, his eloquence,
and his military genius, coupled with
personal tragedy and a photogenic
appearance, made Chief Joseph the
perfect example of a "good Indian" in
the eyes of the whites. To them, his fate
was regrettable, but unavoidable.

Opposite page:

Chief Joseph, 1900. Photograph:
DeLancey Gill. National
Anthropological Archives,
Smithsonian Institution,
Washington, DC.

Four years before his death, Joseph was
granted the right to visit his father's
grave in Wallowa Valley. The pastures
of the Nez Perce had meanwhile been
turned into farms with flowering fruit
groves, and towns had been erected.
The white farmer on whose land the
grave was located had fenced it and
taken care to maintain it – "in a spirit
too seldom found among people
of his kind," as the official from the
Bureau of Indian Affairs accom-
panying Joseph remarked.

# NORTHWEST COAST

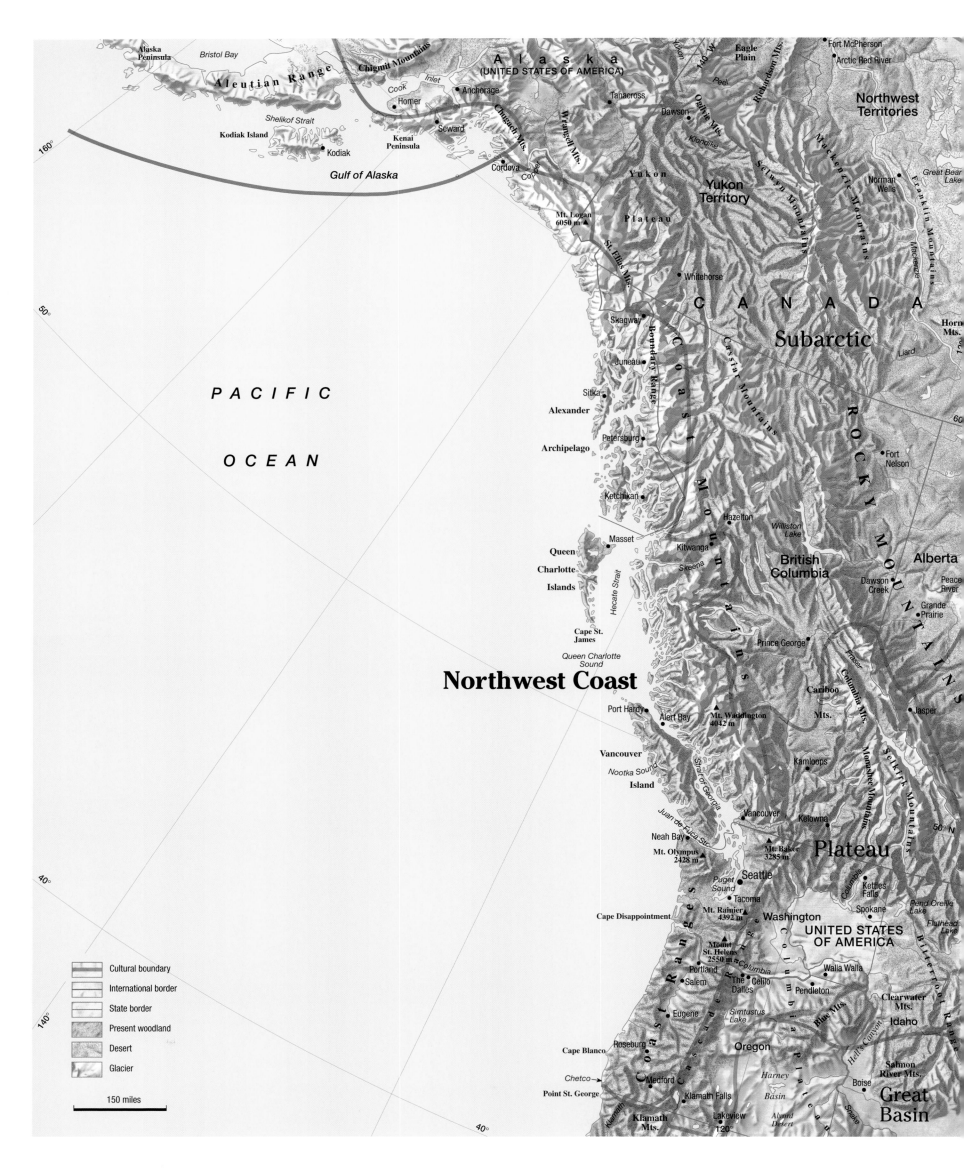

**Alaska Peninsula** · *Bristol Bay* · **Aleutian Range** · **Chigmit Mountains** · A l a s k a (UNITED STATES OF AMERICA)

*Cook* · *Inlet* · Homer · ·Anchorage · Tanacross · Dawson

**Eagle Plain** · *Yukon* · *Peel* · **Ogilvie Mts.** · **Richardson Mts.** · Fort McPherson · ·Arctic Red River

**Northwest Territories**

*Shelikof Strait* · **Kodiak Island** · ·Seward · **Kenai Peninsula** · Cordova · *Copper*

*Gulf of Alaska* · Y u k o n · P l a t e a u · **Selwyn Mountains** · **Mackenzie Mountains**

**Kodiak** · **Mt. Logan 6050 m ▲** · **St. Elias Mts.**

*Klondike* · *Dawson* · Norman Wells · **Franklin Mountains** · *Great Bear Lake*

**Kodiak Island** · Whitehorse · C A N A D A · **Subarctic** · *Liard*

**Horn Mts.**

P A C I F I C · Skagway · **Boundary Range** · **Coast Mountains** · **Cassiar Mountains**

O C E A N · Juneau · Sitka · **R O C K Y** · Fort Nelson

**Alexander** · Petersburg · **Archipelago** · Ketchikan · Hazelton · *Williston Lake* · **M O U N T A I N S** · **Alberta**

Masset · Kitwanga · **British Columbia** · Dawson Creek · **Peace River**

**Queen Charlotte Islands** · *Skeena* · Prince George · *Fraser* · Grande Prairie

*Hecate Strait* · **Columbia Mts.** · **Cariboo Mts.** · Jasper

**Cape St. James** · *Queen Charlotte Sound*

# Northwest Coast

Port Hardy · Alert Bay · **Mt. Waddington 4042 m ▲** · **Monashee Mountains**

**Vancouver** · *Nootka Sound* · **Island** · Kamloops · **Selkirk Mountains**

Vancouver · Kelowna · **Plateau**

*Juan de Fuca Str.* · Neah Bay · **Mt. Olympus 2428 m ▲** · **Mt. Baker 3285 m ▲**

**Puget Sound** · Seattle · *Columbia* · **Kettles Falls**

Tacoma · *Pend Oreille Lake*

**Cape Disappointment** · **Mt. Rainier 4392 m ▲** · **Washington** · Spokane · *Flathead Lake*

**Mount St. Helens 2550 m ▲** · Portland · *Columbia* · **UNITED STATES OF AMERICA**

Salem · The Dalles · *Celilo* · Pendleton · Walla Walla

Eugene · *Simtustus Lake* · **Clearwater Mts.** · **Idaho**

**Blue Mts.** · **Bitterroot Range**

**Cape Blanco** · Roseburg · **Oregon** · *Hell's Canyon*

*Chetco* → · Medford · *Harney Basin* · **Salmon River Mts.**

**Point St. George** · Klamath Falls · Boise · **Great Basin**

**Klamath Mts.** · Lakeview · *Alvord Desert* · *Snake*

*Klamath*

Henry Kammler

# The northern rainforest

## The land of the tree of life

"An indescribable feeling takes possession of the soul at the sight of this ancient and lonely wilderness, where, for numberless centuries, trees have fallen only because of age," Friedrich von Lütke, a German ship's captain in Russian service, wrote in 1835, impressed by the giant trees that shape the coastal landscape of the Pacific Northwest. This region includes the entire stretch of coast from the Copper River delta in southern Alaska down to the mouth of the Chetco River in Oregon. Its eastern border is marked by the Rocky Mountains (more specifically the Chugach and St. Elias Mountains), the coastal mountains of British Columbia, and the Cascade Range in the northwestern United States. At its widest expanse, around Puget Sound, this culture area extends around 220 miles inland.

Where chainsaws and oil rigs have left the "northern rainforest" untouched, the salty sea breeze brought in from the ocean mingles with the odor of tree resin and mould exhaled by the dripping-wet forest. Like two confident rulers, the majestic mountains and the raging sea appear to embrace, leaving only a narrow ledge of coastal forest and shore between the snow-covered summits and the gray-green depths of the Pacific. This narrow stretch of land covered by dark forests and the conglomeration of an infinite number of islands, fiords, and shoals, has allowed an unique culture to mature in relative seclusion. Even without agriculture, the population density was higher than elsewhere, they developed a structure of social classes, and were the only North Americans to produce a group of professional artists – woodcarvers and painters who worked to commission for noble families.

The Kuroshio Current, which flows to these waters from Asia, is the warming lifeline of this naturally wealthy region, providing even sweet nectar for subtropical hummingbirds and a sultry summer climate all the way up to southern Alaska. Salmon is the proverbial daily bread of the region's people, who today jokingly call themselves "Fish Indians," to impress upon disappointed visitors to the region who expect to find Hollywood-style "Feather Indians" the magnificence of the coastal Pacific cultures. Whereas the locals have little in common with the stereotypical bison hunters, another "Indian" stereotype does have its roots here: that of the garishly painted and "grotesquely" carved "totem poles," which actually are crests of noble families. Confused in the European imagination with the stakes for the torture of prisoners, these poles have nothing to

**Skeena River, British Columbia.**

The steep slopes of the mountains rising out of the ocean and estuaries, cause the lifestyle of the region's inhabitants to be focused on the water and its resources. To this day, there are no roads leading along the coast; canoes were the most important form of transport. Inland excursions were avoided where possible, since the dense forests were considered to harbor unpredictable supernatural beings. The Southern and Coast Tsimshian ("Those in the Skeena") and the Gitksan ("People of the Skeena") derived their self-designations from the Skeena River.

Previous pages:

**Howe Sound near Vancouver, British Columbia.**

The narrow river valleys and fiords in the lee of Vancouver Island were home to numerous Coast Salish groups. The Squamish still live north of Howe Sound.

**Peoples of the Northwest Coast.**

Evidence suggests that the Haida are the oldest group among the inhabitants of the northernmost part of the Northwest Coast and that they were driven onto the Queen Charlotte Islands by the Tlingit and by the Tsimshian, who were probably distant relatives of the Penuti of California. Similarly, the Salishan-speaking peoples (Bella Coola, Coast Salish, Tillamook) of the central and southern coast and the Athapaskans in Washington and Oregon (Kwalhioqua, Clatskanie, and others) migrated to the region more recently, possibly between 1,000 BC and 1500 AD, while the Wakashan speakers and those speaking the many isolated languages (Chinook, Chemakum, Alsea, Siuslaw, and Coos) were the earlier inhabitants. In Canada the indigenous peoples have recently achieved the official use of their self-designations such as Nuu-chah-nulth (instead of Nootka), Kwakwaka'wakw (Kwakiutl), or Nuxalk (Bella Coola).

Rocky coastline in Boardman State Park, southern Oregon.

The women of the Athapaskan Tututni, who dwelled here, would climb down these steep cliffs to gather shellfish, edible seaweed, and flotsam. The men would hunt the sea lions and seals that came onto the beaches. Whales washed ashore by the ocean presented a rare opportunity for a feast. In the 19th century, the Athapaskan tribes of Oregon were either wiped out or forced to migrate to the northern parts of Oregon.

# A coast of diversity

The maritime climate of the Northwest Coast produces cool summers and wet, mild winters. The southern Alaskan mountain range, rising 20,000 feet above sea level, receives about 300 inches of rain annually; the coastal regions further south have an annual rainfall of 60 to 150 inches. There are also extensive dry regions (such as the Olympic Peninsula), which, in the lee of the mountains, receive no more than 10 inches of precipitation a year. Many areas have frost-free periods of more than 120 days per year. For the coastal cultures, the frequent storms, which turn the turbulent waters of the ocean into veritable cauldrons, were a serious threat.

Proof of settlement in the region dates back 11,000 years. Evidence for traits of the historical cultures we know today exists in the form of artifacts (notably tools made of bone and stone) dating back 5,000 years and found on Vancouver Island, the Queen Charlotte Islands, and in Puget Sound. While the region offered abundant natural wealth, it was a sometimes hostile environment, which gave rise to the development of sophisticated techniques of seafaring and timber processing. The humid climate, however, has meant that few wooden artifacts survived. It is therefore difficult to reconstruct the early development of whaling, of the first oceangoing canoes, and of the large crest poles.

The Northwest Coast may be divided into three major, culturally distinct regions, plus a transitional zone adjoining the culture area of California. The northernmost part was inhabited by the small Eyak people, wedged in between the Pacific Eskimo and the numerous Tlingit tribes who occupied the entire Alaska panhandle. The Tlingit constitute a linguistic family of their own that is surprisingly uniform, given that they inhabit an extensive territory. The Haida, who have lived on the Queen Charlotte Islands for thousands of years, speak a range of dialects that also belong to one separate linguistic family. The mainland directly opposite the islands is occupied by the peoples of the Tsimshian language family. Their territory extends along the Nass and Skeena rivers and deep inland. It was predominantly the Nisga'a and the Gitksan who, with no access to the coast, maintained close contact (mainly by trade) with the Athapaskan people of the Subarctic, reciprocally influencing one another's culture. Marital ties and trade links were also present with their southern neighbors, the Wakashan-speaking Haisla.

Here, on the northern borders of the central region of the Northwest Coast, the Wakashan peoples and the Salishan-speaking Bella Coola (Nuxalk) were far more oriented toward the ocean than their northern neighbors and developed great skills as sea mammal hunters.

The sheltered mainland opposite Vancouver Island near Puget Sound and on the coast of Washington and Oregon constitutes the southern region of the Northwest Coast. The local inhabitants include many Coast Salish tribes, whose languages spread all along the coast, the Chinook tribes at the mouth of the Columbia River, and

do with torture, except that their owners would agonize over their design and how to best express in them the wealth and dignity of their families.

Timber, available in such abundance, is of elementary inportance for the culture of the Northwest Coast. For the coastal people, the red cedar (not in fact a cedar at all, but a giant "tree of life" and a member of the cypress family) was just as important a source of raw material as was the bison for the peoples of the Plains. This tree, which is truly a "tree of life," provided many useful resources: lightweight timber for houses, canoes, and various other implements of everyday life; its inner bark was used for clothing, its root fiber for basketry.

José Cardero, *Cacique of Mulgrave Requests Peace from the Corvettes*, watercolor, 1791. Museo de América, Madrid, Spain.

Like elsewhere, cultural contact on the Northwest Coast, was shaped by the longing to aquire the possessions of others. In 1791 the theft by the Yakutat-Tlingit of a pair of trousers from a Spanish sailor led to tensions between the indigenous people and the European visitors. The ceremonial return of the garment by a member of the nobility, accompanied by songs and melodramatic gestures, was intended as a display of Tlingit desire for peace. The painting depicts only one of the canoes in a whole convoy of envoys sent on this assignment.

A.F. Postels, *A Forest on Sitka Island, 1827,* lithograph, from Friedrich von Lütke, *Voyage autour du monde,* Paris, 1835. Lilly Library, Indiana University, Bloomington, IN.

The slopes of the coastal ranges facing the ocean can receive up to 240 inches of rainfall a year. Moss and ferns grow on every patch of ground and also cover rocks, tree trunks, and the lower branches of giant trees of the primeval forest. The people portrayed by this Russian artist look more like the Polynesians that he met on another leg of his travels around the world, and that were abducted, albeit in small numbers, to the Northwest Coast of America. The trading companies later officially employed Hawaiians, some of whom intermarried with the indigenous population.

the two groups of Chemakum speakers (Quileute and the Chemakum).

Very little is known about the peoples who settled further south – the Alsea, Coos, Siuslaw, Takelma, Kalapuya, and others – since malaria, smallpox, measles, and forced resettlement destroyed their cultures before they could be recorded in detail. The last survivors of these groups provided anthropologists and linguists with material for now classic works, but little is known about some of the peoples and languages that still exist today. Much the same can be said of the peoples of the region bordering California – the Athapaskans of Oregon, the Tolowa, and the Takelma.

## Of furs and men

The first period of contact between people of the Northwest Coast and Europeans was dominated by the fur trade. By the time Juan Pérez (d. 1774) traveled up the coast in 1774 to claim to the territory for the Spanish crown, Russian entrepreneurs had already been hunting sea otters along the Alaskan coast for decades, using forced labor from the Aleutian Islands, and had sold the furs in Canton, China, for astronomical sums. In the race between the major powers to gain a leading stake in this lucrative source of income on the Northwest Coast, the Spanish lost to the British after a few years. Traders were surprised to find that their indigenous trading partners were clever, sometimes brutal, and even prepared to seize European ships. Keen to aquire valuable metal tools rather than cheap trinkets, the indigenous traders would often dictate the prices by exploiting the competition between the Europeans.

After the elimination of the Spanish competition, three Powers continued the struggle for control of the Northwest Coast trade: the Russians from their possessions on the Aleutian Islands, the British in the central part of the coast, and the Americans in the south. The first permanent trading posts were established by the Russians in 1799 among the Tlingit (with whom they were in a constant state of tension) and in 1811 by the Americans at the mouth of the Columbia River. During the following decades, the British Hudson's Bay Company set up trading posts and the Americans established forts in Oregon, a region jointly used by both nations until 1846. While most of the tribes on American territory ceded their lands through treaties in the mid-19th century, the colony of British Columbia (which joined the Canadian Federation in 1871), did not even consider the possibility that indigenous peoples might have land rights at all. There was a huge influx of settlers to the Washington Territory, which became the 42nd state of the United States in 1889. Puget Sound saw rapid growth and urbanization around such new centers as Seattle and Tacoma, and the reservations established in the 1850s were eventually enclosed by the cities. In 1867, Alaska was transferred from Russia to the United States without the indigenous population being consulted about this issue.

Immediately following the first contact, European diseases caused cruel devastation. In 1775, the first smallpox epidemic killed an estimated one third of the indigenous inhabitants. Population figures declined steadily from around 190,000 to around 30,000 in the early 20th century.

The tribes now became the object of assimilation measures by the American and Canadian governments. Winter ceremonials and potlatch feasts were banned. Missionaries and Indian affairs personnel pressured the larger kinship groups to relinquish the longhouses they inhabited in favor of the nuclear families living on individual allotments of land and to follow the American dream. Until the 1960s indigenous children were sent to special boarding schools, where they were strictly taught to conform to Western culture. Parents who resisted separation from their children and their alienation from their own culture could expect their children to be forcefully adopted into white foster families.

Organizations acting in defense of Native American interests were established at an early stage. The Alaska Native Brotherhood, founded in 1912, was predominantly under the leadership of Tlingit chiefs and represented a self-determined path to "progress" in the Western sense of the term. Various associations in British Columbia have been set up since the early 20th century in the pursuit of land and civil rights. It was not until the end of the 20th century, however, and after a lengthy process of negotiations, that a solution of the land rights issue was outlined in Canada. On the basis of a variety of models for autonomy, individual tribes pursued an improved protection status for their lands and its resources and for a higher standard of living and greater political participation.

Bill Reid

Haida artist Bill Reid (1920–1998) grew up far from the Northwest Coast and only discovered his roots later in life. From the 1960s onward, he was responsible for vital contributions to the renaissance of Northwest Coast art. In addition to reviving traditional carving styles, the art scene in his traditional homeland also profited from his numerous trendsetting innovations, such as the use of metal techniques, and the recognition of Northwest Coast art as a Canadian national art form.

Opposite page:

*The Labeler*, Sitkof Bay Cannery, Alaska, c. 1910. Alaska State Library, Juneau, AK.

Around 1900, fish canneries became the most important provider of jobs for indigenous women on the coast. The men still went to hunt seal and whale – occupations that were, however, already on the decline. The women's work provided an income, which made it possible to stage even larger potlatch feasts with commercial consumer goods, but the old economic dominance of the chiefs waned, as the job market was not interested in lineage or social standing of the workers.

# Salmon and whale

**Spawning salmon.**

During their arduous journey upstream and before finally reaching the upper courses of rivers and the quiet inland lakes in order to spawn, salmon must overcome numerous rapids and escape many a predator. Salmon that have already spawned change their shape: their sides deflate and they soon die. They have fulfilled their mission. In the following year thousands of young salmon will leave their freshwater nurseries and head for the Pacific.

For the peoples of the coast, the arrival of the salmon in their waters in late spring marked the beginning of the year. For it was the salmon around which their economic well-being was centered and which provided the basis for their material and cultural wealth. In addition to the rainbow trout (of the salmon family), the rivers supplied five types of Pacific salmon – chinook (king), pink, coho, sockeye, and dog – until stocks vanished well after the onset of winter.

While in winter people assembled in the large villages located in the sheltered fiords, their summer residences were scattered among their fishing grounds. These locations provided abundant supplies of fish, extracted from the wooden fish weirs that partially or totally blocked off the riverbeds. The weirs were constructed in a such a way as to create an upstream pool, within a rectangular enclosure that proved a deadly trap for fish on their journey upriver. In tidal regions stone walls were built near

estuaries. At high tide, when the walls were submerged, the salmon would pass above them, but they would then be prevented from passing back on their return at times of low tide, thus becoming easy prey for the fishers. In midsummer dense rows of pointed stakes were rammed into the shallow riverbeds so that the salmon attempting to leap over them would impale themselves.

When the Coast Salish fished for salmon in the salt waters of the south, they also used large nets that were stretched out between two canoes and then hauled through a school of fish. A good haul could result in a catch of several thousand fish in one single effort. The leaping salmon of the rivers were caught in midair with hand nets by men in canoes or standing on special platforms positioned over the rapids.

Fish weirs were often made of wickerwork, as were the basket traps installed behind them. Despite its importance as a means of providing food, fishing was

Tlingit fisherman and his candlefish catch, c.1910. University of Pennsylvania Museum, Philadelphia, PA.

Candlefish, or eulachon (locally pronounced like "hooligan" without an h), are a major source of a particularly nutritious oil, which is an important trade item. The fish were placed in troughs where they were fermented for several weeks, after which the oil was extracted. The pungent oil was skimmed off the broth and any remaining oil pressed out of the residue. Candlefish were also dried and stored, since the large quantities of oil that they contained meant that they were flammable and could be used as torches. The Tsimshian and the northern Kwakiutl were the main processors of this fish.

Bottom right:

Makah woman cleaning salmon, Neah Bay, Washington, c. 1907. Washington State Historical Society. Tacoma, WA.

Fishing and hunting were the exclusive responsibility of men. The Nootka even decreed that, during the time of salmon fishing, menstruating women were required to retreat to special dwellings. Once the catch was landed, women were responsible for preparing and conserving the fish, mainly through a process of smoking in special smoke huts that were a part of every household. Women were also responsible for gathering the abundant shellfish and edible algae that the low tides uncovered.

Far right:

Fishing the rapids.

When salmon pass through on their way upstream, there is a buildup of fish in the depressions on either side of a rapid. Here, the fish gather their strength both before and after their strenuous leap, finding plentiful food in the form of smaller freshwater life in the weaker currents.

never considered a very respectable occupation. The nobility, in particular, used slaves to carry out this work. Although they were responsible for preparing the fish after it had been caught, women were excluded from all actual fishing tasks and were always kept well away from all fishing devices.

Fish was roasted in ash, added to stews, or cooked in earth ovens. It was also preserved for winter, either by being cut into thin strips and laid out to dry, or by being smoked in special huts, where the fish, sliced in half, were attached to sticks to prevent them from curling up. They could then be easily bundled and stored. The heads of the fish were, and still are, a favorite food, and there are countless ways of preparing them. A particularly spicy dish was a cheeselike mixture made of fermented fish heads and roe.

The mighty halibut, which frequents the sandy beds of the deeper waters, was caught using large wooden hooks with sharpened bone tips. In general, halibut was not as popular a food as salmon, since its meat was less firm and less fat. The Haida, however, caught larger quantities of halibut than they did of salmon. Other types of fish, for example herring or cod, were generally caught with fish hooks, spears, and nets.

# Whales – the catch of chiefs

Whales, considered to be endowed with supernatural powers, were only rarely hunted despite being a desirable source of food. It was most probably due to the lack of salmon in certain rivers that some peoples of the outer, unsheltered coastlines (Nootka [Nuu-chah-nulth], Makah, Quileute, Quinault) turned to the more difficult task of catching whales (predominantly humpback and Californian gray whales, less often North Pacific right whales and killer whales), hunting them in oceangoing canoes, with experienced crews. This was a dangerous undertaking. A number of canoes would approach the whale, but only the chief, in his capacity as leader of the hunting party, had the right to inflict the first blow. Standing at the bow of the vessel, he would ram the harpoon into this huge mammal's back, trying to reach all the way to the heart. At the same time, a helper would let loose the line to which floats made of inflated seal skins were attached. The next moment was the most dangerous: the whale would dive down at lightning speed, often smashing to pieces the pursuing canoe with its fluke. Slowed by the floats and hampered by the canoe that it was towing, the whale was an easy target for further harpoon attacks accompanied by a quick prayer from the hunters that it would swim toward the coast. If the whale headed toward the open seas, it would be lost. The hunters would also lose it if it landed on a part of the shore belonging to another chief, to whom the whale would then have to be forfeited.

Only chiefs who enjoyed strong support from their supernatural helpers could be good whale hunters. Preparations for hunts required days of fasting and solitary prayer, sexual abstinence, and the support of the deceased; the hunters procured assistance in a shrine that contained the skulls and bones of famous predecessors and of slain enemies, as well as wooden replicas of whales and images of supernatural beings. One skull was usually taken on the hunt as an amulet, in order to maximize its protective and supportive powers.

Other peoples, not skilled in whaling, had to wait for the mammals to be stranded on the shore. When this occurred, a feast was arranged. The meat itself, usually no longer fit for consumption, was of trivial importance, even though it was nonetheless eaten. The animals' huge reserves of fat were extracted in large tubs, the oil being stored in watertight wooden chests for the winter festival season. The stench of the rotting animal would drift inland from the beach for days. For the inhabitants, however, this odor was the promise of future feasts. One Nootka tribe was even named after a beach onto which large numbers of whales were washed ashore: Tseshaht means "Those from the place of putrefaction stench."

Boats were the major means of transport; the ocean and rivers were their highways. These canoes were made of selected trunks of red cedar, which were split and hollowed out; yet they were more than simple dugout canoes. The

Nootka whaling shrine, Yuquot (Friendly Cove), British Columbia, 1904. Photograph: George Hunt. American Museum of Natural History, New York, NY.

This whale hunter's shrine in Yuquot, containing skulls and the wooden replicas of corpses, served Chief Maquinna at the beginning of the 19th century as a place of ritual preparation before he embarked on whaling excursions. This photograph of the strictly secret shrine was taken by the Tlingit George Hunt (1854–1933), who grew up among the Kwakiutl and who posed as a shaman in order to gain access to it. Hunt even managed to purchase this shrine – an important source of tribal well-being – for the American Museum of Natural History. Two chiefs actually claimed rights to this shrine, a fact which caused the purchase price to be inflated, but which also reduced their opposition to the deal, since no-one would be left empty-handed.

The killed whale's mouth was sewn up by a diver while the hunting party was still at sea. The animal would otherwise fill with water and the canoe would no longer be able to tow it in. The seal skin floats can be seen to the right of the carcass. In 1999, amid protests by animal protectionists, the Makah once more began to make use of their treaty right to hunt five Californian gray whales per year.

Wooden frame rattle, Clayoquot (Nootka), British Columbia, second half of the 19th century. American Museum of Natural History, New York, NY.

Rattles were exceptionally important in the ceremonial life of the people of the Northwest Coast. They were used by shamans as a means of communicating with their spiritual helpers. If a rattle was sounded during a potlatch, all conversation would cease, for this signaled the beginning of an important speech or prayer. The significance and function of this unusual Clayoquot rattle, which consists of a whole school of wooden fish attached to a frame, are unknown. Its design may, however, be linked to the annual reproduction rituals for fish.

sides were shaped using hot water, and the bow and stern were sewn to the body construction with spruce root splints and caulked with pitch. On the northern coast, both bow and stern were made of pointed pieces of wood, thus breaking even the waves that crashed onto the stern. By contrast, canoes of the "Nootka" and the "Chinook" types had only an elevated bow. The Salish built low-sided vessels ideal for inland waters. Everywhere boats were built in various sizes – from one-man canoes to large freight vessels – according to their intended usage. War canoes were especially large, streamlined, and fast.

## Gathering food

The most important plant food gathered by the peoples of the coast was the large variety of berries, including cranberries, blackberries, strawberries, black currants, gooseberries, and salal berries (a wintergreen berry). These were dried and pressed into small cakes, and stored for the winter or traded. Wild onions, the roots of ferns, and edible tree bark further supplemented the vegetal diet in this region. In spring, fern and berry-bush shoots were eaten; the shoots of the salmonberry bush, for instance, taste similar to rhubarb. Resin was used as chewing gum. Buffalo berries were beaten to a stiff foam and served as a dessert. Except in Alaska, where potatoes were introduced by the Russians, the only plant originally cultivated to a small extent was tobacco.

In tidal regions, women equipped with digging sticks and large carrying baskets extracted shellfish, including limpets, gooseneck barnacles, and mussels from the mud or broke them off the rocks. Algae and seaweed were also part of the diet, and even today dried seaweed is used in many households as a salty snack.

Herring roe was considered a delicacy. During spawning times, people would hang spruce branches in the shallow waters. In no time, the branch would be full of thick clumps of fish eggs laid by the schools of herring. Sometimes it would suffice to pull large-leaved seaweed, on which the fish would also spawn, out of the water. Herring roe was eaten raw, grilled, roasted, or fermented, and often in combination with seal oil. Dried, it was also an important trade item.

Land animals contributed only a small proportion to the diet, especially as hunting was difficult in the dense woods. Mule deer, bear, mountain goat, beaver, marmot, and sea birds, however, were often on the menu. Mountain goats were a source of both meat and wool; their fat was also used as a condiment and in medicines. Grizzly bears and black bears could be caught in traps or killed with spears during hibernation, Sea lions and seals were clubbed to death. Dogs often accompanied people on goat and deer hunts, although deer meat was considered to be dangerous for women.

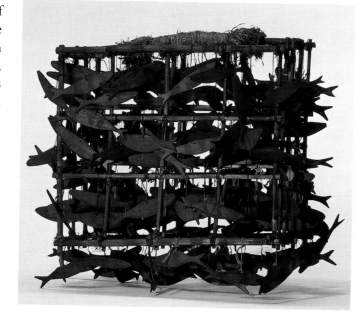

# The world is a house

The villages of the coast consited of plank houses, whose gabled sides and entrance usually faced the ocean. They were 50 to 65 feet long, with a rectangular or square floor plan, and could accommodate half a dozen families, or about 50 people. In exceptional cases the feasting houses of major chiefs could be up to 325 feet long. Houses in northern parts of the Northwest Coast normally had flat gabled roofs, supported by a framework and pierced by a rectangular smoke hole with a contraption allowing it to be opened and closed.

In the central parts of the coast, the territory of the Wakashan and Coast Salish, the framework of the roofs of houses was supported by posts onto which two heavy beams were mounted. Numerous smaller posts formed the framework of the walls, which usually consisted of planks arranged horizontally and overlapping from top to bottom so that rainwater would run down and off the walls. Gaps between the planks provided ventilation, since these houses were built without windows. When people moved from their winter homes to their summer camps at the fishing grounds, they took the planks of their houses with them, leaving only the heavy skeleton construction behind. When the time came to return, the planks were stacked over two boats, and the platform thus created was used to transport household goods and also provided seating for children.

In the central and southern parts of the coast, many of the houses had almost flat, only slightly sloping roofs. The further south one came, the more one would see of these flat-roofed houses as opposed to gabled ones. In the area that today lies in the states of Washington and Oregon, houses were commonly of the smaller, semisunken form.

A longhouse accommodated all the relatives of a lineage (those people with a common ancestor, after whom they were often named) and their spouses. Whereas in the north descent was traced through the female line, in the central regions of the coast individuals were able to choose whether to join the group of their mother, or of their father. It was sometimes even possible to join the lineage of a grandparent. Marriage within one's own lineage was prohibited. The same applied to the clans which existed in the northern part of the region. A clan always consisted of several lineages that could generally each be traced back to a single mythical ancestor. Clans, in turn, grouped themselves into two moieties, and marriage partners were selected among the people of the opposite moiety.

Clans and moieties were named after their respective animal crests: the moieties of the Tlingit were Raven and Wolf; those of the Haida were Eagle and Raven. Clan members also regarded themselves as related beyond tribal boundaries, and marriage between them was likewise prohibited. Visitors would be given accommodation by

Opposite page, above:

Masset, one of the main Haida villages, Queen Charlotte Islands, British Columbia, 1881. Photograph: Edward Dossetter. British Columbia Archives, Victoria, BC.

A forest of totem poles, both free-standing and attached to house fronts, dominates the view of Masset, the largest Haida village, which in 1860 consisted of 33 houses. The so-called Monster House of Chief Wiah is located in the center of the village. It covers an area of 2900 square feet. Inside, a staircase leads up to two lofts and down to a sunken floor some 10 feet below ground level. The house in the foreground is already built according to white American design. By 1905 all the houses built to the traditional fashion, and considered to be not sufficiently "civilized," had completely vanished from Masset.

John Webber, *An Inside View of a Native Habitation,* engraving, 1778. Peabody Museum, Harvard University, Cambridge, MA.

Wooden seating and sleeping platforms are mounted along the walls of this Mowachaht-Nootka house. Clothing and other possessions are stored in wooden boxes stacked behind these platforms. The planks on the right serve to mark the individual living sections for each family. The carved posts in the background display the crests of the chief. The carved whale fin in front of the left-hand post identifies the chief as a successful whale hunter. Fish are smoked above the fire, and are then suspended from the ceiling. Hot stones are used to heat the water in the wooden box next to the fireplace.

their "clan relatives" and prisoners of war were never enslaved by them, but mercifully passed on to southern tribes that used them as slaves.

The inhabitants considered their house to be the basis of their identity. As a social unit, it represented the essential elements of community: home, clan, family, ancestors, health, security, and economic and spiritual well-being. It is only logical, therefore, that in many languages of the region there is no verbal distinction between "house," "village," and "people." Primary reference was always on one's own house group and the inherited land rights to which it held claim, and for the administration of which the highest-ranking individuals in the lineage were responsible. Even the large winter villages rarely acted as a single political unit, since the actions of any individual were determined by his loyalty to his own house group. Each house had its own sacred stories (which the Nootka called "that to which the old is linked") which were not divulged to others and which explained the origin of the family line, the magical powers connected with the crests, and the rights of family members to practice particular forms of art.

House building was commonly a task undertaken by the entire lineage, and when the highest-ranking chief's family built a new house, the whole village would help in order to show their loyalty. On the northern coast, houses were erected, at least theoretically, by the opposite moiety. Lineages would often commission renowned artists from other villages to furnish the interior of their homes, thus adding to the fame of their houses. Housewarmings were celebrated with a major potlatch feast at which high-ranking representatives of other lineages and tribes were lavishly regaled. For their services as witnesses to such ritually exceptional events or as builders of the house, these guests were richly rewarded with gifts.

The houses had names which often referred to specific events in the family legends of the resident house group, and also served as a form of address. The Tlingit gave their houses names relating to an animal (such as Bear Cave, Raven Nest, Killer Whale, or Beaver Dam), describing their location within the village (such as Far Away or Middle of Village) or the surrounding area (such as Treeless Island or Mount Saint Elias), or referring to a celestial phenomenon (such as Rainbow or Moon).

Property rights for the house were clearly defined. Among the Tsimshian, with their matrilineal descent groups, the house itself belonged to the men, while the women they married were responsible for procuring and paying for the furnishings. The bearer of the lineage name lived in the house, with his wife and children, his brothers and unmarried sisters, and the sons of his sisters along with their families. Title and house were passed down to the next-younger brother or to the eldest nephew.

High-ranking families bore few descendants, of whom generally only two or three would in turn reach a marriageable age. The demands of spiritual purity placed on chiefs in conjunction with whaling, trading, and war often required years of sexual abstinence. Children were

breast-fed for a period of up to three or four years, and the bearing of new offspring during this time was generally frowned upon.

Each nuclear family occupied a section of the house according to their rank and occupied designated seats in the ceremonial seating plan. Similar seating arrangements applied in large canoes. The canoes and houses of many peoples also had in common the fact that they were given individual names and crests, and thus were viewed as entities with their own history and identity.

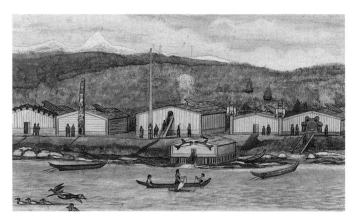

Frederick Alexie (Tsimshian), *Indian Village of Port Simpson*, watercolor, before 1926. Art Gallery of Ontario, Toronto, ON.

Frederick Alexie (1853–1939) recollected his home village of Port Simpson around 1870 as a peaceful and austere-looking place. After the Hudson's Bay Company had established a trading post there in 1831, nine local Tsimshian groups settled nearby. With a population of 2,400 in 1857, the old Tsimshian village on the Nass River was one of the largest settlements on the Northwest Coast at that time.

Paul Kane, *Flathead Woman and Child, Caw-wacham*, oil on canvas, 1847. Montreal Museum of Fine Arts, Montreal, QC.

In the central and southern Northwest Coast, the deformation of babies' heads was a common practice. Such deformation was seen by some peoples as a sign of a woman's nobility, as the ultimate sign of nobility in men and women, or as a distinction of all free-born people. While the Koskimo-Kwakiutl and their neighbors wrapped the heads of babies into the shape of an elongated sugar loaf, the Chinook, Coast Salish, and others (this painting depicts a Cowlitz woman and child) only flattened the children's foreheads and the backs of their heads, which is why they were called Flatheads.

# Rank and name

In no other part of North America do we encounter people to whom status, names, and privileges are as important as to the people of the Pacific coastal forests of the Northwest. They lived in a class society with strict division between the free and the unfree (slaves). A more subtle difference existed among the large group of free people. This group included an upper class of hereditary bearers of name titles, the nobility. Between the ranks of nobility and slavery were the majority of the population, the free commoners, who were closely related by kinship ties and across classlines to the nobility, but held no titles and thus none of the privileges associated with them.

The majority of slaves were prisoners of war who belonged to a foreign ethnic group and who normally had no kinship ties to their owners. The latter predicament alone meant that they had no rights whatsoever, since a person's rights were founded exclusively on reciprocal responsibilities between relatives. In contrast to debt slaves (individuals who, for example, were unable to pay their gambling debts and were therefore obliged to put themselves at the disposal of the creditor), prisoners of war had virtually no hope of ever being bought free by their relatives. Anthropologists had long suggested that slavery had little economic relevance on the Northwest Coast, since the keeping of slaves was no more than a matter of prestige for the nobility and the slaves themselves were considered part of an individual's personal wealth – to be put on display, made a gift of, or even destroyed at potlatch feasts. Generally, however, all the free-born members of Northwest Coast societies (including the nobility) were self-sufficient, donating to the house group all food not required for their own needs. Such donations were distibuted according to need by the highest-ranking chief of the group, often in connection with a potlatch. Within this system, slaves were often used for the procurement of food for their owners and took care of the most difficult and unpleasant tasks within their house group. Thus, the nobility gained additional free time for the cultivation of diplomatic contacts, communication with supernatural powers, and artistic activities. Finally, slaves were also a readily available labor reserve when, for example a whale had been caught or beached, and had to be secured or divided.

Although commoners were also obliged to offer their labor (called "help" by those concerned) to higher-ranking relatives, they were not always at hand, besides which even chiefs had to take care not to overburden and thus cause resentment in their inferiors, who were, after all, free to join another group to which they were related through their grandparents.

If a village community consisted of several lineages, a ranking of the various descent groups was established, and the principal chief of the highest-ranking lineage was appointed to represent the entire village. He was followed in rank by the nobility of other house groups and the lesser chiefs of his own lineage, followed by the commoners of his lineage. The nobility of the lowest lineage could thus, theoretically, be of lesser standing than the commoners of the highest-ranking house group.

Due to the limited number of available name titles, the inheritance of noble status from one generation to the next was only possible to a limited extent. If the leading member of a lineage had more rightful successors than the number of titles available, some members of a noble family would ultimately end up as commoners (as would their descendants), unless a title bearer died before he was able to pass down his standing to his own offspring.

On the central Northwest Coast, hereditary succession was based on the principle of primogeniture. This meant that the oldest child inherited the highest of the available titles (there were normally two to five titles), irrespective of whether it was received from the mother or the father; the second child was given the second-highest title, and so on. This practice may well be compared with the rules of

Right:

"Copper" of the Kwakiutl carver Mungo Martin, early 20th century. Royal British Columbia Museum, Victoria, BC.

"Coppers" were plates with a T-shaped ridge that were made of the copper sheathing taken from the hulls of ships. Among the nobility they were the epitome of wealth and were presented as a gift during potlatch feasts, whereby their value increased to the total value of all other gifts made at the event. The front side was painted with a design (here with a depiction of a killer whale), which often gave it its name and emphasized its splendor. Breaking off pieces of such coppers in front of others was considered to be a bold gesture of affluence, which neither diminished its value, nor destroyed it.

Far right:

Nootka hat depicting a whaling scene, late 18th century. Museo de América, Madrid, Spain.

This basketry hat depicts several identical scenes of a whale hunter standing at the bow of his canoe ready to aim his harpoon and of a harpooned whale towing a line and floats. The fact that no other hunters are shown bears tribute to the decisive role of the noble hunter. Late 19th-century portrayals of this scene, produced for the souvenir market, also show rowers towing the whale back to the shore.

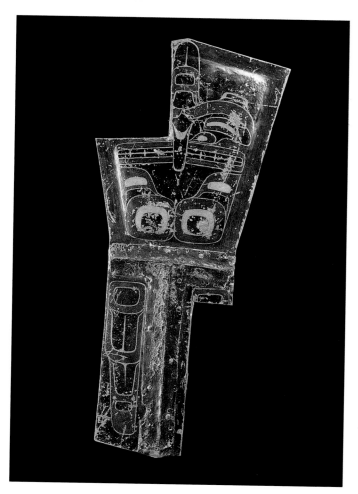

Interior of the Whale House in Klukwan, a Chilkat-Tlingit village, 1895. Alaska State Library, Juneau, AK.

Each Tlingit lineage occupied a house named for its clan. The rear part of the house was the chief's designated living area, usually closed off by a magnificent screen. The other members of the lineage were allotted sections along the walls; the higher the ranking, the closer to the chief's section a family would be positioned. Slaves slept by the entranceway. Here, in front of the screen, the area where guests would normally be received, some of the material privileges of the resident chief have been put on display; there are painted hats and leather shirts, a Chilkat dance apron, masks, and wooden boxes adorned with crests.

succession among the European nobility of the Middle Ages. The house groups aspired to retain and increase the number of titles that they possessed by attempting to interpret to their advantage the privileges and titles spanning all principal and auxiliary bloodlines. Needless to say, this was also a permanent source of contention. Titles could likewise be inherited by the daughters or sisters of chiefs. Only in rare cases, however, did women temporarily take up the role of chief, but generally passed these positions on to their sons.

On the northern Northwest Coast, where marriage was permitted only with members of the opposite moiety, partners were predominantly chosen from the nobility within the father's descent group, who – based on the rule of matrilineal descent – were not considered to be blood relatives. Members of the nobility only married people of their own standing in order to secure through the new combination of the privileges and titles of both sides the status of the next generation. Marriages between nobles and commoners were disapproved of. When, in 1885, Tlingit chief Anaxúúts (Brown Bear) from the Kaagwaantaan of the Wolf moiety planned to marry a commoner from the Raven moiety, the Raven chiefs invited to the wedding refused to participate with the harsh words "No good can come of mating a chief and a clam digger."

Chiefs had to meet high expectations with respect to their conduct. The Tsimshian term for "chief" is "true man," since the ideal chief was said to be a person who possessed all the positive traits of mankind, including a well-balanced disposition, unlimited generosity, respectful manners, above-average language skills in his own tongue, physical stamina, and even magical powers to attract whales, or salmon runs. From their earliest childhood onward, possible candidates for the position were raised to meet these standards. Legend had it that, if a chieftain was not able to live up to expectations or if the commoners in his own house group suffered as the result of his inabilites, he would die under mysterious circumstances.

Nobility and affluence went together, for titles of nobility were linked to rights to the best fishing and food-gathering sites, to stretches of shore on which whales were washed up and shellfish could be gathered, and to other sources of wealth. This type of affluence, however, was used to be given away only in order to validate one's status as a "true man," a nobleman. No distinction was made between material and immaterial wealth – equal to those material rights were the possession of sacred sites or magical powers, and the right to stage mystical dramas, to dances and songs, to conduct gambling games, or to the manifestation of these privileges in the form of masks, crests, and names.

Opposite page, left:

Kachucte (Qaadjaaqí), chief of the Hutsnuwu-Tlingit, in front of his house in Killisnoo, c. 1895. Alaska State Library, Juneau, AK.

Once an American administration was established in Alaska, Tlingit chiefs laid claim to the prestigious positions within the newly created Indian police force. In this photograph Kachucte of Killisnoo poses in police uniform in front of his American house. The verse above the door identifies the chief as the leader of several neighboring Tlingit tribes, and also mocks one of his rivals.

were unadorned, with only an emblematic animal majestically positioned at the top. The majority of crest poles, however, were richly decorated with images in which family emblems were linked to symbols of privilege and to images that indicated their legendary and mythical origins.

The cultural antecedents of these crest poles were presumably the carved interior house posts as well as the funeral poles used to carry boxes containing the ashes of deceased chiefs. The poles created after the arrival of Europeans fall into three groups: those still being used as funeral poles, either to carry the wooden urns or as a receptacle for the ashes themselves; those that served simply as a reminder of the deceased at major potlatch feasts; and those used to express ownership of houses and sections of shore. Some poles even had multiple functions.

Gitksan (Tsimshian) crest poles in Kitwanga, British Columbia, 1978.

The animal- and humanlike images carved one above the other refer to the content of mythical stories detailing the origin of families and their privileges. The high degree of humidity in the region means these monumental wooden statues rot easily; free-standing poles have a natural life expectancy of about 50 years. The only region in which numerous old poles still stand is the somewhat drier Tsimshian region further inland.

Ownership of a section of shore, could be tied to the rights to a certain song, which in turn was linked to the privilege of wearing a specific mask and having the support of a spirit helper, or which might even include the right to perform a particular dance during the winter ceremonial. The combination of all wealth and its relative value was the basis upon which chieftains were ranked; and this ranking was expressed in the seating arrangements at ceremonies.

A more permanent demonstration of status was the display of crests derived from name titles on the walls of the house. Anyone entering the village from the shore would immediately recognize the status of the resident chief. The crests would also appear on household goods, canoes, and hats, which were also used as a symbol of status on travels outside the village. The most conspicuous expression of the nobility's proud display of their privileges are the crest poles, which the earliest European observers already noted, at least briefly. In the 19th century, when European steel blades facilitated the carving of such poles, the village beaches featured veritable forests of these impressive status symbols. The artists who created these poles further refined their skills in no more than a few generations and were thus responsible for a new boom in the art of woodcarving. Some of the poles

# Maquinna –
# a diplomat on dangerous shores

When James Cook (1728–1779) anchored off the shores of Nootka Sound on the west coast of Vancouver Island in 1778, he was to meet one of the most exceptional diplomats in these parts. He was Maquinna, recent successor to the highest position of chief in the tribal confederation of the Yuquot-Tahsis. Despite his youth, Maquinna was quick to recognize the opportunity that presented itself: contact with foreigners who appeared ever more frequently on his shores could help him consolidate and increase his power. As the number of ships arriving for the sea otter trade grew in 1786, exchange activities increased at Yugot. Its proximity to the trade route from Tahsis on the east side of Vancouver Island, meant Maquinna's confederation was always well supplied with sea otter furs obtained from the Kwakiutl. Now it was vital that he secure supplies of European goods by establishing permanent, peaceful relations with the whites. This was not easy, since the Spanish, British, and Americans each had very distinct interests and strategies.

Coexistence with these foreigners was difficult. The boorish European sailors and soldiers ravished Nootka women, stole furs and supplies, and were themselves robbed and assaulted by Nootka men. There were a number of violent deaths on both sides. When, in the summer of 1792, the situation reached such a peak that influential chiefs began to devise an alliance aimed at driving all Europeans out of their waters, Maquinna focused on diplomacy rather than war and convinced the others to relinquish their plan. During that same year, he was party to an agreement that served to avert open conflict between Spain and Great Britain over their claims to Nootka Sound.

Maquinna directly benefited from his policy of détente, since the Europeans felt far safer in his waters than in those of his southern neighbor, Wickaninnish, who headed a confederation of tribes around Clayoquot Sound. Of lesser status than Maquinna, he had fought for power through war and wealth. Wickaninnish had compensated for his lowly birth by accumulating wealth, stopping at nothing to achieve his goals and even seized passing ships.

When the sea otter population had been exhausted, fewer trading ships appeared. In 1795, the Spanish abandoned their fort near Yuquot to the British. It can be attributed to Maquinna's far-sightedness that he made it known that the rights of land use granted to the Spanish would not automatically be transferred to the British. The importance of Yuquot nonetheless diminished and, as ships now rarely passed through his waters, Maquinna could no longer present himself as a statesman to the foreigners.

In 1803, he consolidated his position for a short while by seizing the American ship *Boston* and massacring its crew.

The rewards of this undertaking were plentiful, proving to his neighbors that he could maintain his top ranking among potlatch hosts. Even more valuable than the stolen goods was the human treasure: two prisoners. John R. Jewitt (1782–1821), the smith of the *Boston*, now served Maquinna as a slave, producing highly desirable trade goods from scrap metal. After two and a half years, Jewitt managed to escape. His memoirs, *A Narrative of the Adventures and Sufferings of John R. Jewitt, Only Survivor of the Ship Boston, During a Captivity of Nearly Three Years Among the Savages of Nootka Sound* (1815), were a bestseller; they offered a vivid portrayal of the Nootka during the time of the declining fur trade – and they immortalized Maquinna's fame abroad.

Maquinna was unable to enjoy his success for very long, for the frightened traders now ultimately stayed well clear of his stretch of coast. Further acts of piracy by other chiefs turned the once booming trading center into unsafe waters. Maquinna was equally incapable of stopping the decline of his own power. In 1837, his son finally admitted that Wickaninnish had outranked him. The following generation saw Maquinna's people, who now called themselves Mowachaht, decimated both by war with their neighbors and by disease. Today, his descendants hold claim to the position of the highest chief's seat among the Mowachaht and proudly bear the family name of Maquinna.

# Of trade and war

The wealth of natural resources and abundance of food, but also the local diversity, formed the basis of trade both along the coast and with the interior over mountain passes and on rivers. Chiefs eagerly protected the rights of passage that guaranteed their huge profits, and for a long time they managed to prevent European traders from penetrating beyond the river mouths. In return for ocean products such as blubber and seal oil, mother-of-pearl, and dried herring roe, the inland tribes supplied the coastal peoples with copper, furs, and much sought-after moose and deer hides. Later, European goods were added to the range of items traded between east and west, and the prices of such goods were marked up considerably. Along the coast itself, copper and valuable Chilkat blankets, woven by Tlingit women from the wool of mountain goats, were supplied to the south; dentalium shells (shaped like tiny elephant tusks) from the waters off Vancouver Island were used as a measure of value and as adornment by peoples from southern Alaska to northern California; the thick and shimmering layer of mother-of-pearl that lined haliotis shells made them a popular item that the northern Californians traded with

peoples of the north. Slaves procured through acts of war were often sold to distant tribes to reduce the risk of their fleeing or otherwise being freed.

But even thriving trade could offer no guarantee of peace. People were constantly on the alert in case of surprise attacks by enemy bands, for armed conflicts were an everyday occurrence. Such conflicts were as frequent between neighboring village groups as they were between distant tribes. While raids were often conducted to procure slaves, the predominant goal of war was to increase power and influence, for it was a chief's right to adopt the name and privileges of the lineages that he conquered. Even relatively trivial occurrences could serve the nobility as grounds for exacting compensation, and often by the use of force. For as long as such accounts remained unsettled, surprise assaults were to be expected. The main focus of peace negotiations, therefore, was on fixing compensation payments. Willingness to settle was expressed by sacred eagle feathers or white fur.

The warriors of the coast were no advocates of "knightly" warfare, regardless of the fact that they had been raised to be courageous and tough. A foreign village or the crew of a

Tlingit women selling beadwork on a pier, Alaska, c. 1907. Special Collection Division, University of Washington Libraries, Seattle, WA.

Radical cultural change on the Northwest Coast also had an impact on the role of the sexes. While men signed up to serve on seal- and whale-hunting expeditions, the women were left to organize community life. Deprived of any form of income and because of heightened competition between family groups, women increasingly became involved in the business of trading, formerly the domain of their men.

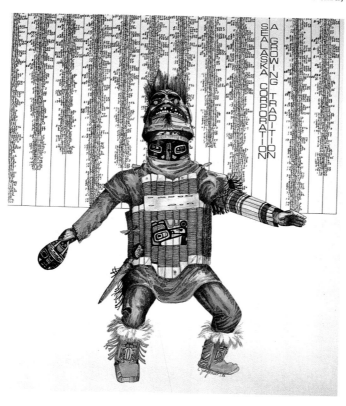

Tlingit warrior on a poster for the Southeast Alaska Corporation, 1982.

In battle, Tlingit warriors wore protective clothing made of thick leather, breast armor made of cedar planks, and a wooden helmet set on a high wooden collar, the upper edge with a slit for the wearer to see through. The warrior on this poster for the Southeast Alaska Corporation (the shareholder company into which the Tlingit tribe was reorganized in accordance with the *Alaska Native Claims Settlement Act* of 1971) is also wearing wooden arm protection around his left arm as well as a belt with a typical war dagger of beaten copper.

canoe would be ambushed, and the attackers would quickly flee before the enemy could gather its strength anew. Upon returning home, the triumphant warriors would display the severed heads of their enemies on long poles for all to see.

During the long-lasting battles for predominance in Barkley Sound, on the western coast of Vancouver Island, the Uchucklisat-Nootka used a sort of "Trojan Whale" to eliminate the enemy Ohiat of Kihiin (also Nootkans). They tied four large canoes together and covered them with dark-dyed bark mats. They made dorsal and pectoral fins of the same material so that, from afar, their contraption looked like a whale floating on water. They even threw pieces of salmon into the water to attract the seagulls that would normally gather around the carcass of a whale. Having spotted what they presumed to be a whale, the Kihiin men raced to their canoes in excited anticipation of a feast and headed out to the whale. By the time they realized their mistake, it was too late and they paid for it with their lives, while other Uchucklisat stormed the village in an ambush attack and massacred the men who had been left behind, taking the women and children as slaves.

The introduction of firearms and competition in the fur trade and among seal hunters added momentum to the already existing disputes. Villages that by then had been decimated by disease ultimately annihilated each other. Because of the high mortality rate, confusion began to arise with respect to hereditary titles, which led to fierce fights for privileges and often to all-out war.

The battle logic of the Pacific coast inhabitants made them unpredictable to the white settlers who felt threatened by them. The British and American navies went to great lengths to pacify the region, razing whole villages to the ground during punitive expeditions. It was only around 1882 that native warfare was finally brought to an end.

Paul Kane, *King Comcomly's Burial Canoe*, watercolor, 1847. Stark Museum of Art, Orange, TX.

Chinook burials in canoes placed on platforms or in trees were reserved for high-ranking individuals. The keel of the vessel was pierced with a hole through which rainwater could drain away. Corpses were covered by a smaller inverted canoe. Items of prestige as well as articles of everyday use were first made unusable and then deposited along with the deceased. Even individual slaves that had belonged to the deceased were killed. Since it was prohibited within the community and the neighborhood to utter the name of deceased persons, it was often necessary to find replacements for everyday words that had been part of a dead person's name.

# The Chinook Peoples – traders along the Columbia River

When the first Europeans reached the mouth of the Columbia River in 1792, they found it to be the hub of a well-organized trade network in which dentalium shells and, to a lesser extent, beaver and sea otter furs were the common items of exchange. The foundation of the trading posts of Astoria (1811) and Fort Vancouver (1825) strengthened the role of the small local Chinook tribes as middlemen with trade links with the peoples of the inland and coastal regions of the Columbia Plateau. While providing valuable services for British and American fur traders all the way into Puget Sound and up the Columbia River, Chinook interpreters also maintained control over all transactions.

One particular Chinook chief by the name of Comcomly (c. 1766–1833) distinguished himself as an especially skilled politician. He arranged for his daughters to marry fur traders, and used both diplomacy and intimidation to consolidate his profitable trading activities. He also benefited from disputes between the British and the Americans over the coastal territories. Because he considered alcohol the prime enemy of his people,

he repeatedly tried to prohibit the trade in rum. In 1833 Comcomly died of smallpox, as did the majority of his people. Several years after his death, an employee of the Hudson's Bay Company extracted his skull from its burial place and brought it to England. In the 1950s, it was returned to Chinook descendants, who reburied these last remains.

By 1850, epidemic diseases had wiped out 90 percent of the tribal population around the Columbia River, and the American government went about resettling groups of the survivors on reservations. Many of the women married white and Hawaiian employees of the fur trading companies. Among the ensuing ethnical mix, the Chinook jargon, a trade language, became the mother tongue of whole generations, while the language of Chief Comcomly (Chinook proper) eventually ceased to exist, having been totally eradicated within less than 100 years of the first white settlement.

The existence of a diversity of languages and the fact that trading activities spanned extensive territories had probably necessitated the use of a trade language even before whites arrived at the Columbia River. This common language was

Mountain sheep horn bowl, Chinook, Washington, before 1890, Field Museum of Natural History, Chicago, IL.

Horn bowls imported from the Columbia Plateau were adorned with relief carving and used by the Chinook for ceremonial purposes. The figure portrayed here, with its protruding ribs, appears to represent a guardian spirit and is typical of the lower Columbia River valley.

"Open Your Mouth Wide and Say Aaaah!", cartoon by Duane Pasco from *Tenas Wawa*, 1991.

This cartoon, with the speech balloon in Chinook jargon, was drawn by a white artist, Duane Pasco (b. 1932), publisher of *Tenas Wawa* ("small word"). Published from 1990 to 1995, this magazine aimed to revive the Chinook jargon. Meanwhile, several local projects have been initiated to research and keep alive the language. One such project is a language course on the Grand Ronde Reservation in Oregon, where the tribes view this former trade language as a feature of their common cultural heritage. Several websites offer comprehensive material for those interested in learning the language. Few outsiders can relate to the wit contained in this caricature. The sketch portrays an indigenous healer in the role of a typical white practitioner, prompting his patient to say "Aaaah." The contrast that this picture symbolizes is an irreconcilable one for many Native Americans.

based on a simplified version of the language spoken by coastal Chinook tribes. It is likely that slave trading played a major role in its development, since it was predominantly among the Chinook slaves, who originated from a myriad of different peoples, that an isolated caste was formed, the members of which were not taught the Chinook language, but who nonetheless needed to be able to communicate with one another as well as with their owners.

When white traders began to make regular trips to the Columbia River area, they brought with them from Vancouver Island a scanty knowledge of Nootka, a language they considered to be the Indian language as such. The Chinook soon adopted these imported words, in the simplified pronunciation of the white traders, as part of their lingua franca. In 1805, the American explorers Lewis and Clark noted a sentence which they believed to be Chinook: "Clouch Musket, wake, com ma-tax Musket" (Nice rifle, I've not seen one of those before). What they did not realize was that all elements of this sentence, with the exception of "musket," originated from the Nootka language.

The numerous fur traders and colonizers that had by then penetrated the region from the interior contributed French and several Cree words to the mixed language (pidgin), and later increasingly introduced English. At the same time, Chinook jargon was spreading into Puget Sound and up the Thompson River, where a unique dialect developed, under the influence of Salishan languages. A form of writing also evolved that was used in missionary

work. While the number of words used was relatively limited and many words had several meanings (*tuš* can mean 'good, beautiful, agreeable, correct, or clean'), the language contains a range of synonyms (*skúkum, pišak*, and *mesahči* all mean 'bad') passed on from the different languages contributed by diverse peoples. New words were formed through combination; for example *man* (meaning 'man') was the basis for *úlman* ('old man,' meaning 'husband') and *tənasman* ('small man,' meaning 'boy').

Local whites tended to simplify complicated sounds and used their own pidgin version of the trade language. During the 20th century, English replaced the Chinook jargon. In the 1980s, the last remaining individuals who had learned Chinook jargon as their mother tongue died.

A name-giving potlatch of the Coast Salish, Quamichan, British Columbia, c. 1913. Royal British Columbia Museum, Victoria, BC.

Adorned with ribbons made of mountain goat wool, a boy and a girl wait to be given their hereditary names. The array of potlatch gifts laid out around them ranges from woven mats to photographs, trade blankets, Salish weavings, and canoes. Before the ceremony comes to a climax, all participants will undergo a ritual cleansing through a performance by two masked Sxwayxwey dancers that will later emerge from behind the curtain of mats visible in the background to the right.

# Potlatch feasts

No institution more epitomizes the quintessence and diversity of all aspects of the social and cultural life in the coastal regions of the American Northwest more than the potlatch. At first sight, the potlatch is a feast hosted by a chief in the name of his house group, which other house groups from near and far are invited to attend. The guests are treated to a banquet and a profusion of gifts is bestowed upon them (especially the attending chiefs, in strict accordance with the guests' rank). The goal is to confirm, increase, and cement the renown and social standing of the host. The potlatch can be interpreted as a "feast of giving," and indeed the word can be traced back to the Chinook jargon, the trade language of the Northwest Coast, where it simply means "to give." As it was a common practice to prepare for a potlatch by accumulating a wealth of impressive possessions, often over a period of many years, and as guests felt compelled eventually to reciprocate or even outdo the "generosity" of their hosts, it was assumed that these events were no more than an act of self-destructive rivalry among the chiefs; this is why the Canadian government legally banned potlatches in 1884.

Almost all the indigenous peoples between southern Alaska and the Columbia River make a significant distinction between a potlatch and other feasts. Both involve the feeding of numerous guests and the distribution of gifts. It is only during potlatch, however, that hereditary rights are conferred. A good chief would host a number of smaller and larger feasts (depending on food supplies) during the course of a year. Neighboring village groups were often invited to attend, a practice that could ensure the survival of a group during times of food shortage. Potlatches, however, were far less frequently held than other feasts; many chiefs hosted only one or two during their entire lifetime. When they did take place, they would often be talked about for generations to come. A potlatch or a feast was held on the occasion of a member of the

*Kwakiutl Potlatch in Alert Bay*, British Columbia, c. 1910. Photograph: William Halliday (?). Royal British Columbia Museum, Victoria, BC.

Apart from objects of native manufacture, the Hudson's Bay Company's woolen blankets were the most common potlatch item in the 19th century. The transition from the credit and exchange economy of the fur trade to a money based economy meant that other goods (such as tin and chinaware, plates, or sewing machines) were added as give-away items. At this potlatch the gifts include sacks of flour, piled up in the background. The guests are surrounded by a veritable wall of gifts.

The Coast Salish (here the Halkomelem) used the flat roofs of the host's house as a stage for ceremonial speeches, which often went on for several hours. It was also from these rooftops that gifts were distributed to the individually named recipients. One of the family privileges was to conduct tests of courage and skill. If a man asked for the hand of a chief's daughter in marriage, the girl's father would arrange for such tests to be conducted at a potlatch. The suitor might be required to climb up a greased rope or to pass through a course of blazing flames.

*Grand Potlatch (or distribution of blankets, guns and money) at Fort Hope Rancherie, Fraser River 1859.*

nobility entering a new life stage (maturity, marriage, the birth of a first child, the death of a high-ranking relative, or the erection of a new house) which involved passing on or acquiring hereditary titles, requiring public validation through the distribution or exchange of gifts. If a high-ranking chief died, a mourning potlatch was held, followed by a memorial potlatch a year later, at which the deceased's relatives gave away everything they owned. Many missionaries understood the religious character of potlatch more clearly than did government representatives and thus branded these events as heathen "ancestor worship."

Potlatches not only had the effect of distributing wealth, which was surely welcomed by the Northwest Coast peoples; they were also a means of maintaining the world through the reanimation of mythical ancestors and their spiritual powers in the here and now. The act of passing on hereditary chief's titles and privileges within the descent groups demonstrated that the links between the ancestors and present and future generations were intact. The larger the number of high-ranking guests in attendance as witnesses to such acts, the more valid was a successor's eligibility to the name title that was his given right. Every potlatch was an opportunity to publicly display and consolidate family rights and privileges in the form of masks, screens, dances, and songs. Host families could also hire dances and masks from other families. These families not only received payment, but were also reconfirmed as the owners of the rights to those dances and masks.

Such privileges might include magical and spiritual powers, presented in an entertaining contest of skills, as reported by Frank Allen, a Twana Salish, to anthropologist William Elmendorf (1912–1997) around 1940. At a potlatch held by a Cowichan chief on Vancouver Island around 1910, Kwakiutl guests gave a dramatic exhibition of their powers by, among other things, making a large rock (two feet in diameter) float on water in a washtub. "Then they called head people from each tribe to come and look at the rock. [...] And all three of us went up and looked at the rock and it really floated. I had a pocket knife with me and I tested the rock with it and it was really a rock. That was the power of the Leqwiltox [-Kwakiutl] keeping it up that way, and that beat anything that the [Puget] Sound people could do. By God, it's no wonder those people [Leqwiltox] were bad ones in the early days, with power like that."

During the 19th century, potlatches became exaggerated. Initially the good profits from commercial fishing and trading activities meant that large quantities of European goods were available. At the same time, war and disease reduced the ranks of the chiefs, so young pretenders began pushing their way into the hereditary offices that they would normally only have been invested with at a mature age and when they possessed considerable life experience. The potlatch thus became a battleground for the attainment of chiefly titles. Some social climbers bundled up their newly accumulated wealth and privileges and embarked on potlatch tours, traveling from village to village in order to put other chiefs to shame and outdo them in generosity. The flexible rule of ambilineal descent of the central Northwest Coast with membership in either the maternal or paternal

Chilkat blanket, Tlingit, Alaska, before 1832. Peabody Essex Museum, Salem, MA.

Chilkat blankets, worn on festive occasions, were adorned with strongly abstracted motifs linked to the privileges of their aristocratic owners. On this blanket the main motif is a bear, flanked by coppers symbolizing wealth. A blanket like this, made from cedar bark and mountain goat wool, using a complicated twining technique, would take a woman a year to complete. Because heraldic art was a male prerogative, the craftswoman who fashioned this blanket would have copied the motif it depicts from a pattern board painted by a male artist; he would have provided one half of the design, the other half being an exact mirror-image. Chilkat blankets, the production of which was revived in the late 20th century, are still among the most spectacular gifts a host can bestow upon his guests at a potlatch.

Opposite page:

Kaw-Claa, a Tlingit woman, Taku, Alaska, 1906.

One of the privileges publicly displayed at potlatches is symbolized by a bear claw headdress that refers to the son of Kats, a mythical hero, and a bear woman. The color around the girl's mouth represents blood. The silver nose ring and the beaded "octopus" bag (so called because of its tentacle-like lobes), were worn by both sexes among the Tlingit.

Tlingit ceremonial wooden bowl with opercula inlay, Angoon, Alaska, before 1887. American Museum of Natural History, New York, NY.

Guests and family members were served their food in a variety of receptacles, depending on their status. Food for high-ranking guests was served in dishes of up to 6 feet long. This bowl, 3 feet long, is in the form of a beaver with faces protruding from its body in classical Northwest Coast manner. The inlay of opercula (the lids of Prosobranchia snails) was attached with an adhesive made of boiled fish skin.

group according to which title inheritance was settled, encouraged strategic marriages. Chiefs aspired to secure as many titles as possible for their descendants. Debts piled up, and women were sometimes forced to prostitute themselves to secure the means for these aims. Slaves and commoners were sent to work in canneries and on whaling boats, and were expected to hand over their earnings.

The decline of potlatching was due much less to the official ban (only enforced with any emphasis in the 1920s) than to the Great Depression, when noble families had to face the fact that they would no longer be able to pay their "debts." Moreover, young people who had been raised in boarding schools had other values in mind, and the impact of Christian teachings played an additional role in almost completely eradicating the potlatch (at least among the Tlingit, Haida, Tsimshian, and Coast Salish). However,

during the past decades, in which indigenous heritage has experienced a revival, many Northwest Coast communities have been returning to the tradition of potlatch.

"Potlatching makes you feel so good because you learn who you are." Comments such as this are made by guests who attend modern-day potlatches. Preparations for the feast include making exact lists of those to be invited and clearly defining the order of rank. It is important to ascertain each individual's kinship to the other guests as well as the rank of each of the chiefs of the families invited in relation to the others. Guests related to more than one of the families invited need to decide which of these families they will represent. All these details are of consequence for establishing a precise protocol for the event, and they influence the personal conduct of each participant. In this way, modern potlatches help tribal members to gain a better understanding of their own culture, a culture which, based on the high demands it places on each individual to have precise knowledge of his heritage, can be likened to the maze of thousands of islands and inlets with sometimes surprising currents and shallows that are its natural environment. Should a guest unwittingly make a gesture or utter a word that is the prerogative of the host and thus bring shame upon the host, or should dancers begin to perform the dance of a certain family on the wrong side of the screen at the back of the house (behind which the dancers take up their positions), official apologies and sometimes even compensation payments will be unavoidably due. It is by no means easy to be of Northwest Coast origin.

# Dream of twins

## The Kwakiutl and the treasures bestowed by supernatural beings (1925)

Thanks to anthropologist Franz Boas, the Kwakiutl and their potlatch became known well beyond the field of science alone. As well as bringing fame to the Kwakiutl, he also originated the method by which a people's culture is presented by texts written by themselves in their own language. He was assisted in this by George Hunt, who over many years provided him with thousands of manuscript pages in Kwak'wala, the language of the Kwakiutl.

The longest of a series of accounts of dreams (most of which deal with similar issues) centers around the subject of supernatural beings, wealth, and death. The "treasure" that the married couple (each of whom was a twin) received from the salmon woman in their dreams was a child together with a name. For the Kwakiutl, both children and the abilities that supernatural beings could bestow upon humans were considered "treasures," as each of these gifts enhanced one's standing in society. The fact that a "treasure" was bestowed upon them during a spontaneous dream rather than after ritual cold baths or a rubbing with hemlock branches or a shroud, is atypical of the Kwakiutl.

But twins in themselves were something special for the Kwakiutl and were considered to have supernatural powers right from the time of their birth. The salmon woman's gift might be explained by the fact that twins are regarded as salmon in human form. They were able to influence the weather, heal the diseased, and call forth salmon when the runs failed to pass through their waters to spawn. Twins do, however, need to take the responsibilities assigned to them as seriously as anyone else or otherwise risk losing their "treasures."

"I was lying in our house in Knight Inlet with my husband, Wäleed," said Hayosdeeselas. And then she told me her dream, for Hayosdeeselas was one of twins, and her husband, Wäleed, was also one of twins. She said: "I dreamed that we were sitting on the floor of our house, I and Wäleed, in the morning at the time when the olachen were running. We heard the sound of a song at the mouth of the river of Knight Inlet. It was coming up the river. Then we began to understand the words of the song which was being sung." And these are the words of the song heard by Hayosdeeselas and her husband:

The treasure of the salmon comes to you, the great treasure. Ha$^e$yo, ha$^e$yo, ha$^e$yo.

Beautifully he comes, the treasure of the salmon, this Maamenla'ya of the salmon.

Then the singing in front of the house of Hayosdeeselas stopped and in her dream Hayosdeeselas saw a small woman coming from the place where the singing had been. In her arms she carried something like a new born child, and she placed the child in the lap of Hayosdeeselas. Then the child disappeared in the body of Hayosdeeselas. Then the salmon woman said to Hayosdeeselas, "You will call this treasure which you received from me Maamenla'ya," thus she said and disappeared. "From that time on my wife was pregnant with this child," said Wäleed when he was telling me this dream. Now that is the end of this. When Hayosdeeselas had been pregnant the right length of time she gave birth to a boy. As soon as night came she dreamed again of the little salmon woman. "She came and sat down on the floor of the house at my right side. She was carrying this little child Maamenla'ya in her arms and she spoke. She said to me, 'Now be careful, friend, of this your treasure, you and your husband. Always paint yourself with ocher, you and your husband, and also this Maamenla'ya. And also put on the sides of the head two feathers of a gull, and the painting on the cradle shall be a

whale. And furthermore, if you do not obey what I tell you, I am going to come and take back this child.' Thus she said to me in my dream," said Hayosdeeselas to me as she was telling me her dream.

Then a cradle with a notched head piece was made and gull feathers were placed on each side of the head of Hayosdeeselas and her husband Wäleed. They were not able to get any ocher. Now the child of Hayosdeeselas was four months old. Then Wäleed, the husband of Hayosdeeselas, came into my house and said, "Oh friend, last night I had an evil dream relating to this child." And so he told me his dream. He said, "All kinds of salmon came to me in canoes here to Fort Rupert in the morning when day was dawning. Then she of whom my wife spoke, the salmon woman, came into my house. She was very angry with us,

particularly with my wife Hayosdeeselas. She said, "We have come to take away Maamenla'ya, according to what I told Hayosdeeselas, namely, if you did not follow all my instructions relating to the dress which Maamenla'ya should wear (which I gave you at the time) when he came to you.' Thus said the salmon woman, and she took the child in her arms and went out of the door. Then the salmon woman went aboard the canoe from the side of the canoe which was towards the shore. Then the many canoes of the salmon went away.

"As soon as I awoke I looked at Maamenla'ya. I saw he was lying in the house. Then I called Hayosdeeselas and told her my dream. As soon as I had told my dream to her Hayosdeeselas spoke and said, 'Right from the beginning I was afraid on account of what she said in the beginning when she brought Maamenla'ya to us. For the salmon woman said "If you do not do everything I tell you, if any of these is not taken for the dress of Maamenla'ya, I shall come back and take him."' Now it seems the salmon woman means that we never got ocher for him.'"

Three days after this the child died. I have got the notched cradle with the painting of the whale. That is all.

(Franz Boas, *Contributions to the Ethnology of the Kwakiutl*, New York, 1925)

Kwakiutl Chief Lagius delivering a speech, American Museum of Natural History, New York, NY.

If anthropologists wish to win the respect of the people in the societies that they study, they themselves must hold feasts. Franz Boas held feasts for the Kwakiutl (not a potlatch, however, since he had no claim to hereditary privileges) at which speeches were made and gifts were distributed. One of the speakers at such an event referred to the scholar, in a typical exaggeration, as "a loaded canoe that has anchored in front of a mountain, from which wealth is rolling down upon all the people of the whole world; you are the pillar supporting our world."

Painted house front of a Kwakiutl house, Nimpkish, Alert Bay, before 1899. National Anthropological Archives, Smithsonian Institution, Washington, DC.

In accordance with local family rights, the Kwagiulth Museum in Cape Mudge, founded in 1979, and the U'Mista Cultural Center, founded in Alert Bay in 1980, hold joint responsibility for the care of the Potlatch Collection, which was returned from Ottawa in 1973 and to which additions have since been made from collections in Toronto in 1987 and New York in 1996. This building is a copy of a house of a Nimpkish kinship group. The house front depicts a thunderbird lifting a whale (its food).

# The Kwakiutl, or Kwakwaka'wakw

Hardly a people in the world has influenced the public image of a region as much as the Kwakiutl of the Northwest Coast. But who are they? In 1849, the Hudson's Bay Company founded a trading post, Fort Rupert, on the east side of Vancouver Island, in the territory of a tribe by the name of Kwakiutl. The 30 tribes that were their immediate neighbors spoke two dialects of the language spoken by the Kwakiutl. For simplicity, the traders referred to all these tribes as the Kwakiutl; later, linguists even used the term to refer to the entire branch of the northern Wakashan languages, which include Kwakiutl, Haisla, Haihais, and Bella Bella. From the 30 original tribes, 15 independent groups evolved. They still exist, and the Canadian government eventually combined them to form the Kwawkewlth Agency. However, since the tribes have no common name for themselves, but no longer wish to be known as Kwakiutl, they have decided on a new name – Kwakwaka'wakw, meaning "speakers of Kwak'wala" (the language of the Kwakiutl).

The fame that the Kwakwaka'wakw achieved under the name of Kwakiutl is attributable to Franz Boas (1858–1942), the founder of modern American anthropology. In 1888, Boas found an ideal collaborator among the Kwakiutl in

Chief Jack James and Chief Bill Cranmer, Kwakwaka'wakw (Kwakiutl), Kingcome Inlet, 1988.

The present-day Kwakwaka'wakw are once again producing large numbers of traditional masks, frontlets, and blankets, which are worn on public occasions even in combination with jeans and business suits as a symbol of dignity. Chief Jack James (behind) is wearing a thunderbird frontlet and a button blanket; Chief Bill Cranmer (grandson of the chief who hosted the potlatch that was broken up by police in 1921) is wearing a Chilkat-style woven blanket.

Fort Rupert: George Hunt, son of a Tlingit woman and a Scot, had been raised among the Kwakiutl and was well informed about many details of their culture. Over the following decades, he sent Boas thousands of pages describing a variety of aspects of Kwakiutl life at Fort Rupert. As with the majority of reports on the cultures of the Northwest Coast, Hunt's material related almost exclusively to the aristocratic upper class – the "high culture" of the Kwakiutl.

Using this material and drawing upon his own observations, Boas published studies and texts of encyclopedic proportions, which aroused intense interest among other scholars. His description of the potlatch, the rivalry upon which it was based, and the traditional credit system that it entailed constantly triggered new interpretations. A book titled *Patterns of Culture* (1934) by Boas's student Ruth Benedict (1887–1948), of which millions of copies were sold, characterized the Kwakiutl as self-aggrandizing and megalomaniac, and made them in the minds of the public the epitome of a "Dionysian" culture – a term Benedict borrowed from German philosopher Friedrich Nietzsche (1844–1900).

Given the cultural significance of the potlatch, the government ban on it was bound to be opposed by the Kwakiutl. This resistance led the Canadian Indian Affairs agency to set a statutory example in order to promote the enforcement of their potlatch law. In 1921, the participants in a potlatch held on Village Island were arrested and released from prison only after they had handed over all the potlatch items. About 500 pieces – including 20 coppers of immeasurable value to the Kwakiutl – were passed on to museums in Ottawa, Toronto, and New York; Indian Commissioner D. C. Scott kept eleven pieces as personal spoils. The tribes involved have never forgotten this confiscation. Attempts to regain their treasures began in 1958, achieving their goal bit by bit over the following decades. The objects, however, were returned not to the families from whom they had been taken, but to the Kwakwaka'wakw – that is, to the entire population of all the tribes who had in the past competed in the ranking system. One condition for the return of the artifacts was that the "Potlatch Collection" would be placed in a museum. This responsibility was divided between two organizations founded around 1980: the U'Mista ["return"] Cultural Society in Alert Bay and the Nuyumbalees ["at the beginning of all myths"] Society in Cape Mudge. These new institutes stimulated cultural life in the Kwakiutl communities in a variety of ways and helped promote the revival of ceremonial traditions. For the Kwakiutl, the establishment of their own museums was an important step on the path to self-determined management of cultural and economic resources, at a time when efforts to create an increasingly autonomous indigenous communities in Canada were gradually achieving a measure of success.

Far left:

Atlak'am mask, Kwakiutl, British Columbia, before 1882. Ethnologisches Museum, Staatliche Museen zu Berlin – Preussischer Kulturbesitz, Berlin, Germany.

The Atlak'am was one of the numerous dancing groups that performed at winter ceremonials. It consisted of 26 men and 14 women, each of whom wore masks that represented mythical beings and that were precisely identifiable to the initiated spectators. Atlak'am masks were used for a period of four years, after which they were usually discarded; this is why many of them were only roughly fashioned in the first place. The cage covering the face of this very rare object probably represents a fishing basket.

Left:

Ceremonial dagger topped with the image of Dzunuk'wa, Kwakiutl, Kingcome Inlet, British Columbia, second half of the 19th century. American Museum of Natural History, New York, NY.

Daggers with exquisitely carved handles were used during winter ceremonials in scenes enacting the decapitation of Túxw'id, and also to cut the sacred bark strips that were distributed among the guests. Dagger-owners bought the steel used to make the blades for the price of one slave. For the Kwakiutl, Dzunuk'wa was a savage female giant, constantly on the look-out for little children whom she would take back to her house, smoke-process, and then devour.

Bak'was mask of the Oowekeeno (Bella Bella), British Columbia, c. 1880. Denver Art Museum, Denver, CO.

The mask's protruding cheekbones and hollow eye sockets point to the association between the wild forest dweller Bak'was and the world of the dead. Bak'was tempted mortals to eat his food; in so doing they themselves become Bak'was. He also lured the souls of the drowned to his ghost house, which is why the coloring of Bak'was masks (gray, blue-green, sometimes white and red) may have been chiefly inspired by rough seas.

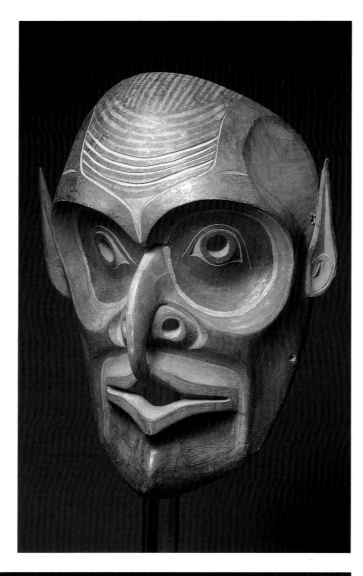

Below:

Raven helmet worn by the Tuknaxadi clan, Sitka (Tlingit), Alaska, early 19th century. University Museum, University of Pennsylvania, Philadelphia, PA.

The raven helmet that the Tuknaxadi clan (the Silver Salmon People) chose as their emblem relates to a myth in which a raven killed a salmon king, depriving other animals of their share. ("Nobody has the right to claim someone else's success for themselves.") The Ganaxtedi, or Raven clan, of Yakutat considered their exclusive right to use of the raven as their crest to have been infringed upon and started a five-year war that ended with the marriage of the Ganaxtedi chief to the daughter of the Tuknaxadi chief.

# Light, spirits, and thunderbirds

"She became aware, as though awakened from sleep, that there were two people, one an old man and the other a shaman with bars painted across his eyes. She realized she was a young woman. The old chief stood on a wide board and cut into the front of his thighs. The shaman wiped the blood on his hand. He blew onto it. He did that to the blood and it turned into a boy. The girl watched; they were doing this inside a house at the rear. Both the little girl and the little boy were growing rapidly. 'You shall be named Day-Dawn (N'aasii!atu),' they told the boy. 'You shall be named Sky-Day (N'aasayilim),' they told the girl."

This was how Tom Sayach'apis, a successful Nootka trader who had never converted to Christianity, imagined in 1922 the creation of the first people of his tribe. Origin myths of this kind existed for every lineage. Each was specially construed and had an individual style. According to the peoples of the Northwest Coast, there was a divine creator who had supremacy over all things. The Kwakiutl prayed to the Old Man and the Salish and Nootka to (Chief) Daylight. The Nootka nobility also prayed to Ka'uuts (Grandchild).

In virtually all parts of the Northwest Coast, light is the most immediate and most significant manifestation of the Creator and his blessings. However, the specific evolution of the world as we know it was attributed to the culture heroes, notably Raven – a being that possesses all the traits of a trickster who creates things in an unintentionally comical way. He is cunning and roguish, but most of all greedy, always bringing harm onto himself because of his greed. Another culture hero that appears in place of Raven is the "Transformer," a no less foolish being, often appearing in the guise of a man or a giant and identifiable by certain features, such as a hole in his cheek. Raven's place is sometimes also taken by Jay or Mink, beings who act in much the same way as Raven, but which are portrayed as even nastier and more lecherous.

According to the Tlingit (and a belief shared by most of the peoples of the region), the three fundamental elements of living human beings were body, vital energy ("breath"), and soul ("shadow"). Breath abandoned men afflicted with disease or who became unconscious, but could be recaptured by powerful shamans or their guardian spirits. When a person died, he would be abandoned by his

Opposite page:

Stikine (Tlingit) shaman from Wrangell, Alaska, c. 1900. Alaska State Library, Juneau, AK.

Shamans were primarily healers. But they were also capable of using their supernatural powers to cause harm, and thus they were very much feared by the people. The essential attributes of a shaman were a hand-held rattle and an apron with rattles and bells. The apron worn by this shaman is adorned with dentalium shells. During their séances, healers wore masks. A typical feature of Tlingit shamans was their matted hair. If their hair fell out, whether through a natural cause or by force, they had to relinquish their office.

462

Wrangell Medicine Man.

WDC
Juneau.

"shadow" and would wander around one of several realms of the dead, depending on the type of death he had suffered, but sometimes returned to life in the body of a newborn child.

The entire universe was populated by supernatural beings that commanded respect. While these beings were known to be benevolent at times, for the most part one had to beware of them. On the mountaintops lived the thunderbirds who would rise from their snow-covered eyries to hunt the double-headed sea serpent or the whales, on which they lived as people live on salmon. The forests were full of wild men with hooked noses and long hair, giant women who devoured children, and the restless spirits of the drowned. The realm beneath the earth was home to tribes of midgets, while the ocean was the domain of the salmon people – people in the guise of salmon who traveled up the rivers to feed their human brothers and sisters.

The first-salmon ceremony was a ritual practiced in various forms all along the coast. The ceremony highlighted the close ties between people and salmon. It was of particular significance for the Coast Salish, for whom it has again become increasingly important in recent years. Children carry the fish from the first catch of salmon in spring to the women of the family of the chief hosting the ceremony. The women then proceed to prepare them in a special way. Served at the festivities that follow, all the salmon (to this day) are devoured to the bones and the remains ritually thrown back into the river.

The universe consists of three spheres: heaven, sea, and land - the human habitate - with its forests, mountains, and rivers. Moving from one world to another was an ominous adventure that boded danger and chaos as personified by the monster of the sea otter spirit, who lured people into the ocean and then drowned them. Among humans, only shamans endowed with very special powers, were capable of undertaking such journeys as they had been performed in mythical times especially by the Transformer.

Oral traditions describe a mythical age in which animals appeared in the shape of humans and in which the environment was first given its present form. This was followed by the age of the human race as we know it, the era of legends, and of historical awareness. It was not hard for traditional myth tellers to believe that the mythical world might one day begin anew or that another one possibly existed alongside the one they knew.

The help of the supernatural powers was summoned for all undertakings in everyday life. The support of personal guardian spirits was the best possible guarantee of success. Hence, everyone sought opportunities to come into contact with benevolent spiritual beings, so as to be endowed with "treasures," as the Kwakiutl say. Treasures, in this sense, were

Far left:

Thunderbird mask, probably Bella Coola (Nuxalk), British Columbia, c. 1880. Museum für Völkerkunde, Vienna, Austria.

When mythical dramas were performed as part of the winter ceremonial, some masks were used to create special effects. They consisted of movable parts (in this case the beak and tongue) or were fitted with mechanical devices that made possible an on-stage transformation. By pulling a string, the face of the mask was raised and an underlying face revealed.

Left:

Sxwayxwey figure, Coast Salish, British Columbia, before 1880. Ethnologisches Museum, Staatliche Museen zu Berlin – Preussischer Kulturbesitz, Berlin, Germany.

Sxwayxwey are mask costumes in the form of an animal with cylindrical eyes and a face devoid of a lower jaw, crowned with the heads of two animals. For the Coast Salish, the privilege to wear such masks in dances was originally bestowed on an ancestor and then passed on to his descendants. Sxwayxwey were displayed on most ceremonial occasions as the privilege of the families who owned them. They also served important ritual purification purposes. According to contemporary belief, these masks when in use represent such overwhelming power that photography is usually forbidden.

supernatural powers. Such encounters could occur at any time; usually they were initiated by those seeking protection and "treasures." For this purpose, individuals would spend days in solitude, rub their skin with cedar branches until it bled, fast, or bathe in cold water, all of which indicated to the spirits the seriousness of one's request and ensured that the individual ready for the encounter with the spirits would be in a purified state – for there was no greater danger than impropriety in the face of a spirit.

Before setting out on hunting expeditions, hunters would communicate in dreams with the spirits of their prey. It was strictly forbidden to abuse animals in any way. It was especially important to be wary of bears, since they were considered to resemble man and could thus understand his every word and guess all his thoughts.

The Coast Salish cultivated the belief in guardian spirits in a very special way. From an early age children were schooled in how to gain the protection of a personal guardian spirit. Once the vision quest finally bore fruit and the desired contact had been made, this fact would manifest itself during the nights of the coming winter, when a supernatural being took possession of the novice in the course of "spirit dancing" to which the house groups invited guests. On these occasions, the older dancers, too, renewed their relationships with

their guardian spirits, who only came to Salish villages in wintertime.

The powers of supernatural beings that entered men and women had them dancing and singing their personal spirit songs for nights on end. Those for whom such occasions marked their first spirit dance wore special costumes and were subjected to the stern supervision of shamans, ensuring that their spirit song could properly unfold in their person without causing any harm. These shamans themselves possessed extremely powerful spirit helpers, who were at their disposal throughout the year and who endowed them with the powers required not only to heal, but also to harm.

Since the 1970s, spirit dancing has experienced a major revival, having long been suppressed by both government and the churches in much the same way as the potlatch. Indigenous therapy centers even apply this ritual for the treatment of depression and addiction which, for many members of traditional communities, are afflictions ultimately brought about by racist rejection and cultural alienation. Spirit dancing integrates participants in a ritual community and endows them with a guardian spirit, thus enabling them to gain a sense of self-value, to experience self-refinement both an individual and in a traditional context, and to acquire a feeling of new vitality.

Ron Hilbert Coy (Tulalip-Upper Skagit), *Spirit Dancing: The Practice of Our Ancestral Religion*, acrylic on canvas, 1988. Burke Museum of Natural History and Culture, Seattle, WA.

For many Coast Salish today, winter spirit dancing represents one of the strongest emotional ties to their native communities. This dance is also being adopted by members of other groups, such as the Nootka or the Makah, as a means of resolving personal crises. Over recent decades, interest in spirit dancing as a form of therapy has even been aroused among orthodox psychiatrists, who seek to explore the functioning of these healing methods and, in isolated cases, to integrate them into specific forms of therapy.

Wolf mask, Mowachaht (Nootka), British Columbia, 18th century. Ethnologisches Museum, Staatliche Museen zu Berlin – Preussischer Kulturbesitz, Berlin, Germany.

The Nootka winter ceremonial was the Wolf dance (*tlukwaana*), in which all members of the tribe could be initiated. Dancers dressed as wolves abducted the novices, taking them into forests where they were kept for several days, were instructed on the origin myths of their kinship groups, and from whence they returned as fully-fledged members of the community. In contrast to the Kwakiutl, the Nootka did not keep up the illusion that the mask dancers were the very spirit beings that they portrayed.

# Wintertime - cannibal time

The onset of the dark days of winter, enveloping in its misty clouds the crest poles and houses along the sheltered fiords, and of damp, cold snowstorms, the season when fathers chase their sons into icy waters to toughen them in preparation for life, meant the time had come to recount anew stories of the mythical dawn of history. Secret societies took command of the villages. The normal fabric of society appeared to lose its validity. The Nootka even prohibited (and punished) the wearing of symbols of status such as hats during this time of the year. The seating order for chiefs, so meticulously observed in summer, lost all validity during the winter months. Slaves participated in the rituals as equals. Even everyday names were relinquished in exchange for ceremonial names with humorous or obscene meanings. All disputes were prohibited, since it was believed that the spirit beings had now returned to the villages. There was no mourning the deceased. The world was turned upside down. While people hunted animals throughout the year, they were now themselves the prey of spiritual beings associated with the animals.

The so-called winter ceremonials were, however, directly related to potlatching, since, despite the supposed rejection of all differences in status, the rights to hold the rituals and to perform the dances were linked to the names of the chiefs of descent groups. The attendance of guests who bore witness to these rights and thus ensured their continuity was also a prerequisite for these ceremonials. Thanks to the many years of cooperation between the anthropologist Franz Boas and George Hunt, we have very detailed descriptions of the winter ceremonials conducted by the Kwakiutl (Kwakwaka'wakw).

For the Kwakiutl, the *Ts'eka* dance cycle, the sacred insignia of which are the bark of the giant tree of life and eagle down, was the centerpiece of winter cult dramas in which the sons of high-ranking families were initiated into

Dancer with a Huxwhukw mask during the Hamats'a ritual, Kwakiutl, Fort Rupert, British Columbia, 1894. American Museum of Natural History, New York, NY.

In myths, the Huxwhukw (cannibal birds) break open their victims' skulls with their powerful beaks and devour their brains. The long strips of cedar bark hanging from the mask at least partially covered the dancers' bodies.

the secrets of this cycle and performed dances which had been bestowed on their forefathers by Báxbakwalanuxsiwe', the "Cannibal at the north end of the world," and the war spirit Wínalagalis. The cannibal dancers (*hamats'a*), it was said, disappeared from the village for several weeks before the beginning of the ceremony. Spirits had devoured and then discharged them again as cannibals, in which capacity they now wandered through the forests.

A Ts'eka required lengthy preparation: stocks of food and cedar bark were accumulated; all dance costumes, masks, and rattles that were part of hereditary privileges and of certain dances had either to be newly made or repaired. With a flair for melodramatic effect, Ts'eka hosts would invite other tribes to attend by having delegations of the highest-ranking chiefs dressed in full chief's regalia travel to those villages to be invited on magnificent catamarans, made by tying individual canoes together. As they neared their destination, they would begin to chant songs of invitation, accompanied by the tapping rhythm produced by the paddlers (also noblemen) on the cross planks. The extending of reciprocal invitations meant that not all of the lineage groups eligible to hold an annual Ts'eka were actually able to do so. This allowed the groups several years to prepare for their next event.

The high-ranking kinship groups would form a committee – the "sparrows" – responsible for the coordination of the many dances and performances of the families. Sparrow harbingers would walk through the village announcing the start of Ts'eka festivities which, over the following four nights, would take place in various houses. The previously abducted heirs of certain dances would

return from the forests wild and in need of "taming." On the fourth night the spectacle would attract the Hamats'as, whose appearance brought the dances to a dramatic climax. Their presence was first discerned when the Hamats'as blew the spirit whistles. This was followed by a thud on the roof of the house (marking the return of a Hamats'a from the realm of the "Cannibal at the north end of the world").

Judith P. Morgan (Tsimshian), *Hok-Hok Dance*, pastel on paper, c. 1950, British Columbia Archives, Victoria, BC.

The dancer depicted here is accompanied by musicians using sticks to beat a rhythm on wooden planks. He wears a three-headed mask featuring a raven and a cannibal bird (Huxwhukw) perched on the image of a crooked-beaked bird. Crooked-beaked birds and cannibal birds are among the flying assistants of the "Cannibal at the north end of the world." Although the artist is a Tsimshian, her depiction primarily reflects Kwakiutl culture.

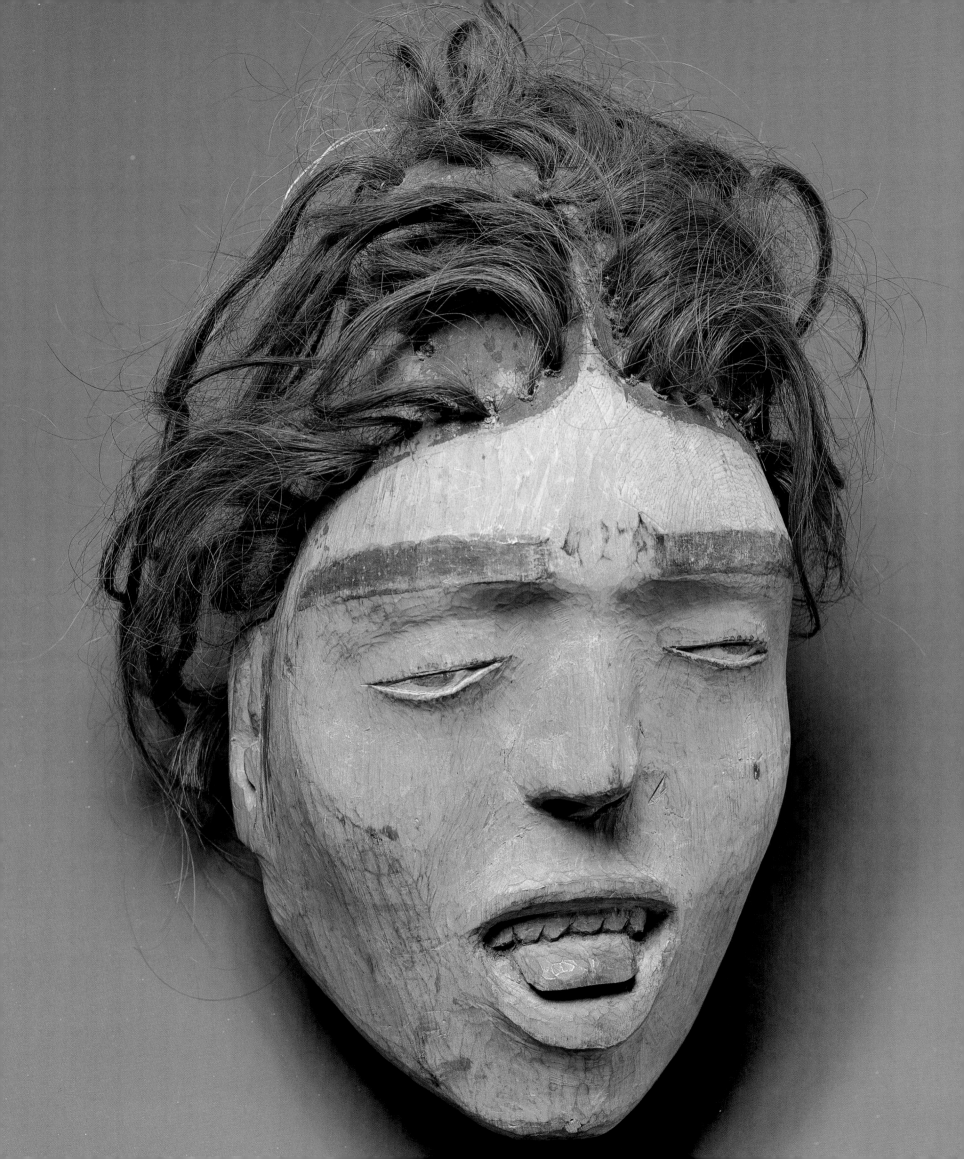

In a corner of the house, a roof plank would noisily fall to the ground, leaving a gap through which appeared a cannibal's head greedily yelling "Hap!" The same thing occurred in the other three corners of the house. Finally, the Hamats'a would fall to the floor. Clothed in hemlock twigs (with even more twigs caught in his matted hair), an unmistakable symbol of his wild state, he crawled on all fours. He then raced around the fire and around the room in a state of possession, frightening the onlookers. Anyone who got in the way of this cannibal when he was in search of human flesh risked being severely bitten. Or so it seemed, for the directors of this performance had positioned preselected victims throughout the room. In the light of the flickering fire, the frightened audience watched as the dancer nibbled at the corpse of a person recently deceased. (Whether the Hamats'a did actually eat human flesh remains a matter of dispute.) The Hamats'a's four assistants, wearing bird demon masks, followed him when he left the house and fled to the shore, where he was captured at dawn.

The performance was an enactment of shocking realism. The dance of the cannibal was the climax of a whole series of dances in which all participants wore masks. His dancing was accompanied by a display of fools throwing firebrands, who posed a very real danger inside the timber houses. One spirit dancer disappeared through a hatch to the underworld, reappearing at the side of the bay opposite the village. Here he enacted a struggle in which he was freed from the clutches of the inhabitants of the underworld.

Flutes were placed into the mouthpieces of the masks and symbolized the breath of the spirits. The bird masks had movable beaks that dancers could open, and their rattling sound mingled with the fast rhythmic beats of the songs, the whistling coming from the masks, and the hungry roars of the beings portrayed by the possessed dancers to create a deafening noise.

Possession is also a central feature of war dances (*hawinalal*) in which the skin of the dancers' backs was pierced by wooden skewers on which they were lifted, dangling, through the air, wantonly destroying objects which they were later required to replace. The *Túxw'id* dance was particularly melodramatic. A woman endowed with supernatural powers would give birth to a giant wooden frog or make wooden birds, attached to an invisible string, fly through the room. She would be decapitated and her head burned in the fire. In the end, however, her supernatural powers enabled her to return – alive and well.

During the following nights, the Hamats'as would appear as half-tamed cannibals, identifiable by their red cedar-bark shoulder rings to which hemlock twigs were attached. Certain words in the songs and speeches would rekindle their appetite for human flesh and make them leap wildly through the house. Their state of possession would also stimulate some Hamats'as of the past to join in. Finally, they disappeared behind the screen. The fourth night saw their rebirth as human beings, brought about by a female healer and indicated by red shoulder rings, forehead rings, and shoulder blankets, and their faces now being painted black.

Having survived this cannibalistic onslaught, and the dark, negative powers having been banished and in their place positive earthly order restored, the participants were now confronted with the usual displays of status rivalry. The objects put on display by the host during the ceremony were now distributed among the participating guests who had contributed with their dances and masks and, to a lesser extent, among the other guests.

The winter ceremonials conducted by other peoples also focused on the element of illusion. A Nootka chief once told of having owned a large model of a wolf that spewed out four real dancers with wolf masks. The Tsimshian had a model of a killer whale that was operated by a team of men who, upon instruction by the host, performed swimming and even diving motions in the waters off the shores of the village. When their contraption capsized, revealing the trick, the young men operating it, shamed by the accident, committed suicide.

Tommy Joseph, a Tlingit, working on a carving at Totem Park, Sitka, Alaska.

A range of cultural projects have been set up to enable young artists from the Northwest Coast to perfect their skills while making a living from their work. Carving, silk screen printing, and metalwork, all based on traditional styles, are not only a visible mark of modern Northwest Coast society, but also have a significant influence on the self-image of young people within the communities. In the right foreground is an unfinished mask representing a bear.

Bear-mother group, argillite, Haida, British Columbia, c. 1880. Rautenstrauch-Joest-Museum für Völkerkunde, Cologne, Germany.

From about 1820 onward, small objects carved of argillite, a material found only on the Queen Charlotte Islands, became increasingly popular among European sailors. The Haida thus came to hold a monopoly on the production of an early form of souvenir art that continues to this day. The bear-mother motif refers to a myth that tells how a noble woman once insulted the bears. As a punishment, she was seduced by a bear, was forced to give birth to his cubs, and to live a life in the wilderness, far from her fellow humans.

# Art and craftsmanship

Just as salmon provided the basis for live on the coast, so the trees of the rainforest were an ever-present source for virtually all the material possessions of the coast people. Bark was spun into yarn that was used to make clothing, or was cut into strips for the fabrication of mats. Root splints were the main material used in basketry. The straight trunks of the giant trees of life ("red cedars") that grow to heights of over 200 feet were ideal for making canoes. From the hard wood of the Nootka cypress ("yellow cedar") masks and other ritual objects were carved using adzes, knives, and burins of beaver tooth. Since this timber was easy to split by means of a wedge, native builders were able to produce planks of all sizes. Heat and steam were used to bend wood into all conceivable shapes.

It is surprising how intricate some of the wooden items were, given the modest range of tools. The richly carved or painted boxes made in this region are technically impressive: the vertical panels consisted of a single board, three corners being made by grooving and folding the wood at right angles, and the fourth secured by wooden pegs. These boxes were used for storage, as "drums" (percussion idiophones), and as cooking vessels in which liquids were heated by red-hot stones.

All male adults were able to make the wooden items they used in daily life. However, the creation of exquisite works of art, whose purpose was to display the privileges of the nobility, required the skills of trained artists. A noble family's emblems were exhibited not only on crest poles; their chests, spoons, and rattles were also marked with

Joe David (Nuu-chah-nulth [Nootka]), *Thunderbird and Killer Whale*, screen print, 1978. Hamburgisches Museum für Völkerkunde, Hamburg, Germany.

On the Northwest Coast, the gigantic thunderbirds were thought to feed mostly on whales and were thus considered an ally of human whale hunters. These two antagonists, the thunderbird and the whale, the mightiest beings on land and in the sea respectively, are combined into a single being in this print. While thunderbirds are normally portrayed with curled ears and sharply hooked beaks, here it is recognizable as such only through its connection to the whale. The revival of traditional Northwest Coast painting styles in the 1960s was mainly in the form of silk screen prints.

references to their hereditary privileges. In addition to their skills as craftsmen, it was also necessary for artists to be familiar with the myths surrounding the family crests and with the secret knowledge of the societies in order to produce the masks used in winter ceremonials. Because of their wealth, nobles were able to pay the best artists very handsomely and thus release them from other kinds of work.

It was on the basis of such specialization in carving and painting that characteristic styles evolved. Classic formline designs, based on the principle of symmetry, with flat areas of unbroken color (black, red, blue/green), flowing outlines, and a limited range of forms producing stylized representational images, were a feature of the style of the northern coast. The austere principles of composition espoused in these pieces produced symbolic items in which one single stylized part of the body often represented the entire being. Killer whales, for instance, are represented by their typical breathing hole and awesome jaws; beavers are typically depicted with large incisors and a diamond pattern representing their tail. Often, the works of these artists were, quite intentionally, of ambiguous symbolism, creating a sort of puzzle that baffled even the most practiced eye and revealed a talent for abstraction. These artists also produced naturalistic portrait sculptures, whose importance increased significantly in the 19th century when white buyers began to show a keen interest in them.

The rather relief-like crest poles of the Haida, and even more so those of the Tsimshian are testimony to the great skill with which artists combined two- and three-dimensional representations. The mastery they developed in the production of monumental sculptures was also applied to miniature carvings in horn, ivory, and argillite. Contact with whites made it easier to acquire the

extremely valuable copper, and silver became a material for their crafts for the very first time. Metal ornaments and tools were adorned with exquisitely engraved designs.

The women of the Northwest Coast produced twined basketry and textiles. In this wet climate, wide-brimmed, watertight rain hats made of spruce-root fibers were indispensable. Other everyday clothing was often limited to capes or blankets made of cedar bark yarn. These products of female craftsmanship generally featured geometric patterns. One exception is the Chilkat blanket, made of twined cedar bark and mountain goat wool and decorated with a typical the Northwest Coast formline design. Named after a Tlingit tribe that supplied such blankets to peoples throughout this coastal region, Chilkat blankets are considered to have originated among the Tsimshian. From 1850, button blankets made of woolen cloth and Chinese mother-of-pearl buttons began to replace Chilkat blankets as ceremonial attire.

Paul Kane, *Clal-lum Woman Weaving a Blanket*, oil on canvas, 1847. Royal Ontario Museum, Toronto, ON.

Using a framework with two warp-beams, Coast Salish women produced both twined and twilled blankets made of cedar bark, mountain goat wool, and dog hair. For the latter, they especially bred a type of dog that had an exceptionally woolly coat. With the extinction of the dogs in the 19th century, production of these half-woven textiles almost completely ceased (although it was revived as a craft in the 1960s). Scottish settlers, however, introduced the Cowichan on Vancouver Island to sheep's wool and ever since the Cowichan have knitted warm sweaters, both for themselves and for sale.

# The Tsimshian – artists and visionaries

Tsimshian women spinning wool, Metlakatla, British Columbia, 1881. Photograph: Edward Dossetter. British Columbia Archives, Victoria, BC.

As part of the traditional method of textile production, the women of the Northwest Coast used spindles with relief-carved spindle-whorls to make thread from animal hair and vegetal fibers. In William Duncan's Metlakatla colony, Tsimshian women were taught to use spinning wheels so as make the transition from home production to commercial manufacture. The primary source of income at Metlakatla was derived from a fish-processing plant whose products were sold directly to Japanese trading ships.

From the perspective of the Tsimshian, the "kinship" between certain clans constituted the basis upon which intertribal relationships between the various peoples of the northern parts of the Northwest Coast were founded. Whereas the Haida, with a long history of habitation in the region, were viewed as paternal relatives, the Tlingit, having probably arrived on the coast after the Tsimshian, were their "younger sisters." Within this network of relationships, the Tsimshian acted as intermediaries between the peoples of the inland, and those of the central and northern coast, enriching the cultural inventory of the entire region, not least through the contribution of their own developments.

Tsimshian society, in contrast to that of other peoples of the Northwest Coast, was divided into four classes, for which their language had specific terms. The highest title bearers of the first-ranking lineage of a village constituted a separate class of village chiefs, higher in status than the remaining upper class. They also had authority over the chiefs of daughter villages which had been established away from the main villages. By the early 19th century, their status had evolved to become that of tribal chiefs. To keep their illustrious titles and privileges within their own ranks, marriages were entered into only between members of families with equal status. They even created new emblems that distinguished them from the "common" nobility. An estimated population of 8,000 in the early part of the 19th century contained more than two dozen such elite chiefs.

It was all the more surprising, therefore, that English lay preacher William Duncan (1832–1918) managed, in 1862, to settle his Tsimshian converts in the Anglican showcase colony of Metlakatla, a settlement in which ideals of equality prevailed. His followers built standardized row houses and financed the community and its schools by setting up small businesses such as bakeries, smith shops, trading posts, and a shipyard. Duncan's excellent knowledge of the Tsimshian language, the diplomatic concessions that he made to traditional authorities, and the general upheavals in society as a whole fueled the rapid

House in the museum village of 'Ksan, Gitksan (Tsimshian), Hazelton, British Columbia, 1978.

Wooden boards on the gabled side of the house create a false front, which suggests a larger building. The crest painted in classical Northwest Coast style on the house front was visible from a long distance and indicated the clan owning the house. Access to the house is provided by an oval opening at the lower end of the crest pole attached to the house.

growth of his community. However, Duncan was opposed to the Tsimshian receiving Holy Communion. He felt that their own history of cannibalistic ceremonial practices would hinder them from truly understanding the receipt of the consecrated wafer as a symbol of the body and blood of Christ. This and other issues of dispute led to massive discord between Duncan and Anglican clerics and, in 1880, to the foundation of New Metlakatla on Annette Island in Alaska, where Duncan's followers were recognized and taken up by the American government as religious refugees.

Since no treaties were ever concluded with the coastal peoples of British Columbia, the indigenous population has never officially ceded its territory. The Canadian government, however, denied the existence of any rightful claims to precolonial land ownership. The Nisga'a, a Tsimshian tribe, were the first people, in 1890, to press for a court decision on the issue of land rights. In 1913, their chiefs cofounded the first pan-Indian organization in British Columbia, and it was from their ranks that the first native parliamentary representative, Frank Calder, was elected to a provincial parliament in 1948. Although the suit filed by the tribe claiming return of territory on the Nass River was rejected by the Supreme Court in 1973, it was the first time a court acknowledged the existence of such land rights. The issue left undecided was whether these rights had lapsed or not. This lawsuit constituted the start of a movement for land rights by the tribal councils of British Columbia. It has since achieved considerable success. The Nisga'a themselves signed an agreement with the government in 1998, by which a part of their territory was returned to them.

Menesk, chief of the Nisga'a village of Gitlakdamkis, British Columbia, 1927. Canadian Museum of Civilization, Hull, QC.

Chilkat blankets, which the Tsimshian called "dance blankets," frontlets adorned with sea lion whiskers and strips of ermine fur, and rattles in the shape of a raven were the symbols of chiefly rank among the Tsimshian. These insignia eventually spread northward and southward. Beards were far more commonly worn on the Northwest Coast than in most other regions of North America, where the sparse growth of facial hair was removed by depilation.

GREAT BASIN

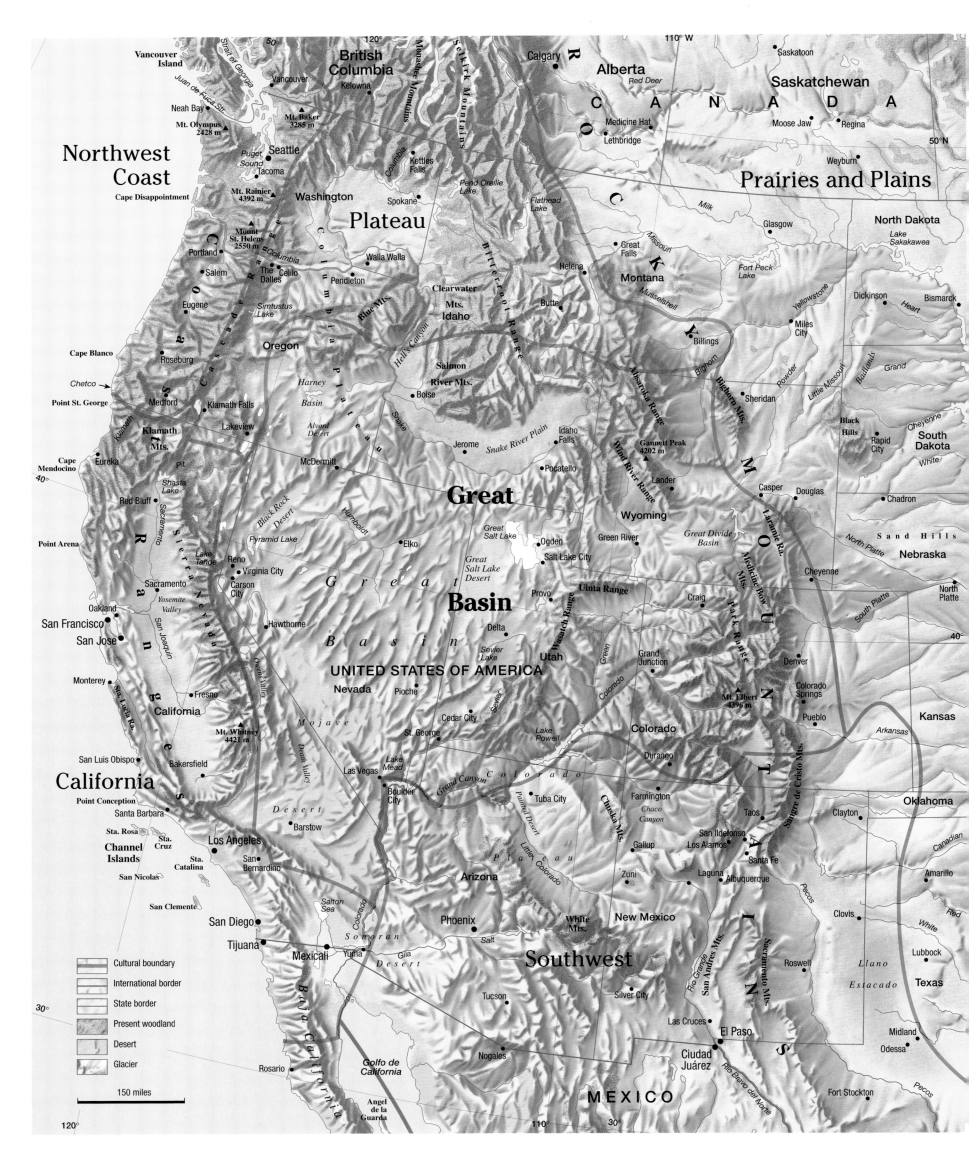

**Northwest Coast**

Vancouver Island
Vancouver
Neah Bay
Mt. Olympus
2428 m
Cape Disappointment
Cape Blanco
Chetco →
Point St. George
Cape Mendocino
Point Arena
Point Conception
Channel Islands
San Nicolas
San Clemente

**California**

San Francisco
San Jose
Oakland
Monterey
San Luis Obispo
Santa Barbara
Sta. Rosa
Sta. Cruz
Sta. Catalina
San Diego
Tijuana

Strait of Georgia
Juan de Fuca Str.
Mt. Baker 3285 m
Seattle
Tacoma
Puget Sound
Mt. Rainier 4392 m
Washington
Mount St. Helens 2550 m
Portland
Salem
The Dalles
Celilo
Eugene
Roseburg
Medford
Klamath Falls
Klamath Mts.
Eureka
Red Bluff
Shasta Lake
Sacramento
Lake Tahoe
Reno
Virginia City
Carson City
Sacramento
Yosemite Valley
Hawthorne
San Joaquin
Fresno
Bakersfield
Mt. Whitney 4421 m
Death Valley
Los Angeles
San Bernardino
Barstow

**British Columbia**
Kelowna
Columbia
Kettles Falls
Spokane
Pend Oreille Lake
Flathead Lake

**Plateau**
Walla Walla
Pendleton
Blue Mts.
Clearwater Mts.
Idaho
Oregon
Simtustus Lake
Harney Basin
Alvord Desert
Lakeview
McDermitt
Black Rock Desert
Pyramid Lake
Humboldt
Elko
Pioche
Cedar City
St. George
Mojave
Desert
Salton Sea
Yuma
Mexicali
Sonoran
Gila Desert
Desert
Phoenix
Tucson
Nogales
Golfo de California
Rosario
Angel de la Guarda
Baja California

Columbia
Hell's Canyon
Salmon River Mts.
Boise
Snake
Jerome
Snake River Plain
Idaho Falls
Pocatello
Bitterroot Range
Helena
Butte

**Great**
**Basin**

Great Salt Lake
Ogden
Salt Lake City
Great Salt Lake Desert
Provo
Uinta Range
Delta
Sevier Lake
Utah
Nevada
Sevier
Lake Powell

**UNITED STATES OF AMERICA**

Grand Canyon
Colorado
Boulder City
Lake Mead
Las Vegas
Tuba City
Painted Desert
Little Colorado
Chuska Mts.
Chaco Canyon
Arizona
White Mts.
Salt
**Southwest**
Silver City
Las Cruces
El Paso
Ciudad Juárez
Nogales

**R O C K Y   M O U N T A I N S**

Calgary
**Alberta**
Red Deer
**Saskatchewan**
Medicine Hat
Lethbridge
Saskatoon
Moose Jaw
Regina
Weyburn
**CANADA**

**Prairies and Plains**

Milk
Glasgow
**North Dakota**
Lake Sakakawea
Great Falls
Missouri
Montana
Musselshell
Fort Peck Lake
Dickinson
Bismarck
Heart
Billings
Yellowstone
Miles City
Badlands
Grand
Absaroka Range
Bighorn
Bighorn Mts.
Powder
Little Missouri
Sheridan
Gannett Peak 4202 m
Wind River Range
Lander
Black Hills
Rapid City
**South Dakota**
White
Casper
Douglas
Chadron
**Wyoming**
Green River
Great Divide Basin
Laramie Ra.
Medicine Bow Mts.
Park Range
Sand Hills
North Platte
**Nebraska**
Cheyenne
North Platte
Craig
South Platte
Grand Junction
Denver
Green
Colorado
**Colorado**
Colorado Springs
Mt. Elbert 4396 m
Pueblo
**Kansas**
Arkansas
Durango
Farmington
Sangre de Cristo Mts.
Taos
Clayton
**Oklahoma**
San Ildefonso
Los Alamos
Santa Fe
Gallup
Zuni
Laguna
Albuquerque
Canadian
Amarillo
Clovis
**New Mexico**
Sacramento Mts.
San Andres Mts.
Rio Grande
Pecos
Roswell
Lubbock
Llano Estacado
**Texas**
Rio Bravo del Norte
Midland
Odessa
Fort Stockton
Pecos
White
Red

**M E X I C O**

Golfo de California

Legend:
- Cultural boundary
- International border
- State border
- Present woodland
- Desert
- Glacier

150 miles

Henry Kammler

# The grass hut people

In the western parts of the North American continent lies an endless landscape of arid semidesert with over 400,000 square miles of scorching sunshine, salt lakes, and thorny desert vegetation extending from the Rocky Mountains to the ridges of the Sierra Nevada. The rivers that flow from the mountains never reach the ocean, but are soaked up by the salt lakes like drops in a trough. Its geographical name, the Great Basin, fittingly describes this landscape, even though it embraces only the heartland of the greater cultural area that includes the Colorado Plateau in the south, parts of the Columbia Plateau in the northwest, and the Snake River Plains in the north. The Rocky Mountains (rising up to a height of 15,000 feet), the high plateaus, and the expanse of territory all the way to the continental divide in the present-day state of Colorado, make up the eastern part of the region. The western Basin, deprived of humidity by the mountains of the Sierra Nevada, receives only about three inches of rain a year. Further east rainfall increases, reaching averages of over 40 inches on the western slopes of the Rockies (the Wasatch Range, the Uintah Range). As is typical in arid regions, rainfall is highly unpredictable. Some areas may receive no rain for several years, only to be deluged with massive downpours in other years.

**Pyramid Lake, Nevada.**

The abundance of fish in the waters of Pyramid Lake and the many birds and edible plants that live and grow on its shores provided the Northern Paiute who lived there with not only a relatively secure, but also a privileged means of sustenance in comparison to the other inhabitants of this semidesert region. In 1844, explorer John Charles Frémont (1813–1890) wrote of the inhabitants: "These Indians are very fat and seem to lead an easy and happy life." At the beginning of the 20th century, farmers began to divert water from the lake to irrigate their fields. The water level sank, and the fish gradually died. The indigenous people have often enough come to realize just how important water rights are for their survival in the Great Basin.

Previous pages:
**Valley of the Gods, Utah.**

In the south, the arid landscapes of the Great Basin join up with those of the Southwest. Although no natural boundaries divide the two neighboring regions, the contrast in existence between the sedentary irrigation farmers on the one hand and the nomadic hunters and gatherers on the other could not be greater.

**The peoples of the Great Basin.**

Only the peoples of the central Great Basin (the Western Shoshone and some of the Southern and Northern Paiute) actually conform to the Desert Culture commonly considered typical for this region. The Northern Shoshone and their Bannock neighbors subsisted on the salmon in the Snake River and its tributaries, and, like the peoples of the Plateau, began to use horses and hunt bison in the 18th century. The Eastern Shoshone and the Ute had already come to possess horses in the 17th century and had also become highly dependent on bison hunting for their sustenance. In the southernmost regions of the Basin, simple farming methods had been introduced along the tributaries of the Colorado under the influence of the neighboring Yuma tribes. The Owens Valley Paiute and the Washoe shared some cultural characteristics, such as the use of acorns for food, with the peoples of central California.

Map labels: Northern Shoshone, Bannock, Eastern Shoshone, Northern Paiute, Washoe, Western Shoshone, Ute, Owens Valley Paiute, Southern Paiute, Kawaiisu

The Rocky Mountains south of Aspen, Colorado.

The Rocky Mountains, which here rise 15,000 feet above sea level, constitute the Great Basin's eastern border. Once horses had been introduced to the Ute, traditionally inhabiting this area, they had ideal access to the Plains and thus adopted some of the characteristics of the lifestyle of the bison hunters.

As hostile as this high basin may appear to be (its depressions lie at 3500 to 5000 feet above sea level), the peoples of the region succeeded in exacting from it a means of existence by their resourcefulness and close adaptation to their environment. Securing the survival of what in the late 18th century was an estimated population of 40,000 did, however, require the use of vast expanses of territory (around 10 square miles per person). Small family bands roamed the countryside, living chiefly on vegetable foods. No fewer than 350 types of plants are known to have been used for food in one way or another. These included first of all the pinyon trees (or nut pines) that grow on the mountain slopes, a variety of reeds from the shores and marshlands (the water levels of which were contingent on the amount of rainfall received), numerous varieties of grass, and, in the southwest, acorns and wild beans (such as mesquite beans). The available game was far more limited and more difficult to come by. They did, of course, hunt mule deer, pronghorn antelope, bighorn sheep, and black bears, if they were able to get hold of them. But most often the staple diet of vegetable food had to be supplemented by rabbits, hares, prairie dogs, small lizards, and birds.

Because of the barren environment and their nomadic lifestyle (for most of the year, they remained in one place for no more than several weeks), the material possessions of the people of this region were necessarily rather limited. The first Anglo-American travelers considered these people to be very poor and wretched figures. In this era marked by the rise of evolutionary thought, the American public was inclined to consider the native inhabitants of the Basin as representatives of an early stage of "savagery." In the travel accounts and the media of the 19th century, they were commonly referred to as "grass hut people" or "diggers" (from their practice of digging up roots). Even the well-known American writer, travel journalist, and humorist Mark Twain (1835–1910), in a display of unveiled prejudice, described the Gosiute (a group of Western Shoshone) as the "wretchedest type of mankind I have ever seen, ... considerably inferior to all races of savages on our continent."

The natural poverty of this region had not always prevailed in this form. As the last Ice Age receded around 12,000 years ago, it left behind huge lakes whose surface covered almost half of the Basin. The people who migrated to the region at the time lived a life of abundance – at least for a short while. They hunted big game (bison, mammoth, wild horses, camels) in rich, subtropical landscapes. Gradually, however, the lakes evaporated, for several thousand years the barrenness was even more severe than it is today, and the large mammals became extinct. For approximately the last 5,000 years, the climate in the Great Basin has been how we know it today. The development of the historical cultures was based on the exploitation of the different vegetation zones characteristic of the various altitudes: the sagebrush-grass zone of the lower levels gives way at higher elevations to the pinyon-juniper zone and other pine forest zones, followed at progressively higher altitudes by sub-alpine and montane zones.

The languages spoken in this huge region were surprisingly homogeneous. With the exception of one group, all the bands belonged to the Numic group of the Uto-Aztecan language family, the most southern representatives of which were the Aztecs who populated the regions extending deep into the Mexican highland. The Numic languages, in turn, are divided into three branches that fanned out over the Great Basin from their southern Californian point of origin. "Numic" refers to the word for "people" common to these languages, which is rendered *nima, nimi,* or – in a simplified English version – "Numa." The low fragmentation of the Numic languages leads to the assumption that these peoples had come fairly recently to the region from the west or the southwest, and quickly spread all over the territory. Archeologists, however, consider them to be the last representatives of the 10,000-year-old Desert Culture that, in the course of time, has constantly adapted to the changing environment.

The three branches of the Numic language group each consisted of two individual languages. Since widely scattered, politically independent groups used the same mother tongue (for example, the north-to-south extension of the Northern Paiute language covered 450 miles), numerous names have come to be used for the groups inhabiting the several regions that, after 1848, were gradually united under the administration of the Bureau of Indian Affairs. Ethnological and linguistic designations thus tend to be confused. Whereas the Southern Paiute, for instance, speak a southern Ute dialect, the Northern Paiute (in Oregon referred to as "Paviotso") and Bannock speak a western Numic language, as do the Owens Valley Paiute, who use a Mono dialect. Central Numic languages are Shoshone (including Comanche of the southern Plains) and Panamint.

The only exception in the Great Basin are the Washoe at Lake Tahoe. They have a completely separate language that is related, if at all, to the Hokan group of languages beyond the Sierra Nevada in California. The Washoe have certainly inhabited their territory for a very long time, a fact supported by the many place names in their language, which are no longer translatable. To some extent, place names are the "fossils" of a language. Originally descriptive of a place, they remain in the vocabulary for much longer than other words which undergo changes in phonetics or meaning from one generation to the next.

Baptism of Southern Paiutes in the Jordan River near St. George, Utah, 1875. Photograph: Charles R. Savage. Museum für Völkerkunde, Vienna, Austria.

Having fled to the desert of Utah, the Mormons strove to maintain friendly relations with their Numic neighbors, gaining most notably the support of the Eastern Shoshone chief Washakie (c. 1802–1900). In 1858, they even sought to establish an alliance against the common threat posed by American troops. They also attempted to convert the Numa to their religion, although these missionary endeavors met with only limited success. The mass baptism of 200 Southern Paiutes in the Jordan River was a major exception, but had little long-term effect.

Alvord Desert, Oregon.

The combination of short, sometimes heavy rainfalls followed by heat produces cracks in the saline ground. Only vegetation especially adapted to these conditions can exist here. Animals and humans alike withdrew to the mountain slopes covered with juniper and nut pines that surrounded the barren valleys. When water was sparse in some of the driest areas, the obligatory daily bath had to be taken by using clean fine sand.

# The history of people without history

Northern Paiute camp on the tailings dump of the Ophir Mine near Virginia City, Nevada, c. 1890. Bancroft Library. University of California, Berkeley, CA.

In the course of the progressive exploration of the Basin by the Americans, the Numa were left the losers of this cultural encounter. Ultimately, they were either reduced to a cheap, readily available labor reserve on the fringes of the national economy, or to recipients of government charity. Their growing culture of poverty was based on a combination of traditional forms and the waste of the "civilization" that was prescribed to them by the government. At the same time, however, they retained a strong sense of their autonomy, and opted for "integration" only to an extent that they deemed absolutely unavoidable.

In the 17th century, most of the inhabitants of the Great Basin were largely unaware of the fact that they were part of a Spanish viceroyalty. Before 1650, some Ute groups came into the possession of runaway or stolen horses that had belonged to the Spanish, which enabled them to extend their military punch and reach. They traded with the Spanish, sold to them children abducted from the Southern Paiute, but they also raided Spanish trading posts.

It was the Mormons who, in 1847, first established permanent settlements in the region. From their base at Salt Lake City, they founded villages in the surrounding fertile depressions that also served as the primary subsistence base for the Numa. The Mormons, however, were intent on avoiding conflict, an objective which, at times, they more or less achieved. In contrast to the Mormons, the large treks of emigrants that passed through Utah and Nevada from 1848 in search of gold, had total disregard for both the native people and their environment. They occupied watering places, set up mail stations and trading posts, and their livestock trampled the food plants used by the Numa. From 1860, seeing their existence threatened, the Numa increasingly took to their weapons – on Pyramid Lake, in the valley of the Humboldt River, in Owens Valley, on Snake River. In response, the army established forts, land cession treaties were negotiated (and quickly broken), and reservations were allocated that were quickly settled by the whites, before the Numa had chance to create on them a basis for their livelihood. The indigenous population soon found itself on the social fringe of an expanding mining and ranching economy of the Americans, who, in 1864, created the state of Nevada. Many Western Shoshone and Paiute did, however, choose to stay near their traditional homelands, rather than be bundled off to one of the large reservations which in fact belonged to the local groups.

Only 20 years after the arrival of white settlers, the Great Basin presented a sorry sight. Like voracious worms, gold and silver mines had burrowed through the mountains, spewing out toxic mercury. Waterholes dried out under

PIUTE INDIAN HARVEST SCENE.

COPYRIGHT, 1897.
SAGE BRUSH ART, CO.

Northern Paiute harvest scene, Nevada, 1897. Nevada Historical Society, Reno, NV.

The women used the same baskets and winnowing trays for harvesting that they used for gathering grass seeds. They were vigorously supported in their task by the men. This type of cooperation was new, for in former times men had only contributed to gathering activities upon their return from an unsuccessful hunt, so as not to arrive home empty-handed. Most farming projects on the reservations in the Great Basin failed in the long term. Not only are the lands on which the reservations were established too poor for intensive use, but the Bureau of Indian Affairs also lacked both competence and the necessary resolution to see such projects through properly.

the hooves of thousands of cattle. Railroads cut into the landscape like steel blades. The traditional lifestyle seemed irrevocably lost. The last hope to which many people clung were the teachings of Wodziwob, a Northern Paiute visionary, according to whom the whites would go away if all Numa regularly held five-night ecstatic round dances throughout the region. The deceased ancestors would then return and the land would recover. This notion was based on the old cycle of mourning (traditionally common only among the inhabitants of the westernmost part of the Great Basin) which entailed holding a second feast of the dead one year after a person's death. Other Numic peoples avoided all contact with the dead. The new religion (called Ghost Dance) spread quickly, but lost influence after only a few years, when the whites not only remained in the area, but their numbers even increased.

Two decades later, the Ghost Dance flared up again. This time it was Wovoka (c. 1856–1932), a Northern Paiute, who around 1887 heralded an era of health and good fortune in friendship with the whites if all Numa regularly took part in the Ghost Dance. Like a prairie fire, Wovoka's happy tidings were carried all the way to the peoples of the Plains (who, however, understood his vision of conciliation as

a call for resistance against white invaders). In the Great Basin, the Ghost Dance was totally integrated into the existing ritual practices and today is a normal part of other ceremonies. Wovoka died in 1932 as a medicine man widely respected, without, however, having received any further visions.

Many of the scattered groups were eventually given small reservations at their places of abode. Even today remote and impoverished, the traditional language and culture remain very much alive in these communities. For decades, the government did not take these tribes seriously, since they had no big chiefs and warriors, and saw fit to turn Nevada (in their view an unpopulated area) into a huge military testing ground. Radioactive waste, low-level flights, and aggressive mining have made the land and its people sick. But the Numa are becoming less tolerant of this treatment, are insisting that old treaties (never ratified and, therefore, considered by the American legal system to be null and void) be honored, are taking mining companies and the army to court, and are seeking their own alternatives, whether by building casinos or through the establishment of eco-tourism projects.

Bannock Sheep Eater brush shelter erected on Medicine Lodge Creek, Idaho, 1871. Photograph: William Henry Jackson. Peabody Museum of Natural History, Yale University, New Haven, CT.

In 1870, the Bannock erected brush shelters reminiscent of the tipis of their Northern Shoshone neighbors. Though the framework of these shelters consisted only of slender saplings, they did cover the frame with lengths of canvas sewn together. Bison, which had been the subsistence base for the mounted Bannock, disappeared from the region around the same time that the Mormon settlers arrived and the gold rush started, leading to conflicts with the settlers and the government that ultimately triggered the Bannock War of 1878.

# Between abundance and famine – the year in the Great Basin

The inhabitants of the Great Basin lived and worked primarily in small family bands that each exploited a specific territory. The herds of bison that sporadically appeared at the eastern edge of the Basin required a tighter form of organization among the local Ute, which enabled several matrilineally related families to cooperate economically under the leadership of an experienced chief. In other parts of the Great Basin, however, firm tribal structures were absent. Respected males assumed leadership roles only in times of food abundance, when several families would join to go on hunting or food gathering expeditions or to retreat to a more permanent winter camp. Each family could leave the group at any time or even join a different group. The flexible structure of such groups allowed people to make the best possible use of this barren territory.

Many of these local groups of families became known by names of the major food resources available in their particular region. Western Shoshone groups were thus known as the Fish Eaters, Buffalo Eaters, or Rice Grass Eaters. Since these groups also referred to themselves by such names, these names underscored their claim to a certain territory and its natural food resources. Depending on the season, a family could join one or another group to get access to a variety of different foods. Neighboring groups would extend invitations to one another when a particular type of plant produced high yields. Pinyon trees, for example, bear ample quantities of nuts only every three to four years. It was never predictable just how abundant the yield on a particular mountain slope would be. If it was very good, the people of one group alone would not be able to consume all the available nuts. Reciprocal invitations also reduced the risk of conflicts between the groups, and were a welcome opportunity to make new friends and seek marriage partners.

At the start of the year, when the weather was icy cold, food was at its scarcest. The supplies in the storage pits were depleted, and the only other sources of food were the occasional trout that passed through the waters under the ice on their way to the spawning grounds, or emaciated rabbits. In such times of famine, the Western Shoshone might leave the old and sick behind (often on their own request) in a sheltered spot and with a little food at their disposal, so as not to put the survival of the group at risk.

The hard time of scarcity drew to a close in February when squirrels came out of hibernation. Soon after migratory birds from the south returned to the shores in great numbers. A variety of ducks, snow geese, Canada geese, and mud hens were hunted with bows and arrows or with nets. Throughout the semidesert, a sparse growth of vegetation suddenly reappeared, the fresh leaves and the root tubers of which were often eaten raw.

## New life unfolds

The people could now leave their protected, bark-covered winter quarters. With a solid juniper frame and measuring more than 30 feet in diameter, these shelters could accommodate a dozen or more people. The lighter, grass-covered *kahni* ("house") was sufficient shelter in the hot summers. During nomadic treks, bushes were covered with hides to provide simple brush shelters.

Alfred Jacob Miller, *Lassoing Wild Horses*, watercolor and gouache, 1837. Joslyn Art Museum, Omaha, NE.

The Eastern Shoshone on the western edge of the Plains already owned horses in the 17th century, which were either stolen directly from the Spanish or, more often, taken from the rapidly growing herds of wild horses. During the 200 years that followed, the Eastern Shoshone engaged in flourishing trade with the animals that they caught and tamed. Once horses had been introduced to the Ute, they too soon changed their traditional lifestyle, embarking on extended raids to the Pueblo region and northern Mexico in the south.

The introduction of tipis brought major advantages. The use of this form of shelter, along with the use of horses, spread gradually westward from the Ute and the Eastern Shoshone. By about 1850, even the Paiute groups possessed modest herds of horses. Roaming over great distances according to the seasons of the year, the inhabitants of the Great Basin, happily adopted the tipi since it was easily erected and provided ideal shelter in both summer and winter. Horses could easily transport the long tipi poles and the heavy leather coverings and also made it much easier to hunt the bison that provided the hides used for tipis. A normal cover of bison leather could only be used for a period of two to four years, during which time enough bison had to be hunted with which to fabricate a new one.

Hunters generally went stalking alone. Sometimes, however, depending on the terrain, it was advisable to

Balduin Möllhausen, *Chemehuevis*, color lithograph, 1858, from J. C. Ives, *Report Upon the Colorado River of the West*, Washington 1861. Amon Carter Museum, Fort Worth, TX.

The Chemehuevi, the southernmost Numic group, lived along the Colorado River in California in the immediate neighborhood of the Mohave, with whom they later shared a reservation. Around the mid-19th century, the cotton shirts worn by the men bore obvious testimony to contacts between whites and the indigenous peoples of the Southwest. The woman shown here, however, is wearing a traditional grass skirt and a basketwork cradle with a rollover bow to protect the head area.

The Numa made fire by twirling a hardwood-tipped reed between the palms of their hands. The tip of this device was placed into a cavity on a yucca stem that began to smolder as a result of the friction caused by the rotating hardwood tip. Blowing onto the spot eventually produced a flame. Campfires were relatively small, since the availability of firewood was limited.

hunt mule deer, pronghorn antelope, and big horn sheep in groups. Such hunting expeditions were supervised by an experienced hunting leader who usually specialized in certain animals and who had the gift of dreaming about good hunting grounds prior to the hunt. While the game was shared among the participating hunters, the hides always belonged to the hunter who had killed the animal. If the meat was plentiful, the women would cut it into wafer-thin strips and dry or roast it for storage and use in the winter months.

Hunters would take a sweat bath both before and after a hunt, thus ritually purifying themselves and ensuring success on future hunts, but hunting rituals were far less extensive than in other parts of North America. If a hunter or a specialist with supernatural powers dreamed of the desired game, this was considered a good omen. Under no circumstances were women allowed to behold the hunting devices – for they harbored powers which men thought it best to beware of.

Although the hostile environment meant that its inhabitants could afford to be anything but choosy about their food, there were some exceptions. The Southern Paiute, for example, never consumed the flesh of wolf, coyote, crow, or magpie, since each of these animals were carrion eaters and the inhabitants of the Basin avoided anything that had come into contact with death. Contrary to the practices in other regions of North America, neither dogs nor horses were part of their diet.

Small reptiles as well as insects, however, were eaten (although preferences varied from one region to the next). The swarms of grasshoppers that appeared in late summer (as many as 12,000 of these insects have been counted in an area of 10 square feet) would be driven by a circle of people toward a fire, where they were scorched. Often these very nutritious insects would simply fall into the Great Salt Lake in Utah, to be washed ashore – already salted – in huge numbers. They would then be roasted or mashed and mixed with grass seeds. A single person could thus gather 1.5 million calories per hour. Caterpillars, flies, bugs, ants, and an array of snakes added variety to the diet. For some groups, insect foods were such an important part of their diet that their names reflected this (the Mono, for instance were called "Eaters of Brine Fly Pupae").

# Summer: fishing in the semidesert

From May, the larger expanses of water provided an abundance of fish, and the first berries and grass seeds were ripe for harvesting. Throughout the summer, women gathered rice-grass seeds and a dozen other varieties of grass seeds (depending on the region), various kinds of berries, and reed pollen (a delicacy that was pressed into small cakes). Always equipped with a digging stick and

large carrying baskets, they used any given opportunity to extract root tubers from the ground. Women thus contributed the greatest portion of food. Hunting was a far more precarious source of food, and game was only sporadically added to the diet of the peoples of the western Great Basin. Up to fifty percent of the Ute diet, on the other hand, consisted of game meat.

Despite their high salt content, the larger waters and marshy lowlands were excellent fishing grounds, defying the description of the region as a barren semidesert. Fishing platforms were erected along the banks of rivers, from which fishing was done with dip nets or fishing spears. Nets made of plant fibers were pulled through the mud flats of the riverbeds to catch trout, whitefish, lampreys, and other sorts of fish. Dams were erected in some places, which narrowed the passageway for the fish and made it easier to spear them. Women and children would catch smaller fish with their bare hands in the shallow waters below the dams. The peoples that inhabited the area around the only large "freshwater lakes" of the semidesert (Pyramid Lake and Walker Lake) were particularly privileged, since these waters held an abundance of trout, carp, and catfish. Both these lakes are quite deep and, despite the fact that they had no outlets, contained relatively low average saline levels in the 19th century. Pyramid Lake, for instance, is the habitat of a type of sucker weighing more than 25 lbs that today is a regional specialty called Cui-ui (a Paiute word also used in American English).

Among the Southern Paiute the men wore caps made of deer hide that gave them protection from the summer sun, a breechclout, and, during the colder months, also a simple leather shirt combined with either leather leggings and moccasins or basketwork sandals. A man was considered a poor hunter if he and his family possessed few leather garments and dressed, instead, in rough bark clothing. The simple bows shown here were typical of the Moapa; elsewhere in the Great Basin sinew-backed bows predominated.

Mary Lent, an Owens Valley Paiute, sorting pinyon seeds, California, 1910. Photograph: Andrew A. Forbes. Los Angeles County Museum of Natural History, Western History Collection, Los Angeles, CA.

Once the pine nuts had been extracted from the pinecones (which were knocked off the trees with poles), they were spread out in winnowing baskets and cleaned of debris. Red-hot charcoal was then placed on the raw nuts to break their hard shell, after which the charcoal rests were cleaned away, the nutshells crushed open, and either picked out or winnowed clean of the nuts.

Opposite page:
**Wunavai, a Moapa (Southern Paiute), gathering grass seeds, Nevada, 1873.** National Anthropological Archives, Smithsonian Institution, Washington, DC.

Fruits were normally gathered by hand and seeds knocked off with woven seed beaters. The foods were collected in baskets which were then emptied into conical carrying baskets worn on the gatherer's back. In good gathering grounds these carrying baskets would be filled in one to two hours. Back at the camp, the seeds were separated from the chaff by winnowing, then roasted and ground on a stone. The flour was either eaten immediately, cooked to a mash in a basket, or (more rarely) baked in ashes to a flat cake.

# Fall:
# the pine nut eaters

For most peoples of the Great Basin, the seeds, or "nuts," of the pinecones of the single-leaf pinyon tree that is found on the higher mountain slopes were the most popular food, and an important store for winter. These pistachio-sized nuts are not only tasty and nutritious, they are also easy to gather in large quantities and can be easily stored.

Some weeks before the harvest, the scattered families would arrive at a large camp. At the end of August, a group of Northern Paiute scouts would head for the mountains in search of the most fruitful pinyon groves, since the yields would differ greatly from one year to the next. If the yields were poor, another type of pine nut, *pinus edulis*, would be gathered. These seeds are not as tasty and are very oily.

The scouts would return with some still unripe nuts which they had already roasted in anticipation of the larger ones to come. They also brought with them a small pinyon tree, which became the center for an all night round dance. Having formed a close circle, the people would move in small dance steps around the tree, while a so-called "guardian of song" (who knew the important songs used in the ceremony and who acted as the lead singer) sang the prayers and was joined in song by the others. Using a branch of sagebrush (considered sacred), a wise woman would sprinkle water onto the ground as a gesture to ensure that the rains would come and the harvest would not dry up. In a second round, she scattered nuts, symbolically returning to the earth what people had taken from it. The following morning would be filled with gambling, which

was a very popular pastime. The actual harvest began only weeks later, when the nuts were ripe. Groups of gatherers would then work their way up the slopes, since the cones in the lower elevations ripened before those in higher, cooler regions.

# Winter:
# the close of the year

Thanks to the supplies of pine nuts gathered, it was possible for people to remain together in larger groups in the late fall. Thus, this was a time of celebration, and also communal rabbit hunting (only possible in larger groups since the animals had to be driven in the direction of an ambush). Large parties of men would gather, led by one individual who specialized in rabbit hunting, the gift of which he had received in a dream or vision. The leader of the hunt was called "rabbit chief," and he mobilized as many men as possible, instructed them, and divided them into groups. In good hunting grounds, thousands of feeding rabbits and hares could be taken by surprise in the valleys. Surrounded by the men, the animals would crowd together in the center. When a rabbit tried to jump free of the human circle, it would be clubbed with a curved throwing stick, and then belonged to the person who had killed it.

An alternative method was the use of nets of up to 300 feet long and as tall as a man. Forming a semicircle, the hunters would drive the rabbits and hares into the net. Those animals caught up in the net could be easily clubbed to death. Considerable skill was required to make these nets of wild hemp fiber. When the owner of such a net died, it was often divided into smaller nets and distributed among his heirs. Even a net 150 or 100 feet long sufficed to catch considerable quantities of rabbits. The rabbits caught by this method were distributed among all the hunters. They would be skinned immediately, and while the men continued to hunt, the women would roast the catch at the camp. The meat would be served at a feast and the rest dried and stored for winter. It was crushed and mixed with grass seeds or the pinyon mash that was the staple dish.

When winter came, people retreated to small family camps set up in sheltered locations. The men often went hunting, though with little success. When they stayed at their camp, they would spend their time making nets and other hunting equipment. The women spent the winter months making basketry. Virtually all household goods used by the Paiute, Shoshone, and Washoe were made of basketwork: conical carrying baskets, hats, watertight bottles and bowls, seed beaters, flat winnowing baskets used for cleaning the threshed seeds (by throwing them up into the air and having the wind carry away the lighter chaff), and the framework for cradle boards (sometimes reinforced with a leather-covered cherry-wood frame). While the women wove willow rods and bulrush, the storytellers would weave words into tales with their tongue. This was the time to tell the tales of the near and distant past.

# Paths of life

Marriage partners were generally chosen during the pinyon-gathering and rabbit-hunting season, since this was the only time of the year that groups of several hundred people came together. Most tribes made little fuss about choosing a partner. A young Paiute man would bring his sweetheart a hunting catch. If she accepted the gift, this was considered to signify her consent. Young girls could themselves take the initiative as well, by taking a bowl of clear water to the man of their choice. If he took hold of her wrist rather than drinking the water, this gesture meant that he was asking for her hand in marriage. Northern Paiute grooms simply moved in with their brides. As long as they had no children of their own, they would live in the bride's parental kahni. Once children were born, the young couple would set up their own household and could choose freely whether they wanted to join a different family group.

Childbirth was accompanied by important rituals to protect children from misfortune. Midwives with strong spiritual powers were selected. The mother-to-be gave birth to her child in a birthing hut that was furnished with heated stones or warm ash. Women gave birth in a squatting position. All the while, the attending women recited prayers for both mother and child. A midwife cut the umbilical cord with a stone knife and then tied it with animal sinew. The afterbirth was immediately and unceremoniously buried.

The Kaibab told a story that Coyote, the culture hero, had once given birth to a child and specified what was to be done on such occasions: The woman who was to give birth was required to retreat to a special hut. She was to refrain from drinking cold water and was to spend several weeks scratching herself with sticks (one for her head and one for her body) and warm her belly with hot stones. During solitary confinement lasting about one month, women were not allowed to eat meat. Young fathers also had to observe restrictions (at least on the birth of their first son or daughter), although these applied only for a few days. Among the Southern Paiute they were prohibited from eating meat and from gambling. If a son was born, the father was required to place the umbilical cord on the tracks left by a mountain goat or in a rabbit burrow, to ensure the boy would become a good hunter. If a daughter was born, the umbilical cord was placed on an anthill or in a prairie dog hole, to ensure that the girl would become as diligent as those animals.

The very mobile and scattered lifestyle meant that the ceremonial activities of the Numa were limited. Puberty rituals were performed (if at all) for young girls only. At their first menstruation, they were required to live in solitude for a whole month. In many regions, they were expected to observe rules similar to those that applied to

The erection of a small, temporary house by one or two people, Northern Paiute, Nevada, 1958. Their construction is almost the same as that of the larger winter houses (kahni).

Along the circular outline of the house, a dozen thin willow poles were thrust into holes in the ground.

Three poles were then tied horizontally around the structure, creating a domelike framework. A smoke hole was left open at the top. The lowest horizontal pole needed to be positioned high enough to allow people to crawl into the house.

Finally, the structure was covered with overlapping mats sewn together with bulrush (tule) and attached to the framework.

women after the birth of a child. After this initial period, they retreated to their own huts outside the camp during menstruation. The plant foods gathered by menstruating women were considered among most of the tribes to be unfit (even dangerous) for consumption. Such food could impair the spiritual powers of men and cause women to experience menstruation and birthing pains.

There was virtually no comparable period of initiation in a boy's life. The most significant time for a young adult male would be his first kill, which he was not allowed to eat himself, but would ceremoniously hand to his grandmother or great aunt. Boys were not allowed to eat the game they caught (nor were the boys' parents) until they married. Their prey was distributed among the old of the camp.

Throughout the Great Basin, people were extremely fearful of death. Most Numic-speakers believed in the existence of two kinds of souls which lived in every person: the ghost, *tso'apa* (that haunted the living survivors), and the soul, *mugua* (that disappeared into the hereafter). For many peoples, however, the evil spirit of the dead was no more than a soul that did not reach the hereafter and therefore tried to take the living into the realm of the restless spirits of the dead. When people died, their bodies were passed through a special opening in the kahni or buried under the ruins of the dwelling destroyed after their death; their possessions were burned or buried with them. Among those peoples who kept horses, it was customary for some animals of the deceased to follow him into death and along the Milky Way to the other world. During the burial, prayers were recited to make the soul benevolent and

encourage it to take up its journey along the Milky Way quickly and leave the living alone. The Numa believed it was difficult for souls to reach the land of the dead – where day was night and night was day, but where souls hunted and gathered in much the same way as did the living. Uncrossable abysses or a chasm between heaven and earth, at the edge of the world, were obstacles for the *mugua*.

The survivors expressed their grief by cutting off their hair or inflicting injury on themselves. In many regions, the period of mourning ended after about one year. The names of the deceased were henceforth not to be uttered and even words that sounded similar were banned from use for long periods of time. People kept away from burial grounds, and when leaving the grounds after a burial ceremony, no one was allowed to look back in the direction of the grave until everyone had safely returned to the camp.

A grass hut and a shade, Northern Paiute, Nevada, 1958.

The supporting framework of these grass huts is identical to that of the mat-covered houses, except that here additional poles are placed against the framework which is covered with bundles of long grass tied to it in the manner of a grass skirt.

If people were planning to stay in one place for a longer period of time, they would also build a shade, whose roof was likewise covered in grass. This construction included a drying rack used to hang meat and fish up to dry. Women carried out most of their daily tasks under the shade.

# Toward civilization – Sarah Winnemucca

Sara Winnemucca (1844–1891) influenced Native American policy in the United States to an extent otherwise unheard of in a system which conceded rights neither to women nor to indigenous people. Her success may have been due to the fact that she was the daughter of the Northern Paiute chief Old Winnemucca and that Paiute women, the breadwinners within their families, were extremely self-confident. Sarah Winnemucca became a popular advocate of the rights of her people – and one of the most controversial figures in the history of native North America.

Influenced by her grandfather, who had always been well-disposed toward the whites, she was raised as a Paiute, but from the age of ten spent a considerable amount of time in white households in California. Thus Sarah Winnemucca was predestined to take on the role of mediator between the two cultures. She worked for Indian agencies and the army, and she founded a school which showed the Paiute a path to "civilization." Present-day political activists would probably label her an "apple Indian": red on the outside, but white on the inside.

Sarah Winnemucca did, however, have a very personal notion of the path the Paiute should take into American society. In interviews and speeches she never tired of criticizing the patronizing attitude taken toward her people by corrupt officials of the Bureau of Indian Affairs who exploited their positions for their own benefit. "If this is the kind of civilization awaiting us on the Reserves," she once said, "God grant that we may never be compelled to go on one." She would gladly have shipped her people to Ellis Island to secure for them the status of immigrants and all the unquestioned civil rights linked to such status.

In 1876, after the Northern Paiute were removed to the (fittingly so-called) Malheur reservation in Oregon, they fell into the clutches of Agent William Rinehart, who confiscated the meager earnings of their still fledgling farming activities and who found it unnecessary to consult the Paiute before leasing the best part of their lands to whites. In doing so, he drove many of them into the arms of the Bannock, who in 1878 revolted against the whites. While Sarah as an interpreter for the army was able to keep her father's group from becoming involved in the military conflict, the majority of her relatives were deported to the Yakima reservation in Washington after the end of the Bannock War, where they led a life of misery. Although Sarah had the assurance of the Secretary of the Interior that the Paiute could return to their homeland, Washington decreed that the Paiute were not to be freed under any circumstances.

The extent to which the government in Washington feared Sarah's public criticism is revealed by the vulgar campaign by which the Bureau of Indian Affairs tried to slander her – that she was constantly drunk, sexually permissive, and a violent gambler. Her explosive temper, four unhappy marriages, and the inclination among the Paiute for gambling provided ample fuel for such malicious rumors.

In 1883/84, she gave more than 300 lectures in East Coast towns and cities, making the public at large more aware of the concerns of her people and also collecting donations. Thanks to her acquaintances with the wealthy sisters Elizabeth Peabody (1804–1894), a renowned reformer of the school system, and Mary Mann, she was introduced to the political and intellectual establishment of New England. The sisters helped Sarah finance her school project in Nevada, where the Paiute children she taught bilingually made remarkable progress. The *General Allotment Act* of 1887, which Sarah had endorsed both in a personal discussion with the man responsible for it, Senator Henry Dawes (1816–1903), and before the Senate subcommittee, did however mark the end of her school, since this legislation proclaimed that indigenous children were no longer allowed to attend independent Indian-run schools.

Her book, *Life Among the Piutes*, published in 1883 with the vigorous support of Mary Mann, was well received by her followers. The book, in which she took up the cause of American Indian civil rights, also represented (though unintentionally) the first self-written Native American autobiography in the history of American literature.

Sarah Winnemucca died, sick and disillusioned, in her homeland in eastern Idaho in 1891.

# Brother Coyote, Father Wolf, and the sung land

**Coyote.**

Coyote heard people's voices from afar, laughing and playing. "Why are you laughing?" he asked. "We are throwing our eyes up in the air. It's fun. They make such a funny noise when they slip back into their sockets!" "I want to try that, too!" They showed him how to do it, but warned, "Never take your eyes out in a yellow willow grove. You will not get them back!" They went on their way. Coyote had fun throwing his eyes in the air; they felt good. He came to a yellow willow grove. "Pshaw! I do not believe the eye throwers." He threw his eyes up in the air, but they did not come back. Thus the blind fool was forced to rely solely on his sense of smell and would have starved if brother Wolf had not killed a mountain goat and given him the goat's eyes. That is why coyotes have yellow eyes, still see poorly, and rely very much on their sense of smell.
(After an Ute tale.)

For the Numa, the world was the result of complex events that took place in the distant past, in which there were no firm boundaries between animal and human life. People told the tales of their ancestors, prudent and courageous Wolf and his brother Coyote, a queer character whose moody, lecherous, and antisocial behavior unwillingly released creativity into the world. While these tales had educational aims, they were also told with a substantial degree of mirth. The Southern Paiute consider it to be no coincidence that one of their words for "coyote" sounded very much like the word for sexual intercourse. Many animals were often not called by their name, but were referred to in kinship terms: Wolf was "Our Father"; Bear "Father's sister"; Coyote "Cousin" or "Brother." None of these characters was "good" or "evil" as such categories did not exist in Numa mythology. Coyote's infantile and completely aimless behavior stood in stark contrast to the Numa ideal of personality: foresight and prudence were regarded as elevated virtues and are found in myths predominantly associated with Wolf. In the language of the Northern Paiute, the word for a myth or tale means "telling one another something." In fact, however, it was only the men who narrated the texts to women and children.

Most Numa consider Coyote to have been the creator of the first humans. He had begotten them with a young woman who had been asked by her mother to look for a husband. Her search yielded no-one, save for Brother Coyote, who now went about cleverly knocking the teeth out of his wife's vagina with a digging stick, thus endowing mankind with the ability to procreate. His wife later secretly gave birth to tiny children, whom she slipped into a sack. Since Brother Coyote always did just the opposite to what he was told, he opened the leather sack that his mother-in-law had forbidden him to open. Out came tiny beings – his children – which fled in all directions. The Southern Paiute claim they were the last to leave the sack, since all that was left for them was their poor semidesert home. The Gosiute, too, were convinced that their ancestor had been the last one remaining in the sack. He was a tough, dusty little fellow, "a true Gosiute." The Ute explained to their Indian agent that the whites had been the first to tumble out of the sack and had immediately turned pale with fear. Thus, they said, it was right that the whites should farm potatoes and grains, leaving the dangerous business of hunting to the Ute.

The people also had a strong and intricate relationship to their land. On closer inspection, it is evident that the expulsion from or the destruction of even a single part of this land must be viewed by them as a catastrophe. Each tribe's territory was like an open book in which

each page turned revealed a new layer in the richly structured cultural map. For the Southern Paiute, their land (extending from northern Arizona to the bottom of the Grand Canyon) is not only the means of their subsistence, but Puaxant Tuvip ("Power Land"), bestowed upon them by the Creator when he created them on Mount Charleston in present-day Nevada.

Every site in Puaxant Tuvip has its meaning, one that is linked to that of other sites. On the floor of the Grand Canyon stands a huge rock of volcanic origin, bathed in the rapids of the Colorado River. Now known as Vulcan's Anvil, it is a unique monolith in a canyon that spans hundreds of miles. For the Paiute, it represents more than spiritual power because of its unusual form, the site on which it stands (just a short distance downstream, the waters of the Colorado plunges down steep cascades), and the medicinal spring in its direct proximity. It is the center of a network of spiritually linked sites, including the cave located nearby, where pilgrims to Vulcan's Anvil prayed and made tobacco sacrifices in spiritual preparation; the site at which purifying sweating rituals were performed before entering the shrine; the outcropping of yellow mineral pigments for rock painting and the body painting of the pilgrims; and, finally, the mineral spring already mentioned, that has the power to heal a person's body and soul.

In addition to its spiritual landscape, this territory also consists of a variety of environments, the categorization of which is in no way limited to the types of foods they supplied. To this day, Kanab Creek Canyon has special significance for the Southern Piaute, for instance, since it provided them with a refuge from the whites. For the Paiute, the waters of Kanab Creek (and likewise the waters of other creeks and rivers) are the blood of the earth, and the riverbeds are the veins through which it flows. At the

The Sun Dance and Bear Dance of the Ute, painted on muslin by an anonymous Ute, c. 1895. Denver Museum of Natural History, Denver, CO.

The Sun Dance spread from the Plains region to the Shoshone and the Ute, who believe it to be a powerful healing ritual. The ceremonial brushwood enclosure is additionally covered by linen sheeting to protect the dancers from the wind. The Bear Dance performed in spring served as an act of reconciliation with the bears, who had taught the Ute this dance. Men and women line up in two rows facing each other, taking two large steps forward and three small steps back in the same direction. The women choose their dance partners and are confident leaders in the dance. A dancer in a bear costume enacts the awakening of the bear after hibernation.

Hand game during a Ute Sun Dance ceremony on the Uintah and Ouray reservation, Utah, 1951.

The people of the Great Basin are enthusiastic gamblers. The hand game involves two teams sitting opposite one another. One of the teams passes both a marked and an unmarked piece of bone back and forth behind their backs, until the leader of the other team guesses which hand is holding the marked bone. The opposing team sings game songs and pulls faces to distract him. Each team has ten counters. Every incorrect guess results in a point loss, until one of the teams has no points left. The stakes can be very high – for example, a horse.

end of the 19th century, the Kanab lived there in almost complete seclusion from the whites. Hunting, gathering, and some modest farming in this fertile canyon were the means of their subsistence for several decades. Chalky white rock paintings in the canyon bear witness to the optimistic Ghost Dance ceremonies performed at the end of the 19th century in anticipation of a better world.

Finally, Puaxant Tuvip is covered with a fine network of routes and paths that enabled cross-country messengers to maintain contacts between the scattered family groups who communicated using simple knotted strings. The messengers never lost their way. They were familiar with every tiny waterhole or point of orientation – for they used special maps: the songs they had been taught by their teachers over the course of many years. The songs not only described the various places, but they explained which ancestors had been there on which occasion and whether or not spirits dwelled there. The knowledge these sung legends contained was so precious that the owners of the songs took great care to safeguard them, only passing them on within their own families. The taking of a path and the singing of the appropriate song created that path anew each time. Puaxant Tuvip is not only the land of the Southern Paiute – it is their home put into song.

CALIFORNIA

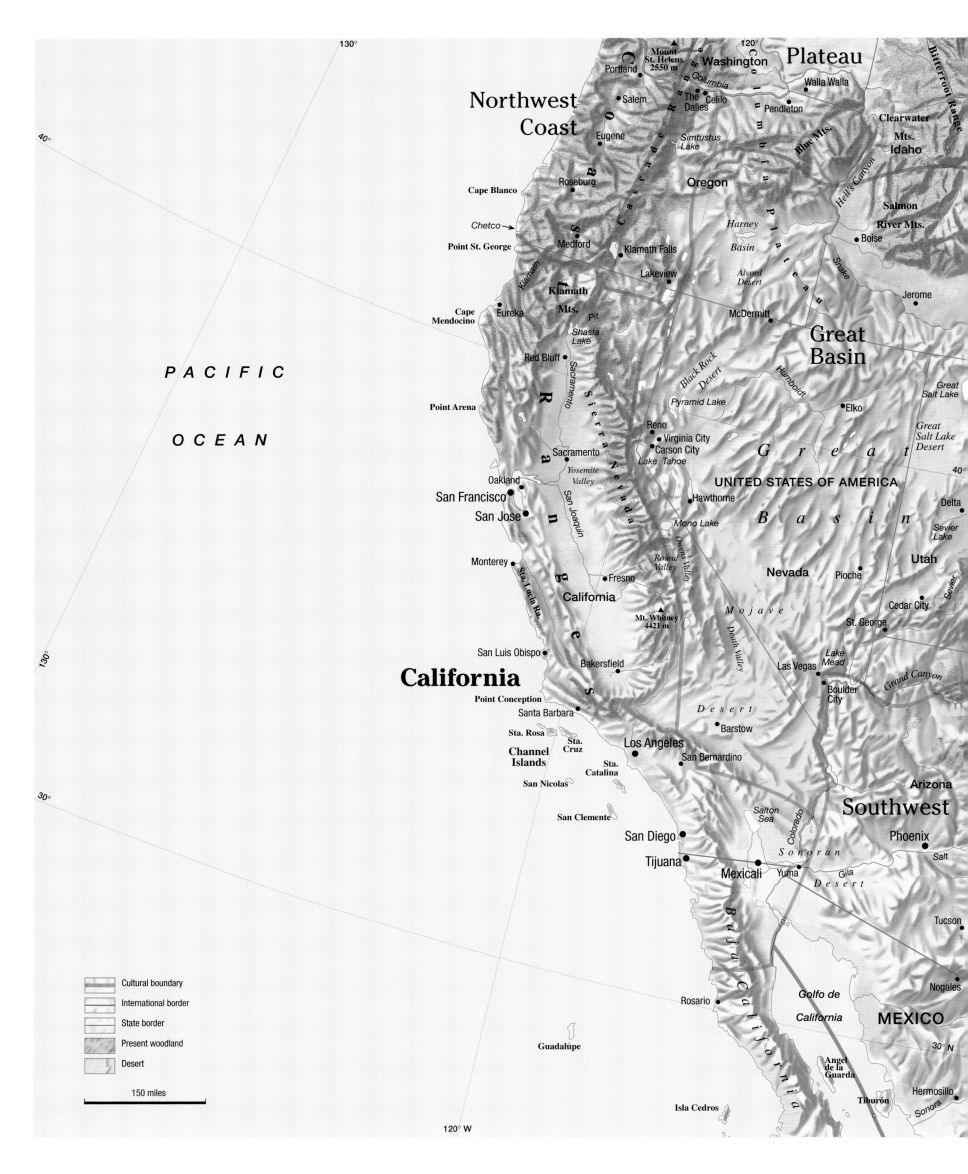

130°

40°

**Northwest
Coast**

Cape Blanco

*Chetco* →

Point St. George

Cape
Mendocino

**PACIFIC**

**OCEAN**

Point Arena

130°

30°

Mount
St. Helens
2550 m ▲

120°

●Portland

**Washington**

**Plateau**

Columbia

●Salem

The
Dalles ●Celilo

●Walla Walla

●Pendleton

**Clearwater
Mts.**

**Idaho**

●Eugene

*Simtustus
Lake*

**Oregon**

Blue Mts.

*Hell's Canyon*

**Salmon
River Mts.**

●Roseburg

*Harney
Basin*

●Boise

S
e

*Klamath*

●Medford

●Klamath Falls

●Lakeview

*Alvord
Desert*

Snake

Klamath

**Klamath
Mts.**

●Eureka

Pit

●McDermitt

●Jerome

*Shasta
Lake*

**Great
Basin**

●Red Bluff

*Black Rock
Desert*

*Humboldt*

R

*Sacramento*

*Pyramid Lake*

●Elko

*Great
Salt Lake*

a

S
i
e
r
r
a

Reno●
●Virginia City

●Sacramento
Oakland●

*Yosemite
Valley*

N
e
v
a
d
a

●Carson City
*Lake Tahoe*

*Great
Salt Lake
Desert*

40°

n

**San Francisco**●

**UNITED STATES OF AMERICA**

G
r
e
a
t

●San Jose

*San Joaquin*

●Hawthorne

g

*Mono Lake*

B
a
s
i
n

e

Monterey●

*Round
Valley*

**Nevada**

●Pioche

**Utah**

●Delta

*Sevier
Lake*

●Fresno

**California**

*Owens Valley*

Sta. Lucia Ra.

Death Valley

r

▲ Mt. Whitney
4421 m

*Mojave*

●Cedar City

Sevier

San Luis Obispo●

●St. George

s

●Bakersfield

*Desert*

●Las Vegas

*Lake
Mead*

*Grand Canyon*

**California**

Point Conception

●Barstow

●Boulder
City

Santa Barbara

Sta. Rosa

Sta.
Cruz

●Los Angeles

**Channel
Islands**

Sta.
Catalina

●San Bernardino

**Arizona**

San Nicolas

*Salton
Sea*

**Southwest**

San Clemente

●San Diego

Colorado

*Sonoran*

●Phoenix

Salt

●Tijuana

**Mexicali**

●Yuma

*Gila*

**Tucson**

*Desert*

B
a
j
a

*Golfo de*

**MEXICO**

●Rosario

C
a
l
i
f
o
r
n
i
a

*California*

30° N

Nogales

**Guadalúpe**

**Angel
de la
Guarda**

**Hermosillo**

*Sonora*

**Tiburón**

**Isla Cedros**

120° W

| | Cultural boundary |
| --- | --- |
| | International border |
| | State border |
| | Present woodland |
| | Desert |

150 miles

Yosemite Valley, California.

The Yosemite Valley was home to a branch of the Southern Sierra Miwok. They formed a "tribelet" that spanned six settlements, one of which was Awani. With its central meeting house, this settlement was probably the group's social center. The Yosemite Miwok were integrated into a network of trade relations. Salt and obsidian (the volcanic glass used to make blades) were imported from east of the Sierra Nevada; the coastal regions beyond the Coast Ranges in the west provided the coveted shells of ocean animals – notably olivella shells. Shells of marine mollusks, especially of olivella snails and abalone (haliotis) shells were used as shell money and to make ornaments. Baskets were traded in all directions, since each region had very distinctive styles and skills.

Henry Kammler

# Between mountains and ocean

A look at a map of California will reveal in its center a long valley framed by the Klamath Mountains to the north, the Sierra Nevada to the east, and the Coast Ranges to the west. The Valley, as this region is known, extends over a length of approximately 450 miles, has an average width of 50 miles, and is closed in by mountain ranges of up to 13,000 feet high. The Valley has only a single gateway to the ocean, through which the Sacramento River that comes from the north and the San Joaquin River from the south force their way together into the Pacific Ocean. These two rivers are the arteries of the Valley, fed by many veins from the narrow side valleys in the east and west. These natural niches were an ideal environment for the development of a variety of lifestyles, which, however, were never isolated, but part of the cultural metabolism of the whole region.

From a bird's-eye view the Valley not only looks like a cradle – in fact, it turns out to be a proverbial cradle of a civilization which has defined "California" as a pre-European culture area.

Previous pages:
Rock and cactus landscape in the Joshua Tree National Monument, California.

The San Bernadino Mountains in southern California were the habitat of a people that the Spanish called Serrano ("mountain dwellers"). The eastern slopes of the mountains fade into the inhospitable zone of the Mojave and Sonoran deserts.

The peoples of California.

The heart of California, the Valley, and the adjoining coastal zone around San Francisco Bay were firmly in the hands of peoples who belonged to the extensive Penuti language family. They had evidently spread a long time ago at the expense of the Hokan-speakers who were pushed into the northern mountain regions, but also lived in several coastal sections. The area southeast of the Valley was populated mainly by Uto-Aztecan peoples, the northwest was home to a number of Athapaskan groups, the Wiyot and Yurok (related to Algonquian), and the linguistically isolated Yuki.

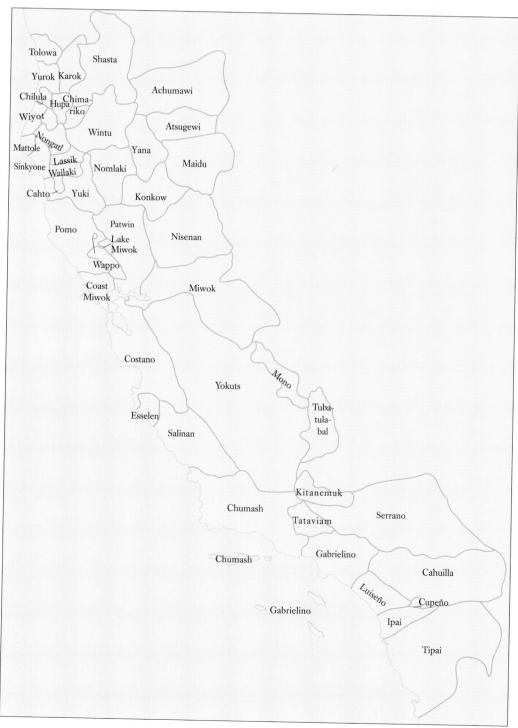

But the multifaceted Californian culture area is not limited to the Sacramento and San Joaquin valleys in its center. Distinctive cultural provinces also developed on the margins under different geographical conditions, which often stood in contrast to those described above. To the northeast of the Valley lies a mountainous landscape with rapids, deep lakes, swampy lowlands, and coniferous forests on the mountain slopes. Petrified streams of lava have created lunar landscapes that often served their inhabitants as fortification against their enemies. Hunting, fishing, and gathering the roots of certain species of water lilies and camas bulbs provided the local Shasta, Chimariko, Achumawi, and Atsugewi with food, while acorns were often unavailable.

Toward the coast, in the far northwest of California, the environment is shaped by a humid marine climate that produces 40 inches of annual rainfall on the coast and up to 70 inches in the mountains. The dense forests of redwood, pine, and fir; large shoals of salmon travel up the rivers, providing a reliable source of food for the people along their shores. It is therefore hardly surprising that the cultures of this region – those of the Yurok, Wiyot, Karok, Hupa, Tolowa, and others – have many features in common with those on the Northwest Coast immediately to the north.

The long stretch of coastline that leads down to San Francisco Bay and further south to Point Conception (across from the Santa Barbara Islands) also receives copious rainfall which progressively decreases toward the south. The proximity of the Coast Ranges gave the inhabitants – the Coast Yuki, several Pomo tribes, the Coast Miwok, Costano, Salinan, and Esselen – access to a large number of different resources: rivers, dense

Oak groves and grasslands were the most dominant features of this fertile landscape that was once home to numerous Yokuts, Miwok, and Nisenan tribes. Across the millennia, the peoples of this region enjoyed a mild, Mediterranean climate in which a society whose economy was based primarily on the gathering of acorns and salmon fishing developed in relative peace. This economy permitted a high population density, but did not foster the formation of large-scale political entities beyond the boundaries of individual villages. Some of these had populations of 1,000 inhabitants and more, but still remained largely independent of one another. Although agriculture was absent, the natural environment provided such a diversity of foods that even a poor harvest of acorns did not lead to food shortages. Armed conflicts were rare, since there was no need to fight over resources, and thus it was unnecessary to form permanent alliances.

**Round Valley, California.**

The hilly landscape in and around the Round Valley Reservation in the northern parts of central California was a part of the territory originally inhabited by the Yuki, a people who owed their wealth to the rich vegetation (actually improved by frequent brush fires) that grows on fertile, mellow soils. The reservation, founded in 1858, soon also became home to members of other Californian peoples of diverse linguistic backgrounds. Having been severely decimated through the genocidal campaigns of their white neighbors, the Yuki eventually merged into this ethnically diverse group. Of 7,000 Yuki estimated to have populated the region in 1850, only 300 had survived by 1864.

**Seals on the Pacific coast of northern California.**

Seals and sea lions were one of the diverse natural sources of food along the Californian coast. They were hunted on land with bows and arrows, spears, or clubs. In some cases they were also harpooned from boats.

coniferous forests, bush and grasslands, and the ocean offered a corresponding diversity of fauna and flora. The region to the south of San Francisco Bay, however, is lined with precipitous cliffs, posing substantial obstacles to the exploitation of the available maritime food sources.

The southernmost section of coast and its hinterland – inhabited by the Chumash peoples, the Gabrielino, Luiseño, Ipai, and Tipai – are relatively dry zones, the inhabitants of which lived in small, widely scattered settlements, and had to subsist mainly on a variety of acorn considered inferior. Those with access to the ocean, supplemented their rather poor vegetable diet with fish, shellfish, and stranded whales.

To the east of the Coastal Range lies the Mohave Desert, a hot zone that receives little rain. The Uto-Aztecan

Cahuilla, Serrano, and Cupeño peoples who lived here exploited especially the oak and pinyon trees of the mountain slopes.

California as a culture are is distinct from the state of California, primarily because the semidesert area east of the Sierra Nevada is considered part of the Great Basin. The southwestern boundary of Californian cultures is marked by the beginning of agriculture on the west bank of the Colorado River. Toward the north, the cultural differences to the neighbouring regions are not, however, as clear-cut. A common feature of California is the environmental and cultural diversity that exists within a geographically confined area which is also reflected in the linguistic diversity, greater in California than in any other region of North America.

Mammoth trees, Redwood Forest, California.

Gigantic mammoth trees (redwoods) can grow to heights of over 300 feet, making them the tallest plants on earth. The Huchnom of this region (a member of the Yukian language) as well as the neighboring Chilula and Whilkut (both Athapaskan) were all known to white settlers and gold prospectors, (who did not bother to differentiate), simply as "Redwood Indians."

# Salvation and suffering

Ferdinand Deppe, *Mission San Gabriel*, oil on canvas, 1832. Santa Barbara Mission Archive-Library, Santa Barbara, CA.

The Uto-Aztecan people of the region around Los Angeles, who had inhabited the area for over 2,000 years, were forcibly resettled in San Gabriel and several other stations in 1771. When the mission was closed in 1833, the majority of Gabrielinos worked as paid laborers for Spanish landowners in southern California. Whereas their style of dress now conformed completely to that of their European masters, they did for some time maintain the design of their houses (which was both inexpensive and adjusted to the climate).

Opposite page, below:
Louis Choris, *A Game of the Inhabitants of California*, color lithograph from his *Voyage pittoresque autour du monde*, Paris 1822. University of Washington Libraries, Seattle, WA.

All cultural expressions on the part of the Mission Indians were initially suppressed. Later, however, the priests gradually relaxed their stringent rule, allowing chiefly the young men to engage in gambling and dancing (always, however, under supervision) as a means of releasing their aggression and conquering boredom. But the painter Louis Choris (1795–1828) observed: "I have never seen one laugh. I have never seen one look one in the face."

In 1542, only 50 years after Columbus had opened the gate to America for Europeans, Juan Rodríguez Cabrillo (d. 1543) sailed along the shores of southern California and declared the entire country to be Spanish property. In 1579, the English buccaneer Francis Drake (1540?–1596) also claimed for the English crown the section of central Californian coast that he had discovered. However, since this remote territory did not appeal to a Spanish colonial economy interested in mineral resources and tropical farming, serious efforts to colonize the region did not begin until 1769, when the San Diego de Alcalá mission was founded.

San Diego was the first of a total of 21 Spanish missionary stations organized according to a system of "reductions," whereby the widely scattered indigenous population was concentrated in newly established, compact settlements subjected to permanent monitoring and control. It was only with the help of the military, however, that the padres were able to round up enough souls to be converted within the reductions. The path these native people were forced to take to a Christian heaven was sheer hell. The monks whipped, branded, or incarcerated them for insignificant breaches of camp discipline. At night, unmarried men and women were separately crammed into barrack dormitories, in the humidity of which European diseases quickly spread. Infectious diseases that posed no threat to Spaniards and Mexicans often proved life-threatening for the Native Americans. Several epidemic outbreaks of measles, diphtheria, and pneumonia killed hundreds of Indians.

Venereal diseases quickly spread in the vicinity of the Spanish garrisons set up to "protect" the missions. A poor diet (mainly *atole*, a watery gruel), strenuous labor, and the lethargy brought on by the hopelessness of this life of imprisonment all contributed to the high rate of mortality within the missions. Of the 53,600 Native Americans baptized between 1770 and 1836 barely one third survived; and countless mission infants died even before they could be christened. These coastal missions were the bridgeheads from which deadly diseases spread into the interior.

The original inhabitants of California, often described as peace-loving and tolerant, did not submit to the conquistadors without a fight. The Ipai and the Tipai opposed the establishment of San Diego from the start; in 1775 their combined forces managed to destroy the mission totally. Under the female leadership of Toypurina, the Gabrielino fought the Spanish in San Gabriel in 1785/86. The Chumash of La Purísima and Santa Barbara revolted in 1824, destroyed the missions, and then retreated into the mountains.

There was a brief period in which Russians tried to establish themselves as a colonial power in California. In 1811 they founded Fort Ross on the territory of the Pomo-speaking Kashaya, where members of various Pomo tribes were employed as farm workers, some intermixing with the Aleut fur hunters who had accompanied the Russians from Alaska. Within little more than 30 years, however, the stocks of fur animals had mostly been exhausted, and the Russians retreated.

After Mexico had obtained its independence from Spain in 1822, it adopted a new constitution, influenced by the ideals of the French Revolution, which prescribed the separation of church and state. The missions were secularized and the surviving native inhabitants declared to be free citizens – at least officially. Many of them, however, ended up as debt slaves on the estates of the new landowners who had been given comprehensive properties by the new government to secure the Mexican claim to these border territories. As in most other parts of the Spanish-speaking Americas, the local "Indios" of this region took their place at the lowest level of the neofeudalistic social order as a cheap and lowly labor force. The term "Indio" indicated a social stigma rather than ethnic identity. Those who abandoned their Native American community or managed to climb the social ladder were no longer labeled "Indios"; those who returned to their homelands were often no longer in possession of the skills needed to survive in the wilderness and lived in a state of constant enmity with the Mexicans, who had taken possession of the best land. While the tribes of central California fought Mexican landowners, they were as yet unaware of an

Tomás de Suria, *The Manner of Combat of the Indians of California*, pencil drawing, 1791. Museo Naval, Madrid, Spain.

In 1770 the Spanish founded Monterey, the capital of the province of Alta California, in the southernmost part of the territory of the Costano tribes. The Costano, consisting of around 40 independent groups speaking eight different languages, accepted neither that their land was being settled nor the subsequent forced missionization. However, they were no match for the mounted and better-armed conquerors. Within 60 years, their numbers declined from at least 10,000 to less than 2,000.

*Modo de pelear de los Indios de Californias.*

*par Norblin d'après Chorus*

*Lith. de Langlumé, r. de l'Abbaye N.4*

*Jeu des Habitans de Californie.*

# Gold rush and bloodshed

In 1848, the United States took control of California, and the discovery of gold brought thousands of unscrupulous adventurers into the new territory. Prospectors destroyed the natural balance of the salmon rivers, and their cattle and pigs devoured the acorns and grasses and thus directly competed for their food with the indigenous population, who in turn retaliated by stealing the livestock. State authorities made substantial funds available for volunteer corps to "pacify" the Native Americans. With payments being provided for such militiamen, the practice of genocide became a creditable means of income.

Opinion leaders (mainly journalists, businessmen, and politicians) of the fledgling state portrayed the indigenous population as dirty beings, devoid of intelligence, that fed on grass and insects and were more akin to animals than to humans. Having thus bestialized their victims, persecution was no longer thought abominable. Entire villages were destroyed and their inhabitants butchered. Young women and children were sold to unmarried farmers. Legislation passed in 1850 even sanctioned the practice of declaring any Native American a vagrant and

forcing him to work for nothing. This enabled white farmers to find seasonal forced labor as they desired. At the onset of winter, many indigenous people faced famine, since these changed circumstances no longer allowed them to procure food for the winter months.

The Bureau of Indian Affairs, responsible for the indigenous population, was a cesspool of incompetence and corruption. Whole herds of cattle allocated to feed famine-stricken tribes disappeared on the black market. Reservations were established, but not surveyed, so it was easy for white settlers to seize the best property for themselves. With the approval of the Indian agents, they drove cattle over the modest fields of the natives or simply chased them away at gunpoint.

In 1864, after years of fierce battle, the Hupa of northern California were finally granted the greater part of their homelands as a reservation – the largest in California in both area and population. Their neighbors, the Karok and Yurok, profited from the support of influential settlers, some of whom were married to Yurok women, and were for the most part spared persecution and terror. For a long time, the

19th-century American school, *Forty-niners washing gold in the Calaveres River, California*, 1858. Private collection.

The discovery of gold on the land of settler John Augustus Sutter (1803–1880) in the Sacramento Valley attracted 40,000 prospectors ("forty-niners") to California in 1849 and 1850. For these fortune hunters, the indigenous population was no more than an annoying obstacle on the way to anticipated wealth. But the gold rush was only the start of a campaign of eradication, the like of which is unique in the history of North America. Within a period of 50 years, the indigenous population was decimated by 95 percent.

Mission Indians in the south had been overlooked by the American government. Only their protests at being driven from the lands that, according to the Mexican land registry records, belonged to them eventually caught the attention of the authorities. During the final years of the 19th century, numerous small settlements, known as rancherias, were turned into reservations of often no more than a few hundred acres.

Around 1900, the number of indigenous Californians reached its all-time low. Whereas the population prior to the time of missionization is estimated to have been about 280,000 to 340,000, the survivors of the genocide numbered less than 17,000 in 1900.

Since the 1920s, rural Native Californians have tried to earn a living in urban centers, but have often retained close ties to their traditional communities. The Catholic descendants of the Mission Indians, for example, celebrate annual fiestas in honor of their patron saints. These are an ideal opportunity to get together with friends and relatives and to acquaint younger generations, growing up in the cities, with the traditions of their homeland.

When the government introduced programs for the relocation of unemployed reservation inhabitants to larger towns and cities in the 1950s, many went to California. At the end of the 20th century over a quarter of a million Native Americans were living in California, more than half of them in metropolitan areas. The majority came to California from other parts of the country. They developed a unique urban culture that has since produced generations of Native American artists, intellectuals, and political activists. Among those who belong to Californian tribes are the painters Fritz Scholder, a Luiseño (b. 1937), Harry Fonseca, a Maidu (b. 1946), and Rick Bartow, a Yurok; writer Wendy Rose, a Miwok/Hopi (b. 1948); and poet and publisher William Oandasan, a Yuki.

**Modern house in the Pit River region, northeastern California.**

Today, the Achumawi and Atsugewi (jointly known as the Pit River Indians) are one of the largest indigenous groups in California. They live in small settlements and rancherias in the northeast of the state. In their battle for land rights – one that is continuing to this day – they have refused to accept compensatory payments for the homelands of which they have been deprived and, instead, have attempted to reappropriate at least parts of their lost territory through land occupation and legal proceedings.

**Raymond Lego in front of his house, 1980.**

In 1963 almost half the Pit River Indians who were entitled to vote refused an offer of compensatory payment for the land which had been taken from them. One of the leaders of this minority group (which, in an act of protest against the official tribal leadership, formed the Legitimate Pitt River Nation) was Raymond Lego, son of an immigrant Ojibwa. Even 20 years after Raymond Lego's death in 1980, the land-rights issue remains unresolved.

# The land of the acorn eaters and fishers

California was the land of the acorn eaters. The abundance of oaks and the fact that their nut fruits could be easily stored made them a basic food all year round for many Californian peoples. Of the ten different varieties of acorn found in the region, however, not all were particularly popular, since some contain high levels of a bitter tannic acid. Individual tribes preferred different varieties and were even willing to travel longer distances to gather the acorns they liked most. Wintu men were allowed to stake personal claim of particularly fine oak trees and mark them for a later harvest. In the fall, people would go to the oak forests and gather the acorns that had fallen to the ground. If there were still plentiful supplies of acorns on the trees, they would use sticks to knock them to the ground. Back at the village, everyone would be involved in breaking open the shells and extracting the fruit, which would then be laid out to dry in the sun for several days.

Although each species contains different amounts of tannic acid, none is edible before its bitterness has been removed. This was done by the women, who pulverized the fruit and poured the meal into clean depressions in the sand (some groups lined them with leaves or a specially woven basket). Warm water was then poured over this powder several times. The water seeped through it, and the bitter substances it contained were washed away into the sand.

Acorn meal, virtually tasteless on its own, was the basic ingredient for soups and mashes. It was also used to make bread, which was wrapped in leaves and placed between hot stones or in a pit oven to bake. This hard bread could be stored for a long time. The Pomo and Coast Miwok added pulverized hematite (a mineral containing iron) to the dough to vary the taste and color.

The Californians also used other plants as a source of food. Pine seeds, pinyon nuts and chestnuts (in the southwest only), and a variety of other nuts and grass seeds were all pulverized to make soups and breads. They also gathered roots (such as those of bulrush and reed). By far the most popular raw vegetable was clover, available in abundant supply in the fields from spring.

The Wintu distinguished five kinds of clover, one of which is said to have tasted salty. Clover was generally picked and then eaten right away. Children would have a great time crawling over the fields and "feeding" on clover directly from the stem. A part of the harvest was sometimes dried and the leaves cooked either to make a winter stew with deer meat or fish, or to be added to acorn mash. The Pomo mixed clover and a species of edible algae, forming the mixture into bite-sized balls.

On the coast, women gathered a variety of clams and edible seaweed. The men used clubs to kill seals and

Opposite page:
Seth Eastman, *Gathering Grass Seed*, watercolor after a drawing by Edward Kern, 1846/47. W. Duncan MacMillan Collection, Afton Historical Society, Afton, MN.

A basic division of labor according to gender also prevailed among indigenous Californians. Men were responsible for hunting, fishing, war, and politics; women devoted their time to gathering and processing food, basketry, and childcare. But there was also a form of professional specialization in some native Californian societies. Among the Patwin, for instance, the right to make arrowheads of obsidian, to extract salt from a particular type of grass, or to hunt ducks with traps were privileges inherited by certain families.

Acorn granaries of the Yosemite Miwok, California, c. 1875. Museum für Völkerkunde, Vienna, Austria.

An annual surplus of acorns made possible a leisurely village life during the winter months. Dried acorns were stored in baskets, in bark-lined pits, or in granaries above ground. Such constructions included bushes that were tied into place on the outside and hollowed out on the inside. In eastern California, receptacles were placed on stilts to preserve the harvest from attack by vermine and to protect it against the elements. It was part of the genocidal strategy of white settlers to destroy such acorn stores.

S. Eastman U.S. Army from a sketch by E.M. Kern.    Pl.

GATHERING GRASS SEED
San Joaquin Valley. California.

Fishing salmon with a dip net, Karok, before 1898. National Anthropological Archives, Smithsonian Institution, Washington, DC.

Salmon was an important part of the diet of the peoples of northwestern California. Ceremonies were held on the occasion of the first catches of the year. To catch salmon, fishers would position themselves on platforms erected over rapids. The salmon, heading upstream, would be scooped out of the water with a wooden-framed dip net. The fish could be dried and stored for winter.

Yokuts pigeon trap, before 1924. Photograph: Edward S. Curtis. National Anthropological Archives, Smithsonian Institution, Washington, DC.

The Yokuts were skilled bird catchers. To catch quails, they would construct fences that spanned distances of several thousand feet. This photograph shows a bird catcher's hideout. When a pigeon was attracted to the spot by the pigeon decoy positioned in front of the hide, it would be caught with a noose attached to a pole.

sea lions that gathered on the shores to rest. Small fish were taken from the pools left behind by ebbing tides. Some coastal tribes became very skilled at using dip nets to fish in the surf.

Salmon were the most important source of food along the rivers. They were caught with spears or with the help of weirs. Canoes or rafts made of bulrush were used for fishing on the lakes with nets and with fishhooks. Some groups added vegetal poison (for example, crushed horse chestnuts or Californian soap roots) to confined sections of creek water or to pools in order to numb the fish, which could then be picked easily out of the water.

Deer were abundant in all areas except the grasslands of the San Joaquin and Sacramento valleys and contributed significantly to the diet of many peoples. They were often caught during hunts that might last several days and in which the animals were driven over cliffs or into narrow canyons, where a separate group of hunters could easily kill them with bows and arrows. The deer meat from such hunting expeditions was dried, sometimes providing supplies that would last well into the winter.

Black bears and grizzlies were also targeted by hunters, except among tribes which observed a taboo against eating these creatures. Smaller animals were caught with nooses or traps and clubs. Some tribes, such as the Miwok, even used bolas to catch birds. These devices consisted of a leather string, to the end of which pieces of bone were attached. They were thrown at the birds, entangling them, after which the hunters would break the birds' necks.

Rock mortars, Grindstone, California.

Instead of using portable wooden or stone mortars, the women would often crush shelled acorns in the natural hollows of nearby rocks which would increase the depth of the cavities. Baskets with openings at the bottom were placed over them and held in place between the knees of the women's outstretched legs. This prevented acorn splinters from escaping during the crushing process.

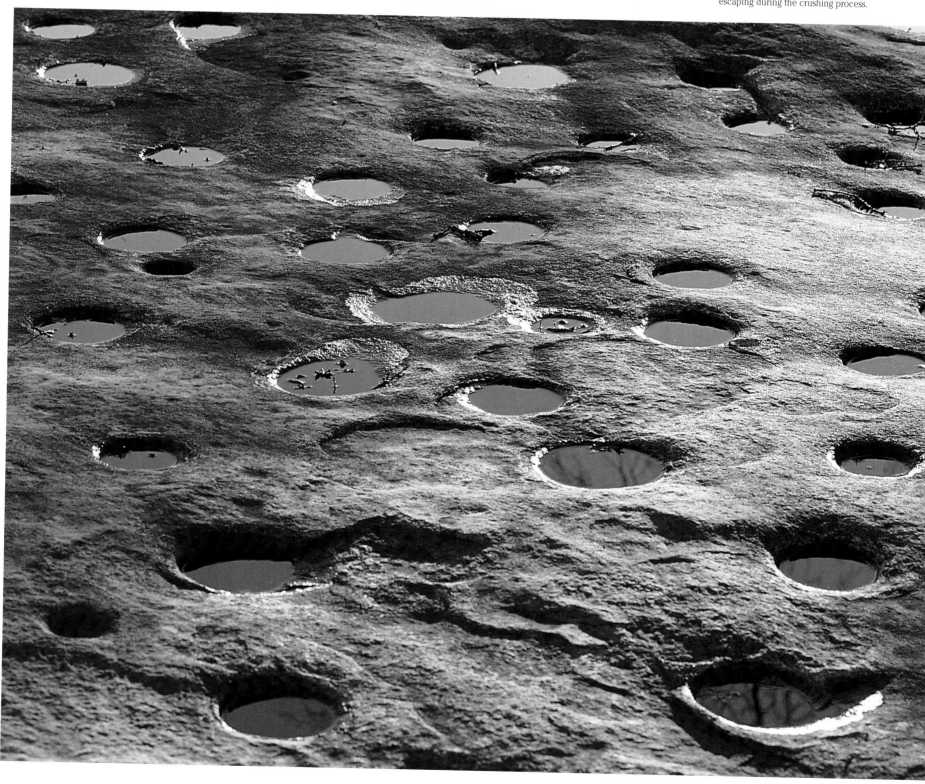

# Dreams of wealth –
# the Yurok and their neighbors

What do we make of Indians for whom wealth is a mythical trio of brothers named Big Money, Medium Money, and Small Change who experience all sorts of adventures? Of a people who reject blood vengeance and war on the grounds that it is "too expensive"? Of men and women who dream of wealth to keep and not to give away? This, at least, was how anthropologist Alfred L. Kroeber (1876–1960) portrayed the Yurok, on the basis of several seasons of fieldwork between 1901 and 1908 in the humid river valleys of Northwestern California; a study which forms the basis of our knowledge of "traditional" Yurok culture. This surprisingly rational world view is confirmed in a comprehensive collection of myths with which this scholar supplemented his own observations.

The Yurok ("the downstream people") on the Klamath River and along a 60-mile stretch of coast on both sides of the river mouth were the center around which the cultural and political life of northwestern California revolved. Because of their close ties to the Wiyot (who spoke a distantly related language), the Hokan-speaking Karok, and the Athapaskan Hupa, these groups displayed a very similar culture to that of the Yurok. Several hamlets (small groups of houses beyond the settlement centers) were populated by members of different cultural groups, whose inhabitants could communicate in three or four languages.

The Yurok of old appear to have been true individualists. They acquired personal property, over which they were free to dispose independent of any kinship ties. There was, however as among the peoples of the neighboring culture area on the Northwest Coast, an upper class of noblemen (*pegherk*) who sometimes kept slaves. The *pegherk* were given an education befitting their social standing and which enabled them more easily to accumulate treasures, especially the highly valued insignia of rank. Treasures were rare objects such as albino deer hides, pairs of

INDIAN VILLAGE, TRINIDAD.

15-inch blades made of volcanic glass, or costumes for major dances. A wealthy *pegherk* was in a position to stage one of the main dances (the Jump Dance or Deerskin Dance, for example) and equip all the participants with the appropriate head dresses and dance skirts. The *pegherk* would act as host, providing food for the numerous guests from other villages. The most visible expression of high social standing were the houses of the nobility, which were erected on elevated ground.

The nobility recruited its members from noble families. Each new member would receive a six-year course of instruction from a master teacher on the lifestyle and habits befitting his social standing. Some of the standards required of the nobility were to work hard, to frequent the sweat house often, to practice the art of a specific form of hand-to-hand combat, and to request the support of supernatural powers that would manifest themselves to the student in the form of visions received during the lonely visit to the mountains. Members of the nobility spoke a high-class variant of the Yurok language that even had its own vocabulary. They undertook long trading expeditions to neighboring tribes in order to increase their wealth but also to expand their horizons, and they saw it as their duty to speak the language of one or several neighboring peoples. Noble girls received the same kind of education, although they did not use the sweat house (a male perogative) and were not taught to fight. Many noblewomen became powerful healers.

The wealthiest *pegherks* laid claim to the best hunting and fishing sites near the village and in the river valleys. Apart from material wealth, however, individual nobles had little political power. *Pegherks* would display their prestigious possessions at ceremonies, which also served to represent their village, its affluence, and hospitality. While *pegherks* had despotic powers over their own family groups, their powers did not extend to other members of the village or

As one of the world-renewal
ceremonies of northwestern
California, the White Deerskin
Dance was performed at the
time of the acorn harvest and
the second salmon run in the fall.
The albino deer hides used in
the dance as well as large obsidian
blades were the most prized
possessions of the nobility. Even
distant village groups would
reciprocally invite each other to
attend these ceremonies, and
regularly compete for the
reputation as to who could
stage the grandest ceremonies.

district. Political decisions – primarily the settlement of disputes – were taken by an informal council of noblemen from all over the region. Compliance with such collective resolutions was, if necessary, achieved by force. Generally, however, it would suffice to refer to the supernatural powers of the *pegherks*, who also held all ceremonial offices within a community.

The only visible distinctions between common free people and the *pegherks* were the commoners' paltry possessions and the fact that their houses were built on lower ground in the village. In contrast to the cultures of the people on the Northwest Coast, the slaves kept by the Yurok were not prisoners of war, but debtors who had overextended their means and were thus obliged to become laborers in the service of their creditors. They formed an extremely small part of the community, and it was only the wealthiest *pegherks* who occasionally owned slaves.

The Yurok territory was divided into five districts, each of which was ruled by a council of local *pegherks*. Council meetings mostly served to organize the major ceremonies. These were also the occasions on which conflicts were arbitrated. In historic times, there were some

two dozen villages of up to 30 large scattered houses situated above the rivers. Several villages might form a federation, especially when they had house groups of common ancestry as confirmed by the legends relating the origins of each house group, which were passed on in the communities. Each federation of villages competed with other federations within the district for fishing grounds and oak groves.

The Yurok had a rich tradition of storytelling, including many tales about mythical beings such as Wohpekumeu and Pulekukwere, who survived exciting adventures in which they fought monsters and other evil inhabitants of the mythical world and during which they invented all sorts of useful and useless things. Surprisingly, there are no myths that could be said to explain the creation of the world. Instead, the Yurok assumed the world as they knew it had been arranged in primeval times by a race of immortal spirits. Everything was more or less predestined, and the act of creation itself was of no significance. Many of the myths or local legends are full of strong emotions: love, pity, greed for wealth, and even the sorrow felt by the original spirits upon the arrival of the first humans are vividly and compassionately portrayed.

# The tribelets of the west

INTERIOR OF INDIAN HUTS, CALIFORNIA.—p. 30. vol. 9.

It is often difficult to apply the terms "people" and "tribe" when describing the social order of other cultures. This becomes evident in view of the structures apparent in traditional Californian society. "Peoples" in the sense of historical communities of fate with a common language and culture and a sense of "national" identity were absent in aboriginal California; and "tribes" in the sense of politically organized ethnic groups were a rare phenomenon.

Large parts of the Californian culture area were multicultural and multilinguistic in the best sense of these terms. Of the neighboring Yurok and Karok, whose languages differ entirely, it is said that their members could chat for hours – each in his or her own language. Northern Hill Yokuts and southern Sierra Miwok often lived together in mixed villages. We know of one village on Clear Lake where speakers of five different Pomo languages and of Patwin lived together. It was, in fact, only the tragic course of colonization in California that resulted in many of the groups being reduced and concentrated into "tribes." Often, tribal organization was a legal necessity, for example, to secure land rights or to gain government recognition and thereby become eligible for social welfare.

The most common political entity in the western part of traditional central California was probably what we would call the "village group." It consisted of a collection of hamlets, grouped around a main village that was its political center. This was usually the residence of a commonly recognized political leader, who headed a council of dignitaries from the individual settlements. A village group of this kind, also known as a "tribelet," could consist of several hundred to well over 1,000 people. It would act as a landowning unit, whose territorial rights other groups were obliged to acknowledge.

Among the Nomlaki, a Wintu group that inhabited the northern parts of the Valley, the main village was located within shouting distance of the other villages of the local group. In its center stood the house of the chief, who usually had inherited this office from his father. The doors of all other houses faced the chief's residence, where the villagers assembled for games and dances, for smoking, and for storytelling. Every morning, the chief would climb onto the roof of his house and call out: "Do the right thing! Do not get into trouble! Help your neighbors!" He was also responsible for assigning work within the village, settling disputes, helping needy families, managing the village's supplies of acorn, and distributing the profits of communal hunting expeditions. His powers were restricted by the necessity to seek consensus with other influential men. This required good rhetoric skills, which he practiced from a very early age in the isolation of a neighboring forest.

In Nomlaki villages, all the men were related, while the women had married into the community. But there were no descent groups or clans as frequently occurred, especially further south. Among the Yokuts, for example, everyone belonged to the clan of his or her father, symbolized by a clan emblem such as an eagle, a crow, a beaver, a dove, or a coyote.

Such clans were also a frame of reference when it came to choosing marriage partners as well as providing legitimation for the inheritance of political offices. Village-group chiefs were normally members of the eagle clan, while heralds and assistants to the chief belonged to the pigeon clan. Upon entering his territory, village guests would always first announce their arrival at the house of the eagle chief – irrespective of whether they had come to trade or to take part in the acorn harvest. Chiefs were furthermore responsible for conducting the annual mourning ceremonial. This central ceremony lasted about six nights and released all those mourners of the previous period from this state, during which they were forbidden to eat meat or to partake in official ceremonies.

The Yokuts, like some other groups, had a system whereby village halves (moieties) were each allotted certain ritual tasks. For example, they alternately conducted the annual mourning ceremonial and invited the other half to attend. For the Central Sierra Miwok, the entire world was structured according to the moieties. One half was the land side, represented by the jay, while the water side was represented by the frog. All species of plants and animals and all humans belonged to either one side or the other, no recognizable system of logic determining the allocation. For instance, deer, quails, and coyotes were also considered to belong to the water side. Personal names likewise referred to the side to which someone belonged. Thus, the names of people from the water side would include elements such as "deer," "salmon," or "water."

Pomo man wearing stick armor, c. 1903. Field Museum of Natural History, Chicago, IL.

Although wars were a rare occurrence prior to the arrival of the whites and battles were normally fought rather as acts of personal blood revenge, Native Californians were equipped for all eventualities. A hero's death was not the favored solution to a conflict if there were other options available. If there was no alternative to fighting, however, this stick armor at least offered some form of protection against enemy arrows. Some groups had peacemakers who would attempt to reconcile disputes with neighboring groups by initiating trade relations.

Ceremonial Bole-Maru dance house, Grindstone, California.

In contrast to the old semi-subterranean dance houses, those of the Bole-Maru religion were built on level ground. Grindstone is situated within Nomlaki territory, but has long been visited by the Pomo, Maidu, and other neighboring groups as well. Numerous ceremonial "roundhouses" have been restored or reconstructed in California in recent years.

# Dream helpers and world renewal

Like those in many other regions of North America, the peoples of California sought special powers and support through contact with supernatural beings. The Yokuts performed ceremonial vision quests on mountaintops; but Yokuts hunters could also contact their supernatural helpers in a daydream during a hunting expedition when the animal to be hunted would turn to them and offer its power to the hunter. In return for hunting or gambling fortune, health, and longevity, dream helpers demanded respect, discretion, and obedience. A skunk that had endowed the gift of invisibility upon the Chumash bandit Valerio, forbade him to take human life during the course of his professional undertakings. When on one occasion Valerio became responsible for the death of a man, his helper abandoned him and he was caught and jailed.

Visions were also caused by a drug that was a central element of ritual life among the peoples of southern California: thorn apple or datura, also known by the Aztec term toloache. The root of this plant is the source of a potent hallucinogenic narcotic that can intoxicate a person for an entire week. Since this thorn-apple extract causes powerful visions, it was considered to have supernatural powers and was the prerequisite for the solemn initiation of Yokuts young men into the community. A cult leader gave the 12-to-15-year-old initiation candidates, who had not yet had their first sexual contact, a dose of thorn-apple extract. Retreating to a site outside of the village, the young men were forced to fast for about a week, and were given no more than a thin acorn soup to eat. All the while they were lectured on their future responsibilities as male adults within Yokuts society and instructed in important cultural knowledge such as the creation of the world. Older women took care of the narcotized boys who, after an initial period of numbness and immobility, began to wander about and, under the influence of the vision, were in danger of inflicting injury on themselves.

The visionary experiences were kept secret, but we do know that datura enabled the intoxicated to recognize diseases, suffered either by themselves or by others, and provided instruction on how to get rid of them. Further on in their lives, they (and also the women) were free to use this drug if they deemed it necessary in their search for supernatural support.

Datura had an even more sacred character in the culture of the Uto-Aztecan groups in southwestern California, where thorn-apple extract was used for the initiation of young men (an event that took place every two to three years). When the clan elders decided that a sufficient number of boys had reached the age of initiation, the time had come to dig up the sacred datura mortar, to repaint it, and to prepare the thorn-apple roots that would cause the novices to have meaningful visions. With the support of one adult helper each, the intoxicated youths danced themselves into a state of trance until they broke down in the enclosed temple area and now received the visions that would help them contact their personal guardian spirits. Their dancing continued for a period of three to four nights and was followed by a period of fasting that lasted several months. During their initiation, a part of the clan secrets was disclosed to the boys and they were taught songs and myths of origin.

As a new cult that worshiped the high god Chingichngish increasingly spread throughout southeastern California, its teachings became an integral part of the initiation. This religion had originated among the Tipai and Ipai at the time of the arrival of the Europeans, and had quickly spread to the Chumash and Luiseño. For the Luiseño, Chingichngish occupied a position between mankind and the original Creator, Wiyoot. They believed that Chingichngish had turned the first humans into spirits and then created humans as we know them today.

The individual attainment of powers through dreams or visions was rarely obligatory for all. In many tribes, however, there were distinctive religous specialists, for whom the visions served to confirm their inherited religious qualifications. While in the southern parts of California the only difference between laymen and specialists was often the number of supernatural helpers and the superior powers they possessed, in the northern parts there were very marked distinctions between laymen and specialists. Yurok medicine women inherited their responsibilities from their mothers, but first in the course of a vision were obliged to swallow a "pain," the healing of which, combined with intensive training, qualified them as healers. They were just as much members of the upper class as the prayer doctors whose inherited or purchased healing formulas became effective only after a period of fasting and self-castigation. Yurok warriors were also religious specialists who, thanks to the helping spirits they had aquired through their visions, would enter a state of ecstasy during battle, and who made their powers available to others in return for payment.

This specialization and the systematic cultivation of esoteric knowledge in the religous associations among the peoples of central California is comparable to the development of elaborate annual rituals in the north. In northwestern California, these events are called world-renewal ceremonies, which attracted numerous members of the Yurok, Karok, Wiyot, Hupa, Chilula, and other peoples to certain cult centers every year. Ceremonial leaders from wealthy and respected families recited formulas that related to mythical texts about the ancient time when semispirits

Pomo Indian Dancers and Fire Eaters Lakeport, California

Pomo Xintil dancers, c. 1906. Historical Society of Lake County, Lakeport, CA.

Subsequent to the emergence of the Bole-Maru cult in 1872, its followers described the dances performed at traditional Pomo ceremonies as secular dances (*xintil xè*) that were now only conducted as a form of entertainment following the Bole-Maru ritual. Today, it is the Bole-Maru followers themselves who are considered to be the traditionalists.

inhabited the earth and created the present world order. According to Yurok belief, the act of reciting mythical events created the world anew. The spoken word itself contained the magic to create things and establish order. The recitation of the mythic formulas corresponded to the ceremonial (re)construction of ritual houses and sites, sweat lodges, and sacred fire places. Ceremonial dances were held over a period of several weeks – notably the Jump Dance and the White Deerskin Dance, performances which included the display of valuable ceremonial objects.

Another ritual complex named after Kuksu, a Pomo creator god, was found throughout north-central California and was organized by secret societies with a strongly hierarchical membership that included between 10 and 12 ranks and complex initiation rites. Because of dual memberships and their distribution beyond tribal and village boundaries, secret societies established a tight ritual network that integrated people across large regions. It was their belief that the secret societies were part of the world order, and that their dissolution would result in the world coming to an end. The dances they performed brought rain, prevented disease, or cured the sick.

The Patwin recruited members for the Kuksu Society by kidnapping youths of eight to 16 years old, symbolically killing them, and subjecting them to the seclusion of a bush school where they were instructed in the basic doctrine of the society – the dances, the meaning of masks, the origin of the world according to the secret knowledge of the society, and so on. Women and girls from distinguished families were occasionally accepted. The close of the initiation was celebrated in the village dance houses, and was followed by a whole cycle of dramatic presentations. Among the Patwin, certain responsibilities were assigned to two dance societies (the Hesi Society and the Northern Spirits). Public appearances of the Kuksu Society were considered to have healing powers. Its cult leaders, whose impersonations in the masked dramas included the Creator God, were able to talk in their dreams to supernatural powers and spirits of the dead.

The most spectacular dances were performed by the Hesi Society. The thumping rhythm of the log foot drums emitted from the dance house heralded the climax of the ceremonial season that had begun in the fall. At the start of the four-day performance, a dance leader positioned himself on the roof of the house and summoned the "Big Head" (T'uya) dancers. Upon his command they would emerge from the bushes, walking backward through the dancers' entrance of the semisubterranean roundhouse. They wore a bushy crown of feathers (hence their name) and held a rattle in each hand. Each dancer gave an extended solo performance, accompanied by a drum and rattles, or moved in or out of sync with the dance leader. Their performance was interrupted by short breaks in which only the rattles and the voices of the singers could be heard. The dance leader held a bow and a quiver of arrows used for the ritual wounding of candidates.

During the second night of ritual, guests from other villages would arrive, and were given special seats in the

Luiseño healer José Alvarez calling for rain, 1904. Photograph: Edward H. Davis. National Museum of the American Indian, New York, NY.

Along with the Chingichngish religion, religious specialization also survived among the Luiseño. Among the specialists were notably the village heads whose office combined political, religious, and military authority. These individuals had assistants who served as heralds and conducted ceremonies themselves. All village heads and their assistants were in charge of healing, rainmaking, and of conducting the rituals related to the cycle of life. Their paraphernalia included feather ornaments and wooden wands which they swallowed and then vomited up again as a display of their supernatural powers. They also possessed small stone tubes which they used both for smoking and for sucking disease out of their patients.

dance house. Every morning, a large fire was ignited in the house, turning the room into a dry-air sauna, and after some sweating, the participants plunged into the river.

Other supernatural beings appeared among the Big Head dancers: the powerful and evil Moki and Sili, identifiable by their crane-feather cape and a fishnet wrapped around their body, and the female Dado spirit, represented by young men. An important role was played by ritual clowns, who held this position for life. They imitated the cult leader in a falsetto voice and incurred his anger by making obscene gestures. As masters of protocol, they also denounced any breach of the stringent ritual rules.

The most respected people of each village were members of all secret societies (from two to four), and generally held elevated positions within them. High social standing and membership were interlinked: societies preferably elected respected individuals to join their ranks, but membership and rank within that society also enhanced a person's social standing. The Patwin's Hesi Society, for example, had a hierarchy of four levels, each defined by the scope of ritual knowledge of that rank's members.

Opposite page:
Leather cap adorned with feathers, central California, c. 1830. Deutsches Ledermuseum, Offenbach am Main, Germany.

The dramatic decline of the native Californian population has meant that a considerable body of knowledge which once existed about traditional ceremonies has been lost. Thus the precise meaning and purpose of the few remaining early 19th-century headdresses used in dances is unknown, especially since most of these paraphernalia have no reliable provenance. We can only presume that this particular cap was part of the costume worn by the members of a men's secret society.

# Living diversity – the Pomo people

Southeastern Pomo village, Lake County, California, c. 1875. Photograph: R. E. Wood. Bancroft Library, University of California, Berkeley, CA.

The houses covered with bulrush mats are crowded around the village square, where groups of women are seated. The houses generally accommodated single families of up to 10 people. It was common for several households in a village to be related through the paternal line. However, there were great differences in social organization throughout the Pomo region.

The seven different peoples that made up the Pomo nation populated the region between the Pacific coast and the marshy shores of Clear Lake. Although their languages were related, they were not mutually intelligible. The cultures of each of these peoples often had more in common with those of their immediate neighbors than with those of other "Pomo" groups.

The Pomo villages along the rivers and around Clear Lake comprised large, oval multiple-family houses covered with timber planks or bulrush mats. Each village had its own semisubterranean roundhouse in which the major ceremonies took place. The peoples of the coast lived in conical shelters made of a framework onto which oak planks were leaned, which accommodated one family of eight to 12 people, and which were often fenced in by brushes. In summer, the families lived scattered throughout the group's territory in light brush shelters. They spent the summer gathering and storing food for the winter months – acorns from seven different species of oak and the seeds of 15 varieties of grass. The coastal waters provided an all-year-round supply of shellfish, fish, and edible algae, while the Clear Lake Pomo hunted and fished from rafts made of bulrushes. Their staple diet consisted of grain or acorn mash, rich in starch, mixed with dried fish.

Pomo villages consisted of kinship groups under the leadership of a speaker. The villages were interconnected through membership of the adults in the ubiquitous secret societies which cooperated to organize the major ceremonies. In some river valleys, kinship and village groups formed alliances in which individual chiefs retained their local authority but were subordinate to one or more overall leaders. The reputation of the leaders did not exclusively depend on their ancestry and wealth, but often also on their membership or office within, secret societies such as the Kuksu Society.

The various religious specialists were often required to undergo extended training. The Pomo distinguished between four types of specialists: the cult leader of the Ghost Dance, the sorcerers, and two types of healers – the song healer ("who treats the poisoned") and the dream healer (*madu*). The song healer had already begun in his childhood to watch the practices of his master and learn about as many herbs and songs as possible. Once he had developed sufficient skills, his master would pass his own equipment on to him, including a rattle, an obsidian blade, a sharpened stick, strangely shaped stones, a headdress, and other utensils. When the song healer was called to attend to a sick person, he would attempt to diagnose the cause of the illness, touching his patient with one of his stones or the obsidian blade (which he had first heated and rubbed with herbs), all the while singing and praying.

Dream healers often received their calling at a late age, during a severe illness. The Creator would appear to that individual twice, instructing him to become a *madu,* and teaching him a song. *Madus* treated patients by localizing their illness and bleeding that spot or by sucking the disease out of their body with their mouths.

To be able to take up the powerful but secret position of the feared "bear doctor," men and women not only had to undergo instruction; they were also required to pay their predecessors. Singing a song, the owner of the magic power would slip on the bear costume, at which moment, so the Pomo believed, the power of the bear took possession of him. A Pomo woman, who had been considered by some to be a bear doctor herself, once described what happened to people under the influence of bear power: "You could even go along with the bears to distant places. You could get there without tiring ... Now when the bear leads people he lets them go ahead of himself ... they become just like feathers; they just trot along all the time without getting tired. The bear keeps on giving a series of short whistles ... The body feels like it's floating off the ground ... You act like the bear does. And (when you go along with the bear) you should abstain from fat, abstain from meat, abstain from fish." "Bear doctors" were feared and at least the male ones were notorious for killing people, even though not a single such case has been documented. Female "bear people" were said to be especially good at finding food.

The apocalyptic religion of the first Ghost Dance movement, which merged with the Kuksu cult, reached the Kashaya Pomo in 1872. They used it as a basis on which to develop their own religion, the Bole-Maru cult. Each of several female spiritual leaders consecutively gathered a dedicated community of followers, which were successful in resisting government plans to relocate them and take their children away to boarding schools.

Pomo dancer performing in an urban setting, 1980.

The number of traditional dancers has again increased in recent times, since this is a visible way of showing that the Californian people have survived despite the systematic genocide to which they were subjected in the 19th century, and are proud of their specific ancient traditions.

# Woven dreams – the magic of baskets

"Now, when Moon had run a little way along, by magic he thought into being a stand of willows – a stand of willows, wonderful to see ... The old woman, coming along behind, ran up to the stand of willows, still holding bunchgrass in her mouth, when she saw the willows, she said, 'Well! I have never seen anything so big and wonderful!' And she stopped in her tracks and gathered some [willows]. For a while she went around breaking them off, one by one."

In this way, Maidu myth reports, Moon, a perfidious devourer of children who had kidnapped the grandchild of Old Woman Frog, was able to prevent her from following him. This particular episode in the tale only becomes comprehensible when we bear in mind the central role that basket weaving and design had, and to some extent still have, in the life of indigenous Californian women. Basketry is the most important and the best known native art form in the region, in which several Pomo groups developed this art to its probably most diverse and elaborate form. Pomo basket weavers relied on a precise knowledge of suitable raw materials and their whereabouts. They were prepared to travel long distances to find the best sources of willow twigs, sedge, or bulrush. Their art required numerous preparatory steps such as soaking, splitting, and dying their materials. Heavy-duty carrying baskets, fish traps, and grass-seed beaters were made by plaiting, and since these objects included hunting and fishing utensils, this was the only kind of basketry that was also made by men. The other basic techniques of basketry – twining and coiling – were the exclusive domain of women.

The specialized Pomo basket weavers developed six main types of twined basketry, some of which they often combined within a single piece for aesthetic and technical reasons. In twining, vertical strands of fiber (such as spruce roots) are held in place by two or three horizontal threads, which are twisted around them. Most of the thin, watertight household baskets used for cooking soups and mashes (with the aid of hot stones), for storing acorn meal, and for transporting water are made in this technique. Specially adorned gift baskets, canoe baskets for storing valuable items or magical implements, and medicine baskets that contained a dream, a song, or magical powers were made using the coiling technique, which involves stitching together a spiralling foundation of rigid material, such as willow rods, with soft material, mostly bulrush and sedge. Some Pomo women had so refined the art of basketry that the individual stitches are barely visible. Already before the arrival of the Europeans, Pomo baskets were popular trade items. Even within Pomo country several regional styles of

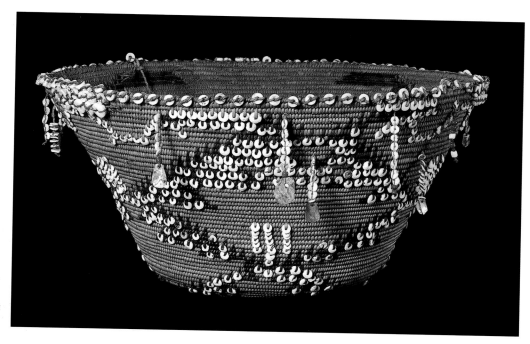

design and technique developed, from which the best Pomo basket weavers created their personal styles, so that experts are able to identify the basket styles of individual women.

Basketry is not only a form of artistic expression and craftsmanship, it also has spiritual significance. In their dreams women often received inspirations for certain patterns and techniques. Small medicine baskets were carried as a charm. When a basket weaver died, the entire collection of baskets she owned was burned along with her. This practice was abandoned only in the 20th century, when, despite the interests of white collectors, the craft came close to being forgotten.

Even today, basket weavers adhere to a principle of spiritual purity that prohibits basketwork from being performed while under the influence of alcohol and drugs or during the "moon time," since menstruating women have both a right and an obligation to withdraw from all arduous physical and spiritual tasks.

Coast Miwok coiled basket adorned with mussel shells, c. 1800. Völkerkundemuseum der Universität Zürich, Zurich, Switzerland.

The shell beads, which are held by the coiling stitches, heighten the effect of the serrated geometric design. This piece was collected in San Francisco Bay during the Russian circumnavigation of Adam Johann von Krusenstern (1770–1846), in 1806.

Yokuts woman making a coiled basket. Tule River Reservation, c. 1900. California Historical Society, Los Angeles, CA.

Californian basketry rarely displays representational designs. They appear, however, on baskets produced by the Yokuts and their southern neighbors. The bowl shown here is almost finished; the willow strands protruding from it will be spiral-stitched onto the rim. The bone awl in the bowl was used to make the stitch holes and to thread the soft bulrush and sedge through the willow rods.

Opposite page:
Lucy Telles (Miwok) and her largest basket, 1933. Yosemite Museum, Yosemite National Park, California.

Standing in front of one of the conical houses of several layers of outer bark used by the Miwok of the Sierra Nevada, Miwok basket weaver Lucy Telles proudly displays the largest coiled basket ever documented, on which she worked from 1931 to 1933. Yosemite National Park, in which the photograph was taken, was not only a tourist attraction, but also a good marketplace for the basket weavers' coveted wares.

Frank La Pena (Wintu), *Olelbis*, from L. J. Bean (ed.), *California Indian Shamanism*, Menlo Park, CA 1992.

Olelbis ("he who is above") is the Creator in Wintu tales. According to Wintu belief, he will one day bring his own creation to an apocalyptic end. Wintu-speakers sometimes respectfully avoided using this powerful word, employing in its stead the innocuous term "Boolaheres" ("he of whom is talked" or "tale"). In the 1970s, Frank La Pena (b. 1937) was one of the leading members of a movement within California's Native American art scene that called itself "Nonconformist."

Opposite page:
Harry Fonseca (Maidu),
*Du – Earth Mother*, 1979.
Oakland Museum of California,
Oakland, CA.

The female character of Du (in its original form *dy*) appears in the Maidu's Kuksu cycle and is identifiable by the diamond-shaped ornament on her forehead. All supernatural beings, including Du, were represented in dances by men.

# Old Man Coyote and his world

"And Earthmaker, they say, when the world was covered with water, floated and looked about him. As he floated and looked about, he did not see anywhere, indeed, even a tiny bit of land. No various creatures of any kind – none at all were flying about. And thus he traveled over this world, over the engulfed land. It seemed transparent, like the land in the Meadows of Heaven."

This is how the Maidu version of the report on the totally empty beginning of all time opens, when only Earthmaker and Old Man Coyote existed and, tired of being bored, they set about creating the earth and humankind. They were already playing their eternal roles, like an old married couple, always bickering but nonetheless bound to one another. Everything that Earthmaker wanted to make pure, white, and ethical could not be sufficiently dirty, colorful, and wicked to suit Old Man Coyote's tastes. It was he who added fun, sensuality, and suffering to Earthmaker's sublime creations, and he who kept everything flowing all the way into the narrative present, while Earthmaker has long resigned and withdrawn to the center of the earth, forced to see how many people worship Old Man Coyote as the Creator.

Thus Old Man Coyote creates not only the joy of sexual desire, but also death. The Yana consider Rabbit, Gray Squirrel, and Lizard to be Old Man Coyote's opponents, who create a heavenly existence on earth. Humans die, but are soon resurrected, Coyote, however, wants to see mankind grieve, with white clay and resin smeared on their faces, as is befitting for mourners. When a man dies, his fellow men take very little notice of it, and only give him a makeshift burial that will suffice until the time of his resurrection. However, Old Man Coyote guards the grave. The dead man begins to move: "Coyote leaped up, jumped on the dead man and pushed him down into the grave. 'Die!' said Coyote. ... 'What are you coming back to life for? Die! Die!' Thus he did, trampling him down with his feet. The people did not say anything. Coyote (went back to where he had been sitting before) took his seat again (on the south side). He still looked at the grave but it no longer moved. ... 'Now!' said Coyote, 'Cry! Weep! Now that this person is dead. We shall never see him again. Go ahead! Mourn with pitch! Go ahead! Smear pitch all over your faces! Go ahead!'" Some time later, the humans take Old Man Coyote's son out hunting and engage Rattle Snake to execute their plan of revenge. Coyote junior dies of poisoning from the reptile's bite, and all the lamenting of Old Man Coyote at his son's death cannot soften the heart of the creators Rabbit and Lizard. They command Coyote to smear himself with white clay and pitch and to chant death laments, just as he has himself prescribed.

Even though the character of the pert, roguish, yet clumsy Old Man Coyote is especially popular, the variety of mythical figures in California is just as profuse as the natural diversity of the region. Bugs, ants, toads, salamanders, the heavenly skies, nasty contemporaries such as skunks and minks, mice, ground squirrels, groundhogs, badgers, beavers, birds, and large four-legged animals all have their own particular place in the mythical order of things.

The mythical characters hold large council meetings. Ground Squirrel steals flint for arrowheads. The small creatures wage war against the large ones. Turtle retrieves the earth from the bottom of the ocean. Old Woman Toad weaves a rescue vessel for the survivors of the great flood and the fire that swept the earth before the creation of mankind.

But no myth teller could ever sidestep Old Man Coyote, who was forever recreating the world order. When the Pomo-speaking peoples talk of myths, they always speak of "Coyote tales," even if Old Man Coyote himself is not involved.

Coyote tales were just as much a part of the long winter nights as were the warming fire and the deep snow on the roof of the pit house. It was improper to tell mythical tales in summer or during daytime hours. "They say that it is dangerous to relate Coyote stories while sitting up." Essie Parrish (1902–1979), a female spiritual leader of the Kashaya Pomo, recalls of the story nights of her childhood. "'You will all lie down,' the storyteller would say to us, lying down himself."

# Mariners and Rock Painters – the Chumash peoples

Our knowledge about the wealthy and peaceful Chumash peoples of southern California is incomplete, pieced together from historical reports and archeological findings. A rich supply of acorns, pinyon nuts, sea mammals, and shellfish provided these coastal dwellers with a secure subsistence base. Their settlements consisted of large, beehive-shaped family dwellings, covered with grass mats, as well as store houses and at least one semisubterranean sweat house. An enclosed shrine was situated in the spacious dance area at the center of the village. The

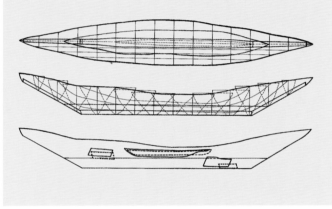

C.F. Richie, Lines of the Chumash plank canoe shown below, 1973.

Lines represent the shape of a boat by measurements of equidistant longitudinal, horizontal, and cross sections. A conspicuous feature of this vessel, over 22 feet long and weighing more than 250 lbs, are the two lengths of wood protruding on either side; they were probably used as handles to pull the boat ashore.

Chumash year was divided into two parts, marked by a thanksgiving festival and a winter solstice celebration. A secret society, to which all tribal leaders belonged, held rituals for the worship of the sun and the earth, at which people used a thorn-apple decoction to put themselves into a trance. In some Chumash languages, the thorn-apple plant was designated by the same term as an important female deity. This was no coincidence, since it apparently played a considerable role in the religious life of these peoples.

The Chumash welcomed the first Spanish arrivals, and the efforts of Catholic missionaries initially seemed to meet with success. But the Chumash considered Christianity supplementary to, rather than a replacement for, their own religion. Despite the severe punishment meted out for "heathen practices," missionaries continued to find secret altars dedicated to the creator Chupu or Achup.

Surviving artifacts relating to Chumash life indicate a high degree of craft specialization and suggest the presence of professional trades. One such trade was practiced by the members of the canoe-faring guild. Only those who dreamed of a peregrine falcon were permitted to paddle oceangoing canoes, which were made of wooden planks, sewn together and sealed with asphalt. When the Spanish

Rock painting of the Emigdiano Chumash, probably AD 1000–1850, from Campbell Grant, *The Rock Paintings of the Chumash*, Berkeley, CA 1965.

Despite the major damage they have suffered as the result of wind erosion and vandalism, the rock paintings of the Emigdiano Chumash display impressively brilliant colors and bold compositions. Beyond the purely abstract elements, stylized human figures, stars, fish, and caterpillars can be recognized. The white dots are reminiscent of the clamshell adornments on Chumash stone figurines. This art bears the closest similarity to the rock paintings of neighboring Chumash groups, who also used a thorn-apple decoction for ritual purposes.

Opposite page:
Chumash plank canoe, 1913.

The only surviving Chumash plank canoe was built in 1913 by Fernando Librado (1804–1915), an old Chumash man of nearly 90 years, on commission by anthropologist John P. Harrington (1884–1961). At the time that it was built, such vessels had long been out of use. The construction of these canoes is nearly unique in the world; similar frameless plank boats are only known from Chile.

first beheld these vessels, they were very impressed by the technical skills of the Chumash.

Soapstone was used by the Chumash to produce polished pots and hotplates. Chumash women were widely renowned for their exquisitely patterned baskets. But they also made simple asphalt-impregnated basketry bottles used to transport water. The lining was made by placing small pieces of asphalt in the basket and then melting it with hot stones. The bottles were turned so that the melted asphalt could spread to seal the gaps between the fibers.

Chumash rock paintings are unusual and enigmatic. Mainly found in the remote caves of the coastal mountains, they bear little resemblance to the historical art of neighboring peoples. Often abstract, they sometimes show representational features, many of them traced with multiple outlines and multiple layers of overlapping color. There are indications that these paintings were executed under the instruction of religious specialists during certain rituals, possibly inspired by thorn-apple visions.

The fact that the various Chumash peoples have been arbitrarily given a collective name should not lead us to ignore the diversity of the individual cultures to which it refers. The Spanish designated most indigenous groups according to their respective missionary stations.

While they had a rather contemptuous view of the poor fishing peoples on the Channel Islands, they had high regard for the affluent coastal inhabitants of the Santa Barbara Channel, whose wealth subjected them to constant raids by the Yokuts and Mohave, but also by inland Chumash people. The mountain dwellers (Cuyama and Emigdiano), responsible for the most magnificent of the rock paintings, only became known to the Spanish in 1800, shortly before the end of the colonial era.

Massive efforts on the part of missionaries to convert the Chumash tribes to Christianity contributed to the rapid disappearance of these peoples. Contrary to popular belief, however, they did not become extinct. During recent decades, several local families have (belatedly) declared themselves to be of Chumash origin. This has evoked problems that go beyond mere administrative issues, as during the first half of the 20th century anthropologists and linguists worked with the last remaining speakers of the Chumash languages (known by names such as Ventureño or Tejón Indians), and the descendants of these people themselves now use the name Chumash to emphasize that they, the "real" Chumash, still exist and that their traditional territory is not fallow land that any neo-Indian new-age clan can simply cultivate as it sees fit.

# "America's last savage" – Ishi

Ishi (c. 1862–1916), "the last Yahi," 1914. Bancroft Library, University of California, Berkeley, CA.

In 1914, Ishi accompanied three scientists on a four-week expedition to his homeland, demonstrating to his new friends his hunting and fishing skills and his ability to fashion utensils. He wore a breechclout and almost everything was the way it used to be; but then again, it was not. Having spent his life fleeing from the enemy, Ishi himself could have no memory of the lost paradise that existed before the arrival of the whites.

On August 31, 1911, the San Francisco morning papers spread the sensational news that a savage Indian had been caught and arrested while trying to steal food at Oroville, in northern California. Since he spoke neither English, Spanish, nor the language of the "tame" local Wintu and Maidu, the anthropologist T. T. Waterman headed for Oroville. With the help of a vocabulary of a related Yana language, he deduced that the prisoner was Yahi, whose tribe was thought to have been extinct for the past 40 years.

Waterman was not entirely surprised, however. Back in 1908, he had spent a month at Deer Creek, attempting to find four "wild Indians" who had recently encountered a party of surveyors, and in panic had fled in all directions. Ishi, as the imprisoned man was named, had lost contact with his comrades, all of whom, it seemed, had died soon after the encounter. He lived alone for three years, until hunger and despair had ultimately driven him to Oroville.

The traditional home of the Yahi were two steep canyons at the foot of Mount Lassen, which were densely covered with dry vegetation. In contrast to the neighboring tribes in the Sacramento Valley, they kept their distance from the Spanish-Mexican and American invaders, for whom the Yahi as well as their northern Yana relatives were the epitome of a barbaric and fearsome mountain tribe; this was in fact more a figment of their imagination than a real danger to the rapidly growing immigrant population. Civilian militiamen undertook to dispose of these Indians, offsetting every cow that had been stolen with the corpses of Yanas and Yahis. In a premeditated campaign in 1865, the entire Yana population was massacred, including those who worked in the households or fields of white farmers. Ishi was about three years old at the time, and survived the annihilation of the only remaining large Yahi village. The Yahi had hidden in caves, but were attacked twice again by militiamen who killed more than 30 people. The survivors, numbering fewer than 20, retreated deep into the canyons and avoided all contact with the outside world. The appearance of a footprint, a vanished sack of flour, or a missing calf kept alive the legend of the "wild Indians" who were still believed to inhabit the Deer Creek area.

Raised in constant fear of the white man, Ishi expected to be killed when he was discovered. Instead, the stranger from San Francisco took him on a train ride to the city, where the streets swarmed with people, and arranged for him to be given accommodation at the university museum, where Ishi became a source of information for the scientists whose ward he was and whose friend he became (at least to the extent that this can be said of someone who had become a living museum specimen). A stream of curious visitors came to shake the hands of "America's last savage," to take pictures for their family albums, or to gape at him while he performed the everyday tasks of his former life. The scientists learned to speak the Yahi language passably, Ishi acquired a limited knowledge of English vocabulary, and together they documented Ishi's culture on photographs and wax cylinders. The Yahi texts recorded by Edward Sapir and Ishi in the summer of 1915 are a remarkable monument to a remarkable language that actually consisted of two languages – one for men and one for women – which is an extremely rare and fascinating linguistic phenomenon.

Ishi in the service of scientific research, c. 1914. Bancroft Library, University of California, Berkeley, CA.

Ishi's skills as a maker and user of bows and arrows were met with special interest. As "the last survivor of his tribe," he willingly demonstrated his expertise to Saxton Pope, a doctor and archer, who published Ishi's medical history (after his death) as well as a booklet on Yahi archery.

Frank Day (Konkow Maidu), *Ishi and Companion at Iamin Mool*, oil on canvas, undated. Herb and Peggy Putter Collection, Oakland Museum of California, Oakland, CA.

Maidu painter Frank Day (1902–1976) twice met Ishi during his early childhood years. Together with his father, he had observed this mysterious scene from a distance, later recording it on canvas. His second encounter with Ishi was at the Oroville prison where crowds of red and white neighbors gathered, only to find out that nobody actually understood Ishi's language.

Ishi rarely and reluctantly spoke about his own life, in which he had seen the death of everyone he had ever known. Not even his name has been passed down. In Yahi, Ishi means "man," and the name was nothing more than an improvisation. It must have been of no significance to Ishi, however, as the Yahi did not address each other by name.

In the last years of his life, Ishi worked as a helper at the museum and was thus freed of day-to-day concerns. He maintained no close contacts with anyone except the scientists. When he met with Sam Batwi, Alfred Kroeber's Yana informant (Kroeber was Waterman's boss), Ishi was extremely disappointed. The bearded half-Maidu spoke the language of the Northern Yana, which Ishi could barely understand, apart from which Batwi looked down on Ishi with the contempt of someone converted to "civilization." Ishi, in turn, considered Batwi to be a traitor devoid of all manners.

Before Ishi died in March 1916, probably at the age of 54, his guardian-friends took him on a trip back to his homeland in order to do fieldwork with this "Stone Age Man" in the course of a summer outing. Ishi left behind a comprehensive collection of objects that bear eloquent witness to his fine skills and that are now displayed alongside the artifacts that militiamen took as souvenirs after the massacre and later donated to the museum.

SOUTHWEST

Cora Bender

# The living desert –
# the Southwest in the imagination of its inhabitants

The Papago tell a story of how Earth Maker created the land. Even before the earth had been completely spread out, he put mountains on top of it; and in each mountain he placed a magician. On the summits was birds' down – precious, life-giving rain clouds. As the earth spread out, the mountains and the magicians were distributed all around. The American anthropologist Morris Opler (1907–1996) learned that many Apache believed that their landscape was endowed with a soul: "Some say that the earth talks to them. Some say the wind has life. Some say the mountains, like the San Andreas, have life. Anyone who gets power from it says, 'That mountain talks to me.' The old people tell stories that show that all things have life – trees, rocks, the wind, mountains. One believes that there is a cliff where the Mountain People stay and that they open the cliff and talk to him. I have heard old men say that trees, rocks, and mountains have life." Talking trees, and a magician for every mountain.

In the latter part of the 20th century, the tourist industry started to advertise the American Southwest, home to the Pima and Papago, Hopi, Zuni, Navajo, Apache, and many other peoples, as a "land of enchantment." Such a sentimental generalization would have had little meaning for the first inhabitants of the Southwest, and would have been equally meaningless to the first white colonists. The

North rim of the Grand Canyon, Arizona.

The deep gorges of the Grand Canyon are among the natural wonders that have given the Southwest a reputation as a land of enchantment. Yet few visitors know that this had once been the land of the Havasupai, who now live on a 500-acre reservation at the foot of the deepest of the canyons.

land was vast and the distances that they could travel were somewhat limited, so they were unlikely ever to experience the numerous "enchanting" attractions that enthrall today's tourists. What they needed was a clear head to avoid succumbing to heat, thirst, and animal or even human predators. They had to travel on foot between those tourist attractions that today's four-wheel-drive vehicles can reach in a matter of a few hours, and they prepared themselves accordingly. From one Apache we know that "There is a ceremonial place on that mountaintop. The people go there before they leave on a long or dangerous journey. It is believed that if you go to the place and drop a stone on the pile already there or throw a sprig of a juniper tree, you will return safely." In the Southwest, magic was a vital ingredient of Native American reality; its inhabitants certainly considered that their environment was beautiful, but equally feared its unpredictability.

Previous double page spread:
"The Mittens", Monument Valley Tribal Park, Arizona.

In the course of increased autonomy on the reservations, the Navajo have begun their own marketing of tourist attractions like the bizarre erosion landscapes of Monument Valley.

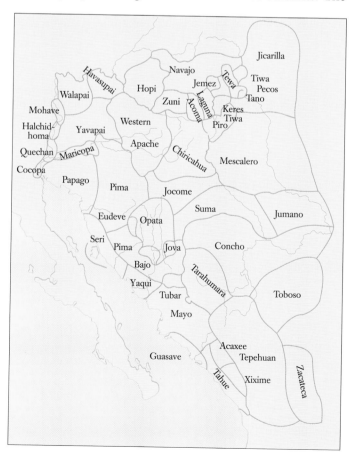

Peoples of the Southwest.

The Southwest forms a variegated link between the hunter-gatherer peoples of the Great Basin to the north and the Mesoamerican civilizations to the south. With its linguistic diversity (from Hopi to Tiwa) and common cultural tradition the Pueblo region stands out as a clearly demarcated and integrated region. During the historic period, it was almost entirely surrounded by immigrant Athapaskans, while Yuman tribes were found toward the Colorado River, and Uto-Aztecan peoples dominated from the Sonoran Desert deep into the Sierra Madre.

it was the Male River. The Male River flowed through the Female River and on; and the name of this place is 'Where the Streams Come Together.'"

The Papago have a song about the beauty of the land in summer after a rain shower: "They saw the earth lie beautifully moist and finished [for new life]."

Prehistoric cultures that have long since disappeared have left their mark on the myths of their descendants: "I have heard the old men tell of one cave," reported an Apache, "which has sun, moon, stars and Mountain Spirits on the walls ... They pray when they see this."

Yet the land is a historical landscape on which the violence of conquests, raids, and retaliations have also left their scars, records of which can be found in archives, at archeological sites, and also in the memories of the descendants. "I have read," recalled Jason Betzinetz, an Apache, "that a slaughter of Apaches at Santa Rita del Cobre in 1837 and another at Janos twenty years later were notable occurrences in the history of my people. We have little remembrance of what happened [there]. So far as we are concerned, the ghastly butchery of our families at Ramos and the terrific revenge raid which followed constitute the greatest and bloodiest conflict in which Apaches were ever involved."

A relative of his mother who was abducted from near Douglas in Arizona in the early 19th century and sold into slavery, escaped captivity and made her way on foot from Baja California, the Californian peninsula,

Pine forest in the White Mountains, Arizona.

The prevailing image of the Southwestern landscape is that of a magnificent, endless desert. In fact, the area is divided into numerous small zones, each with their own climatic conditions and particular flora and fauna, which facilitated a diverse human exploitation and settlement of the land. At high altitudes even forests may be found. They provided timber for the construction of the Pueblos, the wood sometimes having to be transported over hundreds of miles.

Many of the myths about the land concern sexuality and fertility. In the oral tradition of the Navajo there are five worlds. Into the current, fifth world the people saved themselves from a great flood by ascending inside a reed that was growing high into the sky. The Navajo storyteller Sandoval told how in the third world, the yellow world, the sacred mountains of the Navajo were created, and the sexes divided in order that they would always have to reunite according to the eternal principle of life: "A great river crossed this land from north to south. It was the Female River. There was another river crossing it from east to west,

to Arizona. She traveled about 1000 miles. The fact that the story of this spectacular escape has remained more alive in the memory of her descendants than that of the massacres may partly be related to the fact that places of killing and speaking of the dead are strictly taboo among the Apache. A raid resulting in a high casualty rate or an epidemic could literally silence a whole Apache community, because they were prohibited from using any words that sounded even vaguely like the names of those who had been killed in the tragedy.

Irrespective of contemporary international boundaries, anthropologists regard the Southwest as one culture area. It encompasses the US states of New Mexico and Arizona and reaches deep into northern Mexico, down the coast of the Gulf of California to the Tropic of Cancer. The southern boundary runs through the Mexican provinces of Colima and Aguascalientes, and its eastern border along the Sierra Madre Oriental and across the province of Coahuila.

The climate of the Southwest is mainly dry, with cold winters during which temperatures can remain below freezing for long periods, and extremely hot summers. Large-scale agriculture was possible in the valleys of the Colorado and Gila rivers, and along the Rio Grande. In other regions, the inhabitants of the land had to exploit ecological niches in order to grow corn and beans.

Navajo reservation near Ganado, Arizona, 1989.

Even the dry land at the center of the Navajo Reservation can sometimes experience heavy summer showers and the rainbows that come in their wake. For the Navajo, rainbows are the bridges between humans and the supernatural Holy or Knowing People; mythical heroes are said to have walked along rainbows on their way to adventure.

Opposite page, right:

The Painted Desert in the Navajo reservation, Arizona, 1993.

Erosion has exposed the red and yellow bands in the cliffs that run along the northeastern banks of the Little Colorado River.

# Ceramics, canals, and kivas

Since 9500 BC, or perhaps even earlier, the Southwest has been discovered and settled by many different peoples. Around 8000 BC, Ice Age big-game hunters were followed into the territory by the hunter-gatherers of the Cochise culture. They explored and exploited the deserts and canyons that were devoid of game and therefore of no use to the big-game hunters. As agriculture gradually spread north from Mexico, the Cochise culture advanced and eventually developed into the Hohokam, Mogollon, and Anasazi cultures, which are sometimes spoken of as if they had been "peoples."

The term "Hohokam,'" which refers to the prehistoric inhabitants of the Sonoran Desert in central and southern Arizona, has its roots in the language of the Pima and Papago and means "those who have vanished." The name describes the flourishing and, more especially, the slow decline of these masters of irrigation which took place between 300 BC and AD 1450. The Hohokam farmed the desert, where they developed a clever and intricate network of canals by which they channeled water from the rivers to their fields. More than 300 miles of major canals and some 900 miles of secondary canals have been discovered in the valley of the lower Salt River alone. Snaketown, on the Gila River, is merely the best-known of the agricultural areas

that were irrigated in this way. However, after 1450, no more Hohokam settlements were built, and the system of canals disintegrated. Surface irrigation caused evaporating water to leave mineral deposits on the fields that eventually made the land too salty to yield sufficient amounts of food.

The Mogollon people lived in the mountains and deserts of the vast area between the Verde and Little Colorado rivers in Arizona, the Mexican state of Chihuahua in the west, and the Pecos River in New Mexico to the east. This culture was named for the Mogollon Mountains east of the San Francisco River. Natural food sources in the mountains were sufficiently plentiful for the Mogollon not to rely very heavily on agriculture. They hunted, and gathered wild plants, and generally lived an inconspicuous life. Yet toward the end of their 1,000 years of history they suddenly became noticeable through a spectacular cultural achievement, the famous Mimbres ceramics. Probably influenced by their Anasazi neighbors in the north, the Mogollon people in the valley of the Mimbres River between AD 900 and AD 1200 produced ceramics with imaginative and elaborate decorations that bespeak the richness of their spiritual life.

We still do not know the cause of the gradual disappearance of the Mogollon and their Mimbres pottery after about AD 1100. One theory suggests that the Mimbreños who lived along the trade route running

**Cliff Palace, Mesa Verde, New Mexico, AD 1200–1300.**

When the Cliff Palace of Mesa Verde was discovered in 1888 it seemed as if it had only recently been deserted by its occupants. There were kitchenware and tools in the houses, ready for use. About 200 to 250 people lived in 217 rooms and 23 kivas. A kiva is an underground ceremonial room – evolved from the earlier pit house – with a bench along its walls and a *sipapu*, a hole of 4–6 inches in diameter in the floor, symbolizing the hole through which humans are said to have ascended from the underworld into the present world.

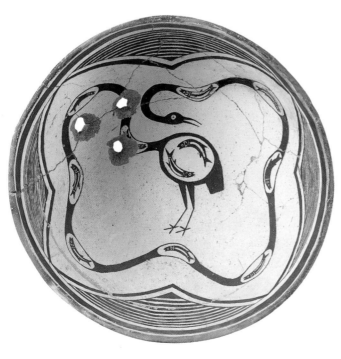

**Mimbres bowl decorated with a snake-necked crane and a fish. New Mexico, AD 1000–1150. Rautenstrauch-Joest Museum für Völkerkunde, Cologne.**

Most Mimbres bowls are painted with fine, generally black, brushstrokes on a white background, although red and polychrome decorations are also known. Realistic depictions of hunting, childbirth, or mourning the dead provide a lively image of the Mimbres people and their world. Half-human, half-animal creatures and mythical monsters provide insights into their imagination. The holes are the result of "killing" the pot before using it as a grave good.

between the Anasazi pueblos in Chaco Canyon and the Mexican trading center of Casas Grandes in Chihuahua adopted, either voluntarily or forcibly, the culture of Casas Grandes, which eventually obliterated any distinguishing features of their own cultural tradition.

The Anasazi settled in the Four Corners region of Utah, Colorado, New Mexico, and Arizona. They were given their name by an archeologist who used a Navajo word he believed to mean "ancient people." Yet, literally translated, it means "enemy ancestors." The descendants of the Anasazi, the peoples of the Western and Rio Grande pueblos, now object to the name, but so far no alternative has been agreed upon. From the Navajo point of view, however, the name makes sense. War often raged between the ancestors of the Pueblo people and the Navajo and Apache who were latecomers from the north.

The Anasazi tradition goes back to the time of the birth of Christ. It was not until 1100 that large centers arose with trade routes that provided the Anasazi with constant contact with the cultures around them and probably also with Mexican cultures. Mesa Verde in the west and Chaco Canyon in the east are the most important of these centers. Pueblo Bonito, in Chaco Canyon, bears witness to the architectural skill, industry, and religion of its inhabitants; its buildings are up to five stories high and with 800 rooms, including numerous circular ceremonial chambers (kivas). In about 1300, the Anasazi deserted the old settlements and gradually founded the pueblos. Leigh Jenkins, a Hopi and modern-day inhabitant of one of these pueblos, expresses his unease about the claim that the Anasazi are a bygone culture with the words "The Anasazi didn't go anywhere. We're still around!"

Pueblo Bonito, Chaco Canyon, New Mexico.

Most of the rooms in Pueblo Bonito, which may have served as an outpost for Mesoamerican traders, are not thought to have been for domestic use. The total population is estimated to have numbered fewer than 3,000.

Apache scouts demonstrate their readiness to fight, Arizona, 1886. Photograph: J. C. Burge.

Without the active assistance of those Apache who preferred to act as scouts for the American army rather than suffer a painfully restricted way of life on the reservation, the Americans' wars against groups of Apache considered to be hostile could never have been won. These perceived enemies had, however, also fled to escape the unbearable conditions that prevailed on the reservations.

# "Cactus people" and "foot-sole foreigners"

For almost 500 years the ancient peoples of the Southwest have held their own in the face of European expansion. Only 100 years ago the land that lay between deserts and mountains, and whose climate and landscape varied so greatly, was still regarded as hardly "civilized." To this day, the Southwest is characterized by a diversity of indigenous cultures and ways of life not found in other culture areas of North America. Many indigenous societies have fought hard to remain in their ancestral territory. Some have succeeded in preserving almost unchanged ancient cultural traditions that elsewhere have survived only in books, integrating them into their modern way of life.

Six cultural and, to a certain extent, linguistically different groups of societies can be distinguished in this region. The farming Yuman speakers, including the Mohave and others, and their ancestors have been settling along the banks of the Colorado River for at least 1,000 years. The agricultural Pueblo peoples, descendants of the Anasazi, belong to four different linguistic families, yet they have many cultural similarities. The Western Pueblo peoples include the Hopi, who speak a Uto-Aztecan language; the linguistically isolated Zuni; and the inhabitants of Acoma and Laguna, where Keres is spoken. The Eastern Pueblo peoples along the Rio Grande cultivate corn with the help of irrigation canals; five of them – Zia, Santo Domingo, Santa Ana, San

Felipe, and Cochiti – speak dialects of Keres; the others, who speak southern and northern Tiwa, Tewa, and Towa, belong to the Tano-Kiowa linguistic family and are thus distant relatives of the Kiowa of the Plains. The Pima and Papago in the Sonoran Desert speak two different dialects of a Uto-Aztecan language; while the Pima maintained an extensive system of canal irrigation along the Salt and Gila rivers, the Papago lived in the desert by hunting and gathering, or by planting fields moistened by the run-off of the heavy rains which occured twice a year. The Navajo and Apache are Athapaskans, and are as much newcomers to the Southwest as are the Europeans, having migrated from the north shortly before the latter's arrival. Like their neighbors in northwestern Mexico, the Tarahumara speak a Uto-Aztecan language. Their home in the jagged mountains seems little suited to agriculture, yet they have stood their ground, farming the mountainsides and valleys. Finally, there are the Seri, who live on the coast of the Gulf of California and who seem to have never tried their hand at farming, having preserved an archaic way of life focussed on gathering food and catching fish.

This classification is broadly based on differences perceived by Europeans when they first came into contact with the peoples of the Southwest. The distinctions made by the peoples themselves appear to be less systematic, yet their own observations are equally precise. For example, in

the Navajo language, the Pima are described as the "foot-sole foreigners," which is probably a reference to the sandals worn by the Pima and which stood in contrast to the Navajo's knee-high moccasins. The latter were a cultural reminder of the Navajo's origins in the snow-rich north of Canada. In the eyes of the Yavapai, the Pima were "the enemy par excellence," and to the Western Apache they were the "sand-house people" – the Western Apache living in simple dwellings built of twigs.

The Apache were called "cedar seeds" by the inhabitants of Picuris Pueblo, and "cactus people" or "grass beds" by the Hopi, who probably wanted to stress the distinction between their own sedentary lifestyle and the nomadic ways of the people from the cactus country. The Mohave, Pima, and Papago called them "the enemy." The Navajo, to whom they are most closely related linguistically, had different names for each Apache subgroup, yet they had no word to describe the Apaches as a whole.

Although the agricultural cultures of the Southwest are often described as oases in the semidesert, the Southwest was never entirely isolated from neighboring regions. For instance, the Pueblo peoples of the northern Rio Grande perform bison dances and their clothes also show elements borrowed from the Plains peoples with whom they traded, and the corn, squash, and beans that came originally from Mexican cultures are grown everywhere in the Southwest.

Taos, New Mexico, c. 1990.

Taos, inhabited by the Tiwa, is the northernmost pueblo on the Rio Grande. To a much greater extent than the other Pueblo peoples, their culture and economy have traditionally been influenced by their contact with the Plains cultures. Because of the relatively short growing season in this area, more importance was attached to hunting and gathering than to agriculture as a basis of subsistence. However, the influence of the neighboring inhabitants of the Plains is also evident in the dress, dances, and music of the Tiwa.

# War and peace in the "land of enchantment"

With sword and crucifix in hand, the Spanish invaded the Southwest in the 16th century. Yet, they also brought wheat, grapes, chickens, and most importantly sheep and horses, which rapidly aroused the intense interest of the nomadic Apache and Navajo. The Spanish introduced the system of encomienda whereby simple soldiers could become landowners and exploiters of Native American labor. They also built churches and missions in order to share with their indigenous day laborers the one true doctrine of salvation. Jesuit and Franciscan missionaries worked to suppress the traditional religions of the indigenous peoples until the Pueblo Revolt of 1680, when more than 1,000 Spaniards were killed, thus bringing Spanish rule to an abrupt end.

Led by General de Vargas, who exploited the lack of unity among the Pueblo peoples, the Spanish returned to Santa Fe in 1692. Many rebels subsequently fled the Spanish dominions; others surrendered. On the surface, the colonized Pueblo peoples appeared submissive, and their leaders collaborated with the Spanish administration. However, they secretly continued to conduct the important ceremonies on which their culture and social cohesion were based. In 1821, the indigenous subjects of the Spanish crown became citizens of the independent state of Mexico.

As a result of the Mexican-American War of 1846–1848 and the Gadsden Purchase of 1853, which sealed the predatory peace with the defeated Mexico by means of symbolic payments, the United States obtained the huge area west of the Rio Grande from New Mexico to California. They assumed control over the Pueblo peoples as Mexican subjects, and not as the original and rightful owners of the land. The legal system distinguished between "civilized" Pueblo peoples and "Indians," thus denying the former the opportunity to claim the special rights due to recognized Native American communities, such as protection of their lands from uninvited intruders and from land sales to white people. The army was deployed against the Navajo and Apache – with mixed success. Following the military appeasement of the Southwest in the late 1880s, Protestant missionaries and agents of the Bureau of Indian Affairs (BIA) began Americanizing the population by means of education and conversion to Christianity, and by redirecting their economic life toward small-scale, family farming. While the Navajo, Pima, Papago, and the Pueblo peoples were largely able to maintain their ancient way of life, or modernize it in a way that suited their culture, the Apache were severely affected by the experiments of forced resettlement, appalling mismanagement, and ruinous agricultural projects conducted by the BIA.

Spanish horsemen. Rock painting in Canyon del Muerto, Arizona, early 19th century.

In popular history, the conquest of the Southwest by the Spaniards is often linked to the legend of the Seven Golden Cities of Cíbola which the Spanish were seeking when they came across the Pueblo peoples. A rock painting in the Canyon del Muerto, which had long been interpreted as a Native American depiction of these early invaders, is today understood to be the work of Navajo artist Tall Lamb and to depict a Spanish attack on the Navajo in 1805.

The interior of the old church in the pueblo of Laguna, New Mexico, 1901. Photograph: Adamson Clark Vroman. Los Angeles County Museum of Natural History, Los Angeles, CA.

During the 18th and 19th centuries, Pueblo peoples and Spanish colonists would frequently join forces in defense against Apache and Navajo raids. Simultaneously, a diverse regional culture developed, blending Castilian, Moorish, and indigenous elements, as in the local architecture. However, while Christianity as practiced in the pueblos was clearly combined with pre-Christian practices, the ancient religion, which continued to be practiced in secret, remained generally untouched by Spanish influences.

Woody Crumbo (Creek-Potawatomi), *Land of Enchantment*, watercolor, 1946. Philbrook Museum of Art, Tulsa, OK.

The picturesque native peoples of the Southwest have always played an important part in the advertising campaigns of the tourist industry. The stream of no less picturesque vacationers may have found edification in cross-cultural roadside encounters with a disappearing world; the indigenous craftsmen, however, were no more than marginal participants in the profits of the tourist industry. Tourism can create its own problems within reservations and pueblos, yet today their inhabitants, particularly the Apache, lure great numbers of outdoor-loving tourists onto the ski slopes of their mountainous homeland and into tribally owned hotels.

A matter of major importance in the period around 1900 was the question of land claims. In 1913 the Pueblo peoples were given the same legal status as other indigenous communities in the United States, and could therefore reclaim land that had already been sold or occupied by settlers. The Apache in Arizona lost three quarters of their reservation land after the discovery of copper deposits. The Navajo even gained a few areas, yet after the great livestock reduction of the 1930s, when overgrazing and subsequent soil erosion made it necessary to destroy a large portion of the Navajo's sheep herds, many left the reservations to find work in metropolitan Albuquerque, Los Angeles, and San Francisco. In 1948, the indigenous inhabitants of the states of Arizona and New Mexico had to litigate for the right to vote – after having been citizens of the United States for 24 years and having served in the army during two world wars.

For a long time, the indigenous population in the remaining Mexican part of the Southwest had to survive without any special protection or government recognition. The "liberal" Mexican constitution of 1857 prohibited churches from owning land, but it also declared any form of communal land-ownership illegal – a catastrophic legal situation for the traditionally communal economies of the indigenous farmers. The situation during the rule of Mexican dictator Porfirio Díaz (1830–1915) was so intolerable that the Yaqui of Sonora staged numerous revolts. Following bloody skirmishes, their leaders were executed, their land was divided into small parcels, and part of the population was deported to the Yucatan peninsula at the opposite end of Mexico, where many Yaquis perished in the heat and humidity. A few hundred Yaquis fled to

the United States, where their descendants are today recognized as "Indians" and where they own a reservation on the outskirts of Tucson. Insofar as they have not been driven from their land nor blended in with the mestizo majority, other indigenous populations in northern Mexico have survived by retreating into the mountains (like the Tarahumara) or the desert (like the Seri) or by fleeing to the United States (as did some Yaquis). The indigenist policies adopted after the revolution of 1910 eventually derived from Mexico's native heritage the paternalistic obligation to assimilate the "first Mexicans."

# Red earth, green fields of corn

Hopi cornfield in the Oraibi Wash, Arizona, 1989.

The word "wash" (for the Spanish term "arroyo") illustrates the fact that the greatest threat to cornfields planted in floodwater drainage areas lies in the floodwaters washing away the fields or in the tender plants being buried under mud. In the arroyo fan delta, however, water spreads evenly across the fields. Removing weeds allows sand between the corn plants to be blown to the edges of the field, thus creating protective banks. If the fields are large, the Hopi also distribute the water from the wash evenly across the soil with the help of irrigation channels.

Opposite page, below:

Hopi woman grinding corn, 1913. Photograph: Joseph K. Dixon, William Hammond Mathers Museum, Indiana University, Bloomington, IN.

Every Hopi household possessed three millstones, on which corn was first ground into small pieces, and subsequently in two steps into fine flour. Before their wedding, young women had to spend three days in the house of their mother-in-law, grinding corn from morning until night. Corn tortillas with beans, and an occasional portion of meat or wild vegetables, formed the traditional main meals. Blue corn is still used to make piki, a flat bread that has the appearance of blotting paper. A Hopi woman explains that "very straight, flat fingers" are needed in order to spread the dough on the red-hot stove.

Almost every society in the Southwest grew corn for at least some of the time. However, agriculture was the main food source for the Pueblo peoples, the Yuman tribes along the Colorado River, the Pima and Papago in southern Arizona, as well as the Tarahumara and their neighbors in northwestern Mexico.

In the arid Southwest agriculture implies, above all, a constant struggle for water. Routines and ritual, world views and technology, aesthetics, artistic expression, and celebrations are all deeply affected by this vital endeavor. The importance of agriculture to the livelihood of the native population has markedly declined in the last 50 years, yet the culture that went with the cultivation of the land is still alive – albeit in modernized form.

Traditional agriculture in the Southwest could only have been possible with the assistance of irrigation technology. Either the water was taken to the fields – or the fields to the water. The Pima of the Sonoran Desert had an extensive system of canals to divert water from the Gila and Salt rivers to their fields. In the Eastern Pueblos on the Rio Grande and its tributaries, the fields were also irrigated by means of canals, whereas the Western Pueblo peoples in the arid foothills of the Colorado Plateau and the Papago in Arizona were dependent on seasonal floods for the cultivation of their soil. They made use of the heavy,

twice-yearly rainfalls by locating their fields at the mouths of arroyos (deep rainwater gullies and stream beds) through which the water rushed down the mountainsides. The Mohave and other Yuman speaking groups used the relatively reliable spring floods of the Colorado River in a way similar to the way in which Egyptian peasants use the Nile floods. The rich mud from the mountains fertilized the fields planted in the alluvial land, and saturated the soil with sufficient moisture for the plants to grow to maturity.

Almost everywhere, men did most of the work on the fields, even though among the Hopi it was the women who owned the land. This form of division of labor by gender was unusual in comparison to other parts of North America, and was probably caused by the fact that the fields were irrigated – the men also dug the canals and kept them clean. On the other hand, Hopi women built and maintained the houses.

Neither fertilizing nor plowing existed before the arrival of Europeans – this was because the domestication of animals, which is a prerequisite for these activities, was unknown. Today, the Tarahumara take their cattle and sheep out to graze on the fields after the harvest, thereby fertilizing the fields; Spanish influence also brought a gradual introduction of ox-drawn wooden plows.

Other than that, the indigenous inhabitants use very simple tools for all forms of agriculture: a dibble and perhaps a hoe for weeding and harvesting. Much more important than tools was an understanding of the growing conditions for the cultivated plants, the nature of the soil, the strong variations in the local climate, the ritual lore surrounding the communication with supernatural beings, and a willingness to cooperate with relatives and other villagers.

Cultivated plants, especially corn, are sacred. Every Hopi newborn is given a "corn mother," a perfect cob of corn that every person keeps throughout their life in remembrance of the spirit sisters, Blue Corn Woman and Yellow Corn Maiden, who first brought them corn. Cornmeal is sprinkled over ceremonial dancers, and the ceremonial leader scatters a path of cornmeal leading from the kiva to the plaza. The sacred "mudhead-clowns" of the Pueblo peoples attach kernels of corn to the protrusions of their masks, and Salako Mana, the Corn Maiden, wears the checkerboard corn symbol at the center of her forehead.

Hopi man tilling a cornfield, Arizona, 1902. Photograph: Adamson Clark Vroman. Los Angeles County Museum of Natural History, Los Angeles, CA.

The Hopi begin to sow their corn in the middle of May: "Every two or three steps, a dibble is used to make holes about 8 inches deep. The upper, dry layer of earth is carefully separated from the lower layer, which still retains some moisture. About eight kernels of corn are inserted into the hole, then covered with the moist soil and then the dry soil." The farmers use hedges, windbreaks, and empty cans to protect their seedlings from the scorching heat of the desert wind.

# Cooperation between the sexes – hunting and gathering in the Southwest

*Papago Women Harvesting the Fruit of the Saguaro Cactus*, 1853. Lithograph after a drawing by Arthur Schott from A. W. Whipple, *Report upon the Indian Tribes*, Washington, DC. 1855. Arizona State Museum, Tucson, AZ.

The fruit of the giant cactus, which were harvested by knocking them off with long sticks, were an important source of food not only for the Papago. They were eaten raw, preserved in the form of syrup, and used to make wine. The seeds were ground to make flour. During harvest times, the nourishing fruit caused visible weight gain ("seasonal fattening") among the Seri. The Seri also had a "second harvest" when they collected undigested seeds after excretion from the body.

The Apache referred to the course of a year as "a harvest." They were raiders and hunters, but primarily food-gatherers, or at least the women were. During the entire growing season women gathered fruit and plants that grew at various altitudes. As soon as there was news of cactus fruit, pinyon nuts, mulberries, or wild grass seeds ripening in a particular area, they would set off either alone or in larger groups with an armed escort of warriors, depending on how far they would have to travel. Family groups often traveled to suit the women's food gathering calendar, and the men, who followed the women, would make themselves useful by hunting in the area where food was being gathered.

"While the man is hunting," Morris Opler was told by an Apache, "the woman gets up before sunrise, builds the fire, if the man hasn't already done so, and cooks the morning meal, using meat if there is some, vegetables if not. Then she goes out to gather seeds or plants, leaving the small children with another woman." A great variety of meals can be prepared with wild vegetables. Papago women pounded the seeds of wild grass to make flour for porridge, soup, or tortillas. Even today, Papago families leave their homes for several weeks when the fruits of the saguaro cactus are ripe. They eat them fresh or use them to make syrup. The Apache gathered yucca fruits (datil) and dried or cooked them as biscuits that could be stored through the winter.

Agricultural communities also supplemented their diet with wild plants. Even the Pima, thanks to whose irrigation techniques two harvests could be grown each year, obtained at least 40 percent of their daily food requirement by gathering wild plants. However, the native inhabitants of the Southwest not only gathered food plants but also collected eggs, honey, and materials for all kinds of ceremonial and utilitarian objects. The evergreen branches of the Douglas fir, for example, are still used in Pueblo ceremonies and have to be fetched from the canyons of the distant mountains. For this purpose, among the Tewa the leader of the ceremony walks to the canyons on the preceding day, whereas the Hopi send a fast runner.

"Titoi made the deer," according to the oral tradition of the Papago, "giving it no gall bladder so that it could not get angry. He gave it the wind for its friend to tell of human approach, but he also caused it to know when its time was come, so that it would submit itself willingly to the hunter." For the Papago, the deer hunt was a matter for religious specialists, who employed masks and magic in their pursuit. They were called "head carriers" and the other men in their kindred helped to till their fields.

In return, they supplied meat for the community throughout the year – except in January ("Moon of thin animals") and February ("Moon when the deer smell bad").

Not every family could afford the cost of having a son trained as a hunter. An apprentice would follow his master, who was paid by the parents, carry his quiver, and help with the tasks of gutting and carrying the game. The master would make him a mask with the first deer killed by the apprentice himself. The young man was not permitted to eat the meat from this deer if he wished to become a successful hunter.

Altruism and generosity when distributing the prey within the community were the prime duties of every Apache hunter. Occasionally, people would try to evade this duty, as Morris Opler was told by a hunter: "If you go through the camps with a deer, they take it from you. You can't say anything. I used to sneak in at night. That's what some do."

However, the most successful method of obtaining meat was by hunting small animals such as rabbits. This did not generally require any magic precautions. Thus the American anthropologist Ruth Underhill (1884–1984) wrote of the Papago: "No man ever left the village without his bow and the light wood-tipped arrows which were used for small game."

Hopi rabbit hunters with throwing stick, bows, and arrows, Arizona, 1900. Photograph: Sumner W. Matteson. Milwaukee Public Museum, Milwaukee, WI.

The flat, slightly angled throwing stick is similar in appearance to a boomerang, but it does not return to the thrower. Originally, this weapon was widespread in western North America and survived in the pueblos until the 19th century, mainly for hunting rabbits, although it may have been used as a weapon of war in the past. The Hopi regarded the throwing stick as a replica of the wing of the sparrow hawk, which was esteemed as a great hunter. They also compared it to a scorpion's tail.

Apache hunting pronghorn antelope, c. 1875. Photograph: D. F. Mitchell. Sharlott Hall Museum, Prescott, AZ.

An Apache describing deer-stalking reported that "The hunter acts like a grazing deer. Some careful men could come within six feet of the deer this way." The necessary hunting disguise had to be made by a hunter with special supernatural powers. During the Apache's antelope and deer ceremonies, held on the night preceding a hunt, the deer was implored through prayer and songs to submit to the hunter. Elements of this ceremony were also used in love magic.

# No two Pueblos are alike

Taos in winter, c. 1990.

Situated at an altitude of 7000 feet before the backdrop of the Sangre del Cristo Mountains, Taos is widely regarded as the most picturesque of all the Eastern Pueblos. On both sides of the plaza, two massive buildings rise four to five stories into the sky. While the center of the town is now open to visitors, the traditional life of Taos generally remains closed to outsiders.

Their villages lie just a few miles apart, strung like pearls along the silver ribbon of the Rio Grande. The Spanish, who first made contact with them in the 16th century, noticed one thing in particular: their village life. It reminded them of their own rural, peasant lifestyle, and so they simply named both the people and the settlements "Pueblos," the Spanish word for "village." Common to the Hopi, Zuni, Keres, and Tano are their dismissive-looking stone or adobe houses, the cultivation of corn, and their secretive ceremonial life, characteristics that distinguish these peoples from every other society in the Southwest.

Yet the manifold characteristics of each village were given scant attention, and we "non-Pueblo people" still know little more about the details of their religious life than we did 100 years ago. One reason for this is the seclusion of many of the pueblos, where strangers – especially white people – are not accepted; another one is found in the historical experiences that the peoples along the Rio Grande had with Spanish colonial rulers, Protestant missionaries, researchers, and romantic admirers of the Native Americans. However regrettable their self-imposed isolation may be for anthropology and tourism alike, this policy has enabled the Pueblo peoples to survive five centuries of changing governments, raids, and well-meaning reeducation measures without in the process losing their own culture.

The greatest influence on traditional Pueblo cultures was wielded by Spanish colonists, their missions, and popular Catholicism, although the Southwest's Spanish period was characterized by forced labor, brutal religious repression, and the abduction of hundreds, perhaps thousands, of people into slavery.

Yet in the 21st century examples of wealthy pueblo inhabitants employing their Spanish-American neighbors as domestic servants are not unknown. Every pueblo along the Rio Grande has a Catholic patron saint who is venerated on his or her holy day. In some pueblos, like Santa Ana, this is the only day of the year on which the presence of tourists is tolerated.

The main difference between the Western Pueblos and those along the Rio Grande lies in the way their buildings are constructed and in the social order of the people who live in them. Nearly all the Rio Grande Pueblos consist of adobe houses, whereas in the Western Pueblos mortar-plastered stone buildings are more common. The stone, terraced, multistory buildings built by the Hopi, Zuni,

and Acoma are fascinating not merely because of the bold construction methods used; they have been in uninterrupted use for around 700 years and are thus the oldest continuously inhabited settlements in the whole of North America.

Despite such unusual continuity, a pueblo is never completed. New rooms are added, and the walls of a pueblo house have to be newly rendered each year to enable it to withstand the summer downpours. The houses are arranged in long rows, as multistory terraces, or around a central village courtyard, demonstrating to strangers that they are not necessarily welcome. In times of war, the windowless rooms were accessible only through a hatch in the roof, via ladders that could be drawn in when necessary. A large part of village life took place on the roof under the open sky: this was where fruit and vegetables were dried, where firewood was stored, where people cooked and chatted, and also where they slept if the weather permitted.

The people in the pueblos are bound together by family ties and close-knit social and political organization.

Until 1934, all the pueblos except the Hopi villages were governed according to a political system of self-rule introduced by the Spanish, whose officials (mayordomos, fiscales, and the like) were appointed by the village chief (cacique or governor) to serve for one year. Although the system outwardly appeared to stand for the new order in village and church, it usually served as a mere facade for the continuing pre-Hispanic form of government. The *Indian Reorganization Act* (1934) was intended to make amends for the forced dissolution of the tribes aimed for in previous decades, and to provide them with communities formed in accordance with the American model of elected government. Thus the formation of elected tribal councils was strongly promoted, although not accepted by every pueblo.

In the 20th century, several pueblos saw a further increase of political factionalism. For instance in the Pueblo of San Ildefonso, a land dispute caused the village to be split into mutually hostile southern and northern sections. Since both village sections are grouped around a central plaza, people now speak of the northern and southern plazas. In other pueblos, there are dividing lines running between traditionalists and modernists. However, it is very rare for internal conflict to lead to the complete dissolution of a village. This may be due to the myriad institutions that bind together their inhabitants and that have always been

important to them, regardless of current government Indian policies: in the Western Pueblos these were the descent groups (or clans), and in the Rio Grande Pueblos the ceremonial associations and the moieties, as the two halves of a socially and symbolically divided community are termed.

Like all Tano pueblos along the Rio Grande, San Ildefonso was divided into a summer and a winter moiety, membership of which was generally passed down through the father. Each half would take turns to provide the cacique, or village leader, and his assistants – "right-hand man" and "left-hand man." The ceremonial associations – which included medicine, hunt, warrior, and two women's societies – had their own leaders and performed their own rituals. The Koshare society stood outside the general dual organization of the village. Koshare were clowns who had the power to bring rain and who also exerted a kind of police authority over the pueblo inhabitants.

In San Ildefonso the oldest building was the large round kiva, which was used in common by everyone. In addition, the summer moiety and the previously noted inimical northern and southern plazas, which were not identical with the old moieties, had their own kivas. Altogether the kivas as meeting rooms of the men counterbalanced the predominance of the women within the families. Women were only welcome in the kivas when

The governors of the pueblo of Zuni, New Mexico, 1879. Photograph: Jack Hilers. National Anthropological Archives, Smithsonian Institution, Washington, DC.

Like the Zuni, all Pueblo peoples were originally led by priesthoods whose activities were generally conducted in the background. Public order and communication between the leader and his people were the responsibility of "bow priests" who, as representatives of a warrior society, were permitted to use force. This is why the Spanish entrusted them with governing the pueblos. The striped blankets were woven by men on vertical looms.

Opposite page, below:

Church and kiva in the pueblo of San Ildefonso, New Mexico, 1898. California Historical Society, San Francisco, CA.

A kiva is a room found in every pueblo, built either partially or completely underground, in which the secret or semipublic parts of ceremonies take place and where the various societies meet. The kivas in the Western Pueblos are rectangular; in the Rio Grande Pueblos they are round. Kivas are entered via ladders through a hatch in the roof. In San Ildefonso, access to the roof is by a staircase. With only a few exceptions, the Rio Grande Pueblos exclude all outsiders from their ceremonies.

they actively participated in the ceremonies or when the women's societies held their own meetings there.

In the Western Pueblos, a large part of social life was decided by the clans, who also owned the land reserved for the cultivation of corn. At birth, everyone became a member of their mother's clan and, after marriage, men would move in with their wives, into a room that would be added to the house of their mothers. The kinship groups – and the ceremonial associations of the pueblos along the Rio Grande – were not immutable institutions. A clan might become reduced through illness or through the vagaries of reproduction, and their sections of the pueblo would decay while others grew.

The close cohabitation and cooperation of women in a single household extending across several rooms has become more difficult in recent years. Many families now make their living by pottery making, by manufacturing artifacts for craft shops, or by taking jobs in administration or in the local tourist industry. As people have started to take jobs that are based outside the reservations, and as urban migration has increased, many Pueblo people now live in ordinary, single-family homes as do so many other Americans, but contact with and concern for and among relatives are still not only an important part of life, they also guarantee the continued existence of Pueblo societies.

Seth Eastman: *Interior of an Estufa* [kiva]. Steel engraving after a drawing by Richard H. Kern from Henry Rowe Schoolcraft, *Historical and Statistical Information Respecting the History Conditions and Prospects of the Indian Tribes of the United States*, Philadelphia, PA 1854.

Shortly after the American acquisition of New Mexico, painter Richard H. Kern (1821–1853) accompanied a government expedition to the land of the Pueblo peoples and of the Navajo. As the guest of honor of the governor of Jemez Pueblo, he was granted the rare privilege of visiting the kiva, usually inaccessible to strangers, and was even allowed to draw it.

# The girl who was stolen by a Navajo

## A story from Cochiti (1924)

Cochiti is a relatively small pueblo on the Rio Grande, not far from Santa Fe, the state capital of New Mexico. Its inhabitants spoke one of the seven Keresan languages, which began to decline in importance during World War II. Up until then many people also spoke Spanish, although English has now become the dominant language.

When Ruth Benedict, a student and successor of anthropologist Franz Boas, made a collection of the oral traditions of Cochiti in 1924, the population of the village numbered around 300 people. Although the ancient myths were still known at that time, short stories that referred to everyday events, stories about animals, and European fairy tales predominated. The following text, which originated with a well-known local storyteller, was classified by Benedict in the group of "true stories," although it unquestionably contains features of the novella. The enmity between the Pueblo peoples and the Navajo (whom the Cochiti, themselves reluctant Catholics, liked to call "heathens") forms the background to the story about the personal fate of a woman who entered a foreign world against her will.


While the Pueblos were at war with the Navajos and Apaches and the Plains Indians, a Cochiti girl was stolen by the Navajos. One evening as it was getting dark the girl went out to the corral. She was leaning against the east side of the stockade. A man in a blanket came around the stockade. She thought it was her lover and she put her arms around him. He covered her in his blanket. As they were embracing he pulled her toward the west. He put his hands over her mouth so she couldn't scream. He took her to the Navajo country. There they tormented her and ridiculed her and the women whipped her with whips and sticks. After a while the Navajo boy could not stand the ridicule the girl had to bear. He put a stop to it. He said, "I took her. I shall live with her – she shall be my wife." She lived with him and had four children, two boys and two girls.

One of the Navajo women was a good friend of the Pueblo girl. One time the friend asked, "Aren't you lonesome for your father and mother and for your brothers and sisters?" "Yes, but I don't know the way home." "Will you take my plan?" "Yes." "This year there are plenty of piñons and yucca fruit on the mountains. We will invite our husbands to go out to help us gather these. When we camp I will tell you in what direction to go, what to do." They invited their husbands. The Navajo woman said, "When you are ready and going to start, choose the two best riding horses." When they were near the place where the piñons grew, the Navajo woman said, "Tell your husband to look for a place to camp where the piñons are thick. I will give you medicine to put your husband to sleep. When he is asleep take a knife and cut off his head. Have no pity, just as he had no pity when he was bringing you to the Navajo country. When you have cut his head off, have the horses ready. Ride as fast as you can. Do not stop anywhere. When my husband discovers that you have killed your husband and goes with his head, you will have a good start."

When the Navajo woman's husband found out, he went to his wife to ask her where the other had gone. She told him that she did not know. He had to take the message to the Navajos before he could follow the girl. The girl did as she was told; she had no pity for the horses. When one was tired she rode the other. She traveled all night. Next day the Navajos gave chase. That evening they nearly caught her at a narrow place. She left her two horses there and escaped down the cliff on foot. When she was almost down to the river level she heard horses' hoofs behind her. She jumped aside and left the trail. There was a little cave there and she hid. The horsemen passed her. They thought the girl had reached the pueblo and they went back to the very place where she was hiding. There they met the Navajos who were coming up behind. They quarreled among themselves, for the relatives of the man who had been killed wanted to take revenge on the pueblo, but the rest were not willing. Those in authority said, "Our horses are tired and if we are pursued by fresh horses none of us would escape." They turned back. The girl could hear the Navajo man's relatives crying. She stayed there all night. In the morning before dawn, she came out of the cave and instead of taking the road, she went down an arroyo and came in from the northeast side into the village.

That morning one of the Cochiti men had risen early to get wood. He was tying his wood ready to put it on his back, and the girl followed him till he was close to the pueblo. She said to him, "Father, where are you going?" He turned and saw that she was a stranger. "Who are you?" "My poor father, don't you know me? I am the girl who was taken by the Navajos. I am the one who is coming back again now to my people." The old man threw off his load and embraced the girl. He said, "Wait here. I will take word back home." He ran to the pueblo and called to all the people that his daughter had come back. So the girl returned home who had been stolen by the Navajos. The rest of her life she lived among her people.


(Ruth Benedict, *Tales of the Cochiti Indians,* Washington 1931)

# The balanced cosmos –
# religion and ritual in the Pueblos

A Pueblo ceremony is prayer, spectacle, religious service, act of meditation, dance, and entertainment in one. "Each person in the village gives offerings and blessings," is how the American artist Virginia M. Roediger described a dance in the Western Pueblos in the 1930s. "For the final performance the people stand silently in solid blocks, looking down from the terraced house tops, or they sit motionless upon the plaza ledges. Between the dances there is quiet conversation, gossip, or the subdued hailing of visitors from a far-off Pueblo."

Both audience and dancers carry an enormous responsibility since, with every ceremony, they help to maintain the equilibrium between man, nature, and supernatural beings. If a ceremony goes wrong, there is a fear that it may not rain, that the universe, at the center of which each pueblo stands, will be thrown into disorder.

And a ceremony can fail if anyone who should be participating – dancer or spectator alike – is missing, if anyone harbors bad thoughts, or if anybody behaves in an unseemly or careless manner. For these reasons alone it is understandable that many Pueblo peoples prefer not to have too many strangers in the audience.

The dancers themselves can cause the greatest damage if they have not achieved a mental state of a "good heart" before the dance. For this meditation they retreat into the kivas and spend a number of days in total isolation from the outside world and in the semidarkness of the ceremonial room, partaking of neither meat nor salt, and undergoing spiritual purification.

A great ceremony can last at least nine, sometimes even up to 20 days, and is led by a ceremonial association in charge of the secret religious knowledge. Membership in

Fred Kabotie (Hopi), *Pueblo Green Corn Dance*, tempera, 1947. Thomas Gilcrease Institute of American History and Art, Tulsa, OK.

Many of the Rio Grande Pueblos are characterized by the coexistence of church and kiva, as in San Ildefonso since 1617. In this painting, Hopi artist Fred Kabotie (b. 1900) interprets this coexistence in terms of a surrender to Catholicism by the pueblo inhabitants. The dancers move out of the traditional kiva toward the Christian altar, and the dance becomes a Catholic procession. In the upper left of the scene, clowns follow the events while making agitated gestures.

such associations is either voluntary or taken up from a sense of personal obligation, as may arise, for example, if the rituals performed by a society have cured one from a sickness. However, not all pueblo inhabitants are members of these associations. For the Western Pueblos, rainmaking is a central activity of the associations; the Rio Grande Pueblos, which thanks to their irrigation methods are less dependent on rainfall, have associations for healing and for good fortune in hunting and in war.

Very little is known about the religious activities of the Rio Grande Pueblos, since the knowledge owned by their associations continues to be secret. In the face of their encounter with the haughty Catholicism of the Spanish, this has enabled them successfully to withstand all further attacks on their traditional religion. In public, there is a fascinating fusion of Catholic practice and indigenous interpretation, as can be seen on the patron saint's day of each respective pueblo, at which white people are welcome. The Western Pueblos, some of which are even a little more open toward outsiders, have adopted very little from the Europeans.

The annual ceremonial cycle of the Hopi, for example, is divided into two periods, that of the masked and that of the unmasked ceremonies. The masked dancers embody the kachinas, which appear in the villages in January or February and take their leave in July. The first great kachina ceremony is Powamu (from *powa*, "supernatural power"), the bean feast in the spring when children are initiated into the kachina associations; the last is Niman (from *nima*, "going home"), the homecoming ceremony at the start of the impatiently awaited rainy season.

The Antelope dance and the famous Snake dance are performed at the beginning of the second half of the year, when specially prepared dancers perform while holding live snakes in their mouths, which they subsequently release back into the wild. The Bison and Butterfly dances are events that are primarily dedicated to enjoyment, while the ceremonies of the women's and men's associations (Maraw and Wuwuchim) that are held in the fall serve to promote the community's fertility and good fortune in war.

Every four years in the fal,l boys are initiated into the men's associations, otherwise they cannot participate in the Soyal, the most important celebration of the year, held at the winter solstice. The Hopi determine the exact date for these central ceremonies by observing the precise point in the landscape at which the sun rises. Only the Powamu ceremony is determined by the appearance of the new moon during the holy month of Powamuyaw.

Deer dance in the pueblo of San Juan, New Mexico, c. 1985.

The Deer dance and other animal dances of the Rio Grande Pueblos reflect the continuing importance of hunting even for farmers who make use of irrigation to cultivate their crops. The dances are generally held at Christmas or at Epiphany. The dancers wear antler headdresses, imitate the animals' movements, and are led by the Deer Mothers who, as the "owners of the deer," allow the people to hunt them.

# Messengers of the gods, toys, and crafts – kachinas and clowns

They are supernatural beings, the friends and allies of humans, and conveyors of their prayers to the gods. They are the spirits of the ancestors, yet they also embody the spiritual essence of all things, from ashes to stars. The kachinas come to visit humans during the period between the winter solstice and their return to the underworld in July when, impersonated by members of men's associations, they stay in the villages. Every village has kachinas, but the greater religious openness of the Western Pueblos has enabled us to learn much more about them there than we know of kachinas in the other Pueblos.

Researchers have counted between 170 and 335 different, named kachinas among the Hopis, but it is impossible to ascertain the precise number of kachinas in each individual village; just as rooms may be abandoned in the pueblos, so kachinas have also been forgotten and forsaken, while others have been added in the course of contacts with other Pueblos, the Navajo, and the Europeans. Furthermore, each mesa – the Hopi inhabit three of these table mountains and have developed corresponding variations in their culture and dialect – and each village may have a different understanding of the nature of a kachina.

For Powamu and Niman, fathers gave their daughters kachina figures, which were treated like dolls, although they also assisted the girls in learning about all the different beings, each of which has its own characteristics and responsibilities.

During kachina dances, the heads of the supernatural beings are represented by masks. These usually envelop the whole head, and consist of a wooden framework covered with fur, cotton, or leather, painted with characteristic designs and may have head boards (also known by the Spanish term *tablitas*), feathers, birds' wings, ears, horns, cloud formations, and beards attached to them.

Shortly before the dances take place, the decorations on the masks are renewed or even changed. Only the masks of the Mong, or leading kachinas, which are kept safe by the eldest women in the clans, may not be altered; these kachinas also do not dance on the plazas, but only appear for special events.

Between December and April, the kachinas perform at night in the kivas; between April and July, the dances take place publicly on the plazas. The dancing is accompanied by songs, chanted either by the dancers themselves or by a drummer and choir, to transmit the people's prayers or a message from the kachinas. Every dance has a leader who also organizes the activities that take place between each dance by appointing the clowns who are to perform.

The clowns (*tsutskut*) are the antithesis of the harmoniously dancing kachinas. Once upon a time, their mythical ancestors Clown Boy and Clown Girl had to make amends for an incestuous indiscretion by making a public confession, this explains why the primary task of their contemporary incarnations has continued to be the demonstration of people's failings. The clowns wear a conspicuous body painting of clay and soot. During the performance they act out a fixed sequence of episodes illustrating the passage of humans from paradisical beginnings followed by decline, punishment by warrior kachinas, and finally to purification and betterment.

Like the beautifully made kachina dolls, the kachina dances and the clowns have changed during the last few decades – thereby preserving their relevance to the people. German anthropologist Hans-Ulrich Sanner (b. 1958) writes: "When, for example, clowns lecture a doll that represents their 'sister' on the duties of women, they are formulating and handing down timeless values of the society. The additional, humorous warning that they should not fall in with drinkers or dope-heads, places the 'Clown Girl' in a relation to contemporary problems and makes her a symbol of modern Hopi girls."

Koyemshis on the plaza of a Hopi village, Arizona, 1904–1906. Photograph: Joseph Mora. John R. Wilson Collection, Tulsa, OK.

Just like the kachina impersonators, clowns in the Rio Grande Pueblos (and in the past among the Hopi) were members of ceremonial associations. Unlike the real, unmasked clowns, the koyemshis ("mudheads") wear masks. As the mythical children of an incestuous relationship between siblings, they embody the inversion of appropriate human behavior. Yet they are jesters and wise men at once, whose special duty it is to act as the servants and speakers of the mute kachinas.

Opposite page:

Ahöla, a Hopi kachina doll (*katsin tihu*) made of cottonwood, Arizona, 1900. Carnegie Museum of Natural History, Pittsburg, PA.

Ahöla is a Mong, or leading kachina. He represents Alosaka, god of germination, and is very important for the growth and thriving of cultivated plants, but he is also linked to the sun. Ahöla is always represented wearing a large feather headdress, with a face divided by painting into two halves, and a triangle with the apex facing downward out of which protrudes a beak.

# Prayers in clay

Nampeyo making a pot, Hano, Arizona, 1901. Photograph: Adamson Clark Vroman. Southwest Museum Collection, Los Angeles, CA.

Hano is a village situated on the first Hopi mesa and was settled by Tewa refugees from the Rio Grande at the time of the Pueblo Revolt. It was the home of Nampeyo (c. 1852–1942), who developed a ceramic style inspired by the pot shards of the prehistoric Anasazi (Sikyatki). In the past, women carried on their heads large pots full of water from distant springs back to their villages, without spilling a single drop of the precious liquid.

Pottery in the North American Southwest is mainly the art of Pueblo women. For hundreds of years they have made their household pots and in the 20th century some even became world-famous for their work. Yet pottery is more than mere household objects or craft. One potter from Laguna remarked that "Some people do not think that pottery is anything, but it means a great deal to me. It is something sacred."

The women did not need a wheel to make their pots. Starting with a flat piece for the base, they applied narrow strips of clay in spirals around the edge, progressively building up the walls of the pot. Round stones or scrapers made from gourds were used to finish the pot. When the pot had dried, the potters would burnish it once more before decorating it. Designs were painted onto a priming color that could vary from pale white to strong orange red, depending on the region. These women artists made their own paintbrushes by chewing yucca leaves until soft. Finally, the pot was fired in a shallow pit. The most difficult stages of the work are the preparation of the surface and then the painting of it with the greatest of care to ensure a decorative, durable, and harmoniously formed vessel.

The Zuni use terms for parts of the body to describe the different parts of a clay pot: the lower part of a jug is the "stomach," the upper part the "neck," and the opening the "lips." The potter draws a line between stomach and neck, which is the most important design feature and is not crossed by any other line or figure. It is called *onane* ("path") and symbolizes the potter's life span.

The artist is not bound to any rules regarding the choice and execution of the traditional patterns and figures. "I am always thinking about designs even when I am doing other things," remarked one particular potter to anthropologist Ruth Bunzel (1898–1990), "and whenever I close my eyes, I see designs in front of me. I often dream of designs, and whenever I am ready to paint, I close my eyes and then the designs just come to me." Patterns do not necessarily symbolize anything, but may be interpreted as the occasion demands.

The pottery of the Anasazi is the ancient source from which even contemporary indigenous ceramic art takes its inspiration. Anasazi pottery was first produced in large quantities in around AD 500, but it was not until between AD 700 and 1100, a period of rapid population growth, that numerous distinct regional styles developed. Patterns may also have served as social markers, used to differentiate between various groups.

Women made pots, bowls, jugs, even mugs for domestic use, and they also produced special vessels for ritual purposes, such as bowls to hold the sacred corn meal. The basic element of decoration was the line. The artists did not limit their art to ceramics: adaptations of their designs also appeared in basketry and textiles.

Zuni pot with polychrome decoration, New Mexico, c. 1825–1840. Taylor Museum of the Colorado Springs Fine Arts Center, Colorado Springs, CO.

The history of ceramics in the pueblos has been subject to a great deal of research and illustrates a constant transformation of styles and methods. Yet each village maintained its own recognizable characteristics, some of which (fine crosshatching of decorative zones) can be traced back to the beginnings of Anasazi ceramic art. Far into the 20th century techniques of manufacture have remained conservative: neither potter's wheel, nor glaze or kilns were adopted from the whites.

Today we find it hard to imagine that by 1900 this exquisite art form had almost vanished from the Pueblos. At that time potters had almost ceased to supply their own needs, but were producing more and more for the unsophisticated souvenir market of the tourist industry, where a cheap candlestick was easier to sell than an expensive, well-made bowl with a traditional motif. Working as assistants on archeological digs, Pueblo people came across ceramics produced by their ancestors, and their growing interest in the old techniques found support among museums and serious collectors. Potters could now sell high quality products at a fair price, and had the opportunity to exhibit their work and make contact with wealthy patrons. The revival of the ancient art of the potter was therefore also a multi-cultural movement. Today, pottery is a highly specialized craft which is often handed down in the family from one generation to the next and which assists in feeding the family.

Potter from Acoma, New Mexico, 1959.

Since the arrival of the transcontinental railroad in Santa Fe in 1880, new markets for the Pueblo women's traditional wares sprung up at railroad stations. However, the railroads brought not only customers, but also cheap industrial products that competed with the utilitarian pots of the villages. Today's ceramics are produced almost exclusively for sale to tourists and collectors. Not all are as valuable as a pot made by the famous potter María Martínez (1887–1980) from San Ildefonso, which was sold at auction for $250,000 in 1990.

# A people with vision – the Hopi of the three mesas

In northeastern Arizona, three mesas stretch out from the Colorado Plateau into the desert, like three splayed fingers of one hand. On the flattened summit of these table mountains (*mesa* means "table" in Spanish) the Hopi built their villages. They originally settled in the area of the present-day city of Flagstaff, and along the Little Colorado River close to their fields. In the mid-13th century they moved to the table mountains, although the fields and springs still lie at the foot of the mesas. Since then, the Hopi have had to carry every drop of water, cob of corn, and squash up the steep, dusty paths. Yet this seemed a price worth paying for their elevated residences which gave them a good view across the landscape. Raids by Apache, Navajo,

and Ute were easier to fend off from the almost inaccessible mesas and, until the 20th century, even Europeans made few attempts to penetrate the closed world of the Hopi.

The Hopi adopted animal husbandry from the Europeans, keeping burros and sheep in particular. They supplemented their traditional cultivation of corn, beans, and squash by growing peach and apricot trees. Other than that, indigenous and European ways of life seem barely to have affected each other. Awatovi, the only Christian Hopi village, stands on a fourth table mountain, Antelope Mesa, and was devastated by other Hopis from Oraibi in 1700. The close links between Awatovi and the Franciscan missionaries had been a thorn in the flesh of the people of

View of the Hopi village of Walpi, on First Mesa, Arizona, 1879. Photograph: Jack Hillers. National Anthropological Archives, Smithsonian Institution, Washington, DC.

Traditionally, Hopi villages are economically and politically independent communities. On top of each mesa, three villages in the past formed a greater unit consisting of principal village, secondary village, and guard village. Hopi villages are fragile social structures. During droughts lasting several years, individual groups, clans, or factions split away – a form of social crisis management in times of shortage and a means of survival. Internal political tensions would also frequently be resolved in this way.

Oraibi. This is not the only episode to demonstrate that the Hopi's reputation as peace-loving people does not necessarily accord with the facts. Even the name they use to describe themselves, Hopisinom, does not mean – as is often claimed – "the small people of peace" but merely "well mannered people." Until the 20th century, government officials and missionaries referred to the Hopi as Moqui. Although this is based on a genuine ancient name, the Americans took it for a Spanish word and pronounced it moki instead of the correct *mokwi*. But *moki* means "dead" in Hopi, and thus the name was considered offensive and, with the support of anthropologist Jesse Walter Fewkes, the Hopi succeeded in making the government understand that they would prefer to be called "the well-mannered people" rather than be known as "the dead."

The traditional economy, religion, and social structures of the Hopi are closely interwoven. Religion penetrates every aspect of life and holds it together. It also ensures that the experiences gained over centuries of irrigation agriculture are remembered throughout the annual cycle. This has enabled the Hopi to survive independently as irrigation farmers in a hostile semidesert landscape, surrounded by enemies.

An important part is played by village ceremonies, to which the Hopi dedicate a great deal of time. A fixed ritual calendar determines when and which ceremonies must be performed, and through individual interpretation each mesa has developed its own characteristics. The purpose of the ceremonies is to bring about exchanges between the people and the deities in order to secure adequate rainfall. The Hopi's various ceremonial associations are responsible for staging these ceremonies, and accept new members only after a comprehensive initiation into their special rites, prayers, and dances. Such associations are linked to particular clans that control them, but are also open to others. The links between clans and associations can differ from village to village; for example, the Horn society in Mishongnovi is controlled by the Patki clan, whereas in Walpi it is controlled by the Bear and Reed clans.

The clans are not equally important, and their relative positions are derived from Hopi mythology. The god Maasaw, who in fact owns the land that he has only loaned to the Hopi for their use, gave the clans the task of traveling through all four quarters of the world before they were permitted to settle in their future homeland. Those clans who were the first to arrive at their present settlement locations are regarded as village founders and therefore have a preferential status in the community. On the Third Mesa, it was the Bear clan who founded Oraibi. As the other clans arrived, they had to prove to the Bear clan that the ceremonies they had brought with them were effective. Thus the Badger clan contributed the Powamu ceremony that ensures plant growth in the spring. Important ceremonies are increasingly becoming restricted to weekends – because many Hopis are employed outside the villages and can return only at weekends.

Political life was also inseparably bound to religion. Pueblo societies as a whole are occasionally described as theocracies. The priests, who were the leading officers in the secret societies and inherited their positions, had the greatest authority within the villages. Yet their already limited power ended at the boundaries of the village. This independence of people and villages was one of the reasons why it was so difficult for an elected tribal government to find wide acceptance among the Hopi.

# Dreamers, warriors, ferrymen – the Mohave

The Mohave, the largest group among the Yuman-speaking peoples, live along the lower Colorado River in the states of Nevada, California, and Arizona. Their ancestors moved there 850 years ago. During the Californian gold rush of about 1850, their land became a passageway for tens of thousands of Anglo-Americans and Mexicans. The Mohave were thus able to establish a new, albeit risky, source of income by offering their services to ferry people across the Colorado River, made treacherous by rocks, drifting sandbanks, and twice-yearly floods.

The indigenous traditional culture and economy, based completely on life along the river, were rapidly relegated to history. Formerly their cornfields were flooded and fertilized in the spring, and men and women worked together to sow the fields with simple tools. When the harvest had been disappointing, the Mohave could rely on fishing, hunting, and gathering food. They were one of the few groups in the Southwest to resort to fishing. They erected their settlements just above the high-water level and near their fields, although in summer the extreme heat forced them to sleep under awnings that were open on all four sides. In the Southwest these are now known as ramadas. Individuals had few material possessions, and whatever they owned joined them on their funeral pyre. Cremation was the only way to ensure that the prayers and wishes uttered during a funeral ceremony would accompany the departed soul to the realm of the dead. The soul remained in the vicinity of the grave for four days, after which it existed contentedly in the land of the dead, having to suffer neither hunger nor sickness until it died as well, was burned, and ceased to exist. The Mohave did not believe in eternal life. The names of those who were dead were not to be spoken, and the worst of all possible insults was to slowly utter the names of a person's dead relatives in his or her presence.

Personal religious experience was more important to the Mohave than were possessions. In the mythical past, Mastamho, whom some Mohave regard as the son of the creator god Matavile, completed the creation of the world and taught man how to grow corn, how to wage war, and how to dream. The Mohave had no public ceremonies – they dreamed. The Mohave dreamed their first important dream, the "good dream" that would determine the course of their lives, while still in their mother's womb. They forgot it, although its return was expected during puberty. Their religion taught the Mohave that there was almost nothing to be learnt in life, that there was nothing one should acquire or practice. An individual's path as a healer, warrior, maize grower, or fisher on the Colorado River would be revealed in dreams through powerful spirit beings who imparted all the knowledge required to survive.

Balduin Möllhausen, *Mohave Playing the Hoop Game*, watercolor, 1853. Ethnologisches Museum, Staatliche Museen zu Berlin – Preussischer Kulturbesitz, Berlin, Germany.

The Mohave's winter houses were semisubterranean structures with clay-daubed, wattle walls and a straw roof covered with a thick layer of sand and soil. The awning in front of the entrance was a much-frequented space in summer. In the area in front of the house, where the men are playing the hoop game, is a corn granary with clay pots resting against its walls.

Opposite page:

Mohave couple, Arizona, c. 1890. Photograph: Henry Buehman. John H. Burkhalter III Collection.

As with many other peoples, the Mohave intensely disliked being photographed. They were afraid that it would cause their souls to remain in this world after death, while their physical body and possessions were cremated. The extensive nudity of the Mohave had already become a thing of the past by the late 19th century. However, tattooed chins remained, because a Mohave without tattoos would be unable to enter the land of the dead.

Balduin Möllhausen, *Mohave Indians*, watercolor, 1853. Stiftung Preussische Schlösser und Gärten, Berlin-Brandenburg, Germany.

The winters in Mohave country are mild and the summers extremely hot. Their scanty attire was a reflection of this climate. Women wore short skirts made of bark or cotton cloth, and the men long breechclouts. By contrast, facial and body paintings and tattoos were lavish. The man carries a bow and a pestle-shaped club; the latter was held close to the thick end, which was thrust upward against the chin or face of an opponent.

Mohave society, like that of all Yuman tribes, was centralized and politically organized around the office of a chief who had a great deal of authority. Villages sent representatives to a council subordinate to the chief. The strategic position of the Yuman groups as middlemen between the Californian coast and the interior of the Southwest gave them temporary economic advantages, but also caused considerable tensions, war, and distress in the region.

The Mohave's frequent wars, particularly against the Pima and allied Yuman peoples, were rarely waged for economic reasons. The men whose dreams, especially of falcons, had enabled them to become part of an exclusive warrior class (*kwanami*), were interested only in satisfying social needs; they sought to confirm the superiority of the Mohave as a people and of the warriors within their own society. In addition to the raids and revenge attacks common all over the Southwest, formal and bloody battles were fought between opposing groups which went on without interruption for up to two days and could end with the complete annihilation of the enemy. Scalping was a task reserved for a religious specialist known as "enemy-dreamer" who was also entrusted with curing those who had fallen ill through contact with the enemy.

Today the Mohave live together with a few Hopis, Navajos, and Chemehuevis on the Colorado River and Fort Mohave reservations established between 1865 and 1870. Corn cultivation on the alluvial land along the Colorado River has given way to modern agriculture; cotton, animal feed, and melons are now the main crops. Every year, the river attracts large numbers of vacationers, enabling the people who live on the reservation to make a living from the tourist industry. Thus the Mohave ferrymen have preserved their role as mediators between the land and the strangers, and even the dreams are still a part of their lives.

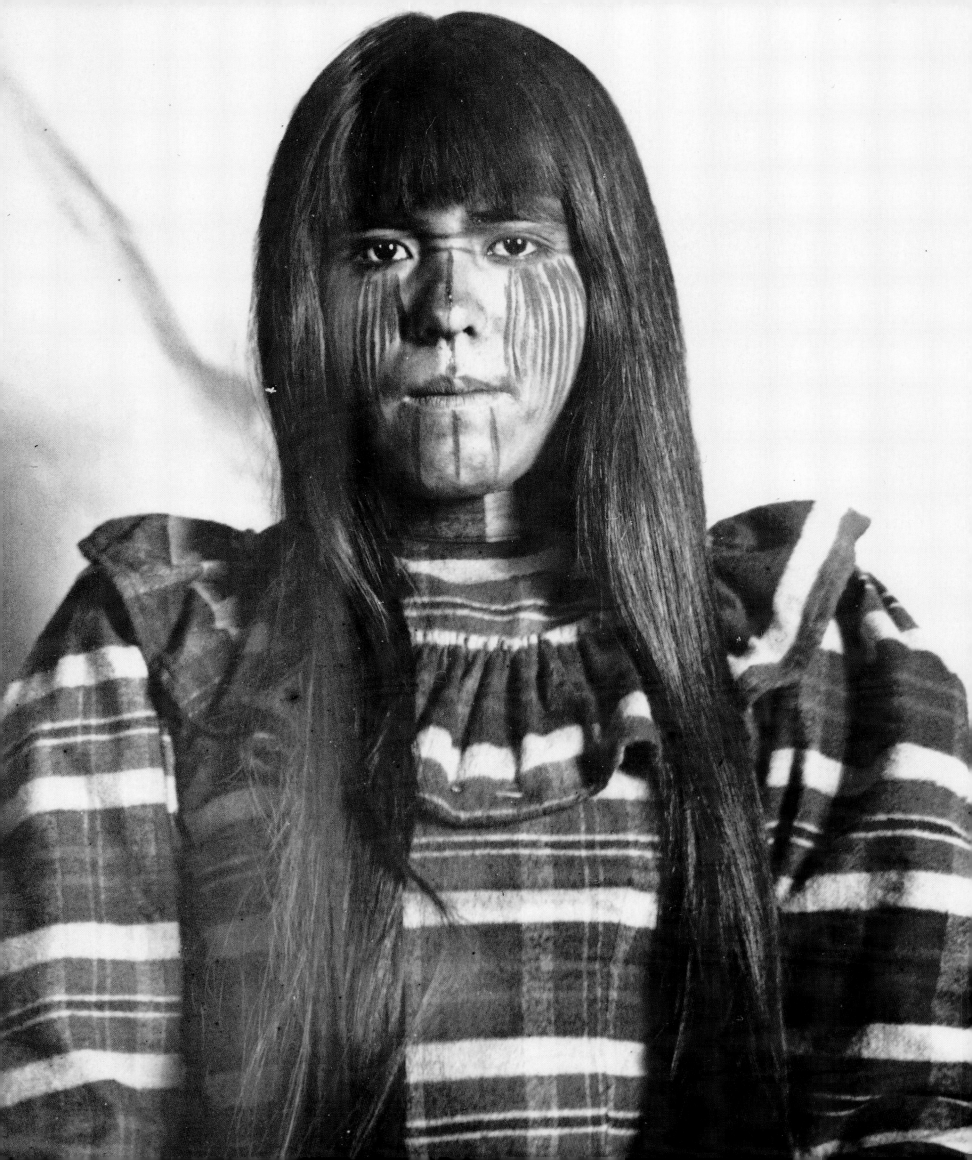

# River people and desert people – the Pima and Papago

Papago women with pots in carrying nets, Arizona, c. 1900. Arizona Historical Society, Tucson, AZ.

The pots of the Papago were simply decorated and never attracted as much attention among collectors as did the ceramics of the Pueblo peoples. The Papago did, however, sell some pots to whites, mainly because the porosity of the vessels helped to keep their contents cool. Evaporation of the water filtering to the outer surface cooled the pot and its contents to 15 to 25° F below the ambient temperature. The women carried their pots in nets supported by four connected wooden poles.

Opposite page:

Lieta, a Pima woman with face painting, Arizona, 1902. Photograph: Frank Russell. National Anthropological Archives, Smithsonian Institution, Washington, DC.

Not unlike their traditional enemies, the Mohave, the Pima originally wore little clothing and valued well-groomed hair as well as face and body decoration. Toward the end of the 19th century, the men were forced to cut off their splendid dreadlocks because the Indian agent threatened to withhold some carts that they had been promised. Women were permitted to keep their long hair because they needed a long fringe to protect them from the glare of the sun, and only cut it off as a sign of mourning when a death occurred.

Nobody knows when they migrated to their settlements in southern Arizona. They may be descendants of the Hohokam canal builders, or may equally have been their enemies and the cause of their disappearance. The Spanish colonists who arrived in their land in the late 17th century called them the Pimas Altas (Upper Pima) to distinguish them from the Lower Pima in southern Sonora. Many of the small groups of Pima-speakers along the Gila River and in the Sonoran Desert became the victims of history, were driven away by Apache raiders, died of diseases brought by the Europeans, or merged with other groups. Today's Pima and Papago, their descendants, are scattered among the Gila River, Salt River, Ak Chin, Papago, San Xavier, and Gila Bend reservations and the various cities of the Southwest.

The tribes were probably named by the Spanish. "Pima" is based on a word from this language group meaning "nothing," and "Papago" meaning "bean." In their own language the Pima call themselves "river people" (Akimel O'odham), and thereby distinguish themselves from the Papago, the "desert people" (Tohono O'odham). The natural environment's influence on the way of life of these two peoples could not have been more aptly described.

The Pimería Alta, the area of the Upper Pima, is one of the hottest and driest areas of North America. A huge desert area, which in some years receives less than one tenth of an inch of rainfall, stretches westward and southward from the present city of Phoenix. When the water comes it is accompanied by roaring storms that form over the Gulf of Mexico in July/August and December/January. The desert soil, which has been baked to a hard crust, cannot hold so much rainfall in such a short time, and the precious water runs in torrents through the arid arroyos. These are the conditions under which both the Pima and the Papago became masters of water supply and distribution.

The Sand Papago (Hia C'ed O'odham) of the western Pimería Alta, the hottest part of the area, were hunter-gatherers who roamed the land in small groups and used their camps only for short periods. They traded salt and shells for pottery and agricultural products with the Yuman tribes on the lower Colorado River. The Papago of the central Pimería Alta, on the other hand, made use of the flash floods for cultivating the soil. Finally, the Pima along the Gila River lived in large permanent settlements and maintained an extensive irrigation system. They supplemented corn, beans, and squash with the winter wheat introduced by the Spanish, and managed to obtain two harvests per year in the desert.

In the 18th century, wealthy Pima villages were a favorite target for Apache raids. In defense, the various Pima villages began to join forces, and the position of chief became hereditary and grew in importance. The Pima also introduced general military service for men, and organized punitive raids based on the Spanish military model. To the American army they sold wheat and corn.

Following the military pacification of the Southwest, the situation became more relaxed; social cohesion declined, and large numbers of white farmers moved into the region.

Pima basket tray, Arizona, c. 1900. Museum für Völkerkunde, Vienna, Austria.

Pima women combined a limited number of geometric forms to create numerous patterns, many of which were based on the designs painted on ancient Hohokam pots. The rigid, coiled basketry trays and bowls were used to prepare food. Inverted, they could be used as percussion instruments ("basket drums").

In order to direct the groundwater to their fields, the whites dug deep canals, but these were unable to withstand the inevitable heavy floods of the rainy season, and within a few years the floods had eaten deep into the desert floor. Precious agricultural land along the Santa Cruz River was swept away, and white farmers along the Gila River simply diverted the water away from their Pima neighbors.

The situation deteriorated rapidly during the 20th century, despite several government-funded irrigation projects like the San Carlos Project with its monstrous Coolidge Dam on the Gila River. Misguided planning, bureaucracy, and indifference on the part of the authorities conspired to turn a formerly independent community of desert farmers into impoverished itinerant laborers and welfare recipients.

As early as 1973, the governor of the Gila Reservation, Alexander Lewis Sr., no longer believed in the possibility of a return to an agriculturally based way of life: "In the past the O'odhams were able to live satisfactorily on the crops they harvested from their land. Today this is not possible, for no longer can we work the land as in the past. For this reason the O'odhams recognized the need for education; the need to learn new skills; the need for employment opportunities in well-paid jobs. All of this will change our way of life, how we live, and how we will live in the future."

In point of fact, by 1980 only 8.8 percent of the working population of the Gila River was employed in farming. Everyone else worked for the tribal administration or in the local manufacturing and tourist industries.

Of all the Pima-speaking groups, those whose traditional culture we know most about are the Papago, thanks to research conducted in the 1930s by anthropologist Ruth Underhill. Papago religious and social life was conducted within the village community, which moved to the "spring village" in winter and to the "field village" situated near

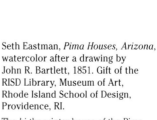

Seth Eastman, *Pima Houses, Arizona*, watercolor after a drawing by John R. Bartlett, 1851. Gift of the RISD Library, Museum of Art, Rhode Island School of Design, Providence, RI.

The *ki*, the winter house of the Pima and Papago, was erected over a shallow pit. The domed roof structure was covered with straw, grass, and shrubs. Its top was usually daubed with mud and sand was poured around the outer walls. A roofless windbreak stands between the houses and protects a cooking area. In front of it, a man is working on a horizontal loom; like the Hohokam (and the Anasazi), the Pima grew cotton long before the arrival of the Europeans.

their fields in summer. Each village had a "smoke house" or "rain house," where the men would assemble at night for councils. Public ceremonies – the corn-harvest ritual, the sacred deer hunt, the midsummer Wíígida ceremony which "kept the world going" – were conducted in the village plaza. Various purification rituals for those who had ritually defiled themselves through war, salt expeditions, and eagle hunting were also held in public.

The rainmaking ceremony in July was particularly important as it "brought down the clouds." Part of this ritual was the making and ample enjoyment of a weak alcoholic beverage made from the fruits of the giant cactus. The satiation of the parched soil by rain was symbolized by the satiation of the body by the "cactus wine." Every step in the preparation of the drink was accompanied by chants and speeches about rain and growth. The song "Be strong!", for example, is addressed to the as-yet-unfermented cactus syrup. "Let us get well drunk! Hither bring the wind and its cloudiness!"

The Papago possessed a rich treasury of myths which, according to tradition, could only be related in winter, when all "biting creatures" like snakes and ants had gone into hibernation. The best time for storytelling was during the four days of the winter solstice, "when the sun stands still." A good storyteller was presented with consecrated cornmeal and requested to relate the entire body of myths, in which he was well versed, during the four nights. During this period, the storyteller practiced abstention,

renouncing meat, fat, and salt. His audience would listen all through the night, sitting upright and in deep silence. Dozing or falling asleep were prohibited and would lead to the storyteller suspending his performance on the spot.

Thus the Papago would hear their traditions each winter, but each time they heard a new version, colored by a different personality. One of these stories is the myth about the origin of the world: Earth Maker and Yellow Buzzard were the first beings and existed in darkness. Earth Maker made the world out of a little bit of dirt and sweat which he scraped off his skin. The flat earth collided with the sky with a thunder and this created I'itoi, the Papago's culture hero. "He brought the people up like children," but in the end he became hostile and they killed him. As he was very powerful, he came back to life and invented war. He decided to destroy the people he had made and went below the earth to fetch the Papago in order that they should help him. While they fought, I'itoi made up chants for everything, for war, for the hunt, and for farming. The Papago say that I'itoi is now a little old man who lives in seclusion in a mountain cave.

Until 1960, about 60 per cent of Pima and Papago spoke only their ancient language. The children were taught in English, and with the ascendancy of a new generation the old language began to die out. By 1990, only 37 per cent of the O'odham could still speak their old language, and only one in 100 was unable to communicate in English.

Opposite page, right:

Papago (Tohono O'odham) calendar stick from Sil Nakya. Arizona State Museum, Tucson, AZ.

Opposite page, left:

Joseph Head explaining the contents of a calendar stick to Henry Soalikee, 1921. Photograph: Edward H. Davis. National Museum of the American Indian, New York, NY.

The calendar sticks of the Pima and Papago were personal mnemonic devices that marked the passing of time. Years were represented by abstract symbols that stood for the year's most notable event. These symbols were separated by grooves. The owners of calendar sticks had to memorize the meaning of the symbols and therefore were able to tell their inquisitive audiences about the history of decades gone by. The stick shown here in part begins in 1841 and ends in 1939.

Modern reconstruction of a rectangular Papago house, Arizona, 1978.

When pressure from the Bureau of Indian Affairs caused the Papago to give up their *kis*, they built houses with walls made of clay-covered dried cactus stems. The awning was supported by forked posts and seamlessly blended into the roof of the house. Modern versions have walls made of alternating layers of timber boards and adobe (air-dried clay).

Tarahumara house with thatched roof and round granaries, Chihuahua, c. 1895. Photograph: Carl Lumholtz. American Museum of Natural History, New York, NY.

The widely scattered compounds of the Tarahumara consist to this day of one house and various outbuildings. The thatched winter houses without side walls that were still to be seen 100 years ago have given way to log cabins or stone houses. Also increasingly rare are the wooden plank houses with gable walls made of loose boards. The storage buildings were used to keep clothes as well as corn and beans.

# Brewers of beer and protectors of God – the Tarahumara

The Tarahumara, who call themselves Rarámuri, have probably been growing corn and living in the western part of the Mexican state of Chihuahua for around 2,000 years. Between 1610 and their expulsion from Mexico in 1767, Spanish Jesuits tried to convert them to Christianity and founded about 50 missions, small settlements with churches at their center. Their attempt at developing an administration was only moderately successful because the authority of the Tarahumara *gobernadores* (Spanish for "governors") was very weak without the direct support of the padres. Under the Franciscans, who replaced the Jesuits, missionary zeal decreased noticeably and, by the 19th century, it had almost disappeared entirely. In the 17th and 18th centuries, several bloody rebellions against foreign rule and revenge attacks by the Spanish military forced many Tarahumara to retreat to the mountainous country in the southwest that was not claimed by Spanish-speaking farmers and ranchers.

Here in the Sierra Madre, Mexico's "mother" mountain range, the Tarahumara have been living in tune with their own rhythms – not without external influences, but unimpressed by cultural contact and historical developments. The Norwegian ethnographer Carl Lumholtz once asked an elderly Tarahumara who a few years earlier had been presented as a "real cave dweller" at the 1893 World's Fair, how he had liked Chicago. The old man thought about the skyscrapers and street canyons in the big city and responded mildly: "It looks very much like here." In fact, some Tarahumara still use the caves in the steep cliffs of their rugged homeland in addition to their rectangular, low-rise stone houses, and in prehistoric times, large groups of families would have lived in the caves.

The Tarahumara have been growing corn, beans, and squash for an equally long period and, apart from the plow, which they adopted from the Spanish in the 17th century together with cattle and sheep husbandry, their farming methods have hardly changed. Fish from the rivers remain a popular supplementary source of food and are caught with traps and spears, but mostly with poison that anesthetizes the fish. Cultivated land belongs to individual family members, who pass it on to their sons or daughters when they die. Whether a married couple with children lives alone or with relatives of the wife or husband depends entirely on individual circumstances.

Nearly all of life takes place on the rancho, the family farm, which tends to be isolated and some miles away from the nearest family farm. The Tarahumara, who from childhood onward shepherd their beasts alone, are used to managing without the assistance and tutelage of others. *Muje machí* ("You know best") is a frequent figure of speech. However, whenever they do not know best, when disputes have to be settled, or when they wish to take part in religious festivals and racing events, they walk to the village.

For some decades now, the Tarahumara have also migrated to the cities in search of work. They sell baskets, belts, woolen blankets, and homemade musical instruments. Yet none of them becomes rich by this trade, and the ownership of money does not carry prestige in the eyes of other Rarámuri. Mexican policymakers, who see the integration of the Indian population into the dominant society as a goal to be achieved on their country's way to full First World status, regard this slow pace of life as a tiresome curtailment of progress. On the other hand, government agencies have not even been able to reduce the extremely high rates of infant mortality and illiteracy. Yet the government will continue to have little success as long as integration measures are linked to the declared goal of destroying the sovereign structure of the indigenous communities.

At least the Mexican constitution was amended in the early 1990s in order to protect the multicultural character of the republic and to enshrine the government's duty to protect and support indigenous cultures. It remains to be seen how long it will take before constitutional rights are realized in the Sierra Tarahumara, which is still regarded by many Mexicans as a borderland between civilization and wilderness.

As in the days of the Spanish missions, it is difficult today to find among the Tarahumara anyone willing to

**The Tarahumara women's running game, Chihuahua, c. 1975.**

The Tarahumara are known throughout Mexico for their stamina as runners, and they are in constant training. Races can last up to two days, with the men running cross-country propelling a wooden ball with their toes. They wear rattle-belts to keep them awake and at night the running track is illuminated by lanterns. Instead of a ball, the women use rings made of yucca which they scoop up using sticks with a slight bend at one end, then throw the ring forward.

take on a formal communal administrative office, as provided by Spanish legal tradition. From the point of view of the Tarahumara, the most important duty of a *gobernador*, a position comparable to that of mayor, lies in giving a sermon on Sundays extolling the community's moral values, particularly peaceful behavior. Carl Lumholtz made a note of the basic tenet of these speeches: "Drink quietly, talk quietly, sing quietly."

The Tarahumara regard themselves as Catholics, and they have merged their traditional indigenous religion with Catholicism and in so doing have formed a new and quite autonomous faith. God and the devil are brothers who created the universe consisting of seven levels. God and his wife María (who is also taken to be the moon and called "mother") live at the top, the devil at the bottom. Humans live at the center, on the surface of the earth. These are divided into Rarámuri, which term the Tarahumara primarily use to refer to themselves but also to other Indians, and Chabóchi, meaning all non-Indian people.

The father of the Rarámuri is God, and the father of the Chabóchi is the devil. His realm is not a place of hellish torment, but rather a mirror image of the world of God, and paradise for the Chabóchi. The devil does not harm the Chabóchi, but he is the enemy of the

Rarámuri and without the protection of God, they would be at his mercy. They secure the assistance of God in three ways: by dancing, making food sacrifices, and leading their lives in accordance with His commandments.

The Tarahumara of Basíhuare believe that God and his wife undergo a period of weakness each year during Holy Week, when they are vulnerable to attacks by the devil. The Easter festival serves to give strength to God and

Lumber truck, wooden toy made by the Tarahumara, Rituchi, Chihuahua, 1977. Arizona State Museum, Tucson, AZ.

Today, a railroad runs across the land of the Tarahumara, bringing tourists to the Barranca del Cobre, a gorge even more monumental than the Grand Canyon. A greater danger to traditional ways of life than that posed by the travelers, who now provide a market for craft souvenirs, is that presented by the loggers whose heavy trucks herald the start of industrial exploitation and the destruction of homelands through the uncontrolled felling of trees.

Plowing a cornfield in Rejogochi, Chihuahua, 1981.

Up to 90 percent of the diet of the Tarahumara consists of corn, added to which is a substantial consumption of corn beer. Corn is the main crop of their relatively small and frequently scattered fields, which are worked with wooden plows pulled by oxen. As several species of large game animals have become extinct in the Sierra Madre, hunting has lost its importance. Only birds and small game still supplement the diet.

his wife, until they are strong again and able once more to protect themselves. The president of Mexico is regarded by the Tarahumara as a superhuman being and is highly venerated as Papa President: "He is always the same man, and merely changes his name."

In addition to Holy Week and Christmas the Tarahumara celebrate many other religious festivals during the course of the year, particularly the corn beer festivals (*Tesgüinadas* in Spanish), to which families invite neighbors, relatives, and friends. On average a single family will take part in 20 to 50 *Tesgüinadas*, often lasting several days. During each one of these events, 20 adults will between them consume at least 200 to 400 quarts of freshly made corn beer, which is about 3 percent proof and is good for only a few hours.

This absolute devotion to intoxication appalled the missionaries. In the late 17th century, a horrified Jesuit Father Johannes Maria Ratkay wrote: "While singing ribald songs they drink so much wine [meaning corn beer], that they lie around like dead people. Out of their minds, some of them abandon themselves to carnal desires ... And when they have thrown their arms up, hopped about, and their blood is sufficiently hot, they challenge each other to fight ... Later, old women dance in a circle, grasp one another's hair and bewail their sons and relatives who have either been killed or wounded. This brings the festivities to an end. Yet this does not cause lasting grief or even improvement, quite the contrary, they are back in a clinch within a very short space of time."

One further aspect of the *Tesgüinadas* was not discerned by the cleric. Before the drinking begins, the guests work for the host, plowing, building houses, and assisting in the healer's ceremonies. The network of drinking parties binds families together, enables men and women to find marriage partners, and allows people to see distant neighbors with whom they would otherwise have very little contact. The Tarahumara explained to Lumholtz: "We pray by dancing and the gourd."

Tarahumara performing the Matachine Christmas dance, Chihuahua, 1975.

With the Matachine dances, held at Christmas and on the occasion of other church festivals, the Tarahumara ask God for a long life, healthy children, and economic well-being. They are prepared by one or several members of the community, who also have to arrange and pay for the subsequent fiesta. The dances that accompany violins and rattles are European in origin and once celebrated the victory over the heathen in remembrance of the recapture of Spain from the Moors and the triumph of the Spanish over the Aztecs – but little of this is now apparent.

# From herdsmen to marines – the Navajo

Navajos accompanied by their Indian agent on a visit to Washington, 1874. Photograph: C. M. Bell. National Anthropological Archives, Smithsonian Institution, Washington, DC.

When conditions in Fort Sumner became unbearable for the Navajo and Congress cut the annual budget from 1 million to $100,000, a delegation was sent to Washington with the camp administration's support with the aim of returning the Navajos to their homeland. A subsequent visit in 1874 was concerned with the clarification of land rights on the new reservation. Seated at the center of the group are Juanita and her husband Manuelito, one of the Navajo's most celebrated leaders.

With more than 220,000 members, the Navajo have now the largest residential population of any Native American nation in North America. Shortly before the arrival of the Europeans, their ancestors, hunter-gatherers from the icy subarctic forests of Canada, migrated on foot to the hot Southwest where, within the relatively short period of about three centuries, they learned to ride horses and became sheep-farmers. They were feared raiders, but their own women and children were often enough abducted, enslaved, and killed by their enemies. They learned to grow corn, and what they did not produce themselves they acquired through trade with their Pueblo neighbors and with the Spanish.

When the Americans took over the Southwest from the Mexicans, violence erupted between the Navajo and the army. As a punishment Washington decided that the scattered Navajo should be herded together like cattle and reeducated in Fort Sumner (Bosque Redondo), southeast of Santa Fe. While the army captured the Navajo, armed bands of whites and Mexicans marauded through their land, abducting women and children into domestic slavery, and driving family groups into the arms of the military. On the 300-mile "Long Walk" of three convoys of captives many Navajo died of hunger, cold, or the brutality of the soldiers, who even stole the Navajo's warm blankets to sell them.

General Carlton, who led the exercise with an iron hand, was surprised that there were at least twice as many Navajo than the estimated 5,000. Eventually, more than 9,000 people ended up in the concentration camp of Fort Sumner, originally intended for 500 Mescalero Apache prisoners. In the overcrowded camp, nothing came of the proclaimed

Hogans on the Navajo Reservation, Arizona, c. 1900.

According to myth, the first hogan, the traditional dwelling of the Navajo, was built by First Man after the arrival of the people in the current, fifth world. The typical 19th-century hogan consisted of a conical structure covered with a layer of branches and slender tree trunks. This was followed by the octagonal hogan with side walls made of tree trunks and an earth-covered roof. The octagonal form is still found today, although it is made of different materials and frequently merely serves as an outbuilding in a compound.

reeducation program. Drought, plagues of locusts, bad planning, and poor soil contributed to disastrous harvests year after year, and imprinted in the Navajo's historical consciousness an enduring sense of horror at the "civilization" supposedly enjoyed by the American farmer.

Only when the dictatorial Carlton, who had imposed martial law on the territory of New Mexico and gagged his critics, was replaced did the situation change. In 1868, after four years of camp imprisonment, the surviving 10,000 Navajo were allocated a reservation in their homeland, and the reservation has been expanded several times since then. It encloses the reservation of the Hopi, who have been embroiled in a land rights dispute with the Navajo for decades. Anyone traveling through the seemingly endless landscape, with scarcely a settlement or farm to divert the eye, would find it difficult to believe that the reservation is overpopulated.

The Navajo Reservation is still an area with one of the highest unemployment rates in the whole of the United States; per-capita incomes are very low, as is the general standard of living. In the 1930s, the American government ordered a drastic reduction in the number of sheep, which had been increasing in parallel with the Navajo population, while continuous drought was having a devastating effect on the growth of vegetation, meager at the best of times. Although this measure put a stop to soil

erosion, it destroyed the economic basis of the Navajo. Since then many Navajos have sought work in towns like Gallup, Farmington, or Tuba City on the edges of the reservation, or with local coal, gas, and uranium companies licensed by the tribe. Others still have migrated to the distant cities of Albuquerque and Los Angeles in the search of employment.

The traditional Navajo way of life is centered on sheep herding. The sheep are usually tended by children who learn at an early age that a good shepherd needs to be vigilant – and to know the correct song: "Early in the morning we take the sheep out of the corral. I sing a song and open the gate. When the sheep are half out, my song is half finished. When they are all out, I stop my song. They eat grass all day. They mustn't eat loco weed or they go crazy [loco in Spanish] and run all around. If they eat sagebrush I mustn't give them water or they will get blown out. ... When you are herding there are songs for the protection of the sheep and to make them increase."

Every sheep in the flock tended by this young man belongs to a member of the family, although people may not do as they like with their livestock. From a certain age onward, children are regularly given gifts of a sheep, but they are also expected to use their flock to contribute wool, milk, and lambs to the family. When a man marries, he moves in with his wife's family, but leaves the majority of

his sheep with his mother's flock for several years until the marriage has proved to be enduring. The land on which the sheep graze belongs to the family in the sense of an inherited right of use. Nobody can sell the land or take it away from the family in any other way.

The strong position of women – through whom descent and rights of ownership are inherited – was weakened a little by the influence of the American legal system, yet within Navajo society this has never been seriously challenged. The division of labor between the genders is adapted to suit the vagaries of animal husbandry, and tends to be flexible rather than rigid. Women run the households, slaughter sheep, look after young children, and weave rugs – for many families the latter was the sole reliable source of income for a long time. Men perform the heavy tasks on the fields, maintain buildings and vehicles, tend the horses and cattle and are in charge of all external contacts, such as those with white traders, authorities, and so on, although it is not unusual to find Navajo couples where the men defer to the women, who take the initiative.

Over and above the family, each Navajo is born into one of about 60 clans to which their mother also belongs; but the father's clan is likewise important as an extension of the social network. Clan members are addressed and referred to in the same terms as family members and marriages within the clan are not permitted.

Despite the cultural shocks suffered as a result of various attempts to "civilize" the Navajo, many facets of the ancient way of life have been preserved. Every new generation finds ways of combining both the traditional and the contemporary. In a sample family – call them the Atcitty, a name roughly equivalent in meaning and frequency to Smith in English – the children may attend college in Phoenix, the parents work for the Navajo Nation administration, and the grandparents live in a new housing development in a reservation village, selling

jewelry at the large flea markets of Window Rock or
Kayenta. Finally, great-grandfather who served with the
United States marines in the Pacific during World
War II, and great-grandmother who does not speak a word
of English, are the heads of the family and custodians of
tradition, and prefer to live in the remote mountains.
Their old house that was built with financial assistance
from the Bureau of Indian Affairs has no electricity or
running water, is 20 miles from the nearest supermarket,
but is close to the flock of sheep that they have never
given up.

Several times a year, the whole family meet at the great-
grandparents' home and help with the livestock. A sheep
may be slaughtered, and the visitors bring along huge stocks
of food and drink, as well as any friends who may be
available at the time to cook a hearty mutton stew. There
are animated discussions surrounding the rodeo being
staged on the occasion of a national holiday, cousin

Marcia's wedding plans, and the new supermarket in
Window Rock. These are conducted in a lively mix of
Navajo-English – a regional variant of English spoken
exclusively by the Navajo – and Navajo.

Nobody would think of painting the old house, which
has been stripped of color by the sandy, arid wind.
Yet the whole family will contribute from their meager
savings because a sister-in-law would like to study for
a degree in social work; they provide child-care for
one another or arrange a purifying, and by no means
cheap, Enemy Way ceremony for a son's return from
military service. This requires a "singer" who has undergone
many years of training to intone a cycle of chants
lasting right through the night to expel any stubborn
foreign spirits and remove any contamination caused
by the killing trade.

The Atcittys' everyday problems are as apparent as
those of any other American family. Nevertheless, the
Navajo are culturally distinguishable from the melting pot
of American society. Their language stubbornly stands its
ground alongside the dominant English language. Because
the population rate continues to rise, the decrease in the
proportion of Navajo-speakers (today it is about 50 per
cent of all Navajos under 18 years of age) still signifies an
increase in absolute terms, even if only a third of children
learn Navajo as their first language.

Even in the 21st century, the Navajo seek and find
solutions to problems within the framework of their
own culture, because the culture has proven to be
adaptable. This may explain why the flexible Navajo are
now regarded as one of the most traditional and least
acculturated indigenous groups in North America.

Although their past as Subarctic hunters dates back more than 500 years, the Navajo have retained many of their hunting ancestors' ethical principles. The unnecessary slaughter of animals is regarded as immoral, and where it is unavoidable, the reasons are explained to the animal and it is asked for forgiveness. The deer hunt, for instance, had to be performed in a ceremonial manner and was linked to particular rituals, such as the Night Chant (Nightway).

# Holy people and healing images

Opposite page, below:

Navajo dry painting: "Whirling Logs" for the Nightway ceremony.

The Navajo have between 600 and 1,000 different motifs that may be used in their ceremonial dry paintings. Most of the paintings used in curing rituals depict several "Holy People" standing next to each other or grouped like rays around a center, or themselves standing in the center. The image is framed by an elongated guard figure and there is an opening toward the east to allow good to enter and bad to leave.

According to Navajo oral tradition, the Holy or Knowing People, Diyin Dine'é, had to cross four imperfect worlds before rising into the current, fifth world – only to discover that it was a flooded place of chaos, populated by monsters. Coyote had stolen the child of Water Monster, master of destructive floods. The child was returned and the waters subsided. Only then did the chaos clear, and the stars, the sun and moon, and animals and plants were created, and time was divided into day and night, and spring, summer, fall, and winter.

The two sons of Asdzáá Nádleehé (Changing Woman who embodies seasonal changes), Born For Water and Monster Slayer, took up the victorious fight against the monsters allied to Water Monster.

The first hogan was built after this victory. The holy people gave humans all the knowledge that they needed to survive, along with the way to achieve *hózhǫ́*, a state of universal harmony, beauty, and goodness. This balance can be undone by several factors, including contact with the spirits of the dead, particular animals such as coyotes, snakes, or bears, natural phenomena like lightning or tornadoes, or by exaggerated devotion by a person to a single thing, be it gambling, sex, or weaving blankets. The result is sickness, the healing of which is the goal of most of the complex and lengthy ceremonies that take place among the Navajo. Families organize ceremonies for ailing relatives, and religious specialists (*hataali*, "singers") lead them.

There are three different ritual patterns for healing rituals ("Chantways"): Lifeway, Evilway, and Holyway, the last of these being the most common. A Holyway ceremony is dominated by chant, accompanied by the singer's rattle. Anyone present may join in – if they have fully mastered the songs. The "singer" needs to know several hundred chants for a complete healing ritual lasting several days, a feat comparable to knowing by heart the score of one of Wagner's operas. The patient, or person being "sung over," has to behave with care and restraint towards the other participants because he or she is endowed with the powers of the Holy People during the ceremony and could therefore be of harm to others.

Other important elements of a Holyway ceremony are the unbinding ritual, by which a patient is released from negative powers, a purifying sweating ritual, and the offering of pieces of turquoise, cigarettes, and prayer sticks to the Holy People. Each of these elements is repeated altogether four times, four being for the Navajo a sacred and auspicious number.

After the sacrifice, the men are permitted to contribute to the making of a dry painting under the supervision of a "singer." It is made by sprinkling pigments derived from colored sandstone, charcoal, cornmeal, and pollen on the floor. The patient strips down to his or her underwear and sits on one of the figures of the sand painting while the "singer's" touch transfers the powers of the Holy People depicted to the patient.

The curative work of art, created through many hours of work, is destroyed by the "singer" at the end of the ceremony, the contaminated sand being removed and scattered north of the hogan, where it can do no harm to anyone.

The Navajo steadfastly resisted Christianization until well into the 20th century. However, since the 1970s, Mormon missionaries have become increasingly successful, although the Mormon practice of admitting young people into foster families and providing them with the education that impoverished Navajo families could never afford is often criticized by the young people themselves, who feel that they have thus been alienated from their homeland and language.

Since the enforced sheep stock reduction of the 1930s, which caused a deep existential insecurity among the Navajo, the number of adherents of the Peyote religion has grown rapidly. About half of the Navajo population now consider themselves adherents of this new religion, which came to them from the Plains. Even the Navajo generally stage their peyote ceremonies in tipis.

Talking God, Shooting God, and Fringed Mouth, New Mexico, c. 1905. Photograph: Simeon Schwemberger. National Anthropological Archives, Smithsonian Institution, Washington, DC.

The Nightway is one of the most important and common Holyway ceremonies. It can only take place after the first frost and before the first thunderstorm of spring, when the snakes are in hibernation and there are no lightning flashes in the sky. During the last of nine nights, the *yé'i* deities appear, whose leader is known as Talking God, or Maternal Grandfather of the Gods (*yé'i bichei*), which is why the Navajo increasingly refer to the Nightway as *yeibichai* when speaking in English. The ceremony is said to be particularly curative of all ailments of the head. The masks and costumes of the *yé'i* performers shown here do not match. Talking God wears Female God's costume, Shooting God wears Gray God's mask, and Fringed Mouth wears Female God's mask.

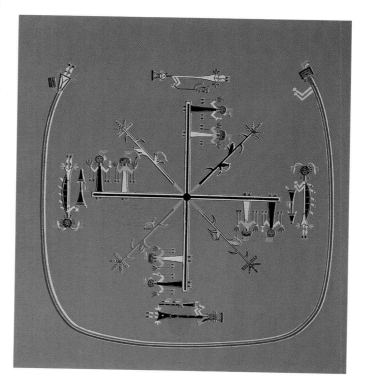

# Weaving and silversmithing

The Navajo's decorative woven blankets and splendid shining silverwork are universally renowned for their beauty and as an expression of cultural distinctiveness. Diverse accounts of the origins of weaving and silversmithing are contained in myths, historical testimonies, and oral traditions. While much remains unknown, the fact that the Navajo crafts of weaving and silversmithing, often described as ancient traditions, have only been practiced since the 17th and 19th centuries respectively, is indisputable.

Spider Woman is said to have taught the Navajo how to weave, and mothers pass on their craft to their daughters. Archeologists and ethnologists hold that the Pueblo peoples who fled to the Navajo for shelter following the

revolt of 1680 brought with them the art of weaving. The Navajo, who had already adopted sheep herding from the Spanish, linked one to the other and began to manufacture blankets, dresses, and belts made of wool on their wide vertical looms. They sold these products to the Spanish and also in neighboring Pueblos; in the mid-19th century, Navajo textiles were traded as far as the northern Plains.

By the late 19th century, the Navajo preferred to wear modern dresses, skirts and blouses made of gleaming velvet, jeans and cotton shirts, so that weaving for their own needs declined considerably. After a creative low period at the turn of the century, caused by commercialization, the

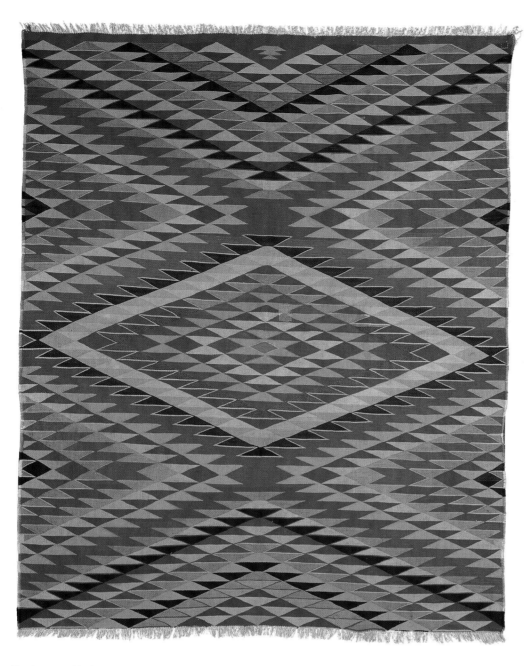

Navajo woven blanket, c. 1885. Museum für Völkerkunde, Vienna, Austria.

The introduction of synthetic dyes combined with the Navajo familiarity with Spanish-American examples of the Rio Grande weaving tradition, resulted in the dazzling designs of the late 1860s, a veritable explosion of color and jagged diamond patterns ("eyedazzler"), now interpreted as an artistic coming-to-terms with the trauma of the Navajo's deportation to Fort Sumner.

Zuni silversmith, New Mexico, c. 1990.

In the 20th century, the Hopi and Zuni adopted the Navajo's silversmithing craft and gradually developed their own style. In the beginning, a silversmith's equipment would have consisted of a stone and adobe hearth, sheepskin bellows, an iron anvil, a clay crucible, sandstone molds, a soldering pipe, hammers, files, and embossing hammers to stamp the patterns into the silver. Today modern soldering equipment and electric polishing and frosting tools are used.

influence of local traders, who introduced new patterns and materials, enabled the Navajo to develop an extremely fine craft tradition which has now expanded to encompass numerous varied regional styles.

The Navajo adopted blacksmithing from the Mexicans of the upper Rio Grande. The memory of the first Navajo blacksmith, Atsidi Sani ("Ancient Smith"), has remained alive in their oral tradition. He mostly made iron bridles for sale, but he also taught his sons how to work silver, a metal that quickly replaced the brass jewelry prevalent at the time. Knowledge of the techniques of this craft spread rapidly, especially in the southern Navajo territory.

A Navajo silversmith remembers: "When I first heard about some women over near Gallup making silver, I felt sort of silly. I thought that I was better than a woman because I could make silver jewelry and they couldn't. But when I heard this, I had to admit that women were just as good as I was. I think that it is all right if women make silver. They can earn good money that way."

The Navajo traded their silver jewelry with the Zuni and Hopi for the mother-of-pearl and turquoise which

they had begun to incorporate into their jewelry designs by 1880. They obtained silver by smelting Mexican pesos and working the metal in modest workshops, where many a silversmith ruined his eyesight in the dim kerosene light. Nowadays, silversmithing is taught at the Navajo Community College, and smiths use modern equipment and tools.

After 1910 tourism helped to spread the fame of Navajo jewelry to such an extent that white manufacturers began to copy Navajo designs and undercut the prices of native craftsmen. Even today, silver is unlikely to make a Navajo's fortune, since the souvenir and jewelry market in the Southwest is firmly in the hands of non-Indians, although buyers are beginning to demonstrate their growing trust in tribally owned jewelry outlets.

Unlike weaving, where the products are now sold almost exclusively to tourists, silver jewelry continues to be immensely popular amongst the Navajo themselves, whether young or old, and is still worn in accordance with the motto "the more the better." Silver, like a large flock of sheep, is a visible way of expressing a family's wealth and social standing.

*Wikiup* is the name given to the
domed or conical abodes of the
western and southern Apaches
(the northeastern groups preferred
the tipi), which provided space for
the immediate family and could be
erected in just under an hour. Camps
consisted of several such houses
belonging to related families. A
basket and a woven water bottle
sealed with resin – an important
item for nomadic populations in
an arid environment – lie next to
the campfire.

Apache women collecting firewood
rations, Arizona, c. 1885. National
Anthropological Archives,
Smithsonian Institution,
Washington, DC.

Western Apache women held a
prominent position within the family.
Women sent men on raiding parties
if their supplies were running low, or
to war if a relative's death had to be
avenged. During the long years of war
against the Americans, the women
joined the men in pursuit of the
enemy, reloaded guns in the heat of
battle, or took on difficult missions
between the fronts.

# Raiding and old wives' tales – the Apache

No North American poulation has been subject to such
a colorful array of modern old wives' tales and legends
as have the Apache. Novels, history books, and movies
either maligned or glorified them. In the early 20th
century, anthropologists spoke to elderly Apache who
reminisced on the way that life was lived in their youth.
These interviews present quite a different picture.

The Navajo and the Apache are descendants of
the southern Athapaskan people who migrated to the
Southwest between 1300 and 1500, adapting their way
of life to suit entirely different conditions and later
developing into known historic tribes: the Jicarilla, Lipan,
and Kiowa Apache, who adapted themselves more closely
to the Plains cultures, and the Chiricahua, Mescalero,
and Western Apache.

Their lives revolved around gathering, hunting, and
raiding. The Apache left their winter camps in April to
move to less arid places at higher altitudes, where
they cultivated small fields of corn, squash, and beans.
In May they split into groups and fanned out to gather
food. Throughout the summer adult sisters and their
daughters worked together, searching for plants that
ripened in large quantities at particular times, such as

mescal in May, saguaro fruit in June, or pinyon nuts
in October. While the younger men accompanied the
women searching for food or went off hunting, the older
men and women stayed behind with the children, and
tended the fields that would be harvested in the fall.

Consequently, the Apache were unable to store large
amounts of supplies, and in winter, when the women
worked on the hides that their men had brought home

to make clothes and utensils, the men took sole responsibility for the community's livelihood and set off in small groups on raiding parties, where their main objective was to steal other people's cattle.

Looked at this way, raiding was an economic activity embedded in the annual cycle that enabled many Apache groups to survive during the hard winter months. Just as mescal gathering was accompanied by ritual and prayer, raids fitted into a strict ritual framework. This included the initiation of young men during their first four raids and the use of a sacred language of war. The cattle seized were distributed among relatives, although widows who did not belong to the family and other people in need would also receive their share if they sang or danced for

the successful raider, thus giving him a sense of obligation towards them.

For the largest part of their history, the Apache have not regarded themselves as one single community. Large groups of related families would migrate and settle together; some tribes reckoned their descent through the mother's side. Local groups would contain between 30 and 200 people and owned exclusive rights of use of particular fields or hunting grounds.

Contrary to the prejudice that has taken hold both in the United States and Europe, according to which the Apache were subject to a form of totalitarian leadership, Apache leaders were not tyrannical eccentrics, but affable, experienced men who made consensual decisions and preferred to solve internal conflicts rather than to

Chasi, son of Bonito, a Warm Springs Apache, with an Apache fiddle, 1882. Photograph: A. Frank Randall. National Anthropological Archives, Smithsonian Institution, Washington, DC.

The Apache fiddle is the only stringed instrument of indigenous America, apart from the Californian musical bow, which has a single plucked string, and for which the player's mouth is used as a resonance box. Musicologists describe the instrument as a heterochord tubular zither because the strings are made of a foreign material and attached to the instrument rather than being cut from its surface. There are some indications that the Apache fiddle, made from a yucca stalk, originated in the Philippines and was brought to America by the Spanish.

exacerbate them. The leader had no other means of bringing pressure to bear on his followers than the success of his endeavors and his own good example. Many of them were also believed to be endowed with a range of supernatural powers (*diyi*) which enabled them to cure the sick, trick the enemy and predict future events.

When the Spanish introduced horses into the Southwest, these nomads rapidly recognized their value as a means of transport (and also a source of meat), which could hugely increase the distances that they were able to cover. We do not know precisely when the Apache began to cultivate corn, a custom learned from the Pueblo peoples and practiced only occasionally, because almost nothing is known about their way of life during the 17th century. By the 18th century, the horse had become essential for their dealings with indigenous and colonial peoples, whether by trade or by raid, both of which were necessary for stocking up on any items that they did not produce themselves. This was particularly true of the Western Apache and of the Chiricahua.

When all Spanish attempts to conquer the Apache had failed, efforts were made to bind them to military posts (presidios) by distributing gifts and alcohol, and thereby

Allan Houser (Chiricahua Apache), *Apache Family*, tempera, 1938. Fred Jones Jr. Collection, Museum of Art, University of Oklahoma Museum of Art, Norman, OK.

Among the Chiricahua, marriage was a sober institution, characterized by social and economic considerations. Nevertheless, love had some role to play in the choice of partner and in a couple's future life. Some Chiricahuas used love magic to win the heart of their desired partner. A Chiricahua explained to the anthropologist E. M. Opler: "They sing to the sun. They think that the sun can stretch a net like a spider's net and catch a person in it." Marital life was marked by strict etiquette, especially for the man who generally lived in his wife's household. He had to keep to an absolute avoidance rule with respect to his in-laws. He was compelled to stay out of their way at all times and was not permitted to speak to them. Other relatives could demand that he behave the same way toward them to indicate his respect.

Dance of the Mountain Spirits. Drawing by Naiche (Chiricahua) on a doe skin, c.1900. Oklahoma Historical Society, Oklahoma City, OK.

The Apache have always celebrated the coming of age of their daughters with great confidence, even during the war against the Americans, during their time of exile in Florida, and under the miserable conditions of the early years on the reservation. This drawing by Naiche (c.1857–1921) shows the Ga'an dancing around a fire and two small clowns entertaining the audience. The costs of entertaining a large numbers of guests were born by clan relatives, which demonstrated their solidarity.

corrupting them. However, once Mexico became independent, the presidio system broke down, and the Apache went back to making a living by launching raids on their neighbors. They regarded alien settlements within their territory as a form of renewable resource that could be raided but should not be destroyed or, as in the case of the small town of Janos in Chihuahua, they used them as trading posts where they could exchange stolen horses and cattle for other goods.

After 1853, the Americans began to develop the region. The recalcitrant, nomadic population stood in the way of mining projects, road and rail links to the West Coast, and the allocation of land to veterans of the Mexican War. The aim was to concentrate them in an area that was not subject to claims by any white party. This was the prelude to a protracted war, described as "bitterly immoral" by American ethnolinguist Keith Basso (b. 1940).

In the course of President Grant's pacification policy, four reservations were allocated to the Apache in 1871/72. However, a relocation program in 1874 determined that all Western Apache, Chiricahua, and Yavapai were to be concentrated in San Carlos, a strip of desert that was utterly unsuited to agriculture or cattle farming, but had the dubious advantage of being easy to control by the military. The Chiricahua and their leaders Victorio, Nana, Chihuahua, Naiche, and Geronimo became famous for their reckless breakouts from this reservation, and the subsequent pursuits by several thousand cavalrymen that could continue for months.

The war in the Southwest finally came to an end in 1886 when the last rebels led by Geronimo capitulated and all Chiricahuas were deported to Florida. In 1913, the last surviving 271 Chiricahuas, who by then had been relocated to Oklahoma, were released from their prisoner-of-war camp and were permitted to choose whether to stay in Oklahoma or to settle in New Mexico, where their descendants have formed a new community with the Lipan and Mescalero. Nowadays, the Western Apache live on the reservations of Fort Apache, San Carlos, and Tonto Apache, near Payson; in 1873, the Mescalero were given their final reservation in southeastern New Mexico, and the Jicarilla were given theirs in the northwest part of this state in 1887.

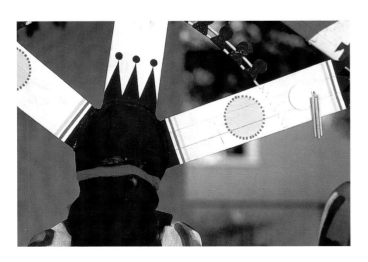

Despite the ghastly living conditions on the reservations in the late 19th century, a few Apache groups began to farm particularly strong breeds of cattle which have become the main source of income at San Carlos, where a cooperative of private owners keeps around 20,000 cattle. The Fort Apache Timber Company runs four sawmills; the White Mountain Apache and the Mescalero and Jicarilla in New Mexico have also had success with tourism by running ski, camping, and outdoor pursuit centers.

It is a popular misconception that the Apache disappeared from history with the end of the frontier period. Those who are willing to learn otherwise could do worse than spend a vacation with them.

Western Apache Ga'an Dancer, c. 1985.

The Ga'an are supernatural beings who have lived in mountain caves ever since the world was created by Yusn. They are the Apache's protectors and teachers, share their way of life in their own otherworld, and sometimes visit them bodily in order to do good. They appear as dancers during ceremonies and are also known as crown dancers because of their headdress. They always appear in groups of five, four symbolizing the four quarters of the earth, and the fifth to lead the dance and mediate between the dancers and the humans.

# Pleasure and promise

According to Apache oral tradition, a great ceremony of celebration was founded by White Painted Woman (ˈIsdzánádleeshé): "When the girls first menstruate, you shall have a feast. There shall be songs for these girls. During this feast, the masked dancers shall dance in front. After that there shall be round dancing and face-to-face dancing." With these sparse words, the goddess instructed the Apache how they were to celebrate the young girls' passage into adult womanhood.

Preparations begin as soon as the first signs of physical maturity become apparent. The family puts aside supplies and suitable deerskins for the girl's sumptuous leather dancing costume. During the course of the ceremony, she will be accompanied at all times by an older woman who will, from that time, remain her godmother for life. The second important person that the parents must select is the "singer," a ritual specialist who will lead the family and guests in four days of celebration.

First, the girl needs to have a new set of clothes made her, then a ceremonial room, similar to a tipi, has to be erected. The girl is now in a special transition stage, during which everyone addresses her as White Painted Woman, the originator of this ceremony. During this period she can also bless children and cure the sick. On the first day the girl is "shaped" by her chaperone, who massages her to endow her with health and strength. As if to prove her growing powers, the girl runs four times to a basket containing important ceremonial objects, including a rattle and an eagle feather. Her family distributes food, nuts, and fruit among the guests.

In the evening, a large fire is lit to illuminate the dancing area. With a distinctive cry, black-painted dancers suddenly leap from the darkness into the bright light surrounding the fire. They hold long, decorated staffs and their faces are concealed beneath leather or cloth hoods. Small bunches of sticks are suspended from their towering, antlerlike headdresses, making a rattling sound during the dance.

The audience's welcome is boisterous, but care must be taken not to touch the dancers or address them by name because they represent the mountain spirits, the Apaches' protectors and teachers, and their dance is performed to ward off sickness and evil. Meanwhile, the girl dances too, although she is in the ceremonial tipi, away from the spectacle, where songs are intoned at the behest of White Painted Woman to guide her on her path through adult life until she reaches old age.

The ritual dance is followed by a public dance party which lasts until the early hours of the morning, when even the most tenacious dancers have to have a rest. Women and girls are clearly at the center of things, and they can choose who they want as their dancing partner – as long as it is not their own husband or any other relative. Their partners have to pay for the dance when it is over.

The course of the following days and nights runs along similar lines, except during the fourth night, when the girl herself is given leave to dance through the night. In the light of the rising sun the ritual is concluded with the girl once more running around the basket while she is decorated with abalone shells and white paint, the symbols of the White Painted Woman. A rich meal is eaten before the ceremonial tipi is taken down and the guests finally depart.

Popular culture, kitsch, and Coca Cola have diluted the celebrations, or they may have added something to them, but they have certainly not made them redundant.

Gifts are distributed among the guests, 1981. Arizona State Museum, Tucson, AZ.

Toward the end of the celebration, the ritual leader blesses the girl and, from a small basket, he pours candy, corn kernels, and coins over her head. This action endows these objects, and those in the large baskets and boxes all around her, with supernatural powers. Male relatives can now distribute candy and fruit among the guests, and anyone lucky enough to receive a coin can expect never to have to go without money.

Leather dress used in the girl's puberty ceremony of the Western Apache, Arizona, 1935. Arizona State Museum, Tucson, AZ.

Ceremonial dresses used in puberty rituals originally consisted of a poncho and a skirt made out of six deerskins decorated with fringes and small metal cones. Since these outfits were very valuable, they continued to be worn on special occasions until a girl's first pregnancy, and were subsequently handed down to other relatives. In recent times, leather has been replaced by textiles, and increasingly by synthetic fibers.

Opposite page:

Western Apache puberty celebration for a girl, Bylas, Arizona, 1981. Arizona State Museum, Tucson, AZ.

During the ceremony, the girl sits and dances on a deerskin spread out over several blankets. The hide refers to the supply of meat – this young woman should never have to suffer hunger. Her demeanor is that of her ancestor White Painted Woman when the sun impregnated her during her first menstruation.

# Geronimo, scourge of the Southwest

Glowing black eyes, lips pressed into a determined line, hands clutching a rifle which was already regarded as an antique by most Americans of the time – this is the now famous image of Geronimo. The photograph was posed and the props belonged to the photographer; yet this face continues to cast its spell on people the world over.

Geronimo's Apache name was Goyaalé ("He Who Yawns"), and he was born in 1825 into the Bedonkohe-Chiricahua tribe. One of the key events of his life, later described in his memoirs, was when his mother, his wife, and three young children were murdered by Mexican soldiers in 1858. This marked the beginning of his seemingly endless revenge campaign of murder and mayhem in the villages south of the border. He was captured only once, in 1877, when John Clum, the San Carlos Reservation's agent, caught him unawares and had him chained and brought to the reservation.

Eyewitness accounts describe conditions on the reservation as unbearable. In addition to the heat, insects, harassment by the administration, and conflict between various Apache groups crowded together on the reservation, they had to bear the machinations of their new agent, who was defrauding the government of money and the Apaches of rations. Geronimo stayed a little while, then escaped and covered his tracks in Mexico. He returned in 1880, but by the spring of 1881 he and about 70 followers left for Mexico once more after soldiers in Cibecue had begun firing their guns indiscriminately, apparently to put a stop to a religious ritual they regarded as threatening.

In 1883, General George Crook was ordered to capture the escaped Chiricahuas. With the support of 200 Apache scouts Crook's men were able to penetrate deep into the Chiricahua's area of retreat. Geronimo entered into negotiations and returned to San Carlos in March 1884, where the Chiricahua were placed under army supervision. Although this initially seemed successful, it led to conflict with the civil administrators of the reservation, who felt their own authority to be under threat.

"Soon ... Geronimo rode into camp unarmed, and dismounting approached General Miles, shook hands with him, and then stood proudly before the officers waiting for General Miles to begin conversation with him. The interpreter said to Geronimo, 'General Miles is your friend.' Geronimo said, 'I never saw him, but I have been in need of friends. Why has he not been with me?'"

(Official government report of Geronimo's capitulation, 1886)

Geronimo and his sixth wife Zi-yah and children, after 1894. National Archives and Records Administration, Washington, DC.

In the end the Americans managed to turn Geronimo into a farmer. When he saw an Igorot group from the Phillipines at the 1904 World Exhibition in St Louis he found them to be rather uncivilized. The following year he told his biographer, "They did not wear much clothing, and I think that they should not have been allowed to come to the Fair. But they themselves did not seem to know any better."

When the liquor ban imposed on the Apache was extended to include their own corn beer, Geronimo and his friend Naiche, the son of Cochise and the real leader of the Chiricahua, led another reservation breakout. Crook pursued them with 3,000 cavalrymen and scouts; when he finally caught him, the rebel promised to surrender, but disappeared during the night. By this time he was accompanied by only 20 warriors and as many women and children. Crook was officially censured for his carelessness and, offended, asked to be relieved of his duties. He was replaced by Colonel Nelson Miles, who increased the number of his troops to 5,000. Despite his one hundredfold superiority, the absconding Apache were not to be caught, and panic ensued in the American Southwest. Geronimo did not finally lay down his guns until September 1886.

All the Chiricahua, including those who had escaped, were deported from San Carlos to Florida, and Geronimo and Naiche were separated from their families, despite having been promised that this would not happen. Nearly 500 people arrived in Fort Marion, which had space for a maximum of 75. In no time at all, more than 100 deportees were dead as a direct result of the appalling living conditions. In 1894 the survivors were taken to Fort Sill, in Oklahoma, where they tried to rebuild their lives. The septuagenarian Geronimo farmed and supplemented his income by exploiting his popularity, producing souvenirs and selling autographs. In 1905, while still a prisoner of war, he dictated his life story. According to his nephew and interpreter Daklugie, Geronimo never ceased to regret his surrender. He died in 1906, after contracting pneumonia during a drinking spree.

Opposite page:
Geronimo in 1886. Photograph: Ben Wittick. National Archives and Records Administration, Washington, DC.

Geronimo may have been surprised when he was handed a gun for this photograph, taken shortly after he was disarmed. It is not entirely clear why the Mexicans called him Geronimo. It may have been an inaccurate rendering of his Apache name, Goyaalé. Alternatively the Mexicans may have been calling on Saint Jerome (Jerónimo or Gerónimo in Spanish) for help when the feared Chiricahua appeared in the vicinity of their villages.

PRESENT
AND FUTURE

Christian F. Feest

# THE PRESENT AND FUTURE OF INDIGENOUS NORTH AMERICA

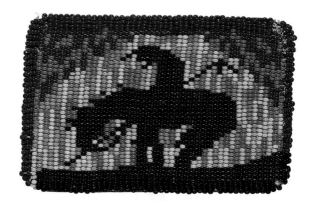

*The End of the Trail*, Sicangu Lakota beaded belt buckle, Rosebud Reservation, South Dakota, c. 1980. Museum für Völkerkunde, Vienna, Austria.

*The End of the Trail*, James Earle Fraser's sculpture for the Panama Pacific International Exposition of 1915 in San Francisco, was intended to express the anguish of "a weaker race ... steadily pushed to the wall by a stronger one." This symbol of decline is now a popular theme in Lakota painting and crafts, despite the fact that the end of the trail has long since disappeared from view.

Opposite page:

Andy Warhol, *The American Indian: Russell Means*, synthetic polymer, 1976. Andy Warhol Foundation for the Visual Arts, New York, NY.

The "noble savage" as a pop-culture icon. For Russell Means (b. 1939), leader of the American Indian Movement and lately actor for Disney Studios, militant actions were media events as much as they were political protests.

## The Last of the Mohicans?

By 1900, ten years after the end of the Indian wars, few would have wagered even one cent on the future prospects of "the Indians." Politicians, officials, scientists, and even many of those affected agreed that the "Red Man" was dying out. Since the first days of their involuntary confrontation with European colonists, the numbers of the indigenous population had rapidly decreased, whole nations had disappeared completely, and the original inhabitants of much of the continent at best survived in place names such as Chicago ("place of skunks" in the Ojibwa language), Canada ("large settlement" in Mohawk), or Sioux City. To white Americans it seemed as if divine providence had paved the way for the progress of civilization by the demise of the "barbarous tribes." By 1900 only 237,000 Native Americans were registered in the United States census, and only 101,000 were counted in Canada a year later.

The reasons for the dramatic decline of the indigenous population were obvious. Whites had brought diseases to the New World, against which Native Americans had no immunity: measles, whooping cough, smallpox, cholera, and other epidemics often preceded the advancing frontier and had a disasterous effect. Acts of violence and accidents resulting from previously unknown alcohol abuse took a heavy toll of lives in many places; the number of Native American war victims is estimated at up to half a million in 400 years. Although premeditated genocide was rarely part of official Indian policies, it was all too often tacitly accepted; the forced removal of many peoples not only cost the lives of the old and infirm, who were not equal to the exertion, but indirectly contributed to the population decline as much by uprooting and despair as by the loss of the old economic systems and the fragmentation of traditional communities under the pressure of policies of assimilation. Life expectancy and birth rates on the reservations dropped drastically because of poor medical services and overall destitution.

In any discussion of the depopulation of indigenous North America, it is necessary to consider the size of the aboriginal population before the arrival of the Europeans. This question, however, cannot be answered easily – and certainly never accurately. For a long time, the most accurate estimate, based on the earliest eyewitness reports, was thought to be about 1 million. This figure began to be placed into doubt sometime after 1960, when demographically and environmentally based, but also ideologically colored, projections suddenly came up with figures of up to 18 million. Because such a population mass would have left behind quite different and, above

Crow women and children, Montana, c. 1990.

The growth of reservation populations in the US during the last 50 years has been mainly the result of an increase in the number of children. Of all Native Americans living on reservations, 33 percent are under 15 years old, and the average age is 24 (the overall US average is 33). However, life expectancy continues to be lower among Native Americans: only 6 percent of Native Americans live beyond the age of 64 (the US average is 13 percent).

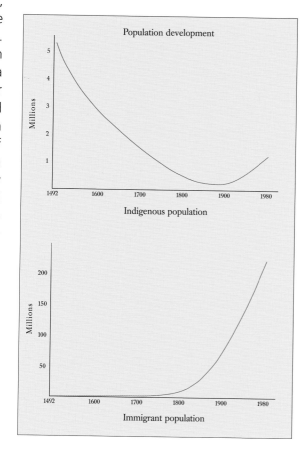

**Indigenous population development in North America**

The decline of the indigenous population of North America from between 2 and 8 million in 1500 to less than 500,000 in 1900, and its growth to about 3.5 million in 2000, is eclipsed by the growth of immigrant populations in the United States and Canada from zero to more than 300 million in the same period. The way that indigenous populations have fared have varied enormously: in eastern North America, even large peoples were completely destroyed within the space of 200 years, whereas the Navajo population has grown continuously throughout its history.

all, much more numerous traces in the prehistoric record than have actually been found, these estimates are no longer thought to be credible either. All we are left with is the rather vague statement that the indigenous population figure was probably somewhere between 2 and 8 million.

Anyone accustomed to thinking in terms of "the last of the Mohicans" may be surprised to find that the indigenous population has grown during the last decades. In 1950, 350,000 "American Indians" were counted in the United States; according to the 1990 census, numbers had risen to just above 2 million (in Canada the total number, including the Métis, was around 800,000 in 1996). Although such a vast population increase in 40 years is welcome, it also seems rather improbable. Growing optimism and improved medical services have contributed to higher birth rates and lower mortality rates and therefore to considerably

**Powwow in Wikwemikong, Ontario (1984).**

Only 10 percent of the indigenous population of the United States regard themselves primarily as "Indians"; for all the rest, membership of a particular tribe (sometimes of several) is more important. During special events like powwows, at which the beauty and otherness of the participants' culture is celebrated with pride, patriotic manifestations especially by indigenous war veterans play an important role. Tribal member, Indian, or citizen of the United States or Canada – identity is multifaceted and frequently determined by context.

increased numbers. More than half of the increase, however, is attributable to the "identity migration" of people who have made a conscious decision to become "Indians" in the course of this period. Statistics compiled by the Bureau of Indian Affairs in 1990 show that only 1 million Indians are under its jurisdiction. In the final analysis, we do not know how many indigenous people there were in 1492; neither do we know exactly how many there are today.

## Who is an "Indian"?

The discrepancy between the population figures offered by the census and the Bureau of Indian Affairs is easily explained. Whereas the census asks citizens to identify themselves by "race," the BIA only counts people who fall within its sphere of responsibility on the basis of treaty or legal obligations. These are primarily the members of tribes recognized by the federal government, as well as persons having more than half (sometimes only one quarter) of "Indian blood" of tribes indigenous to the United States.

Not all the tribes are recognized by the federal government, however. Remaining without official acknowledgment are those who only signed contracts with the British during

the colonial period, and who have since maintained official relations with their respective states but not with the government in Washington, as well as a few tribes who did not enter into any treaty relations, and those released from the government's trusteeship. Although it is still possible to be recognized as a tribe today, it is very difficult.

There is no single set of rules governing membership of a tribe, because this is determined by each tribe individually. Originally, a tribe was a group of people linked by kinship ties (through descent, marriage, or adoption), who lived together and who regarded themselves as part of the same group. Therefore, an adopted white prisoner could, if he was assimilated into a tribe, become a member and thus an "Indian." Conversely, serious crimes were often punished by exclusion from the tribe.

Rules of descent varied from tribe to tribe: many tribes acknowledged people as members regardless of whether they had inherited membership from their mother or from their father; others reckoned descent only through either the mother's or the father's line. In the 19th century, so many children of white American fathers had been born to women of the patrilinear Ojibwa that they were allocated their own clan – the eagle clan – named for the American heraldic eagle, and therefore as it were adopted. In the Seneca Nation in New York, where descent continues to be strictly reckoned through the mother's side, many members have white fathers and grandfathers,

whereas the children of Seneca men cannot become members if their mothers are white,

**Hulleah Tsinhnahjinnie (Seminole/Creek/Navajo): *"Don't Leave the Rez Without It!"* from *Photographic Memoirs of an Aboriginal Savant*, Davis, CA, 1994. Private collection.**

The *American Indian Arts and Crafts Act* of 1990 was passed to protect indigenous craftspeople against unfair competition, and threatens any non-Indian Americans who attempt to pass off their products as "Indian" art with high penalties. This legislation also affects the million Americans who, like the indigenous peoples of Canadian and Mexico, regard themselves as "Indians" although they are not recognized as such by the federal authorities. The course of history might have been different if Wovoka, Geronimo, or Sarah Winnemucca had required official documentation to be accepted as real Native American activists.

**"American Indians. You Count! Be Counted ...," United States census poster of 1980 based on *Generations*, a work by Ward Churchill (Creek/Cherokee)**

To some people figures for the indigenous population of the United States may appear too high; others think it is far too low. Based on the census of 1980, Jack Forbes, historian and Native American activist of mixed ancestry, calculated that there were in fact approximately 19 to 28 million "Indians": 1.4 million self-declared Native Americans, plus 4.8 million non-declared descendants, 7 to 8 million descendants of Latin American Indians, and 6 to 14 million African Americans with Native American blood.

even if both the mother and the child live on the reservation and follow the Longhouse religion. Interestingly, according to this strict rule, the famous British statesman Winston Churchill (1874–1965) would have been considered a Mohawk since he was the descendant of a Mohawk woman on his mother's side.

Another criterion for membership of a tribe was residence within the community. Although such communities continue to exist on the reservations, migration of members to towns and cities since the early 20th century, but particularly after 1950, has increasingly caused the criterion of kinship to come into conflict with that of cohabitation. For example, the 1935 tribal constitution of the confederated Salish and Kootenai tribes on the Flathead reservation made it a condition of membership, that a person's parents had been residents on the reservation at the time of the birth of their child. Since 1960 however, it has only been necessary to be a descendant of a member of the tribe and to have at least one quarter Salish and/or Kootenai blood to qualify for membership.

The United States introduced the "blood quantum" as a criterion of "Indianness" in

**Canadian Native Friendship Center, Edmonton, Alberta, c. 1985.**

Urban Indian centers were set up to provide assistance to migrants adapting to a new way of life and work. In the long run, however, they were much less supportive of integration than they were of raising a Panindian consciousness. With 33,000 Indian inhabitants in 1996, Edmonton (after Winnipeg) had the second-largest urban Indian population in North America.

1918. To reach the quantum, it is insignificant whether the required portions all derive from the same tribe and whether forebears were "full-blooded Indians" or not, as long as they appeared as members on a tribal roll. Because of the high proportion of marriages to non-Indians, some tribes have since also adopted this problematic criterion. On the other hand, in the mid-1970s the Cherokee Nation of Oklahoma opened its tribal rolls to all persons who in one way or another were descendants of people who had been members of the tribe in the 19th century. Consequently, membership suddenly increased from around 12,000 to 180,000, culminating in the 1990 census, in which some 308,000 Americans designated themselves as "Cherokee."

## Indians of all nations, unite!

Unlike in Europe, where the centuries preceding the conquest of America saw the emergence, at least among the cultural elite, of a common identity based on Christianity and the beginnings of an encompassing Western civilization, the native peoples of America had no supraregional sense of unity. There was no word to designate the indigenous population of America as a whole, and cultural similarities were limited to comparable regional adaptations to the environment and the equally regional diffusion of ideas and practices. It ultimately required the

**John Mix Stanley, *International Indian Council, Tahlequah,* oil on canvas, 1843. National Museum of American Art, Washington, DC.**

In June 1843, Cherokee chief John Ross called an International Native American Council which took place in Tahlequah, capital of the Cherokee Nation in present-day Oklahoma. For four weeks, about 4,000 delegates from 18 tribes of the Indian Territory discussed the future form of their peaceful coexistence in their new, common homeland. Not until 1944, 101 years later, did the establishment of the National Congress of American Indians provide a relatively representative and supraregional Panindian lobbying organization.

**Robert Penn, *Urban Indian,* casein on paper, 1972. Sioux Indian Museum, Rapid City, SD.**

After 1945, the Bureau of Indian Affairs began to systematically relocate people from reservations to urban areas. Since employment opportunities on the remote reservations were in short supply, it was hoped that this would assuage the problem of native unemployment while also promoting the integration of the indigenous population into American society. Although more than 50 percent of all Native Americans now live in cities, the desired goals were not achieved. Rural destitution was merely replaced by urban poverty and discrimination.

shared threat caused by the invasion of pale-faced strangers to gradually bring to fruition the realization that the indigenous peoples, regardless of their many differences, had become a community of fate.

The common experience to be recognized across tribal boundaries was the loss of land. By the 18th century vast portions of eastern North America had been alienated from native ownership. It was also apparent that European trade goods and the comforts of the White Man's way of life were estranging more and more tribal members from their own traditions.

It was around 1760 that the prophet Neolin (c. 1725–1775) made his appearance in the Ohio Valley among the Delaware, who had been driven out from their homeland, and predicted that God himself would assist in restoring their land. He propagated intertribal peace and preached social reforms, which included a rejection of the white man's trade goods, especially of alcohol, and the abolishment of the ancient medicine societies and of polygamy. This supratribal doctrine contains at its core the aims of most of the subsequent "Panindian" movements: the

defense of shared "Indian" interests and a pointed separation from whites, accompanied by an adaptation to their value systems. Here and subsequently, the spiritual unity that was invoked was rapidly transformed into organized political activity.

Nevertheless, such attempts were generally without significant results because united military resistance in the end always remained unsuccessful, and because contact between most of the tribes was not permanent enough to cement their solidarity. This changed in 1830 when the American government tried to settle most of the indigenous peoples of eastern North America in a compact Indian Territory in Oklahoma. Even when the dream of an "Indian" state aspired to especially by the Five Civilized Tribes had faded, Oklahoma and its mix of different peoples continued to provide a fertile soil for a political, and also cultural, Panindianism. Dance costumes, musical styles, and the Peyote religion spread from Oklahoma across large parts, although not all, of North America.

The whites inadvertently also contributed in other ways to the promotion of Panindian tendencies. The 19th-century Indian stereotype

based on the lifeways of the equestrian warriors of the Plains became a model for others, particularly when the intention was to present oneself to white people as an "Indian." The boarding schools for Indians that were estabished from 1879 onward further contributed to children of different tribes growing up together and creating a network of relationships which provided a basis for the political Panindianism and the "Indian Movement" which became a major influence during the 20th century.

Ultimately all these movements were championed not so much by those people who were still attached to the old way of life, but by those who stood between indigenous and Euro-American traditions, and who recognized that only unity could provide strength for confrontation with a more powerful opponent.

Even today, the vast majority of North America's indigenous inhabitants regard themselves primarily as belonging to particular nations. The fact that they are all also "Indians" is a social and legal reality which they have come to acknowledge with varying degrees of enthusiasm.

Opposite page:
**Powwow in Washington, DC., 1976.**

One of today's most visible manifestations of "Panindian" culture is the powwow. This public event, with dancing competitions accompanied by singing and drumming, is equally an expression of an attachment to unique traditions and an opportunity for exchanges between members of different peoples. The dances are based on the ceremonies of the warrior societies of the Plains that over the past 100 years have spread to other (but not all) regions of North America, where they have frequently been adapted to local requirements.

Right:
**Headdress and hair ornaments of a powwow dancer.**

Roaches of dyed deer hair and porcupine quills, with two bobbing feathers attached to the center, were once the insignia of a warrior society whose rituals had spread to many Plains tribes. Today they have become the typical headdress of male powwow dancers. Although ownership of eagle's feathers is prohibited under wildlife protection laws, this is not enforced in the case of Native American owners because of the religious importance of feathers.

Below:
**Powwow dancer in "traditional" costume.**

Dancing competitions at powwows are held in different age, gender, and dance style categories. The judges assess not only the dancing itself, but also the costumes for which dancers invest considerable amounts, because cash prizes of several hundred dollars can be won. The first powwow dancing world championship was held in Oklahoma in 1925.

Below right:
**Powwow participant and the American flag.**

As a symbol of power, the Stars and Stripes became a popular motif in the arts and crafts of the Plains peoples of the 19th century. When the precursors of the first modern-style powwows were held in the 1870s, the government permitted these "heathen" dances to take place only on the Fourth of July. Ever since Indians have been fighting for and not against the American army, a dance of the indigenous veterans in honor of "their" flag has become part of every powwow.

Cora Bender

# From smoke signals to the Internet – voices from "Indian Country"

"KTNN Radio station, o-o-okay! A-a-all right, well, folks, good evening, you're tuned to KTNN AM 660, Window Rock, Arizona!" This is how Lori Lee, music editor and presenter of the Navajo station KTNN, introduces her popular live show *Drums of Summer*. Every Thursday evening in summer, KTNN travels to a different place on the large Navajo reservation according to the concept, "Live, free, and outdoors." Today they are the guests of NCI, a therapy center for drug and alcohol addicts in Gallup, New Mexico. "We have a lot of folks coming in," Lori entices her audience, "and you're more than welcome to come on in and join us, and of course if you're traveling throughout the great Southwest or maybe at home or at work, keep it right here on KTNN, we'll be here with some beautiful pow-wow drum and singing tonight here on KTNN with Drums of Summer, proudly sponsored by NCI here in Gallup, New Mexico."

"Hosting KTNN's Drums of Summer is like a way for us to talk to the community," explains Matthew Kelley, the center's director. "And it allows people an alternative to drinking." Whether at community centers, schools, supermarkets, or gas stations, "when we have a remote on the weekend," comments

After Charles Bird King, *Sequoyah*, 1828. Color lithograph from T.L. McKenney and J. Hall, *The Indian Tribes of North America*, Philadelphia, PA, 1836.

In 1819, disabled after a hunting accident, the Cherokee Sequoyah (c. 1770–1843) invented a writing system for his language which consisted of 86 syllabics. This system was rapidly accepted and was taught in tribal schools until 1903. Thanks to its success, Sequoyah's syllabary became the model for a series of other writing systems for indigenous languages. After the Cherokee were removed to Oklahoma, the *Cherokee Advocate* and the *Cherokee Messenger*, both of which were bilingual publications temporarily replaced the *Cherokee Phoenix*.

a shopkeeper, "we get people from, like I said, a hundred miles coming in, because they heard there is something going on here." The station provides culture, music, information, and also entertainment, for 12 hours a day in Navajo. The white media's news reporting generally takes the position of the white majority on such issues as land rights and alcohol problems. It is therefore important that the inquisitive and bemused view of outsiders be supplemented by an internal perspective.

Indigenous newspapers and radio stations see providing this as their primary task. The first such newspaper, the *Cherokee Phoenix*,

was published from 1828 to 1834. Until 1832 it was edited by Elias Boudinot (1804–1839), and accompanied the Cherokee during the dramatic years preceding their expulsion from Georgia and their forced relocation to Oklahoma. The young editor of the *Cherokee Phoenix* wrote articles both in English and in Cherokee, and people subscribed from all over North America and even from as far afield as Europe. In 1834, the pressure of imminent removal and the effects of political infighting among the various Cherokee factions put an end to publication of the *Cherokee Phoenix*.

*Wassaja* ("Signal" in English) was the brainchild of maverick Carlos Montezuma (1866–1923) and appeared monthly from 1916 until 1922. Montezuma was a Yavapai, had studied medicine in Chicago, and worked for a time as a doctor in the service of the Bureau of Indian Affairs. His work for the Yavapai of the Fort McDowell reservation made the sharp-tongued and ardent activist a radical opponent of the BIA. As he wrote in the newspaper's first issue, *Wassaja* was intended to be published only for as long as the BIA remained in existence and to contribute to the BIA's abolition – a hopeless venture. Nevertheless, his clearsightedness has earned Montezuma the lasting respect of the Native American community, something that was always denied the BIA.

Stimulated by the civil rights movement, Native American media really took off during the 1960s. In the course of campaigns organized by the American Indian Movement, Native Americans discovered that they could use the power of the media for their own ends. Between 1960 and 1969, Native Americans in North American produced more than 300 newspapers, including such well-known journals as *Akwesasne Notes*. The first

Technology conquers the powwow, 1987.

Dance music at powwows is supplied by drum groups, and good drummers not only have their fans, but also their imitators. Portable cassette recorders have enabled people to learn new songs, but the fact that the musicians' copyright was sometimes being infringed only became apparent when the Ponca tribe in Oklahoma expressly prohibited the imitation of Ponca music. The songs of 19th-century warrior societies had also been the exclusive property of their members.

Radio KTNN, Navajo Reservation, Arizona, 1998.

Although all indigenous languages of North America still in use can now also be written, these writing systems have not become fully established in practice. Thus newspapers on the Navajo Reservation are almost entirely in English, while the radio is dominated by spoken Navajo. Tribal council meetings are also held in Navajo – but the minutes are recorded in English.

Native American radio stations, KYUK in Alaska and KTDB in New Mexico, went on the air in the early 1970s. Today there are 30 stations, and all tribal governments contribute financially to the operation of many local media, supporting professionally made local newspapers and websites.

Such a development can, of course, never be entirely free of conflict. Native American journalists in the employ of tribal governments complain about political exertion of influence and political pressure. With regard to sensitive issues such as gambling casinos, journalists have been accused of harming their reservation community by washing dirty laundry in public. Thus Native American news reporting is often a difficult balancing act between the frontlines.

## The new Indian wars

After the Indian wars, white North America ceased to regard the pacified inhabitants of the reservations as a threat and patiently awaited their extinction or eventual assimilation into the dominant society. In the 1930s, a short-lived surge of enthusiasm for the "red" minority gave rise to the rebirth of tribes as democratic organizations, but this eagerness was already evaporating during World War II. The exemplary service provided by many indigenous soldiers during the war convinced politicians that the time had come for the Indian Question to be solved once and for all. Large-scale urban relocation programs, the attempt to settle tribal claims arising from treaties made in the 19th century, and measures to terminate the special relationship between the tribes and the federal government were a clear indication that attitudes were changing. Yet these are precisely the steps that would eventually lead to the reawakening of Native American resistance against the nation state.

The Indian Claims Commission was established in 1947 to investigate the peace and land cession treaties of the past, and the resultant protracted negotiations provided the tribes with a clear picture of just how much they were owed. Good lawyers helped them win significant compensation, which contributed to strengthening the indigenous communities. The tribes rightly saw the termination of their relationship with the federal government, and thus of their direct administration by the BIA, as a threat to their existence. Despite its inherent paternalism, this relationship had protected their political autonomy and remaining land base from the covetous grasp of the individual states on whose territories they resided. The example of tribes (such as the Menominee in Wisconsin) that had been officially dissolved because of their "degree of civilization" and whose members subsequently found themselves in dire economic need encouraged skepticism and active resistance. Finally, Native American urbanization, which had not proceeded quite according to plan, introduced Native Americans from isolated reservations to an environment in which they were able to observe and emulate the aims, strategies, and successes of the civil rights and student movements of the 1960s.

The first spokespeople of the "new Indians," as they were called, were themselves students

"This is Indian land." Graffiti on a bridge near Kahnawake, Quebec, c. 1990.

The roots of many contemporary conflicts between the First Americans and the white nation-states lie in unresolved land questions that have arisen over the last five centuries and for which there are no solutions which would be satisfactory for all parties. Regardless of whether it is a claim for the return of sacred land, for damages for illegally expropriated land, or for a fundamental clarification of land rights, the native peoples are constantly reminded that their close links to, and common ownership of, the land are the basis of their collective survival.

# "As long as the sun shall shine ..."
## The proclamation of the occupiers of Alcatraz (1969)

In the 1960s, a young generation of mostly urban "new Indians" began to proclaim to the world that the "Indian problem" was by no means resolved. In the wake of the government's relocation program, Californian cities like Los Angeles and San Francisco had attracted large numbers of indigenous people from all over the United States, who were looking for work. The San Francisco Indian Center provided the focus for the formation of the United Bay Area Council of American Indian Affairs, where problems arising from their common legal position as "Indians" as well as strategies for their solution were discussed. Land questions, poor welfare services, and the remaining rights of sovereignty were at the forefront of these discussions. Feelings ran high when the United States offered to pay damages of 47 cents per acre of land expropriated in the 19th century. The Indian Center was destroyed by fire in October 1969.

Under the leadership of Adam "Fortunate Eagle" Nordwall, a Chippewa originally from Minnesota, this triggered a spectacular protest action. The high-security prison on the island of Alcatraz, near San Francisco, had been closed down in 1968. Referring to the Fort Laramie treaty of 1868 between the Sioux and the United States, according to which the government was to return to the Sioux "surplus" land no longer required by the federal government, the abandoned prison island was occupied on November 20, 1969. Initially this peaceful occupation received a great deal of positive media attention and it continued until June 1, 1971. Although the protest action was not directly successful, it became a model for similar, increasingly militant actions in the 1970s.

The proclamation distributed by the occupiers to the press illustrates the use of irony as a means of nonviolent resistance.

## To the Great White Father and all his people:

We, the native Americans, re-claim the land known as Alcatraz Island in the name of all American Indians by right of discovery. We wish to be fair and honorable in our dealings with the Caucasian inhabitants of this land, and hereby offer the following treaty: We will purchase said Alcatraz Island for 24 dollars ($24) in glass beads and red cloth, a precedent set by the white man's purchase of a similar island about 300 years ago. We know that $24 in trade goods for these sixteen acres is more than was paid when Manhattan Island was sold, but we know that land values have risen over the years. Our offer of $24 per acre is greater than the 47 cents per acre the white men are now paying the California Indians for their land. We will give to the inhabitants of this land a portion of that land for their own, to be held in trust by the American Indian Government – for as long as the sun shall rise and the rivers go down to the sea – to be administered by the Bureau of Caucasian Affairs (BCA). We will further guide the inhabitants in the proper way of living. We will offer them our religion, our education, our life-ways, in order to help them achieve our level of civilization and thus raise them and all their white brothers up from their savage and unhappy state. We offer this treaty in good faith and wish to be fair and honorable in our dealings with all white men.

We feel that this so-called Alcatraz Island is more than suitable as an Indian Reservation, as determined by the white man's own standards. By this we mean that this place resembles most Indian reservations, in that: (1) It is isolated from modern facilities, and without adequate means of transportation. (2) It has no fresh running water. (3) The sanitation facilities are inadequate. (4) There are no oil or mineral rights. (5) There is no industry and so unemployment is very great. (6) There are no health care facilities. (7) The soil is rocky and non-productive and the land does not support game. (8) There are no educational facilities. (9) The population has always been held as prisoners and kept dependent upon others.

Further, it would be fitting and symbolic that ships from all over the world, entering the Golden Gate, would first see Indian land, and thus be reminded of the true history of this nation. This tiny island would be a symbol of the great lands once ruled by free and noble Indians.

What use will we make of this land? Since the San Francisco Indian Center burned down, there is no place for Indians to assemble. Therefore, we plan to develop on this island several Indian institutions:

1. A Center for Native American Studies will be developed which will train our young people in the best of our native cultural arts and sciences, as well as educate them in the skills and knowledge to improve the lives and spirits of all Indian peoples. Attached to this Center will be traveling universities, managed by Indians, which will go to the Indian Reservations in order to learn from the people the traditional values which are now absent from the Caucasian higher educational system.

2. An American Indian Spiritual Center will be developed which will practice our ancient tribal religious ceremonies and medicine. Our cultural arts will be featured and our young people trained in music, dance, and medicine.

3. An Indian Center of Ecology will be built which will train and support our young people in scientific research and practice in order to restore our lands and waters to their pure and natural state. We will seek to de-pollute the air and the water of the Bay Area. We will seek to restore fish and animal life, and to revitalize sea life which has been threatened by the white man's way. Facilities will be developed to desalt sea water for human use.

4. A Great Indian Training School will be developed to teach our peoples how to make a living in the world, improve our standards of living, and end hunger and unemployment among all our peoples. This training school will include a Center for Indian Arts and Crafts, and an Indian restaurant serving native foods and training Indians in culinary arts. This Center will display Indian arts and offer the Indian foods of all tribes to the public, so that all may know of the beauty and spirit of the traditional Indian ways.

5. Some of the present buildings will be taken over to develop an American Indian Museum, which will depict our native foods and other cultural contributions we have given to all the world. Another part of the Museum will present some of the things the white man has given to the Indians, in return for the land and life he took: disease, alcohol, poverty, and cultural decimation (as symbolized by old tin cans, barbed wire, rubber tires, plastic containers, etc.). Part of the Museum will remain a dungeon, to symbolize both those Indian captives who were incarcerated for challenging white authority, and those who were imprisoned on reservations. The Museum will show the noble and the tragic events of Indian history, including the broken treaties, the documentary of the Trail of Tears, the Massacre of Wounded Knee, as well as the victory over Yellow-Hair Custer and his Army. In the name of all Indians, therefore, we reclaim this island for our Indian nations, for all these reasons. We feel this claim is just and proper, and that this land should rightfully be granted to us for as long as the rivers shall run and the sun shall shine.

Indians of All Tribes, November 1969, San Francisco, California

Untitled, 1969. Photograph: Vince Maggiora, *San Francisco Chronicle*, San Francisco, CA.

The outline of a lone tipi on the prison island of Alcatraz stands out against the skyline of San Francisco, and embodies the occupiers' demand for an authentic, "First American" alternative to the late capitalist world. For American citizens whose certainties had been shattered by the Vietnam War, this idyll promised the security of a traditional lifestyle: "Peace and freedom," proclaimed graffiti on the prison's water tower "Welcome. Home of the Free. Indian Land."

The occupation of Wounded Knee, South Dakota, 1973.

The most sensational action taken by the American Indian Movement was their occupation in February 1973 of the historically sensitive area of Wounded Knee on the Pine Ridge Reservation. The occupation was intended to overthrow the elected, although allegedly corrupt, tribal government, and was also staged as a valuable public relations exercise. The press gratefully published photographs of armed Lakota warriors and drew parallels between the Indian wars, both old and new, and the recent Vietnam War. The "Wounded Knee Nation" proclaimed by the sticker on the rifle butt remained a publicity gimmick of AIM, the palpable results of the action remained poor.

Negotiations at Wounded Knee, Pine Ridge Reservation, South Dakota, 1973. University of Utah, Salt Lake City, UT.

Treaty negotiations between the United States government and the American Indian Movement were intended to demonstrate the continuing sovereignty of the native nations. Here a round of negotiations is opened with a ceremony led by the two medicine men Leonard Crow Dog and Wallace Black Elk. AIM leaders Dennis Banks and Russell Means (third and fourth from left) and their lawyer Ramon Roubideaux (second from right) sit opposite government representative Kent Frizzell. Instead of positive results, the occupation led to several years of civil war on the reservation and lengthy legal proceedings for the activists.

Mohawk "Warrior" on the barricades of Kanehsatake (Oka), Quebec, 1990. Canapress Picture Archive, Toronto, ON.

In 1990, after decades of unsuccessful pleading by the people of Kanehsatake for a reservation of their own, plans for a golf course on an old Mohawk burial ground resulted in a confrontation between the Mohawk of Kanehsatake (Oka) and the Canadian army. The Mohawk Warriors responsible for escalating the military conflict, refer to as their model the ancient social order of the Iroquois which existed before the reforms introduced by prophet Handsome Lake. At the same time, they are the most vociferous supporters of the gambling casino developments that finance their weapons.

militant groups, the American Indian Movement (AIM) was founded in Minneapolis in 1968 and kept the public in suspense for a decade with its spectacular actions.

The Native American student and urban protest movement was opposed to white society and its institutions, but it was also particularly scornful of "Uncle Tomahawks," the integrated and compliant tribal politicians on the reservations whom they named in allusion to Uncle Tom in his cabin. Their radical message found little approval from the generally conservative populations on the reservations. In areas where conditions were so atrocious that some members of the community felt themselves compelled to join the militant camp, existing rifts within communities were further entrenched by radical action. The media, however, were hardly interested in the armed conflicts within the tribes, which occasionally followed the AIM's telegenic appearances, nor did they want to know about the power struggles within the movement.

Already by the 1980s, radicalism had become far less significant to Native American national politics. Many rebels turned away from the movement and others gradually drifted into tribal politics. Nevertheless, the spirit of resistance has survived and is an integral part of the new confidence of indigenous Americans at the beginning of the third millennium.

who used humor and their powers of persuasion to foster the indigenous population's new sense of identity and tried, by nonviolent means, to realize the dream of a "Red American" renaissance. Their media-effective actions of passive resistance were modeled on the Afro-American civil rights movement and its figurehead Martin Luther King, and they found favor with a contrite public. However, many rootless urban Native Americans found the Black Power movement more attractive and used it as their model. Their subsequent violent actions forced the politicians to respond rapidly. One of many

Seth Eastman, *Chippewa Indians Playing Checkers*, oil on canvas, 1848. Regis Collection, Minneapolis, MN.

Games of chance, often played with high stakes, were popular in pre-European North America. It is not surprising, therefore, to find that European card and board games were quickly adopted and played inside or in front of the wigwam or tipi. However, white observers saw in this disposition for gambling a regrettable lack of work ethic, and the government was unstinting in its attempts to remove this obstacle on the path to "civilization" by means of prohibitions.

## Bingo!

Dire economic conditions on the reservations were fuel to the fire of the "new Indian wars." Especially peoples that had previously lived as hunters, fishermen, or gatherers suffered particularly badly because they were deprived of the traditional foundations of their existence while being forced to settle on land that could barely sustain them as farmers. Located far from industrial areas and markets, and with inadequate transportation links to the outside world, the reservations had little to offer in the way of commercial or industrial employment and, despite every effort, they were almost entirely unsuccessful in attracting industry. The continuous population growth was yet another impediment in the struggle against economic deprivation. With unemployment rates of up to 90 percent, many of the reservations were black spots of poverty on the prosperous American landscape.

When the reservations were established in the 19th century, their land was generally barren and desolate. It gradually emerged, however, that the government had un-intentionally given the Native Americans land that held an unusually high proportion of the United States' energy reserves. The Department of the Interior was responsible for general matters pertaining to land use, and for a long time its role as trustee of Native American land enabled it to negotiate particularly favorable coal and uranium mining and oil extraction contracts for the energy industry.

As tribal self-determination became stronger, income from these leases improved, and when energy prices soared during the oil crises of the 1970s and early 1980s, many tribal politicians began to hope for the big money. Some people even began to talk of an Indian OPEC that would have the power to dictate pricing. However, when world market prices for oil dropped again, reservations were left with little more than land destroyed by strip

Peter B. Jones (Onondaga), *Horns of a Dilemma*, clay, wood, and bison horn, 1992. Museum für Völkerkunde, Frankfurt am Main, Germany.

The beneficial effect of bingo and gasoline smuggling on the finances of at least part of the reservation population is set against the dangers of encroaching materialism, Mafia-like machinations, and deep divisions in the indigenous community. The Iroquois have already had unfortunate experiences in this respect, and they see this dilemma as reminiscent of Thadodaho, the man-eating arch magician of Onondaga who became the leading chief of the newly-founded League of the Iroquois after snakes were combed out of his hair. Can the miracle be repeated with bingo?

mining and drinking water polluted by uranium. At around the same time, some tribes remembered that Native American land enjoyed a special legal status. Although situated within state territory, it is not subject to state laws. Tax-free gasoline and cigarettes which should have benefited the reservation population, also attracted many white customers, especially on reservations close to towns. The amount of tax lost to the states was minimal, but the police were tireless in their law enforcement against smugglers. A new idea of the 1970s was to build casinos on the reservations. Bingo is a game of chance, but is generally seen as a harmless pastime, often used by churches and charitable organizations to raise funds; thus the first Native American casinos to be set up were so-called "bingo palaces."

As in the case of gasoline and cigarettes, the state authorities doggedly tried to prevent the

Gambling machines in the Mystic Lake casino, Minnesota.

When,in 1992 the Mdewakanton Dakota opened a casino with more than 1,000 slot machines and a huge bingo hall near Minneapolis-St. Paul, the most strident opposition came from leaders of the American Indian Movement, who objected to the use of a (sacred) white buffalo in the advertising logo. Prescott, the chairman of the tribal council, responded that the days of buffalo hunting were over and that gambling was the Dakota's "new buffalo."

Carson Waterman (Seneca), *The Seneca Have Landed*, acrylic on canvas, 1982.

The Seneca are not afraid of the future. Should they ever land a person on the moon, their astronaut will wear a beaded breechclout, belt, and armbands, and his helmet will sport a *gastowe*, the traditional Iroquois chief's headdress.

development of a Native American gambling industry, and warned of the dangers of possible infiltration by organized crime syndicates. The federal government, on the other hand, supported the tribes in the legal proceedings initiated by the state authorities, probably in the hope that gambling might ameliorate conditions for the many Native Americans who were dependent on public funds. After the courts consistently found in favor of the new casino owners, these enterprises became subject to federal legislation in 1988.

Since then, an almost incalculable number of Indian "bingo palaces" have sprung up all over the country. Not all are as successful as the Foxwoods Resort casino run by the Mashantucket-Pequot in Connecticut, whose small state reservation was almost deserted 20 years ago because of the lack of opportunities available for its population. The Mashantucket-Pequot are a mixed people who have finally been recognized as a tribe by the federal government. Thanks to the location of their reservation between New York and Boston, their gambling paradise makes an annual profit of several hundred million dollars. However, not all reservation dwellers have found this form of income generation in keeping with their traditional cultural values.

## "Indian time"

When making appointments with Native Americans today one should always inquire as to whether the time agreed corresponds to real time or to "Indian time." Several hours may lie between these two possibilities. This is the type of experience which seems to confirm the opinion held by many whites that "the Indians" live deep inside the eternal cycle of a mythical world, devoid of linear time. Ric Glazer Danay (b. 1942), a Mohawk painter and director of a Native American Studies program at an American university, sees the matter differently. When his students try to excuse their tardiness by referring to "Indian time" he tells them "The Mohawk were always on time!"

The idea that a cyclical sense of time precluding "progress" and cognizant only of circular renewal is "typically Indian" is a modern cliché. Most of our watches have hands that rotate in a circle, and Christmas reoccurs each year just as our daily and annual routines do. Equally, Native Americans experienced human existence as having a beginning and an end, and as stretching between the past, the experience of the elders, and the as-yet-untrodden path of the future. The lack of writing systems may have prevented the creation of documents which could serve as a basis for a historiography, but pictographic records were kept in some places, while in others notches were carved in wooden sticks and knots tied in strings to record the linear passing of time. It is not a coincidence that the Iroquois derived the word for "minute" from their term for the notches on a calendar stick.

Navajo bracelet with digital watch, c. 1985. Museum für Völkerkunde, Vienna, Austria.

Thanks to their extraordinary ability to learn and to adapt to new circumstances, the Navajo have entered the third millennium as the largest reservation population with the highest percentage of speakers of the old language. Their conciousness of tradition – and this includes silver jewelry, which has formed part of Navajo culture for only the last 150 years – is organically linked with progress.

Not all indigenous peoples were equally interested in the measurement of cyclical time. Calendrical timing was of greater importance to agricultural groups than to hunters or fishermen. The precise points on the horizon at which the sun appeared provided a reliable calendar from which the Pueblo peoples could tell when it was time to plant corn. Hunters, on the other hand, could generally make do with the far less precise lunar calendar, the months of which were named after recurring events such as the return of migrating birds. Hunters had no fixed working hours either, since hunting only became necessary when stores of provisions were exhausted; on average hunters worked many hours less than peasants or even factory workers.

All peoples distinguish between real events of the past and those of a mythical age, even where historic fact entered the world of myth. Thus the 19th-century inhabitants of Greenland were able to recount that they had attacked the Vikings in the 14th century, and the Athapaskans of Alaska remembered an 8th-century volcanic eruption as a story of the beginning of time. Many peoples regarded mythical time as being more important than historical time, perhaps because the order of the present world could only be explained through myth or because mythic time was also alive in the present.

The concept of progress was not an invention of the 19th century, nor was it unknown to indigenous North Americans. The Canadian Cree tell of a primitive people whom they supplanted in the distant past; the Navajo regard their rise out of a series of underworlds as a gradual process of improvement. In the course of their contact with whites, indigenous peoples have repeatedly demonstrated their willingness to accept useful innovations, even where they challenged ancient traditions; they have made use of progress when it served their own goals. This is one of the reasons why nothing is as it used to be; after all, we look back on our own 20th-century history with mixed feelings of mild forbearance and utter bewilderment. At the same time, these changes also demonstrate the vitality of indigenous America. Only dead things cease to change.

Opposite page:
*Kills Two, a Brule Medicine Man, Painting the Big Missouri Winter Count*, c. 1926. Photograph: John A. Anderson. Nebraska State Historical Society, Lincoln, NE.

Many peoples of the Plains (and apparently of the Eastern Woodlands as well) used pictographic representations of the most significant events of the year to produce what is known as a "winter count," which seved as a linear timeframe of sometimes up to 150 years, into which historic events could be positioned by the chronicler.

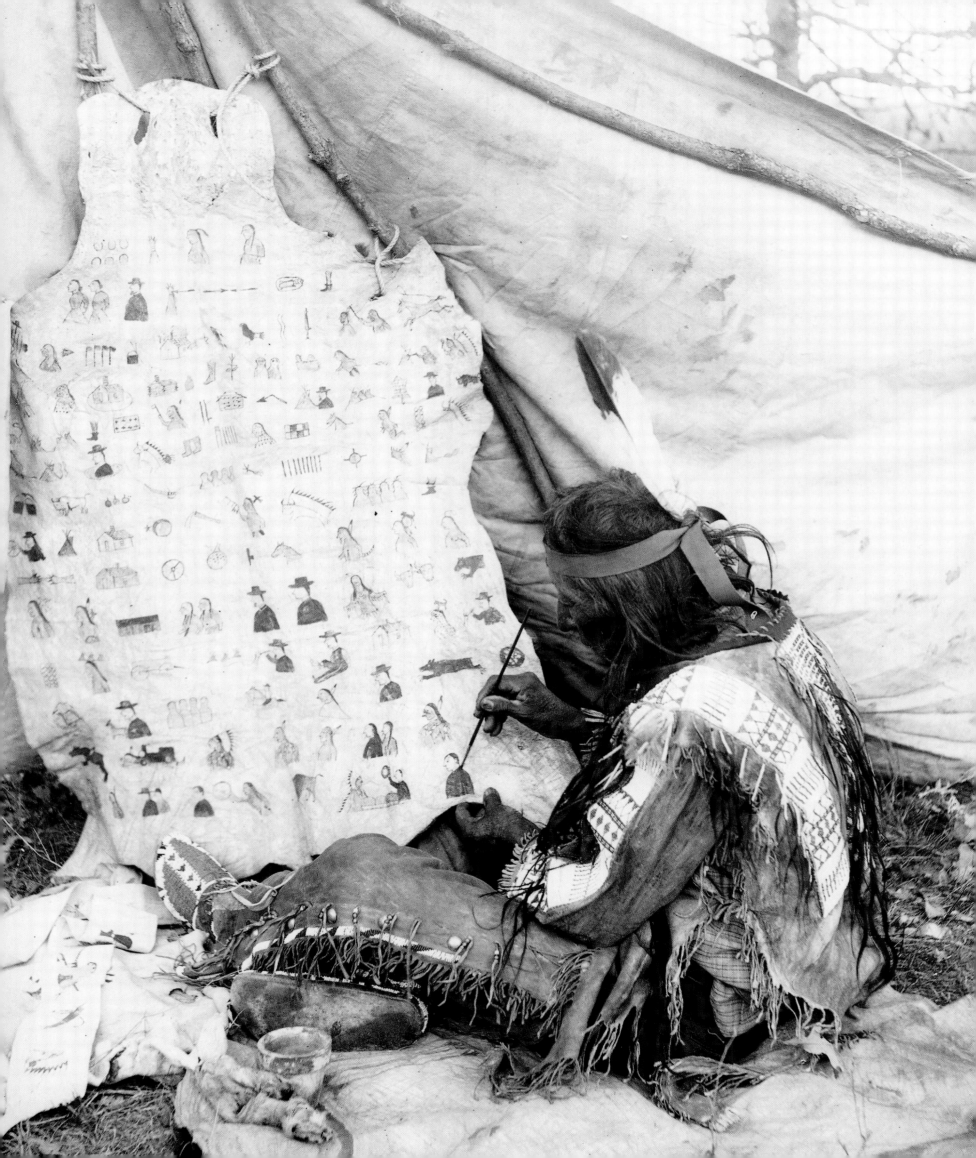

APPENDIX

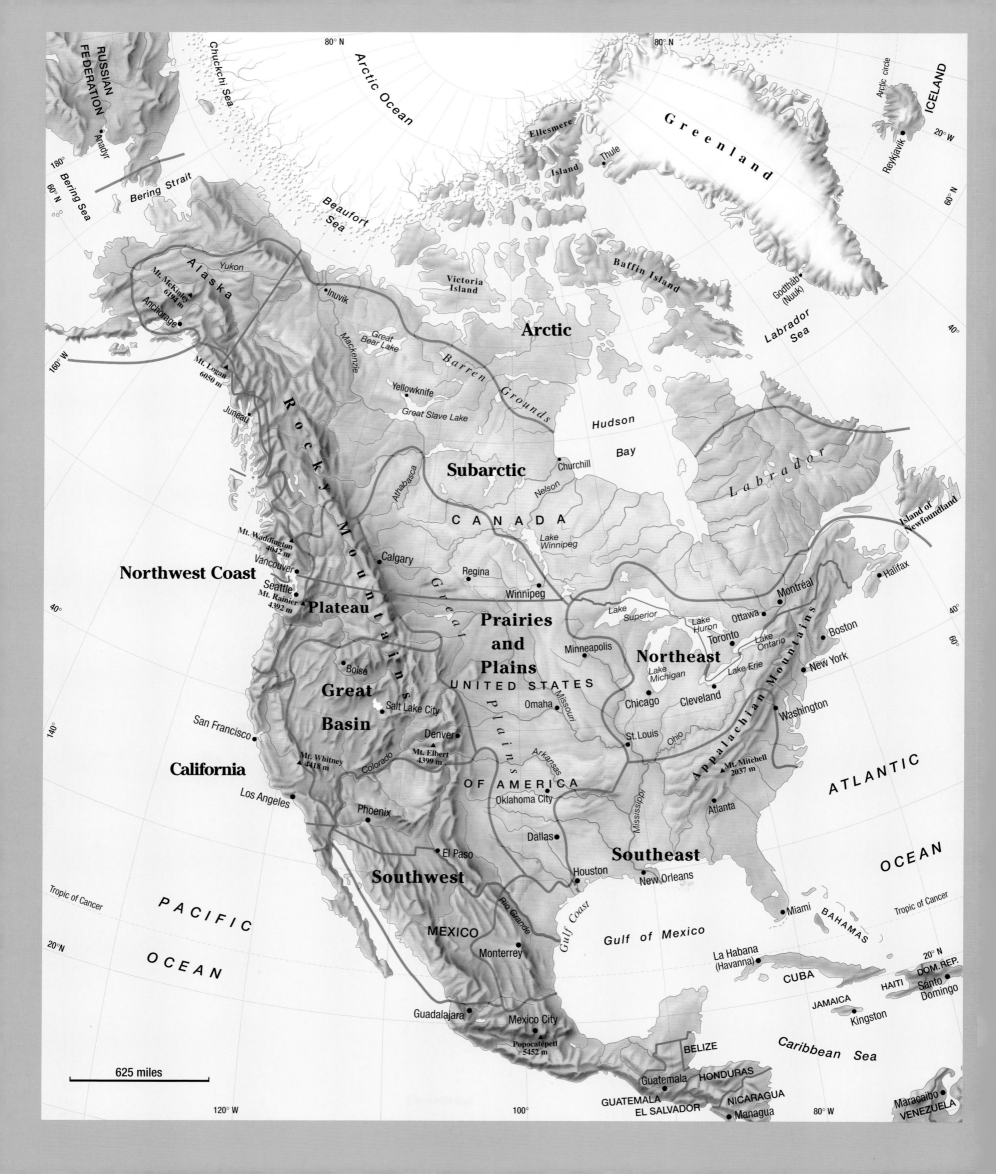

# GLOSSARY

Christian F. Feest

**Abelone** → Haliotis.

**Acculturation**, process of mutual cultural influence between two different groups in long-term contact. The extent and direction of cultural transfers depend on a variety of factors, including power relationships. Unlike *assimilation*, acculturation does not require basic identities and values to change; changes caused by cultural transfer often bring forth entirely new forms and/or meanings (see, for example, *tomahawk*).

**Adena**, prehistoric culture that flourished c. 500 BC– AD 100 in the Ohio Valley. Typical of this sedentary agricultural society were 60-foot-high conical mounds built over the cremated remains of distinguished individuals, and engraved stone slabs with depictions of birds of prey.

**Adobe** (Spanish, derived from Arabic), sun-dried clay bricks used as a building material by the Pueblo peoples. After the arrival of the Spanish, the previously handmade bricks were produced with the aid of wooden molds.

**Age groups.** Men and women of the Mandan and Hidatsa tribes on the upper Missouri River were organized into a series of associations whose membership changed with age. Graduation to a higher grade was achieved by acquiring from a relative in one of the higher grades the knowledge and ritual objects required for membership.

**Akicita** (Lakota, "warrior"), members of male warrior societies (e.g. the Prairie Fox society and the Strong Hearts), who policed the Lakota's large summer camps, ensuring order and discipline during the hunt.

**Akwesasne Notes**. Local newspaper of the St. Regis Reservation Mohawks, established in 1968. During the 1970s it became one of North America's leading Panindian publications, a mouthpiece for "native and natural people" that defined the image of the "new Indian" as an alternative model beyond the boundaries of indigenous North America.

**Alaska Commercial Company (ACC)**, American trading company founded in 1868, a year after the USA acquired Alaska, to replace the Russian-American Company. As a monopoly it became the most important instrument of the USA's colonial exploitation of the new USA territory. Since 1977, the ACC has been owned by a non-profit development organization in the interest of the indigenous population.

**Alaska Native Brotherhood (ANB)**, organization founded in 1912 to protect indigenous rights. Led by Tlingit brothers Louis and William Paul, the ANB was able to achieve full citizenship for native Alaskans (1922), protect fishing rights, achieve equal legal standing with indigenous peoples of other states, and led the struggle to have indigenous land rights acknowledged. Originally, the ANB advocated assimilation into American society but since the 1960s they have contributed to the resurgence of traditionalism.

**Alaska Native Claims Settlement Act (ANCSA)**. In 1971, 104 years after the USA acquired Alaska from the Russian Tsar, ANSCA was passed to regulate indigenous land rights in the northernmost US state. Thanks to this legislation, some 40 million acres of land and a payment of $926.5 million in compensation were transferred to the newly founded regional corporations whose shareholders were the former tribal members. Some of the hunting and fishing rights terminated in the wake of ANCSA were reinstated by later legislation.

**American Indian Arts and Crafts Act**, legislation passed by the US Congress in 1990 with the aim of protecting indigenous arts and crafts by imposing serious penalties on artists and dealers for wrongly describing as "Indian," work produced by persons, who are not members of federally recognized tribes. This legislation in fact discriminates against many indigenous peoples who do not match the government's definition. It also makes tribal people vulnerable to the imitation of their typical products by other tribes (kachina dolls of the Hopi, for example, are produced by the Navajo at cut-rate prices).

**American Indian Movement (AIM)**, organization founded by urban Native Americans in 1968 in Minneapolis (Minnesota) to combat police harassment. In the 1970s it developed into one of the most influential militant Native American organizations thanks to its involvement in spectacular actions carried out under the leadership of Russell Means, Dennis Banks, and others. Partly funded by Libya, the organization gained little support on the reservations and soon lost importance in the 1980s.

**American Indian Religious Freedom Act (AIRFA)**. Despite constitutional guarantees of religious freedom, indigenous people were repeatedly hindered from practicing their traditional religions by legislative measures, court decisions, and bureaucracy. The AIRFA was passed in 1978 to once again confirm the right to religious freedom, although without providing a recourse to court action. In the years that followed, further court decisions on the use of sacred sites and peyote were regarded by many Native Americans as additional restrictions on their religious rights.

**American Revolution** (1775–1783), rebellion of 13 British colonies in North America against the British crown, which led to the independence of the USA. Among the causes of the rebellion were the consequences of the Peace of Paris (1763), which marked the end of French colonial presence in North America and paved the way for the crown's increased taxation and patronization of the colonies. At the same time, the crown promised indigenous peoples that white settlement would not be permitted west of the Appalachians, thereby curbing the colonists' expansion. Initially neutral, indigenous peoples fought on both sides of the American Revolution, although overall they and the British were the major losers.

**Amerind**, hybrid term (from *American Indian*) coined in 1899 to distinguish between Indians of the Indian subcontinent and American "Indians." The term has found little application except in French-speaking regions and in some disciplines marginal to anthropology.

**Anasazi** (Navajo, "ancestors of the enemies"), term introduced in 1936 to designate the culture of the prehistoric ancestors of the present-day Pueblo peoples of Arizona, New Mexico, Colorado, and Utah, after becoming sedentary around the time of the birth of Christ. Distinctions are made between the early "Basketmaker" phases (until AD 700) and the later "Pueblo" phases, which were characterized by the emergence of pottery and stone or adobe architecture.

**Ancestors**. ascendants, as defined by the respectively valid *descent rules*, play a central role

Cooking basket, northwestern California, c. 1900. Rautenstrauch-Joest Museum für Völkerkunde, Cologne, Germany. → *Basket weaving*.

in indigenous North America, particularly for sedentary peoples, since it was they who founded the social groups and rituals of the communities. In the *chiefdoms* of the Virginia and the North Carolina Algonquian, the mummified ancestors of rulers were preserved in temples. The *kachinas* of the Pueblo peoples represent the ancestors of religious leaders and act as mediators between humans and the gods during rituals.

**Angakoq** (Inuktitut), religious specialist similar to a *shaman* who is possessed by spirits while in a state of ecstasy. He can command these spirits, or his own soul, to travel in search of solutions to the tasks with which he has been entrusted. These tasks may serve the entire community or individual members, and can include securing the success of the hunt, curing the sick, influencing the weather, predicting the future, or the expulsion of ghosts (→ *Sedna*). Generally, angakoqs pursued normal socio-economic lives, although they did enjoy a special status.

**Animal-calling ceremonies**. Many of the hunting peoples of North America performed rituals designed to attract game. Among the Blackfoot, the owners of particular sacred bundles and their wives disguised themselves as bison and performed a dance which imitated the animals' mating behavior. Eskimo umiak crews in northern Alaska chanted enticingly, while the umiak owner kept magical amulets, and his wife used certain behavior patterns to entice whales into allowing themselves to be killed.

**Animal souls**. The idea that animals have souls was widespread in indigenous North America. In contrast to the conception of human souls, animals were generally said to possess only one soul, which was often not held individually but regarded as the expression of a common inhabitant, owner, or master of a particular animal species (→ *inua*).

**Anorak** (West Greenlandic, "clothing"), tailored Eskimo shirt with a hood and long sleeves, usually made of seal skin or caribou hide. From Greenland to Siberia many different designs exist. There are also differences between the anoraks of men and those of women; the former are hunting garments while the much larger hoods of the latter often serve to carry infants.

**Antelope** → *Pronghorn antelope*.

**Apache fiddle**, instrument made from a hollowed stalk of mescal agave, strung with one or two strings of horsehair, and played with a horsehair bow. It is particular to the Apache and is used mainly for the performance of love songs. It is possibly derived from similar Filipino instruments which may have been brought to western Mexico by the Spanish. See *Musical bow*.

**Appaloosa** (from the tribal designation "Palouse," or the river named after it), breed of horse with typical patches on the rump, bred by the Nez Perces and/or their neighbors on the Plateau.

**Arctic fox** (*Alopex lagopus*), species of fox which occurs north of the timberline, with a dense white or slate gray winter coat that was highly prized by the fur trade. In pre-European times, the arctic fox was a relatively unimportant source of meat and skins for the Eskimo, although it was sometimes caught in pitfalls or nooses; these were later replaced by the metal traps used for commercial fur hunting.

**Arctic hare** (*Lepus arcticus*) → *hare*.

**Argillite**, generic term for various kinds of shale or slate used for carving (e.g. catlinite), which hardens rapidly in air. Specifically, the term argillite describes a black clay slate found only on the Queen Charlotte Islands in British Columbia and used by the Haida from about 1820 to produce "tourist art" (such as pipes, bowls, and models of crest poles).

**Arrow**, projectile discharged by a bow (or, less commonly, a blowgun), used in hunting and warfare. The great differences in the length, material, shaft construction, point and feathering of arrows in use were determined by the size of the bows in use, available raw materials, and their usage. Arrows used in warfare were often fitted with barbed heads to prevent easy removal from a wound. From the 19th century onward, iron arrowheads replaced those made of stone or bone. Arrows could also carry symbolic or

Previous pages:

Powwow camp.

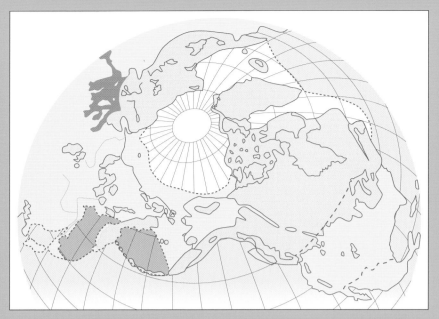

The Bering Strait theory.

Toward the end of the last Ice Age, large areas of the northern hemisphere (the gray areas on the map) were covered by glaciers. The Arctic Ocean (white) was covered by ice throughout the year and the Bering Sea and the Sea of Okhotsk (blue) for only part of the year. Glaciation caused a reduction in sea levels of approximately 900 feet; this created a wide land bridge in the area of the Bering Strait which connected Alaska and Siberia. At the height of the Ice Age (c. 18,000–12,000 BC), the two great North American glaciers merged to form an impassable barrier; before and after that time, however, migration would have been possible by going south and passing through a corridor on the east side of the Rocky Mountains. → *Bering Strait theory*.

religious meaning; the gift of four sacred arrows by the culture hero Mutsoyef is represented by one of the Cheyenne's two tribal bundles which must be cared for and kept safe to ensure the continued survival of the tribe.

**'Asdzáá Nádleehé**, "Changing Woman," an important mythical figure among the Navajo and Apache, sometimes also referred to as "White Painted Woman" or "White Shell Woman." She represents the changes that women undergo during their life cycle as well as those of the earth and its vegetation in the course of a year. As the creator of corn she provides humans with food. The culture hero twins Monster Slayer and Child of Water are born out of her union with the sun. She is personified by young women during the ceremony held to mark their first menstruation.

**Assembly of First Nations**, Canadian Panindian organization which replaced the National Indian Brotherhood of Canada in 1982, and is the official negotiating partner of the Canadian government with regard to affairs affecting the legal status of indigenous peoples.

**Assimilation**, process of adaptation whereby people and groups adopt the customs and values of a different group with the aim of achieving acceptance as members of that group. The assimilation of "the Indians" was a frequently proclaimed political aim of most colonial powers and nation-states; it generally failed because of the majority society's rejection, on the grounds of race or ethnicity, of the people who were to be assimilated (see *Acculturation*).

**Association (societies)**, groups of people based on common experiences or goals play an important part in binding together kinship groups in societies that are based predominantly on kinship. Associations were the keepers of ceremonial lore and of special knowledge generally kept secret from outsiders. Membership in an association was connected to social status, as were the various offices to which members could aspire. Membership could be acquired through a dream, by purchase, by invitation,

when a society's secret had been inadvertently discovered, or by belonging to an age group. According to their function, e.g., warrior societies, medicine societies, craftsworkers associations (guilds) may be distinguished. Membership might be restricted to either men or women, or could be open to both. Associations were most common in the Eastern Woodlands, in the Prairies and Plains, in the Southwest, in California, and along the Northwest Coast.

**Babiche** (Canadian French derived from Algonquian languages), narrow straps made of *rawhide*, used particularly in eastern and central North America for snowshoes, lacrosse sticks, and gaming hoops, as well as for making nets and netted bags.

**Badger**, (*Taxidea taxus*), musteline animal found in central and western North America, rarely hunted and then only for its fur. Yet the badger frequently lent its name to clans and was regarded as an animal with strong supernatural powers. According to the Cheyenne, badgers had at an earlier time spoken to humans, warning them of coming dangers; in Hopi mythology the badger was the first creature to emerge to earth from the underworld; the Micmac regarded the badger as a → *trickster*.

**Bald eagle** (*Haliaetus leucocephalus*) → *eagle*.

**Ball-headed club**, type of wooden club widespread in the Northeast, used for hand-to-hand combat, often slightly curved, with a carved ball in the form of a face or animal head at one end. After the European introduction of iron, these clubs began to feature thornlike metal spikes. The shafts often feature pictographic records of the owner's war deeds.

**Band**, anthropological term for a small and loosely organized political unit of fewer than 150 people, made up of several families who, in the course of a year, sometimes work alone and at other times cooperate. In North America, bands are typically found in the Arctic, Subarctic, Great Basin, and marginal zones of the

Southwest. In Canada, the term "band" is the official designation for indigenous groups living on *reservations*.

**Basket weaving**, various techniques used for making woven receptacles, were found across indigenous North America, albeit of differing regional importance. In addition to plaiting with active warps and wefts, baskets were made by *coiling* and *twining*. In California, the Great Basin and parts of the Plateau, baskets were used for cooking (→ *cooking with stones*). On the Northwest Coast and elsewhere they were also used for gathering wild plants, for storage purposes, and as hats. Together with pottery vessels, baskets were of great importance in the Southwest and in the Eastern Forests. Among the Hopi, basket weaving was the privilege of the women's societies (→ *Maraw*).

**Bast**, the innermost layer of tree bark. It consists of long fibers that can be peeled off in wide strips, and be worked in one piece by beating with mallets made of bone (as on the Northwest Coast), or be cut into narrow strips and plaited. Bast was also spun to make thread and used to produce cloth (→ *Chilkat blanket*).

**Bear cult**, in northern North America (as in northern Eurasia), a form of ritual behavior adopted when killing bears (→ *polar bear, grizzly bear, black bear*), which are regarded as having many human characteristics. The hunter speaks to the animal as he would to a relative, asking for forgiveness and subsequently decorating and anointing the carcass. The distribution of the meat and treatment of the bones are also subject to strict ritual rules. In Alaska a similar ceremony is dedicated to the whale.

**Beaver** (*Castor canadensis*). The beaver was the most important animal for indigenous fur hunters in the Subartic and the Northeast who supplied European and American trading companies. Beaver furs were widely used as a measure of value for trade goods. The use of steel traps and *castoreum* (the excretion of the beaver's sexual gland) as bait contributed to its extinction over a wide area.

**Berdache** (from Persian), term inappropriately applied to indigenous men and women who, usually as a result of a vision, adopt the opposite gender role to that of their natural sex (e.g. men as clothes-makers, women as warriors). The practices included under this term were not unusual, though by no means universal, and were not necessarily linked to homosexuality, although homosexual Native Americans today like to refer to the tradition of the "people with two souls."

**Bering Strait theory**. Scientists agree that America was populated as a result of migration during the Ice Age, when the lower sea levels allowed a land bridge to form between Asia and America in what is now the Bering Strait area. The exact period at which migration began (23,000–18,000 BC at the latest) is subject to disagreement. In contrast, however, many indigenous peoples believe that they were created on the American continent itself.

**Bighorn** → *Mountain sheep*.

**Bingo**, game of chance commonly organized by white American churches and charitable foundations to raise funds for good causes. Since the 1970s, reservation-owned "bingo salons" and casinos have been offering high stakes to their white customers – a growing source of tribal income. Commercial gambling on reservations is a source of controversy among the inhabitants and since 1988 has

been regulated by the Indian Gaming Regulatory Act.

**Birch bark**. According to an Ojibwa story, the culture hero Nanabozho gave humans the birch tree (which, being a child of the thunderbirds, is never struck by lightning). In the Subarctic and the Northeast, boats and containers were made from the bark of the paper or canoe birch (*Betula papyrifera*). Wide strips of bark were used to cover *wigwams*. After it was removed from the tree, the bark was heated to make it supple; it was sewn together with root splints and decorated by incising the inside, scraping the outside, or with embroidery of dyed porcupine quills.

**Bison** (*Bison bison* or *Bison americanus*), a close relative of the European bison and the most widespread wild cattle in North America since the early buffalo (*Bison antiquus*) became extinct at the end of the Ice Age. The forest bison originally spread almost as far as the Atlantic coast. Its economic importance rapidly declined as whites penetrated further inland (small numbers survive in the Subarctic). Prairie bison, whose numbers stood at some 30 million c. 1800, were the Plains peoples' main source of food until they were driven to the brink of extinction in the 1880s. They were also important big-game animals on the Prairies and were often equated with power and fertility.

**Bison-hunting culture**. In pre-European times, small groups of nomadic peoples hunted the bison which migrated between the open grasslands in summer and the sheltered edges of the Plains in winter. The bison-hunting culture flourished from late 17th century as a result of the introduction of the horse, which increased mobility and facilitated intensive exploitation of the herds. The bison-hunting culture was also characterized by a mounted warrior system, and a widespread and almost exclusive dependence on the bison. Its end came, after 200 years, when the bison herds were finally almost wiped out.

**Bison robe**, tanned bison hide worn by the peoples of the Plains and Prairies in winter or for ceremonial purposes. The robe was made by cutting a hide lengthwise and sewing it back together. It often featured a strip of porcupine quillwork or glass beads covering this seam and/or gender specific designs, for examples war deeds or a sun motif of painted feathers for men, an abstract bison symbolizing the earth and fertility for women.

**Bitterroot** (*Lewisia rediviva*), plant of the purslane family and a native of the Plateau region, where it grows at various altitudes. Its fleshy roots are gathered between April and June and dried for winter. Bitterroot is mentioned in third place after water and salmon in the Harvest Thanksgiving ceremonies of the Sahaptin.

**Black bear** (*Ursus americanus*), the most common type of American bear, whose coat, despite its name, varies from light brown to black, gray, or white. This generally nocturnal animal lives in the forests and swamps of the east and in the mountains of western North America and was highly prized for its meat, fat, and fur. The killing of black bears was almost invariably linked to elements of the *bear cult*.

**Black Drink**, also known by the Timucua name "cassina" and by the southeastern Algonquian term "yaupon". A decoction made from the leaves of the *Ilex vomitoria*, a holly used in rituals in the Southeast. In the 17th century the potion, which contains caffeine, was a popular drink in Europe, although it was supplanted by coffee and tea. In the Southeast, the black potion was used as an emetic exclusively by adult men for internal purification before Green Corn ceremonies, ball games, and other events. It was also used medicinally as a diuretic.

**Bladder Festival** (Yupik: Nakaciuryaraq), Yupik festival held at the beginning of the winter ceremonies when the bladders (regarded as the seat of the soul) of seals killed during the preceding year are returned to them. After ritual purification with sweatbaths and smoke, the men would compete in sporting events, song, and distribute gifts in the *qasgiq* where the inflated bladders were hung on the walls. At the end of this ten-day ceremony, the bladders were taken from the *qasgiq* through the smoke hole and returned to the seals through a hole chipped in the ice; thus ensuring their return the following year.

**Blowgun**, weapon used for hunting birds and small mammals in the Northeast (among the Iroquois and Maliseet) and Southeast (among the Cherokee, Creek, Choctaw, and Houma). It may have been introduced by the French in the 18th century. In the Southeast, the pipes are made from river cane (*Arundinaria*) and the arrows from splinters of cane wrapped with plant fibers at one end.

**Body painting.** Alongside tattooing, body painting is an important form of human adornment. Painting was generally used to mark temporary personal or social circumstances such as mourning, war, or ceremonial tasks to be performed by the painted person. However, some body painting, for example on the Northwest Coast, was regarded as the privilege of particular social groups. Body painting also served as protection from wind and sun.

**Bola** (boleadora), set of strings with weights attached at the ends, used for hunting birds and other small prey. Before being thrown, a bola is swung, causing the spinning weights to stretch the strings while in flight and wrap around the prey on contact. The bola of the Alaskan Eskimo consisted of seven strings with walrus ivory weights; the Californian bola took the form of a single rope with wooden weights at both ends.

**Bole-Maru** (Patwin, *bole* and Pomo, *maru*, "dreamer"), religion that developed in central northern California in 1872 through the amalgamation of the *Kuksu* cult with the *Ghost Dance*. Ceremonies led by dreamers who received instructions from the Creator were held to heal the sick. They also served to preserve ancient beliefs while also adapting them to suit new social and political circumstances. In the 20th century most Kashaya-Pomo dreamers have been women.

**Booger masks** (from English bogey, "ghost"), masks made of wood or gourd and used in a dance of the Cherokee of North Carolina to represent strangers who enter the perfect world of the Cherokee and are driven out at the end of the dance. This dance was originally performed expel sickness, and was performed only in winter because the spirits of strangers could cause frost.

**Bow**, in many parts of North America the most important weapon for hunting and war; originating in Asia, it spread over the continent during the 1st millenium BC. It is less important in the central Arctic and the Southwest where wood was scarce. There are numerous variations, including man-high

wooden bows in the Eastern Forests, short, reinforced bows used by the mounted bison hunters of the Plains, similar forms found in California, soldered bows made of horn and antler in the northern Plains and Plateau, and bone bows in the central Arctic (see *Arrow*).

**Breechclout**, garment covering the genital area which in North American took various forms. Breechclouts could take the form of a single or double apron attached to a belt either at the front only, or at back and front. Other types were made of a longer piece of material pulled between the legs and folded over a belt at front and back.

**Bull boat** (from French *boule*, "ball"), usually a hemispherical boat made of untanned bison hide stretched over a willow frame; used on the Plains for crossing rivers.

**Bundle**, collection of ritual objects used in public and private ceremonies, and kept wrapped together in leather or cloth when not in use. Sacred bundles and their rituals were based on visions (→ *vision quest*) or dreams of a person (or of a mythical ancestor); the objects they contained (feathers, stones, animal hides, and musical instruments, for example) were gifts from the being who had appeared in the vision or dream, or were assembled on their instruction. Some peoples permitted the buying and selling of personal bundles.

**Bureau of Indian Affairs (BIA)**, federal government agency responsible for the affairs of the USA's indigenous peoples. Formed in 1824 as part of the War Department and integrated into the Department of the Interior in 1849, the BIA was, for most of its existence, an instrument of the USA's internal colonial administration, responsible for implementing the government's "program of civilization," administering the reservations, inefficiency, and regulating all tribal relations. Despite preferential staff recruitment of indigenous Americans since the 1930s, and its management by Native Americans since 1966, most indigenous people regarded the BIA as a symbol of government patronization, inefficiency, and nepotism. In 1972, militant members of the *American Indian Movement* occupied its central administration offices in Washington. Since the 1980s, many administrative tasks have been performed by the tribes themselves, while the BIA's activities are generally limited to the government's trust obligations to the tribes.

**Burial mound**, monumental mound of earth up to 60 feet high piled over the remains of a dead person. Characteristic of the pre-historic Adena and Hopewell cultures of the Northeast.

**Busk** (from Creek *poskita*, "to fast"), Creek Green Corn ceremony lasting four or eight days, which also celebrates the annual renewal of the world. Busks are held in July or August, when all the misdeeds of the previous year are forgiven, the ceremonial plaza is cleaned, a new fire lit, and old household items exchanged for new. Before and during the ceremony, participants had to undergo spiritual purification by fasting and drinking the *Black Drink* which caused nausea and vomiting.

**Buzzard Man** (Chitimacha *oshácna*; called by the Choctaw "he who loosens the flesh from the bones"), burial specialist among some tribes of the lower Mississippi, whose task it was to scrape off the semidecomposed flesh from the bones of the dead laid to rest on raised platforms, and to bundle the bones.

The Buzzard Man lived in the tribe's charnel house and kept his fingernails long to facilitate his work.

**Cacique** (from *kazike*, in the language of the Arawak of Hispaniola and Cuba), term introduced to the Southwest by the Spanish to describe village chiefs recognized by the colonial administration.

**Cactus wine**, alcoholic drink made from the fermented juice of the *saguaro* cactus, drunk during the annual rain ceremonies of the Pima and Papago in Arizona and Sonora in order to ensure that the soil receives sufficient water and will be fertile.

**Calendar stick**, wooden stick with incised mnemonic signs used by the Pima and Papago to record the passing of the years and important events during the year. Similar aide memoires were used in other regions of North America, although far less is known about them.

**Calumet** (French *chalumeau*, "reed"), wooden pipe decorated with feathers and bird skins used in adoption rituals during which kinship relations between individuals or groups were established. The term is also used to describe a long-stemmed "peace pipe." The Calumet dance originated in the *Southeastern Ceremonial Complex*, and spread to the Prairies, Plains, and Eastern Woodlands following the example of the Pawnee's Hako ritual (→ *Hunka*), whereby two calumets symbolize the wings of an eagle. Dancing and singing underline the desire for a supernatural blessing of the new relationship.

**Camas** (Chinook jargon from Nootka, "sweet"), lily (*Camassia quamash*) whose sweet and nutritious bulbs were gathered in great numbers by the peoples of the Plateau area and neighboring Northwest Coast (Flathead women, for example, collected over 2 tons per year) and subsequently prepared by slow steaming.

**Camp circle.** The arrangement of the tents in the Plains peoples' summer camps repeated the circular floor plan of their conical tents, including the opening to the east. The position of each tent within the circle marked the respective status of each local group within the tribal community (the seating order within each tent also corresponded to the hierarchical position of each family member).

**Canada goose** (*Branta canadensis*), large, brown waterfowl, whose V-shaped migratory

flight formation is sometimes interpreted as a sign of the approach of winter or is used to describe that season (Virginia Algonquian *cohonks*). Canada geese are a popular, but difficult to catch game bird, inducing hunters to use decoys, bait, and screens.

**Candlefish (eulachon)** (Chinook jargon *ulakan*), small salmon-like migratory fish (*Thaleichtys pacificus*), native to the Pacific Northwest Coast, especially the Nass River. Thanks to its high oil content, it is flammable when dried and can be used as a torch. An oil was produced by fermenting, boiling, and pressing the fish.

**Cannibalism**, the habitual consumption of human flesh. In North America, as elsewhere, this custom is frequently ascribed to alien peoples, and is reflected by the appellation "man-eater" (e.g. the Mohawk as seen by the Narragansett, or the Tonkawa as seen by the Cheyenne). Cannibalism is also a characteristic of some supernatural beings (→ *Hamats'a*; *Windigo*) and finds its symbolic ritual and linguistic form in the ritual and rhetoric of war. The consumption of corpses (including intentional killing for this purpose) as a survival strategy was reported from the Subarctic during times of famine. The term "cannibal" derives from the Arawak name for their Carib neighbors.

**Canoe** (Carib, "dugout"). The word is frequently used as a collective term for all Native American boats, especially the bark boats of the Subarctic and the Northeast (→ *birch bark*), the dugouts of the Northwest Coast and the Eastern Woodlands as well as plank boats and other types of vessel.

**Cardinal directions**, a widely (although not universally) employed principle of ordering the world by quartering the horizon into east, south, west, and north; *zenith* and *nadir* are sometimes added as a fifth and sixth direction. Cardinal directions are frequently associated with different winds. In symbolism they are often linked with colors and particular roles in rituals. Ritual sequences in clockwise or counterclockwise directions are also conceived in relation to the cardinal directions.

**Caribou** (derived from Abenaki), American species of reindeer. Sometimes a distinction is made between the woodland caribou of the Subarctic (*Rangifer caribou*), and the tundra caribou (*R. arcticus*) of the Arctic. In both regions, caribou were important game animals although

Man's underpants made of seal skin with leather appliqué, eastern Greenland, c. 1900. Rautenstrauch-Joest Museum für Völkerkunde, Cologne, Germany → *Seal*.

their season and effective use could vary enormously. The domesticated reindeer of northern Eurasia (*R. tarandus*) was introduced to Alaska (1891), Canada (c. 1940), and Greenland (1952) as a draft animal and source of meat, although with limited success.

**Carlisle Indian School**, the first nonreservation boarding school established by the American government (1879). This school was committed to implementing General R. H. Pratt's ideas of turning indigenous peoples into American citizens through strict educational methods. Until its closure in 1918, thousands of boys and girls from hundreds of tribes were given training, mainly in agricultural and vocational skills. Although the school was frequently described as an instrument of "ethnocide," many of its alumni became well-known campaigners for Native American rights and Panindian aims.

**Carving**. Woodcarving was particularly well developed in the forested regions of the Northwest Coast (including among the Eskimo of southwestern Alaska) and the Eastern Woodlands. The emergence of a class of professional artisans and artists along the Northwest Coast contributed to a particular refinement which was further promoted by the introduction of European metal tools. In other areas, wood carving had little significance or was limited to a few forms (e.g. *tihus* in the Southwest, masks in Greenland). Stone carving exploited the occurrence of soft stones (*argillite, catlinite, soapstone*) and also developed in regions, like the Plains and Arctic, where wood was scarce.

**Castoreum**, excretion from the sexual gland of the beaver. It was applied to traps to attract other beavers. This bait was so successful that the beaver population was entirely wiped out in whole areas.

**Catlinite**, red clay slate (see *argillite*) used mainly to make the bowl of pipes, and therefore also known as "pipestone." It is named after American painter George Catlin (1796–1872), who visited, and was the first to describe, the great catlinite quarry (now Pipestone National Monument) in southeastern Minnesota in 1836. This quarry was used by several different tribes and was treated as a neutral zone in times of war. Smaller amounts of catlinite are also found in North and South Dakota and in Canada.

**Cayuse**, a type of horse bred by the tribe of the same name. The name is sometimes used to describe all "Indian ponies" and even *mustangs*.

**Cedar** → *yellow cedar, red cedar*.

**Ceramics** → *pottery*.

**Ceremonial ax**, weapon with a stone or metal blade (war hatchet), used primarily on ceremonial occasions, rather than in battle, as a symbol of rank or power. Ceremonial axes made out of a single piece of polished stone were used by the prehistoric Mississippian cultures of the Southeast. *Tomahawks* were often also used as ceremonial axes after the end of the Indian Wars.

**Ceremonial dance** → *dance*.

**Cherokee Phoenix**, the first Indian tribal newspaper. It appeared between 1828 and 1834 in the Cherokee Nation in Georgia, published by Elias Boudinot (1804–1839) in both English and the Cherokee syllabary.

**Chickee**, type of housing among the Seminole of Florida. The ridge roof was covered with *palmetto* leaves, and the walls either similarly covered or left open. The internal sitting and sleeping platform was raised about three feet above the ground. Four or five such chickees, each measuring about 18 square yards, were grouped into compounds which could each house up to 12 people.

**Chief**, colloquial term for all political leaders of societies below the level of states. However, there are more differences than similarities between such leaders. In principle, chiefs aquire their office through their achievements (e.g. as hunters, warriors, or orators), or are assigned to it through membership in a family or other kinship group. Their power of persuasion was often all the

Blackfoot bison-horn headdress denoting rank in a men's society, c. 1880. Ethnologisches Museum, Staatliche Museen zu Berlin – Preussischer Kulturbesitz, Berlin, Germany. → *Buffalo; Horned headdress*.

political leverage that they possessed, although they occasionally were able to rely on force or religious legitimization in exercising their power. Many tribes had different leaders for times of war and for times of peace (→ *Miko; Sachem*).

**Chiefdom**, anthropological term for a form of political organization in which political, economic, and ceremonial life is centralized, and a (usually hereditary) leader is endowed with extensive powers as well as being actively involved in the redistribution of economic wealth. Chiefdoms are regarded as an intermediary stage in the evolution of states.

**Child carriers**, cradle-like devices for protecting and transporting infants. Child carriers were not used in the Arctic and the Southeast, where infants were either carried in anorak hoods or in slings on the hip in cloth. On the Northwest Coast, child carriers consisted of wooden boxes fitted with a board which deformed the infant's skull while serving as a sunshade. Basketry child carriers were widespread, from the central Northwest coast to California and the Southwest. Leather bags reinforced with wooden slats were common on the Plains, as were bark cradles in the western Subarctic and wooden cradleboards in the Northeast. Child carriers were generally carried on the back by means of tumplines.

**Chilkat blanket**, ceremonial robe worn by high-ranking men among the Tlingit and their neighbors on the northern Northwest Coast. The twined blankets were made of cedar bark and mountain goat wool by the women after designs painted on pattern boards by the men, and depicted the stylized crests of noble families. They were first made at the beginning of the 19th century and their production was largely restricted to the Tlingit village of Chilket. The craft was abandoned in the late 19th century but reemerged in the late 20th century.

**Chingichngish**, high god in a religion that originated in the 18th century among the Ipai, Tipai, Luiseño, and Chumash of southern California. He was believed to be the creator or transformer of a previous world, and stood at the head of a pantheon. Chingichngish was credited with the invention of the initiation ceremonies at which the roots and leaves of the thorn apple *Datura innoxia* (*toloache*) were used as a narcotic.

**Civil War**, American (1861–1865), During the war between the Northern States (the Union) and the Southern States (the Confederacy) of the United States, the conquest of the West necessarily became of secondary importance. In 1862 the Dakota of Minnesota, believing the white Americans to be distracted by their internal conflict, staged an uprising (which ultimately proved unsuccessful). Many indigenous peoples of the Eastern Woodlands fought on both sides of the conflict.

**Clan**, kinship group consisting of several *lineages*, whose common ancestor (or the common past from which the group's relationship derives) is mythical and not historical. As with the lineage, distinctions are made between matrilineal and patrilineal clans that are determined by *descent rules*.

**Coiling**, looping and sewing technique in basketry. Bundles of fibers or twigs are coiled in a spiral fashion, and fastened together by sewing or by wrapping thread around them. Patterns can be created by changing the shape and color of the threads or by applying decorative material to the exterior (e.g. shell beads in California). Coiling is the oldest known form of basket weaving in North America. It is particularly typical of the cultures of the Southwest, California, the Great Basin, and the Plateau.

**Colonial period**, period in American history when European settlement was politically and economically controlled by European governments or by the private companies authorized by them. The colonial period lasted until the establishment of the nation-states of the USA (1776), Mexico (1821), and Canada (1867), and until those regions that were still under European dominion were integrated into these new states (e.g. Louisiana 1803, Florida 1821, Oregon 1846, Alaska 1867). For the indigenous peoples the colonial period has never ended, since they continue to be under the economic and political control of a foreign power.

**Colonization**, process of taking possession of a foreign country, including the subjugation or expulsion of its original inhabitants. Indigenous peoples of North America have also been colonizers in the course of their histories, but from the 16th century onward all of them became the victims of colonization by European powers and Euro-American nation-states.

**Cooking with stones**, cooking method whereby liquids are heated by hot stones like those used in sweat lodges. This method is used wherever fireproof cooking vessels made of pottery, stone, or metal do not exist. For cooking, leather containers were used on the Plains, wooden boxes on the Northwest Coast, baskets in California and the Great Basin, and vessels of birch bark in the Subarctic.

**Copper**. Pure copper is found along the northern shore of Lake Superior and around Great Slave Lake in the western Subarctic. The smelting process being unknown, copper was hammered to make ornaments, emblems of rank, and (in the Northwest) daggers. The "coppers" of the Northwest Coast were valuable ceremonial objects which were given away or destroyed during potlatches. The peoples of the Great Lakes region believed the metal to be a gift from the supernatural beings of the underwater world. The value ascribed to copper made it a coveted trade item which white people began to supply after their arrival.

**Corn beer,** was widely produced in pre-European times in the Southwest south of the Pueblo region, by fermenting the sugar produced from the starch by the germination of corn.

Corn beer continues to play a central role in the social life of the Tarahumara of Chihuahua. The southern Athapaskans (Apache and Navajo) also learned to make corn beer in the 18th and 19th centuries (→ *Tulipai*).

**Coup** (French, "blow"), among the peoples of the Plains, the act of touching a living or dead enemy with either the hand, a weapon, or a coup stick. The coup was the Plains peoples' most highly regarded war deed, rewarded with the greatest honor. The number of coups that could be counted on each enemy varied from tribe to tribe.

**Cowry** (*Cypraea moneta*), the shell of a marine mollusk, native to the Indian Ocean, which was used as currency in southern and southeastern Asia and in Africa, and which reached North America as a trade good. Cowries were used as magical projectiles for the symbolic killing of initiates to the *Midewiwin* ritual.

**Coyote** (Spanish loanword from Nahuatl), species of wild dog (*Canis latrans*) common everywhere south of the Arctic with the possible exception of the Southeast. In the oral tradition of the Plains, Plateau, Great Basin, central California and parts of the Southwest, the coyote is a *trickster* and/or creator or *culture hero*. He frequently appears in the company of another animal or the real Creator, whose intentions he generally thwarts.

**Cradleboard**, form of *child carrier*, particularly common in the Northeast and in the Prairies. The child is strapped to a wooden board, which has a wooden "roll bar" to protect the head.

**Cranial deformation**. The artificial deformation of the soft cranium of infants was either an unintentional consequence of strapping babies to *cradleboards*, or was performed intentionally to produce an aesthetically pleasing head form which would also serve as a marker of social status. A flattening or elongation of the forehead, achieved by attaching a board to the front of the head, was common in parts of the Southeast and on the central and southern Northwest Coast. The Koskimo Kwakiutl and their neighbors produced elongated, conical skulls by firmly wrapping their infants' heads.

**Creole**, in Alaska a term designating the offspring of marriages between Russian settlers or traders and indigenous people. In the Southeast the word refers to the culturally conservative descendants of French or Spanish settlers, although it is also used to denote the offspring of such settlers with African Americans.

**Crest pole**, popularly known as "totem pole," tree trunk carved with figures representing the hereditary privileges of a person or kinship group, common along the Northwest Coast. The images generally refer to mythical events related to the privileges' origins. Crest poles stood in front of a house to indicate its ownership and also served as grave posts (which could contain the ashes of the deceased). As memorial poles erected during potlatches they marked the privileges of the organizer.

**Cross-cousin marriage**, form of marriage in parts of the Subarctic and on the northern Northwest Coast in which "cross-cousins" are preferred marriage partners. Cross-cousins are the children of siblings of the opposite sex, i.e., a person's mother's brother's child or father's sister's child. In the Subarctic cross-cousin marriage strengthened the social cohesion of small hunting groups. On the Northwest Coast it reinforced links between high-ranking members of particular clans.

**Cult of the dead**. The ceremonial practices connected with death which, together with mourning rituals, help the living to deal with separation from the deseased, document the remaining links to the dead, or facilitate the transition of the dead into another world. This may include the deposition of grave goods, sacrifices at the burial site, the erection of monuments such as burial mounds or crest poles, and memorial services for the deceased. Fear of the ghosts of the dead was prevalent among many peoples (e.g., the Apache and Navajo) and prevented them from developing

Pukwubis masks depicting victims of drownings who have been transformed into forest spirits. Opetchesaht-Nootka, British Columbia, c. 1890. Ethnologisches Museum, Staatliche Museen zu Berlin – Preussischer Kulturbesitz, Berlin, Germany. → *Mask*.

an elaborate cult of the dead.

**Culture hero**, mythical person who is believed to have been responsible for the renewal of an existing world or for its completion for use by human beings, including the creation of social and religious institutions (→ *I'itoi*; *Mastamho*; *Motseyoe*; *Tharonhiawagon*). The cunning this requires can at times develop into mischief, thereby turning a culture hero into a *trickster*.

**Dall's sheep** (*Ovis ammon dalli*). This animal inhabiting the mountain regions of Alaska, northern British Columbia, and the Yukon Territory, was hunted by the Tlingit for its fat and for its horns, which were used to make spoons and bowls. The Athapaskans of the interior also used its hide to make moccasin trousers.

**Dance**, ritualized form of movement to music with symbolic meaning. In indigenous

North America dance was predominantly of a religious nature, yet in more recent times it has also become an expression of a group's identity. A dance can be a form of prayer, a demonstration of supernatural powers, a magical imitation of desired goals, or a dramatic reenactment of mythical events. The meaning of the dance movements may be reinforced by the use of special dance attire (e.g. animal disguises, *tablitas*), *masks* or dancing wands (→ *animal-calling ceremonies*; *Ghost Dance*; *calumet*; *Okipa*; *powwow*; *Prophet Dance*; *Snake Dance*; *Sun Dance*; *winter ceremonial*).

**Datil** (Spanish, "date"), the sweet, banana-shaped fruit of the palm lily (*Yucca baccata*, *Yucca glauca*) gathered by the Apache and Yuma in the fall and either eaten raw or roasted and dried for storage.

**Dawes Act** → *General Allotment Act*.

**Deer**, in a wider sense this term encompasses *caribou*, *moose*, and *wapiti* as well as deer of the genus *Odocoileus*, including the white-tailed deer (*Odocoileus virginianus*) of southern Canada and the USA (excluding California and the Great Basin), and the mule deer (*O. hemionus*) which is restricted to the western half of the continent south of the Northwest Territories. Both were game animals and a particularly important source of meat and skins in the Eastern Woodlands. Among the Iroquois, deer antlers symbolized the chief's office, and in western North America the dew-claws of deer were used to make rattles

which were widely used during female puberty rites.

**Dentalium** (tooth shell), mollusk of the Pacific Ocean whose conical, pipe-shaped, slightly curved shell was used for ornaments and traded as far inland as the Plains. In northwestern California dentalium shells were strung and used as a measure of value and means of exchange ("shell money").

**Descent rules**, determine membership of kinship groups. Where descent is reckoned equally through both mother and father (as it is in Western society), we speak of bilateral kinship, whereby every person is at the center of a network of maternal and paternal ancestors, their descendants and his or her own descendants. *Clans* and *lineages* occur when descent is defined exclusively through either the male or female line (patrilinear or matrilinear) or, as with the Kwakiutl and Nootka, where there is a choice to define it either through the mother or the father (ambilinear).

**Digging stick**, implement used by gatherers for digging up roots, usually in the form of a straight or slightly bent stick made of wood or antler or, after contact with whites, iron. The lower end was pointed, while the upper end sometimes had a crossbar handle attached.

**Dip-net fishing**, form of fishing in which a bag-shaped net attached to a long pole is used in waters containing large numbers of fish.

**Diyin Dine'é** (Navajo, "Knowing People"), the supernatural beings of the Navajo. They include "persuadable deities" whose intentions are always good, the unpredictable "unreliable deities," the messengers of the gods, the heroes standing between gods and humans, the "unpersuadable deities" (mainly dangerous monsters), the "dangers," and the "beings between good and evil" (e.g., cold, sleep, and poverty).

**Dog** (*Canis familiaris*), domesticated relative of the *wolf* and coyote. The earliest archeological indications of a close link between dogs and humans in North America date from c. 5000 BC in the Eastern Woodlands. Since that time the use of dogs spread to all parts of North America and spawned innumerable breeds. In the Arctic, the Subarctic, peripheral zones of the Northeast, on the West Coast, and in the Southwest, dogs have become particularly important hunting companions. Dogs have served as pack and draft animals (for *dog sleds*, *toboggans*, and *travois*) in the Prairies and Plains, the western Subarctic, and the Arctic. Despite a widely held belief that dog meat was poisonous, it was almost universally eaten in times of famine; the Iroquois, the peoples of the southern Great Lakes region, the Cheyenne, and the Californian Yokuts fattened dogs for food; especially in the northern Prairies and Plains, in the Northeast, and on the Northwest Coast, dogs were eaten without fattening for ceremonial reasons.

**Dog sled**, a vehicle with runners drawn by dogs, used as a means of transportation on snow. In North America it was originally used only in the western Arctic, later spreading eastward with the expansion of the Thule culture c. AD 1000. These dog sleds had low runners made of wood, bone, ivory, or frozen leather which directly supported the cargo area, and were drawn by individually harnessed dogs whose traces were arranged in a fan shape. The Siberian dog sleds that were introduced to Alaska in the 18th century had an elevated cargo area to increase clearance and a central trace to which the dogs were harnessed in tandem.

**Drum**, any musical instrument from which sound is produced by vibrating a stretched hide (membranophone). Except in California and parts of the Southwest, drums, such as used in rituals by the *angakoq* and other religious specialists, had low wooden frames. In the Northeast and Southeast, some drums consisted of covered vessels partly filled with water. These are still in use today in Peyote religion rituals. Wooden cylinder drums with hides covering both ends were predominant in the Southwest, and in a different form are also still used by powwow drumming groups.

**Eagle**, collective term for various types of hawklike birds of prey, e.g., the golden eagle (*Aquila chrysaetos*) and bald eagle (*Haliaetus leucocephalus*). Many North American cultures endowed the eagle, the largest bird of prey, with great religious and symbolic importance. It is often associated with the sun, whose rays the Hopi and peoples of the Plains interpreted as feathers, which were also widely regarded as symbolizing success in warfare. In the Northeast and along the Northwest Coast, eagles were seen as thunderbirds in constant conflict with the animals of the sea, and were regarded as helpers of warriors and whalers. Some tribes (e.g., the Pueblo peoples and Hidatsa) captured live eagles and kept them in cages for their feathers.

**Earth lodge**, term for the earth-covered, circular *pit houses* of the sedentary peoples of the Prairies. The buildings had low, conical roofs, measured up to 90 feet in diameter, and featured along the walls sleeping cabins, space for storing firewood and domestic and ceremonial objects, and a corral. Pits were dug into the floor to store corn and squash.

**Endogamy**, prescription or custom of marrying only within one's own local, social, or ethnic group. Endogamy frequently occurs where there are social classes (e.g., the Northwest Coast and the Southeast), though not universally (e.g., not among the Natchez). Endogamy strengthens solidarity within a group while limiting the network of external relations. See *Exogamy*.

**Eskimo roll**, technique developed by the Eskimo whereby the paddler of a capsized *kayak* can right his vessel without assistance. The most sophisticated form of the Eskimo roll developed in the eastern Arctic. In the western Arctic it appears either to have never existed or to have been a skill that was lost long ago.

**Ethnogenesis**, the evolution of new peoples, particularly when ethnic groups are divided or merge with one another. The Seminole in Florida, for example, originated in the late 18th century when factions of the Lower Creek and remnants of earlier indigenous peoples of Florida amalgamated. Hybrid populations (e.g., the Lumbee in North Carolina and the Métis in Canada) have developed their own identities to distinguish themselves from the groups from which they derived and especially in reaction to discrimination and oppression.

**Eulachon** → *candlefish*.

**Evening star**, for nine months of the year, the planet Venus is in superior conjunction (behind the sun as seen from the earth) and appears as a bright star in the western evening sky (see *Morning star*). However, as there are also other planets appearing on the morning or evening sky, identification is not always unambiguous. The Chumash of California considered the evening star to be linked to the land of the dead, and the sun as connected to the eagle. The Pawnee of the Prairies believed that the evening star ("Female White Star") and morning star ("Large Star") were the parents of the first Pawnee girl.

**Exogamy**, prescription or custom of marrying only outside the limits of one's own local or social group. Because of the almost universal incest taboo, the smallest exogamous units are usually formed by the nuclear family. Exogamy is frequently practiced in clans or moieties as a means of linking such kinship groups through exchange. This form of exogamy often exists alongside local endogamy.

**Eyedazzler**, term used to describe a popular Navajo blanket design of the period between 1870 and 1890 which features colorful zigzag lines arranged in a diamond pattern.

**False face** (or simply "face"), Iroquois term for a mask, often with distorted facial features, used by members of an Iroquois medicine society to embody a supernatural being. The origin of such masks is said to date from the mythical past, when the leader of the supernatural forest dwellers ("Great Humpbacked One") challenged the Creator to a test of strength. As punishment, the giant was given the task of helping humans combat sickness. The masks are ideally carved from the wood of a living tree, and since the 19th century they have also been produced for a white market. Traditionalists are attempting to stop not merely the sale of such masks but their depiction and exhibition in museums.

**Fasting**. In many parts of North America, going without food for long periods of time formed part of religious life (→ *busk*; *purification rituals*). In the Southeast, for example, fasting served to purify the body before ceremonial events or during life crises. In the Northeast and in the Prairies and Plains it formed part of the *vision quests* undertaken to seek the assistance of supernatural beings. The physical weakening brought about by voluntary starvation facilitated a vision seeker's state of mild ecstasy. From an indigenous point of view, fasting aroused the pity of the spirit helpers.

Harpoon point for hunting walrus, Eskimo, Alaska, 19th century. → *walrus*; *harpoon*.

**Feather headdress**, head decoration usually made of eagle feathers which served to denote rank in particular warrior societies among the peoples of the Prairies and Plains. There were major differences in the form of the headdress and in the number and arrangement of the feathers. A circle of eagle's feathers often symbolizes the sun. Today, the feather headdress has become a symbol of "the Indian" and has spread to peoples where it was previously unknown.

**Fire making**. In indigenous North America fire was produced either by striking stones against each other or by friction. The former method was used in the Arctic and northern Subarctic and on the Northwest Coast; sparks were produced by striking flint against iron pyrite. The friction method, using a fire drill, was widespread; friction produced by rotating a stick between the hands in a depression of a wooden hearth heated the dust produced by the twirling until it glowed. (A less common implement was the fire plow, in which a wooden stick was moved back and forth in a groove cut into a block of wood.) The sparks or smoldering wood dust would then set alight tinder such as dried sponges, bark, or dried grass.

**Firewater**, term for "alcohol," probably derived from French, in the Algonquian languages of the Northeast and Subarctic, and in some Siouan languages of the Prairies.

**First Nations**, a term used in Canada since the late 20th century to refer to the country's indigenous peoples, whose umbrella organization is known as the Assembly of First Nations.

**Fish-in**, demonstration held by indigenous people, particularly along the Northwest Coast, in support of their legal claims to fishing rights outside the reservations and for using traditional fishing methods prohibited by state laws. Since the 1960s fish-ins have been media-friendly and effective actions against social discrimination, and have been supported by such popular movie stars as Marlon Brando.

**Fishing spear**, widely used fishing implement, usually consisting of several barbed bone points attached to a wooden shaft so as to improve the fisherman's chances of spearing fish.

**Fishing wheel**, device for catching fish consisting of a paddle wheel operated by the force of the water and designed to lift fish out of the water with no human intervention. Originally a European device, it was adopted by the Yupik in southwestern Alaska in the 19th century and is now regarded as a "traditional" fishing implement.

**Five Civilized Tribes**, Euro-American collective term for the Cherokee, Chickasaw, Choctaw, Creek, and Seminole of southeastern North America. As sedentary corn farmers with the beginnings of territorial political organization, they showed the greatest potential for adopting many characteristics of European civilization, which they did during the 18th and early 19th centuries under the influence of an elite consisting of the descendants of white fur traders and indigenous women. Despite this adaptation to the white American way of life, they were forced to remove to Oklahoma in the 1830s (→ *Trail of Tears*).

**Five Nations** → *Iroquois League*.

**Flute**, the most common indigenous wind instrument in North America (trumpets were known only in the Southeast and shawms only on the Northwest Coast). "Pipes" without finger holes were used mainly for signalling and during ceremonies such as the Sun Dance of the Plains and the winter ceremonials of the Northwest Coast. Panpipes are known only from the *Hopewell* culture, where they were a form of insignia of rank. Melodious flutes with finger holes were used mainly by courting young men in the Northeast and the Prairies and Plains (see *Kokopelli*).

**Food-gathering economy**, economy based on gathering the edible parts (seeds, fruit, roots, leaves, etc.) of wild plants and catching small animals (insects, reptiles, mollusks, etc.). This activity tends to be reserved for women (with the assistance of children andthe elderly) and only requires the use of simple tools such as digging sticks, wooden or basketry beaters to beat down seeds or fruit, and baskets or bags to transport the food. This form of food provision was particularly important in the Great Basin, on the Plateau, and in California, but also in parts of the Southwest and eastern North America.

**Forest bison** (*Bison athabascae*), originally a type of bison adapted for life in the forest. It became extinct in the east. A small herd still survives around Great Slave Lake, while elsewhere it has interbred with the prairie bison.

**Fort Laramie treaty**. In 1868, after five years at war, the USA signed a treaty at Fort Laramie (Wyoming) with various Lakota tribes, awarding them a large reservation in what is today North and South Dakota as well as hunting rights further westward. Under the terms of the treaty, the army was to withdraw from Lakota land; future land cessions required the agreement of 75 percent of the adult men. The breach of this treaty in 1874 by the USA, when the Black Hills were annexed following the discovery of gold, gave rise to military resistance which culminated in the Battle of the Little Bighorn.

**Franciscans**, members of three Catholic mendicant orders founded by St Francis of Assisi in the early 13th century; they include the Minorites, the Capuchins, and the Franciscans proper, who form the second-largest Catholic order after the Jesuits. In the late 16th century, the Franciscans worked as missionaries in the Spanish Southeast and Southwest of the present USA. From the late 18th century they also became active in California, later also in other parts of North America.

**Gastowe**, Iroquois term for a man's headdress consisting of a bentwood headband, above which fabric is stretched over two intersecting strips of wood forming the cap. After the 18th century, the headband was often adorned with silver (instead of copper or porcupine quills), and the cap was covered with a bunch of small feathers from the center of which protruded a single large feather.

**General Allotment Act** (1887), also known as the *Dawes Act* after its author Senator Dawes, American legislation by which remaining tribal lands were transferred from communal ownership to the private ownership of individual tribal members. It was hoped that this measure would help to develop a sense of personal material ambition among the "Indians" and to thereby "civilize" them. The actual result, however, was the loss of two thirds of the land in indigenous ownership, the dissolution of tribal organizations, and the further impoverishment of the indigenous population.

**Ghost Dance**, name of two religious movements which emerged in the last third of the 19th century as a result of the rapid changes in indigenous life. The Ghost Dance movements offered their adherents a return of or reunion with their deseased relatives and a restoration of the indigenous past. The first Ghost

Dance movement of 1869/70 was based on the teachings of the Paiute Wodziwob and spread to the Plateau and California where the Ghost Dance contributed to the evolution of the *Bole-Maru* religion. In 1889, the Paiute Jack Wilson (Wovoka) had a vision which triggered another Ghost Dance movement, this time attracting and giving hope to the Plains peoples who experienced an existential crisis as a result of the extermination of the bison. The Lakota interpreted Wovoka's pacifistic teachings as a call to military resistance; the suppression of the Ghost Dance movement by the American army culminated in the massacre of *Wounded Knee* (1890).

**Glass beads** were introduced since the 16th century to North America by Europeans who used them as bartering goods in trade with indigenous peoples. They rapidly replaced disk-shaped shell beads and porcupine quills in the decoration of leatherwork. Glass-bead work rapidly came to be regarded as a typical "Indian" craft. The beads were sewn onto leather with sinew (later also yarn), worked into baskets or belts, or loom-woven to make large decorative panels.

**Gluskap** (Micmac, Maliseet, and Passamaquoddy), *culture hero* and *trickster*, equivalent to the Ojibwa's Nanabozho.

**Goosefoot** (*Chenopodium spp.*), one of several wild plants cultivated in eastern North America since the 1st millennium BC, some of which were still being used at the time of European contact. The leaves can be eaten as a vegetable and the seeds were made into a porridge.

**Gourd** (*Lagenaria vulgaris*), species of the gourd family with a lightweight yet strong shell used for making vessels (calabashes). The bottle gourd is among the cultivated plants that reached North America from Mesoamerica since the 2nd millennium BC. It is grown in the Eastern Woodlands and in the Southwest where it was used to make water containers, ladles, and rattles.

**Great Sun**, title given to the supreme leader of the Natchez of Louisiana, who was regarded as the descendant of the *culture hero* whom the Creator, who is associated with the sun, had ordered to arrange the world for the use of the Natchez. The Great Sun, whose family members were known as Suns, was at the center of the Natchez state and enjoyed the adulation usually reserved for deities. Each morning he welcomed the sun on behalf of his people by offering smoke from a sacred pipe.

**Grizzly bear** (*Ursus horribilis*), an American species of brown bear, originally widespread in western North America, from Alaska and the Northwest Territories to Mexico. Grizzly bears stand up to 8 feet tall and can weigh as much as 800 lbs; in size they are surpassed only by the kodiak bear of the Pacific coast of Alaska. Grizzly bears were highly prized game animals, and their killing was a source of great pride to successful hunters. Especially bear claws were used as emblems marking a hunter's courage.

**Groundnut** (*Apios tuberosus*), the edible, sweet-tasting tuber of a wild legume. It was gathered and eaten raw in eastern North America, boiled with *maple sugar* to make syrup, or peeled, parboiled, and sliced for storage.

**Guardian spirit (spirits helper)**. Many indigenous peoples in North America believe in supernatural beings that appear in dreams and visions, thereby endowing humans with special knowledge or powers (e.g., healing powers, good fortune in war, success during

the hunt, etc.), and promising lasting assistance. The relationship between humans and guardian spirits is often embodied in a sacred *bundle*. Individuals who can summon one or several particularly powerful spirit helpers may use their special abilities for the good of others or to cause harm (→ *witchcraft, medicine man, shaman, vision quest*).

**Gunstock club**, wooden weapon, wider at the front and slightly angled, somewhat similar to a gunstock. The gunstock club was mainly used in the western Great Lakes and among the peoples of the Prairies, and often featured metal blades and brass tack decorations.

**Half-breed**, American term for people of mixed white and Native American descent. The fundamentally negative value inherent in this term is based on 19th-century ideas, which ascribed to half-breeds the worst characteristics of both races. Unlike the Métis in Canada, half-breeds in the USA have never been granted collective indigenous rights (→ *Mestizization*).

**Halibut** (*Hippoglossus stenolepis*), flat fish of the Pacific Ocean weighing up to about 650 lbs. The people of the Northwest Coast of North America used large wooden fishing hooks with bone points to catch halibut. A slightly smaller species was also caught off the coast of California.

**Haliotis** or **abalone**, sea mollusk native to the Pacific coast of California, the meat of which is regarded as a delicacy. The shells, lined with mother-of-pearl, were particularly popular along the Northwest Coast for making ornaments and were a coveted trade good.

**Halves** → *moieties.*

**Hamats'a**, cannibal dancer of the Ts'eka dance dramas performed during the Kwakiutl winter ceremonial. The Hamats'a are members of a secret society and are abducted during their initiation by a mythical cannibal monster who devours them, thereby turning them into cannibals. On their return to the village, the Hamats'a demonstrate their appetite for human flesh; they enter a state of possession and are finally tamed and turned back into human beings through the efforts of the village community.

**Hare** (*Lepus spp.*), a rodent of which there are many species across North America, including the arctic hare of the western Arctic, the snowshoe hare of the Subarctic, the Northwest Coast, the Plateau, and the Northeast, as well as several species of long-eared jackrabbits in the Great Basin, the Plains, and the Prairies. In the Great Basin, hares were particularly popular as game animals. The hare appears as a *trickster* in the mythology of the Ojibwa and Winnebago (→ *rabbit*).

**Harpoon**, a spear, lance, or arrow fitted with a point that detaches itself from the shaft on impact while remaining tied to it by a line. Harpoons are used for hunting marine mammals on the coasts of the Arctic, Atlantic, and Pacific oceans (→ *toggle harpoon*).

**Hatchet** → *tomahawk.*

**Headhunting**, practice of severing the heads of fallen enemies and taking them as trophies in connection with collective or individual raids. It was frequently linked to the belief that the head was the seat of magical powers. Pre-European records of headhunting are contained in the imagery of the *South-eastern Ceremonial Complex* and the *Mimbres* culture. Historical evidence is available for headhunting in the Southeast and on the Northwest Coast. *Scalping* is regarded as a development of headhunting.

**Hemlock fir** (*Tsuga*), a member of the pine family, various species of which grow in eastern

Mask for the Nutlem dance, Tlatlasikwala-Kwakiutl, British Columbia, c. 1880. Ethnologisches Museum, Staatliche Museen zu Berlin – Preussischer Kulturbesitz, Berlin, Germany. → *masks;*

and northwestern North America. Its branches are used in various rituals of the Northwest Coast and the Plateau, e.g., to make headdresses for the *Hamats'a* dancers of the Kwakiutl, for the female puberty rite of the Thompson, or for the painful rubbing down of the body during the Nootka's sea otter hunting rites.

**Hickory** (from Virginia Algonquian), tree belonging to the walnut family (*Carya spp.*), of which several species grow in North America. Its nuts were gathered in the fall, dried over a fire and ground and moistened before being eaten. Its timber served as a building material for houses and for making pestles and mortars and bows and arrows, as well as providing firewood. In the Southeast, hickory bark was used as a roofing material and for firing pottery.

**Hodenosaunee** ("those of the longhouse"), self-designation of members of the Iroquois League. The *longhouse* and its inhabitants were

a reflected the idea of the tribal league whose members thought of each other as relatives with mutual obligations.

**Hogan** (Navajo, "house"), generally polygonal to circular houses with domed or conical roofs. Their walls were originally built of horizontally stacked tree trunks (rarely of stone), and the roof was constructed as a corbelled vault. This "female" form was once inhabited by 'Asdzáá Nádleehé and stood in contrast to the conical, "male" form, with an earth-covered roof. Both types of hogan were originally built by Speaking God for First Man and First Woman after their emergence into the present world.

**Hohokam**, prehistoric culture that flourished c. 300 BC–AD 1450 in the Sonoran Desert in the Southwest of North America. The Hohokam used an extensive system of irrigation for their fields, in which they cultivated corn, beans, squash, and cotton. Copper bells and metal mirrors, clay figures and ceramic forms, ball courts and temple pyramids are clear indications for the influences that reached them from Mesoamerica.

**Hominids**, order of primates, the only living example of which are humans. In the Americas no trace has been found of any of the other, long extinct members of this family, including the forebears of humans. Therefore, from a scientific point of view, humankind cannot have originated in the Americas.

**Hominy** (from Virginia Algonquian), corn kernels that have been stripped of their skin by immersion in an ash lye, cooked whole, or ground and eaten as a porridge or baked as biscuits.

**Hopewell**, prehistoric culture that flourished 200 BC–AD 500 in Illinois and the Ohio Valley. It is characterized by large burial mounds erected over the cremated remains of high-ranking individuals accompanied by grave goods such as zoomorphic stone tobacco pipes and clay figurines, as well as extensive embankments of earth enclosing ceremonial plazas. The use of exotic raw materials (e.g., mica and copper) suggests the existence of extensive trade links.

**Horned headdress**, insignia of office among some warrior societies of the Plains, consisting of a cap with two horns made of split bison horn and a train that was sometimes decorated with feathers. Horned headdresses could also take the form of a piece of bison hide with horns attached. Horns are a wide-spread symbol of power; among the Iroquois, headdresses featuring deer antlers were emblems of chiefs.

**Horse** (*Equus*). The horse originated in North America, whence it spread to the Old World. It was hunted by the early inhabitants of North America where it became extinct 10,000 years ago. The Spanish reintroduced horses to America as domesticated working animals in the 16th century. The colony of New Mexico was the starting point for the spread of naturalized mustangs as far as the northern Plains and the Plateau region, where they were tamed by indigenous peoples for their own use (→ *Appaloosa*; *Cayuse*). This facilitated the intensive exploitation of the great bison herds, the development of mounted warfare and the emergence of the classic Plains culture whose end coincided with the extermination of the bison herds.

**Hudson's Bay Company (HBC)**. Founded by royal charter in 1670, this British company was charged with creating settlements on Hudson Bay, conducting trade with the native inhabitants, checking French influence in Canada, and finding a route to the Orient. The HBC has held a long-standing trade monopoly in the north and northwest of the continent (interrupted by the North West Company between 1779 and 1821, after which the two companies merged). However, until 1869 it also performed administrative duties on behalf of the British crown in sparsely populated areas until they were transferred to the Canadian dominion, which was founded in 1867. The HBC continues to be an important trading company for indigenous peoples in northern Canada.

**Hunka** (Lakota, "ancestor"), Lakota adoption ceremony (*hunka lowanpi*). Hunka wands, decorated with eagle feathers and horsehair, were important ceremonial objects that symbolized the powers of the sun and the sky. The Lakota regarded the Hunka as one of seven ceremonies given to them by the mythical *White Buffalo Calf Woman*. There are some indications that the ceremony was not introduced until c. 1800, and that it was based on the Pawnee's Hako ceremony (→ *calumet*).

**Hunter-gatherers** (foragers), collective term used to describe societies of hunters, gatherers, and fishers whose food production was limited to naturally occurring resources and who did not produce food by either agriculture or animal husbandry. Especially hunters as well as some gatherers were forced to live a nomadic way of life since sufficient food was rarely available at one single location.

**Hunting fence**, converging fences or heaps of stone, into the wide opening of which game animals were chased. The fences prevented game animals from escaping sideways as they were driven to the narrow end where hunters could kill them with ease (→Inuksuit).

**Hunting hat**, asymmetric, conical headdress made of bentwood and decorated with eye symbols and baleen, worn by the Aleut when hunting in kayaks to protect them from the glare of the sun on the water. Similar conical visors used by the Aleut and Pacific Eskimo (Koniag) served the same purpose; the Inuit had snow goggles of wood or leather with slits to protect their eyes from the light reflected off the snow.

**Ice Age** (Pleistocene), cold period in the Earth's history, lasting approximately 2 million

Wooden mask, Yupik, Kuskokwim, Alaska, 19th century. Eugene Chetrow Trust.

years and ending c. 9000 BC. Humans emerged during this period and, during the fourth and final stage of the Ice Age, some migrated to the American continent (→ *Bering Strait theory*). The glaciation of the northern half of North America during the Ice Age had a lasting effect on the habitat of its later inhabitants, particularly by creating the Canadian Lakes. Climatic change at the end of the Ice Age caused the extinction of many large game animals (e.g., the *mammoth*), forcing the cultures of the period to adapt to new conditions.

**Igloo** (Inuktitut, "house"), Eskimo dwelling made of snow bricks laid in spiral fashion. It is the only true vault construction in pre-European North America. Blocks of ice built into the walls permit light to penetrate into the buildings. In the central Arctic, igloos were used as winter dwellings; Eskimo groups of other areas used them as temporary shelters while traveling. A slightly lowered entrance tunnel served to keep out the cold. Heating and lighting were provided by oil lamps.

**I'itoi** ("Elder Brother"), the *culture hero* of the Pima and Papago of the Sonoran Desert. I'itoi, a small bearded man with white hair, was one of the first creations of Earth Maker who remade the world after flooding it. He gave his creations, the Hohokam, their culture, but after he had offended them they had him killed by Buzzard . When I'itoi came back to life, he led the Pima and Papago, who had been hiding in the underworld since the flood, to the surface of the earth, but later withdrew from human society.

**Indian carrot** (*Perideridia gairdnieri*), a parsley plant of the Plateau which was dug up in spring for its edible roots. The Indian carrot is sometimes called "yampa," a Shoshone term for a potato-like tuber (*Atenia spp.*). It lent its name to the Comanche section of the Yamparika (Yampa eaters).

**Indian celery** (*Lomatium spp.*), various members of the parsley family used for food by the peoples of the Plateau. The stalks and stems were eaten, as were the subterranean sprouts of a species which, when fully grown, provided medicine and a poison for fishing.

**Indian Claims Commission (ICC)**, commission set up in 1946 by the U.S. Congress to examine outstanding claims of indigenous peoples resulting from land cessions to the USA. In over 30 years of activity, the ICC considered hundreds of applications and recommended compensation payments which the tribes partly distributed among their members and partly used for tribal investment. Although the ICC's work was intended to pave the way for dissolving the tribes (→ *termination*), the compensation payments actually strengthened the position of the tribes.

**Indian hemp** (*Apocynum cannabium*), American plant of the dogbane family, and for indigenous people in many parts of the USA and in southern Canada one of the most important wild fibrous plants. Especially in the Northeast and California, Indian hemp was used to make thread for burdenstraps, belts, and bags.

**Indian Removal Act**, American legislation passed in 1830 to provide the financial means for relocating all indigenous peoples living east of the Mississippi to Oklahoma and Kansas. Its implementation, particularly under Presidency of Andrew Jackson (1767–1845), achieved the given goal almost completely in the Southeast, and led to the Cherokee *Trail of Tears* and to the second and third Seminole wars.

**Indian Reorganization Act (IRA)**, American legislation passed in 1934 to provide tribes, particularly those dissolved under the General Allotment Act, with an opportunity to reestablish themselves under democratic constitutions following the American model with elected tribal councils and leaders. Many tribes accepted this offer, although it led to continuing conflicts between the new system and the traditional ways which were often still in existence. The IRA formed part of the new Indian policy (Indian New Deal) of Commissioner of Indian Affairs John Collier (1884–1962), as well as of the reforms (New Deal) instituted by President Frederick Delano Roosevelt (1882–1945).

**Indians**, historical term for the indigenous peoples of the Americas, excluding the Eskimo, derived from Christopher Columbus' assumption that he had discovered the western sea route to India. The general use made of this misleading, collective term by colonial powers and subsequent nation-states for fundamentally different cultural groups, particularly when applied in a political and legal context, and the common fate of these groups under colonial rule, has given the word new meaning. Many members of indigenous peoples now refer to themselves as "Indians," sometimes as a synonym for the real name of their group, sometimes as a collective term (Panindianism). Others prefer to use such terms as *First Nations*, or *Native Americans* (→*Amerind*).

**Indian Wars**, conflicts which took place between the 17th century and 1890 between the colonial powers (later the USA and Canada) and indigenous peoples, who in military terms tended to be less well organized and armed with inferior weapons (→ *Wounded Knee*). Revenge, the conquest of land, and subjugating the native population – or, conversely, defending territory against white invaders – were the main reasons for the Indian Wars. Many indigenous peoples of North America were never involved in the Indian Wars, others fought on the side of the whites as allies or scouts.

**Indigenous** (from Latin "native"), existing in an area before the arrival of colonial powers. In North America this includes all the people subsumed under the terms "Indian" and "Eskimo," as well as the mixed population of the Métis in Canada. Since the 1970s, a global movement of indigenous peoples has been fighting within the framework of the United Nations for recognition of their particular legal rights. The indigenous peoples of North America play a central role in this struggle.

**Initiation rite**, ritual marking the acceptance of an individual into a social group, including that of adults, where the emphasis lies on the acquisition of gender roles at puberty, but which may also take place in steps. Acceptance into societies (associations) also frequently requires initiation. As initiations are events of great importance they are often accompanied by special tests of courage or artificial deformations of the body such as ear piercing or circumcision (the latter being rare in North America), and are sometimes staged as symbolic dramas portraying death and rebirth in the new social role.

**Inua** (plural: *inue*; Inuktitut, "inhabitant"; Yupik *yua*), a western Arctic term used to describe the breath souls of humans; in other parts of the Arctic, the word refers to the common life principle which inhabits all animals, plants, stones, and other natural phenomena, a single *inua* inhabiting all members of a particular species. Important for the success of the hunt, the *inue* were also represented in the western Arctic by wooden masks.

**Inuit Circumpolar Conference**, association of the Eskimo populations of Greenland, Canada, and Alaska (as well as of Russia since 1989) founded in 1977 to exchange ideas, coordinate political activities, and strengthen a pan-Eskimoan identity.

**Inuksuit** (singular: *inuksuk*; Inuktitut, "they look like human beings"), heaps of rock shaped like people which the hunters of the tundra built and arranged in converging lines, between which herds of caribou into an impasse or river where they could be killed more easily.

**Iroquois League**, confederation of tribes, originally of five Iroquois-speaking peoples (the Mohawk, Oneida, Onondaga, Cayuga, and Seneca), founded in the 15th or 16th century by Deganawida (assisted by Hiawatha), who was sent by the Creator to overcome the state of war and feud that existed between the tribes and to establish the "Law of the Peace". Through this confederation, the Iroquois (or Five Nations) became the leading political power in the Northeast during the colonial era. After 1715, the Tuscarora joined the league as the sixth nation. After the *American Revolution* a split occurred, with the Canadian and American Iroquois continuing the league separately.

**Iyatiku** (also Uretsete), among the Keresans the primeval mother in the underworld before their emergence into the present world, and the provider of corn. On the orders of the Creator, she and her sister Nautsiti (Naotsete) completed the forming of the world. Conflict developed between the sisters, leading to the belief by some that Nautsiti is the mother of white people.

**Jerusalem artichoke** (*Helianthus tuberosus*), the edible, potatolike rhizome of a species of sunflower found in eastern North America, where women and children gathered it for eating either raw, boiled, or roasted.

**Jesuits (Society of Jesus)**, Catholic missionary order founded in 1540 to lead the Counter-Reformation. In Canada, French Jesuits began to carry out sporadic missionary work in 1609, and then continuously from 1632 until order was suppressed in Canada in 1791. From 1620 until their expulsion in 1767, most of the Jesuits working in northwestern Mexico came from German-speaking countries. The Jesuits' missionary work based itself on learning indigenous languages, and their success was due to their relatively tolerant attitude toward indigenous cultures and their defense of the rights of their congregations. From their black habits derives the term "blackrobe" for Catholic missionaries in northeastern North America.

**Joke relationship,** a socially required intimate form of behavior between relatives which can range from practical jokes to sexually explicit humor. In North America the milder form of joke relationship is often found between grandparents and grandchildren, whereas the explicit variety may occasionally occur between a brother and sister-in-law since they are the potential marriage partners under the levirate and sororate. The joke relationship is a counterpart to the avoidance behavior of the mother-in-law taboo.

Pipe tomahawk, central Plains (c. 1870). The British Museum (London). → *tomahawk*.

**Kachina** (Hopi *katsina*), in the religion of the Pueblo peoples, supernatural beings who are embodied by members of Kachina societies during ceremonies between the winter solstice and July. There are more than 200 distinct kachinas in the Western Pueblos, each with their own dress and specific tasks, and together they represent the mythical ancestors of human beings while acting as mediators between humans and gods and ensuring an adequate supply of rain. As moral authorities they also admonish humans to follow the social norms → *Tihu*.

**Kahni** (Numic, "house"), grass-covered summer dwelling of the peoples of the Great Basin.

**Kamleika** (Siberian Russian), outer garment of the Aleut, Koniag, and Yupik of the western Arctic, made of sea lion or walrus gut. Due to their waterproof properties, kamleikas were particularly suitable for use as kayak shirts.

**Katsina** → *Kachina*.

**Katyutayuk**, in the imagination of the Inuit of Quebec a class of man-eating, female monsters. With their heads set on their feet, they cause thunder when they walk. Although Katyutayuks can walk through walls, they nevertheless cause a great deal of noise when they bump into buildings and other objects at night.

**Kayak** (from West Greenlandic Inuktitut), slender boat, 15 to 18 feet long, made of sealskin stretched over a wooden frame. The kayak, the typical hunting boat of the Eskimo, Aleut, and neighboring peoples of northeastern Siberia, is usually designed for one person, whose outer garment (*kayak shirt*) is attached to the frame of the circular cockpit so as to prevent water seeping in. It is propelled by a double-bladed paddle. Leather straps and other fittings are attached to the outside of kayaks to facilitate the transportation of hunting equipment.

**Kayak shirt**, outer garment made of greased leather, fish skin, or sea mammal gut (→ *kamleika*) attached by the paddler of a kayak to the edge of the cockpit to prevent water entering the boat in rough seas or during the *Eskimo roll*.

**Ketoh**, Navajo term for a leather bracer worn on the wrist to protect it from the returning bow string. Following the introduction of silver-

Walrus ivory fat scraper, northwestern Alaska, 19th century. British Museum, London. → *walrus*.

smithing, ketohs began to be adorned with silver panels, sometimes inlaid with turquoise. These became a popular form of jewelry among Navajo men and also appear as accouterments in the kachina dances of the Pueblo peoples.

**Ki** (Papago, "house"), traditional winter dwelling of the Pima and Papago built over a shallow pit with a domed roof covered with straw, grass, and shrubs. Since the late 19th century, the Papago have built houses of dried cactus trunk walls daubed with clay with a canopy for shade. Modern versions are made of alternating layers of timber and sun-dried clay (adobe).

**Kinnikinník** (Ojibwa, "I mix together a variety of things"), term for various mixtures of *tobacco* and other leaves and barks (particularly dogwood) added to eke out and improve the flavor of tobacco and to give it additional healing properties. Kinnikinník was particularly popular at, and beyond, the northernmost borders of the tobacco growing regions.

**Kiva** (from Hopi), circular or rectangular rooms built partly or fully underground, found in pueblos, and used as meeting places for members of societies or of the ceremonial organizations of kinship groups (clans, moieties), as well as venues for secret religious ceremonies. Access is usually via a ladder from a hatch in the roof. → *sipapu*.

**Kokopelli**, hunch-backed Hopi kachina with a large penis who, together with his female counterpart Kokopell Mana, imparts dramatic expression to the importance of fertility by exhibiting aggressive sexual behavior. Images of Kokopelli have featured on pottery and in wall paintings since the 14th century. Rock paintings depicting a hunch-backed flutist are also thought to be representations of Kokopelli.

**Koshare (Koshairi, Kossa)**, ceremonial clowns of the Rio Grande Pueblos represented by members of one of the two clown societies (→ *kwira(i)na*). Koshare are characterized by their black and white striped body paint and horned headdresses. They are associated with summer by the Tewa, and with winter by the Keres. In some pueblos, they have eclipsed the *kwiraina* in

importance or even entirely supplanted them. They are not identified with either of the seasonal moieties. Following the Pueblo Revolt of 1680, Tewa refugees introduced the *Koshare* to the Hopi of the first Mesa ("Hano clowns").

**Kuksu**, among the Pomo of northern central California, the Creator who is the focus of ceremonies conducted by a men's society during which he is represented by a dancer with an elaborate feather headdress ("big head"). In winter, Kuksu cult activity serves the initiation of new members and to renew the world. It has spread to the Yuki, Miwok, Maidu, Patwin, and Wintu and spawned numerous variations. It became the basis of the *Bole-Maru* religion.

**Kunti**, generic term of the Creek and Seminole for a starchy root. Red kunti, the root of greenbrier (*Smilax spp.*), was widespread in the Southeast, while white kunti (*Zamia integrifolia*) was found only in southern Florida. To prepare either, the roots were chopped, ground in wooden mortars, and mixed with ample quantities of water. White kunti was left to ferment to remove any poisonous or bitter substances. The flour was added to water to make a jelly, popular with children and the elderly.

**Kwira(i)na**, ceremonial clowns of the Rio Grande Pueblos, represented by members of one of the two clown societies (→ *koshare*). Among their tasks is weather control, but they also alternate with the *koshare* in the organization of rabbit hunts.

**Labret**, circular or oval lip ornament inserted in piercings around the mouth. Among the Haida, only high-ranking women were permitted to wear labrets in their lower lip. Among the Eskimo of northern Alaska, men generally wore labrets in the corners of their mouth or in their lower lip.

**Lacrosse** (French, "crosier"), French Canadian word for an indigenous *stickball* game; now a Canadian national sport.

**Legend painting**, indigenous school of painting founded in the 1960s by Norval Morrisseau (Ojibwa) in Ontario. Themes from Algonquian (Ojibwa, Ottawa, and Cree) mythology are depicted in bright acrylic colors and flowing lines.

**Leggings**, most common form of legwear in indigenous North America, consisting of two separate tubes for the legs, attached to the belt or tied with garters above the calves. Men generally wore hip-length leggings while those worn by women were of knee-length. Leggings were originally made of leather, which was eventually replaced by cloth. Crocheted cotton leggings were also known in the Southwest.

**Levirate**, custom by which a widow marries the brother of her deceased husband. This practice was widespread in North America and served to maintain trade relations between two kinship groups originally connected by marriage (→ *sororate*).

**Lineage**, a descent group whose members are genealogically related to a male or female ancestor through an exclusively male or female line. All the men and women who are descended from the male descendants of a male ancestor belong to a patrilineage, and all men and women descended of the female descendants of a female ancestor belong to a matrilineage (→ *clan*).

**Little Bighorn, the**. On June 25, 1876 an allied force of Lakota, Cheyenne, and Arapaho defeated the 7th US cavalry regiment led by the popular Civil War General George Armstrong Custer, who had attacked the joint camp of these tribes on the Little Bighorn River in Montana.

The defeat was humiliating for the American army, but the radical Indian movement of the 1960s regarded it as the embodiment of the possibility of successful resistance against American society.

**Longhouse**, collective term for various domestic or ceremonial buildings of elongated form common in various parts of North America. Best known are the barrel-roofed longhouses, up to 400 feet long, of the Iroquois in the Northeast, which contained several compartments for individual nuclear families. The external appearance of the coastal Algonquian long-houses was similar, although these were no more than 100 feet long and were inhabited by extended families, the size of each house representing the wealth or social standing of each family. Temples and meeting houses could be up to 150 feet long. The mat-covered, ridge-roofed houses of the Plateau were of similar dimensions, while some of the ceremonial longhouses built of wooden planks on the Northwest Coast were twice as long. On the Plateau, as among the Iroquois, ceremonial buildings constructed by Euro-American methods are also referred to as longhouses.

**Longhouse religion**, among the Iroquois, the term is used for the traditional religion as reformed c. 1800 by the prophet Handsome Lake, which revolves around giving thanks to the Creator and strengthening the community through a seasonal cycle of ceremonies. Christian elements have been assimilated into this religion, as also into the Longhouse religion of the Plateau (or Washat religion, from the Sahaptin word *wáashat*, "dance") which evolved around 1830 from first-fruit rituals and was again amended by the Wanapam prophet Smohalla.

**Long Walk**, the forced removal of more than 9,000 Navajos under military supervision from Fort Canby (Fort Defiance)

in Arizona to Bosque Redondo (Fort Sumner) in New Mexico in the winter of 1863/64, during which several hundred Navajos lost their lives. After their release in 1868, a Navajo reservation was established in New Mexico and Arizona which has since been enlarged several times.

**Lynx**, a short-tailed wildcat of which two species (*Lynx rufus* and *L. canadensis*) are widespread across North America. It was hunted mainly for its coat, and, although rarely available, was prized for its meat by the Kutchin of Alaska.

**Maasaw**, Hopi god of death and ruler of the realm of the dead. He helped to bring human beings into the present world and is the owner of the land used by the Hopi. Maasaw is thought of as a young man with long hair, beautiful clothes and splendid turquoise jewelry who, however, wears a gruesome blood-smeared mask and threatens people with a club. As the master of fire and light, Maasaw taught humans how to make fire and also contributes to the fertility of the fields by producing warmth. As the protector of the land of the Hopi and the god of death, he is also instrumental in destroying the enemy in times of war.

**Maheo**, Cheyenne creator god who made the universe and, living together with his natural and supernatural creations, taught humans to hunt, cultivate corn, dig for roots, work stone, and make fire. He then retired to the Blue-Sky-Space above the clouds. The Cheyenne reenact Maheo's creation of the world each year with the Massaum ceremonies.

**Mammoth** (*Mammuthus jeffersonii*) and mastodon (*Mammuthus americanus*), proboscideans related to the Indian elephant, which became extinct in North America shortly after the Ice Age. The big-game hunters of the Clovis or Llano culture (c. 9600–8700 BC) hunted them extensively and seem to have disappeared at

Woolen leggings with glass-bead appliqué, Athapaskans, upper Yukon, Alaska, c. 1900. Rautenstrauch-Joest-Museum für Völkerkunde, Cologne, Germany. → *leggings*.

the same time as their prey. The cause of the mammoth's extinction may equally lie in climate warming or in the efficiency of the hunters.

**Manitou** (from Algonquian languages, "supernatural being"), a plurality of supernatural beings among the central and eastern Algonquians, who appear in the form of humans, animals, plants, natural phenomena, or objects and who can endow people with extraordinary abilities (→ *vision quest*). The northern Algonquian (Cree, Montagnais-Naskapi) concept of a "Great Manitou" may go back to an ancient high god, but under the influence of Christianity it has also become a heavenly creator. The "Evil Manitou" is definitely the product of contact with missionaries.

**Maple sugar**, the juice of the sugar maple (*Acer saccharum*), which in the area around the Great Lakes and in the eastern Subarctic is tapped from the trees in late winter and thickened by boiling in metal kettles. Before the European introduction of suitable containers, only a thick syrup was produced. Maple sugar was generally packed in birch-bark boxes and was sometimes poured into wooden effigy molds. It played an important role in trade relations with whites in the first half of the 19th century.

**Maraw**, the most important of the Hopi's three women's societies, whose ceremonies are held annually, before or after the *Wuwuchim*. Their secret and public rituals are primarily concerned with rain and fertility. One of the privileges of the maraw is basket weaving.

**Marsh elder** (*Iva spp.*), plant of the Compositae family. It was first cultivated in eastern North America during the *Hopewell* period and, together with the *goosefoot* and *sunflower*, is one of the few indigenous cultivated plants of North America.

**Mask**, facial disguise used to represent or embody supernatural beings during rituals. The *false faces* of the Iroquois and the *kachina* masks of the Pueblo peoples transformed their wearers into the being represented. For the Yupik of Alaska, wearing a mask was a form of prayer through which what was represented by the mask could be obtained; others represented shamanic spirit helpers. While Yupik masks expressed personal experiences and a relationship with the supernatural, on the Northwest Coast or in the Pueblo area they represented the secret knowledge of the ritual associations.

**Maskalataq**, masking tradition of the Koniag of Kodiak Island inspired by a Russian custom,

in which processions held between Christmas and New Year represent the search for the infant Jesus.

**Mastamho**, among the Mohave of the borderland of California and Arizona the son of the Creator Matavilye and the culture hero who, after his father's death, made the world ready for humans, teaching them language and customs and inventing the clan system. On completing his work, he turned into an osprey and flew away.

**Mastodon** → *mammoth*.

**Matachine** (from Arabic, "masked people"), dance introduced by the Spanish that has been endowed with new meaning in wide areas of Mexico. The Tarahumara in Chihuahua dance the Matachine on important Christian holidays as a prayer for health and prosperity.

**Ma'toki**, the "Buffalo Women" society among the Blood and Northern Blackfoot on the northern Plains. The society was divided into four grades and held ceremonies each summer during which members wore various feather, horn, and snake headdresses. Their fertility rituals were designed to promote the growth of the bison herds.

**Matriarchy** ("government by women") or "mother right," a stage of development in human society, posited by 19th century science as a precursor of patriarchy. This view is no longer tenable, partly because government by women cannot be proven to have existed in any known historic society. For a long time, Iroquois society was regarded as an example of matriarchy yet, despite matrilineal succession and the right to nominate chiefs, the rights of men and women were generally balanced.

**Matron**, oldest woman of a matrilineage and head of the household; also applied to the "clan mother", i.e., the matron of the leading (oldest) matrilineage of a matriclan. Iroquois matrons had rights over the names (titles) of the *clan* and were therefore entitled to nominate chiefs.

**Medicine (bundles)**. "Medicine" is a frequently used term for the supernatural powers that supernatural beings can give to a person through dreams and visions, especially when they provide physical or spiritual healing. Since these powers or abilities are usually hypostatized in the form of sacred *bundles*, the term "medicine bundle" is also used.

**Medicine man**, equivocal, therefore no longer acceptable, term for "healer." Some medicine men apply herbs to cure their patients, some use traditional rituals, and others draw on the supernatural abilities that they acquired through visions. However, the term "medicine man" is also used to describe all religious specialists whose powers are derived from a supernatural *medicine*; it is of little importance whether they have healing or other powers such as those of prediction or of influencing the weather.

**Medicine societies**, *associations* dedicated primarily to curing the sick are found in many parts of North America, including the medicine societies of the Rio Grande pueblos, the *Midewiwin* of the Ojibwa, and the *false face* societies of the Iroquois. Medicine societies increased in importance after diseases imported from Europe ran rampant through indigenous communities.

**Menstruation hut**, building erected outside a settlement to house women during their menstruation and to facilitate their observance of the rules of avoidance that commonly apply in relation to menstruation.

War shirt with beaded bear-paw motifs, Omaha c. 1898. Ethnologisches Museum, Staatliche Museen zu Berlin – Preussischer Kulturbesitz (Berlin). → *glass beads*.

Menstruation taboos and menstruation huts are widespread in North America, but are by no means universal. Whereas the Hopi do not have a menstruation taboo, the Chiricahua Apache have strict taboos, yet do not isolate menstruating women. Menstruation huts are frequently used as places for giving birth.

**Mesa** (Spanish, "table"), mountain with precipitous sides and flat summit, created by erosion and a common feature of the Southwest of North America. In the Pueblo area, mesas were often chosen for settlement because their inaccessibility provided protection from attack. An added advantage was that the rainfall running off its slopes watered the fields at the foot of the mesa.

**Mescal** (Spanish loanword from Nahuatl) generic term for the agaves (*liliaceae*) of the Southwest and the food provided by their roots and stalks. The edible parts of the plant are fried, roasted, or sun-dried for storage. The Apache sometimes use them to make beer (→ *tesgüino*).

**Mesoamerica**, area of Middle America occupied by pre-European civilizations. Mesoamerica is characterized by intensive agriculture (corn, squash, beans, and other cultivated plants), predominantly Stone Age technology (late emergence of metallurgy), and the absence of animal husbandry. An aristocratic elite lived in ceremonial centers and directed the fate of villagers and citizens with the assistance of a bureaucracy, promoting a class of craftsmen whose status was superior to that of the peasantry, and the creation of an elitist art form. Markets provided the points of intersection for networks marked by regional differences. A frequently fatalistic world view combined with the development of mathematics, writing systems, astronomy, and a calendar. Mesoamerica influenced its neighbors, particularly the agricultural cultures of southwestern and southeastern North America, through trade relations and by the diffusion of ideas.

**Mesquite bean**, edible pulse of the honey mesquite (*Prosopsis juliflora*), one of the most important wild foods in the Southwest, consumed by the Yuma peoples along the Gila River and the Apache. Mesquite beans were gathered in July and August and could either be ground to make flour, eaten as a vegetable, or turned into a sweet porridge.

**Messenger Feast** (Yupik: Kevgiryaraq), important Alaskan Yupik and Inupiaq winter celebration. Two messengers would invite the inhabitants of another village to a feast where gifts were distributed and expected in return. The Messenger feast served to redistribute wealth within and among the villages while simultaneously allowing the conspicuous exhibition of social status.

**Mestization** (from Spanish *mestizo*, "half-breed," i.e., a person of white and Native American descent). Mestization is understood not as a biological process by which races become mixed, but as the emergence of new social groups consisting of people who have broken away from the communities to which they were originally linked by kinship, without being accepted as equal citizens by Euro-American nation-states. In the USA in the 19th century, for example, inhabitants of reservations who adopted a white American lifestyle, regardless of their biological origins, were often called "mixed bloods" and stood in contrast to the more traditional "full bloods."

**Methodism**, Protestant Christian movement based on the teachings of John Wesley (1703–1791), and influenced by the pietism of the *Moravian Brethren*, at the core of which stands sinful man's pursuit of a state of holiness through the grace of faith. In America, the spread of Methodism began in 1766; from 1818 onward Methodists became actively involved in missionary work among indigenous peoples in pursuance of the American policy of "civilization."

**Mica (schist)**, a group of crystalline slates, consisting mainly of quartz or mica in thin, easily separated layers. It occurs in various colors and may be translucent or iridescent. From natural deposits in the southern Appalachians, the trade in mica schist spread far and wide, and the material was regarded as a luxury item by the ruling class of the *Hopewell* culture in the Ohio Valley. In the northern Rio Grande Pueblos, mica was added to clay to give it a glittering finish.

**Midewíwin** (Ojibwa, "association of *mide*"), *medicine society* of the Ojibwa and their neighbors. The purpose of membership of the society was to cure ailments or to prevent sickness. Admission into this society, which was organized in four grades of secrecy, was conditional on the acquisition of the required knowledge from someone who was already a member. The initiation ritual symbolized the death and rebirth of the novices and publicly demonstrated the power of *medicine*.

**Miko** (Muskogee, "leader"), title given to the hereditary "peace chiefs" of the Creek and Seminole of the Southeast. Among their duties were the distribution of food from the communal corn store, attending to envoys and other visitors, organizing feasts, and leading council meetings whose always unanimous decisions they had to support.

**Mimbres**, late regional variant of the Mogollon culture in southwestern New Mexico, dating between AD 1000–1150. Especially noteworthy and highly prized on the contemporary art market are their black and white or polychrome pottery bowls decorated with mythological and ceremonial motifs.

**Mink** (*Mustela vison*), musteline, fur-bearing animal, occurring almost universally across North America (except in the eastern Arctic and in and around the Southwest). It was of importance to the fur trade, especially in the Subarctic and on the Northwest Coast. In the mythology of the central Northwest Coast the mink occurs as a lascivious *trickster*.

**Missionary work**. The propagation of the Christian faith according to Biblical command was a popular justification for the expansion of European and American settlers in America. Catholic and Protestant missionaries acted as harbingers of Western civilization, the fundamental acceptance of which was regarded as a precondition for successful conversion. Missionary work was particularly successful where indigenous religions were unable to deal with the existential crisis caused by contact with Europeans, or where indigenous peoples or groups wished to aquire the superior quality of life promised by the whites. Although the majority of indigenous Americans became Christians in the long term, there were repeated massive movements for a return to ancient religions or for new, autonomous forms of faith.

**Mississippian cultures**, Pre-European cultural tradition which flourished in southeastern North America c. AD 800–1500. An intensive system of agriculture (corn, squash, beans) gave rise to urban centers with temples built on truncated earth pyramids. Mesoamerican influence is apparent in the *Southeastern Ceremonial Complex* of the late Mississippian

Ceremonial warrior dress, Arapaho, c. 1880. Deutsches Ledermuseum, Offenbach am Main, Germany.

period. Besides the city of Cahokia (near St. Louis), centers like Spiro (Oklahoma), Moundville (Alabama), and Etowah (Georgia) flourished in the 13th and 14th centuries. When Europeans arrived in the 16th century, the Mississippian cultures were already in decline. The Sun kingdom of the Natchez is regarded as a descendant of this cultural tradition.

**Moccasins** (from Algonquian languages, "footwear"), collective term for indigenous North American shoes. The dominant forms in the Eastern Woodlands and the Subarctic had no separate sole: the soles and uppers were made from one piece (sometimes with an oval insert at the instep). On the Plains and in the Southwest soft leather uppers were generally sewn onto stiff rawhide soles. Numerous variations of cut and decoration may indicate where a moccasin originated from. High boots are not regarded as moccasins.

**Moccasin trousers**, item of clothing of the Athapaskan peoples of the western Subarctic whereby the footwear and legwear are made out of one piece (like tights).

**Mogollon**, prehistoric culture that flourished on the borders of New Mexico, Arizona, and Chihuahua 250 BC–AD 1150. The first cultivated plants from Mexico (corn, beans, squash, gourds) appeared in this region as early as 1250 BC, and became established among a people already displaying sedentary tendencies. The Mogollon people originally lived in pit houses (later also in buildings with clay walls) and produced pottery vessels.

**Moiety**, anthropological term for the organization of social groups (a tribe or village) into complementary halves. This frequently refers to the grouping of *clans* into one of two moieties, in which case individuals are born into one or the other half according to *descent rules*. In other cases, allocation is by birth sequence (first and third, second and fourth children) or by season of birth (summer and winter moieties). Sometimes, moiety affiliation was changed upon marriage. The most common task of a moiety is the organization of marriages (generally by *exogamy*; moieties with *endogamy* tend to be equivalent to social classes). Moieties also provided mutual assistance, e.g., in building houses, funerals, or rituals.

**Moose** (*Alces alces*). The largest type of deer in North America; the male has palmate, flat antlers. Moose (the term derives from an Algonquin word) are solitary, timid animals that live in the woodlands of the Subarctic (and adjacent areas of the Northwest Coast and the Northeast) near lakes and rivers. They were hunted by lone huntsmen, sometimes using lures. Since the 18th century dyed moosehair has been used to decorate leather and bark objects.

**Moravian Brethren**, members of a Hussite community from Moravia who in 1722 founded a community in Herrnhut, Saxony. In 1731 they began intensive missionary work in America.

Apart from their activities among the Eskimo of Greenland and Labrador, they successfully worked among the Delaware, whose peaceful community at Gnadenhütten in Pennsylvania was massacred by an American militia in 1782.

**Mormons**, followers of the Church of Latter Day Saints founded by Joseph Smith (1805–1844), in whose holy scripture, the Book of Mormon, the indigenous peoples of America are described as the descendants of the prophet Lehi, who arrived in America in 589 BC, and of his son Laman (hence Lamanites). After establishing their settlement near the Great Salt Lake in Utah, they began missionary work among the peoples of the Great Basin. Among their major achievements in this regard was the conversion of almost the entire Catawba

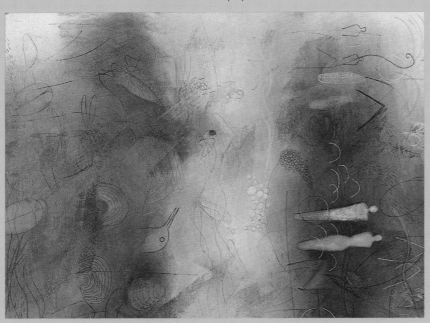

Emmi Whitehorse (Navajo), *White Corn and Yellow Corn*, Mashantucket Pequot Museum and Research Center, Mashantucket, CT. → *American Indian Arts and Crafts Act*.

population in South Carolina after 1883, and a placement program for Navajo and Hopi children started in 1949.

**Morning star**. For nine months of the year the planet Venus, in inferior conjunction (between the earth and the sun), appears in the eastern morning sky as a bright star (→ *evening star*). The Pawnee of the Prairies regard the morning star ("Great Star") as a warrior who heads the council of the gods and who owns a garden with cultivated plants and a herd of bison. Sun is his younger brother. The Blackfoot of the Plains regarded the morning star as the son of the sun, symbolize him by a motif similar to a Maltese cross, and direct to him prayers for nourishment and longevity.

**Mother Earth**, the concept of a maternal deity equated with the earth is known from European antiquity. Although the earth was frequently thought of as female, particularly among the agricultural societies of indigenous North America, it does not appear as a personal deity until the early 19th century in connection with efforts to explain to the whites how important the land was to its native inhabitants. Since that time, Mother Earth has become a Panindian concept.

**Mother-in-law taboo**, various rules demanding complete avoidance or reserve, which regulate the social interaction between sons-in-law and mothers-in-law, especially when living in the same household. Among the Creek and Choctaw of the Southeast, this prohibits men from talking to or looking at

their mothers-in-law, while the Apache regard complete avoidance of mothers-in-law, fathers-in-law, and their parents as an expression of respect, which may be voluntarily extended to include other relatives by marriage. The mother-in-law taboo serves primarily to avoid conflict between different members of a household (→ *joking relationship*).

**Motseyoef** ("Sweet Root Standing," "Sweet Medicine"), Cheyenne *culture hero* who, together with the Suh'tai Tomsivisi ("Erect Horns"), received teachings and cult objects from the Creator *Maheo* in the interior of the Sacred Bear Butte in South Dakota, and who gave the Cheyenne their great ceremonies. When he took leave from human beings, he prophesied the arrival of the whites, the extermination of the buffaloes, and a hard future for the Cheyenne.

**Mound**, term for a variety of earthworks built by various pre-European cultures in eastern North America. Mounds either served as large burial tumuli (*Adena, Hopewell*), to represent particular animals, or as platforms on which temples were erected (*Mississippian cultures*).

**Mountain goat** (*Oreamnos americanus*), white goat inhabiting the snowline of the Rocky Mountains and coastal mountains of British Columbia, southeastern Alaska, and Washington State. Along the Northwest Coast its wool was spun into thread for making *Chilkat blankets* and other textiles and its horns were used to make spoons.

**Mountain lion** (also cougar, panther, or puma), largest North American wildcat (up to six feet long) with a long tail and a plain (tawny to gray) coat. Originally widely distributed in the regions south of the Subarctic and east of the Rocky Mountains, it has been extinct there since the 19th century. The *underwater panther* is an important figure in the cosmology of the Algonquian peoples of the western Lakes.

**Mountain sheep** (*Ovis ammon canadensis*), also known as bighorn sheep, native to the mountains of the western USA and southern British Columbia. Rocky Mountain sheep were not widely hunted as game, although, from the Northwest Coast to the Plains, their horns were used to make spoons and bowls, and on the Plateau and Plains they were also used to make bows. The Chinook used the wool for textiles.

**Mourning wars**, wars waged in the Northeast to avenge losses suffered in warfare and to obtain prisoners to replace these losses by adoption into the tribe. As in economic exchange, the aim was to achieve a state of equilibrium between warring parties.

**Mukluk** (from Yupik, *maklak*, "bearded seal"), material initially used by Americans for manufacturing boots, from the late 19th century it became synonymous with seal skin boots themselves (Yupik *kamak*).

**Mule deer** → *deer*.

**Mummy**, corpse that, either naturally or by human intervention, is prevented from putrefying. In some chiefdoms (Virginia and North Carolina Algonquian, Biloxi) of eastern North America, the corpses of deceased rulers were preserved by drying or taxidermy and kept in the temples. Among the Nootkan peoples of the Northwest Coast noble owners of whale shrines stole the corpses of the deceased for use in their animal-calling ceremonies and stored them in the shrines after preserving them by smoking and drying.

**Musical bow**, probably the only pre-European stringed instrument in North America. Similar in form to a hunting bow, the musical bow is held at the mouth, which serves as a sound box, while the string is made to vibrate by being hit with a stick or arrow. Musical bows were used in western North America, particularly in California, occasionally also from the Southwest and British Columbia.

**Musk ox** (*Ovibos moschatus*), woolly wild cattle, contemporary of the mammoth, whose habitat during the Ice Age extended to almost the entire circumpolar region, although in historic times it was restricted to the area between the central arctic west of the Hudson Bay, northern Greenland, and northern Alaska, where it was hunted by the Inuit with the help of dogs. Because the musk ox is easy prey, it became almost extinct in the 19th century.

**Muskrat** (*Ondrata zibethica*), amphibious rodent, about 14 inches long, found throughout most of North America (except the extreme north and south). The English term is a distortion of the Virginia Algonquian word *musquash*. It played an important role in the Indian fur trade until the 19th century, when several million muskrat skins were annually exported to England alone (see *Nanabozho*).

**Mustang** (from Mexican Spanish, *mesteño*, "unbranded horse"), a naturalized horse originally of North African extraction that had belonged to Spanish settlers in the Southwest. Mustangs rapidly multiplied on the Plains and developed into a distinct breed which was characterized by smallness of stature, speed, and stamina. Native breeds such as *Appaloosas* and *Cayuses* are derived from the mustang.

**Myths**, stories relating to the time before the current state of the world, describing its creation or preparation for human use by supernatural beings; therefore also used to justify the way of life regarded as appropriate by a community. These stories were sacred and were often passed on by specialists, and their telling was generally restricted to particular occasions or seasons and accompanied by particular rules of behavior: e.g., among the Coast Salish, the storyteller and his audience must lie flat on the floor, and the Jicarilla Apache were not permitted to sleep during the day that followed a night of storytelling.

**Nadir** (Arabic), lowest point in the sky opposite the zenith. Among some peoples (e.g., of the Southwest) nadir and zenith are counted

among the six cardinal points. The term is also used figuratively to denote the lowest point of population development which, in North America, was achieved around 1890 when only about 350,000 people still lived in traditional communities.

**NAGPRA (Native American Grave Protection and Repatriation Act)**, American legislation passed (1990) to allow the return from federally-funded museums of human remains taken from burial grounds as well as of objects that either originated in grave sites, or are regarded as sacred or as contributing to a people's sense of identity. Since its enactment, thousands of objects have been "repatriated" to indigenous applicants.

**Naja** (Navajo *najahe*, "crescent moon"), horseshoe- or crescent-shaped silver pendant, originally used by the Navajo to adorn horse harness, later worn on necklaces. The form has Spanish-Mexican and, ultimately, Arabic roots.

**Name soul**, in Eskimo belief the breath soul of the deceased which becomes part of the soul of a newborn infant who is named after the deceased person, and is said to acquire some of their personality traits. The same name soul may enter several people, who thereby become related to each other.

**Nanabozho** (also, *Mänapos*, **Weenaposo**), *culture hero* and *trickster* of the Ojibwa and Menominee of the Great Lakes (see *Gluskap, Wisakechak, wolverine*) who appears in the form of a hare. Nanabozho is one of a set of quadruplets born to a virgin who dies in childbirth. He is raised by his grandmother, steals fire from a neighboring people and kills the brother responsible for his mother's death. He is accompanied by a wolf on his adventures, and seeks revenge against the underwater manitous after the wolf drowns. The manitous then cause a great flood, after which Nanabozho recreates the earth with the help of a *muskrat*. Nanabozho was also widely regarded as the founder of the *Midewiwin* and benefactor of his nephews, the humans, although he is also responsible for a number of mischievous and indecent acts.

**Native Americans**, since the 1960s the politically correct term for indigenous people in the USA. It has become established among white people and indigenous intellectuals, but not on the reservations, where the term "Indians" still predominates.

**Negative painting**, technique used for decorating ceramics, whereby a pattern is applied in wax to the surface of a vessel before being completely covered in pigment. When the vessel is fired the wax melts away and the pattern appears in the color of the fired clay against a colored background. Negative painting is found on prehistoric pottery of the Southeast as well as in specific cultures of ancient Middle and South America.

**Niman**, ceremony held at the beginning of August, concluding the annual cycle of the Hopi's *kachina* dances, during which supernatural beings return from the world of humans to their home in the San Francisco Mountains. Within the framework of the Niman, the Hemis kachinas, adapted from those of the Rio Grande Pueblo of Jemez, dominate with their *tablitas* representing clouds.

**Nobility**, social class whose members are characterized by the possession of inherited privileges of an economic or social nature and who frequently have a different lifestyle from that of other members of the community. The acquisition of material and nonmaterial possessions (e.g., name titles, crests, songs, or myths), and the display of special garments, ornaments and, in some cases, languages, was characteristic of the nobility of the Northwest Coast and in parts of the Southeast. While members of the nobility usually married within their own class, among the Natchez in Louisiana members of the ruling classes were forced to marry members of the lowest class ("stinkards").

**Nomads**, anthropological term for pastoralists (an unknown way of life in pre-European North America) who have a completely or partly mobile way of life. Although hunters are not nomads, they are metaphorically described as living a "nomadic" way of life.

**Northwest Passage**, direct route in the north of the continent linking the Atlantic and Pacific Oceans, the existence of which was assumed by early European discoverers of North America. The search for the Northwest Passage began from the east in the 16th and from the west in the 18th century and provided many Eskimo groups with their first contact with white people.

**Oak** (*Quercus spp.*), generic term for numerous species of a tree of the beech family widespread south of the Subarctic and west of the central grasslands. In the east and in California, the oak's fruits, or acorns, were gathered and processed to make food. After the introduction of metal tools, oak splints were used for basket weaving in the Northeast.

**Obsidian**, black volcanic glass occurring in California, Oregon, and Wyoming, as well as other parts of western North America, which was of great importance in the long-distance trade; finds of obsidian in the area of the *Hopewell* culture in Ohio around the 1st millennium BC indicate the existence of trade links with Wyoming. Thanks to its conchoidal fracture, obsidian is a highly suitable material for arrows and spear points, and tools. Large obsidian blades were also used as a standard of value in northwestern California.

**Oil lamp**, among the Eskimo, usually a shallow oval or rectangular soapstone bowl with a wick of moss floating in seal blubber. Oil lamps were the only source of heat or light in Eskimo tents and houses; their tending was an obligation of the women.

**Oka Crisis**, military conflict between the Mohawk of Kanehsatake (Oka) near Montreal and the Quebec police and Canadian army during the summer and fall of 1990. The Oka Crisis was triggered by plans for the extension of a golf course on a Mohawk burial ground, although its origins lie in an old conflict regarding the land rights of the Mohawk who, as the wards of missionaries, settled on church land in the 17th century. The militant action was led by a faction known as the Mohawk Warriors, and mirrored the conflict within the Mohawk community regarding the authorization and control of casinos located on the reservation.

**Okipa**, annual four-day ritual drama enacted by the Mandan of the upper Missouri, at the center of which lies a dramatization of the creation of the world by First Creator and the *culture hero* First Man, the rescue of humans from the great flood, the release by First Man of game animals from captivity inside a hill, and the introduction of the buffalo dance to increase the size of bison herds. Self-torture by young men also occurred during the Okipa, which is comparable to that during the *Sun Dance* of the Plains peoples.

**Olelbis** ("he who sits above"), name of the god and creator of the northern Wintu in

northern central California. Comparable to the creator deities of the neighboring Yuki (Taikomol) and Maidu (Kodoyanpe), he – a condensate of the clouds rising from the water and therefore himself a product of his own thoughts – created the world from nothing, but subsequently withdrew to the sky where he sits in benign and elevated enthronement, yet without exerting his influence on the world.

**Opercula**, the white horny plates of prosobranchiate snails, used on the Northwest Coast for inlays on wooden objects.

**Opossum** (*Didelphis marsupialis*), North America's only marsupial, native to the Southeast. In North Carolina and among the Natchez, its wool was spun and used to make belts.

**Paho**, Hopi prayer stick made of poplar wood, about six inches long, adorned with painted decorations, feathers and corn husk. As a carrier of prayers, it is laid on shrines and altars, serving as a messenger to the appropriate deity. Similar prayer sticks are also used by other peoples in the Southwest.

**Paleface**, allegedly a Native American term for white people (the counterpart of *redskin*). It first appeared in the English language in the early 19th century. Besides comparable terms such as Pale Skin People (an Ojibwa term) and White Meat People (Choctaw), there are numerous other descriptions, including Yellow Eyes (Osage), Mule People or Pubic Hair People (Kiowa), and Spider (Cheyenne and Arapaho).

**Palmetto**, generic term for various species of palm trees native to the Southeast, particularly *Sabal palmetto*, the leaves of which are used to cover the roofs of houses, and *Serenoa repens*, which bears fruits that are eaten raw or dried for storage.

**Panindianism**, the intended or actual process of achieving political or cultural unity among North America's indigenous peoples. Precursors emerged since the mid-18th century in the form of intertribal alliances led by Pontiac, Joseph Brant, and Tecumseh. After the end of the Indian Wars, peaceful intertribal meetings on the reservations increased, leading to the widespread development of such cultural phenomena as the *powwow* and the *Peyote* religion. Contacts forged in the government's schools for Indians in the early 20th century provided fertile soil for political Panindianism, which aims to improve the social and legal position of indigenous persons and peoples. Several characteristics of Panindianism have been borrowed from the white conception of "Indians" (e.g., feather bonnets as typical headdresses). The language of Panindianism is English. Panindianism does not generally stand in opposition to tribalism but is closely linked to it.

**Panther** → *mountain lion*.

**Parfleche** (French *parer* "to ward off", and *flèche* "arrow"), usually a folded and painted container made of rawhide and used in the Plains and neighboring regions to transport food and clothing. The term "parfleche" refers to the use of rawhide for making shields.

**Parka** (from Aleut), hooded fur jacket, synonymous with *anorak*.

**Peace pipe** → *calumet*.

**Peccary** (*Pecari angulatus*), Native American wild boar found only in the southern areas of the Southwest and on the Gulf Coast, where it was a game animal of the indigenous foragers.

**Pemmican** (Cree, "manufactured fat"). Meat preserve of northern and central North America made of dried and pounded caribou, moose, or bison meat, often flavored with berries and covered with hot fat.

**Persimmon** (Virginia Algonquian, "dried fruit"), the fruits of the wild date plum tree (*Diospyros virginiana*), which were gathered in many parts of the Eastern Woodlands and dried on platforms. Since the 18th century also used in the Southeast to make a fruit wine known as "persimmon beer."

**Peyote** (Spanish loanword from Nahuatl), a button-like cactus (*Lophophora williamsii*), whose stimulating and sedative alkaloids can cause visions when consumed. It grows only as far north as the borderlands of Texas and New Mexico. Already in use in pre-European Mexico, this cactus only came into use in the Southwest and the southern Plains since the 18th century. Around 1870, the ritual consumption of peyote among the Comanche and Kiowa led to the

Myra Kukiiyaut (Inuit, Baker Lake, NWT), *The Shaman Flies with his Helpers*, stenciled print, 1980. Canadian Museum of Civilization, Hull, QC. → *shaman*.

emergence of the Peyote religion, which cult leaders ("road men") rapidly disseminated across the Plains and their peripheries. Influenced by Christianity in varying degrees, the Peyote religion as organized in the Native American Church (founded in 1918) is today the largest Panindian religious community.

**Pictogram** → *pictograph*.

**Pictograph**, pictorial symbol, often in the form of a stylized image. Pictographs, which often record events or achievements, are mnemonic aids rather than writing systems which can be read and understood without prior knowledge of the contents. East of the Rocky Mountains they were inscribed on wood, bark, or leather and served to record rituals and the achievements of warriors, and to chronicle the passing of the years (→ *winter count*).

**Pidgin**, trade language used for communication between speakers of different languages, usually by combining characteristics of each. Pidgins have a limited vocabulary and very simple grammatical rules. They are not native languages, i.e. all pidgin-speakers have to learn to speak it as a second language. Among the best-known North American pidgins are the Chinook jargon, a hybrid language containing elements of Chinook, Nootka, Salish, English, French, and Russian, and the Mobilian trade language used along the lower Mississippi, which combines aspects of Choctaw and Alabama with features of European languages.

**Piki**, the thin, pale blue corn bread of the Hopi, consisting of a dough made of ash lye, and

blue cornmeal, placed on a stone slab oiled with melonseed, and cooked over an open fire. The dried breads are eaten on special occasions (such as weddings), either flat or rolled up, with or without additional ingredients, but when available, they are also eaten as an everyday food.

**Pine nuts**, or pinyons, the edible seeds of various types of American pines (*Pinus edulis, P. sabiniana*) commonly known as pinyon pines. In the Great Basin, pine nuts were the only form of food that grew in sufficient quantity in one place to feed large groups of people over several weeks. This meant that the gathering of pine nuts in the fall became the social highlight of the year, when important religious ceremonies were held. Pine nuts were also eaten in parts of California and by the Apache in the Southwest.

**Pit house,** building type with sunken floor produced by a shallow to wall-height pit. In the latter case the roof rests directly on the surface of the ground. Frequently the roofs of pit houses are covered with earth (→ *earth lodge*). The pit houses of the Prairies and California have an entrance from the side, those of the western Arctic and the ceremonial rooms of the Pueblos (→ *kiva*) are entered through a smoke hole in the roof.

**Plank boat**, oceangoing boat of the Chumash of California, constructed of planks of wood sewn together with fiber threads and made watertight by a coating of asphalt.

**Platform burials**, disposal of human corpses by exposure on platforms set in trees or on scaffolding. A platform burial could be the final form of a burial (as on the Plains, where the ground was too hard or frozen to permit inhumation) or (as in the Southeast) the first of several stages, in which the bones cleaned of the flesh would eventually be buried. Along the southern Northwest Coast wooden boats were raised in the same way as platforms.

**Polar bear** (*Thalarctos maritimus*), carnivorous animal found from eastern Greenland to northern Alaska and southward to Hudson Bay. A good swimmer, it lives on ice floes or on rocky Arctic coasts and feeds principally on sea mammals. The polar bear is hunted by Eskimos of all parts of the Arctic (→ *bear cult*).

**Polyandry**, rare form of marriage in which a woman has several husbands, preferably brothers (fraternal polyandry). The need for

Wolf mask used in winter ceremonial, Mowachaht-Nootka, British Columbia, 18th century. Ethnologisches Museum, Staatliche Museen zu Berlin – Preussischer Kulturbesitz, Berlin, Germany. → *mask*; *winter ceremonial*.

polyandry in the Arctic arose from a shortage of women (caused by female infanticide); in the Great Basin, those women who were particularly adept food gatherers, and thus able to feed several men, would enter into polyandrous marriages. Polyandry was not regarded as a desirable form of marriage but was accepted as a transitional solution.

**Polygyny**, polygamous marriage between one man and several women. It was desirable because of its economic advantages and the fact that it augmented birth rates, although only a limited number of marriages could be polygynous due to the ratio of men to women. Polygyny was therefore most common in areas where wars were frequent (Prairies and Plains), because the practice of capturing wives and the loss of large numbers of men on the warpath resulted in women outnumbering men, or where there was great prosperity (Northwest Coast). Polygyny did not exist in areas where women had a strong social position (e.g., among the Hopi and Iroquois).

**Poor People's March**, protest march to Washington by African-American civil rights organizations during the election year of 1972. It served as a model for the *Trail of Broken Treaties* organized shortly afterwards by militant Indians.

**Porcupine**. The American tree-dwelling porcupine (*Erethizon dorsatum*), a native of the north and west of the subcontinent (as far as the Northeast and the Plains), is particularly important to the indigenous peoples of this region for its quills, which are dyed and used to decorate leather or birch bark. The soft interior of the quills absorbs the pigment, while the quills themselves are flattened and folded over stitches made with sinew or plaited on warp frames.

**Potlatch** (Chinook jargon, "to give"), gift-exchange feast held by the peoples of the Northwest Coast on occasion of the transfer of titles or privileges to new owners. It forms part of a system of exchange between kinship groups and provides an opportunity to demonstrate

wealth and inherited privileges. Despite a ban imposed by the Canadian government in 1884 to curtail what was regarded as a wasteful use of goods, potlatches continued to be held in parts of the coastal areas of British Columbia and have seen a revival since the ban was lifted in the late 20th century.

**Pottery**. Pottery was common in agricultural areas (the Eastern Woodlands, the Southwest) and in Alaska, where it was introduced from Siberia in the 2nd millennium BC. The oldest instance of pottery in North America (3rd millennium BC) occurs in the Southeast and in form is similar to that of Colombia. In the Southwest, where it first appeared c. 100 BC, pottery found its most sophisticated expression in vessels painted with polychrome representational motifs and in sculptural forms, which continue to be an important source of income. Across North America, pottery was made without the potter's wheel, the kiln, or the use of glazes, and was almost always produced by women.

**Powamu**, first in the Hopi's annual cycle of ceremonies, in which masked dancers embody *kachinas*. It takes place during the new moon in the fourth lunar month ("purification month," January or February). Corn and beans are planted in the *kivas* and children are initiated to the kachina and Powamu societies responsible for organizing the ceremony.

**Powwow** (Natick, "medicine man"). Powwows originated in the late 19th century on reservations of the Plains on the basis of public dances of warrior societies and developed during the 20th century into the most important Panindian expression of identity in the cities as well as on the reservations. Dance competitions (with prizes awarded in categories defined by gender, age, and dance form) are accompanied by drumming and singing. In addition there may be honors for participants, memorial services for the deceased, games, or the sale of food and crafts.

**Prairie dog** (*Cynomys spp.*), marmot-like mammal of the squirrel family. Large numbers live together in underground colonies in the Plains and parts of the Great Basin and the Southwest. In the Plains, prairie dogs were only eaten in emergencies. In the Basin they were regarded as a delicacy.

**Presbyterian**, reformed church of Calvinist character led by a hierarchy of presbyters (elders). In Scotland, the Presbyterian church is the state church, and since the 18th century it also became widespread in the USA primarily through Scottish colonists. Presbyterians have been involved in active missionary work with indigenous peoples of North America since 1802.

**Presidio**, Spanish garrison of 30 to 50 soldiers, established particularly in Sonora during the 18th century. Pima and Opata auxiliary troops deployed against the Apache often settled in the area surrounding a presidio and thus became familiar with Spanish civilization.

**Prohibition**, ban on the manufacture, transport, and sale of alcohol. It was subject to state legislation from 1846, but an amendment to the constitution made it a federal law from 1919 to 1933. On Indian land, individual colonial prohibition laws were applied from the 17th century onward, and a general ban was imposed in the USA from 1802 to 1953 and in Canada from 1874 to 1951. Since that time the tribes themselves regulate access to alcohol on the basis of local option. Prohibition has proved unhelpful in the fight against alcohol abuse.

**Pronghorn antelope** (*Antilocapra americana*), type of ruminant exclusive to North America. It was hunted in the Plains, the Great Basin, and parts of the Southwest.

**Prophet**, person who acquires the ability to make predictions after an encounter with supernatural beings or by invoking their assistance. The gift of prophecy frequently formed part of the repertoire of religious specialists in indigenous North America (→ *tent-shaking ceremony*). As contact with white

people increased, prophecy increasingly became a means for reviving indigenous religions hit by existential crises, and for adapting to a rapidly changing social and natural enviroment (→ *Ghost Dance*; *Longhouse religion*; *Prophet Dance*).

**Prophet Dance**, early 19th century religious movement of the Plateau area, based on the purported personal meeting between indigenous prophets and the Christian God, during which the imminent end of the world and the return of the dead were announced. The Prophet Dance combined Christian and indigenous religious elements, formed part of the tradition of similar 18th-century movements in the Northeast, and was a precursor of the *Ghost Dance* movement.

**Puma** → *mountain lion*.

**Purification rituals**, rituals performed in preparation of important religious ceremonies, to overcome life crises, or for encounters with the supernatural which require a state of physical and spiritual purity. This may include fasting and other forms of mortification, the consumption of medicine to cause vomiting (→ *Black Drink*), or a visit to the *sweat lodge*.

**Puritans**, Calvinist followers of a movement to reform the Church of England, which began to expand in 1560. Central to Puritan doctrine was the belief that humans were predestined to eternal salvation or to damnation. Because of their rejection of the Episcopal constitution of the church, they were subject from 1585 onward to religious persecution and emigrated first to the Netherlands and, from 1620, to North America, where they founded competing colonies in New England. Their belief that they were a chosen people and that the damnation of the Indians was predetermined contributed to their warfare against neighboring indigenous peoples, whose extermination was, at least, accepted and condoned.

**Qarigi** → *qasgiq*.

**Qasgiq** (Yupik; Inupiaq *qarigi*), large house for meeting, living, and sleeping used by men and boys more than five years of age in the winter villages of the Yupik and Inupiaq in Alaska. All ceremonies took place in the qasgiq, which like the other houses was semisubterranean and covered with soil. It was also used as a sweat lodge. The place of each man within the qasgiq was determined by his social rank (dictated by age, marital status, and wealth).

**Rabbits** (*Sylvilagus spp.*), several species of harelike mammals found south of the Subarctic, including several species of cottontail, marsh, swamp, and pygmy rabbits. They are important game animals, especially in the Great Basin, but rabbits also play a prominent role in mythology. In the Basin, the cottontail rabbit stole the sun for the human beings, and in the Southeast, indigenous stories about the rabbit as *culture hero* became interwoven with African trickster stories (→ *hare*).

**Raccoon** (derived from Virginia Algonquian), nocturnal predator (*Procyon lotor*), widespread across the USA and southern Canada. In some mythologies (e.g., Abenaki, Kathlamet) the raccoon appears as a *trickster*. The Iroquois used to make oil from raccoon fat to grease their hair.

**Rainmaking** → *weather control*.

**Rancheria**, term for a small reservation of a few acres established in northern California in the late 19th and early 20th centuries by the Secretary of the Interior for the survivors of those tribelets with which the USA had not entered into treaties. As part of the policy of termination, some rancherias were dissolved in the 1950s and transferred to the private ownership of their occupants.

**Rattle**, percussion instrument used to accompany dancing and singing. The sound is produced by causing rigid objects to vibrate. Most often these are hollow containers such as gourds, insect cocoons, turtle shells, or carved wooden vessels containing grains of sand, small pebbles, or corn kernels. Other rattles consist of frames from which several objects are suspended (e.g. wooden disks, dewclaws) or of strings or sticks strung with such objects. Most rattles are shaken by hand; others are attached to belts or garters and rattle at every move of the body.

**Rawhide**, hard, flexible material made from cleaned but untanned animal skins that are stretched while still damp and then left to dry. Particularly common in the Plains and Plateau regions as a material for making shoes (*moccasins*) and receptacles (*parfleches*), rawhide was also used in the Subarctic to make strong thongs (*babiche*).

**Red cedar** (*Thuja plicata*), the giant tree of life of the cypress family, native to western North America, one of the most important sources of timber for the peoples of the Northwest Coast. The long, thick trunks lend themselves to the construction of dugouts and can be split into wide planks for building houses.

**Red Power**, political movement of the late 1960s and 1970s which arose among urban Native Americans under the influence of the radical African-American Black Power movement (→ *American Indian Movement*). Red Power fought in the urban environment against racism and discrimination, but also affected those reservations with a high degree of labor mobility.

**Redskin**, red man, term inaccurately used to describe North America's indigenous peoples, based partly on early European observations of the red body painting of the Beothuk in Newfoundland, and partly on the description of the skin of Native Americans as "copper red." In the first classification of human races, written in 1758, Linnaeus also described *Homo sapiens americanus* as being "red." Frequently used derogatively, the militant Indian movement of the late 20th century has reclaimed the word as its own (such as in *Red Power*, the counterpart of Black Power or the self-designation Skins from Redskins).

**Reincarnation**. The rebirth of a deceased person's soul in another body forms part of most indigenous North American peoples' conception of the nature of humans. Generally, souls are reincarnated as humans, except in California where human souls can transmigrate into animal bodies. The concept of the *name soul* among the Eskimo represents a specific form of re-incarnation.

**Repatriation** (restitution), the return of objects, especially those of a religious nature, of central importance to the preservation of a culture or to an indigenous group's sense of identity, which, in the past, had been taken more or less illegally from such a group (e.g., masks or other embodiments of supernatural beings, *wampum* belts, sacred pipes and bundles). Demands for repatriation have become increasingly insistent since the 1960s. To some extent this has now been regulated in the USA by an act passed in 1990 (→ *NAGPRA*), and in Canada by an agreement between museums and indigenous groups.

**Reservation** (USA: reservation; Canada: reserve), land in the common ownership of an indigenous group, which is subject to special governmental protection and where remnants of the group's original rights of sovereignty apply (e.g., exemption from taxation). Most reservations were established through treaties or by executive order of the president of the United States. Reservations created in colonial times, some of which date back to the 17th century, are subject to the authority of the governors of their respective states. All others are protected by the federal governments of the USA or Canada.

**Ritual**, strictly prescribed activity, frequently of a religious character, the precise observance of which is regarded as vital for its intended purpose while mistakes are punished by supernatural retribution. On a social level, rituals confirm the permanence of the social group and the protection of the individual by the community.

**Roach**, hairstyle in which a brushlike strip of hair is left standing along the center of an otherwise shaved head, or a similar hairpiece made of deer hair and porcupine quills. The hairstyle is similar to the "mohawk" favored by punk rockers in the late 20th century, and in indigenous North America it was particularly used by the agricultural peoples of the Northeast, Southeast, and the Prairies. As a hairpiece, it has become a widespread emblem of warrior society membership, the dances of which form the basis of the Panindian *powwow*.

**Rock paintings**, pictures created by scratching lines or applying pigment onto rock faces. Rock paintings have a wide distribution in North America, and they show great stylistic variation. It is difficult to determine their age and their meaning, and the cultures that produced them. Some rock paintings served to record war deeds, some were the result of spontaneous artistic desire, and others had a religious meaning: young people among the Salish of the Plateau continued to produce such images well into the 20th century as part of their vision quest.

**Russian Orthodox Church**. The Orthodox Church led by the Patriarch of Moscow made efforts to convert indigenous people during the period of Russian possession in North America (until 1867). They were most successful with the Aleut and the Yupik of the Pacific Coast; the results of their efforts with the Tlingit and Athapaskan of Alaska were negligible. The Tlingit did not turn to Orthodox Christianity until after the end of Russian rule, when they used the church fraternities for their own political ends and discovered parallels between the Orthodox church and their own cult of the dead.

**Sachem**, **sagamore**, term for hereditary leaders derived from northeastern Algonquian languages, in the 19th century also wrongly applied to hereditary chiefs of the *Iroquois League* (the proper term for whom is in Seneca *hoya:ne:h*, and in Mohawk *roya:ner*). Unlike the Iroquois, whose chiefs had to be male, among the coastal Algonquians women could also take office as a sachem.

**Sacred bundle** → *Bundle*.

**Saguaro**, **sahuaro** (loan word from Latin American Spanish), giant cactus (*Carnegia gigantea*) of Arizona and parts of California and Sonora. Together with other giant cactii (e.g., pitahaya), these plants were a major food source for the hunter-gatherers who populated the arid regions of western North America. The fruits of this cactus were eaten raw, preserved in the form of syrup, or used to make cactus wine.

**Salmon**, family of fish (*Salmonidae*) that includes many different species of soft-finned, bony fish widespread across the northern hemisphere in the form of saltwater, freshwater, and migratory fish. Salmon were particularly important to the inhabitants of the Northwest Coast, where it was a staple food and formed the basis for sedentary life and social development. However, various species of salmon also played an important role in parts of the Arctic, the Subarctic, the Northeast, the Plateau, and California. Along the Northwest Coast, salmon were thought to be immortal supernatural beings who lived in a house in the ocean, and who offered themselves to humans as food during their annual migration.

**Sand painting** (dry painting), technique used in the Southwest, southern California, and on the Plains for creating ceremonial images by sprinkling colored sand, cornmeal, pollen, pulverized petals, and charcoal on a level surface. The Pueblo form of sand painting used on the altars of kivas was taken over into Navajo healing rituals. The sand paintings, which could vary from one foot to over 14 feet in diameter, were destroyed immediately after use in order to prevent their abuse. Today the Navajo make sand paintings for sale by sprinkling pigment onto boards covered with adhesive.

**Scalp**, war trophy usually made by stretching a piece of the scalp of an enemy, including hair, on a frame. It was most prevalent among the peoples of eastern North America, although it also occurred in the Plains and the Southwest. The scalp, which is a form of head trophy, is commonly used in fertility rituals and is demonstratively exhibited by women during scalp dances. Scalping is a pre-European practice, but was further encouraged by the introduction of sharp metal knives and the payment of scalp bounties – an idea which was ascribed to New Netherlands governor William Kieft around 1640.

**Scout**, indigenous person in the service of Euro-American military troops during the Indian Wars. White armies used indigenous expertise in traditional warfare and tracking and exploited ancient enmities between tribes for their own ends. During the *Sioux Wars*, most of the scouts were recruited from the Lakota's traditional enemies such as the Crow, Pawnee, and Arikara. However, in the late 19th century many Apache auxiliary troops fought other Apache. In 1866 the USA army established a special Indian scout section which continued to exist until 1943 and was deployed against Pancho Villa's rebels in Mexico and during World War I.

**Seal,** marine mammals with webbed feet, which can only move with difficulty on land; includes the common seal (*Phoca spp.*), which is typical of the Arctic, the sea elephant (*Miruonga angustirostris*) of the West Coast, and the hooded seal (*Cystophora cristata*) of the North Atlantic. Seals were the Eskimo's most important source of skins, meat, and fat. In winter seals were caught through breathing holes in the ice, and by harpoon from kayaks on the open sea. Along the Atlantic and Pacific coasts, seals are regarded merely as a supplementary source of food.

**Sea otter** (*Enhydra lutris*), musteline animal, up to 3 feet long without the tail, which has adapted to life in the sea by developing flippers. Originally widespread from western Alaska to California, after c. 1780 it became one of the most valuable animals on the Northwest Coast because of the high prices paid in China for its fur, and was subsequently nearly exterminated by overhunting. The related land otter (*Lutra canadensis*), which was common almost

Wooden warrior helmet with opercula inlay, Chilkat-Tlingit, Alaska, early 19th century.
Ethnologisches Museum, Staatliche Museen zu Berlin – Preussischer Kulturbesitz, Berlin, Germany.
→ *opercula*.

everywhere south of the Arctic, also became a victim of the fur trade. In the Prairies its pelt was used to make turban-like hats.

**Sedna** ("the one down there"), Baffin Island Eskimo name for the mythological mistress of all marine animals, known by other Eskimo groups under different names and in slightly different manifestations. Sedna is sometimes conceived as being as half-seal, half-woman, sometimes as a cyclops, and occasionally as a giantess. The animals she rules were created from her finger joints, which her father had severed. When game animals are scarce, an *angakoq* must bring them back by traveling to the underwater world where he combs Sedna's hair to remove the taboos that have been broken by human beings and then cleans her house. In Eskimo folk religion, Sedna is frequently regarded as the supreme being in the pantheon.

against the settlement of white Americans along the border. Their defeat by General Andrew Jackson led to Spain's loss of Florida to the USA. A second war (1835–1842) erupted when the Seminole resisted forced removal to Oklahoma, although most were unable to avoid this fate.

**Shaking tent**, ritual performed by the Algonquian peoples of the eastern Subarctic, the western Great Lakes, and the northern Plains, during which a ritual specialist summons his spirit helpers, among them *Turtle*, whose arrival becomes apparent when his cylindrical, open-topped tent begins to shake violently. The ritualist remains in the tent and on behalf of his audience asks the spirit helpers about the causes of illnesses, the location of lost objects, the fate of distant people, and events in the future. A related ritual is the Yuwipi of the Lakota.

possessed by them. Sometimes the term "shaman" is used to encompass all religious specialists who were not "priests," i.e., persons who routinely perform complex ceremonies in accordance with a ritual calendar, and whose religion is characterized by permanent cult sites, an organized clergy, and ordered ritual sequences. The fact that in many North American cultures, every man (and woman, on occasion) has access to the supernatural through dreams or visions (→ *vision quest*), draws many religious practices within the field of shamanism, although in many cases the application of these acquired powers does not require a state of ecstasy. The greatest similarities to Siberian shamanism are found in the Arctic and in parts of western North America. However, the use of the term shaman to describe every medicine man or ritual specialist is not appropriate.

to the incest *taboo*. This exception to the taboo is known to have existed among other societies with marked social stratification, where it was thought to help maintain the purity of the ruling bloodline. It is a particularly notable phenomenon among the Calusa because they were hunter-gatherers, and would therefore have been expected to lack social differentiation.

**Sign language**, method of communication using a set of standardized hand gestures. Sign language was frequently used in indigenous North America for trade and other purposes where the ability to communicate across language barriers was important. Although the introduction of horses, which increased mobility, promoted the expansion of sign language on the Plains, sign language in North America has pre-European origins; there is incontrovertible evidence that it was used in southern Texas in the early 16th century.

**Sila** (Inuktitut; Yupik; Ellam yua), the *inua* of air, wind, and weather, which is embodied by the breath souls and in the mind of human beings. Songs and words as expressions of the breath can therefore have a supernatural effect. As a life-giving being, Sila sometimes also appears as a creator god.

**Silk ribbons**. As a European trade good silk ribbons became widespread in eastern North America during the late 18th century, where they were used to adorn clothing of leather and textiles. The most sophisticated form of silk ribbon appliqué work was found among the peoples of the western Great Lakes region and the eastern Prairies (Winnebago, Menominee, Potawatomi, Fox, Delaware, Osage, and others). Today cotton shirts decorated with a few ribbons ("ribbonshirts") are part of a Panindian form of dress.

**Silver**, precious metal which the indigenous peoples of North America first acquired in the 17th century in the form of jewelry through trade with Europeans. The Iroquois began to make their own silver jewelry after the decline of the fur trade in the early 19th century, while at around the same time the Tlingit learned from Russians how to engrave silver. In around 1860, Mexican blacksmiths taught the Navajo the skill of working silver, while nickel silver (made from copper, nickel, and zinc) was preferred by some Plains peoples as a metal for jewelry.

**Sioux Wars**, violent military confrontations (1862–1881) between the Dakota, Nakota, and Lakota and the American army. The conflict began when the Dakota in Minnesota rebelled against white domination. When the Americans began to pursue the tactic of forward defense in 1863, the conflict escalated to include the western Sioux, who defended themselves under the leadership of Red Cloud, Crazy Horse, and Sitting Bull. The *Fort Laramie treaty* (1868) was followed by a short-lived period of peace, shattered by the army's penetration of the Black Hills and the Battle of the *Little Bighorn* (1876). The Sioux Wars came to an end when Sitting Bull returned from exile in Canada.

**Sipapu** (Hopi), Shipap (Keres), Sipofene (Tewa), the place where humans emerged from the underworld, or the underworld itself, as imagined by the Pueblo peoples. The Hopi represent Sipapu by a covered hole in the floor of their kiva; among the Tewa each moiety had a room attached to the kiva. According to the belief of the Rio Grande Pueblos the real Sipapu is located north of the contemporary settlements.

Bison robe with depictions of war deeds, Lakota, c. 1830. Ethnologisches Museum, Staatliche Museen zu Berlin – Preussischer Kulturbesitz, Berlin, Germany. → *buffalo cloak.*

**Self-determination**, policy pursued in the USA since the 1980s, by which tribes living on reservations are given more extensive powers of self-government and administration, including greater control over education policies. The main problem in implementing self-determination has been the tribes' generally weak financial position, which has only partly improved as a result of the income generated by gambling (→ *bingo*).

**Seminole Wars**, two military conflicts between the Seminole in Florida and the USA. During the first (1817/18), when Florida was still a Spanish dominion, the Seminole fought

**Shalako**, among the Zuni, 12 large, birdlike figures with long snouts, who participate every December in a ritual at the center of which stand the six *cardinal directions*. Among the Hopi, at intervals of many years, the conclusion of *Niman* sees the appearance of kachinas, who are also known as shalakos (or salakos), equipped with large tablitas; in this case, each shalako is accompanied by a female salako mana.

**Shaman** (from the Ewenk language of Siberia), a person who, in an intentionally induced state of ecstasy, interacts with supernatural beings by sending his *soul* to the other world, by summoning his spirit helpers, or by being

**Shell beads,** were widely used to decorate clothing and jewelry before the introduction of European glass beads. Thanks to their durability and the value ascribed to them, on account of the work involved in making them, the use of shell pearls as a medium for exchange, as a standard of value, in ceremonies, and as a trade good extended deep inland. → *dentalium, cowry, wampum.*

**Shipap** → *sipapu.*

**Sibling marriage**. Marriage between brothers and sisters within the ruling house was not unusual among the Calusa in Florida, although such liaisons were generally subject

**Sky Woman**, mythological figure among the peoples of the Northeast (the Huron,

Iroquois, Mahican, and Delaware), who is said to have plunged from an upperworld through a hole in the sky and landed on a world carried on the back of a turtle. There she became the mother or grandmother of the *culture hero* and the ancestor of mankind.

**Slavery**, a condition of domination in which one person has complete power of disposal over another. As a social practice, slavery is especially known from the Northwest Coast and the Southeast, where those prisoners of war who were not integrated in the kinship group through adoption were deprived of all rights. Those forced into slavery by debt were often bought free by their relatives. While the *Five Civilized Tribes* of the Southeast soon also turned to keeping African slaves, here and in the Southwest indigenous persons were also sold to white masters through the slave trade.

**Sled dog**, Arctic breed of dog particularly suited to drawing sleds, which spread from Alaska to Greenland since the first appearance of *dog sleds* in the *Thule* culture. In the western Subarctic, dogs were used to draw *toboggans* only after the fur trade began.

**Smallpox**, dangerous and highly contagious viral infection of frequently epidemic proportions until its eradication in 1979. Between the 16th and 19th centuries, smallpox, together with influenza, measles, cholera, and typhoid fever, was responsible for most of the indigenous population decline in North America. Death rates caused by smallpox often surpassed 75 percent and exterminated entire peoples. During the last great smallpox epidemic (1836–1840), at least 20,000 people died in the Prairies and Plains alone. From this point on, vaccines against smallpox, available since 1796, were increasingly used to immunize indigenous peoples.

**Smoke signals**, mainly used in the steppes of the Plains, where the view was unobstructed by trees, to transmit messages by feeding a fire with damp grass or leaves. Pillars of smoke of various sizes could be produced by covering the fire with a blanket, and the addition of certain plants could alter the color of the smoke. Under optimal conditions, smoke signals could be seen from a distance of up to 50 miles.

**Snake Dance**, ritual performed every two years in the pueblos of the Hopi, when members of the Snake and Antelope societies conclude eight days of secret ritual within the kiva by publicly dancing while holding live rattle snakes in their mouths and subsequently letting them go free. The Snake Dance is regarded as a form of rain dance and was in the past also practiced in other pueblos. A similar ceremony was held by the Yokuts in California.

**Snowshoe hare** (*Lepus americanus*) → hare.

**Snowshoes**, footwear that, by increasing the base area of the foot permits walking over deep snow. The most widely used snowshoes in subarctic North America and its southern neighborhood (Northeast, northern Plains, Plateau) had frames consisting of one or two pieces of bent wood reinforced by cross-braces across which lengths of *babiche* were stretched to form a net. The great variety of frames (e.g., "swallow tail," "bear's foot," and "hourglass" forms) reflected regional differences and uses (for hunting, long journeys, etc.). Oval board snowshoes are known from the Naskapi of Labrador. The Eurasian plank form (skis) was only rarely adopted from whites.

**Soapstone** (steatite), a soft stone consisting mainly of talc, easy to cut and used since pre-European times in many parts of North America to make bowls, tools, and effigies.

Since 1948, soapstone has become the preferred material of the Canadian Inuit for making commercial stone carvings.

**Societies** → associations.

**Sofki**, Muskogee term for *hominy*. It was eaten with blue corn dumplings, mashed hickories, or mixed with bone marrow.

**Sororate**, custom by which a widower marries the sister of his deceased wife. It served to maintain the relationship established between two kinship groups through marriage (→ *levirate*).

**Soul**, generally invisible principle of life and consciousness within human beings and those other living beings who become persons by having a soul. Most North American peoples assumed the existence of at least two such principles: a "breath" or "vital" soul, tied to the body and manifesting the principle of life, and a "free" soul, which embodied the principle of consciousness and could leave the body, for instance in a dream. The fate of these souls after death varies, although it is common for one to remain in the proximity of a grave as a ghost for some time, while the other enters the world beyond (→ *name soul*, *reincarnation*). Animals generally have a single, collective soul, embodied by an "owner of species" or master/mistress of the animals (→ *inua*).

**Southeastern Ceremonial Complex**, term for a regional belief system (AD 1200–1500), of the Mississippian cultures at the center of which stood agriculture, fertility, war, and chiefdom. The Southeastern Ceremonial Complex is known only through its visual images, preserved on shell, copper, and stone objects.

**Spanish moss** (*Tillandsia usneoides*), mostly rootless plant that grows on trees, hanging in long clusters. It is found in the coastal regions of the Gulf of Mexico and the Atlantic Ocean; local indigenous peoples used it to a limited extent as a source of textile fibers.

**Spear thrower**, board or stick used to elongate the lever arm when throwing a spear, thereby making better use of the throwing force. Before the introduction of bows and arrows, the spear thrower was widely used in North America. More recently it has been used mainly for hunting marine mammals in the Arctic.

**Spirits**, supernatural beings with superhuman abilities although less powerful than gods (e.g., guardian spirits), but not the souls of the dead that have remained in the world (ghosts).

**Squash** (from the Massachusett language, *Cucurbita pepo* and *C. maxima*), together with corn and beans, squash is one of the three cultivated food plants introduced to eastern and southwestern North America from Mesoamerica. It first appeared c. 1200 BC in southern New Mexico and in the 1st millennium BC also in the Eastern Woodlands. The flesh was boiled, fried, or cut into strips and dried for storage; the flowers and seeds were also eaten (→ *gourd*).

**Stickball**, team game played in the Northeast, Southeast, and in the Prairies, with one or two wooden sticks fitted with nets and a stuffed leather ball. The teams – frequently the entire village or tribe – have to convey the ball past the ends of the playing field or onto wooden posts. The game, sometimes referred to as the "little brother of war" is rich in religious symbolism, as is the preparation that players have to undergo before the game can begin.

**Stone hammer** and **Slung shot** clubs were used as weapons of war on the Plains, where wood was in short supply. Either a stone

shaped like a pointed egg was fastened to a slender shaft covered in rawhide (stone hammer club), or a round stone together with a wooden shaft was encased in wet rawhide, which shrunk as it dried and thus held the parts firmly together.

**Storage economy**. The preservation of a seasonal surplus of food for use in times of need has often been the foundation for a sedentary way of life. A variety of storage buildings were found in indigenous North America, including larders built on platforms above ground in California (for acorns) and in the Southeast (for corn and other agricultural products), as well as underground storage pits in the Northeast and the Prairies. On the Northwest Coast dried or smoked fish would be hung under the roofs of houses, and the preserved meats of the Plains peoples (→ *pemmican*) were stored in rawhide containers (→ *parfleche*). In the Arctic, fish and meat could easily be frozen in winter.

**Succotash** (from Narragansett, "corncob"), white American term for a dish of corn and beans that may be eaten with or without meat.

**Sugar maple** → maple sugar.

**Sun Dance**, the most important religious ceremonial among the Plains peoples, held during the summer bison-hunting period to serve the wellbeing of individual participants as well as of the entire community. The ceremony is performed in a specially built Sun Dance lodge, and lasts several days. During this time, dancers fulfill solemn vows by making personal sacrifices in gratitude to the supernatural beings who have undertaken to help them. The U.S. government prohibited the Sun Dance in 1881 as barbaric because of the self-torture that was sometimes involved. Nevertheless, it has been widely practiced again since the 1960s.

**Sunflower** (*Helianthus spp.*), plant grown by agricultural peoples of eastern North America from the 1st millennium BC. Various varieties have been cultivated in historic times by the peoples of the Northeast, Southeast, and the Prairies. The Iroquois press the seeds to extract an oil used mainly for cosmetic purposes, but also as a polish for masks. The Virginia Algonquian used the seeds to make broth, bread, and dried dumplings (→ *Jerusalem artichoke*).

**Sweat lodge**, building commonly used in many parts of North America for physical and spiritual cleansing. In northern and southwestern Alaska, and in California and the Pueblo region, sweating was induced by the direct heat of a fire, and the sweat lodges also served as men's houses in the winter (→ *qasgiq*). In the Southeast, women also lived in such winter houses ("hot houses"). Much more widespread were steam baths in small, dome-shaped buildings where water was poured onto hot stones. These were generally used by individuals, although they have recently been used as places where rituals are conducted under the direction of a ceremonial leader.

**Sxwayxwey**, zoomorphic masks of the Coast Salish in British Columbia and Washington, featuring stalk eyes and a long tongue, but no jaw. Sxwayxwey are regarded as hereditary privileges of families who acquired them in the mythical past.

**Syncretism**, the merging of beliefs and ritual acts from different religions to form a new religion; in North America this particularly applies to the amalgamation of indigenous religions with Christianity (e.g., *Peyote religion*). The Pueblo peoples of the American Southwest, on the other hand, observe both their indigenous religion and Christianity, albeit separately.

**Tablita** (Latin American Spanish, "board"), wooden board worn as a headpiece by kachinas and female dancers in dances like the Hopi Butterfly Dance and the Rio Grande Pueblo Corn Dance. Tablitas generally have the appearance of stylized clouds and feature symbolic paintings referring to rain and fertility.

**Taboo** (from Polynesian), anthropological term for a collective prohibition, the infringement of which often brings about supernatural punishment. The incest taboo (prohibition of sexual relations with parents, siblings, and children; but → *sibling marriage*) is almost universal in North America. The prohibition of sexual activity before war and rituals was also common. Various forms of the *mother-in-law taboo* have been recorded, as have food taboos and the widespread taboo against menstruating women (→ *menstruation hut*).

**Taime**, sacred stone objects central to the Kiowa *Sun Dance* and kept safe by a designated keeper in a small *rawhide* box. According to oral tradition, the Kiowa acquired three taimes some time around 1765. Two of them, one a painted human bust, the other a bear kidney, were lost in 1868 during a revenge raid on the Ute when three taboos linked to their handling were broken: a skunk crossed the warriors' path, and the Comanche who accompanied the Kiowa on this raid carried mirrors and ate bear meat.

**Tattoo**, permanent decoration of the face or body produced by applying pigment beneath the skin. In North America, a widely used method consisted of piercing the skin with pointed, sometimes comb-shaped, tools and rubbing the pigment (usually charcoal) used for sketching the design on the skin into the wounds. In the Arctic and along the Northwest Coast, threads blackened with soot were drawn beneath the skin. The predominantly linear and often abstract designs served as markers of permanent social roles, such as gender or membership of a kinship group.

**Tawiskaron** ("flint"), in Iroquois mythology, *Tharonhiawagon's* younger twin, who killed his mother by being born through her armpit, and later, while collaborating with his brother on arranging the world, frustrated his good intentions. Thus, when Tharonhiawagon arranged for the rivers to flow in both directions, his brother made them flow in only one direction thereby making it extremely difficult to travel upstream. Under the influence of Christian ideas, Tawiskaron eventually became the embodiment of evil.

**Temple**, permanent place of ritual activities tended by a priesthood whose religious and ritual knowledge has primarily been received from their predecessors. In a wider sense this includes the shrines where Nootka chiefs ritually prepare for whale hunting, or the *kivas* of the Pueblo peoples. In a more restricted sense, the cult sites of the Southeast, where a "state religion" with close links to the political leadership was practiced, are also referred to as temples.

**Temple mound**, artificial earth mound, generally in the shape of a truncated pyramid, characteristic of the Mississippian cultures of the Southeast, on which temples of perishable material were built following the model of Mesoamerican pyramids. Large ceremonial centers such as Cahokia in Illinois and Spiro in Oklahoma featured numerous such temple mounds.

**Termination**, US government policy pursued after World War II which aimed to end the special legal relationship between indigenous tribes and the federal government (dissolution of communally owned reservations and tribal governments, transfer of some rights to the state governments, suspension of federal assistance for education and healthcare etc.). Problems resulting from termination rapidly became apparent, and the policy was abandoned in the 1960s.

**Tesgüino**, Spanish-American term for corn beer, also known as *tesvino* or *tiswin* in the Southwest. Hence the term "tesgüinada" to describe the Tarahumara's drinking feasts. Tiswin can also denote an Apache mescal beer.

**Tharonhiawagon** ("He who Grasps the Sky"), Iroquois *culture hero* and grandson of *Sky Woman*. He and his antithetical twin brother *Tawiskaron* were born to a virgin. In the present-day belief system of the Iroquois, Tharonhiawagon has developed into a creator god, to whom calendric thanksgiving rituals are dedicated.

**Thorn apple** → *toloache*.

**Throwing stick**, curved, flat hunting weapon made of wood, similar to a boomerang, but without its ability to return to the thrower. Throwing sticks were widely used for hunting small animals by the peoples in the Pueblo region and in southern California.

**Thule**, the culture of the direct ancestors of modern Inuit or Inuktitut-speaking Eskimo, whose sophisticated means of transport (*kayak*, *dog sled*) enabled them to spread from Alaska to the east coast of Greenland in the period between AD 1000 and 1200, absorbing older Eskimo populations (*Dorset culture*) in the process. The culture was named after the legendary kingdom of the Far North.

**Thunderbird**. In large areas of eastern North America, the Plains, the Plateau, the Northwest Coast, and northern California, thunder was thought to be the sound created by the wings of a large bird (an eagle, hawk, or partridge) from whose eyes lightning shot to earth. These powerful, supernatural beings, living in permanent struggle with the beings of water and of the underworld, were sometimes regarded as the patrons of warriors, as well as those of certain healers

**Tihu** (Hopi, *katsin tihu*), carved and painted cottonwood figurines representing *kachinas*, best known from the Hopi and Zuni, but also made by other Pueblo peoples. Among the Hopi, these dolls were originally carved by fathers for their daughters and given to children by the masked kachina dancers. Since the 19th century, tihu have become an important branch of Hopi arts and crafts production.

**Tipi** (Dakota, "domicile"), term for the leather-covered, conical tent of the Plains. A tipi consists of a supporting framework made up of three or four inclined wooden poles, about 20 feet long, tied together near the top, between which additional poles are positioned, the lower ends of which form the circular floor plan of the tent. The outer covering, sewn of a dozen or more bison hides, was fastened with wooden pins at the front side. Tipis had to be small enough to be transported; after the introduction of horses, they could measure up to 35 feet in diameter. Thanks to the form of its construction, the tipi is quick and easy to erect and dismantle, and thus facilitated the Plains people's mobile lifestyle.

**Tirawahat** (Pawnee, "The Wide Expanse"), the Pawnee's supreme being, also known as "our father above." He stands at the beginning of all things and is thought to have also created the star gods, whom he ordered to create the world. Because of his great power, Tirawahat has

moved away from humans who nevertheless acknowledge his omnipotence, pray to him, and offer him smoke and other sacrifices. He is not, however, central to the Pawnee's ritual worship.

**Tobacco**, the dried leaves of various kinds of *Nicotiana*, members of the nightshade family, used by all the peoples south and west of the Subarctic, especially for ceremonial purposes. Particularly in the East, some species (especially *N. rustica*) were grown in gardens, mainly by men, others grew wild and were gathered, especially by peoples in the west of the country. North American peoples were introduced to the South American *N. tabacum* by Europeans, who brought tobacco as a trade item as

far north as the Arctic. Tobacco was smoked in pipes, in the form of cigarettes or cigars, chewed, and some-times drunk as a decoction (→ also *kinnikinnik*).

**Tobacco pipes**. Evidence suggests that tobacco pipes were first used in the 1st millennium BC. Initially made of stone and having a tubular shape (as they were in California until recently), they were later made in eastern North America, also of clay and with an angular bowl and a long wooden stem shaft. As contents of sacred *bundles* and as ceremonial instruments for communicating with supernatural beings, tobacco pipes could become sacred pipes of great symbolic and spiritual value. As "peace pipes," they embodied the concepts of kinship and exchange (→ *calumet*).

**Toboggan** (Canadian French from Abenaki), sled without runners used by the peoples of the Subarctic and adjacent regions of the Northeast and Plains to transport heavy loads over snow, made of one or several boards bent upward at the front. Toboggans were drawn by humans using a tumpline or by teams of dogs. It is probable that drags made of deer hide were used originally.

**Toggle harpoon**, improvement on the "bearded" harpoon with lateral barbs and a

line attached near the end of the detachable point to secure the prey once it has been hit. In the toggle harpoon invented by Alaskan Eskimos in the 1st millennium BC, a line is attached to the center of the point which upon entering the prey pivots sideways under the pull of the escaping animal and thus firmly lodges itself in its body.

**Toloache** (Spanish loanword from Nahuatl), consciousness-altering drug extracted from the roots and leaves of the thorn apple *Datura innoxia*. This drug was used by southern Californian peoples (Yokut, Chumash, Luiseño) during collective initiation ceremonies of boys into adult society, in the initiations into secret

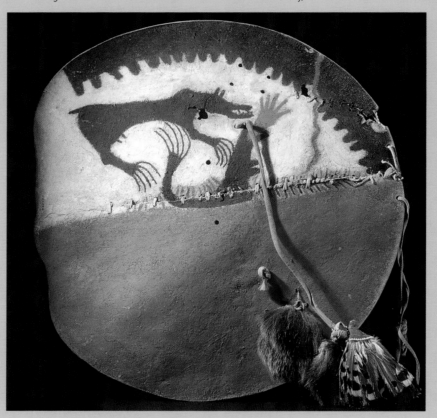

Shield decorated with the image of a bear, c. 1880, Crow, Montana. Field Museum of Natural History, Chicago, IL. → *bear cult*.

societies, and as part of the Chingichngish religion. In the neighboring Southwest, toloache was occasionally consumed by ritual specialists as part of their religious practices.

**Tomahawk** (from Virginia Algonquian, "tool for cleaving," adopted through English by other languages in its extended meaning), in the more restricted sense a metal ax imported to North America as a trade good and used as a weapon for throwing and striking, although in the wider sense, the term is used for all indigenous American forms of clubs. From the early 18th century, ax and pipe were combined to form the pipe tomahawk; a pipe bowl was fitted opposite the blade and the hollowed shaft served as the stem.

**Torture stake**, post rammed into the ground and sometimes surrounded by a raised platform. Prisoners of war who were not adopted by the victorious tribe would be tied to this and tortured to death. While the stake was used by the Iroquois and their neighbors, the peoples of the lower Mississippi used a scaffold on which victims were tied. Although generally a form of revenge, killing people on the stake can also be regarded as a human sacrifice related to the fertility of the fields (as can *scalping* and *headhunting*).

**Totem** (English, derived from Ojibwa), originally a northern Algonquian kinship term used among siblings and, in a wider sense, among members of a patrilineal *clan*. Hence the derivation of "totem" as a designation for the clans themselves (Ojibwa *nintotem*, "my family sign"). A series of mistakes and mis-understandings resulted in the word "totem" being used to refer to the guardian spirits acquired during vision quests, and being linked to particular taboos pertaining to the killing, touching, and consumption of the totem animals which are unrelated to the Ojibwa totem.

**Totem pole** → crest pole.

**Traditionalism**, adherence to patterns of thought and behavior handed down from generation to generation, generally accompanied by a rejection of innovations regarded as progressive by the Euro-American world. Traditionalism does not necessarily bring stagnation, although its followers tend to use models of the past to justify cultural change. Contradictions between traditionalism and adaption to a changed reality have caused deep rifts within many indigenous communities.

**Trail of Broken Treaties**, march on Washington organized by several US and Canadian Panindian organizations in the fall of 1972 which concluded with the occupation of the *Bureau of Indian Affairs* by some of the demonstrators .

**Trail of Tears**, the forced removal of the Cherokee from their homelands in Tennessee, Georgia, and North Carolina to Oklahoma in the summer and fall of 1837/38, following the implementation of the *Indian Removal Act*, caused the death of about a quarter of the 16,000 persons affected. Around 1,000 Cherokees managed to escape the deportation by fleeing into the mountains, whereas about 5,000 had previously voluntarily migrated westward.

**Trapper**, hunter whose livelihood depends on selling the pelts of animals caught with traps. As European and American fur-trading companies (e.g., the *Hudson's Bay Company* or the Russian-American Company) penetrated deeper into the continent, increasing numbers of indigenous hunters, particularly in and around the Subarctic, became trappers rather than hunting animals for food. The efficiency of trapping was greatly increased by the introduction of European metal traps and scent baits such as *castoreum* and by the division of hunting grounds into family hunting territories.

**Travois** (Canadian French, *travail*, "tripod"), transportation device used by the peoples of the Plains, consisting of two long, inclined, and usually crossed poles connected near the lower end by a platform; the other ends were attached to a draft animal (dog, later horse). Travois were used to transport tents, household equipment, and small children.

**Treaties**, the basis of the legal relationship between indigenous peoples and the British crown and the postcolonial nation-states, the USA and Canada. Treaties recognize tribes as largely sovereign entities subject to international law, and promise to provide them with annuities, assistance for educational, health, and economic development, and special protection against third parties in exchange for the cession of land rights. Between 1789 and 1871 the USA signed about 800 treaties with indigenous tribes, of which less than half were ratified by the Senate. Canada signed 11 collective treaties between 1871 and 1921 with tribes in Ontario, Manitoba, Saskatchewan, and Alberta. Several of the many treaties drawn up during the colonial period are also still valid today.

**Tribalism**, adherence of indigenous peoples to the tribal community as the main focus of identity. Fundamental to the close ties between tribal members are the bonds of kinship from which arise mutual rights and duties, communication usually based on a common language, a common worldview, and common ritual → also *Panindianism*).

**Tribe**, ambiguous term, used with great reluctance in contemporary anthropology. In the more restricted sense, a tribe is a political unit of several connected kinship groups, although the term is sometimes applied to whole peoples or *bands*. In the USA, tribe is the official designation for most of the political units with which the federal government maintains a special legal relationship.

**Tribelet**, term used for the politically autonomous, but generally very small, sedentary village groups of California.

**Trickster**, mythical figure, widespread in North America, who embodies the contradictory characteristics of a benevolent *culture hero* and those of a cunning deceiver, excessive in his gluttony and libido, whose behavior is distinguished by buffoonery and serious breaches of taboo. In western North America the part was often played by Coyote and on the Northwest Coast by Raven or Mink; in the east, Rabbit and hare-like beings (→ *Nanabozho*) embody tricksters. Tricksters can also appear in the form of humans or of other animals.

**Tulipai** (Apache, "gray water"), weakly alcoholic corn beer of the southern Athapaskans (Apache and Navajo) drunk for nourishment (including by children), in times of need, during the performance of arduous tasks, and also for its intoxicating effect. In the 20th century the term tulipai was also used for a fermented drink made from raisins and yeast.

**Turkey** (*Meleagris gallopavo*), species of fowl, with at least six wild forms known in North America, hunted for its feathers as well as for its meat. The Anasazi began to domesticate the turkey in AD 500, and like the peoples of the Eastern Woodlands used turkey feathers to make cloaks. Turkey burials are known from the Southwest. The type of turkey bred for food in present-day North America originated in Mesoamerica, was introduced to Europe in the 16th century, and subsequently to North America.

**Turquoise**, blue gemstone of the Southwest used for making jewelry since the Anasazi period. It became the main gemstone used by Navajo and Zuni silversmiths during the late 19th century. The Navajo regard turquoises as representing prosperity and good fortune and associate it with the south and invincibility.

**Turtle**, any one of a large order of terrestrial and aquatic reptiles with horny or bony shells, of which there are many in eastern North America. Indigenous peoples used the meat for food while the shells were widely used for rattles. In the mythologies of the peoples of the Northeast, the turtle frequently played a major role as carrier of the earth, yet is also often the victim of a trickster's mischief. Turtle is regarded as a leading spirit helper in the *Shaking tent*. It is linked to longevity (and healing rituals), and in the Pueblo region to rain and fertility.

**Twining**, textile technique by which passive elements are bound by two or more active threads. Used in basket weaving and to produce flat textiles, especially in California, on the Northwest Coast, and in the Northeast (→ also *Chilkat blanket*).

**Uktena**, a spotted, winged and horned snake monster of the Cherokee underworld, engaged in permanent conflict with the hawk Tlanuwa, into which humans are involuntarily drawn. Winged and horned snakes are featured in the imagery of the *Southeastern Ceremonial Complex*, although they also occur in the imagination of the peoples of the Northeast.

**Umiak** (from Inuktitut), an open boat, up to 35 feet long, consisting of a lightweight wooden framework over which seal hides were stretched. Umiaks were generally rowing boats, although some were fitted with sails. In Alaska (and earlier also in the eastern Arctic), they were used mainly for the whale hunt, the decline of which led to

Shield relating to a vision of Chief Arapoosh, Crow, Montana, 19th century. National Museum of the American Indian, Washington, DC. → *vision quest.*

the umiak becoming especially in Greenland purely a "women's boat," because on journeys it is rowed by the women.

**Umialik**, owner of an umiak and leader of a group of Eskimo whale hunters in northern Alaska, whose central role in the whale hunt ritual and in distributing the proceeds of the hunt also endowed him with a high rank in society.

**Underwater panthers**, group of mythical beings in the belief system of the Algonquian peoples of the western Great Lakes and some of their neighbors. They are recognizable as mountain lions by their long tails, and the horns on their heads symbolize their outstanding power. Together with other beings of the underworld they are regarded as opponents of the thunderbirds. They can help humans to success with the hunt or (in their role as keepers of the subterranean copper) to wealth. The comparable water cougars of the Florida Seminole had shaggy coats, long fishtails, and legs without paws.

**Urban Indians**, term for that section of the indigenous population of North American that moved to the cities, either voluntarily or in the course of US government relocation programs in connection with the policy of termination. Today, urban Indians are in the majority as compared to the inhabitants of the reservations.

**Vision quest**, the purposeful attempt by an individual to bring about a vision of a supernatural being (*guardian spirit*), by fasting and other forms of castigation, in order to acquire from the being special skills and a promise of future assistance. In the Northeast, on the Plateau, and among the Coast Salish, the vision quest was a common practice among adolescent boys (and sometimes girls); in southern California it formed part of a collective ritual and included the use of drugs. On the Plains and in the Great Basin, it was mainly grown men who thereby qualified as specialists for healing or war. Vision quests share certain similarities with the practices of *shamans* and other religious specialists.

Among the Mohave and the Iroquois supernatural experiences may be gained through spontaneous dreams.

**Wakan** (Lakota, "mysterious, inexplicable, sacred"), term used to describe all that is supernatural and inexplicable in the world, including the powers that could be acquired through contact with supernatural beings. In their personified form, the Wakan were 16, or four times four supernatural beings from a much larger number, the existence of which was assumed, and which in its entirety was known as Wakantanka ("the great secret"). This systematic view probably reflects the teachings of the religious specialists or wakan people, and was not shared by all Lakota.

**Wall painting**, form of predominantly ritual art restricted to the Pueblo region of North America, best known through archeological finds of the *Anasazi* culture, where *kivas* with over 100 layers of paintings, in the fresco secco technique and dating from the 14th and 15th centuries have been discovered. Because the Pueblo religion is today shrouded in secrecy, little is known about modern wall painting.

**Walrus** (*Odobaenidae*), two species of large marine mammals (→ *seals*) of the eastern and western Arctic, and unknown in the central Arctic. The walrus supplied Eskimo with meat and blubber and a thick hide, which was split and used to cover kayaks and umiaks. Walruses were hunted with harpoons. The long tusks provided walrus ivory for carved tools or engraved objects, which eventually developed under white influence into a commercial art form.

**Wampum** (from New England Algonquian, "white string"), white and purple cylindrical beads made from the shell of the sea snail *Venus mercenaria*, which were made into strings and belts by the peoples of the Northeast. These were used for jewelry but also served as standards of value in ritual exchange. The introduction of European metal drills promoted the spread of wampum at the expense of earlier disk-shaped shell beads. The Iroquois integrated wampum strings and belts into their rituals and, more importantly, used them in diplomacy to record agreements.

**Wapato** (Chinook jargon derived from Cree, "white sponge"), the root balls of one of several species of arrowhead or swamp-potato (*Sagittaria spp.*) which was gathered along the Columbia River and traded into the interior.

**Wapiti** (Shawnee, "white rump"), type of large deer (*Cervus canadensis*), once widespread in North America only found today in small scattered areas. The wapiti was a prized game animal which was hunted either individually or in collective drives. On the Plains its antlers provided a useful material for making whip handles, and in California containers for shell money. The teeth of wapiti were used on the northern Plains and the Plateau as a measure of value.

**War of Independence** → *American Revolution.*

**Washat religion** → *Longhouse religion.*

**Wassaja**, Panindian periodical published between 1916 and 1923 by Yavapai physician Carlos Montezuma, who used it as a platform from which to fight for the rights of Native Americans and for the abolition of the *Bureau of Indian Affairs*. A new *Wassaja* was among the many publications which appeared in the 1970s.

**Weather control**, a matter of concern across North America common to both hunting and agricultural peoples. This ability was widely regarded as a gift from a supernatural being to particular persons who used their powers for the good of the community, e.g., to bring about rain or to influence the direction and speed of the wind. Traditional rituals like the Pueblo peoples' representations of *kachinas* also served to control the weather.

**Weaving**, the production of cloth on a loom. Originally, this form of textile production was only known in the cotton-growing regions both of the Pueblos in the Southwest and of the Sonoran Desert in northwestern Mexico. After the Spanish introduced sheep, the Navajo in particular, who had adopted the Pueblo loom, also began to use sheep's wool for weaving. Under the influence of Europeans in the 19th century, people in the northeastern Great Lakes region began to weave narrow bands using hole-and-slot heddles. A half-weaving method developed by the Salish and Chinook on the Northwest Coast enabled them to weave yarns of dog and mountain goat wool on warp frames without mechanic sheds. Other textiles were produced by *twining*.

**Whale**, order of marine mammals hunted by indigenous peoples in the western and eastern Arctic and on the coasts of the Pacific and Atlantic oceans. There are more than 40 different species of whale, ranging in size from 15 feet to 60 feet in length. They include the

Rawhide silhouette of a male figure for the top of the Sundance pole. Oglala Lakota, South Dakota (before 1882). The Peabody Museum, Cambridge, MA. → *Sun Dance*.

blue whale, gray whale, humpback whale, sperm whale, and numerous type of dolphin, including porpoises and the killer whale (*Orcinus orca*), which occupies a central place in the mythology of the Northwest Coast. *Umiaks* (→ *umialik*) were used to hunt whales in the Arctic, whereas along the Northwest Coast, where whale hunting and the exploitation of beached whales were a privilege reserved for chiefs, dugouts were employed in whaling. The Aleut used poison (aconite) to hunt whales.

**White Buffalo Calf Woman** (Wohpe), culture heroine of the Lakota. The beautiful daughter of the Sky (Skan), who can also take on the appearance of a bison calf, taught the Lakota the use of the sacred pipe and its symbolic importance as well as the seven sacred ceremonies (*sweat lodge, vision quest,* keeping the ghost of the dead, *hunka,* female puberty ceremony, ball throwing, Sun Dance).

**White-tailed deer** (*Odocoileus virginianus*) → *deer*.

**Wigwam** (Massachusett, "house"), term used for various northeastern Algonquian forms of dwelling, especially the circular or oval domed structure consisting of a frame made of branches and covered with bark or mats. Colloquially, "wigwam" also denotes other Native American forms of housing.

**Wikiup** (probably an English loanword from Sauk or Fox, "house"), term used in the late 19th century, particularly for Apache and Numa (→ *kahni*) dwellings.

**Wild rice** (*Zizania aquatica*), species of wild aquatic grass with long, gray to black seeds that grows along the shores of lakes and rivers in the Northeast. Wild rice represents a major portion of the food resources in the western Great Lakes region. The seeds, which ripen in late summer, are harvested by people threshing the grass seeds with wooden sticks directly from the stalk into their boats. Wild rice is dried in the sun or parched over a fire, and then stored.

**Windigo**, supernatural being among the Algonquians of the eastern Subarctic, frequently appearing as a giant consisting entirely or partly of ice. In winter, windigos develop a ravenous appetite for human flesh. People who, under the influence of the Windigo, themselves were turned into such had to be deprived of their power by tent shakers ( → *Shaking tent*) and then killed. There is disagreement as to whether the

transformation of people into windigos is a culturally specific mental illness (Windigo psychosis) or whether it is merely a concept arising out of a fear of *witchcraft* triggered by the threat of hunger.

**Winter ceremonial**, collective term for the dance dramas of the Northwest Coast held during the ceremonial period of winter, when supernatural beings are represented by masked members of secret societies. In the Arctic and on the Plateau, the dark and generally unproductive winter was also regarded as a sacred period during which important ceremonies (e.g., *Bladder Festival, Messenger Feast)* took place.

**Winter count** (from Lakota *waniyetu yawapi*, "they count winters"), pictographic chronicle in which each year is represented by a pictogram of a memorable event. The symbols were painted in spiral or snake form on leather (later also on muslin or paper), and were accompanied by short sentences which were memorized by the chronicler. Winter counts are known to have been kept by the Lakota, Blackfoot, Kiowa, and other Plains peoples, but originally also were known in the Northeast (e.g., Virginia Algonquian).

**Winter house,** form of housing for the winter period among seasonally mobile peoples, often built more solidly than summer dwellings (e.g., *igloos*) and occasionally semisubterranean (*pit houses*).

**Winter village**, permanent winter settlement of peoples either with a mobile way of life during the rest of the year or who establish their summer villages in other ecozones. In the Arctic and along the Northwest Coast, winter villages were usually established near the coast, and in

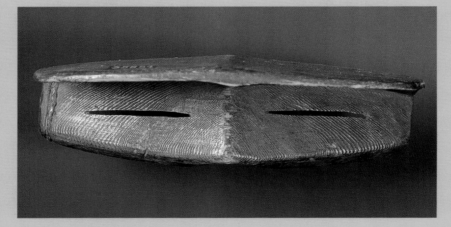

Wooden snow goggles with visor. Inuit, Canada (19th century). Rautenstrauch-Joest Museum für Völkerkunde, Cologne, Germany. → *Hunting hat.*

the central Arctic they could also be set up on the frozen sea. The peoples of the Plateau, Plains, and Prairies sought the shelter of wooded areas with rivers nearby.

**Wisakechak** (Cree, Saulteaux), Wisakeha (Sauk, Fox, Kickapoo, Potawatomi), Vasaagijik (Kutchin), *culture hero* and *trickster* corresponding to the Ojibwa's Nanabozho. The name "Wisakechak" was corrupted as "Whiskey Jack."

**Witchcraft**, the use of supernatural powers to the detriment of others. Supernatural beings who could endow humans with varying degrees of power or abilities, were generally believed to be neither good nor bad. Powerful healers were therefore easily suspected of using their knowledge for witchcraft. In fact, witchcraft is generally nothing more than an assumed action, and the danger of being accused of practicing it is a powerful means of social control. Such accusations tend to increase when societies are in crisis. Because of the influence of

Christianity, indigenous people also began to associate witchcraft with the concept of evil.

**Wolf** (*Canis lupus*), largest of the wild dogs and ancestor of the domestic dog (*Canis canis*), originally widespread across North America, now found in large numbers only in Canada, Alaska, and Greenland. In the mythology of the Great Lakes Algonquians, Wolf is the brother of culture hero *Nanabozho* and the lord of the realm of the dead. In the Great Basin and in California, the wolf is the brother of the *trickster Coyote*. The embodiment of the wolf is at the center of the Nootka's winter ceremonials and a reminder of the mythical transformer of the world who acquired his healing powers by killing the wolf. Many peoples name clans after the wolf, and the Tlingit name one of their two moieties after it.

**Wolverine** (*Gulo luscus*), predatory musteline mammal of northern and western Canada. The wolverine feeds mainly on small mammals, and it is notorious among trappers for devouring animals caught in their traps. The wolverine was sometimes equated with culture hero *Nanabozho* in the mythology of the Naskapi, Montagnais, Cree, and Ojibwa.

**Woodland Period**, prehistoric period of eastern North America (1000 BC–AD 1500), characterized by the emergence of agriculture, the general use of pottery, and the development of forms of political organization on the basis of sedentary life. The Woodland Period is also characterized by the development of local cultures and by the regional influence of the *Adena, Hopewell,* and *Mississippian cultures.*

**Woodpecker**, any of the many species of common North American birds of the *Picidae* family. In California the feathers and skin of the flicker (*Colaptes cafer*), the pileated woodpecker (*Dryocopus pileatus*), and the acorn woodpecker (*Melanerpes formicivorus*) were used to make ceremonial belts and headbands. Woodpecker skins were used in eastern North America to decorate *calumets*. Woodpeckers feature in the imagery of the *Southeastern Ceremonial Complex* and were regarded by the Pawnee as subject to special protection by the high god Tirawahat because of their fearlessness in storms and their building of nests in the crowns of dead trees.

**Wounded Knee**, village along the creek of the same name on the Pine Ridge Reservation of South Dakota where, at the height of the *Ghost Dance* movement, on December 29, 1890, the American army massacred more than 200 Lakotas led by Chief Big Foot, although they had previously surrendered and were about to be disarmed. The massacre is seen as marking the end of

the *Indian Wars*. This deeply symbolic place was occupied in February 1973 by members of the militant *American Indian Movement* in protest against a corrupt tribal government and the USA's Indian policies. The military confrontation lasted several months and attracted much international interest while endowing the AIM and its leaders with temporary celebrity status.

**Wuwuchim**, Hopi men's society, and a term for the ceremonies of all four men's societies (Wuwuchim, Agave, Horn, and Singers) into which adolescent boys are initiated once every four years. The Wuwuchim and Singers societies are concerned with promoting fertility, whereas the Agave and Horn societies concentrate on war and hunting. Wuwuchim and the women's *Maraw* are based on a mythical brother and sister to whom secret knowledge was imparted by their father Sun.

**Ye'i**, group of mute supernatural beings (*Diyin Dine'é*) within the Navajo belief system, who are embodied by masked persons during certain ceremonies. Their leader is Speaking God, also known as *ye'i bichai* ("maternal grandfather of the ye'i"), for whom the Night Chant ceremony (which can last for nine nights) is named and during the last night of which the ye'i appear. Among them are Calling God, two Fringed Mouths, Hunchback (an embodiment of the bighorn), the clown Water Sprinkler, the Black God, the Great God and a series of male and female ye'i.

**Yellow cedar, Nootka cedar** (*Chamawecyparis nootkaensis*), tree of the cypress family found on the Northwest Coast. Its soft wood is particularly suitable for making carved masks, bowls, and other household items.

**Yucca** (*Yucca spp.*), species of succulent *Liliaceae*, widespread in the Southwest, but also on the Plains and in the Eastern Woodlands. Whereas one kind of yucca bears fruit eaten by the Apache (*datil*), the leaf fibers of *Y. filimentosa* (bear grass) were used by the Virginia Algonquian and especially in the Southwest to make string, woven items (bags, baskets, sandals), and implements (e.g., brushes, paint brushes). Their flowers were eaten and the roots used to make soap with which Pueblo women washed their hair. Yucca roots were used to tan leather; the leaves and flowers could yield a variety of pigments.

**Zenith** (Arabic), highest point of the firmament, directly overhead, and opposite the nadir. Among some peoples (e.g., of the Southwest) zenith and nadir are counted among six *cardinal directions*. The term is also used figuratively to denote any high point (e.g., of population growth).

# INDIGENOUS PEOPLES AND LANGUAGES OF NORTH AMERICA

Henry Kammler

Only the names of those peoples, languages, tribes, and subgroups that are mentioned in the text and appear on maps of this book are listed below. A complete inventory of all the groups that make up indigenous North America would be much larger in scope. Population figures are based on various census methods; they are not strictly comparable and merely serve to give an idea of approximate numbers.

**Abenaki**, collective term for various Algonquian-speaking groups in Maine, New Hampshire, and southeastern Quebec. Population: c. 15,000 (1600), c. 2,000 (2000).

**Abitbi**, Algonquian band in Amos, Quebec.

**Acaxee**, Uto-Aztecans (probably related to the Cahita) in northern Sinaloa on the borders of Mesoamerica. Believed to have become extinct long ago.

**Achumawi**, people in northeastern California. Language: Palaihnihan (Hokan). Together with the Atsugewi, they are known as Pit River Indians. Population of Pit River Indians: 3,000 (1770), 2,000–2,500 (1995).

**Acolapissa**, small chiefdom in southeastern Louisiana. language family: Muskogean. Population: c. 1,000 (1700). Ceased to exist as an autonomous group in the 18th century.

Man from the pueblo of Taos, New Mexico, c. 1990. → *Taos.*

**Acoma**, Pueblo on a mesa in Valencia County, New Mexico. A Western Keresan language is spoken in Acoma. Population: 2,000 (1630), 6,400 (1995).

**Adai**, member group of the Caddo Confederation in northeastern Texas. language family: Caddoan. The remnants of the Adai merged with other Caddo groups in the 19th century. Population: 400 (1698).

**Ais**, tribe in southern Florida, thought to be related to the Calusa. Believed to have become extinct in the 18th century.

**Akimel O'odham** → *Pima.*

**Alabama**, collective term for several independent Muskogean chiefdoms at the upper course of the Alabama River in the state of the same name. Population: 2,000 (1700), around 1,000 Alabama and Koasati in Texas (1995), many of whom still speak their mother tongue.

**Aleut**, people on the Aleutian Islands, and a branch of the Eskimo-Aleut languages. Population: 16,000 (1740); 2,600 in Alaska and c. 500 in Russia (1990).

**Algonquian**, largest language family in North America, widespread in the Northeast: includes the eastern Algonquian languages (e.g. Massachusett, Delaware) on the Atlantic coast; the languages of the central region (Cree, Ojibwa, etc.) are independent branches of this language group; early breakaway groups include the Blackfoot, Arapaho, and Cheyenne in the Plains region. A distant relationship to the Californian Ritwan languages (Wiyot and Yurok) has been proven.

**Algonquin,** historically autonomous Ottawa River valley population who speak a dialect of Ojibwa. Population: c. 5,000 (2000).

Iglulik Eskimo, Baffin Island, Northwest Territories, c. 1990. → *Eskimo.*

**Alsea**, small, linguistically isolated population with two dialects (Alsea and Yaquina) on the central coast of Oregon. Population: 1,700 (1805), the population dwindled as a result of epidemics and in 1875 the Alsea were settled with other tribes in the Siletz Reservation.

**Anishnabe** (various spellings) self-designation ("human being") of most Ojibwa/Chippewa groups.

**Apache**, collective term for southern Athapaskan peoples in Arizona and New Mexico, including Jicarilla, Chiricahua, Mescalero, Western Apache. The Navajo speak an Apachean language.

**Appalachee**, chiefdom with numerous settlements near modern Tallahassee in northern Florida, forming part of the Muskogean language family. In 1764 the remnants of this once numerous people moved to southern Louisiana, where all traces of them disappeared in the 19th century. Population: 7,000 (1630).

**Aranama**, small people in Texas of unknown linguistic affiliation. Population: 125 (1820), believed extinct since the mid-19th century.

**Arapaho**, Plains people who lived in eastern Wyoming in the 19th century. Together with the Atsina, the Arapaho form a separate branch of the Algonquian languages. After the Medicine Lodge treaty of 1867, the Arapaho were removed to Oklahoma with the Cheyenne; the Northern Arapaho were subsequently settled on the Wind River Reservation with the Eastern Shoshone. Population: 3,000 (1780).

**Arikara (Sahnish)**, agricultural people on the upper Missouri in North Dakota. Closest linguistic relatives of the Pawnee (language family: Caddoan). Decimated by war and epidemics, they established a joint village with the Mandan and Hidatsa in the mid-19th century and were eventually settled on the Fort Berthold Reservation. Population: 3,000 (1780), c. 3,000 (1995).

**Assiniboine**, a Plains people from Montana, southern Alberta, and Saskatchewan who split from the Yanktonai (language family: Siouan) in the 17th century. In Ojibwa, their name means "they who cook with stones,"; and they are sometimes referred to as Stoney in Canada. Population: 10,000 (1780).

**Atakapa**, linguistically isolated group on the coast of Louisiana and Texas. The name means "cannibal" in Choctaw. Population: 2,000 (1650).

Believed to be extinct since the early 20th century.

**Athapaskana**, large language family, part of the Na-Dene phylum, spread across northwestern Canada, the interior and the southeastern region of Alaska, in the Southwestern United States (Apache and Navajo), as well as small, isolated groups in California and Oregon which have nearly all died out.

**Atsina**, a Plains people on the Milk River and upper Missouri in Montana, close relatives of the Arapaho (language family: Algonquian). The Atsina were settled with part of the Assiniboine on the Fort Belknap Reservation. Population: 3,000 (1780), the population of Fort Belknap numbers c. 5,200 (1995). The Atsina language is no longer spoken.

**Atsugewi**, northeastern Californian people. Language: Palaihnihan (Hokan). Together with the Achumawi they are referred to as Pit River Indians. Population of Pit River Indians: 3,000 (1770), 2,000–2,500 (1995).

**Attikamek**, language: Cree. Known in the past as Têtes de Boule. The Attikamek are politically united with the Montagnais in the Conseil Attikamek-Montagnais. Population: c. 3,500 (2000). The mother language is still in everyday use.

**Bannock**, group of the Northern Paiute in southeastern Idaho who allied themselves with the Northern Shoshone and adopted their Plains culture. They were consigned to the Fort Hall Reservation in 1853. In 1879 the Bannock fought a desperate war against the misguided reservation policy. Population: 1,000 (1845).

**Beaver**, Subarctic Athapaskan people on the upper Peace River (Alberta and Saskatchewan). Population: 1,000 (1780), c. 1,000 (2000). About a third of the population can still speak their mother tongue.

**Bella Bella (Heiltsuk)**, term for four previously autonomous tribes in the hinterland of Fitz Hugh Sound, British Columbia. Language family: Northern Wakashan (close relatives of the Kwakiutl). Population: 2,700 (1780), 1,500 (2000). Fewer than 300 people can still speak their tribal language.

**Bella Coola (Nuxalk)**, northernmost Coast Salish people in central British Columbia, along the Dean and Bella Coola River. Population: 1,400 (1780), 1,246 (2000). Fewer than 200 still speak Bella Coola.

**Beothuk**, aboriginal population of the island of Newfoundland. Population c. 500 (c. 1700); by 1823 systematic genocide had reduced the population to a total of 14, and the last of the Beothuk died within six years. Their language may have been related to Algonquian.

**Bidai**, Atakapa group of the Trinity River, Texas. Resettled by the Franciscans at San Ildefonso mission. Population: 500 (1690), 100 (1805), now regarded as extinct.

**Biloxi**, a people of the Siouan language family on the coast of the Mississippi around the mouth of the Pascagoula River. The last speakers of Biloxi died at the beginning of the 20th century. Population: 1,000 (1650), descendants of the Biloxi can be found among the 730 Tunica-Biloxi in Louisiana (1995).

**Blackfeet** → *Blackfoot*

**Blackfoot**, a Plains people belonging to the Algonquian language family on the east side of the Rocky Mountains in northern Montana and in southern Alberta. The name is a literal translation of Siksika, the aboriginal name of a constituent tribe of the Blackfoot. Population: 15,000 (1780); 33,000 (2000). About 10,000 in Canada still speak Blackfoot.

**Blood**, self-designation of the Kainah, a constituent tribe of the Blackfoot confederation in Alberta. Population: 8,865 (2000).

**Borrado**, tribe on the Gulf Coast in present-day Tamaulipas, Mexico.

**Brotherton**, last Delaware reservation and Presbyterian mission in New Jersey (1758–1802). The Brotherton emigrated to Wisconsin via New York.

**Brulé** → *Sicangu*.

**Caddo,** language family which includes the Pawnee, Arikara, Wichita, and the Caddo proper.

**Cahuilla**, Uto-Aztecans in southern California. Population: 2,500 (1770), over 1,000 (1995). There are currently fewer than 20 Cahuilla-speakers.

**Calusa**, aboriginal population of southwestern Florida. It can only be assumed that their language was related to Timucua.

**Carrier**, a Subarctic Athapaskan people in central British Columbia. Population: 8,500 (1780). In 1980 they were 5,800, of whom 3,600 could speak their mother tongue.

**Carrizo**, Gulf Coast people in present-day Tamaulipas, Mexico; possibly a collective term used to describe tribes belonging to different language groups. Population: 35 (1885).

**Catawba**, amalgamation of various surviving Siouan tribes of South Carolina and Virginia. The Catawba now have a reservation in South Carolina. Population: 5,000 (1600), 1,600 (2000). Catawba was spoken by some families until the 20th century. The last Catawba-speaker died in 1958.

**Cayuga**, one of the five founding tribes of the Iroquois League. Today the Cayuga live on the Six Nations Reserve in Ontario, in Cattaraugus in New York, and in Oklahoma. Population: c. 1,000 (1600), 3,000–4,000 (2000).

**Cayuse**, small tribe on the Grand Ronde River, Oregon, once renowned for their horse breeding. The inadequately documented language has become extinct. In 1853 they joined the Umatilla on the Umatilla Reservation. Population: 500 (1770).

**Chatot**, Muskogean chiefdom on the Apalachicola River, Florida. Population: 1,500 (1670), 1,000 (1805); the survivors joined the Choctaw and moved with them to Oklahoma.

**Chauí**, Pawnee tribe in Nebraska.

**Chemakum** people of the Chmakuan language family which merged with the neighboring Puget Sound Salish at the end of the 19th century.

**Chemehuevi**, a Uto-Aztecan people (Numic branch) in the eastern Mohave Desert and on the Colorado River, California. Population: 800 (1770).

**Cherokee**, Southern Iroquoian tribe in Tennessee, North Carolina, and neighboring regions. After 1838 the Cherokee were one of the Five Civilized Tribes to be forcibly removed to the Indian Territory, although a part of the population remained in the east. Population: 22,000 (1650), 11,240 Eastern Cherokee, 114,900 Oklahoma Cherokee (1995). In 1990 around 310,000 US citizens identified themselves as Cherokee while the number of people who fluently speak Cherokee has continued to stagnate at around the 20,000 mark.

**Cheyenne**, a Plains people of the Algonquian language family. Resettled to Oklahoma in 1867,

some Cheyenne returned to the old homeland on the Platte River and were eventually granted their own reservation (Northern Cheyenne). Population: 3,500 (1770); 6,700 people regard themselves as Northern Cheyenne, while there are 11,000 Southern Cheyenne and Southern Arapaho (1995).

**Chickahominy**, group of Virginia Algonquians who have succeeded in maintaining their distinctiveness to the present day. Population: 1,000 (1610), over 1,000 (2000).

**Chickasaw**, nation belonging to the Muskogean language family in northern Mississippi and adjacent regions. After 1838 the Chickasaw were one of the Five Civilized Tribes to be forcibly removed to the Indian Territory. Population: 8,000 (1600), 34,000 (1995). Only about 1,000 elderly people still speak Chickasaw.

**Chilcotin**, a Subarctic Athapaskan people of the upper Chilcotin River in British Columbia. Population: 2,500 (1780), 1,800 (1982), of whom 1,200 habitually speak Chilcotin.

**Chilula**, an Athapaskan people of Redwood Creek in northern California who spoke a dialect of Hupa, then merged with the Hupa in the 19th century. Population: 500–600 (1770).

**Chimakuan**, small language family in Washington State which includes the Chemakum and Quileute.

**Chinook**, collective term for the constituent groups of the Chinookan language family within the Penuti language phylum. In a more restricted sense, Chinook refers to the Lower Chinook near the mouth of the Columbia River.

**Chipewyan**, an Athapaskan people of the western Subarctic. Population: 3,500 (1780), c. 6,000 (2000).

**Chippewa** → *Ojibwa*.

**Chiricahua**, Apache tribe with c. 300 members on the Mescalero Reservation in New Mexico (1995).

**Chitimacha**, linguistically isolated people on the Grand River and Grand Lake in Louisiana. Population: 3,000 (1650), 900 (1995). Their language has long been extinct.

**Choctaw**, a people of the Muskogean language family in southeastern Mississippi and in adjacent regions in Alabama. After 1838 the Choctaw were one of the Five Civilized Tribes that were forcibly removed to the Indian Territory. Population: 20,000 (1650), 7,500 in Mississippi, plus 60,000–100,000 in Oklahoma (1995). Only c. 10,000 people are fluent Choctaw-speakers.

**Chugach**, collective term for the eastern groups of the Pacific Eskimo around Prince William Sound in southern Alaska.

**Chumash**, collective term for a number of linguistically and culturally related peoples on the southwestern coast of California and in the adjacent hinterland.

**Cibecue**, subdivision of the Western Apache.

**Clatskanie**, Athapaskan group along the Clatskanie River, Oregon. Merged with other tribes of the Grand Ronde and Siletz reservations.

**Coahuilteco**, barely documented language family in the Gulf region of Texas and Coahuila.

**Coast Miwok**, population north of San Francisco Bay (Golden Gate) encompassing several hamlets. Population: 1,500 (1770). The Coast Miwok language ceased to be spoken in the 1960s.

**Coast Salish**, collective term for all Salish tribes of the Northwest Coast, as opposed to the Interior Salish, who are part of the Plateau culture area and who form an independent linguistic branch within Salishan.

**Cochiti**, Keresan Pueblo on the Rio Grande in New Mexico. Population: 300 (1680), 1,200 (1995).

**Cocopa**, a people in southwestern Arizona and adjacent Baja California. Their language is part of the Yuman branch of the Hokan languages.

Navajo silversmith, Arizona. Photograph: Adamson Clark Vroman, 1901. Southwest Museum, Los Angeles, CA. → *Navajo*.

**Colville**, an Interior Salish people along the Colville and Columbia rivers in eastern Washington.

**Comanche**, a people of the southern Plains who split from the Shoshone in the 17th century bringing northern Texas under their control. Population: 11,300 (1990 census), 9,100 tribal members (1995).

**Comecrudo**, ("raw eaters"), designation for the Coahuiltecan and Karankawan tribes in the coastal regions of Texas and Coahuila (Gulf Coast).

**Comox**, Coast Salish tribe on the east coast of Vancouver Island and the opposite mainland of British Columbia. Population: 1,800 (1780).

**Concho**, collective term for Uto-Aztecan groups in western Chihuahua and along the lower Rio Grande.

**Conoy**, an Algonquian people west of Chesapeake Bay in Maryland who merged with the westward-migrating Delaware and Mahican in the 18th century.

**Coos**, independent branch of the Penutian language phylum in Oregon which includes the now extinct languages Hanis and Miluk. The Coos groups joined the Lower Umpqua and Siuslaw in the 19th century. This joint group now has around 600 members (1995).

**Copper Inuit**, Inuit population in the north of the Northwest Territories (Mackenzie and Franklin District). Their name was derived from the surface copper deposits in the area.

**Costano**, collective term for numerous groups belonging to the Penutian language phylum to the south of San Francisco Bay.

**Cotoname**, group of barely documented Coahuiltecan tribes in the Gulf regions of Texas and Coahuila.

**Cowichan**, Coast Salish group on southern Vancouver Island. Language: Halkolmelem (Central Coast Salish).

**Cowlitz**, southwestern Coast Salish people on the Cowlitz River in the interior of Washington. Population: 1,000 (1812). Some of their descendants have organized themselves into the Cowlitz Indian Nation (1987: 1,412 members).

**Cree**, largest indigenous population in Canada. Language: Algonquian. Population: 25,000–35,000 (1770); more than 70,000 with Indian status in Canada, an unknown number of Cree-speakers do not have Indian status and are counted among the Métis; more than 5,000 in the USA (1995).

**Creek**, large confederation of members of the Muskogean language family in Georgia and Alabama. After 1836 the Creek were one of the Five Civilized Tribes that were forcibly removed to the Indian Territory. Population: 18,000 (1833), 40,000 in Oklahoma and 2,000 in Alabama (1995).

**Croatoan**, a North Carolina Algonquin group on Cape Hatteras. The Croatoan helped British settlers of the "lost colony" of Roanoke (1585–1587) to fight hostile indigenous groups.

**Crow**, a people belonging to the Siouan language family in Montana. Population: 9,300 (1995).

**Cupeño**, Uto-Aztecan group in southern California.

**Cusabo**, group of tribes of unknown linguistic affiliation in southern South Carolina. Became extinct in the 18th century.

**Cuyama**, Chumash tribe in the Cuyama River valley and on the upper Santa Maria River in California.

**Dakota,** alliance of seven tribes belonging to the Siouan language family in the Prairies and Plains region (Sisseton, Wahpeton, Wahpekute, Mdewakanton, Yankton, Yanktonai, and Teton). The name means "allies." In a narrow sense it includes only the first four groups. (→ *Lakota, Nakota*).

**Delaware**, collective term encompassing historically and regionally distinctive groups of speakers of Munsee, Unalatchtigo, and Unami in New Jersey, Delaware, Pennsylvania, and New York. Self-designation: Lenape ("real people").

**Dene**, self-designation ("human beings") of most of the northern Athapaskans, of whom numerous groups have joined together in northern Canada to form the Dene Nation.

**Dogrib**, Subarctic Athapaskan people in five communities in the area between Great Slave Lake and Great Bear Lake. Population: 760 (1825), 3,000 (1994).

**Duwamish**, group of southern Coast Salish whose traditional territory was in the present city of Seattle, named after the famous Duwamish chief. Language: Southern Lushootseed.

**East (Main) Cree**, Cree group on the eastern shore of the Hudson Bay, organized into six bands. Population: 3,325 (1970).

**Eastern Shoshone**, division of the Shoshone in Wyoming and Colorado, which has adopted the culture of the Plains. Language family: Uto-Aztecan, Numic branch.

**Emigdiano**, Chumash population east of the coastal ranges of Southern California.

**Erie**, sedentary people at the eastern end of Lake Erie. Language family: Iroquoian. This nation was conclusively defeated in 1656 in their war with the Iroquois and subsequently scattered. Population estimates for 1600 vary from 4,000 to 14,500.

**Eskimo**, collective term for all the inhabitants of the American Arctic and into Siberia who speak an Eskimoan language. Regionally, the self-designations Inuit (Canada) and Yupik (southern Alaska) are preferred.

**Esselen**, group in the central coastal region of California, whose language is thought to have been related to the Hokan language phylum. Population: 500 (1770); believed to have been extinct since the 19th century.

**Etchemin**, name in 17th-century sources for the Maliseet-Passamaquoddy.

**Eudeve**, Uto-Aztecan population in Sonora, Mexico, perhaps a division of the Opata, long regarded as extinct.

**Eyak**, an Athapaskan people between the Yakutat Tlingit and the Chugash Eskimo at the mouth of the Copper River, with strong cultural links to both sides. The last woman to speak Eyak died in 1990. Population: 444 (1880), 5 (1985).

**Flathead**, self-designation: Salish. A people of the Interior Salish in western Montana. Population: 3,000 (1780), 7,000 members of the Salish and Kootenai Tribe in Montana (1995).

**Fox**, an Algonquian people (culturally and linguistically related to the Sauk and Kickapoo) in southern Wisconsin. In 1857 traditionalist leaders purchased land in Iowa and founded the Tama settlement, which is regarded as particularly conservative and where the majority of the Fox population continues to live today. Population: 2,000 (1820), 1,100 (1995), about 700 of whom habitually speak Fox.

**Gabrielino**, large Uto-Aztecan group in southern California, named after the San Gabriel mission founded in 1771.

**Gitksan**, Tsimshian tribe with seven subgroups in the area around the mouth of the Skeena River, British Columbia. Population: 2,600 (1835), 3,200 (1983), of whom about half still speak their tribal language.

**Gosiute**, division of the Western Shoshone in the area around the Great Salt Lake.

**Guachichil**, Uto-Aztecans in Nayarit, presumably close relatives of the Huichol. Disappeared as an autonomous people.

**Guale**, a people of unknown linguistic affiliation on the coast of Georgia. Population: 4,000 (1600). Traces of the Guale in Florida's Spanish missions disappear after 1726.

Kaibab basket weaver in front of her *kahni* (house), Southern Paiute, Utah, 1873. Photograph: Jack Hillers. National Anthropological Archives, Smithsonian Institution, Washington, DC. → *Kaibab.*

**Haida**, old-established population on the Queen Charlotte Islands, British Columbia, and on Prince William Island, Alaska. It is thought that the otherwise isolated Haida language may be related to the Na-Dene language phylum. Population: 9,800 (1780), c. 3,000 (2000) of whom about a third in Alaska. About 300 Haida-speakers.

**Haihais**, a northern Wakashan people on the Finlayson Channel, British Columbia, close relatives of the Bella Bella and Oowekeeno, whose language they share. Population: 463 (2000).

**Haisla**, a northern Wakashan people along the Kitimat River and Gardner Canal, British Columbia. Population: 367 (1889); 1,457 (2000).

**Halchidhoma**, Yuman-speaking population at the confluence of the Gila and Colorado rivers, Arizona. Population estimates for the late 18th century vary between 1,000 and 3,000. The Halchidhoma merged with the Maricopa after waging wars with the Mohave.

**Haliwa-Saponi**, population in North Carolina who trace part of their ancestry back to the Siouan-speaking Saponi and their neighbors and who regard themselves as Indians.

**Halkomelem**, language of the central Coast Salish once spoken by the Chilliwack, Cowichan, Musqueam, and Nanaimo. Only a handful of old people are still able to speak this language.

**Han**, Athapaskans on the Yukon River on both sides of the border between Canada and Alaska. Most of the Klondike gold rush after 1897 took place in their territory. Population: 1,000 (1780), 300 (2000). There are fewer than 20 Han-speakers.

**Hare**, Athapaskans west of Great Bear Lake, on both sides of the Mackenzie River and on the shores of Colville Lake, Northwest Territories, Canada. Population: 750 (1670), c. 500 (2000).

**Hichiti**, a Muskogean people with their own language, and for some time a member of the Creek Confederation. The Hichiti emigrated to Oklahoma with the Creek and lost their autonomy. Hichiti has remained the mother tongue of the Mikasuki (Miccosukee) in Florida.

**Hidatsa**, agricultural people of the Siouan language family (close relatives of the Crow) along the upper Missouri, between the Heart River and Little River in North Dakota. The survivors of the smallpox epidemic of 1837 united to form a new, single village, and in 1862 they joined the Mandan and Arikara on the Fort Berthold Reservation. Population: 2,500 (1780), 1,200 (1990), of whom around 450 still speak the tribal language.

**Ho-chunk**, self-designation of the →Winnebago, meaning "big fish" or "big voice."

**Hodenosaunee** (from Seneca *hotinonhsyónni*, "those of the longhouse"), one of the self-designations of the Iroquois League.

**Hokan**, language phylum the existence of which has been suspected since 1913, and which includes Karok, Chimariko, and the Shastan, Pomoan, and Yuman languages, among others. The inclusion of individual language groups is subject to controversy.

**Holikachuk**, Athapaskans on the upper Innoko River in Alaska, closely related to the Kolchan and Koyukon. The Holikachuk now live among the Ingalik and Koyukon. Population: c. 160 (1977), of whom about 25 people can still speak Holikachuk.

**Hopi**, Uto-Aztecan Pueblo people on three mesas in northern Arizona who live in nine old pueblos and several modern villages at the foot of the mesas. Population: 2,800 (1680), 9,700 (1995), of whom nearly all speak Hopi.

**Houma**, a Muskogean people, closely related to the Choctaw, on the eastern shore of the Mississippi near the delta, who have remained in their homeland and preserved their autonomy to the present day. The Houma gave up their Muskogean language in favor of French Creole.

**Hunkpapa**, one of the seven divisions of the Teton Lakota. The spiritual and political leader Sitting Bull was undoubtedly the most famous Hunkpapa in history.

**Hupa**, an Athapaskan people in northwestern California whose tough resistance won them a comparatively large reservation in their own territory. Population: 1,000 (1770), 2,100 (1995); in 1990, 93 elderly Hupas could still speak their own language.

**Huron**, tribal confederation of the Iroquoian tribes on the eastern shore of Lake Huron. As allies of the French, they competed with the Iroquois League in the fur trade. The smoldering conflict was decided in favor of the Iroquois in 1649 when the Huron confederation, decimated by epidemics, was crushed. Today's descendants of the Huron are the Wyandots and the Huron of Lorette. Population: 18,000–20,000 (1615).

**Iglulik**, Eskimoan aboriginal population of eastern Baffinland, from Southampton Island and the facing mainland (Northwest Territories, Nunavut). Population: 400–600 (1820).

**Illinois**, collective term for a dozen independent tribes (Kaskaskia, Cahokia, Michigamea, etc.) who shared the same language (part of the Algonquian language family) in the state of Illinois. In the 19th century they and other Algonquians were settled in Kansas and Oklahoma. Population: 2,400 (1735).

**Inuit**, self-designation ("people," singular: *inuk*) of the Eskimo in northeastern Alaska, Canada, and Greenland. Inuit is the official designation for the Eskimo in Canada.

**Inuktitut**, collective term for all the Eskimoan languages of Canada and northern Alaska.

**Inupiaq**, self-designation of the Eskimo in northern Alaska (*iñupiaq*; plural: *iñupiat*).

**Ipai**, a Yuman-speaking people in southwestern California, closely related to the Tipai. language family: Hokan. The historical designation Diegueño for the Ipai and part of the Tipai is derived from San Diego, the mission and modern city. Total Itai/Tipai population: 3,000 (1770).

**Iroquoian**, language family with two branches, Northern Iroquoian (the languages of the Iroquois League, Huron, Tuscarora, Susquehannock, and others) and Southern Iroquoian (Cherokee).

**Iroquois,** a confederation consisting of the Mohawk, Oneida, Onondaga, Cayuga, and Seneca, formed in the 16th century in present-day New York State. In 1722 they were joined by the Tuscarora, who had been driven out of North Carolina.

**Itazipco (Sans Arc)**, one of the seven divisions of the Teton Lakota. (*itazipco*, "without bow").

**Jemez**, Pueblo people on the Rio Grande (language family: Kiowa-Tanoan, Tano branch) who originally inhabited around a dozen settlements, but concentrated in a main pueblo at San Juan de Jemez since c. 1700. Population: 2,500 (1680), 428 (1890), 2,900 (1995).

**Jicarilla**, Athapaskans in New Mexico and Colorado (eastern branch of the Apachean languages). Population: 800 (1845), 3,700 (1995). About 800 people speak the tribal language.

**Jocome**, a now vanished hunter-gatherer people of northern Mexico, frequently mentioned in 17th century Spanish sources. Perhaps an Apache tribe.

**Jova**, Uto-Aztecans in the upper valley of the Rio Yaqui, Sonora, Mexico. Like the Opata they belonged to the Taracahitan branch of the Uto-Aztecan languages. They lost their autonomous existence in the 19th century.

**Jumano**, a people known from 17th and 18th century Spanish sources to have lived in mountains along the Rio Grande in Texas and Chihuahua. They are thought to have spoken a Uto-Aztecan language.

**Kaibab**, Southern Paiute band on the Kanab River, Utah, and in northern Arizona.

**Kalapuya** tribe belonging to the Kalapuyan language group; in 1855 they settled with other peoples on the Grand Ronde Reservation and adopted the Chinook jargon as their habitual language. Population: 3,000–8,000 (1780).

**Kalapuyan**, branch of the Takelman languages (Penuti language phylum?) in northwestern Oregon. It included the Ahantchuyuk, Yamhill, Kalapuya, Yoncalla, and others.

**Kanab**, constituent group of the Southern Paiute on the Kanab River, Utah.

**Karankawa**, collective term for the populations of coastal Texas, between Trinity Bay and Aransas Bay, who are thought to have constituted an independent language group. Population: 2,800? (1690); thought to be extinct since about 1860.

**Karok**, a people on the central Klamath River in northwestern California (language family: Shasta, thought to belong to the Hokan language phylum). Population: 1,500 (1770), 3,700 (1995). About 100 elderly people still speak Karok and a few younger people are learning it as a second language.

**Kashaya**, a Pomo people on the Russian River in western California.

**Kaska**, Athapaskans in northern British Columbia and in the southern Yukon Territory. Population: 500 (1780), 750 (1995), of whom about half still speak the Kaska language.

**Kaskaskia**, one of the largest of the Algonquian tribes, collectively designated as Illinois, south of Lake Michigan. Together with other tribes they were settled in Oklahoma as "Peoria."

**Kawaiisu**, Uto-Aztecans (Numic branch) in southwestern California, linguistically most closely related to the Ute. No longer existing as an autonomous group, although a few elderly people still spoke Kawaiisu in the 1970s.

**Keresan**, language family containing the Rio Grande (Pueblos along the Rio Grande) and Western Keresan (Acoma and Laguna) branches.

**Kickapoo**, an Algonquian people in southern Wisconsin. Divided into three groups during the 19th century: one in Kansas; one in Oklahoma, and one in the village of Nascimiento in Coahuila,

Mexico. Population: 2,700 (1780); c. 4,000 in the USA, 500 in Mexico (2000). All the Mexican Kickapoos and around 500 in the USA still speak their mother tongue.

**Kiowa**, a Plains people belonging to the Kiowa-Tanoan language family. In the 17th century they inhabited Montana and South Dakota, but later advanced into the southern Plains, where they allied themselves with the Comanche. Population: 2,000 (1780), 1,165 (1905), 5,300–10,000 (1995), of whom about 1,000 are Kiowa-speakers.

**Kitanemuk**, Uto-Aztecans of Tejon Creek in the Tehachapi Mountains of southern California. Some descendants live on the rancheria of Tejon.

**Kit'kaháxki**, (also Kitkehaki), Pawnee tribe.

**Klamath**, closest relatives of the Modoc in southeastern Oregon. Conjectured language phylum: Penutian. The tribe was officially terminated in 1958; their case for re-recognition is currently in progress. Population: 1,200 (1780), 3,000 (1995).

**Klikitat**, a people in southern Washington (language family: Sahaptian) who settled in 1855 with their relatives the Yakima on the Yakama Reservation.

**Koasati**, Mukogean chiefdom at the confluence of the Coosa and Tallapoosa rivers, Alabama. Their descendants live on a reservation in Louisiana and on the Alabama-Coushatta Reservation in Texas. Population: 500 (1760), c. 600 (1995).

**Kolchan**, Athapaskans on the upper Kuskokwim River, Alaska. Population: 300 (1780), 50 (1935), 130 (1995).

**Koniag**, western Pacific Eskimo on Kodiak Island and the Alaskan peninsula. Population: 8,000 (1780), 2,450 (1880).

**Konkow**, close relatives of the Maidu in central California with whom they have settled on the Round Valley Reservation. Population: 171 (1905), later merged with the other Maidu.

**Koskimo Kwakiutl**, tribe of the Kwakiutl on Quatsino Sound, Vancouver Island.

**Koyukon**, Athapaskans of the upper Yukon and Koyukuk rivers, central Alaska. Population: 1,500 (1740), 2,500 (1995). With fewer than 10 speakers, the language is almost extinct.

**Kutchin**, collective term for several Athapaskan groups along the borders between the Yukon Territory and Alaska. Population: 5,400 (1750), 2,150 (1968).

**Kutenai (Ktunaxa-Kinbasket)**, a linguistically isolated people in southwestern British Columbia, northern Idaho, and adjoining regions. Population: 1,200 (1780), 1,500 (1990), of whom fewer than 200 speak the language.

**Kwakiutl**, self-designation Kwakwaka'wakw ("speakers of the Kwakiutl language"). Collective term for a number of independent tribes (language family: Northern Wakashan) on both sides of the Queen Charlotte Strait, British Columbia. Population: 4,500 (1780), 3,532 (1983). Despite extensive programs in schools, the tribal language is gradually disappearing; fewer than 300 people still speak it fluently.

**Kwakwaka'wakw** → *Kwakiutl*.

**Kwalhioqua**, the only Athapaskan people in Washington State, on the Willapa River. They were separated from the linguistically related Clatskanie in Oregon by the Chinook tribes along the Columbia River. Extinct after 1850.

**Laguna**, Western Keresan Pueblo in New Mexico. Population: 7,400 (1995). Barely 2,000 people speak Laguna.

**Lake Miwok**, a people belonging to the Miwokan language family, which forms part of the Penutian language phylum, around Clear Lake in California. Population: 500 (1770).

**Lakota**, designation for the Dakota (Sioux), in the western dialect of their common language (Teton or Lakota).

Council between General Crook and Geronimo, 1886. Photograph: Camillus S. Fly. National Anthropological Archives, Smithsonian Institution, Washington, DC.

NO. 176--Council between General Crook and Geronimo.

COPYRIGHT 1886, By C. S. Fly, Tombstone, Ariz.

Eskimo girls in Labrador with dolls given to them by the Greenland expedition led by Donald B. MacMillans. November 17, 1926. → *Eskimo.*

**Lassik**, Athapaskans on the Eel River in northern California. Population: (including the neighboring Nongatl and Sinkyone) 2,000 (1770), 100 (1910).

**Lenape** ("real people"), self-designation of the Delaware, sometimes also Lenni Lenape ("really real people").

**Lillooet (Stl'atl'imix)**, tribe of the Interior Salish in the Fraser River valley. Population: 4,000 (1780), 3,000 (1990), of whom around 400 still speak their mother tongue.

**Lipan**, tribe of the eastern Apache (Athapaskans) along the Pecos River in Texas. Enmity with the Comanche and Texans caused the Lipan to flee to Coahuila, Mexico, in 1850, where they remained until 1905. The remaining population was resettled among the Mescalero Apache, with whom they merged. Population: 500 (1780), 28 (1910).

**Loucheux**, historical term encompassing the Kutchin tribes.

**Luiseño**, Uto-Aztecans (Cupan branch) in southern California. Population: 4,000 (1770), 2,000 (1990), of whom around 40 still spoke Luiseño.

**Lumbee**, large population (c. 60,000) recognized as Indians by the states of North and South Carolina. They can be traced back to local Siouan and Iroquoian peoples, although they also contain African-American and European elements.

**Maidu**, a people of the Penutian language phylum along the Feather and American rivers in northern central California with numerous independent village groups and three strongly differentiated dialects. Population: 9,000 (1770), 300–500 (1990).

**Makah**, southernmost people of the Wakashan language family on the Olympic Peninsula, originally forming at least two independent groups (Makah and Ozette). Population: 2,000 (1780), 1,100 (1990). About 200 people still speak the tribal language.

**Maliseet** (also: Malecite), northern division of the Algonquian-speaking Maliseet-Passamaquoddy, all of whom, except for one group, live on the Canadian side of the border (Quebec, New Brunswick). Population: c. 1,000 Maliseet-Passamaquoddy (1600), now c. 3,000 Maliseet, of whom c. 600 in the USA. About 50 percent of the population still speak the tribal language.

**Mandan**, agricultural Siouan people on the upper Missouri in North Dakota. Reduced to a single village as the result of a devastating smallpox epidemic in 1837, they later formed a close alliance with the Hidatsa and Arikara. Population: 3,600 (1780), 380 (1850), 400 (1990). In 1990 there were eight elderly people who were still able to speak some Mandan.

**Maricopa**, a Yuman-speaking people on the Gila River in Arizona. Population: 2,000 (1780), 400 (1990). About 180 can still speak some Maricopa.

**Mascouten**, an Algonquian people in southern Michigan who merged with the Kickapoo in the early 19th century. Population: 1,500 (1670).

**Mashpee**, descendants of the Massachusett, Pokanoket, and other Algonquian groups in Massachusetts who owned a reservation on Cape Cod until 1869 and have successfully defended their identity to the present day.

**Massachusett**, an Algonquian people in what is now the state of Massachusetts. Decimated by an epidemic in 1617, they were later concentrated in mission settlements, where today some of their descendants still live. Population: 3,000 (1600).

**Mattaponi**, a Virginia Algonquian people who trace their ancestry to Powhatan's chiefdom and maintain their distinct identity on a reservation established in the 17th century. The Upper Mattaponi (no reservation) have different origins.

**Mattole**, Athapaskans in northern California. Population: 500 (1770), 34 (1910).

**Mayo**, Uto-Aztecans (Taracahitan branch) in Sonora and Sinaloa. Population: 25,000 (1600), 50,000 (1990).

**Mdewakanton**, one of the seven divisions of the Dakota in Minnesota. They belong to the eastern Dakota (Santee).

**Menominee**, an Algonquian people in Wisconsin. The tribe was terminated by the US government in 1958, but it and the reservation were restored in 1973 after fierce protests. Population: 3,000 (1650), 7,500 (1995). The language is now spoken by a few old people.

**Mescalero**, an Apachean people (Athapaskan) in New Mexico. Population: 2,500–3,000 (1850), 1,700 (1995), around 70 percent use Apache as their habitual language.

**Mesquakie** → *Fox.*

**Métis** (French, "mixed-bloods"), official designation of the large Canadian population of people of mixed Native American and European descent, including those indigenous persons who have not been granted Indian status. Population: 210,000 (1996).

**Miami**, collective term for several Algonquian peoples (e.g. Piankashaw, Wea) south of the Great Lakes in Indiana who spoke the language of the same name. The majority settled in Oklahoma, though many remained in Indiana. Population: 4,000–5,000 (1650), 1,600 (1995).

**Miccosukee**, (1) Hichiti-speakers among the Seminole; (2) a tribe, recognized by the state of Florida in 1965, which traces its ancestry to the aboriginal population of Florida. Population: 400 (1995).

**Michif**, hybrid language of Cree (verb complex) and French (particularly nouns), spoken by the Plains Cree and the Métis in North Dakota, Manitoba and Saskatchewan. About 300 speakers in the USA; an unknown number in Canada.

**Michigamea**, tribe of the Illinois.

**Micmac**, Algonquians in New Brunswick, Nova Scotia, Maine, Prince Edward Island, Quebec, and Newfoundland. Population: 3,500 (1600), 13,000 (1900) of whom about 8,000 still speak their mother tongue.

**Mingo**, older Algonquian designation for the Iroquois, especially the Seneca and Cayuga in Ohio.

**Minneconjou** (also Mnikwoju), one of the seven divisions of the Teton Lacota.

**Mississauga**, band of southeastern Ojibwa on the northern shore of Lake Huron. The name was sometimes as a collective term for all southeastern Ojibwa.

**Missouri**, a people of the Siouan language family (Chiwere branch); one part joined the Iowa in about 1830 while the majority joined the Oto. Population: 1,000 (1780), 1,460 Oto-Missouri (1995).

**Mistassini**, band of Cree around Mistassini Lake in Labrador. Population: 3,315 (2000).

**Miwok**, collective term for several peoples in central California, along the San Joaquin River, around Clear Lake, and on the coast around San Francisco Bay.

**Moapa**, southern Paiute tribe.

**Modoc**, a people in southeastern Oregon who together with the Klamath form a language family

465

Navajo woman spinning wool inside a hogan. → *Navajo*.

(suspected language phylum: Penutian). Fought a desperate war in 1872/73 against the USA, after which most Modoc were deported to Oklahoma. Population: 800 (1780), 3,000 among the Klamath, around 125 in Oklahoma (1995).

**Mohave**, a Yuman-speaking people on the Colorado River in Arizona and California. Population: 3,000 (1680), c. 2,000 (1990) of whom 10 percent still speak Mohave.

**Mohawk**, the easternmost of the five founding tribes of the Iroquois League in the northern New York State. Since the 17th century they have also lived in mission settlements in Quebec (Kahnawake, Kanehsatake, Akwesasne).

**Mono**, Uto-Aztecans in eastern California. Population: 200 (1990). The language died out in the late 20th century.

**Montagnais**, an Algonquian people in Labrador. Often classed together with the Naskapi, who live further north. Population: 5,500 (1600), 10,000 (1996), 80 percent of whom habitually speak Montagnais.

**Montauk**, an Algonquian people on the southernmost tip of Long Island.

**Moqui (Moki)** → *Hopi*.

**Mountain**, an Athapaskan people of the western Subarctic.

**Mowachaht**, Nootkan tribe around Nootka Sound on Vancouver Island, British Columbia.

**Munsee**, a people belonging to the Delaware (Algonquian) and possessing their own language. Their descendants now live mainly in Ontario and Wisconsin.

**Muskogean**, language family in the Southeast (including the Creek, Choctaw, Chickasaw, and Hitchiti, among others). In a more restricted sense Muskogee refers only to the Creek.

**Na-Dene**, language phylum thought to encompass Tlingit and possibly Haida as well as the Athapaskan languages.

**Nakota**, variant of the name Dakota in the northern dialect of the language (of the Yankton and Yanktonai; Assiniboine is almost identical).

**Nanticoke**, an Algonquian people on both sides of Chesapeake Bay, Maryland. The term encompasses numerous independent groups. Population: 12,000 (1600). Several communities in Maryland and Virginia, with a total population of about 10,000,

trace their ancestry to the Nanticoke. The last Nanticoke-speaker died in 1856.

**Naolan**, a small people with an unclassifiable language in southern Tamaulipas. It died out in about 1950.

**Narrangasett,** an Algonquian people on Rhode Island. Following a war against the colonists in 1675 only a handful of Narrangasett remained in Rhode Island. Population: 4,000 (1600), 424 (1972).

**Naskapi**, an Algonquian people on the Labrador peninsula (→ *Montagnais*).

**Natchez**, a chiefdom in Louisiana. Defeated by the French in 1729/30, the Natchez split in two and found refuge with the Creek and the Cherokee. A few Oklahoma Cherokee still identified themselves as Natchez in the 20th century. Population: 4,500 (1650).

**Navajo**, Athapaskans in Arizona, New Mexico and Utah, today the largest indigenous people in North America living on a common territory, with 200,000–250,000 members, of whom about 70 percent speak Navajo.

**Netsilik**, Inuit in the north of the Keewatin District (Nunavut), Canada. Population: 500 (1880), 1,200 (1980).

**Neutral**, an Iroquoian people between Lake Erie and Lake Ontario, crushed by the Seneca in 1652. Remnants of the population were adopted by the Huron and the Seneca.

**Nez Perce**, a people in northern Idaho, Washington, and Montana (language family: Sahaptian). Population: 4,000–6,000 (1800), 3,300 (1995).

**Nipissing**, an Algonquian people, who speak a dialect of Ojibwa, around Lake Nipissing in Ontario.

**Nipmuck**, an Algonquian people in Massachusetts and Connecticut. Population: 500 (1600).

**Nisenan**, southern relatives of the Maidu of central California.

**Nisga'a**, a Tsimshian people on the Nass River, British Columbia, with no access to the sea. Population: 1,700 (1835), 3,513 (1995).

**Nisqually**, southern Coast Salish (language: Southern Lushootseed) on the Nisqually River, Washington. Population: 3,600 (1780), 500 (1995).

**Nomlaki**, central Californian tribe related to the Wintu (language phylum: Penuti).

**Nongatl**, Athapaskans in northern California (→ *Lassik*).

**Nootka (Nuu-chah-nulth)**, term encompassing a number of independent tribes belonging to the Southern Wakashan language family on the west coast of Vancouver Island. Population: 29,000 (1770), 6,000 (1995). About 150 people still speak one of the three Nootka dialects.

**North Carolina Algonquians**, collective term for the Algonquian peoples of North Carolina (e.g., Croatoan, Neusiok, Pamlico, Roanoke, Secotan).

**Northern Ojibwa**, Subarctic Ojibwa in Ontario, south of Hudson Bay.

**Northern Paiute**, Uto-Aztecs in Nevada, Utah and Oregon. Population: 4,000 (1990), of whom half still speak their mother tongue.

**Northern Shoshone**, a Uto-Aztec people (Numic branch) in Idaho and Wyoming. Population: 4,500 including the Western Shoshone (1845), 7,000 including the Western Shoshone (1990). About half the population still speaks the tribal language.

**Numa** ("human"), self-designation of the Uto-Aztecans of the Great Basin.

**Numunu** ("people"), self-designation of the Comanche.

**Nunamiut**, an Eskimoan people in the Brooks Range in the interior of Alaska.

**Nunavut**, autonomous administrative district in the former Keewatin District of Canada's Northwest Territories. The majority of the population is Inuit.

**Nuu-chah-nulth** ("along the mountains"), self-designation of the Nootka, adopted as the tribe's official designation in 1978.

**Nuxalk** → *Bella Coola*.

**Occaneechi**, eastern Siouans on the Roanoke River in Virginia who merged with the Tutelo in the early 18th century. Population: 1,200 (1600).

**Ofo** (also Mosopelea), a Siouan people in Ohio who moved down the Ohio and Mississippi in the 17th century and settled among the Tunica. Believed to have become extinct since the early 20th century. Population: 50 (1758).

**Oglala**, one of the seven divisions of the Teton Lakota. Today most live on the Pine Ridge Reservation. Population: 38,000 (1995).

**Ohiaht**, official self-designation: Hu-Ay-Aht. Nootkan tribe around and south of Barkley Sound, Vancouver Island.

**Ohlone**, modern self-designation of the Costanoans south of San Francisco Bay.

**Ojibwa**, collective term for the linguistically related Algonquian groups to the west and north of the Great Lakes. Linguistically, the Ottawa, Algonquin, and Nipissing also form part of the Ojibwa. Population: c. 30,000 (1750), 103,000 (1990, USA, of whom 5,000 speakers; in Canada alone about 28,000 speakers).

**Ojibway, Ojibwe** → *Ojibwa*.

**Omaha**, a Siouan people in Nebraska (Dhegiha branch), close relatives of the Ponca. Population: 2,800 (1780), 5,000 (1995). In 1990 about 60 elderly people still spoke the tribal language.

**Oneida**, one of the five founding tribes of the Iroquois League. Today they live in New York, Ontario, and Wisconsin. Population: 7,000 (1980). About 200 speakers.

**Onkwehonwe** ("real people"), one of the self-designations of the peoples forming the Iroquois League.

**Onondaga**, one of the five founding tribes of the Iroquois League: the central tribe, the metaphorical central fireplace of the common longhouse and the League's traditional capital. Population: 1,500 (1990). Fewer than 50 speakers.

**Oohenonpa**,("Two Kettles") one of the seven divisions of the Teton-Lakota.

Navajo weaver near Shiprock, New Mexico, c. 1980. → *Navajo*.

**Oowekeeno**, a Northern Wakashan people at Rivers Inlet, British Columbia. Population: 222 (2000).

**Opata**, an Uto-Aztecan people (Taracahitan branch) in Sonora, Mexico. Population: 20,000 (1600). They no longer exist as an autonomous group, although several thousand people regard themselves as descendants of the Opata. In 1990 there were still 12 speakers of the Opata language.

**Osage**, a Siouan people (Dhegiha branch) in Missouri and Kansas who were removed to Oklahoma. Population: 6,200 (1780). According to tribal membership criteria there are 5,200 Osages, although the Bureau of Indian Affairs has counted 10,500 (1995). In 1991 there were five people who could speak Osage.

**Oto**, a Siouan people (Chiwere branch) of the Platte River region in Nebraska. In the 19th century the Oto absorbed parts of the related Iowa and Missouri. Population: 900 (1780), 1,460 Oto-Missouri (1995). In 1991 five people could speak fluently Oto while another 40 had a limited understanding of the language.

**Owens Valley Paiute**, Uto-Aztecans (western Numic) in Owens Valley, California.

**Pahvant**, local group of the → *Ute*.

**Paiute**, slightly unfortunate generic term for two different peoples and languages: the Northern Paiute and Southern Paiute (Ute dialect).

**Pame**, a people of the Otomanguean language family in the Mexican state of San Luis Potosí. Population: 5,000 (1990).

**Pamunkey**, group of Virginia Algonquians who have managed to preserve their independence to the present day and who live on a reservation established during the colonial period. Population: 1,000 (1610), 333 (1972).

**Panamint** (also Koso), Uto-Aztecans (Central Numic, Shoshone) in eastern California. Population: 500 (1770).

**Papago**, Uto-Aztecans and close relatives of the Pima in Arizona and Sonora. Population: 6,000 (1680), 19,200 (1995). About two thirds of the population habitually speak Papago.

**Passamaquoddy**, name for those Algonquian-speaking Maliseet-Passamaquoddy who live on the American side in Maine. Population: c. 1,000 Maliseet-Passamaquoddy (1600), c. 3,000 Passamaquoddy (1995).

**Patwin**, a people of the Wintuan family of the Penutian languages in central California.

**Paviotso**, name for the Northern Paiute in Oregon.

**Pawnee**, a people belonging to the Caddoan language family in Kansas and Nebraska consisting of several allied tribes (Chauí, Kit'kaháxki, Pitahauírata, Skidí). Removed to Oklahoma in 1874. Population: 10,000 (1780), 2,500 (1995). About 100 still speak Pawnee.

**Pecos**, pueblo of the Tiwa language group (language family: Kiowa-Tanoan) which was abandoned following epidemics and attacks by enemies. The survivors found refuge in Jemez. Population: 2,000–2,500 (1680), 17 (1838).

**Peigan** → *Piegan*.

**Penobscot**, a group which emerged from an historical division of the Eastern Abenaki in Maine. Population: 600 (c. 1700), 2,100 (1995).

**Penutian**, language phylum said to encompass various language families of western North America, including Tsimshian, Chinookan, Sahaptian, Wintuan, Maiduan, Yokutsan, and others.

**Peoria**, one of the politically independent tribes of the Illinois who merged with the Wea and Piankashaw in 1854. Today their descendants live in Oklahoma. Population: 2,500 (1995).

**Pequot**, an Algonquian-speaking people in eastern Connecticut who were driven out in 1637 after a war with the British and who were almost entirely destroyed by the linguistically related Mohegan and the Iroquoian Mohawk. A few descendants are today recognized as a tribe under the name of Mashantucket Pequot (155 members).

**Petun (Tobacco Nation)**, an Iroquoian people, close allies of the Huron, utterly defeated in battle by the Iroquois in 1649, after which they disappeared. Population: 8,000 (1610), 1,200 (1639).

**Piankashaw**, one of the Algonquian tribes subsumed under the name Miami.

**Picuris**, a pueblo (language: Tiwa branch of the Kiowa-Tanoan language family). Population: 3,000 (1680), 300 (1995).

**Piegan**, tribe of the Blackfoot confederation on both sides of the USA-Canada border. Population: 14,600 in the USA and 3,048 in Canada (2000).

**Pima**, Uto-Aztecans in Arizona (Pima Alto), Sonora, and Chihuahua (Pima Bajo). Population: 4,000 (1680); 12,200 in the USA and c. 3,000 in Mexico (1995).

**Piro**, Pueblo people of the Kiowa-Tanoan language family's Tiwa branch. Their independence was lost in the 18th century, and descendants live in Ysleta del Sur, Texas and in Ciudad Juarez, Mexico.

**Pitahauírata**, Pawnee tribe in Kansas.

**Pit River Indians**, name that encompasses the Achumawi and Atsugewi.

**Plains Cree**, Cree groups who penetrated into the northern Plains of Montana and Alberta in the 17th century and closely associated themselves with the Assiniboine.

**Plains Ojibwa**, Ojibwa groups who penetrated into the Plains, particularly in North Dakota, in the 18th century, and adopted the Plains culture.

**Pokanoket** (also Wampanoag), alliance of Algonquian village groups in present-day Massachusetts. Decimated by an epidemic in 1617 before the arrival of whites, they were decisively defeated by the English in the King Philip's War in 1675.

**Pomo**, collective term for seven linguistically related peoples in western central California. Population: 8,000 (1780).

**Potawatomi**, an Algonquian people of the lower peninsula of Michigan, southeast of Lake Michigan. In the course of their eventful history, the Potawatomi split into groups which settled in Oklahoma, Kansas, Wisconsin, Michigan, and Ontario. Population: 4,000 (1680), 9,000–10,000 (1830), 7,500 (1977). About 300 Potawatomi still speak the language.

**Pueblo** (Spanish, "village"), collective term for the agricultural peoples of the Southwest living in the characteristic villages of interconnecting houses of stone or adobe.

**Puyallup**, Coast Salish tribe on Puget Sound. Language: Southern Lushootseed. Population: 2,100 (1995).

**Quapaw**, a Siouan people (Dhegiha branch) from Arkansas who were removed to Oklahoma in 1867. Population: 2,500 (1650), 2,700 (1995). In 1990, 37 people indicated that they spoke Quapaw.

**Quechan** (also Yuma), a Yuman-speaking people on the Colorado River. Population: 4,000 (1600), 2,400 (1995). About 340 speakers.

**Quileute**, a people forming part of the Chimakuan language family, south of the Olympic Peninsula, Washington. Population: 500 (1780), 840 (1995). Fewer than 10 speakers.

**Quinault**, a Coast Salish people near the mouth of the Quinault River, Washington. Population: 1,000 (1805), 2,500 (1995). In 1990, six people could still speak Quinault.

**Quiripi**, Algonquian village group in Connecticut. Population: 250 (1600).

**Rappahannock**, Virginia Algonquian tribe on the Rappahannock River, whose name disappeared from documents during the late 17th century. In the

Cherokee woman working with glass beads, North Carolina, 1973. → *Cherokee*.

20th century the name is a designation for the descendants of various local indigenous tribes.

**Rarámuri** → *Tarahumara*.

**Sahaptian**, language family and possible branch of the Penutian language phylum in the Plateau region, consisting of two languages: Nez Perce and Sahaptin. Numerous Sahaptin dialects were once spoken by various autonomous tribes, e.g. Klikitat, Yakima, Walla Walla, Tenino, and Umatilla.

**Sahnish** → *Arikara*.

**Saint Lawrence Iroquois**, an Iroquoian people, encountered near the St. Lawrence River by the French explorers and colonizers Jacques Cartier and Jean-François de la Roque between 1535 and 1543. They inhabited the large settlement of Hochelaga in the area where Montreal now stands. A century later these Iroquoian had disappeared and their land was taken over by Algonquian and Mohawk.

**Salinan**, collection of village groups with similar languages along the Salinas River south of San Francisco Bay. The inclusion of Salinan in the Hokan language phylum is contested. Population: 3,000 (1770), 16 (1910).

**Salishan**, language group in Washington, British Columbia, Idaho, and Montana, divided into five branches: Bella Coola, Central Salish (Comox, Sechelt, Halkomelem, Lushootseed, and others), Tsamosan (languages in southern Washington), Tillamook, and Interior Salish (Salishan languages in the Plateau region: Thompson, Shuswap, Coeur d'Alêne, and others)

**Salish**, self-designation of the Flathead.

**San Felipe**, Keresan pueblo at the foot of Santa Ana Mesa on the Rio Grande in New Mexico. Population: 600 (1680), 3,000 (1995).

**San Ildefonso**, Tewa pueblo south of the Black Mesa on the Rio Grande, 20 miles southwest of Santa Fe. Population: 800 (1680), 600 (1995).

**San Juan**, Tewa pueblo at the confluence of the Rio Grande and Rio Chama. Population: 300 (1680), 425 (1901), 2,300 (1995); more than half its population live outside the pueblo today.

**Sanpoil**, an Interior Salish people on the Sanpoil and Columbia rivers in Washington. A part of the Sanpoil, the Nespelem, became an autonomous people in the 19th century. Population: 1,600–1,700 (1780), 286 (1910). Today they form part of the Colville Reservation's multiethnic population.

**Sans Arc** → *Itazipco*.

**Santa Ana**, Keresan pueblo in the area near the confluence of the Jemez River and Rio Grande in New Mexico, northwest of Albuquerque. Population: 340 (1707), 750 (1995).

**Santee**, collective term for the four Dakota tribes (Sisseton, Wahpeton, Wahpekute, and Mdewakanton), where the eastern-dialect is spoken.

**Santo Domingo**, Keresan pueblo on the Rio Grande, 30 miles south of Santa Fe, New Mexico. Population: 1,000 (1807), 4,000 (1995).

**Saponi**, a Siouan people of Virginia, close relatives of the Tutelo. Some of them sought refuge with the Iroquois in the 18th century and were assimilated. Today there are possible descendants of the Saponi in North Carolina (→ *Haliwa-Saponi*).

**Sauk**, an Algonquian people around Saginaw Bay, Michigan, who settled in Oklahoma in 1869 after being repeatedly driven away (e.g., in the Black Hawk War of 1832). Population: 3,000 (1820), 2,400 "Sac and Fox" in Oklahoma, Kansas, and Nebraska (1995). In 1990 a dozen speakers of Sauk were still alive; by 1999 there were only three.

**Saulteaux**, originally a name given to the Ojibwa at Sault Sainte Marie, Michigan. Now it particularly denotes the Western Ojibwa around Lake of the Woods and south of Lake Winnipeg in Ontario and Manitoba. Population: 19,000 (1978).

**Sekani**, Athapaskans (close relatives of the Beaver and Sarcee) in central British Columbia. Population: 250 (1860), 600 (1990).

**Seminole**, Collective term groups of Creek (Muskogee- and Hichiti-speakers) who fled to the Everglades in Florida, where they mixed with the remnants of the local population and with runaway slaves. They are counted among the Five Civilized Tribes and many were deported to Oklahoma. Population: 2,000 (1800), 5,000 (1820), (1995): 13,200 in Oklahoma, 2,300 in Florida (→ *Miccosukee*).

Interior of a Hopi house in Sichomovi, Arizona. Photograph: Adamson Clark Vroman, 1902. Los Angeles County Museum of Natural History, Los Angeles, CA. → *Hopi*.

**Seneca**, westernmost of the five founding tribes of the Iroquois League. Population: 4,000 (1771), 8,000 (1980). Fewer than 200 people still speak Seneca.

**Seri**, fishers and hunters on the central coast of Sonora (Isla Tiburón and the coastal strip of the opposite mainland), Mexico. Their language may form part of the Hoka language phylum. Population: 3,000 (1692), 500 (1995).

**Serrano**, Uto-Aztecans from the San Bernardino Range, southern California. Population: 1,500 (1700), 118 (1910). One Serrano-speaker remained in 1990.

**Shasta**, collective term for several linguistically related peoples in northeastern California (Shasta, Okwanuchu, Konomihu, and others). Population: 2,000 (1770), 100 (1910). In 1990 Shasta was still spoken by 12 people.

**Shawnee**, Algonquians south of the Great Lakes. In the 18th century they represented a major political factor in the borderlands. Around 1810 the Shawnee Tecumseh attempted to establish a united Indian front against the advancing white Americans. Population: 2,000–4,000 (1750), 4,700 (1995). About 200 people still speak Shawnee fluently.

**Shinnecock**, Indian community recognized by New York State that has continuously inhabited settlements and a small reservation on Long Island. Their Algonquian mother tongue (Montauk) was lost in the early 19th century. Population: 150 (1890), 400 (1972).

**Shivwits**, local division of the Southern Paiute.

**Shoshone**, subgroup of the Numic branch of the Uto-Aztecan languages. Although they share a language, the Shoshone belong to different culture areas: Western Shoshone and Panamint (Great Basin), Eastern Shoshone and Comanche (Plains). The Northern Shoshone were influenced by Plains and Plateau cultures.

**Shuswap (Secwepemc)**, an Interior Salish people in the Plateau region between the Fraser and Columbia rivers. Population: 7,200 (1850), 6,500 (1990), of whom about 500 still speak the language.

**Sicangu** (*sican gu* 'burnt thigh'), one of the seven divisions of the Teton Lakota, better known by their historic name Brulé. Today most live on the Rosebud Reservation, South Dakota. Population: 30,200 (1995).

**Sihasapa** (*siha sapa* "black foot"), one of the seven divisions of the Teton Lakota, not to be confused with the Algonquian-speaking Blackfoot.

**Siksika**, northernmost section of the Blackfoot in Alberta. Population: 5,188 (2000).

**Sinkyone**, Athapaskans on the Eel River in northern California (→ *Lassik*).

**Siouan**, large language family in central and southeastern North America with two branches: Catawba (extinct) and Siouan with several subgroups.

**Sioux**, the allied Dakota, Nakota, and Lakota, whose Ojibwa name formed the basis for the word "Sioux."

**Sisseton**, one of four Santee (Dakota) tribes in Minnesota. Today some live on the Sisseton Reservation in South Dakota while others live in western Minnesota.

**Siuslaw**, language family including the Siuslaw and neighboring Lower Umpqua on the coast of Oregon. The majority of both peoples live with the Coos at Coos Bay. Total population of all three peoples: 600 (1995).

**Skagit**, a southern Coast Salish group on Whidbey Island in Puget Sound, Washington. Language: Northern Lushootseed. Upper Skagit is a collective name for a further five Coast Salish groups (population: 620 in 1995).

**Skidí**, Pawnee tribe in Nebraska. This self-designation is also translated as Wolf Pawnee or Pawnee Loup.

Annie Osceola using a sewing machine to make dolls, Florida, c. 1950. National Anthropological Archives, Smithsonian Institution, Washington, DC.

**Skokomish**, southern Coast Salish group on the southern side of Puget Sound, where the reservation of the same name is also located. Language: Twana. Population: 250 (1995).

**Slave (Slavey)**, Athapaskan group on the Mackenzie and Liard rivers west of the Great Slave Lake in the Northwest Territories, British Columbia, and Alberta. Population: 1,600 (1880), 4,000 (1980).

**Snohomish**, southern Coast Salish group on whose territory stands the Tulalip Reservation. Language: Northern Lushootseed. Population: 2,900 in 1995.

**Snoqualmie**, southern Coast Salish group on the river of the same name east of Puget Sound, Washington. Language: Southern Lushootseed.

**Solano**, unidentified language of the Terocodame and probably also of the other little-known groups between the Sierra Madre Oriental and the Rio Grande near Piedras Negras, Coahuila. Disappeared in the 18th century.

**Southern Paiute**, over a dozen different groups (Kaibab, Moapa, Shivwits, and others), speakers of a southern Numic language in southern Utah and Nevada and in northern Arizona. Population: 2,000 (1873), 770 (1970, reservation population only).

**Spokane**, group on the upper Spokane River in western Washington; they shared their Salish language with the Kalispel, Pend d'Oreilles, and Flathead. Population: 1,400 (1780), 2, 025 (1994).

**Stl'atl'imx** → *Lillooet*

**Phylumbridge**, Mahican group in western Massachusetts who joined the Oneida in 1785, with whom they moved to Wisconsin in 1833, where they united with a Munsee group.

**Sugpiaq**, language of the Yupiq (Chugash, Koniag) on the Pacific Coast.

**Suh'tai**, relatives of the Cheyenne. In the 18th century they lived between the Missouri and the Black Hills, but eventually united with the Cheyenne.

**Suma**, western neighbors of the Jumano. in northwestern Chihuahua; they may have spoken the same language.

**Suquamish**, one of about 50 southern Coast Salish groups around Puget Sound, Washington. Their language is Southern Lushootseed and their reservation is called Port Gamble. Population: 800 (1995).

**Susquwhannock**, northern Iroquoians in the Susquehanna Valley, Pennsylvania. Heavily decimated by wars against the Iroquois League and the British colonies in the 17th century; most of the survivors merged with the Iroquois of the Five Nations.

**Swampy Cree** (West Main Cree), Cree bands on the west side of Hudson Bay, including the Moose Cree south of James Bay. Population: 6,500 (1980).

**Swinomish**, one of about 50 southern Coast Salish groups (Northern Lushootseed) around Puget Sound, Washington. Population of the reservation of the same name: 630 (1995).

**Tagish**, Athapaskan hunters and fishers in the headwaters of the Yukon in Yukon Territory and British Columbia. Population: 80 (1887), 111 (1978).

**Tahltan**, Athapaskan hunters and fishers on the upper Stikine River in British Columbia; trading partners of the Tlingit. Population: 1,000 (1880), 800 (1978).

**Tahue**, a poulation in the coastal area of southern Sinaloa, which included speakers of various extinct languages probably related to Cahita.

**Takelma**, collective name for the Takelma and Latkawa in the area around the Umpqua and Rogue rivers in southwestern Oregon. Population: fewer than 1,000 (1850), 27 (1884).

**Takelman**, extinct language family of the Takelma and Kalapuya (Penutian language phylum?).

**Tamaulipec**, group of numerous small and now disappeared tribes in central and southeastern Tamaulipas; there is no conclusive information regarding their linguistic affiliation.

**Tanaina**, Athapaskan group on Cook Inlet, southwestern Alaska. Population: over 5,000 (1800), c. 1,000 (1995).

**Tanana**, collective term for several Athapaskan groups in the Tanana River valley in eastern Alaska. Population: 600 (1885); no longer existing as a group.

**Tano**, language family in New Mexico consisting of Tewa, Tiwa, and Towa which, together with Kiowa, form a language phylum.

**Taos**, northernmost pueblo on the Rio Grande in New Mexico, inhabited by Tiwa-speakers. Population: 400 (1890), 2,300 (1995).

**Tarahumara** (Rarámuri), Uto-Aztecan farmers in the Sierra Madre Occidental in southern Chihuahua. Population: 45,000 (1945).

**Tataviam**, mountain population on the upper Santa Clara River in southern California; the language, which was extinct before 1916, probably belonged to the Takic branch of Uto-Aztecan.

**Tejon**, collective term for the heterogeneous inhabitants of the Tejon Rancheria in the upper San Joaquin Valley, California.

**Tepehuan**, a people in Durango, on the eastern side of the Sierra Madre Occidental; their language belongs to the Piman branch of Uto-Aztecan and is spoken by the majority of the northern and southern Tepehuan, of whom there are c. 8,000 (1995).

**Teton**, western Sioux (→ *Lakota*).

**Tewa**, Tano language of which several dialects are or were spoken in the pueblos of San Juan, Santa Clara, San Ildefonso, Nambe, Pojaque, and Tesuque.

**Thompson (Nlaka'pamux)**, Interior Salish in southern British Columbia, with more than 60 small winter villages in 1900. Population: 5,180 (1997).

**Tillamook**, southernmost Salish group consisting of speakers of several dialects (Siletz, Nehalem, Nestucca, and others) on the coast of northern Oregon. Population: 1,000 (1805).

**Timucua**, a people of the Atlantic coast of northern Florida, who spoke an isolated language and were organized into several chiefdoms. They disappeared in the 18th century; remnants of their population probably were absorbed by the Seminole. Population: 20,000–30,000 (1650), 35 (1728).

**Tipai**, various Yuman-speaking groups in southern California and northern Baja California, of whom some also form part of the "Mission Indians" known as Diegueños (→ *Ipai* ); others, e.g., are known as Kamia.

**Tiwa**, two Tanoan languages spoken in the pueblos of Taos and Picuris (northern Tiwa) as well as in Isleta and Sandia (southern Tiwa).

**Tlingit**, a coastal people in southeastern Alaska who include numerous tribes and whose language belongs to the Na-Dene language phylum. Population: 10,000 (1740), 14,000 (1990).

**Tobacco Nation** → *Petun*.

**Toboso**, hunter-gatherers in the interior drainage basin of Bolsón de Mapimi, in the tri-state corner of Coahuila, Durango, and Chihuahua. The language may have been Uto-Aztecan or Athapaskan.

**Tocobaga**, a people of unknown linguistic affiliation who lived on the Gulf coast of Florida in the 16th and 17th centuries.

**Tohono O'odham** → *Papago*.

**Tolowa**, an Athapaskan group on the coast of northwestern California. Population: 2,200 (1828), after 1900 they merged with the Tututni in Oregon, who are also Athapaskans.

**Tonkawa**, a group of various tribes with an isolated and now extinct language on the southern Plains of central Texas. Population: 1,600 (1690), 50 (1937).

**Towa**, a Tanoan language spoken in the pueblo of Jemez, New Mexico.

**Tsetsaut**, an Athapaskan group who spread from the coastal mountains of central northern British Columbia to the coast of Alaska. The Tsetsaut and their language became extinct in the early 20th century.

**Tsimshian**, a group of peoples (Nisga'a, Gitksan, Coast Timshian, Southern Tomshian) in the northern coastal region of British Columbia. Their two languages form a distinct group that is thought to be related to the Penutian language phylum.

**Tubar**, small group in southern Chihuahua, on the western side of the Sierra Madre Occidental; may be a division of the Tarahumara.

**Tubatulabal**, a people on the upper Kern River in the foothills of the Sierra Nevada, California. Their language, a branch of Uto-Aztecan, has nearly died out. Population: 400–1,000 (before 1850), 43 (1972).

**Tunica**, a people on the Yazoo River in Mississippi, who later migrated to the Red River in Louisiana; their language, which is not know to be related to any other, is extinct. Population: 1,600 (1700), 730 (1995, including Biloxi).

**Tuscarora**, southernmost of the Northern Iroquoian peoples on both sides of the fallline in eastern North Carolina. After waging a war against the colonists (1711–1713) part of the tribe fled north and joined the Five Nations of the Iroquois.

**Tutchone**, an Athapaskan group consisting of a few hundred people in southern Yukon Territory. They were trading partners of the Tlingit in Alaska.

**Tutelo**, eastern Siouan-speakers in the piedmont of Virginia. The tribe sought refuge among the Iroquois in the 18th century; the last speaker of the language died in 1898 among the Cayuga in Canada.

**Uchucklesaht**, local group of central Nootkans, north of Alberni Inlet on Vancouver Island.

**Uintah**, Ute group east of the Wasatch Range in Utah, where they have lived on the Uintah Reservation since 1881.

**Umatilla**, speakers of a dialect of Sahaptin on the Columbia River in western Washington and Oregon. Population: 2,500 (before 1805). Their descendants live with the Cayuse and Walla Walla on the Umatilla Reservation in Oregon.

**Unami**, the southern of two Delaware languages of which at least three dialects (including Unalatchtigo) were spoken in Pennsylvania, New Jersey, and Delaware. The population was divided into numerous independent groups.

**Uncompahgre**, a group of Ute south of the Colorado River in Colorado, settled on the Ouray Reservation in Utah since 1882.

**Ute**, speakers of a southern Numic language (Uto-Aztecan), who lived in at least 11 bands in Colorado and Utah. Population: 6,000 (1873), 5,100 (1980).

**Uto-Aztecan**, large language family which extends from the American Southwest into Mexico and into Central America. The northern branch includes Numic, Tubatulabal, Hopi, and the southern Californian languages of the group (Takic). The southern branch includes the Pima languages and Tarahumara-Cahita, among others.

**Ventureño**, southeasternmost Chumash group on the Californian coast and in the hinterland of the San Buenaventura mission. Population: 2,500–4,000 (1770).

**Virginia Algonquians**, collective term for Algonquian-speakers of the coastal region of Virginia, including several independent groups as well as Powhatan's chiefdom. Population: c. 20,000 (1600). → *Chickahominy*, *Mattaponi*, *Pamunkey*, *Rappahannock*.

**Waco**, close relatives of the Wichita, with whom they merged. Population c. 500 in Texas (1824).

**Wahpekute**, one of the four tribes of the Santee (Dakota) in Minnesota who now live with the Mdewakanton on the Santee Reservation in Nebraska.

**Wahpeton**, one of the four tribes of the Santee (Dakota) in Minnesota who now live with the Sisseton on the Sisseton Reservation in South Dakota. Population: 1,500 (1835).

**Wailaki**, an Athapaskan group on the Eel River in northwestern California, consisting of 19 tribelets with c. 2,800 members in about 1800.

**Walapai**, Yuman-speakers in the Colorado River area of Arizona, and neighbors of their relatives the Yavapai and Havasupai. Population: over 1,000 (1850); over 2,000 (1995).

**Walla Walla**, speakers of a northeastern dialect of Sahaptin in southeastern Washington; since 1860 they have lived with the Umatilla and Cayuse on the Umatilla Reservation in Oregon. Population: c. 1,500 (1780).

**Wampanoag (Pokanoket)**, chiefdom which consists of over 30 villages (1620) on Rhode Island and in Massachusetts; the majority of the Algonquian-speaking population was killed in the King Philip's War (1675–1676). A group survived on Martha's Vinyard; they were recognized by the federal government in 1987 and have about 700 members.

**Wanapam**, speakers of a northeastern dialect of Sahaptin, and the northeasternmost neighbors of the Yakima in the Columbia River area around Priest's Rapids, where about 10 families still lived in 1995.

Wichita encampment, Oklahoma. Photograph: Henry Peabody, c. 1904. → *Wichita*.

Inuit woman with stores of water in the form of blocks of ice, Canada, c. 1960. → *Inuit*.

**Wappo**, a people from Napa Valley and south of Clear Lake in northern California, whose language is distantly related to that of the Yuki. Before 1840 there were about 1,000 speakers of five different dialects. Today the language is becoming extinct.

**Wasco**, speakers of the Kiksht language, which forms part of Upper Chinook and is the last spoken form of Chinookan, in The Dalles, Oregon. Today they live on the Warm Springs Reservation.

**Washoe**, speakers of an isolated language in the Lake Tahoe region of the Sierra Nevada in the borderlands of California and Nevada. In 1995, more than 1,995 Washoe lived in and around several settlements in both states.

**Wea**, a tribe of Algonquian-speaking Miami who lived between the Ohio and Wabash rivers in the 18th century. In the 19th century they migrated via Missouri and Kansas to northeastern Oklahoma, where they merged with the Peoria.

**Wenro**, Northern Iroquoians and allies of the Neutral on the southwestern shore of Lake Ontario. In 1638 they sought refuge from the Seneca among the Huron and were integrated into both tribes.

**Western Apache**, five Apache groups (White Mountain, San Carlos, Cibecue, and Southern and Northern Tonto) of eastern central Arizona who share the same language and culture. Population: over 25,000 on four reservations (1995).

**Western Shoshone**, more than 40 groups of speakers of the Central Numic languages Shoshone and Panamint in central Nevada and adjacent areas of California and Utah. Population: 1,950 (1873), 3,650 (1980).

**Whilkut**, an Athapaskan group related to the neighboring Hupa on the upper Redwood Creek in northwestern California. Population: 500 (1850); no longer exists as an autonomous people.

**Wichita**, a group of tribes, as the southernmost of the northern Caddo originally inhabiting Arkansas and Kansas. Since 1867 they have lived on a reservation in Oklahoma. Population: 1,800 (1995).

**Winnebago (Ho-chunk)**, Siouan-speakers (Chiwere branch) who originally lived in the Green Bay area and moved to central Wisconsin in about 1800. Population: 5,800 (1820), c. 10,000 (2000) mainly in Wisconsin and Nebraska.

**Wintu**, a people in the upper Sacramento Valley, northern California, whose language belongs to the Penutian phylum. Population: 12,000 (estimate of 1770), their descendants are now widely scattered.

**Wishram**, speakers of the Wasco-Wishram dialect of an Upper Chinook language, on the Columbia River near The Dalles, Washington. They now live on the Yakama Reservation.

**Wiyot**, Ritwan-speaking group (→ *Yurok*) from the northern Californian coast around Humboldt Bay; the language is now extinct. Two small reservations with just over 100 inhabitants were terminated in 1958.

**Woods Cree**, over 40 Cree bands between Hudson Bay, Lake Winnipeg, Lake Athabasca, and Lubicon Lake in Alberta. Population: 35,500 (1978).

**Wyandot**, descendants of the Petun and Huron who were driven to Michigan by the Iroquois and eventually reached Oklahoma via Ohio and Kansas. The language died out in the late 20th century.

**Xixime**, neighbors and relatives of the Axacee in the borderland of Durango and Sinaloa who were assimilated at an early stage. The origins of the name probably lie in the widespread Aztec term "Chichimec," meaning "uncivilized people."

**Yahi,** Yana subgroup which became famous thanks to Ishi, the "last Yahi."

**Yakima**, a Sahaptin-speaking people on the eastern side of the Cascades in southern Washington, with several dozen independent winter villages. The Yakama Reservation is located within their ancient territory. Population: 7,000 (before 1805), 8,600 (1995).

**Yamassee**, tribe in the southern coastal area of Georgia, the remnants of which fled to Florida after the Yamassee War (1715) where they merged with the Seminole. There is no record of their language.

**Yana**, a people east of the upper Sacramento River in California who form part of the Hokan language phylum. Their numbers declined from 1,900 (1848) to 120 (1905) and then to 20 (1973).

**Yankton**, Nakota (Siouan)-speakers who inhabited the upper Mississippi in the 17th century and advanced to the Missouri in about 1700. Most of them have lived on a reservation in southeastern South Dakota since 1858. Population: 3,000 (1862), 6,800 (1995).

**Yanktonai**, Nakota-speakers who, like the Yankton, migrated to South Dakota, where they split into Upper and Lower Yanktonais who today live on the Standing Rock and Crow Creek reservations.

**Yaqui** (self-designation: Yoeme), speakers of a dialect of Cahita (Uto-Aztecan) in southern Sonora on the coast of the Gulf of California. After a dramatic history, which included deportation to Oaxaca and Yucatan (1887), a part of the Yaqui fled to Arizona, where the Pascua Yaqui in Tucson are now a tribe recognized by the federal government.

**Yavapai**, Yuman-speaking hunters, gatherers, and farmers in western central Arizona. Population: c. 1,500 (1680); over 1,000 (2000) on two reservations (Fort McDowell and Yavapai) in Arizona.

**Yellowknife**, Athapaskan group (c. 200 people) which was identifiable in the 18th and 19th centuries in the area northeast of Great Slave Lake in the Northwest Territories, now merged with neighboring groups.

**Yokuts**, a language family comprising over 40 tribelets in the San Joaquin Valley and the adjacent western side of the Sierra Nevada, California, and forming part of the Penutian language phylum. Population before contact with Europeans: 30,000–50,000 (estimate).

**Yuchi**, a people from eastern Tennessee whose language has no known relatives. Since the late 18th century they have been dominated by the Creek, with whom their descendants live in Oklahoma.

**Yuki**, a group on the upper Eel River and adjoining coastal areas in northern central California. Population c. 10,000 (c.1850), 125 (1910).

Yavapai scouts in Camp Date Creek, Arizona, c. 1880. National Archives and Records Administration, Washington, DC. → *Yavapai*.

Opposite page:
The Ghost Dance prophet Wovoka (Jack Wilson) and General Tim McCoy, governor of Wyoming Territory and Hollywood actor, 1926. National Anthropological Archives, Smithsonian Institution, Washington, DC.

**Yukian**, together with the Wappo a small language family which, with the exception of a very few Wappo-speakers,has almost died out.

**Yuma**, commonly used name for the Quechan, who form part of the Yuman language family.

**Yuman**, language group on the Colorado River and the Californian peninsula, probably part of the Hoka language phylum.

**Yupik**, (1) a group of western Eskimo languages spoken in Siberia and in Alaska south of Norton Sound; at c. 13,000, the number of speakers seems to be stable; (2) self-designation of this group.

**Yurok**, a people on the coast of northern California and in the Klamath River area. Their language is becoming extinct; together with Wiyot it forms the Ritwan language family, which is related to Algonquian. Population: c. 3,000 (before 1850).

**Zacateca**, an agricultural Uto-Aztecan people in Zacatecas who merged with the mestizo population at an early stage.

**Zia**, a Keresan pueblo on the Jemez River west of the Rio Grande. Population: over 5,000 in five villages (1540), 100 (1890), 745 (1995).

**Zuni**, speakers of an isolated language who, in 1542, lived in seven pueblos in the western central region of New Mexico. Of the 6,000-plus inhabitants, only 1,500 still lived in a single pueblo in about 1850 (1995: 9,000).

Mohave man in a rabbitskin blanket beside the Colorado River, Arizona. Photograph: Edward S. Curtis, 1903. Southwest Museum, Los Angeles, CA. → *Mohave*.

# Bibliography

Christian F. Feest

## Introductions, overviews, thematic literature, bibliographies

Adams, David Wallace, *Education for Extinction. American Indians and the Boarding School Experience, 1875–1928*. Lawrence 1995

Ambler, Marjane, *Breaking the Iron Bonds. Indian Control of Energy Development*. Lawrence 1990

Berkhofer, Robert F., Jr., *The White Man's Indian*. New York 1978

Berlo, Janet C. and Ruth B. Phillips, *Native North American Art*. Oxford/New York 1998

Bolz, Peter and Hans-Ulrich Sanner, *Indianer Nordamerikas. Die Sammlungen des Ethnologischen Museum Berlin*. Berlin 1999

Calloway, Colin G. (Ed.), *New Directions in American Indian History*. Norman 1988

Campbell, Lyle, *American Indian Languages. The Historical Linguistics of Native America*. New York/Oxford 1997

Chute, Janet E., *The Legacy of Shingwaukonse. A Century of Native Leadership*. Toronto 1998

Clifton, James A. (Ed.), *The Invented Indian. Cultural Fictions & Government Policies*. New Brunswick/London 1990

Culin, Stewart, *Games of the North American Indians* [1907]. New York Undated.

Deloria, Vine, Jr., *Custer Died For Your Sins*. New York 1969

As above, *Red Earth, White Lies. Native Americans and the Myth of Scientific Fact*. New York 1995

Dickason, Olive Patricia, *Canada's First Nations. A History of Founding Peoples from the Earliest Times*. Toronto 1992

Dillehay, Tom D. and David J. Metzler, *The First Americans. Search and Research*. Boca Raton 1991

Dippie, Brian W., *The Vanishing American. White Attitude & U.S. Indian Policy*. Lawrence 1982

Driver, Harold E., *Indians of North America*. 2nd ed. Chicago 1969

Eggan, Fred (Ed.), *Social Anthropology of North American Tribes*. Chicago 1955

Fagan, Brian N., *Ancient North America. The Archaeology of a Continent*. London 1991

Feest, Christian F., *Das rote Amerika*. Wien 1976

As above, *Beseelte Welten: Religionen des indianischen Nordamerika*. Freiburg 1998

As above, *Native Arts of North America*. 2nd ed. London 1992

As above, (Ed.), *Indians and Europe. An Interdisciplinary Collection of Essays*. 2nd ed. Lincoln/London 1999

Frantz, Klaus, *Indian Reservations in the United States*. Chicago/London 1999

Getches, David H. and Charles F. Wilkinson, *Federal Indian Law. Cases and Materials*. 2. Ed. St. Paul 1986

Gill, Sam D., *Native American Religions. An Introduction*. Belmont 1982

Goddard, Ives (Ed.), *Languages*. Handbook of North American Indians 17. Washington 1996

Gugel, Liane, *Frauenbünde der Indianer Nordamerikas*. Wyk auf Foehr 1997

Hertzberg, Hazel W., *The Search for an American Indian Identity. Modern Pan-Indian Movements*. Syracuse 1971

Hodge, Frederick W. (Ed.), *Handbook of American Indian North of Mexico*. 2 vols. Washington 1907–1910

Hoffmann, Gerhard (Ed.), *Indianische Malerei im 20. Jahrhundert*. Munich 1985

As above, (Ed.), *Zeitgenössische Kunst der Indianer und Eskimos in Kanada*. Stuttgart 1988

Hoxie, Frederick E. (Ed.), *Encyclopedia of North American Indians*. Boston/New York 1996

Hultkrantz, Åke, *The Religions of the American Indians*. Berkeley/Los Angeles 1979

Hurt, R. Douglas, *Indian Agriculture in America. Prehistory to Present*. Lawrence 1987

Jacquin, Philippe, *Les Indiens Blancs*. Paris 1987

Johnson, Try, Joane Nagel and Duane Champagne (Ed.), *American Indian Activism. Alcatraz to the Longest Walk*. Urbana/Chicago 1997

Kehoe, Alice B., *North American Indians. A Comprehensive Account*. Englewood Cliffs 1981

Keith, Michael C., *Signals in the Air. Native Broadcasting in America*. Westport 1995

King, J. C. H., *First Peoples, First Contacts. Native Peoples of North America*. London 1999

Krech, Shepard III, *The Ecological Indian. Myth and History*. New York/London 1999

Leacock, Eleanor B. and Nancy O. Lurie (Ed.), *North American Indians in Historical Perspective*. New York 1971

Liedtke, Stefan, *Indianersprachen. Sprachvergleich. und Klassifizierung*. Hamburg 1991

Lindig, Wolfgang, *Die Indianer Nordamerikas*. 3. Ed. Munich 1985

As above, (Ed.), *Indianische Realität. Nordamerikanische Indianer in der Gegenwart*. Munich 1994

Miller, James R., *Shingwauk's Vision: a History of Native Residential Schools*. Toronto/Buffalo/London 1996.

Mithun, Marianne, *The Languages of Native North America*. Cambridge 1999

Morse, Bradford W. (Ed.), *Aboriginal Peoples and the Law: Indian, Metis and Inuit Rights in Canada*. Ottawa 1985

Murdock, George Peter and Timothy O'Leary, *Ethnographic Bibliography of North America*. 4th ed. 5 vols. New Haven 1975. Supplement: M. M. Martin and T. J. O'Leary, 3 vols. New Haven 1990

Murphy, James E. and Sharon M. Murphy. *Let My People Know. American Indian Journalism*. Norman 1981

Nabokov, Peter and Robert Easton, *Native American Architecture*. New York/Oxford 1989

Nagel, Joane, *American Indian Ethnic Revival. Red Power and the Resurgence of Identity and Culture*. New York/Oxford 1996

Nies, Judith, *Native American History. A Chronology of a Culture's Vast Achievements and their Links to World Events*. New York 1996

O'Brien, Sharon, *American Indian Tribal Governments*. Norman/London 1989

Olson, James S. and Raymond Wilson, *Native Americans in the Twentieth Century*. Urbana/Chicago 1984

Oswalt, Wendell H. and Sharlotte Neely, *This Land was Theirs. A Study of North American Indians*. 5th ed. Mountain View 1996

Peterson, Jacqueline and Jennifer S. H. Brown, *The New Peoples. Being and Becoming Métis in North America*. Lincoln 1985

Pevar, Stephen L., *The Rights of Indians and Tribes*. 2nd ed. Carbondale 1992

Prucha, Francis Paul, *A Bibliographical Guide to the History of Indian-White Relations in the United States*. Chicago 1977. Supplement: Chicago 1983

As above, *Atlas of American Indian Affairs*. Lincoln/London 1990

Schusky, Ernest L. (Ed.), *Political Organization of Native North Americans*. Lanham 1981

Silver, Shirley; Miller, Wick R., *American Indian Languages. Cultural and Social Contexts*. Tucson 1997

Stanley, Sam (Ed.), *American Indian Economic Development*. Berlin/New York 1978

Swanton, John R., *The Indian Tribes of North America*. Bureau of American Ethnology, Bulletin 145. Washington 1952

Thornton, Russell, *American Indian Holocaust and Survival: A Population History Since 1492*. Norman 1987

Trigger, Bruce G. and Wilcomb E. Washburn (Ed.), *Cambridge History of the Native Peoples of North America*. 2 vols. Cambridge 1996

Vennum, Thomas, Jr., *American Indian Lacrosse. Little Brother of War*. Washington 1994

Vogel, Virgil J., *American Indian Medicine*. Norman 1970

Waldram, James B., D. Ann Herring and T. Kue Young, *Aboriginal Health in Canada. Historical, Cultural, and Epidemiological Perspectives*. Toronto /Buffalo/London 1995

Washburn, Wilcomb E., *Red Man's Land, White Man's Law*. 2nd ed. Norman 1995

As above, *The American Indian and the United States. A Documentary History*. 4 vols. Westport 1973

As above, (Ed.), *History of Indian White Relations*. Handbook of North American Indians 4. Washington 1988

Wiget, Andrew (Ed.), *Dictionary of Native American Literature*. New York 1994

## ARCTIC

Balikci, Asen, *The Netsilik Eskimo*. Garden City 1970
Boas, Franz, *The Central Eskimo*. [1888].
Lincoln 1964
Crowe, Keith J., *A History of the Original Peoples of Northern Canada*. 2nd ed.
Montreal/Kingston1991
Damas, David (Ed.), *Arctic*. Handbook of North American Indians 5. Washington 1984
Duffy, R. Quinn, *The Road to Nunavut. The Progress of the Eastern Arctic Inuit Since the Second World War*. Kingston/Montreal 1988
Fienup-Riordan, Ann, *The Living Tradition of Yup'ik Masks*. Seattle/London 1996
Kaalund, Bodil, *The Art of Greenland. Sculpture, Crafts, Painting*.
Berkeley/Los Angeles/London 1983
Malaurie, Jean, *Les derniers rois de Thulé. Avec les Esquimaux polaires face à leur destin*. Paris 1976
Merkur, Daniel, *Powers Which We Do Not Know. The Gods and Spirits of the Inuit*. Moscow 1991
Nelson, Richard K., *Hunters of the Northern Ice*.
Chicago/London 1969

## SUBARCTIC

Brightman, Robert, *Grateful Prey: Rock Cree Human-Animal Relationships*. Berkeley 1993
Helm, June (Ed.), *Subarctic*. Handbook of North American Indians 6. Washington 1981
Marshall, Ingeborg, *A History and Ethnography of the Beothuk*. Montreal/Kingston 1996
Ray, Arthur J., *The Indians in the Fur Trade*.
Toronto/Buffalo 1974
Ridington, Robin, *Trail to Heaven. Knowledge and Narrative in Northern Native Community*.
Iowa City 1988
Savishinsky, Joel, *The Trail of the Hare*.
New York 1974
Tanner, Adrian, *Bringing Home Animals. Religious Ideology and Mode of Production of the Mistassini Cree Hunters*. London 1979

## NORTHEAST

Grumet, Robert S., *Historic Contact. Indian Peoples and Colonists in Today's Northeastern United States in the Sixteenth Through Eighteenth Centuries*. Norman/London 1995
Hauptmann, Laurence M. and James D. Wherry (Ed.), *The Pequots in Southern New England. The Fall and Rise of an American Indian Nation*.
Norman/London 1990
Howard, James H., *Shawnee! The Ceremonialism of a Native American Tribe and Its Cultural Background*. Athens/London 1981
Prins, Harald E. L., *The Mi'kmaq. Resistance, Accommodation, and Cultural Survival*.
Fort Worth 1996
Radin, Paul, *The Winnebago Tribe*. [1923].
Lincoln/London 1990
Rountree, Helen C., *The Powhatan Indians of Virginia. Their Traditional Culture*.
Norman/London 1989
Snow, Dean, *The Iroquois*. Oxford/Cambridge 1994
Sugden, John, *Tecumseh: A Life*. New York 1998
Tanner, Helen H. (Ed.), *Atlas of Great Lakes Indian History*. Norman/London 1987
Trigger, Bruce G. (Ed.), *Northeast*. Handbook of North American Indians 15. Washington 1978
Vennum, Thomas, Jr., *Wild Rice and the Ojibway People*. St. Paul 1988
Weslager, Clinton A., *The Delaware Indians. A History*. New Brunswick 1972

## SOUTHEAST

Hudson, Charles, *The Southeastern Indians*.
Knoxville 1976
King, Duane (Ed.), *The Cherokee Indian Nation. A Troubled History*. Knoxville 1989
Merrell. James H., *The Indians' New World. Catawabas and Their Neighbors from European Contact Through the Era of Removal*.
New York/London 1989
Paredes, J. Anthony (Ed.), *Indians of the Southeastern United States in the Late 20th Century*.
Tuscaloosa/London 1992
Salinas, Martín, *Indians of the Rio Grande Delta*.
Austin 1990
Sider, Gerald M., *Lumbee Indian Histories*.
Cambridge 1993
Swanton, John R., *Indian Tribes of the Lower Mississippi Valley and Adjacent Coast of the Gulf of Mexico*. Washington 1911
As above, *Social Organization and Social Usages of the Indians of the Creek Confederacy*.
Washington 1928
As above, *The Indians of the Southeastern United States*. Washington 1946.
As above, *Source Material on the History and Ethnology of the Caddo Indians*. [1942]
Norman/London 1996
Widmer, Randolph J., *The Evolution of the Calusa. A Nonagricultural Chiefdom on the Southwest Florida Coast*. Tuscaloosa 1988

## PRAIRIES AND PLAINS

Ewers, John C., *The Blackfeet. Raiders on the Northwestern Plains*. Norman 1985
Feest, Christian F. (Ed.), *Sitting Bull. "Der letzte Indianer"*. Darmstadt 1999
Fletcher, Alice C. and Francis LaFlesche, *The Omaha Tribe*. [1911]. 2 vols. Lincoln 1992
Grinnell, George B., *The Cheyenne Indians*. [1923].
2 vols. Lincoln 1972
Hartmann, Horst, *Die Plains- und Prärieindianer Nordamerikas*. Berlin 1973
Kavanagh, Thomas W., *The Comanches. A History, 1706–1875*. Lincoln 1996
Lowie, Robert H., *The Crow Indians*. [1935].
New York 1956
Powers, Marla N., *Oglala Women. Myth, Ritual, and Reality*. Chicago/London 1986
Powers, William K., *Oglala Religion*. Lincoln 1975
Taylor, Colin F. *Catlin's O-kee-pa. Mandan Culture and Ceremonial*.
Wyk auf Foehr 1996
Weltfish, Gene, *The Lost Universe. Pawnee Life and Culture*. [1965]. Lincoln 1977
Wilson, Gilbert L., *Agriculture of the Hidatsa Indians*. Minneapolis 1917

## PLATEAU

Gidley, M., *Kopet: A Documentary Narrative of Chief Joseph's Last Years*. Seattle 1981
Hunn, Eugene S., *Nch'i-Wána, "The Big River". Mid-Columbia Indians and Their Land*.
Seattle 1990
Walker, Deward E., Jr. (Ed.), *Plateau*. Handbook of North American Indians 12. Washington 1998

## NORTHWEST COAST

Boas, Franz, *Kwakiutl Ethnography*. Helen Codere (Ed.). Chicago 1966
Bruggmann, Maximilian and Peter R. Gerber, *Indianer der Nordwestküste*. Zürich 1987
Dauenhauer, Dora Marks and Richard Dauenhauer, *Haa Shuká, Our Ancestors. Tlingit Oral Narratives*. Seattle, WA/London/Juneau 1987
Donald, Leland, *Aboriginal Slavery on the Northwest Coast of North America*. Berkeley/ Los Angeles/London 1997
Emmons, George T., *The Tlingit Indians*. Frederica de Laguna (Ed.).
Seattle/London/New York 1991
Fisher, Robin, *Contact and Conflict. Indian-European Relations in British Columbia, 1774–1890*. Vancouver 1977
Harkin, Michael, *The Heiltsuks. Dialogues of Culture and History on the Northwest Coast*.
Vancouver 1997
Jewitt, John R., *The Adventures and Sufferings of John R. Jewitt*. [1824]. Toronto 1974
Jonaitis, Aldona (Ed.), *Chiefly Feasts. The Enduring Kwakiutl Potlatch*. New York/ Seattle/London 1991
Kan, Sergei, *Symbolic Immortality. The Tlingit Potlatch of the Nineteenth Century*.
Washington 1989
Mauzé, Marie, *Les fils de Wakai. Une histoire des Indiens Lekwiltoq*. Paris 1992
Miller, Jay, *Tsimshian Culture: A Light through the Ages*. Lincoln/London 1997
Suttles, Wayne (Ed.), *Northwest Coast*. Handbook of North American Indians 7.
Washington, 1990

## GREAT BASIN

Canfield, Gae Whitney, *Sarah Winnemucca of the Northern Paiutes*. Norman 1983
D'Azevedo, Warren L. (Ed.), *Great Basin*. Handbook of North American Indians 11. Washington 1986
Hittman, Michael, *Wovoka and the Ghost Dance*.
Yerington 1990
Madsen, Brigham, *The Northern Shoshoni*.
Caxton 1980
Steward, Julian H., *Basin-Plateau Socio-Political Groups*. Washington 1938
Wheat, Margaret M. (Ed.): *Survival Arts of the Primitive Paiutes*. Reno 1967

## CALIFORNIA

Abel-Vidor, Suzanne, Dot Brovarney, Susan Billy, *Remember Your Relations: The Elsie Allen Baskets, Family & Friends*.
Ukiah/Oakland/Berkeley 1996
Bean, John Lowell, *Mukat's People. The Cahuilla Indians of Southern California*.
Berkeley/Los Angeles 1972
As above and Thomas C. Blackburn (Ed.), *Native Californians. A Theoretical Perspective*.
Ramona 1976
Blackburn, Thomas C. (Ed.), *December's Child. A Book of Chumash Oral Narratives*.
Berkeley/Los Angeles/London 1975
Heizer, Robert F. (Ed.), *California*. Handbook of North American Indians 8. Washington 1978
As above, *The Destruction of California Indians. A Collection of Documents from the Period 1847 to 1865 in which are Described Some of the Things that Happened to Some of the Indians of California*. Lincoln/London 1993
As above and M. A. Whipple (Ed.), *The California Indians. A Source Book*.
2. Ed. Berkeley/London 1971
Kroeber, Alfred L., *Handbook of the Indians of California* [1925]. New York Undated.
Kroeber, Theodora, *Ishi in Two Worlds. A Biography of the Last Wild Indian in North America*.
Berkeley, CA/Los Angeles 1961
Rawls, James J., *Indians of California. The Changing Image*. Norman 1984

## SOUTHWEST

Barrett, S. M. (Ed.), *Geronimo. His Own Story*.
[1906] New York 1971
Deimel, Claus, *Tarahumara. Indianer im Norden Mexikos*. Frankfurt 1980
Farella, John R., *The Main Stalk. A Synthesis of Navajo Philosophy*. Tucson 1984
Iverson, Peter, *The Navajo Nation*.
Albuquerque 1983
König, René, *Indianer wohin? Alternativen in Arizona*. Opladen 1973
Lindig, Wolfgang and Helga Teiwes, *Navajo*.
Zürich 1991
Opler, Morris E. *An Apache Life-Way. The Economic, Social, and Religious Institutions of the Chiricahua Indians*. Chicago 1941
Ortiz, Alfonso, *The Tewa World*. Chicago 1969
As above, (Ed.), *Southwest*. Handbook of North American Indians 9–10. Washington 1979–1983
Reichard, Gladys A., *Navajo Shepherd and Weaver*.
[1936] Glorieta 1968
Rushforth, Scott and Steadman Upham, *A Hopi Social History*. Austin 1992
Spicer, Edward H., *Cycles of Conquest. The Impact of Spain, Mexico, and the United States on the Indians of the Southwest, 1633–1960*.
Tucson 1962
Spier, Leslie, *Yuman Tribes of the Gila River* [1933].
New York 1978
Underhill, Ruth, *Social Organization of the Papago Indians*. New York 1939
Witherspoon, Gary, *Language and Art in the Navajo Universe*. Ann Arbor 1977

# Index

# Acknowledgments

The publisher wishes to thank the museums, collectors, archives, and photographers who have given permission for photographic material to be reproduced and for their support in the production of this book. The editor and publisher have made every effort to trace all copyright-owners. Any individuals or institutions that have not been contacted regarding copyright are kindly requested to contact the publisher.

C = center    A = above    B = below    L = left    R = right

**8/9:** National Museum of American Art, Washington, DC./Art Resource, NY; **10:** Archiv Christian F. Feest, Altenstadt; **11:** Studio für Landkartentechnik, Norderstedt; **12 AL:** National Archives of Canada, Ottawa, ON [C-092415]; **12 B:** Christian F. Feest, Altenstadt; **13 A:** Musée du Nouveau Monde, La Rochelle; **13 B:** Glenbow Archives, Calgary, Canada [NA 1811-16]; **14 A:** Courtesy of the Mashantucket Pequot Museum and Research Center, Mashantucket, CT; **14 B:** The Saint Louis Art Museum (Eliza McMillan Fund), St. Louis, MO; **15:** Rochester Museum & Science Center, Rochester, NY; **16 A:** Courtesy of M. Knoedler and Co. Inc., New York, NY; **16 B:** Christian F. Feest, Altenstadt; **17:** 1999 Board of Trustees, National Gallery of Art, Washington, DC. – Photo: Richard Carafelli; **18 A:** Indiana University Museum of Art, Bloomington, IN – Photo: Michael Cavanagh/Kevin Montague; **18 B:** John Borman, Fort Collins, CO; **19:** Rolli Arts, Essen; **20 A:** National Archives and Record Service, Washington, DC.; **20 B:** Buffalo Bill Historical Center, Cody, WY; **21:** Minnesota Historical Society, St. Paul, MN; **22 AL:** Reinhard Mandl, Wien; **22 AR:** Wayne Leidenfrost/Vancouver Sun and Province, Vancouver, BC; **22 B:** Barbara Fahs Charles, Washington, DC.; **23 A:** Archives des Jésuites, St. Jerome, QC; **23 B:** Wanamaker Collection/William Hammond Mathers Museum, Indiana University, Bloomington, IN; **24 A:** Museum für Völkerkunde, Wien; **24 B:** Bibliothèque Nationale de France, Paris; **25 A:** Marquette University Archives, Milweaukee, WI; **25 BL:** The Library of Congress, Washington, DC.; **25 NR:** Courtesy The New York State Library, Albany, NY; **27 L:** The Thomas Gilcrease Institute of American History and Art, Tulsa, OK; **27 R:** National Archives of Canada, Ottawa, ON [C-21765 (observe)] [C-21764 (reserve)]; **28/29:** Archiv für Kunst und Geschichte, Berlin – Photo: Jürgen Sorges; **29 B**: Rolli Arts, Essen; **30/31:** Studio für Landkartentechnik, Norderstedt; **31 A:** Rolli Arts, Essen; **31 BR:** Das Fotoarchiv, Essen – Photo: James Sugar; **32 A:** Special Collections Division/University of Washington Libraries, Seattle, WA [Neg. # NA 3907]; **32 B:** Archiv für Kunst und Geschichte, Berlin – Photo: Werner Forman; **33 A:** Rautenstrauch-Joest-Museum für Völkerkunde, Köln; **33 C:** James H. Barker, Fairbanks, Alaska; **33 B:** Denver Museum of Natural History, Denver, CO – Photo: Alfred M. Bailey; **34 AL:** Wolfgang R. Weber, Darmstadt; **34 AR:** Canadian Museum of Civilization, Hull, QC; **34 B:** Rolli Arts, Essen; **35 A:** A.B. Text & Bilder, Stockholm – Photo: Paul Popper; **35 B:** National Archives of Canada, Ottawa, ON – Photo: Albert Peter Low [PA 053569]; **36 A:** Das Fotoarchiv, Essen – Photo: Robert Semeniuk; **36 B:** National Anthropological Archives, Smithsonian Institution, Washington, DC.; **37 A:** Rolli Arts, Essen; **37 B**: Canadian Museum of Civilization, Hull, QC; **38 A:** Das Fotoarchiv, Essen – Photo: Robert Semeniuk; **38 B:** Canadian Museum of Civilization, Hull, QC; **39 A:** Rautenstrauch-Joest-Museum für Völkerkunde, Köln; **39 BL:** Rolli Arts, Essen; **39 BL:** James H. Barker, Fairbanks, Alaska; **40:** Wolfgang R. Weber, Darmstadt; **41 A:** Das Fotoarchiv, Essen – Photo: Bill Strode; **41 C:** Das Fotoarchiv, Essen – Photo: Bill Strode; **41 B:** Das Fotoarchiv, Essen – Photo: Robert Semeniuk; **42:** Nicolas Vanier, Paris; **43 A:** Das Fotoarchiv, Essen – Photo: Robert Semeniuk; **43 C and B:** Archives Des Chatelets, Ottawa, ON – Photo: Guy Mary Rousselière; **44 A:** Wolfgang R. Weber, Darmstadt; **44 B:** Verena Traeger, Wien; **45 A:** Wolfgang R. Weber, Darmstadt; **45 B:** Verena Traeger, Wien; **46:** Archives Des Chatelets, Ottawa, ON – Photo: Guy Mary Rousselière; **47 L:** Rolli Arts, Essen; **47 AR:** Archiv für Kunst und Geschichte, Berlin – Photo: Werner Forman; **47 B:** Archives Des Chatelets, Ottawa, ON – Photo: Guy Mary Rousselière; **48 L:** Manitoba Museum of Man and Nature, Bishop Marsh Inuit Collection, Winnipeg, Canada [H. 5.231.294]; **48 R:** National Museum of Finland, Helsinki; **48 B:** A.B. Text & Bilder, Stockholm; **49:** A.B. Text & Bilder, Stockholm; **50:** Das Fotoarchiv, Essen – Photo: Bill Strode; **51 AL:** Rolli Arts, Essen; **51 AR:** Wolfgang R. Weber, Darmstadt; **51 BR:** Canadian Museum of Civilization, Hull, QC; **52 A:** Glenbow Archives, Calgary, Canada [NC-1-827t] – Photo: Lomen Brothers; **52 B:** Mitchell Library, State Library of New South Wales, Sydney, Australia; **53 A:** The Library of Congress, Washington, DC.; **53 B:** Verena Traeger, Wien; **54 A:** Trustees of the National Museums of Scotland, Edinburgh; **54 B:** The Field Museum of Natural History, Chicago, IL [Neg. # A 103915]; **55:** Bilderberg, Hamburg – Photo: Hans-Jürgen Burkard; **56:** Alaska State Museum, Milotte Collection, Juneau, AK [Cat.No. # 1098]; **57 A:** Greenland National Museum and Archives, Nuuk; **57 B:** Bildarchiv Preußischer Kulturbesitz, Berlin; **58 L:** Cambridge University Museum of Archaeology and Anthropology, Cambridge [Accs. # 1950-411A]; **58 R:** Canadian Museum of Civilization, Hull, QC [photo # S94-13531]; **59:** Verena Traeger, Wien; **60/61 A:** Canadian Museum of Civilization, Hull, QC; **60 B:** Panstwow Muzeum Etnograficzne, Warsaw; **61 R** and **B:** Panstwow Muzeum Etnograficzne, Warsaw; **62:** Special Collections Division/University of Washington Libraries, Seattle, WA [Neg. # uw 13374]; **63 AR:** 1999 The Heard Museum, Phoenix, Arizona; **63 B:** Erskine Collection, Acc. # 70-28-1190, Alaska and Polar Regions Department, University of Alaska, Fairbanks, Alaska; **64:** James H. Barker, Fairbanks, Alaska; **65 A:** Bilderberg, Hamburg – Photo Milan Horacek; **65 B:** James H. Barker, Fairbanks, Alaska; **66, 67:** Verena Traeger, Wien; **68:** Das Fotoarchiv, Essen – Photo: Robert Semeniuk; **69 A:** Courtesy of the Haffenreffer Museum of Anthropology, Brown University, Bristol, RI; **69 B:** Verena Traeger, Wien; **70/71:** W. Wisniewski/Okapia, Frankfurt am Main; **71 B:** Rolli Arts, Essen; **72 A:** Daniel J. Cox/ OSF/Okapia, Frankfurt am Main; **72/73 B:** Studio für Landkartentechnik, Norderstedt; **73 A:** Rolli Arts, Essen; **74:** Das Fotoarchiv, Essen – Photo: Lee Day; **75:** The Hulton Getty Picture Collection, London; **76 A:** Frobenius-Institut, Frankfurt am Main – Photo:P. Steigerwald; **76 B:** Bilderberg, Hamburg – Photo: Hans-Jürgen Burkard; **77:** Bilderberg, Hamburg – Photo: Hans-Jürgen Burkard; **78:** Frobenius-Institut, Frankfurt am Main – Photo: P. Steigerwald; **79 A:** Bilderberg, Hamburg; **79 B:** Trustees of the National Museums of Scotland, Edinburgh; **80 A:** Rolli Arts, Essen; **80 B:** Look, München – Photo: Christian Heeb; **81 L:** Nicolas Vanier, Paris; **81 R:** Rolli Arts, Essen; **82:** Franz Bagyi, Weil der Stadt; **83 AL:** Henry H. Holdsworth/Wildlife/Okapia, Frankfurt am Main; **83 AR:** Nicolas Vanier, Paris; **83 C:** Nicolas Vanier, Paris; **84:** NAS/ Tim Davis/Okapia, Frankfurt am Main; **85 AL:** Nicolas Vanier, Paris; **85 AR:** Nicolas Gilles, Paris; **85 B:** Rautenstrauch-Joest-Museum für Völkerkunde, Köln; **86 A:** Canadian Museum of Civilization, Hull, QC; **86 B:** University of Alaska Museum, Fairbanks, Alaska; **87:** Adrian Tanner, St. Johns, Newfoundland, Canada; **88:** State Historical Society of Wisconsin, Madison, WI [WHi (X3) 36725]; **89 A:** Joel Savishinsky, Ithaca, NY; **89 B:** John W. Warden/Okapia, Frankfurt am Main; **90:** Photo: Charles Wesley Mathers/Northwest Territory Archives, Yellowknife NT [N-1192-099]; **91:** Photo: Rene Fumoleau/Northwest Territory Archives, Yellowknife NT [G-1979-023]; **92:** Collection of The Dalhousie Art Gallery, Halifax, Nova Scotia; **93:** Frobenius-Institut, Frankfurt am Main – Photo: P. Steigerwald; **94 A:** Nicolas Vanier, Paris; **94 BL:** Rautenstrauch-Joest-Museum für Völkerkunde, Köln; **94 BR:** Bildarchiv Preußischer Kulturbesitz, Berlin – Photo: Dietrich Graf; **95 A:** Rautenstrauch-Joest-Museum für Völkerkunde, Köln; **95 B:** North West Territory Dept. of Information/North West Territory Archives, Yellowknife, NT [G-1979-023]; **96 A:** John Kieffer/P. Arnold Inc./Okapia, Frankfurt am Main; **96 C:** Bildarchiv Preußischer Kulturbesitz, Berlin – Photo: Dietrich Graf; **96 B:** Canadian Museum of Civilization, Hull, QC; **97 A:** Trustees of the National Museums of Scotland, Edinburgh; **97 B:** The Peabody Museum, Harvard University, Cambridge, MA; **98:** Wolfgang R. Weber, Darmstadt; **99:** Frobenius-Institut, Frankfurt am Main – Photo: P. Steigerwald; **100 L:** National Archives of Canada, Ottawa, ON [C-005149]; **100 R:** Frobenius-Institut, Frankfurt am Main – Photo: P. Steigerwald; **101** A: Wolfgang R. Weber, Darmstadt; **101 B:** Frobenius-Institut, Frankfurt am Main – Photo: P. Steigerwald; **102 L:** Rolli Arts, Essen; **102 R:** Das Fotoarchiv, Essen – Photo: Lee Day; **103 A:** National Archives of Canada, Ottawa, ON [C-0011917]; **103 B:** Reinhard Mandl, Wien; **104/105:** Tony Stone Bilderwelten, München; **105 B:** Rolli Arts, Essen; **106:** Studio für Landkartentechnik, Norderstedt; **107 A:** Christian F. Feest, Altenstadt (1984); **107 B:** Rolli Arts, Essen; **108 A:** Christian Carstensen, Edenkoben; **108 B:** Sylvia S. Kasprycki, Altenstadt; **109 A:** Stephan J. Krasemann/Okapia, Frankfurt am Main; **109 B:** Franz Bagyi, Weil der Stadt; **110:** Christian F. Feest, Altenstadt; **111 A:** United States Nation Park Service, Chilicothe, OH – Photo: Michael Bitsko; **111 B:** Ohio History Society, Columbus, OH; **112:** Museum of Art, Rhode Island School of Design, Providence/Gift of Mr. Robert Winthrop – Photo: Del Bogart; **113:** National Museum of American Art, Washington, DC./Art Resource, NY/Scala Group S.p.A, Antella/Firenze; **114 A:** Braunschweigisches Landesmuseum, Braunschweig – Photo: Ingeborg Simon; **114 B:** State Historical Society of Wisconsin, Madison, WI [WHi (X3)18849]; **115 A:** Bibliothèque Nationale de France, Paris; **115 B:** Tippecanoe County Historical Association, Lafayett, IN; **116 A:** The Library of Congress, Washington, DC.; **116 B:** Dementi Studio, Richmond, VA; **117:** Museum of Art at Brigham Young University, Salt Lake City, UT – Photo: David W. Hawkinson; **118:** The Thomas Gilcrease Institute of American History and Art, Tulsa, OK; **119 A:** National Museum of American Art, Washington, DC./Art Resource, NY; **119 B:** Christian F. Feest, Altenstadt; **120:** State Historical Society of Wisconsin, Madison, WI [WHi (W6) 6290]; **121 A:** Rochester Museum & Science Center, Rochester, NY; **121 B:** Sylvia S. Kasprycki, Altenstadt; **122 L:** The British Museum, London; **122 B:** Courtesy W. Duncan MacMillan Collection/Afton Historical Society Press, Afton, MN; **123:** National Archives and Records Administration – Central Plains Region, Kansas City, MO – Photo: Jim Devine, Underwood Studio [image # NRE-75.RL (Pho)-1072]; **124 A:** Ashmolean Museum, Oxford; **124 B:** Christian F. Feest, Altenstadt (1981); **125 A:** The British Museum, London; **125 B:** Christian F. Feest, Altenstadt (1978); **126:** Museum für Völkerkunde, Wien; **127:** Photo: John M. Zielinski; **128:** Milwaukee Public Museum, Milwaukee, WI; **129 AL:** Bibliothèque Nationale de France, Paris; **129 AR:** Cranbrook Institute of Science, Bloomfield Hills, MI – Photo: Tim Thayer; **129 B:** Rheinisches Bildarchiv, Köln – Photo: A. Meyer [Inv. Nr.: RJM 49718]; **130:** Milwaukee Public Museum, Milwaukee, WI; **131 A:** Reinhard Mandl, Wien; **131 B:** National Museum of Ireland, Dublin; **133:** Frobenius-Institut, Frankfurt am Main – Photo: P. Steigerwald; **134 A:** Frobenius-Institut, Frankfurt am Main – Photo: P. Steigerwald; **135:** The British Museum, London; **136:** Art Gallery of Ontario, Toronto, ON. Purchase 1932 – Photo: Carlo Catenazzi, AGO [# 2121]; **137 A:** Milwaukee Public Museum, Milwaukee, WI**;** **137 BL:** The Detroit Institute of Arts, Detroit, MI; **137 BR:** Das Fotoarchiv, Essen – Photo: Andreas Riedmiller; **138:** The Art Archive, London; **139 A:** Gift of Enron Art Foundation/Joslyn Art Museum, Omaha, NE; **139 BL:** Canadian Museum of Civilization, Hull, QC; **139 BR:** Peabody Museum of Archaeology and Ethnology, Harvard University, Cambridge, MA; **140:** Rochester Museum & Science Center, Rochester, NY; **141 A:** Courtesy of the U.S. Department of the Interior, Indian Arts and Craft Board, Washington, DC.; **141 B:** National Gallery of Canada, Ottawa, ON [purchased 1951]; **142 A:** Courtesy of the Southwest Museum, Los Angeles, CA [photo # N. 24963]; **142 B:** Reinhard Mandl, Wien; **143 A:** 1999 Das Fotoarchiv, Essen/Black Star – Photo: Peter S. Mocca; **143 B:** CORBIS/Bettmann, London; **144:** Micmac Mews – Photo: A. Morris; **145 A:** Collection Musée d l'Homme, Paris – Photo: M. Delaplanche; **145 B:** National Gallery of Canada, Ottawa, ON [purchased 1957]; **146:** National Museum of the American Indian, New York, NY – Smithsonian Institution [photo # 2882]; **147 A:** The Historical Society of Pennsylvania (HSP), Philadelphia, PA; **147 B:** National Museum of the American Indian, New York, NY – Smithsonian Institution [photo # 03-2720]; **148/149:** Tony Stone Bilderwelten, München – Photo: Larry Ulrich; **149 B:** Rolli Arts, Essen; **150:** Studio für Landkartentechnik, Norderstedt; **151 A:** Tony Stone Bilderwelten, München – Photo: Stephen Krasemann; **151 B:** Rolli Arts, Essen; **152:** Look, München – Photo: Christian Heeb; **153 L:** NAS/J.L. Lepore/Okapia 1991, Frankfurt am Main; **153 R:** Look, München – Photo: Christian Heeb; **154:** Christian F. Feest, Altenstadt (1973); **155 A:** Courtesy of Frank H. McClung Museum, The University of Tennessee, Knoxville, TN – Photo: W. Miles Wright; **155 B:** Saint Louis Science Center, St. Louis, MO; **156:** Archiv Christian F. Feest, Altenstadt; **157:** Pres. and Fellows of Harvard College. All rights reserved. The Peabody Museum, Harvard University, Cambridge, MA – Photo: Hillel Burger; **158:** The Philbrook Museum of Art, Tulsa, OK [The Museum purchase 1967.24]; **159 R:** The British Museum, London; **160:** National Anthropological Archives, Smithsonian Institution, Washington, DC. [photo # 1102-B-9]; **161 A:** Museum für Völkerkunde der Stadt Frankfurt am Main – Photo: Maria Obermaier; **161 B:** The Art Archive, London; **162 A:** Christian F. Feest, Altenstadt; **162 B:** The Philbrook Museum of Art, Tulsa, OK [The Museum purchase 1950.10]; **163:** The British Library, London; **164:** Pres. and Fellows of Harvard College. All rights reserved. The Peabody Museum, Harvard University, Cambridge, MA – Photo: Hillel Burger; **165 A:** National Anthropological Archives, Smithsonian Institution, Washington, DC. [photo # 44353-A]; **165 B:** National Anthropological Archives, Smithsonian Institution, Washington, DC. [photo # 1000-A]; **166:** Pres. and Fellows of Harvard College 1987. All rights reserved. The Peabody Museum, Harvard University, Cambridge, MA – Photo: Hillel Burger; **167:** Gift of Enron Art Foundation/Joslyn Art Museum, Omaha, NE; **168:** New Orleans Museum of Art, Gift of William E. Groves, New Orleans, LA – Photo: Owen F. Murphy Jr.; **169 A:** Gift of Enron Art Foundation /Joslyn Art Museum, Omaha, NE; **169 B:** Christian F. Feest, Altenstadt; **170:** Gift of Enron Art Foundation/Joslyn Art Museum, Omaha, NE; **171 A:** Musée de l'homme, Paris – Photo: D. Ponsard; **171 B:** Musée d'histoire naturelle, La Rochelle – Photo: J+M Photographes, La Rochelle; **172:** Ny kgl. Saml. 565,4 to, Royal Library, Kopenhagen; **173 A:** National Anthropological Archives, Smithsonian Institution, Washington, DC.; **173 B:** Christian F. Feest, Altenstadt; **174:** Public Record Office, London; **175 A:** The British Library,

**380:** Arizona State Museum, University of Arizona, Tucson, AZ; **381 A:** Milwaukee Public Museum, Milwaukee, WI; **381 B:** Courtesy of Sharlot Hall Museum, Prescott, AZ – Photo: D. F. Mitchell [IN-A 174P]; **382:** Reinhard Mandl, Wien; **383:** Christian F. Feest, Altenstadt; **384:** National Anthropological Archives, Smithsonian Institution, Washington, DC. [photo # 2255C1]; **385 A:** Deutsches Ledermuseum, Offenbach am Main; **385 B:** California Historical Society, Los Angeles, CA; **387:** Courtesy of the Southwest Museum, Los Angeles, CA [photo # N. 20269]; **388:** The Thomas Gilcrease Institute of American History and Art, Tulsa, OK; **389:** John Running/Flagstaff, AZ; **390:** John R. Wilson Collection, Tulsa, OK – Photo: Joseph Mora; **391:** Carnegie Museum of Natural History, Pittsburgh, PA; **392:** Courtesy of the Southwest Museum, Los Angeles, CA [photo # 20319]; **393 A:** Christian F. Feest, Altenstadt; **393 B:** Colorado Springs Fine Arts Center, Colorado Springs, CO; **394:** National Anthropological Archives, Smithsonian Institution, Washington, DC. [photo # 32357-K]; **395 A:** Museum für Völkerkunde, Wien; **395 B:** National Museum of the American Indian, New York, NY; **397 A:** Bildarchiv Preußischer Kulturbesitz, Berlin; **397 B:** Stiftung Preussische Schlösser und Gärten, Berlin-Brandenburg; **398:** National Anthropological Archives, Smithsonian Institution, Washington, DC. [photo # 2629]; **399 A:** Courtesy of the Arizona Historical Society, Tucson, AZ [photo # 24808]; **399 B:** Museum für Völkerkunde, Wien; **400 AL:** National Museum of the American Indian, New York, NY – Smithsonian Institution [photo # 24596]; **400 AR:** Arizona State Museum, University of Arizona, Tucson, AZ – Photo: Helga Telwes; **400 B:** Museum of Art, Rhode Island School of Design – Photo: Del Bogart; **401:** Christian F. Feest, Altenstadt; **402:** American Museum of Natural History, New York, NY [neg. # 44388]; **403:** Claus Deimel, Hannover; **404 A:** Arizona State Museum, University of Arizona, Tucson, AZ; **404 B:** William L. Merill, Washington, DC.; **405:** Claus Deimel, Hannover; **406:** National Anthropological Archives, Smithsonian Institution, Washington, DC.; **407:** Reinhard Mandl, Wien; **408:** 1999 Das Fotoarchiv, Essen/Black Star – Photo: John Running; **409 A:** Reinhard Mandl, Wien; **409 B:** Das Fotoarchiv, Essen – Photo: Jochen Tack; **410:** The Philbrook Museum of Art, Tulsa, OK [1947.40]; **411 A:** National Anthropological Archives, Smithsonian Institution, Washington, DC. [photo # 82-2048]; **411 B:** Bildarchiv Preußischer Kulturbesitz, Berlin; **412:** Reinhard Mandl; **413 L:** Museum für Völkerkunde, Wien; **413 R:** Das Fotoarchiv, Essen – Photo: Harry Redl; **414 A:** National Archives and Records Administration, Washington, DC. – Photo: Camillus S. Fly; **415:** National Anthropological Archives, Smithsonian Institution, Washington, DC. [photo # 2580B-4]; **414 B:** National Anthropological Archives, Smithsonian Institution, Washington, DC. [photo # 43005B]; **416 A:** Collection Fred Jones Jr., Museum of Art; University of Oklahoma, Norman, OK; **416 B:** From the collections of the State Museum of History, Oklahoma Historical Society, Oklahoma City, OK; **417 I:** John Running/Flagstaff, AZ; **417 R:** Das Fotoarchiv, Essen – Photo: John Running; **418:** Arizona State Museum, University of Arizona, Tucson, AZ – Photo: Helga Telwes; **419 A:** Arizona State Museum, University of Arizona, Tucson, AZ – Photo: Helga Telwes; **419 B:** Arizona State Museum, University of Arizona, Tucson, AZ; **420:** National Archives and Records Administration, Washington, DC. – Photo: Ben Wittick; **421:** National Archives and Records Administration, Washington, DC.; **422/423:** Das Fotoarchiv, Essen – Photo: Jim Cammack; **424:** The Andy Warhol Foundation for the Visual Arts, NY/Art Resource, NY/Scala Group S.p.A, Antella/Firenze; **425 AL:** Museum für Völkerkunde, Wien; **425 AR:** Rolli Arts, Essen; **425 B:** Reinhard Mandl, Wien; **426 A:** Johanna E. Feest, Wien; **426 BL:** Peter Schwarzbauer; **426 BR:** Hulle-

ah Tsinhnahjinnie, Arizona; **427 A:** National Museum of American Art, Washington, DC./Art Resource, NY; **427 BL:** Christian F. Feest, Altenstadt; **427 BR:** Courtesy of the U.S. Department of the Interior, Indian Arts and Crafts Board, Sioux Indian Museum, Rapid City, SD; **428:** Christian F. Feest, Altenstadt; **429 A:** Reinhard Mandl, Wien; **429 BL:** Reinhard Mandl, Wien; **429 BR:** Das Fotoarchiv, Essen – Photo: John Running; **430 A:** Archiv Christian F. Feest, Altenstadt; **430 B:** Reinhard Mandl, Wien; **431 A:** Cora Bender, Frankfurt am Main; **431 B:** Reinhard Mandl, Wien; **433:** United States Department of the Interior, National Park Service; **434 AL:** 1999 Das Fotoarchiv, Essen/Black Star – Photo: Michael Abramson; **434 AR:** Manuscripts Division, J. Willard Marriott Library, University of Utah, Salt Lake City, UT; **434 B:** Canapress Picture Archive, Toronto, ON – Photo: Frank Gunn; **435 AL:** Christie's Images, New York, NY; **435 R:** Photo: Heide Kratz, Frankfurt am Main; **435 B:** Das Fotoarchiv, Essen – Photo: Per Breiehagen; **436 A:** 1982 Carson Waterman, Salamanca, NY; **436 B:** Museum für Völkerkunde, Wien; **437:** Nebraska State Historical Society, Lincoln, NE – Photo: John A. Anderson; **438/439:** 1999 Das Fotoarchiv, Essen/Black Star – Photo: Owen; **440:** Studio für Landkartentechnik, Norderstedt; **441:** Rautenstrauch-Joest-Museum für Völkerkunde, Köln; **442:** Rolli Arts, Essen; **443:** Rheinisches Bildarchiv, Köln – Photo: A. Meyer [RJM 41265]; **444:** Bildarchiv Preußischer Kulturbesitz, Berlin – Photo: Dietrich Graf; **445:** Bildarchiv Preußischer Kulturbesitz, Berlin – Photo: Dietrich Graf; **446:** Archiv für Kunst und Geschichte, Berlin – Photo: Werner Forman; **447:** Bildarchiv Preußischer Kulturbesitz, Berlin – Photo: Dietrich Graf; **448:** Archiv für Kunst und Geschichte, Berlin – Photo: Werner Forman; **449:** Archiv für Kunst und Geschichte, Berlin – Photo: Werner Forman; **450 A:** Rautenstrauch-Joest-Museum für Völkerkunde, Köln; **450 B:** Archiv für Kunst und Geschichte, Berlin – Photo: Werner Forman; **451:** Deutsches Ledermuseum, Offenbach; **452:** Courtesy of the Mashantucket Pequot Museum and Research Center, Mashantucket, CT; **453:** Canadian Museum of Civilization, Hull, QC; **454:** Bildarchiv Preußischer Kulturbesitz, Berlin – Photo: Dietrich Graf; **455:** Bildarchiv Preußischer Kulturbesitz, Berlin – Photo: Waltraut Schneider-Schütz; **456:** Bildarchiv Preußischer Kulturbesitz, Berlin – Photo: Dietrich Graf; **458:** Archiv für Kunst und Geschichte, Berlin – Photo: Werner Forman; **459:** Archiv für Kunst und Geschichte, Berlin – Photo: Erich Lessing; **460 A:** Archiv für Kunst und Geschichte, Berlin – Photo: Werner Forman; **460 B:** Rautenstrauch-Joest-Museum für Völkerkunde, Köln; **461 L:** Das Fotoarchiv, Essen – Photo: Thomas Mayer; **461 R:** Das Fotoarchiv, Essen – Photo: Robert Semeniuk; **462:** National Anthropological Archives, Smithsonian Institution, Washington, DC. [photo # 1610]; **463:** Courtesy of the Southwest Museum, Los Angeles, CA [photo # 37826]; **464:** National Anthropological Archives, Smithsonian Institution, Washington, DC. [photo # 43003-A]; **465:** Archiv für Kunst und Geschichte, Berlin; **466 A:** 1999 Das Fotoarchiv, Essen/Black Star – Photo: Peter Korniss; **466 B:** Das Fotoarchiv, Essen – Photo: John Running; **467:** Christian F. Feest, Altenstadt; **468 A:** National Anthropological Archives, Smithsonian Institution, Washington, DC. [photo # 45216-K]; **468 B:** Seaver Center for Western History Research, Los Angeles County Museum of Natural History, Los Angeles, Ca; **469:** Archiv für Kunst und Geschichte, Berlin; **470 A:** Archiv für Kunst und Geschichte, Berlin – Photo: Paul Almasy; **470 BL:** National Archives and Records Administration, Washington, DC.; **470 BR:** Courtesy of the Southwest Museum, Los Angeles, CA [photo # 42455]; **471:** National Anthropological Archives, Smithsonian Institution, Washington, DC.; **480:** Indianermuseum der Stadt Zürich, Zürich.

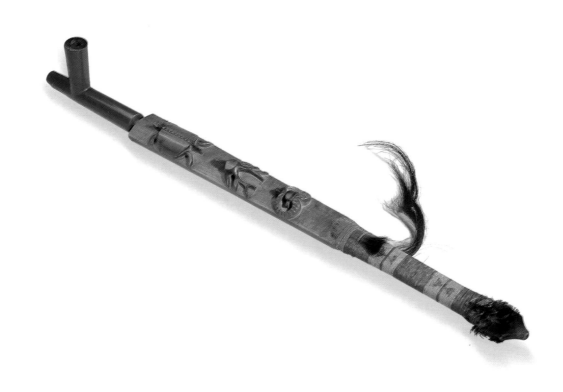